EXLIBRIS

Kristine
From Nana + Gramp
12/25/98

Also by Julia Child

Mastering the Art of French Cooking, Volume I
(with Simone Beck and Louisette Bertholle)

The French Chef Cookbook

Mastering the Art of French Cooking, Volume II
(with Simone Beck)

From Julia Child's Kitchen

Julia Child & Company

Julia Child & More Company

The Way to Cook

Julia Child

The Way to Cook

Photographs by

Brian Leatart

and Jim Scherer

Food Designer

Rosemary Manell

Alfred A. Knopf

New York 1997

This Is a Borzoi Book
Published by Alfred A. Knopf, Inc.

Copyright © 1989 by Julia Child

All rights reserved under International and Pan-American
Copyright Conventions. Published in the United States by
Alfred A. Knopf, Inc., New York, and simultaneously in
Canada by Random House of Canada Limited, Toronto.
Distributed by Random House, Inc., New York.

Library of Congress Cataloging-in-Publication Data

Child, Julia.
  The way to cook.

  Includes index.
  I. Cookery, French.   2. Cookery, American.
I. Title.
TX719.C455   1989   641.5   88-45838
ISBN 0-394-53264-3   Pbk 0-679-74765-6

Manufactured in the United States of America
Hardcover edition published October 1989
Reprinted eleven times
Thirteenth printing, November 1997
Paperback edition published October 1, 1993
Reprinted five times
Seventh printing, November 1997

A Note on the Type

This book was set in a modern adaptation of a type
designed by William Caslon (1692–1766). In style Caslon
was a reversion to earlier type styles. Its characteristics are
remarkable regularity and symmetry, and beauty in the shape
and proportion of the letters; its general effect is clear and
open, but not weak or delicate. For uniformity, clearness,
and readability, it has perhaps never been surpassed.

Composed by Graphic Composition, Inc., Athens, Georgia.
Color separations by Combined Communications Services,
Clearwater, Florida.
Printed and bound by R. R. Donnelley & Sons, Willard, Ohio.
Designed by Janet Odgis & Company, Inc.

Contents

To the memory of
Robert H. Johnson,
dear friend and mentor
who brought so much of this to pass

Foreword and Acknowledgments

The Way to Cook derives its title from the six one-hour videocassettes of the same name; recipes and techniques therein are incorporated in this present book, as well as those of mine from the "Dinner at Julia's" television series, four years of monthly food articles in *Parade* magazine, cooking segments on "Good Morning America," and other recipes and ideas that I have wanted to share.

The cast of characters for these several events remains much the same, and I speak in the plural because we were a close-knit team. Included as hardworking associate cooking and catering friends in Santa Barbara were Catherine Brandel, Ken Davis, Neil Flaster, Paule McPherson, Gloria Paulsen, Linda Schwartz, Karyn Scott, Barbara Sims-Bell, and students from the Hotel and Restaurant Administration of Santa Barbara City College. In Cambridge we were joined at various times by Tim Bunch, Jessica Clendenning, Lori Deliso, Ruth Feinberg, Brett Freschette, Ave Moran, Sara Moulton, and Holly Safford.

Executive Secretary for the "Dinner" series in Santa Barbara was Bitsy Gordy, and for the teaching cassettes was Ennan West, a.k.a. "Video Book." She has also done yeoman research on the hideous task of cross-referencing the text pages for this present volume. Home Secretary in Cambridge was and is Judith Avrett; Comptroller for all enterprises, Ron Bredesen.

Executive Chef for the "Dinner" series and teaching cassettes was Marian Morash, chef in her own right as well as "Victory Garden" chef and author of *The Victory Garden Cookbook* and videocassette. Cooking teacher, food writer, and author Nancy Barr was Executive Chef for the *Parade* articles and "Good Morning America" appearances.

Executive Associate was Elizabeth Bishop, a talented organizer and ready-for-anything friend and colleague; we've worked together on television and cooking demonstrations since the early days of "The French Chef." Food Designer for the photographs in this book, as well as for the videocassettes, *Parade* articles, and the television "Company" and "Dinner" series, was long-time friend Rosemary Manell, who also acted as recipe developer and proofreader.

How fortunate I am to have been given my television experience at ABC, and I am greatly indebted to Sonya Selby-Wright, my producer for "Good Morning America." Her talents for creating a kitchen drama in three and a half minutes are awesome. I am especially blessed to have been with Public Television all these years at WGBH-Boston. Russ Morash, our friendly ayatollah, has been my PBS producer almost continually since the beginning of the "French Chef" days. His grasp of complicated culinary problems and techniques has so often clarified my thinking, and although I speak of him in television terms, his influence has been profound in the making of this book.

Working with friends like these is one of the great pleasures in life for me. We all learn from each other, we eat magnificently, and we've invariably had a wonderfully good time.

Thanks to the great generosity of Walter Anderson, Editor of *Parade,* we have been given the negatives and free use of all our *Parade* photographs—more than six hundred of them. This has been a windfall of immense value, and I express my fond appreciation to Ira Joffe, Art Director for *Parade,* and David Currier, *Parade* Senior Editor.

A reference or teaching book is only as good as its index. This one— by far the most intelligent in any of my books—was prepared by Pat Kelly, one of the founders of The Culinary Historians of Boston.

The dedication to quality of Judith Jones, my editor, and of the Knopf staff of designers and proofreaders is always impressive, as is the vast amount of time needed to put together a complicated book like this. I have been in Judith's stable since the beginning of my cookbook career in the late 1950's and cannot imagine working with anyone else. She is, indeed, a peerless editor and friend.

Introduction

Attitudes about food have changed since the 1960's when my first book came out. More and more of us have less time to shop and cook, and we are becoming more health conscious and more aware of what is in our food. That very awareness is the best of all reasons for learning *The Way to Cook*.

While attitudes about food have changed through these last years, fortunately the principles of good cooking have not. The more one knows about it, the less mystery there is, the faster cooking becomes, and the easier it is to be creative and to embrace new trends and ideas—in addition, the more pleasure one has in the kitchen.

I am aiming this, my seventh book, at the new generation of cooks who have not grown up in the old traditions, yet who need a basic knowledge of good food so that they may enjoy fresh, healthy home cooking. It is also directed to those who would like to cook but who have never dared even to string a fresh green bean. It is aimed, too, at old-timers who will find some new ideas here and certainly a new approach.

A grouping by techniques. I have broken with the conventional organization of a cookbook, where all lamb is together in one section and all beef in another, all carrots or salmon or game hens in their separate places, and so on. Wherever possible, I have put things together by method—veal chops are with pork chops because they cook the same way. Chicken stew in red wine is with turkey-wing ragout and rabbit stew—if you can do one, you can do the others because they are assembled, simmered, and sauced the same way. It makes sense to me, also, that all braised meats be grouped together so that their similarities are clearly evident. And since you can boil-steam butternut squash in the same way you boil-steam carrots, pearl onions, and green peas, I have grouped them together also. You use the same base for clam chowder as you do for corn or fish chowder, and that base can also be used for a fish casserole; they, too, are a group. The technique is what's important here, and when you realize that a stew is a stew is a stew, and a roast is a roast whether it be beef, lamb, pork, or chicken, cooking begins to make sense.

A guide to fish cookery. What to do with a trout, for instance. Look it up in the index under T for Trout and you'll see that it can be sautéed whole, as can any small fish. If it's larger, it can be braised or roasted whole, as can any large fish. It can be filleted, then simmered on top of the stove in lightly salted water, or poached with wine in the oven, or it can be turned into a mousse. How about a shark steak? That, too, can be simmered on top of the stove, but it can also be braised with wine or broiled. Thus, you have master recipes that suit your particular fish-of-the-day, some of them simple, quick, and easy, others more elaborate or fussy or formal. The point is that whether whole, filleted, or cut into steaks, all fish that cook the same way are grouped together. That's the way one learns to cook.

New ideas and treatments. Besides the fundamentals, I have included many new ideas of my own. The all-purpose soup bases are an example, where you start out with onions and chicken stock puréed with cooked rice to make a fat-free cream soup; with the addition of other items, you turn it into chicken soup, a cucumber soup, a broccoli soup, and so forth. Or take the velouté soup base, which can be, among others, a chicken soup but also a mushroom soup, or a curried onion or fish soup.

A vast array of fresh vegetables. Vegetables can be the glory of any meal when lovingly cooked. Here they get that same treatment of togetherness—broccoli, Brussels sprouts, green beans, and spinach—they're all green, they can all get a preliminary blanching in a large quantity of boiling water so that they will remain green and beautiful for serving. Full-flavored winter squashes and root vegetables, which are so good to eat but usually take so long to cook, are ready to serve in a matter of minutes when grated and sauté-steamed, and they all cook the same way—from beets and rutabagas to carrots and winter squash. Leeks, endives, and celery are prime candidates for braising, while many a stuffed vegetable does well using the same technique. Of course, there are beans and lentils, chestnuts and sauerkraut, as well as vegetable mixtures that can make a whole main course.

New ways with turkey, goose, and duck. I've had fun fooling around with turkeys, from the conventional whole roasted bird to butterflied turkey, dis-assembled and re-assembled turkey, almost boneless turkey laid back to roast on its stuffing, turkey hash, and turkey stew. Duck and goose make marvelous eating with their full-flavored meat, but they need special treatment because of the fat problem; I have devised a system of steam-roasting which renders out fat to give a crisp skin, yet tender, succulent flesh. Besides roasting whole, duck offers many enticing possibilities, especially when the breast is done one way and the legs another, including a stir-fry, a *confit*, and duckburgers.

Photographs to complete the text. A picture is, indeed, worth a thousand words, especially when you are trying out something new like the duck pâté enclosed in its own skin on page 254—and we have more than six hundred color photographs in this book. How to make it and how is the finished dish suposed to look? In addition, you not only want to read about splitting a cake in half, you also want to see it. You need a visual

explanation of how to hold the pastry bag when you squeeze out the meringue, how to grasp the spinach leaf as you peel off the stem, how to angle the razor as you slash the dough for a loaf of French bread. With this book, you don't have to turn it upside down to see where you place your hands because the photographs here are taken from the cook's point of view, exactly as you yourself are looking at the chicken when you truss it, or at the fish fillet when you score it. Food photography is a specialized art, and I have been blessed by working with two of the best in the business, Jim Scherer in Boston and Brian Leatart in southern California.

Learn the way to cook by starting simple. If you are a beginning cook, don't try to be too elaborate at first. Concentrate on the main course with, perhaps, a chicken sauté. There are certain simple but all-important steps to follow, such as drying off the chicken parts before they go into the pan so that they will brown rather than steam and, for the same reason, leaving enough air space between pieces. You keep the heat just right so the pieces will color nicely without burning, and you turn them so they will brown evenly before you cover the pan and finish the cooking.

When is the chicken done? Timing will give you an estimate, but what are the real indications? You feel it with your impeccably clean finger—cooking is pleasurably tactile. The flesh is springy to the touch; you pierce it with a sharp-pronged fork to examine its juices—they run clear yellow. It's done! You arrange the chicken on hot plates or a platter, pour the fat out of the pan, and right in that same pan, you make your delicious little deglazing sauce, boiling

up the chicken juices with a chopped scallion or shallot, a dollop of chicken broth and perhaps another of wine. It's a perfect dish, yet it is simplicity itself, and while it's cooking, which takes less than half an hour from start to finish, you prepare the rest of the meal.

Most of the master recipes include ideas for what to serve. You might accompany the preceding chicken, for instance, with the easy-to-make broiled tomatoes Provençale—stuffed with fresh bread crumbs and herbs, and sprinkled with olive oil—on page 306. French bread, a green salad, and either a simple white or red wine would make this a fine main course.

You are becoming a cook. After doing the chicken another time or two, it's part of your repertoire, you know it by instinct, and you can start playing around with the variations. The little deglazing sauce, too, is part of you, and you will be using that same technique with meat, fish, and vegetables for the rest of your cooking life. You gradually build up your knowledge and confidence as well as your store of techniques, and you begin feeling that you really are on the way to becoming a cook.

Dinner in half an hour? Even if you're working all day, why buy Chinese take-out food, or frozen dinners, or eat at a fast-food joint when you can make a fresh, informal home-cooked meal even in a minuscule kitchen—and you will know exactly what you are eating. Pour out a glass of wine, and while you're gossiping about the day and trimming the fish fillets, a big pot of water can be set to boil for skinning the tomatoes and blanching the green beans. Perhaps you'll get some help snapping the ends off those beans and preparing the salad greens, too. While the fish has its short sojourn in the oven, you're all but ready for dinner and everyone is refreshed and happy. Dessert can be cheese and fruit, or ice cream or sherbet from the freezer, and you've an easy, satisfying meal.

Those long-simmered stews and braises need not be saved for weekend rainy days because they can be cooked in stages, as indicated in each of the recipes. You want a beef stew, for instance; brown the meat one morning while having breakfast or while preparing tonight's dinner, then simmer it in wine and aromatic vegetables during another meal. The next day or the day after, it needs only rewarming and final flavoring while you ready the accompaniments, such as boiled noodles for sopping up the sauce and steamed broccoli sautéed with garlic. You now have another satisfying, home-cooked main course, and it takes but a few minutes, once the preliminaries have been staged.

Plan ahead for company, too. You are preparing a frozen dessert over the weekend, perhaps. Double the recipe and keep one batch in the freezer. Or make double the usual amount of pie-crust dough when you are doing a fast batch in your food processor. Turn the extra into the quick mock puff pastry on page 392; cut it into shapes and freeze them. When you need an especially dressy finale, pop them from freezer to oven, and they'll be puffed and brown in the few minutes it takes you to hull the strawberries and whip the cream for the chic little dessert pictured on the same page. Or cut the pastry into disks and freeze them for the almost instant apple tarts on page 432. When you know the way to cook, you can produce wonders in minutes.

Moderation and variety. In this book, I am very conscious of calories and fat, and the major proportion of the master recipes are low in fat or even fat-free. Listings of low-calorie and low-fat recipes are in the index.

For healthy eating, know yourself and those you cook for regularly—which means knowing enough about their backgrounds to determine their nutritional requirements as to fat, salt, sugar, and other dietary needs. I do think a general weekly intake count is more sensible and more easily managed than a strict daily one; then you can afford a guilt-less indulgence on Tuesday, for instance, knowing you must pay for it on Wednesday and Thursday. Most authorities agree that the right diet consists of moderation in all things and a great variety of foods; add to this weight-watching, exercise, and picking your grandparents—meaning that you inherit your family's health history. Moderation includes everything from pâtés and pickles to vitamins and fibrous cure-alls; overdosing on anything brings trouble.

Fear of food, indulgences, and small helpings. Because of media hype and woefully inadequate information, too many people nowadays are deathly afraid of their food, and what does fear of food do to the digestive system? I am sure that an unhappy or suspicious stomach, constricted and uneasy with worry, cannot digest properly. And if digestion is poor, the whole body politic suffers.

An imaginary shelf labeled IN-DULGENCES is a good idea. It contains the best butter, jumbo-size eggs, heavy cream, marbled steaks, sausages and pâtés, hollandaise and butter sauces, French butter-cream fillings, gooey chocolate cakes, and all those lovely items that demand disciplined rationing. Thus, with these items high up and almost out of reach, we are ever conscious that they are not everyday foods. They are for special occasions, and when that occasion comes we can enjoy every mouthful.

Servings indicated in the recipes are for conventional amounts, but for all of us it's sensible, indeed, to make a habit of smaller helpings. I, for one, would much rather swoon over a few thin slices of prime beefsteak, or one small serving of chocolate mousse, or a sliver of foie gras than indulge to the full on such nonentities as fat-free gelatin puddings.

Final words. The pleasures of the table—that lovely old-fashioned phrase—depict food as an art form, as a delightful part of civilized life. In spite of food fads, fitness programs, and health concerns, we must never lose sight of a beautifully conceived meal.

J.C.
Cambridge, Massachusetts
1989

A Short Note
Ingredients and Equipment

Ingredients. With the probable exception of fresh foie gras, which appears only once, all the ingredients called for here can be found in any well-equipped American supermarket. It is obvious to anyone who is interested in food that you choose the freshest and finest—which does not mean the most expensive, just the best, whatever it may be. If you do not find the right quality for a dish you had planned on, change gears, and pick another recipe.

Equipment. I am assuming you have a food processor, stoves and ovens that perform as they should, pots and pans of acceptable quality, and knives that are sharp. If you are new to the game, ask advice from the best cooks in town.

Microwaving. I wouldn't be without my microwave oven, but I rarely use it for real cooking. I like having complete control over my food—I want to turn it, smell it, poke it, stir it about, and hover over its every state. Although the microwave does not let me participate fully, I do love it for rewarming, defrosting, and sometimes for starting up or finishing off. However, I know how popular microwave ovens have become and that many people adore them. I'm delighted to see, therefore, a growing number of excellent books on the subject available in supermarkets and bookstores.

The Way to Cook

Soups

Chicken Soups,
Vegetable Soups,
Low-Fat Cream Soups

Oxtail Soup, French Onion Soup

Chowders and
Mediterranean Fish Soups

Garlic, Pistou, Pumpkin,
and Tripe and Bean Soups

Soup for elegant first courses, soup for lunch, supper soups, main-course soups—almost every kind of a soup is here. But no cold soups? No, no recipes for cold soups—except for a Cucumber Fool, a Chilled Watercress Soup, and the usual Vichyssoise, since almost any soup can be served cold with the addition of a little more milk, cream, or stock, and imagination.

Imagination and a number of the basic springboards are what this chapter aims to present, with its theme and variations, and its soup bases that act as building blocks. It is my hope that you will draw from it a solid background for making up your own combinations.

And what a marvelous resource soup is for the thrifty cook—it solves the ham-bone and lamb-bone problems, the everlasting Thanksgiving turkey, the extra vegetables. In addition, soup is a most attractive and nutritious way to take the edge off insatiable youthful appetites. Now, to start out with the mother family of them all, chicken soup.

THE CHICKEN SOUP FAMILY

In the old days of a chicken in every pot, all households presumably had a rich succulent chicken stock perpetually simmering away on the back of the coal stove—a wonderful resource, but keeping it ever on the stove was your only option because there were no refrigerators or freezers. In those days, too, you could buy a stewing hen—where have all those venerable birds gone? Some time ago I was looking for one and had to order it a week in advance, from a chicken farm!

Perhaps all the old hens go into canned chicken broth, a modern convenience our great-grandparents never knew. However, even though today's cooks are blessed with cans of excellent quality, homemade chicken broth is certainly easy and economical to brew. In our house, I usually make a good quantity, and usually make it perfectly plain, so that nothing but chicken can interfere with the other elements I may wish to put into my soup—or my sauce.

Chicken bones and scraps, and optional vegetables

 MASTER RECIPE

Chicken Stock—Chicken Broth

For soups and sauces

It always has a cleaner, fresher, and deeper flavor when made from raw chicken, but you may use bones and scraps from cooked chicken or a mixture of both. Packaged chicken backs and necks are particularly fine for stock because there's meat on those bones; or if you are one who bones chicken breasts or cuts up whole chickens, save all bones, backs, gizzards, and scraps in the freezer, and boil up a stock when you have an adequate collection.

For about 2 quarts

2 quarts or so raw and/or cooked chicken bones and scraps
Water to cover by 1 inch
2 tsp salt
Optional flavorings: ½ cup each chopped onion, carrot, and celery; 1 medium imported bay leaf; 8 parsley stems

SPECIAL EQUIPMENT SUGGESTED: *A 3-quart stainless saucepan with cover; a fine-meshed skimmer or large metal spoon; a fine-meshed sieve*

Simmering the broth. Chop the bones and scraps into 1-inch pieces and bring to the simmer in the saucepan with the water and salt. As the sim-

mer is reached, gray scum will rise
to the surface for several minutes;
skim it off occasionally until it almost
ceases to rise. Add the optional flavorings. Cover the pan loosely and
simmer 1½ hours, adding a little
water if the liquid evaporates to expose the ingredients. Strain through
the sieve into a bowl, and degrease
(degreasing directions are on page
242).

Ahead-of-time note: May be prepared
in advance; chill uncovered, then
cover and refrigerate or freeze.

VARIATIONS

Turkey Stock

Follow the preceding directions for
Chicken Stock.

Brown Chicken Stock

When you want a soup or sauce with
a good brown color, you brown the
ingredients in a frying pan before
simmering them. Follow the recipe
for brown turkey stock on page 173.

Clear Chicken and Vegetable Soup
Quick version, using boned chicken
breasts

A good chicken soup is easily made
with a package of fresh chicken
breasts and either homemade or
canned broth plus fresh vegetables
cut into julienne matchstick size. The
modest addition of wine gives a little
touch of sophistication.

MANUFACTURING NOTE: *If you are in
a hurry, omit the steeping of the chicken
in its cooking broth—it does subtly flavor the meat but adds another 20 minutes to an otherwise quick recipe. Thin
slices are fastest for the vegetable garnish, but julienne matchsticks are more
chic.*

For about 2½ quarts, serving 6 to 8

The soup base:
2 quarts chicken broth—the
   preceding homemade version, or
   canned chicken broth
2 boned and skinned chicken-breast
   halves

The vegetable garnish:
1 cup each onions, carrots, white of
   leek, and tender celery stalks, that
   have been cut into julienne
   matchstick size, fine dice, or thin
   slices

½ cup dry white French vermouth
   or dry white wine
1 imported bay leaf
Salt and freshly ground white pepper

SPECIAL EQUIPMENT SUGGESTED:
A 3-quart stainless saucepan

The soup base. Bring the broth to the
simmer in the saucepan with the
chicken breasts, vegetables, wine,
and bay leaf. Simmer for 4 minutes,
skimming as necessary; remove the
chicken breasts, and let the vegetables
continue to simmer a few minutes
more, or until tender. Meanwhile cut
the chicken into julienne, and when
the vegetables are done, return the
chicken to the hot soup. If time permits, remove from the heat and let
the chicken steep in the soup—
to absorb its flavors—for 15 to 20
minutes. Taste carefully, and correct
seasoning.

Ahead-of-time note: May be prepared
in advance; chill uncovered, then
cover and refrigerate or freeze.

Serving. Just before serving, bring
the soup to the simmer, taste and correct seasoning again if necessary.
Ladle into warmed soup cups or
plates, and serve with melba toast,
buttered toast points, toasted pita triangles (page 33), or puff pastry fleurons (page 395).

CREAM SOUPS

Soups may be creamed in a number
of ways, including great lashings of
cream itself—an ambrosial item I
shall soft-pedal here in favor of the
velouté system with its flour-butter
roux, and of the following rice purée
system, which looks, feels, and tastes
for all the world like a creamy soup
but can contain as low as zero fat.

Cream Soups: Low-Fat with Rice Purée

Start with onions cooked slowly in a
little butter, add rice and soup liquid,
simmer until the rice is tender. Then
add other ingredients to simmer for a
moment, like cucumbers, zucchini,
broccoli. Put it all through your
purée machine and you have a quick
and delicious soup that is also as low
in fat as you wish it to be. Here is
the base for the soup, and following
it a number of ideas.

⚓ MASTER RECIPE

Rice and Onion Soup Base
For puréed cream soups

For about 2 quarts

1 to 2 cups sliced onions, depending
   on how strong an onion flavor
   you wish, and how much of the
   other ingredients you have
2 Tbs butter
7 to 8 cups liquid: water, plus
   chicken, fish, or vegetable stock,
   and/or milk—4 cups of liquid for
   the base; the rest added later
½ cup raw white rice
Salt and freshly ground pepper

SPECIAL EQUIPMENT SUGGESTED:
*A heavy-bottomed 3-quart stainless
saucepan; an electric blender works especially well here, but a food processor
may be used*

Sauté the onions slowly in the butter
for 7 to 8 minutes, or until tender
and translucent. Add the rice and 4
cups of liquid; simmer about 20 minutes, or until the rice is very tender.
(Then, in most instances, you would
also add whatever else your recipe
specifies, and let simmer 5 minutes
or so more.) Purée the soup in the
blender or food processor, adding
more of the liquid if needed, and you
will have a smooth, creamy, lightly
thickened purée. Return the soup to
the pan, add the remaining liquid,
and correct seasoning. Finish off as
suggested in one of the following
recipes.

Cream of chicken and vegetable soup

Cream of Chicken Soup with Vegetables
Low-fat rice-purée method

Here's an easy and excellent cream of
chicken soup. For 2½ quarts, combine the preceding rice and onion
puréed soup base with the Clear
Chicken and Vegetable Soup on page
5, but using only 4 cups of liquid for
each. Stir in a little sour cream or
heavy cream if you wish, and the
soup is ready to serve.

Additional Vegetables

Cook 1 cup of shelled fresh green
peas separately, and reserve. Peel,
seed, and cut a cucumber into julienne matchsticks, salt lightly, and
reserve. Just before serving the preceding soup, add the peas and cucumbers, simmer for a moment,
correct seasoning, and serve.

Cucumber Fool
A cold cucumber purée

As long as we're on the subject of cucumbers, this soup is a particularly
fast, cool, and comfortable soup for a
summer day. A fool is an English
term usually indicating mashed or
puréed fruits mixed with cream,
gooseberry fool being typical. It's a
catchy title particularly when associated with cucumbers, which might
well be a fruit after all.

The soup mixture. For about a quart,
serving 4 to 6, peel and halve 4 or 5
large cucumbers; scrape the seeds and
juice into a sieve set over a bowl, see
illustration. Toss with a big pinch of
salt and let drain. Cut the cucumber
halves into chunks and set aside.
Chop the tender white and green
parts of half a dozen scallions in the
food processor. Add the cucumber
and chop roughly with a big pinch of
sugar, several grinds of white pepper, droplets of wine vinegar, the cucumber juices, a small handful of
watercress leaves and either fresh dill
or a big pinch of dried dill, and, if
you wish, several tablespoons of sour
cream or heavy cream. This will be a
fairly thick purée; correct seasoning,
and chill.

Serving. Correct seasoning again before serving in chilled soup bowls or
cups. Decorate each, if you wish,
with a spoonful of sour cream, or stir
in heavy cream, and top attractively
with thinly sliced cucumbers and
sprigs of fresh dill or parsley.

Scraping seeds out of cucumber half

Floating on thin slices of cucumber

Cream of Cucumber Soup

For about 2¼ quarts, serving 6 to 8

4 large cucumbers for the soup base
2 tsp wine vinegar
2 tsp salt
¼ tsp sugar
Ingredients for the Rice and Onion
Soup Base
½ cup or so sour cream, optional
Decoration: 1 small cucumber cut
into very thin slices, with green
skin on if edible; minced fresh dill
or parsley

The soup. Before starting the soup
base, peel the 4 large cucumbers,
chop roughly, and toss with the vinegar, salt, and sugar. Let stand until
the base has simmered 15 minutes,
then turn the cucumbers and their
juices into the soup and simmer 5
minutes more. Purée; whisk in the
optional sour cream.

Serving. Ladle the soup into warmed
soup bowls, and top each serving
with 3 or 4 cucumber slices and a big
pinch of minced dill or parsley.

Cream of Zucchini Soup

For about 2¼ quarts, serving 6 to 8

1½ pounds zucchini (5 zucchini,
8 inches long)
Ingredients for the Rice and Onion
Soup Base
¼ tsp fragrant dried tarragon leaves,
or sprigs of fresh tarragon
½ cup or so sour cream, heavy
cream, or *crème fraîche,* optional
Decoration: sprigs of fresh tarragon,
or minced fresh parsley

SPECIAL EQUIPMENT SUGGESTED:
A food processor with coarse grating
disk, or the coarse side of a hand grater

The soup. Trim off the zucchini's
stem and bud ends, and wash but do
not peel the zucchini. Grate them.
Simmer three quarters of the pulp 5
to 6 minutes in the soup base before
puréeing. After puréeing, blend in
the optional cream and the remainder
of the zucchini shreds; simmer 2 to 3
minutes, just until the zucchini is
tender.

Serving. Top each serving with sprigs
of tarragon or a sprinkling of
parsley.

SPECIAL NOTE

Crème Fraîche

This is the typical heavy cream you
buy in France; the culture it contains
allows it to ferment gently so that it
thickens like sour cream or yoghurt
and takes on a pleasant, slightly sour
taste. *Crème fraîche* was all the rage
in this country during the 1960s and
1970s—those happy, guilt-free days
when cream was king. Its advantage
over sour cream is that you can let it
boil, reduce, and thicken without
fear of curdling. In addition, it has a
shelf life of a week or more in the refrigerator. I used to make it by stirring 2 tablespoons of yoghurt or
buttermilk into a cup or heavy
cream, and letting it thicken several
hours or overnight at room temperature. I am now less orthodox and find
the following system quick, satisfactory, and a little less rich.

To make 2 cups of crème fraîche:
Whisk 1 cup (½ pint) of chilled
heavy cream and 1 cup of chilled
sour cream in a bowl until lightly
thickened. If you wish, let it sit out
at room temperature for several
hours to thicken and sour a little
more. Refrigerate in a covered container, where it will keep a week or
so—or until it takes on a bitter taste.

Cream of Cauliflower Soup

Cauliflower soup can be very good, in spite of the dreadful public examples most of us have refused to finish. Perhaps those dreary memories stay with us because the cauliflower was overcooked, or because the soup sat in a steam table. However, even a fine cauliflower soup like the following is very white, and I like to dress up mine with something colorful like the blend of toasted bread crumbs and parsley suggested here.

For about 2¼ quarts, serving 6 to 8

A 2-pound head of cauliflower (about 6 inches across)
Ingredients for the Rice and Onion Soup Base, using only 1 cup of the onions called for, and including 2 cups of milk after puréeing
Salt and freshly ground white pepper
½ cup or so sour cream, heavy cream, or *crème fraîche*, optional

Optional Decoration:
1 cup crumbs from fresh white bread sautéed to brown lightly in 2 Tbs butter; ¼ cup loosely packed minced fresh parsley

SPECIAL EQUIPMENT SUGGESTED:
A steamer basket set in a covered saucepan

The soup. Core the central stem out of the cauliflower and peel off its tough outer skin; cut the remaining stem into chunks. Chop the rest of the cauliflower roughly. Add ½ inch of water to the saucepan, and steam the cauliflower pieces for 3 to 4 minutes, or until barely tender. Remove the steamer basket, and rapidly boil down the steaming liquid to less than 1 cup. Purée the cauliflower with the steaming liquid, plus a little of the

soup base if needed. Pour the purée back into the soup.

Finishing the soup and serving. Shortly before serving, toss the toasted crumbs and parsley in a bowl with a dusting of salt and pepper. Stir the cream, if you are using it, into the soup and simmer 2 minutes. Taste carefully and correct seasoning. Top each serving with a sprinkling of parslied crumbs.

VARIATION

Cream of Cauliflower Soup with Broccoli

A combination of cauliflower and broccoli makes an attractive soup; use about half and half. Treat the broccoli in the same fashion—peeling the stem, chopping the rest roughly, and steaming it with the cauliflower. Top each serving with a dollop of sour cream rather than with the crumbs.

OTHER VARIATIONS

Any of the cream soups in the following velouté group may be adapted to the preceding rice purée system.

Cream Soups: Velouté

Start out with minced onions tenderly simmered in butter, stir in a little flour to make the roux that will lightly thicken the soup, and cook until the butter and flour are foaming nicely; moisten with a delicious chicken stock or milk or wine, then simmer a few minutes more. That's the traditional base for a myriad of

cream soups, be they based on chicken, mushrooms, artichokes, broccoli, or even fish.

MANUFACTURING NOTE: *Velouté soups are delicious and velvety when properly made, but they can be dismal and gluey when prepared by careless or untutored cooks. It is of greatest importance that the roux be sufficiently cooked, as described below, and that the soup have a preliminary simmer of least 10 minutes. Nothing difficult about that!*

CHICKEN STOCK NOTE: *When making vegetable soups, don't be too lavish with chicken stock, particularly canned stock. If it is too strong, you'll muffle the taste of such vegetables as broccoli and zucchini. Dilute the stock with some of the vegetable cooking liquid, as suggested for the broccoli soup farther on. No rules here; have trust in your own judgment of tastes.*

 MASTER RECIPE

Velouté Soup Base

For about 2 quarts

4 Tbs butter
¾ cup to 1½ cups minced onion and/or white of leek—the amount depending on your other ingredients
¼ cup flour
7 to 8 cups liquid: chicken or fish stock and/or milk or vegetable cooking liquid—of which at least 1 cup is hot
Salt and freshly ground white pepper

SPECIAL EQUIPMENT SUGGESTED:
A heavy-bottomed 3-quart stainless saucepan

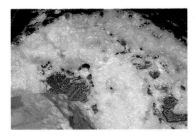

1. Cooking the butter and flour together to make a roux

2. Whisking the hot liquid into the roux

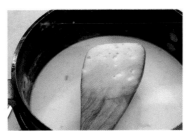

3. The liquid is thick enough to coat a wooden spoon.

4. Folding mushrooms into soup base

Set the saucepan over moderately low heat, add the butter, and, when melted, stir in the onions. Cover and cook slowly 7 to 8 minutes, or until the onions are tender and translucent. Blend in the flour. Stir slowly for 3 minutes, to cook the flour without letting it color, see illustration, step 1. Remove from heat, and in a few seconds, when bubbling stops, pour in 1 cup of hot liquid all at once, whisking vigorously to blend smoothly, step 2. Whisk in 6 more cups. Bring to the simmer, stirring, and simmer 10 minutes—stirring frequently to be sure the soup is not scorching on the bottom of the pan. The soup base should be slightly thickened, enough to coat a spoon lightly, step 3—add dollops more liquid if too thick. Correct seasoning, and continue as your recipe directs.

SPECIAL NOTE

Ahead-of-time note for roux-based soups and sauces: Warm flour-based soups and sauces will form a skin over their surface. The skin will not form if you stir the soup frequently until it is cool. Or fill a large kitchen spoon with stock or milk and lay the spoon just over the surface, tipping it to let the liquid float on top. Or lay a sheet of plastic wrap on top of the surface, pressing it in well.

VARIATION

Cream of Mushroom Soup

Use this as the general model for all velouté soups, and since the base itself is well flavored, the actual amount of other ingredients you add is not too important. For instance, the following recipe calls for 1 quart of mushrooms, but just a handful will give the mushroom impression.

For about 2¼ quarts, serving 6

Ingredients for the preceding Velouté Soup Base, made with 1 cup of hot chicken broth and 6 or more cups of milk
1 quart fresh mushrooms, trimmed, washed, and diced (page 314)
¼ tsp dried tarragon leaves
½ cup or more sour cream, heavy cream, or *crème fraîche*, optional
Salt and freshly ground white pepper
Drops of lemon juice, if needed

Suggested decoration:

Sprigs of fresh tarragon; or slivers of neatly sliced raw mushroom caps tossed in drops of lemon juice; or a fluted stewed mushroom cap (page 312) for each serving

SPECIAL EQUIPMENT SUGGESTED:
A food processor is useful for mincing the mushrooms

Finishing the soup and serving. Bring the soup base to the simmer, and fold in the mushrooms and tarragon, see illustration; simmer 10 minutes, stirring frequently to prevent scorching. Stir in the optional cream, simmer a moment more, and carefully correct seasoning, adding drops of lemon juice if you think they are needed. Decorate each serving, if you wish, as suggested.

Other Cream of Vegetable Soups

Make other vegetable soups in much the same way, either simmering the vegetables in the velouté base as for the preceding mushroom soup, or cooking them separately as for the following broccoli soup. Here the soup is puréed, and given a final decor of broccoli buds.

Cream of Broccoli Soup

For about 2½ quarts, serving 6 to 8

**2 large heads of fresh broccoli
    (1¼ to 1½ pounds)**
Salt and freshly ground white pepper
**Ingredients for the Velouté Soup
    Base**
**½ cup or more sour cream, heavy
    cream, or *crème fraîche,* optional**
Drops of lemon juice, if needed
2 Tbs butter, optional

SPECIAL EQUIPMENT SUGGESTED:
*An electric blender or a food proces-
sor—the blender does a faster and better job of puréeing—or a vegetable mill*

Preparing the broccoli. Wash the broccoli. Trim an inch or so off the
woody ends of each stem, and peel
the stems with a knife up to where
the bud branches begin, taking off a
scant ¹⁄₁₆ inch of the tough outer
green skin. Cut off the tiny branches
and bud ends of the broccoli flowerettes, and reserve. Cut the remaining
stalks into ¼-inch slices.

Preliminary cooking of the broccoli.
Place the sliced broccoli in a saucepan; add ½ inch of water and ¼ teaspoon of salt. Bring to the boil and
boil slowly uncovered 4 to 5 minutes,
adding a little more water if necessary, until the pieces are barely tender and a fine bright green. Drain
through a sieve set over a bowl, and
return the cooking liquid to the
saucepan. Purée the steamed broccoli
with a cup or so of the soup base,
pouring the purée back into the remaining soup—which will now be a

lovely fresh pale green. Simmer the
reserved broccoli buds in the cooking
liquid for 2 to 3 minutes, drain the
cooking liquid into another saucepan,
and boil down rapidly to less than 1
cup; pour the liquid into the soup
base. Meanwhile, run cold water
over the broccoli buds to set the
color, and reserve for the final
decoration.

*Ahead-of-time note: To preserve its
green color chill the soup uncovered.

Finishing the soup. Shortly before
serving, bring the soup to the simmer. Stir in the cream if you are
using it. Simmer 2 to 3 minutes uncovered—always watching that it
does not scorch! Taste carefully for
seasoning, adding lemon juice if you
think it needed. (*The broccoli buds:*
rather than leaving them as is, you
may wish to sauté them briefly in 2
tablespoons of butter.)

Serving. Pour the soup into a warmed
tureen for serving at the table, or
into warmed soup cups or plates.
Decorate with the broccoli buds.

To serve cold. See directions for the
following asparagus soup.

Cream of Asparagus Soup

This uses essentially the same method
as the preceding broccoli soup, but
since there are slight differences, here
are more details than usual.

For about 2 quarts

1 cup sliced onions
3 Tbs butter
**2 pounds fresh green asparagus,
    washed and butts trimmed**

2 quarts lightly salted boiling water
Salt
2 Tbs flour
Freshly ground white pepper
**½ cup or so heavy cream, *crème
    fraîche,* or sour cream, optional**
2 Tbs butter, optional

SPECIAL EQUIPMENT SUGGESTED:
*A food processor and a sieve set over a
bowl*

The soup base and the asparagus. Start
out with the soup base. Cook the onions and butter slowly in the saucepan
until tender and translucent. Meanwhile, cut 2½ to 3 inches of tender
green from the tip ends of the asparagus; drop them into the boiling water
and boil 3 minutes, or until barely
tender. Dip out with a skimmer (reserving water), and refresh the asparagus tips briefly in a bowl of cold
water to set the color; drain and reserve. Chop the remaining stalks into
½-inch lengths and add to the onions
with a sprinkling of salt. Cover and
cook slowly 5 minutes. Stir in the
flour and cook, stirring, 3 minutes
more. Remove from heat, and, when
bubbling stops, blend in the hot asparagus cooking water. Simmer uncovered 25 to 30 minutes, or until
tender enough to purée.

Puréeing the soup. Cut just the tips off
the blanched asparagus tops; cut the
tips lengthwise in halves or quarters
and reserve for final decoration. Add
the lower parts of the tips to the soup
base, and purée the soup. Then, to
remove asparagus strings, strain
through the sieve, pressing juices out
of ingredients. It will be a lovely pale
green color—to keep it that way, reheat it only just before serving. Carefully correct seasoning.

Ahead-of-time note: See Special Note, page 9.

To serve hot. Just before serving, reheat the soup to the simmer, stirring in cream if you are using it. Taste, and correct seasoning again. Decorate each serving with the reserved asparagus tips (use them as is, or sauté briefly in butter, if you wish).

To serve cold. Chill uncovered. Either stir in chilled cream (half a cup or so) and ladle into soup cups, or float a dollop of sour cream on the surface of each serving. Decorate with the reserved asparagus tips.

VARIATION

Cream of Carrot Soup: Potage Crécy

The same idea as the preceding asparagus, where a vegetable is cooked with the onions, then simmered with them and the rice before being puréed. Crécy, by the way, is a small town south of Paris, in the Seine et Marne district, where they would have us know that the best of the best carrots are grown. Thus any time you see Crécy as part of a recipe name you know what it contains. Is Crécy also famous for the French version of a certain cake, so popular in this country?

For about 2¼ quarts, serving 6

6 to 8 large carrots
Ingredients for the Rice and Onion Soup Base, page 6
½ cup or so sour cream, heavy cream, or *crème fraîche*, optional
Salt and freshly ground white pepper

SPECIAL EQUIPMENT SUGGESTED:
A vegetable steamer

The carrots. Trim and peel the carrots; reserve one for final decoration.

Soup carrots. Chop the remaining carrots roughly and stir them into the onions as you are sautéing them for the rice and onion soup base. When tender, continue with the recipe, simmering them with the rice, and puréeing the soup.

Decorative carrot. While the soup is simmering, shave the reserved carrot into strips 3 inches long with a vegetable peeler; steam several minutes over ½ inch of water until tender. Reserve uncovered. Reheat just before serving, and strew a small handful over each cup of soup.

SPECIAL NOTE

Other Vegetables for Soup

Celery, turnips, rutabagas, parsnips, and beets may be treated in the same general way as carrots.

Curried Onion Soup

For 2¼ quarts, serving 6

Ingredients for the Velouté Soup Base (page 8), using 4 cups sliced onions and 4 Tbs butter
1 Tbs fragrant curry powder
½ cup or so sour cream, heavy cream, or *crème fraîche*, optional

Decoration:
Minced fresh parsley, or a dollop of sour cream and faint dusting of curry powder for each serving

The soup. Sauté the onions for the soup base in the 4 tablespoons of butter, and, when tender, stir in the curry powder. Sauté 1 minute longer, stirring, then blend in the flour and continue as usual. Purée the soup or not, as you wish, and simmer a moment with the optional cream.

Serving. Decorate each serving with parsley or sour cream and curry powder.

VARIATION

Curried Fish Soup

For 2⅓ quarts, serving 6 to 8

Ingredients for the preceding Curried Onion Soup, but you may wish to use only 1 to 2 cups onions, and fish or chicken stock plus milk
1 pound (2 cups) or so very fresh-smelling lean fish fillets such as sole, halibut, trout, cod, hake, sea bass, pollack

The soup. Prepare the base for the Curried Onion Soup, and let it simmer its 20 minutes. Meanwhile, cut the fish into smallish bite-size pieces; when the soup is ready, stir in the optional cream and the fish. Simmer 2 to 3 minutes, and correct seasoning.

Serving. Serve as described for the Curried Onion Soup.

Cream of Corn Soup

Here is one of the great solutions for
fresh ears of corn that just aren't
quite fresh and tender enough to
make it alone on the cob.

For about 2¾ quarts, serving 6 to 8

**Ingredients for the Velouté Soup
Base (page 8), using 3 cups
chicken stock, 3 cups milk, plus
more milk or water later, as
needed
6 ears of fresh corn (about 1½ cups,
grated)
½ cup or so sour cream, heavy
cream, or** *crème fraîche,* **optional
Salt and freshly ground white pepper**

Decorative suggestions:

**Rings of red pepper sautéed slowly
in butter (3 per person); or 1 tsp
diced pimiento per serving; or a
mixture of cooked corn kernels
and parsley, floated on a spoonful
of sour cream; or minced chives
or parsley**

SPECIAL EQUIPMENT SUGGESTED:
*A corn grater is useful; a food processor,
blender, or vegetable mill if you wish to
purée the soup*

The soup. While the velouté base is
simmering, grate the corn—if you
have no special tool, run the cutting
edge of a small knife down the center
of each line of kernels, up-end an ear
over a pie plate, and scrape out the
pulp with the back of a knife. After
the velouté has simmered 15 minutes, add the corn and simmer 5
minutes more—stirring up frequently from the bottom of the pan to
prevent scorching. If too thick, add a
little milk and/or optional cream.

Purée the soup if you want a
smoother effect. Carefully correct
seasoning.

*Ahead-of-time note: This soup gains
in flavor when made an hour or more
in advance; see Special Note, page 9.

Serving. Bring to the simmer, stir in
a little cream if you wish, taste again
for seasoning, and serve either as it is
or with a decoration such as those
suggested.

Cream of Artichoke Soup

What to do with all that good arti-
choke-flavored cooking liquid when
you're making artichoke bottoms—
that's the real name of this soup. That
liquid is known as a *blanc,* a lemony
lightly thickened soup designed to
prevent the artichokes from darkening as they cook. It is a shame to
waste expensive artichoke flavor, especially when you could get some
meat off the discarded leaves, and
could easily cook 1 or 2 more bottoms for such an elegant soup.

MANUFACTURING NOTE: *Here the
lightly thickened artichoke cooking liquid serves as the velouté base, but it
needs simmering with sautéed onions to
give it more flavor. If the soup seems too
lemony, dilute it with milk or cream, or
make additional velouté base.*

For about 6 cups, serving 4 to 6

**¾ cup minced onions
2 Tbs butter
Ingredients for the recipe To Cook
Artichoke Bottoms (page 281).
Use the artichokes as you wish,
but cook 2 additional bottoms for
the soup; save the cooking liquid,
and save all the artichoke leaves.
Additional liquid as needed: milk,
cream, and/or light chicken broth**

Final decoration:

**1 to 2 Tbs butter for sautéing the
sliced artichoke bottoms; 2 Tbs
finely chopped fresh parsley**

SPECIAL EQUIPMENT SUGGESTED:
*A heavy-bottomed 1½-quart saucepan;
a vegetable mill with fine blade, or a
food processor and sieve*

The soup base. Sauté the onions in the
butter until tender and translucent—
6 to 8 minutes. Blend in the artichoke liquid and simmer 15 minutes,
stirring frequently and adding more
liquid if necessary, to prevent
scorching.

The artichokes. Meanwhile, drop the
discarded artichoke leaves in a kettle
of lightly salted boiling water, and
boil uncovered 20 minutes or so, until tender. Drain; refresh in cold
water. Scrape the tender flesh off the
inner bottom curves of the leaves—
labor-intensive but worth it—and
drop the flesh into the soup base.
Trim rough edges off the artichoke
bottoms and add the trimmings to the
soup. Place them hollow side down,
cut the artichoke bottoms into thin,
neat, vertical slices, and set aside.

Finishing the soup base. Simmer the trimmings and the flesh from the leaves 5 minutes in the soup base. Purée the base and return it to the saucepan. Add more liquid, if needed, and taste very carefully for seasoning.

*Ahead-of-time note: See Special Note, page 9.

Serving. Shortly before serving, heat the butter until bubbling, and gently warm the reserved artichoke slices, seasoning them lightly with salt, pepper, and a sprinkling of parsley. Ladle the soup into warmed soup cups, and decorate with the artichoke slices.

THE LEEK AND POTATO SOUP FAMILY

Delicious, fragrant, easy to make—that's the abiding charm of the leek and potato soup family. They are vegetable soups, and interestingly enough they are usually water-based, meaning that the fine fresh taste of the vegetables is not obscured by lashings of chicken stock.

Leeks and potatoes simmered in lightly salted water make a perfect soup in themselves even without the addition of a little cream, and are a perfect background for other additions such as watercress, spinach, and so forth. And when you're looking for a cold soup, for instance, chill plain old leek and potato and you have the famous Vichyssoise.

Onion Note: Of course you may substitute onions for leeks, but you won't get that wonderful pervading and special flavor that is the trademark of the leek.

 MASTER RECIPE

Leek and Potato Soup

Here is the mother of the family in all her simplicity. You'll note there's no chicken stock here, just water, leeks, potatoes, and salt in the soup base. However, you may include chicken stock if you wish, and you may certainly include milk. A bit of cream at the end is a nourishing touch, but by no means a necessity.

MANUFACTURING NOTE: *If you are not puréeing the soup, cut the vegetables rather neatly.*

For about 2½ quarts, serving 6 to 8

4 cups sliced leeks—the white part and a bit of the tender green (to clean leeks, see page 298)
4 cups diced potatoes—old or baking potatoes recommended
6 to 7 cups water
1½ to 2 tsp salt, or to taste
½ cup or more sour cream, heavy cream, or *crème fraîche*, optional

SPECIAL EQUIPMENT SUGGESTED: *A heavy-bottomed 3-quart saucepan with cover*

Simmering the soup. Bring the leeks, potatoes, and water to the boil in the saucepan. Salt lightly, cover partially, and simmer 20 to 30 minutes, or until the vegetables are tender. Taste, and correct seasoning.

SERVING SUGGESTIONS

Serving au Naturel

Ladle out the soup, and top each serving with a dollop of sour cream, if you wish.

Puréed Leek and Potato Soup

Purée the soup through a vegetable mill, or in a blender or food processor. Serve with the optional cream.

Cream of Leek and Potato Soup

Use a cup less liquid when simmering the soup. After puréeing, whisk ⅔ cup or more of sour cream, heavy cream, or *crème fraîche* into the soup, simmering a moment to blend.

Chilled Leek and Potato Soup: Vichyssoise

For about 2½ quarts, serving 6 to 8

Ingredients for the preceding Cream of Leek and Potato Soup, but using the white part of the leeks only
Chilled sour cream, heavy cream, or *crème fraîche*, optional
1 Tbs minced fresh chives or parsley

After chilling the soup, you may wish to stir in a little more cream. Taste carefully, and correct seasoning. Top each serving with ½ teaspoon of chives or parsley.

Watercress Soup

Watercress soup, hot or chilled—lovely to look at, delightful to sip, and one of the best versions is made with a leek and potato base.

For about 2½ quarts, serving 6 to 8

Ingredients for Leek and Potato Soup
A big bunch of watercress
½ cup or so sour cream, heavy cream, or *crème fraîche*, optional

Prepare the Leek and Potato Soup as directed. Meanwhile, wash the watercress and chop the stems roughly—you may wish to save out a handful of leaves for decoration. Stir the chopped cress into the soup during the last 5 minutes of simmering. Purée the soup, and serve with a topping of cream and a scattering of watercress leaves, if you wish.

VARIATIONS

Chilled Watercress Soup

Prepare the Watercress Soup as described, then follow the directions for Chilled Leek and Potato Soup.

Spinach Soup

Prepare Spinach Soup like Watercress Soup, roughly chopping 2 packages (20 ounces) of stemmed and well-washed fresh spinach, and simmering the leaves in the soup 4 to 5 minutes before puréeing. (Directions for stemming spinach are on page 277; note that the stems have nothing to recommend them—no color, no flavor, just nongastronomical bulk.)

Soupe du Jour

With your Leek and Potato Soup at hand, consider it as a base to which you can add all sorts of other vegetables either raw or cooked, such as cauliflower, brussels sprouts, carrots, green beans, turnips, broccoli, squash, pumpkin, and so forth and so on. If they are fresh, grate or chop them and simmer a few minutes in the soup before puréeing; if they are cooked, simply purée them with the soup.

THE BOUILLON-BASED SOUPS

Beef stock—beef bouillon—is the base for beef stews, rich brown sauces, and wonderful soups, such as French onion, oxtail, beef and vegetable. There's nothing like your own personal stock to give all of these soups your own special flavor.

 MASTER RECIPE

Brown Beef Stock—Beef Bouillon—Beef Broth

THE BONES TO CHOOSE. *Raw beef bones, some of them meaty, are what you want here, such as the shank, the neck, the knuckle; leg bones, too, plus any raw scraps you may have collected in your freezer—ribs, steak bones, and so forth. If the bones are too big, ask your butcher to chop them up, see illustration, step 1. An oxtail will give extra flavor and a pleasantly slightly gelatinous texture; you can either add the meat to a soup or turn it into the oxtail dumplings described farther on.*

1. Chopping bones with mallet and cleaver

2. Bones and vegetables after browning in the oven

3. Skimming off the scum

MANUFACTURING NOTE: *There is nothing fancy or elaborate about the following home-style stock, and no attempt to make it a production of la grande cuisine. To get a good brown color, however, you do want to brown the bones half an hour or so in a hot oven; the rest of the cooking is simply a matter of quiet and almost unattended simmering.*

For 3 to 4 quarts of stock

3 to 4 pounds (4 quarts or so) meaty
 raw beef bones sawed into pieces
 of 3 inches or less (see the
 preceding discussion of bones)
2 each: large carrots, onions, and
 celery ribs, roughly chopped
6 or more quarts cold water
A large-size herb bouquet plus 4
 allspice berries and 6 peppercorns
 (see Special Note, page 336)
2 large cloves of unpeeled garlic,
 smashed
1 large unpeeled tomato, cored and
 roughly chopped, or ½ cup
 canned Italian plum tomatoes
1½ tsp salt, plus more as needed
 later

SPECIAL EQUIPMENT SUGGESTED:
*A roasting pan for the bones; an 8-quart
kettle with cover for simmering the
stock; a colander and fine-meshed sieve
for straining*

Browning the bones—30 to 40 minutes.
Preheat the oven to 450°F. Arrange
the bones and ½ cup each of the
chopped vegetables in the roasting
pan and brown in the upper third of
the oven, turning and basting with
accumulated fat several times until
they are a good walnut brown, step
2. Scoop bones and vegetables into
the kettle; pour out and discard accumulated fat.

Deglazing the roasting pan. Pour 2
cups of the water into the pan and
bring to the boil over moderately
high heat; using a wooden spoon,
scrape browning juices into the liquid, then pour the liquid over the
browned bones in the kettle.

Simmering the stock—4 to 5 hours.
Add the herb bouquet to the kettle
and the rest of the vegetables listed,
with enough of the water to cover the
ingredients by 2 inches. Bring to the
simmer on top of the stove; skim off
and discard gray scum that will collect on the surface for several minutes, step 3. Add 1½ teaspoons salt.
Cover loosely, and maintain at the
slow simmer, skimming off fat and
scum occasionally, and adding a little
boiling water if the liquid has evaporated below the surface of the ingredients. Simmer until you feel the
bones have given their all.

Straining and degreasing. Strain the
stock through the colander into a
bowl, pressing juices out of the ingredients. Degrease the stock—directions are on page 242—and season
lightly to taste. Strain again, this
time through the fine-meshed sieve
into a clean pan or container.

*Ahead-of-time note: May be prepared
in advance; chill uncovered, then
cover and refrigerate or freeze.

CONSOMMÉS AND ASPICS

Clarification of Stocks

Both consommés and aspics are made
of meat, fish, or poultry stock that is
sparkling clear. All the minute float-
ing particles of this and that which
cloud the stock have been drawn off,
and the clarified liquid not only is
beautiful to look at but has acquired a
subtle refinement of taste. Again
there is nothing difficult about clari-
fying stock—it is heated with egg
whites, then strained—but this really
magical process takes a little time.

 MASTER RECIPE

To Clarify Stock

For about 4 cups

5 cups fully degreased cold meat or
 poultry stock, such as the
 preceding beef stock (see notes
 following for using weak stock or
 canned broths)
4 egg whites (½ cup)

SPECIAL EQUIPMENT SUGGESTED:
*A very clean 2-quart saucepan for the
stock; a large clean ladle; straining
equipment—a sieve lined with 3 thicknesses of washed cheesecloth set in a colander over a bowl (see illustration)*

Combining stock and egg whites. Whisk
1 cup of the cold stock in a bowl with
the egg whites while bringing the
rest of the stock to the simmer in the
saucepan. Remove from heat and
whisk 1 cup of the hot stock by dribbles into the egg white mixture, then
slowly whisk the egg white mixture
into the saucepan of hot stock.

The clarification process. Set the saucepan over moderate heat and, whisking slowly to keep the egg whites in
gentle but constant circulation
throughout the liquid, bring just to
the simmer. At once stop whisking.
(The egg whites will have clung to
the bits of matter that cloud the stock
and will rise to the surface; they must
now coagulate firmly enough so that
when you strain the stock the egg
whites will hold together, allowing
the clear liquid to drip through.) Set
the pan at the side of the heat so the
stock barely bubbles in that area; let
it barely bubble for 5 minutes. Ro-

Ladling cloudy stock through cheesecloth

To Clarify Stock (*continued*)

tate the pan a quarter turn and repeat the process for 5 minutes; rotate the pan again and let bubble a final 5 minutes.

Straining. Making sure that the bottom of the sieve will be well above the level of the liquid once it is strained, gently ladle the stock with the coagulated egg whites into the sieve and let the miraculously clear sparkling liquid drip through undisturbed, as illustrated. (Do not squeeze the cheesecloth, or cloudy liquid will come through.)

*Ahead-of-time note: When the stock is cold, you may refrigerate it for several days in a covered container, or freeze it for several months.

MANUFACTURING NOTE: *To give character to weak stock, blend ½ cup of perfectly lean chopped beef (or chicken or turkey breast), ½ cup of finely chopped leek, and a small handful of chopped fresh parsley with the raw egg whites before you combine them with the cup of cold stock at the beginning of the clarification.*

SPECIAL NOTE

Using Canned Broth or Bouillon

Simmer canned chicken broth for 30 minutes with just enough canned beef bouillon to color it lightly, plus ¼ cup each of minced carrots, celery, onions, and dry white wine or vermouth. Strain, and you have a respectable stock substitute.

VARIATION

Consommé

If your stock was strong and well flavored to begin with, it is now consommé; however, you may wish to add a few tablespoons of Port wine.

Aspic

For 4 cups of aspic, soften 2½ tablespoons of unflavored gelatin in ¼ cup of Port or Madeira wine (or in Cognac or dry white French vermouth for clear chicken stock). Stir the gelatin mixture into the hot clarified stock as soon as it has dripped through into the bowl.

Jellied Consommé

Follow the same system, using only 1 tablespoon of gelatin.

SOUPS USING
A BEEF STOCK BASE

Beef and Vegetable Soup

This colorful minestrone-type soup could well be a main course, especially when you include the meat and beef-marrow croutons in the serving suggestions following the main recipe.

For 2½ quarts, serving 6

2 Tbs butter
1 cup each: finely and neatly diced carrots, onions, leeks, and tender celery ribs
2 quarts Brown Beef Stock—or canned beef bouillon slightly diluted if necessary so it is not too strong
½ cup neatly diced turnips
½ cup orzo (rice-shaped pasta), or quick-cooking tapioca, or raw rice
1½ cups shredded green outer leaves of cabbage
¾ cup peeled, seeded, and neatly diced tomatoes
¾ cup cooked or canned red or white beans, optional
Salt and freshly ground pepper

SPECIAL EQUIPMENT SUGGESTED:
A heavy-bottomed 3-quart saucepan

The soup. Melt the butter in the saucepan, stir in the diced carrots, onions, leeks, and celery, and sauté 2 minutes. Pour in the stock, add the turnips and orzo, tapioca, or rice, and simmer 10 to 15 minutes, or until the vegetables are tender. Meanwhile, drop the cabbage into a pan of boiling water and boil uncovered 2 to 3 minutes, until limp; drain, run cold water over it to set the color, and reserve.

Ahead-of-time note: May be prepared in advance; chill uncovered, then cover and refrigerate.

Finishing the soup. Just before serving, bring the soup to the simmer with the cabbage, diced tomatoes, and the cooked beans if you are using them. Taste carefully, and correct seasoning. Serve the soup as it is, or in one of the following ways.

Ingredients for oxtail soup

Serving Suggestions: Oxtail Soup

If you have included oxtails among the bones for your beef stock, brown them along with the rest of the bones, and let them simmer in the stock for about 2 hours, or until the meat can be removed from the bones—a picky job! Cut off bits of fat and gristle, reserve the meat, and return the remains and bones to simmer with the stock. After sautéing the diced vegetables in the preceding recipe, add all or part of the meat along with the turnips, stock, etc., for the 10- to 15-minute simmer. Finish the soup as described. Or you may wish to turn all or some of the meat into the following dumplings.

Oxtail Variation: Oxtail Dumplings

What else to do with that scrappy, shreddy, but delicious meat that you have dug out of those oxtails? Turn it into oxtail dumplings to garnish the soup, or let it be a meat loaf, sauté it hamburger-fashion, or consider it a stuffing for braised vegetables. The meat of just one oxtail provides the following.

For about 2 cups

1 large clove of garlic
1 large onion
2 Tbs butter
½ cup lightly pressed down parsley
   leaves
1 cup, approximately, cooked oxtail
   meat
3 ounces sausage meat (¾ cup or 3
   links)—for texture and flavor
⅓ cup lightly pressed crumbs from
   fresh white homemade type
   bread—as a binder
1 "large" egg
Salt, freshly ground pepper, and
   thyme
2 to 3 Tbs grated Swiss or Parmesan
   cheese

SPECIAL EQUIPMENT SUGGESTED:
A food processor

Garlic and onions. Peel the garlic and chop roughly by hand; with the machine running, drop it in. Peel the onion, chop roughly by hand, and pulse it several seconds in the machine to dice it. Scrape into a small frying pan and sauté slowly in the butter until tender—5 minutes or so.

The rest of the ingredients. With the machine running, drop in the parsley, then the oxtail meat, sausage, crumbs, egg, sautéed onions and garlic and a modest amount of seasoning. Scrape into a mixing bowl and blend in the cheese; sauté a spoonful in the small frying pan, taste carefully, and correct seasoning. The mixture is now ready to be formed.

*Ahead-of-time notes: Two cups will make 3 dozen or so dumplings, and you'll probably want only 3 or 4 per serving. You may freeze the mixture either at this point or after cooking the dumplings as described in the next step.

To use as dumplings. Rapidly take up tablespoon gobs of the dumpling mixture and nudge with a rubber spatula into a pan of simmering beef stock or of lightly salted water; cook at just below the simmer 5 to 6 minutes. Slip them into a bowl of cold water to firm them for 2 minutes, then drain them on paper towels. Add them to warm in the soup just before serving.

Serving of soup with beef marrow croutons

Removing beef marrow

SPECIAL NOTE

Poached Beef Marrow

Marrow is the fatty filling of beef leg bones. It's a pleasing topping for soup croutons, and it also goes into red-wine sauces and flavored butters. A shame to waste it!

For ½ to ⅔ cup

3 or 4 bone-in beef shin slices ¾ inch thick, or 2 or 3 beef marrow (leg) bones

SPECIAL EQUIPMENT SUGGESTED:
A cleaver or heavy knife and hammer for marrow bones

Removing the marrow. Trying to keep the marrow in big pieces, scoop it out of the shin slices with a small knife. Or stand a longish leg bone on end, poise the cleaver at one side of the bone where it meets the marrow, and whack with the hammer to split bone from marrow. Repeat on another side if necessary, then dig out the marrow with a knife. Before cutting the marrow into ⅜-inch slices or ½-inch dice, first dip your knife in boiling water; refrigerate the marrow until you are ready to use it.

To poach marrow. Shortly before serving, drop it into a pan of hot (not simmering), lightly salted water for a moment to soften; dip it out with a slotted spoon.

Serving suggestion. Arrange marrow slices over Hard-Toasted French Bread Rounds (page 24). After ladling the soup into warmed soup plates, top with the marrow croutons and a sprinkling of grated Swiss or Parmesan cheese.

French Onion Soup

This is certainly one of the all-time favorites. The canned and packaged onion soups I've tried have been very good, and the only way to better them is for you to have your own beautiful beef stock. However, bought onion soup will benefit from the flavor additions suggested here.

TIMING: *For the most delicious results, you want a slow simmer of 2 ¾ to 3 hours.*

For about 2½ quarts, serving 6

3 Tbs butter
1 Tbs light olive oil or fresh peanut oil
8 cups thinly sliced onions (2½ pounds)
½ tsp each salt and sugar (sugar helps the onions to brown)
2 Tbs flour
2½ quarts homemade beef stock, page 14, at least 2 cups of which should be hot
4 to 5 Tbs Cognac, Armagnac, or other good brandy
1 cup dry white French vermouth

SPECIAL EQUIPMENT SUGGESTED:
A food processor with slicing blade or a hand slicer is useful for the onions; a heavy-bottomed 3-quart saucepan with cover for onion cooking and simmering

Browning the onions—40 minutes. Set the saucepan over moderate heat with the butter and oil; when the butter has melted, stir in the onions, cover the pan, and cook slowly until tender and translucent, about 10 minutes. Blend in the salt and sugar, raise heat to moderately high, and let the onions brown, stirring frequently until they are a dark walnut color, 25 to 30 minutes.

Simmering the soup. Sprinkle in the flour and cook slowly, stirring, for another 3 to 4 minutes. Remove from heat, let cool a moment, then whisk in 2 cups of hot stock. When well blended, bring to the simmer, adding the rest of the stock, the Cognac or brandy, and the vermouth. Cover loosely, and simmer very slowly 1½ hours, adding a little water if the liquid reduces too much. Correct seasoning.

*Ahead-of-time note: May be prepared in advance; chill uncovered, then cover and refrigerate or freeze.

Serving. Serve the soup as it is, accompanying it with French bread and a bowl of grated Swiss or Parmesan cheese, or gratiné it as follows.

VARIATION

Onion Soup Gratinéed

When onion soup is a main course, bake it in the oven with cheese and toasted French bread, and bring it all crusty and bubbling to the table. A big salad, more bread and cheese, and fruit could finish the meal, accompanied by a bottle or two of fruity white wine, like a sauvignon blanc or even a gewürztraminer.

MANUFACTURING NOTE: *Be sure you have a homemade type of bread with body here because flimsy loaves will disintegrate into a slimy mass; a recipe for your own homemade French bread is on page 37.*

Onion Soup Gratinéed (*continued*)

For about 2½ quarts, serving 6

**12 or more Hard-Toasted French
Bread Rounds (page 24)**
**1 to 2 ounces Swiss cheese, very
thinly sliced**
**Ingredients for the preceding French
Onion Soup, heated**
**¾ to 1 cup finely grated Swiss or
Parmesan cheese**

SPECIAL EQUIPMENT SUGGESTED:
*A lightly buttered 3-quart ovenproof
casserole or baking dish about 3 inches
deep—good-looking if possible*

*Assembling and baking—about 30 min-
utes.* Preheat the oven to 425°F and
set the rack in the lower middle
level. Line the bottom of the casserole with half the slices of toasted
French bread, and spread over them
the sliced cheese. Ladle on the hot
onion soup and float over them a
layer of toasted bread, topping with
the grated cheese. At once set in the
preheated oven and bake 20 to 30
minutes, until the cheese has melted
and browned nicely. Serve as soon as
possible—if you dally too long, the
toast topping may sink into the soup.

CHOWDERS AND OTHER FISH SOUPS

Although you can serve a cup
of chowder or fish soup to
begin a meal, big bowls of it make a
wonderfully satisfying main course
for informal luncheons and family
suppers. When you follow with a
salad and cheese, and finish off with a
fruit dessert, everyone is happy and
well fed. One of my favorites is the
New England chowder with its base
of salt pork, potatoes, milk, and
plenty of onions. Next is the Mediterranean type with its olive oil, onions, garlic, and tomatoes. We'll start
off with a New England clam chowder, but first here's an all-purpose
chowder base to which you add
clams, fish, corn—and it makes a
dandy soup just as it is.

 MASTER RECIPE

All-Purpose Chowder Base

For about 2 quarts

⅔ cup (4 ounces) diced salt pork
1 Tbs butter
3 cups sliced onions
1 bay leaf
**¾ cup crumbled "common" crackers
or pilot biscuit; or crumbs from
fresh homemade type white bread**
**4 cups liquid: clam-steaming juices
and water; or water and fish
stock; or light chicken broth**
**1 pound sliced or diced "boiling"
potatoes (3 to 3½ cups)**
Salt and freshly ground white pepper
2 cups milk and/or light cream

Clams for chowder

The salt pork and onions. To freshen
the salt pork and remove excess salt,
blanch it by simmering in the saucepan with 1 quart of water for 5 minutes; drain in a sieve and rinse under
cold water. Sauté slowly with the butter in the saucepan 5 minutes or so,
until the pork has rendered fat and
begins to brown. Stir in the onions,
add the bay leaf, cover, and cook
slowly 8 to 10 minutes, until the onions are tender and translucent. Turn
them into a sieve to drain out excess
fat, return them to the pan, and
blend in crackers or bread crumbs.

The potatoes. Pour the 4 cups of liquid into the onion pan. Add the potatoes, bring to the boil, and simmer,
loosely covered, for 20 minutes.
Blend in the milk and/or cream,
bring to the simmer, taste, and correct seasoning. (The milk goes in
now to prevent the possibility of
curdling.)

*Ahead-of-time note: May be completed a day in advance. Refrigerate;
cover when chilled.

Pork and/or fat-free notes: You may
omit the salt pork, and sauté the onions in 3 tablespoons of butter. Or,
for a fat-free chowder, simmer the
onions in 2 or 3 cups of the stock,
and, when tender, continue with the
recipe.

New England Clam Chowder

This is the real old New England type with onions, salt pork, potatoes, and clams—if you can't buy them fresh, minced canned clams will do nicely, or even no clams, because the soup base is a meal in itself.

TIMING NOTE: *Chowders always pick up added flavor when made several hours or a day in advance.*

For 2½ quarts, serving 6 to 8

The clams

24 medium hard-shell chowder clams, scrubbed and soaked (see Special Note, page 22)
1 cup water
Ingredients for the preceding All-Purpose Chowder Base

Decorative suggestions:

2 or 3 whole steamed clams in their shells per person; chopped fresh parsley

SPECIAL EQUIPMENT SUGGESTED:
A kettle or large saucepan with tight-fitting cover; a 4-quart heavy-bottomed saucepan with cover for the chowder; a food processor is useful

The clams. Place the scrubbed and soaked clams in the kettle, add the water, bring to the boil, cover the kettle, and let steam 3 to 4 minutes, just until most of the shells have opened. Remove the opened clams and steam the rest 2 minutes longer, then discard any unopened clams. Remove the meats to a bowl, and, being careful not to include any sand in the bottom of the kettle, decant the steaming liquid—which goes into your chowder base.

New England Clam Chowder

Finishing the chowder. Prepare the chowder base. Meanwhile grind clam meats in a processor or chop by hand—you should have 1½ to 2 cups. Fold the clams into the finished chowder base.

*Ahead-of-time note: May be completed in advance to this point. When cool, cover and refrigerate.

Serving. Just before serving, bring the chowder to below the simmer, thinning out if necessary with more milk—careful here, since clams toughen when overheated or boiled. Taste carefully and correct seasoning. Serve as is, or decorated as suggested.

Suggested accompaniments: Serve toasted and buttered split common crackers, chowder crackers, or pilot biscuit; or English muffins, split, toasted, and buttered.

NOTE: Common crackers can be ordered from a number of New England mail-order houses.

Fish Chowder

Like so many regional dishes, there is no "authentic" one-and-only genuine recipe for a New England fish chowder; however, it should contain onions, potatoes, and salt pork along with the fish—which may be fresh or frozen, as long as it smells and tastes wonderfully fresh. An ingredient that will foster authenticity, though, is fish stock. You can make a fine chowder without it, but here, in the Special Note on page 23, is how to go about cooking a fish stock if you live near the source and can find the only basic requirement, fish frames—the heads and bones that are often thrown out when the fish has been filleted.

New England Fish Chowder

For 2½ quarts, serving 6 to 8

Ingredients for the All-Purpose Chowder Base
2 to 2½ pounds boneless and skinless lean fish cut into 2-inch chunks, such as cod, hake, haddock, monkfish, halibut, ocean pollack, sea bass, catfish— all one kind or a mixture

Decorative suggestions:
A dollop of sour cream for each serving; a sprinkling of fresh chopped parsley

When the potatoes in the chowder base are tender, add the milk and/or cream and the fish. Simmer 2 to 3 minutes, or just until the fish is opaque rather than translucent, and lightly springy. Taste carefully, and correct seasoning.

*Ahead-of-time note: May be completed to this point. When cool, cover and refrigerate. You will take your chances keeping it warm on a hot plate because the milk can curdle.

To serve. Ladle into warmed wide soup plates, top with the optional dollop of sour cream and parsley sprinkle, and accompany with the same suggestions as for the preceding New England Clam Chowder.

VARIATION

Chowder with Dried Codfish or Finnan Haddie

Codfish and finnan haddie are wonderful chowder fish. For codfish, I think it best to de-salt and poach it as described on page 131; use the poaching liquid in the chowder base, and add the fish to the chowder at the end, just before serving. For finnan haddie, poach it first in the milk called for, adding more if needed; add milk and poached fish to the chowder base when the potatoes are tender.

New England Fish Bake
Fish baked with potatoes and onions

As long as we are on a chowder-base spree, the same general method can be used for oven-baked fish fillets or thin steaks. In Down-East Maine I've eaten it with fresh haddock fillets, first lightly salted and left to cure in the refrigerator overnight—a nice touch if it appeals to you. But any fish suitable for baking takes well to this comfortable rusticity.

For 6 servings

Ingredients for the All-Purpose Chowder Base—omit the 4 cups of liquid but not the milk
1 Tbs butter
2 to 2½ pounds thick skinless and boneless lean fish fillets, or ½-inch-thick steaks, such as cod, hake, eastern halibut, ocean pollack, catfish, petrale sole
Salt and freshly ground white pepper
1 cup flour on a plate
Fresh salt pork fat, clarified butter, or peanut oil
½ to ⅔ cup crumbs from fresh homemade type white bread
2 to 3 Tbs melted butter, optional

SPECIAL EQUIPMENT SUGGESTED:
A 10-inch no-stick frying pan; a buttered 2½-quart baking dish, such as a 7½- by 12-inch rectangle 2 inches deep; a bulb baster

The base. Prepare the base with the pork and onions, simmering the sliced potatoes in the 2 cups of milk, adding a little more if needed.

The fish. Meanwhile, prepare the fish, which wants a quick sauté before baking; otherwise it exudes too much liquid and waters down the sauce. Score the fillets on the skin side (page 81) and season lightly with salt and pepper. The moment before sautéing, dredge half the fish in the flour and shake off excess. Film the pan with a ¹⁄₁₆-inch layer of fat, butter, or oil, and when very hot sauté the fish a minute on each side. Repeat with the remaining fish.

Assembling. Spread half of the potatoes and onions in the buttered baking dish. Arrange over them the fish in a slightly overlapping layer. Cover with the remaining potatoes and pour on any milk remaining in the pan. Spread the bread crumbs over all; drizzle on the optional butter.

*Ahead-of-time note: May be prepared several hours ahead to this point; cover and refrigerate.

Baking 35 to 40 minutes at 400°F. About 45 minutes before serving, set in the upper middle level of a preheated 400°F oven and bake, tipping the dish and basting with accumulated liquid once or twice. It is done when bubbling throughout and the crumbs have begun to brown lightly. Do not overcook or the fish will dry out.

Suggested accompaniments: A salad or coleslaw, or fresh spinach steamed and buttered, plus French bread or hot biscuits. What white wine to serve? A Mâcon, Chablis, or sauvignon, a chenin blanc or riesling, or perhaps a blush wine.

New England Corn Chowder

There's no fish here, but it's the same New England base of salt pork, onions, and potatoes. This is a most American recipe, and a fine use for out-of-season corn on the cob.

For about 2½ quarts, serving 6 to 8

Ingredients for the All-Purpose Chowder Base
10 to 12 ears of fresh corn, grated; or 2½ to 3 cups (20 to 24 ounces) cream-style canned or frozen corn

Optional additions:
2 red or green bell peppers, chopped and sautéed briefly in butter; sour cream for topping the chowder

The chowder. When the potatoes in the chowder base are tender, stir in the milk or cream, the corn, and the optional sautéed peppers. Bring to the simmer for 2 to 3 minutes, and correct seasoning.

*Ahead-of-time note: May be completed to this point. When cool, cover and refrigerate.

Serving. Ladle into warmed soup cups or plates, top with optional dollops of sour cream, and accompany with hot biscuits, crackers, or melba toast.

MEDITERRANEAN FISH SOUPS

With this heady base of olive oil, onions, garlic, saffron, and tomatoes almost any fish will take on a Provençal flavor. But not all Mediterranean

Simple Fish Stock

For 2 quarts or so

2 or more fine fresh fish frames (3 to 4 quarts), see illustration, page 81, as large and meaty as you can find, from lean fish such as sole, flounder, cod, hake, haddock, sea bass, halibut
2½ to 3 quarts lightly salted water

Wash the fish frames, cut out and discard the gills (pairs of feathery red tissues attached to either side of the throat). Whack the head and bones into pieces that will fit into a roomy kettle. Pour in the water to cover and bring to the boil. Skim off scum for the few minutes it continues to rise; cover loosely and simmer 20 minutes. Strain, and that is all there is to a fish stock.

*Ahead-of-time note: Refrigerate; cover when cold. The stock will keep a day or two, or may be frozen.

soups have to be the traditional bouillabaisse, which is a real production with its whole fish served on a platter and its soup in a tureen. Much easier to cook, serve, and eat, but equally magnificent in taste, are chunks of fish simmered in a Mediterranean soup base. Serve with red garlic sauce—the classic rouille—toasted rounds of French bread, and you have a first-rate main course. Here's the typical soup base with its nostalgic aromas of garlic, onions, olive oil, and tomatoes.

MASTER RECIPE

All-Purpose Mediterranean Soup Base

For about 3 quarts

½ cup fruity olive oil
2 cups sliced onions
8 large cloves of unpeeled garlic, chopped
3 cups chopped fresh tomatoes, cored but unpeeled
2 cups canned Italian plum tomatoes
Seasonings: ½ tsp thyme, ¼ tsp fennel seeds, 3 pinches saffron threads (or ¼ tsp turmeric), and a 3- by 1-inch piece of dried orange peel (or ½ tsp bottled dried peel)
2 quarts liquid: fish stock (page 23), or water plus bottled clam juice or chicken broth
Salt and freshly ground pepper to taste

SPECIAL EQUIPMENT SUGGESTED:
A 6-quart heavy-bottomed kettle

Heat the olive oil in the kettle, add the onions, and sauté 8 to 10 minutes, stirring frequently, until tender but not brown. Stir in the garlic, tomatoes, and seasonings; simmer 3 to 4 minutes, then pour in the liquid. Salt lightly to taste, and boil slowly, loosely covered, for 45 minutes. Strain, pressing juices out of the ingredients, and return the resulting liquid to the pan. Taste carefully for seasoning.

*Ahead-of-time note: Refrigerate; cover when cold. Will keep several days; may be frozen.

SPECIAL NOTE

Hard-Toasted French Bread Rounds: Croûtes

For 18 rounds

1 loaf of French bread 16 inches long—the homemade type with body
½ cup or so olive oil, optional
1 cup grated Parmesan, hard Jack, or Swiss cheese, optional

Slice the bread into rounds ¾ inch thick, arrange in one layer on a baking sheet or sheets, and dry out for 25 to 30 minutes in a preheated 325°F oven, until a light brown and crisp through. If you wish, baste with the olive oil halfway through the baking. As a final touch, again if you wish, spread the toasted rounds with a ¼-inch layer of grated cheese, drizzle on a few drops of oil, and brown lightly under the broiler.

*Ahead-of-time note: May be done in advance and kept in a warming oven for an hour, or wrap and freeze them.

Santa Barbara Fish Stew

Santa Barbara Fish Stew

This appeared on one of our "Dinner" TV shows, taped in Santa Barbara, and I've kept the name here as a reminder that you can make a fine Mediterranean-type fish soup anywhere, as long as you have the makings for that colorful base.

For 2½ quarts, serving 6 to 8

The preceding All-Purpose Mediterranean Soup Base
2 to 2½ pounds skinless and boneless lean fish cut into 2-inch chunks, such as cod, hake, halibut, sea bass, monkfish, catfish, snapper—can be all one kind, but a variety is preferable
Salt and freshly ground pepper
2 or 3 Hard-Toasted French Bread Rounds per serving (see recipe preceding)

Red Garlic Sauce: Rouille

This marvelous sauce for all garlic lovers makes any fine fish soup even more splendid. Use it also on pasta, boiled potatoes, boiled fish, poached eggs—on anything, in fact, that would enjoy being associated with a big touch of garlic and pimiento. You could, of course, add chili peppers, but I shall leave it for you to provide that touch of the great American Southwest.

For 1½ cups, serving 6 to 8

6 large cloves of garlic, peeled
¼ tsp salt
18 or so large leaves of fresh basil,
or 1½ tsp dried savory, oregano,
or thyme
¾ cup lightly pressed down crumbs
from homemade type fresh white
bread
2 to 3 Tbs hot soup (or milk)
3 egg yolks
⅓ cup canned red pimientos, drained
¾ to 1 cup fruity olive oil
Drops of hot pepper sauce
Salt and freshly ground pepper

SPECIAL EQUIPMENT SUGGESTED:
A mortar and pestle, or a heavy bowl and pounding instrument of some sort; a garlic press and hand-held electric beater are useful

MANUFACTURING NOTE: *It is essential here that the garlic be puréed into a fine paste—the food processor or blender chops rather than purées. Although you could use the processor rather than mixer at the point where you add the egg yolks and oil, it hardly seems worthwhile for a small quantity of sauce.*

The sauce. Purée the garlic in a heavy bowl, add the salt, and pound into a paste. Continue pounding while adding the herbs; when well mashed and blended, pound in the bread crumbs and soup base or milk. When they have formed a paste, pound in the egg yolks, then the pimientos. At this point switch to the electric beater or a whisk, and beat a minute or more, until thicker and sticky. Finally, start beating in the oil by small driblets, as though making a mayonnaise. This should be a thick, heavy sauce. Season to taste with the pepper sauce, and salt and pepper.

*Ahead-of-time note: May be made a day in advance; cover and refrigerate. Let come to room temperature before stirring up, to avoid possible curdling.

1½ cups Red Garlic Sauce (see
recipe above)
1 cup chopped fresh parsley
1½ cups grated Parmesan or hard
Jack cheese

SPECIAL EQUIPMENT SUGGESTED:
A 6-quart heavy-bottomed saucepan or soup kettle with cover

The soup base. While completing the soup base as directed, prepare the fish. Bring the soup base to the boil shortly before serving.

Adding the fish. Fold the fish into the soup base, bring to the boil again, and boil slowly 2 to 3 minutes, just until the fish is opaque rather than translucent, and lightly springy to the touch. Correct seasoning.

*Ahead-of-time note: May be kept warm (but not near the simmer) for half an hour or so on an electric hot plate, but be very careful that the fish does not overcook.

Serving. Place 2 or 3 rounds of hard-toasted French bread in each warmed wide soup plate, top with a spoonful of the rouille, ladle on fish, then soup, and finish with a sprinkling of parsley. Pass the grated cheese separately.

Soupe de Poisson Provençale
Purée of Mediterranean Fish Soup

You'll see this more often than a bouillabaisse in bistros on the Mediterranean coast. It has the same soup base, but the best and fanciest are made of tiny rockfish. However, use any reasonably priced fish like ocean pollack (or fresh fish heads, like cod or hake), whatever is lean (not mackerel!), fresh smelling, and inexpensive.

For 2½ quarts, serving 6 to 8

Ingredients for the preceding Santa Barbara Fish Stew

SPECIAL EQUIPMENT SUGGESTED:
A vegetable mill with medium blade

Do not strain the finished soup base; add the fish to it and simmer 3 or 4 minutes, then purée through the vegetable mill into another saucepan or a hot soup tureen. To serve, ladle the soup onto rouille-topped toasted bread rounds.

Mediterranean Fish in Aspic

Here is a beautiful idea for a summer luncheon, an aspic showing forth all the fine flavors of Provence, served with a red garlic sauce. It's a free-form idea, and here is how this particular version is done—it's a good idea to start it the day before, since an aspic cannot be hurried. It takes its own time to chill and set during its various stages.

For 2½ quarts, serving 8 to 10

Ingredients for the Santa Barbara Fish Stew
4 egg whites (½ to ⅔ cup)
¼ cup unflavored gelatin dissolved in a small bowl with ⅓ cup dry white wine or French vermouth
4 cooked shrimp
⅔ cup diced red pimiento tossed with ½ tsp olive oil
1 medium clove of garlic puréed with ¼ tsp salt (page 350)
½ cup chopped fresh parsley
Salt and freshly ground pepper
6 to 8 slices of tomato, halved crosswise, chilled
Red Garlic Sauce (see Special Note, page 25)

SPECIAL EQUIPMENT SUGGESTED:
A 6-cup mold or dish to hold the aspic

The fish. Make the soup base as described in the master recipe, and poach the fish in it. Let it steep in the soup base for 20 minutes or longer, to pick up its flavor. Remove and drain the fish, flake it with a fork, and refrigerate in a covered bowl.

The aspic. Following the illustrated details on page 16, strain the soup liquid into a stainless saucepan, and degrease it—you should have about 6 cups. Beat 1 cup of it gradually into the egg whites, and whisk it gradually back into the saucepan. Bring almost to the simmer, whisking, and without stirring again let it sit over the heat 15 minutes, rotating the pan a quarter turn twice as the egg whites draw the cloudy particles to them while coagulating. Carefully ladle through a sieve lined with 3 thicknesses of damp washed cheesecloth. While still warm, stir in the dissolved gelatin. You should have a lovely, clear, pink-tinged, and delicious liquid.

Assembling. Pour ½ inch of the aspic into the mold; chill until set. Halve the shrimp horizontally, and arrange decoratively over the aspic layer. Chill ½ cup of aspic until almost set. Meanwhile, mix together the pimiento and garlic. Fold the chilled aspic into the flaked fish along with the pimiento and parsley. Taste, and correct seasoning; chill if necessary. Spoon the chilled fish mixture into the mold, keeping a ⅜-inch space between it and the side of the mold. Chill the remaining aspic until almost set; pour it around and on top of the fish. Cover and refrigerate for several hours.

Serving. Unmold the aspic onto a chilled platter, and decorate with the halved tomato slices. Accompany with the sauce, a bowl of black Mediterranean olives, French bread, and a tossed green salad. A chilled Chablis or Alsatian riesling would go nicely, or a cool red wine, like a light Beaujolais or Gamay.

Mediterranean Fish in Aspic

SPECIAL NOTE

To Unmold an Aspic

Always mold an aspic in a metal bowl or mold; metal reacts quickly to hot and cold, and that's what you want for easy unmolding.

Hot Water Method. Have a chilled serving platter at your side. Fill a much larger bowl with very hot water, and dip the mold in it—up to as near the rim of the mold as you dare—for several seconds. Remove the mold and rapidly run a small thin sharp knife around the inside edge between the aspic and the mold. Turn the platter upside down over the mold and reverse the two, giving the mold a sharp downward shake and a slap on the bottom. If the aspic does not budge, repeat, and repeat again if necessary, running the knife around the edge of the aspic again, and covering the mold with several thicknesses of towel dipped in very hot water. (Too many repeats, of course, and you'll melt the aspic.) Refrigerate the unmolded aspic for 10 minutes or so, covered with an upturned bowl, then clean up any congealed dribbles.

Blowtorch Method. A blowtorch is not just for laughs—it is a legitimate kitchen tool, and marvelous for loosening aspics from their molds. Buy a portable torch with an instant self-igniting nozzle that attaches to a small propane bottle. For aspics, loosen the edges of the aspic from around the bowl with a knife, turn the aspic mold upside down on the chilled platter, and run the flame around the sides and bottom of the bowl for several seconds.

A SELECT GROUP OF NON SEQUITURS

The following group of soups could only fit into the master plan of theme and variations by stretching the fabric too far, and are best presented as the individuals they wish to be. Here, for instance, is soup cooked and served in a pumpkin shell, and another that is enriched with a special garlic and basil sauce. There is also the full-dressed garlic soup, that wonderfully fragrant Aïgo Bouïdo from Provence. Black Bean Gazpacho is followed by a tripe and bean soup that can also turn itself into the Mexican menudo. These are hearty soups, rib stickers, that make the grade as main courses.

Pumpkin soup in a pumpkin

Soup in a Pumpkin

Choose a fine solid pumpkin, scrape it clean, fill it with a hot soup mixture, and bake it until the pumpkin is tender, and a little of the pumpkin flesh goes into each serving. It's a delightful beginning to any fall dinner, particularly the Thanksgiving feast. But be sure to choose a pumpkin to fit your oven—or vice versa!

SEASONAL NOTE: *Pumpkins will keep perfectly well for a number of weeks in a cool place, but they collapse overnight in freezing temperatures.*

For a pumpkin serving 8 to 10 people

2½ **cups lightly pressed down fresh crumbs from homemade type white bread, crust off**
2 **cups minced onions**
4 **ounces (1 stick) butter, plus 2 Tbs or so soft butter**
A 6- to 7-pound healthy and unblemished pumpkin
1½ **cups coarsely grated Swiss cheese**
2 **to 2½ quarts chicken stock, brought to the simmer**
Seasonings: salt, freshly ground pepper, ½ tsp sage
1 **cup heavy cream (or sour cream liquefied with a little milk or stock), desirable but optional**
½ **cup lightly pressed down chopped fresh parsley**

SPECIAL EQUIPMENT SUGGESTED: *A lightly buttered pizza pan to hold the*

pumpkin in the oven; a long-handled ladle for serving

The bread crumbs and onions. Spread the crumbs in a roasting pan and dry them out in a 350°F oven for 15 minutes or so, once or twice tossing them about—they should hardly color. Meanwhile, melt the stick of butter and slowly cook the minced onions in it until the onions are perfectly tender and translucent—about 15 minutes; toss the crumbs into the onions and cook, stirring, for 3 minutes.

Preparing the pumpkin. Cut a neat cover out of the pumpkin, scrape out the seeds and strings, and rub the inner flesh of both the pumpkin shell and its cover with the soft butter. Set the pumpkin on the pizza pan.

Ahead-of-time note: May be prepared in advance to this point. Preheat the oven before proceeding.

Baking the soup—about 1½ hours at 400°F. Turn the crumb mixture into the pumpkin, stir in the grated cheese, and fill the pumpkin to within 2 inches of its top with hot chicken stock. Season to taste with salt, pepper, and sage. Set the pumpkin at once in the lower level of a preheated 400°F oven. Bake until the pumpkin has just softened—but do not overcook, or it will collapse!

Ahead-of-time note: You may keep it warm for half an hour or so in a 175°F oven until ready to serve—too much heat and too long a wait will dangerously soften the pumpkin.

To serve. Just before serving, bring the optional cream almost to the simmer; gently stir it into the soup, followed by the chopped parsley. Correct seasoning. At the table, ladle the soup into hot bowls, scraping off some of the flesh from inside the pumpkin as you do so.

Soupe au Pistou
Provençal vegetable soup with a cheese, garlic, and basil finish

This wonderfully fragrant brew of mixed vegetables starts with a base of potatoes, carrots, leeks, onions, beans, and herbs all simmered together; fresh green beans and other seasonable tender vegetables then go in, and the soup is finally blended with its garlic-flavored sauce. The

base and the sauce may be prepared hours ahead, but to preserve its freshness, the green vegetable garnish is added only at the end.

The soup gets its name from the sauce, whose garlic and basil in the old Provençal days were pounded to a paste in a mortar with a pestle—in an operation known as the pistou. A pesto, by the way, is the Italian version of the French Mediterranean pistou. Fresh basil is marvelous and typical here, but if you can't get it there are secondary wintry choices.

For 6 to 8 servings

The soup base

3 quarts water
2 Tbs salt
2 cups peeled and diced carrots
2 cups peeled and diced "boiling" potatoes
2 cups diced white part of leeks and/or onions
If available: 2 cups fresh white beans or speckled fresh cranberry beans (otherwise add 3 cups of cooked or canned white beans and their juices with the final additions, later)

1¼ cups Pistou Sauce (see Special Note the next page)
2 cups diced fresh green beans
⅓ cup small pasta shapes, or spaghetti broken into ½-inch pieces
Optional additions: 1 to 2 cups diced fresh zucchini; and/or cored, seeded and diced green or red bell peppers; and/or fresh green peas—one or all
1 slice of stale homemade type white bread, crumbed

A large pinch of saffron threads, or ½ tsp fragrant curry powder
Freshly ground pepper
A little boiling water, if needed

SPECIAL EQUIPMENT SUGGESTED:
A 4-quart saucepan or kettle for the soup; a soup tureen and ladle for serving—optional but attractive

The soup base—about 40 minutes. Place the listed ingredients in the kettle, bring to the simmer, skim off scum for several minutes, then cover partially and simmer until the vegetables are tender.

Ahead-of-time note: May be prepared in advance; chill uncovered, then cover and refrigerate. Bring to the simmer before proceeding.

The Pistou Sauce. While the soup base is simmering, make the sauce as described in the Special Note on the next page.

Final additions—10 to 15 minutes. Add the remaining ingredients (except the boiling water) to the simmering soup, and boil slowly uncovered until the green vegetables are tender. Stir in a little boiling water if the soup seems too thick. Carefully correct seasoning, and the soup is ready for the pistou.

Serving. Turn the pistou sauce into the warmed soup tureen, stir in a ladleful of soup, then stir in the rest—or top each bowl with a big spoonful of the pistou. Serve at once, accompanied by French bread or Hard-Toasted French Bread Rounds (page 24).

Pistou Sauce

Use this fragrant flavoring idea in other dishes such as the Beef and Vegetable Soup on page 16, and it is delicious with hot pasta and rice dishes. This pistou is much like the Rouille served with bouillabaisse in the Special Note on page 25—in fact the two are interchangeable.

For about 1¼ cups

4 or more large cloves of garlic
¼ tsp salt
¼ cup chopped fresh basil leaves, or 1½ Tbs fragrant dried basil or oregano
¼ cup tomato paste
½ cup grated Parmesan cheese
½ cup fruity olive oil
¼ cup lightly pressed down chopped fresh parsley

Purée the garlic into a mortar or mixing bowl. With a pestle or the back of a wooden spoon, mash to a fine paste with the salt. Then mash in the basil or other herbs. Next, blend in the tomato paste and cheese. Finally, with a wire whip, whisk in the oil by dribbles to make a thick paste. Blend in the parsley shortly before serving.

*Ahead-of-time note: If made in advance, cover and keep at cool room temperature—it may separate if chilled.

Aïgo Bouïdo
Garlic Soup

Here is another famous Mediterranean soup, and if you didn't know what it was made of you'd wonder what this subtle herbal wonder-broth could possibly be. It is simple indeed to make, as you will see.

For about 2¼ quarts, serving 6 to 8

The soup base
1 or 2 large heads of garlic (2 heads are not too much!), the unpeeled cloves separated and smashed
2 quarts water
Seasonings: 2 tsp salt, a big pinch of freshly ground white pepper, 2 whole cloves, ¼ tsp each sage and thyme, 1 medium imported bay leaf, 6 parsley sprigs
3 Tbs fruity olive oil

Final liaison
3 egg yolks
¼ cup olive oil

Accompaniments
Hard-Toasted French Bread Rounds (page 24)
1 cup grated Parmesan or Swiss cheese

SPECIAL EQUIPMENT SUGGESTED:
A 3-quart saucepan with cover; a soup tureen is attractive but not essential

The soup base. Combine all the listed ingredients in the saucepan, bring to the boil, and simmer partially covered 30 minutes. Strain into a bowl, pressing juices out of the ingredients, and return to the saucepan. Correct seasoning.

*Ahead-of-time note: May be prepared in advance; chill uncovered, then cover and refrigerate or freeze. Bring to the simmer shortly before serving.

The final liaison. Whisk the egg yolks in the soup tureen or a mixing bowl for a minute or two until thick and sticky; by droplets, whisk in the olive oil to make a thick, mayonnaise-like cream.

Serving. Just before serving, and by dribbles, beat a ladleful of hot soup into the egg yolk liaison; gradually whisk in the rest. Serve immediately, passing the bread and cheese separately.

Provençal Garlic and Chicken Soup

Ingredients for the preceding Garlic Soup
2 skinless and boneless chicken breasts
A handful of chopped fresh parsley

While the soup base is simmering, cut the chicken breasts into small slices, ½-inch dice, or julienne. After straining the soup base, add the chicken and let simmer 4 to 5 minutes. Finish the soup as described, whisking the liquid into the egg yolk liaison, and folding in the chicken and parsley.

Provençal Garlic and Fish Soup

Ingredients for the Garlic Soup
1 pound (2 cups) chowder-type fish
such as cod, hake, halibut,
pollack, red snapper, sea scallops
A handful of chopped fresh parsley

Follow the recipe for the preceding
Provençal Garlic and Chicken Soup,
simmering the fish only 1 to 2
minutes.

Provençal Garlic Soup with Poached Eggs

6 to 8 warm poached eggs
Ingredients for the Garlic Soup, but
omit the egg yolk and olive oil
liaison
A handful of chopped fresh parsley

Place a warm poached egg on a
toasted bread round in each warmed
soup bowl, ladle on the soup, and top
with a sprinkling of parsley; pass additional bread rounds and the cheese
separately.

Provençal Garlic and Potato Soup

Ingredients for the Garlic Soup
3 cups sliced "boiling" potatoes
A big pinch of saffron threads, or
1 tsp fragrant curry powder,
optional

After simmering and straining the
soup base, add the potatoes and optional saffron or curry; bring to the
boil and simmer about 10 minutes,
or until the potatoes are tender. Finish the soup as directed.

Black Bean Gazpacho

Black Bean Gazpacho

Guests love to add condiments to
their dishes—consider all the fasci-
nating tidbits that go into a curry—
so let them have fun with their black
bean soup. Since the Spaniards make
a white gazpacho with ground almonds, it seems legitimate to make a
dark gazpacho with black beans,
which you may serve hot or cold accompanied by its colorful garnish.

MANUFACTURING NOTE: *Use a good
brand of canned black bean soup if you
do not want to make your own as described here.*

For 2 quarts of soup, serving 6 people

The bean soup
2 cups black beans
2 quarts water
2 cups chopped onions
½ cup each chopped celery and
carrots
1 tsp salt
A little chicken stock or water, if
needed

Suggested accompaniments, each in a
small bowl—use some or all.

2 cucumbers, peeled, seeded, and
diced
3 hard-boiled eggs, chopped and
tossed with a little salt and freshly
ground pepper
2 green bell peppers, finely diced
2 cups diced tomatoes (fresh
tomatoes peeled, seeded, juiced,
and diced, page 358)
2 cups toasted croutons (page 24)
1 cup or so crumbled crisp bacon

SPECIAL EQUIPMENT SUGGESTED:
*A 3-quart heavy-bottomed saucepan, or
a pressure cooker; a food processor or
vegetable mill for puréeing the soup*

The soup. Wash and pick over the
beans to remove any debris. Bring
them to the boil in the saucepan with
the 2 quarts of water; boil exactly 2
minutes, then cover the pan and set
them aside for exactly 1 hour. (If
beans give you digestive complaints,
pour out the water and add fresh cold
water.) Bring to the simmer, adding
the onions, celery, carrots, and salt.
Either simmer slowly, partially covered, for 1½ hours or so, until the
beans are tender; or pressure-cook
for 5 minutes and let the pressure go
down by itself. Purée the beans with
their liquid, adding a little chicken
stock or water if too thick.

**Ahead-of-time note:* May be prepared
in advance; chill uncovered, then
cover and refrigerate.

Serving. Bring the soup to the simmer, adding again a little more
chicken stock or water if the purée
seems too thick, and taste again very
carefully for seasoning. Ladle into
warmed wide bowls and pass the accompaniments separately.

Soupe aux Haricots et à la Tripe

Tripe and White Bean Soup

A wonderful main-course soup for tripe lovers, and it's a happy initiation for neophytes. This is a close cousin to the Mexican menudo, but uses beans rather than hominy—which you can, of course, substitute for the beans as described in the variations. I have suggested some Mexicanesque accompaniments, which go very nicely here, as would a red wine such as a Beaujolais, Côtes du Rhône, a zinfandel, or a Spanish rioja.

MANUFACTURING NOTE: *There's no telling how long it takes tripe to cook so that it is properly tender—5 to 7 hours, and sometimes 12, of very slow simmering. A Crock-pot (slow cooker) works well for tripe, which will always be somewhat chewy but should not be disagreeably so. Although I've had success at times adding tripe to beans, I conclude it's best to cook each separately and combine near the end.*

For about 2½ quarts, serving 6

2 pounds ready-to-cook honeycomb tripe
1 veal knuckle or 2 pig's trotters, optional
4 cups sliced onions (1¼ pounds)
3 or 4 large cloves of garlic, peeled and chopped

1 cup chopped unpeeled tomatoes, cores removed, or ¾ cup canned Italian plum tomatoes
4 cups beef stock or bouillon
Seasonings: salt, freshly ground pepper, thyme or oregano, 1 large imported bay leaf
2 cups cooked or canned kidney beans with their juices
1 Tbs red wine vinegar, or to taste
Suggested accompaniments (any or all): 2 hard-boiled eggs, chopped; ½ cup chopped scallions or red onion; 1 cup fresh tomato relish (page 359) or salsa (page 200) and/or chopped mild or hot peppers; Hard-Toasted French Bread Rounds (page 24) or Cheese-Toasted Tortillas (see Special Note, page 33)

SPECIAL EQUIPMENT SUGGESTED: *A large square of double-thickness well-washed cheesecloth if using the bones; a Crock-pot is useful, or a bean pot or flameproof casserole, or any 3- to 4-quart covered casserole or baking dish about 3 inches deep*

Preparing the tripe. Wash the tripe and cut it with shears into strips 1 inch wide; cut the strips into longish triangles, and drop into a large saucepan of cold water. Wash the optional veal knuckle or pig's trotters, and add to the tripe. Bring to the boil, simmer 3 minutes, drain, and rinse. Remove the optional bones or trotters, tie in cheesecloth (to keep all the little bones out of the broth), and reserve. Blanch the tripe several times again if you wish to remove more of its tripe-iness.

Cooking—overnight or longer. Turn the tripe into the Crock-pot or casserole, adding the optional bones or trotters, the onions, garlic, tomatoes, stock, and enough water to cover the ingredients by 2 inches. Bring to the simmer either in the Crock-pot or on top of the stove, season lightly, and add the herbs. Cover closely, and cook at medium heat or 275°F—adjusting the heat so the tripe simmers very slowly. Cook slowly until the tripe is tender, adding boiling water if the liquid is low—test by analytically chewing a piece or two. Remove and discard the package of bones or trotters (if using pig's trotters, you may wish to add the meat to the tripe; discard the remains). Add the beans, simmer another ½ hour, and correct seasoning.

*Ahead-of-time note: May be prepared in advance; chill uncovered, then cover and refrigerate.

Serving. Ladle into warmed wide soup bowls and pass the accompaniments separately.

VARIATION

Hominy or Chick-Pea Variation

Omit the beans and substitute 2 to 3 cups of drained and rinsed canned hominy or chick-peas in the preceding tripe soup.

Fresh Corn Variation

Cut the kernels from 2 or 3 ears of boiled fresh corn, and warm them up for several minutes in the soup before serving—or use frozen corn kernels.

With Mini Sausage Cakes

Dipping your hands into cold water for each, form miniature sausage cakes, page 257, about 1 inch across—you'll want 4 to 6 per person, and about ¾ pound of sausage meat. Sauté them to brown nicely, and add to the soup to heat through for 10 minutes before serving.

OTHER SOUPS IN OTHER CHAPTERS

A number of other soups appear where their main ingredient lies:

Lobster Stew on page 108 is a logical continuation of the lobster sauté.

Mussel Soup, page 121, with its variations, *Oyster Bisque* and *Monterey Bay Sole Food Stew*, follows very logically the steaming of mussels in wine.

Scotch Broth, page 215, with its lamb stock and barley, is fittingly part of boning and butterflying a leg, while *Split Pea Soup*, page 233, and the remains of the ham are inseparable.

SPECIAL NOTE

Cheese-Toasted Tortillas

For 6 servings, to go with main-course soups or for a cocktail snack

6 flour tortillas 8 to 9 inches across (or 9 smaller tortillas)
2 Tbs olive oil
A little salt
1 Tbs or so dried herbs such as thyme, oregano, or Italian herb mixture, optional
3 to 4 Tbs finely grated hard Jack or other grating cheese such as Parmesan, Romano, or Swiss

SPECIAL EQUIPMENT SUGGESTED: *2 large baking sheets; a pastry brush*

Baking. Preheat the oven to 400°F. Cut the tortillas into halves or quarters, and arrange in one layer on baking sheets. Bake 7 to 9 minutes in the upper-third and middle levels of the preheated oven, switching sheets halfway through, just until the tortillas are beginning to crisp. Remove and turn them over; paint lightly with the olive oil, sprinkle lightly with salt and the optional herbs. Spread a teaspoon of cheese over each. Return to the oven for 3 to 4 minutes, until the cheese has melted and has barely begun to brown.

*Ahead-of-time note: They will keep in an airtight container for a few days, or wrap and freeze them. Recrisp in the oven if necessary.

VARIATION

Cheese-Toasted Pita Bread

Use the same formula for pita bread, first trimming off the circumference with shears so that you can separate them into 2 layers. Halve or quarter them, and bake them inner sides up.

Breads

French Bread, Whole Wheat, Rye, and Walnut Breads

Hamburger Buns, Rolls, and Sandwich Bread

Spiced Dough for Coffee Cake and Sticky Buns

Pizza, Calzone, and Buttermilk Cornsticks

Bread making is for those who love to cook and to work with their hands. There is a deep satisfaction to be gained from the feel and smell of the dough as it is kneaded and formed, from that wonderful warm aroma of its baking, and finally from the pride of authorship. The art of bread making can become a consuming hobby, and no matter how often and how many kinds of bread one has made, there always seems to be something new to learn.

Although French bread and a number of other breads appear in *Mastering II* and in *Kitchen*, the recipes here speed up the process by using the food processor—a real boon to the bread maker. I am particularly pleased with our full photographic coverage of French bread, and I have also included three favorite whole-grain loaves, as well as brioche dough for spiced bread. Tired of mushy hamburger buns and soggy pizza crusts? I hope you will find the solutions to these problems here, starting out with a few hints from an old-time home baker.

DON'T MURDER THE YEAST AND OTHER RANDOM NOTES

Following are some personal hints I've picked up through the years.

Yeast is alive. Dry-active yeast figures in all the dough recipes here just for convenience, but fresh yeast may be used in its place. Store fresh yeast cakes in either the refrigerator or the freezer. Fresh yeast is healthy as long as it is firm and of an even gray color; if it becomes soft or discolored, toss it out. Store dry-active yeast in the refrigerator, too, but for longer storage use the freezer—I've kept it frozen alive and well for a year or more.

How much yeast to use. In general, you'll want 1 package (a scant tablespoon of dry-active yeast or ½ ounce of fresh cake yeast) per pound or 3½ cups of flour. However, I have used that same amount for 6 cups of flour with perfect success. A smaller proportion of yeast makes a slightly longer rise, of course, but a leisurely rise gives better texture and flavor.

Proving yeast. If you've had dry-active yeast for some time, always make it show you it's alive: dissolve a package or tablespoon of it in 3 tablespoons of warm water (not over 110°F—too much heat will kill it). Whisk in a tablespoon of flour or ¼ teaspoon of sugar so it will have something to eat. In about 5 minutes it should begin to foam. It's alive!

If your dough won't rise. You've given it an hour or more, and it hasn't budged—but have you left it long enough? Is it cold? Or is the room cold (60°F or lower), so the yeast is somnolent? If so, put the dough in a warmer place—set your bowl in the oven, turn it on for 1½ to 2 minutes, turn it off, and close the door. If the dough still lies dormant, perhaps you killed the yeast by dissolving it in too-warm water. Or was it dead to begin with? Break out some new yeast, prove it to make sure, mix it into the dough, and start again. A heavy-duty mixer or food processor will be faster than elbow grease in this case, and your bread may be even better because it has had time to develop character.

Ideal rising temperature. If you let your dough rise in too warm a place—over 80°F, for instance—you'll get a lot of hot air but little flavor and texture. A longer rise at 75°F, or even 70°F, gives the best results.

You've let the dough over-rise, and it has fermented. Don't throw it out. You can still make beautiful bread because the fermented dough will act like an old-fashioned "levain," or starter. If it's only slightly strong and yeasty, use an equal amount of flour, water, and so forth for a new batch; if quite strong, use twice the amount. Mix the required liquid into the old dough—a food processor or heavy-duty mixer is useful here, and you may well have to mix it in 2 or 3 batches. Then knead in the flour, salt, etc., but no yeast—your fermented dough will do the work. You'll probably produce a bread with much more character and texture than usual.

Kneading. The main ingredients of flour are starch and gluten. It's the starch in the dough that feeds upon the yeast, belching forth gas that pushes up the gluten. I think of a well-kneaded dough as being like a fine-meshed plastic sponge, the gluten forming the web that holds it in shape. The purpose of kneading is not only to blend all the dough ingredients together, but to join the gluten particles into that continuous web. You can tell when you have kneaded enough when you hold the ball of dough between your hands and bend it downward—it is smooth and elastic, and it holds its shape.

Hand kneading versus machine kneading. I don't think it makes any difference what system you use as long as you produce a properly kneaded dough. There is certainly an elemental and intimate pleasure in kneading by hand, but it takes time. The hand-crank bread bucket and the heavy-duty mixer with dough hook are tolerably satisfactory, but to my mind the best system is to start with a food processor and to finish by hand. Then you get the best of both worlds. The food processor does a fast job of mixing and preliminary kneading but it does cut the gluten strands; however, the hand-kneaded finish rejoins them quickly and easily. You'll note rest periods in the recipes to come—these allow the flour particles to absorb the liquid in the dough, and make for more efficient kneading.

The free-form loaf vs. the bread pan. A hand-formed loaf that bakes free in the oven is certainly appealing, especially for French bread. But when

must. A passionate baker since his apprenticeship as a seventeen-year-old, he is now in his late seventies, having taught for years at the École Professionelle de la Meunerie. At this writing he is still experimenting, still perfecting, always with a view to adapting the ideal of "le bon pain français" to modern conditions.

Since those early days with him I have also had the good fortune to consult with one of his most talented pupils, the American baker Danielle Forestier. And I, too, have evolved in my own way—as do all home bread makers. These, then, are my findings to date.

Manufacturing Notes:

Baking equipment. Although you can bake your bread on a pastry sheet or in a bread pan, you will not get the big puffy loaf. For that fine effect you must transform your home oven into a baker's oven by lining your oven rack either with ceramic quarry tiles ½ inch thick or with a baking or pizza stone. You can find tiles in most building supply stores and you'll see both tiles and baking stones in some of the specialty stores and mail-order catalogues. You will also need a system for creating steam, plus a board for unmolding the risen loaf and transferring it to a baker's peel or sliding board—these are discussed or illustrated in the recipe to come.

(*continued*)

you have a heavy low-gluten dough, such as the buttermilk rye on page 46, the pan produces a handsomer loaf than the free-form, which in this case tends not to puff very much in the oven.

Baking—when is it done? An underdone loaf has a slightly damp interior, and the unsatisfactory taste of insufficiently cooked dough. Unless you are a professional, thumping to hear a hollow sound is not good enough. The sure way is to take its temperature in the oven, with an instant meat thermometer: turn the loaf over, stick the thermometer into a bottom crease, and wait a few seconds for the needle to stop moving—I consider it done at 200°F.

FRENCH BREAD DOUGH

Flour, water, yeast, and salt—those four elements alone are the official components of French bread. A fine loaf of it is crusty outside while the inside is a creamy off-white with an open, rather chewy texture. It is not baked in a pan—it stands free in the oven, held in shape by its own gluten cloak, created by the very special way you form it.

My experiences began in the 1960's, when my French colleague, Simca, and I had our first session with a master bread maker, Professeur Raymond Calvel, in Paris. That meeting brought forth the recipe for French bread in *Mastering II*—well before the invention of the food processor. Since then our mentor himself has continued to evolve, as professionals

French Bread Dough (*continued*)

Yeast. The recipes here are for regular dried granular yeast, although you may use fresh cake yeast or the so-called instant yeast interchangeably. Just to be safe and sure, I always prove my yeast, whatever the directions say, and I always keep it in the freezer.

White flour. Bread flour should have a reasonably high gluten content so that the loaf will rise and keep its volume. Professional bakers can, of course, order in bulk exactly what they want, but the home baker has to depend on home sources and experience. I look for unbleached all-purpose flour or bread flour, and have had good luck on the East and West coasts both with supermarket types and with flours from the health-food stores, as well as with bromated flour. Some all-purpose flours in the South are low in gluten because they are blended more for biscuits than for bread. If you suspect this to be the case, look for bread flour in your local health-food store or blend some gluten flour into the all-purpose—starting with ⅓ cup of gluten for every 3 cups of all-purpose.

The time it takes. A fine loaf of bread takes a certain amount of time to produce if it is to have the texture and taste you hope for. You'll want 4 to 5 hours in all, but these are almost unsupervised hours—3 to 4 for the several risings of the dough, and about 45 minutes for the baking. Unfortunately you cannot hurry it, but the results are worth every moment spent.

◀▦▶ MASTER RECIPE

Dough for French Bread and Hard Rolls
Food Processor Method

This is a thoroughly detailed tell-all recipe, since it is the master for all the yeast doughs described in this chapter, all of which are made in the food processor.

Enough for 3 cups, making three 18-inch baguettes, 2 fat long loaves, two 9-inch round loaves, or 12 rolls

The yeast mixture

1 package dry-active yeast
⅓ cup tepid water (not over 110°F) in a 2-cup measure
¼ teaspoon sugar
3½ cups (1 pound) unbleached flour—bread flour if possible, or all-purpose (measure by scooping and leveling, page 380)—plus a little additional flour, if needed
1 Tbs rye or whole wheat flour
2¼ tsp salt
1 cup cold water, plus ⅓ cup or so additional water

SPECIAL EQUIPMENT SUGGESTED:
A food processor equipped if possible with a plastic blade, although the metal blade will do; a fairly narrow 4-quart bowl with fairly straight sides—for the dough to rise in; see also the forming and baking requirements that follow, so that you will have everything you need before you begin

Food processor capacity: These recipes are designed for a processor with a 2½-quart container. If yours is smaller, you may have to make the dough in 2 or even 3 batches, and combine them for the final hand kneading.

The yeast. Sprinkle the yeast over the water, and stir it in along with the sugar; let stand for 5 minutes or more until the mixture has foamed up, proving to you that it is active.

The rest of the ingredients. Measure the flours and salt into the bowl of the processor. Stir up the yeast to be sure it has thoroughly dissolved, blend in the cup of cold water and set the mixture by your side, along with the extra water and extra flour. Start the machine.

Preliminary machine kneading—about 60 seconds. With the machine going, rather slowly but steadily pour in the yeast mixture. If the dough does not form into a ball in a few seconds dribble in a little more water, adding more dribbles at several-second intervals until the dough balls on top of

1. Dough balled up on top of blade

the blade, see illustration, step 1, and revolves under the cover 8 to 10 times—don't worry if particles of dough do not join the mass and remain in the bottom of the container.

(If by chance you have added too much water and the dough refuses to ball or clogs in the machine, keep it running and pour in a tablespoon or so more of flour until the revolving ball forms.)

Rest period. Stop the machine, remove the cover, and feel the dough. If it seems damp and wet, start the machine again, pour in a tablespoon or so of flour, and let the ball rotate several times under the cover. Now let the dough rest 4 to 5 minutes; a rest allows the flour particles to absorb the liquids and facilitates kneading.

Final machine kneading. Turn on the machine and let the dough rotate 30 times under the cover, then remove it to a lightly floured work surface. It should be fairly smooth and quite firm.

A note on machine kneading: You do not want to overknead in the machine since that can overheat the dough and break down the gluten—this is particularly true if you are using a steel rather than plastic blade. If you have any doubts, stop the machine, remove the cover, and feel the dough; if it is warmer than room temperature, let it rest and cool off for 5 minutes before continuing.

Final kneading by hand. Let the dough rest 2 minutes, then knead roughly and vigorously—rapidly fold the dough over on itself, push it out with

2. Final kneading by hand

the heels of your hands, step 2, and repeat 50 times. The final dough should not stick to your hands as you knead (although it will stick if you pinch and hold a piece); it should be smooth and elastic and, when you hold it up between your hands and stretch it down, it should hold together smoothly.

Preliminary rise—40 to 60 minutes at around 75°F. Scoop the dough into the clean dry bowl, cover with a sheet of plastic wrap, and set in a warm place free from drafts. (As an example, I turn on my electric wall oven for exactly 1½ minutes, place the dough bowl in the lower third, turn off the oven, and close the door. Note that the bowl is not oiled—the French theory is that dough needs a seat to push up from.) This first rise is sufficient when the dough has definitely started to rise and is about 1½ times its original volume.

Deflating. Turn the dough onto your lightly floured work surface; roughly and firmly pat and push it out into a 14-inch rectangle. Fold one of the

long sides over toward the middle, and the other long side over to cover it, making a 3-layer cushion. Repeat the operation. This important step redistributes the yeast throughout the dough, for a strong second rise. Return the dough smooth side up to the bowl; cover with plastic wrap and again set to rise.

Final rise in the bowl—1 to 1½ hours or longer. This time let the dough rise 2½ to 3 times its original bulk. It is the amount of rise that is important here, not the timing. The dough is now ready to form.

VARIATION

Making Dough in a Mixer or by Hand

When you are making dough in an electric mixer with a dough hook, proceed in the same general way with the rests indicated, and finish by hand. Or mix the dough by hand in a bowl, turn it out on a work surface, and start the kneading by lifting it up with a scraper and slapping it down roughly for several minutes until it has body. Let it rest several minutes, then proceed to knead as illustrated.

French Bread: Long Loaves

Forming a loaf of bread is just as important as making the dough, particularly since French loaves stand free in the oven.

The various flattenings, foldings, and rollings here are traditional in French bakeries when loaves are formed by hand. Their object is to elongate the gluten strands inside the dough so that the loaf will hold its shape under the cloak of gluten that forms on its surface. Work rapidly!

Master recipe for French bread dough after its final rise

SPECIAL EQUIPMENT SUGGESTED: *A little flour for the work surface; a pastry scraper; a lightly floured linen towel set on an upside-down tray; a lightweight lightly floured second towel to cover the dough*

To make the 2 fat loaves shown here, cut the dough in half, and fold each

3. Flattening dough half into rectangle

piece in half end to end. Pat 1 piece (left in the photo) firmly into a 14-inch rectangle, squaring it up as evenly as you can, step 3. (Cover the other piece loosely with a towel.)

4. Folding rectangle in half lengthwise

Keeping your work surface always clean and very lightly floured, fold the rectangle of dough in half lengthwise, its 2 edges toward you, step 4.

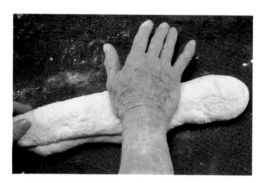

5. Flattening folded rectangle with heel of hand

With the heel of your hand, press and pound the dough firmly where the 2 edges meet, to seal them, step 5. Then pound the rest of the rectangle flat—a firm hand here reactivates the yeast to give your loaf more volume.

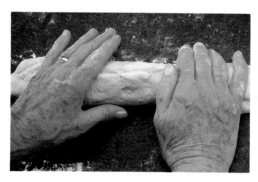

6. Rotating dough forward, seam on top

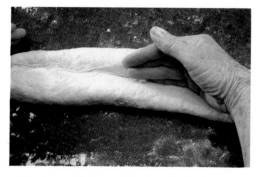

7. Pressing trench in top of dough with side of hand

Roll the dough forward so that the sealed seam is on top, step 6. Pat it firmly again into a rectangle, being sure it is not sticking to your work surface—you do not want to tear the gluten cloak that is forming.

With the side of your hand, press a trench down the central length of the dough, following the seam, step 7.

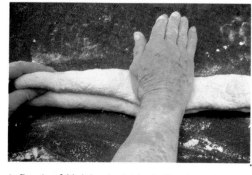

8. Pressing folded dough with heel of hand to seal

Fold the dough again lengthwise, its joined edges toward you. Again press and pound the 2 edges together, pounding and flattening also the rest of the rectangle, step 8. Rotate the dough so the seal is underneath.

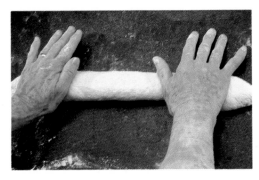

9. Elongating dough by rotating it under palms of hands

Now rotate the dough rapidly back and forth under your palms, starting at the middle and sliding your hands to the ends, step 9—and off the ends, to make them pointed. Repeat several times, extending the loaf as evenly as possible to the length you wish—but not so long it won't fit your baking surface!

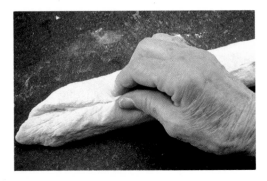

10. Pinching the seam to seal

Rotate the loaf seam side up, straightening it as necessary. I then like to pinch the edges together, just to be sure, step 10. Lift it seal side up onto a lightly floured towel, cover loosely with the second towel, and form the second loaf.

11. Laying second loaf on floured towel

Make a pleat in the bottom towel to separate the 2 loaves, and lift the second loaf into place, step 11. Cover loosely with the second towel. Let rise to more than double—1 to 1½ hours, again at around 75°F. (I again use the warm turned-off oven here.) Meanwhile prepare for baking as follows:

SPECIAL EQUIPMENT SUGGESTED *(to produce a loaf of bread the baker's way):*

A hot baking surface: Set your oven rack in the lower third level and cover with quarry tiles or a baking stone or stones—see the manufacturing notes on page 37. Preheat the oven to 450°F at least 20 minutes before you plan to bake.

Unmolding board and sliding board or peel: These are ⅜-inch plywood boards, pictured in the instructions following—the unmolding board is 8 inches across and about 16 inches long. The sliding board is 2 inches less than the width of the oven and 18 to 20 inches long. Or use a baker's peel or pizza paddle.

Cornmeal: A light dusting of cornmeal on the unmolding and sliding boards prevents the dough from sticking.

For slashing the tops of the loaves: A single-edge razor—art supply stores have these.

Steam: Once the loaves go into the oven, you must fill it with steam the first few seconds of baking. For an electric oven simply throw ½ cup of cold water into the bottom of the oven; for a gas oven, place a heavy frying pan on the floor of the oven as you preheat it, and toss the water into the hot pan after the loaves go in. Steam sets the starch on the surface and helps the crust to brown; steam also humidifies the oven and allows the dough to puff a little longer before the yeast is killed by the intense heat.

An instant meat thermometer: You can't tell that a loaf of bread is done just because it looks brown and crusty, and gives out a hearty thump when you tap it. But you can be sure when your thermometer registers an interior temperature of 200°F.

To bake French bread. The loaves have risen, the oven has been preheated to 450°F, and all equipment is at hand. Work rapidly here, as usual.

Unmolding. Dust the unmolding board lightly with cornmeal and flip

12. Flipping loaf from towel onto board

French Bread (*continued*)

onto it a risen loaf, its seamless side up, step 12. Dust the sliding board lightly with cornmeal and slide the loaf in place at the far edge. Repeat with the second loaf.

Slashing. Holding the razor almost parallel to the surface of the loaf, make 3 quick, sure slashes about ½

13. Slashing top of second loaf

inch deep as shown, step 13. These open up the gluten cloak and allow the dough to swell in the oven. (This is part of the baker's art, and if one slashed 500 loaves a day one should eventually do it perfectly almost every time.) Slash the second loaf.

Into the oven. At once open the hot oven, poise the end of the sliding board at the far end of the baking

14. Sliding loaves into oven

surface and rapidly pull it out, dislodging the loaves onto the hot sur-

face, step 14. Toss the ½ cup of cold water into the bottom of an electric oven or a hot frying pan. Close the door and set timer for 20 minutes.

Baking. Check the bread after 20 minutes. It will have swelled in 5 minutes or so, and the slashes will open. In 20 minutes it should be brown and crusty, but it will need another 10 minutes or so at 400°F to cook through. At this point check the bottoms of the loaves—if they are too brown, slip an oven rack under them to raise them from the hot baking surface. If the tops are browning too much, cover loosely with a sheet of foil, shiny side up; lower thermostat to 400°F and continue.

When is it done? The loaves should feel rather light. Insert the thermometer discreetly through a central slash and wait a few seconds until the needle stops moving. The loaf is done at 200°F.

Cooling. Remove the loaves to a rack, and in a few seconds a sharp ear will hear them crackle—the bread's own music, as Professeur Calvel describes it. Although bread warm from the oven is irresistible, its texture is best when it has cooled. If not eaten soon, store it as follows:

Storing French Bread

Refrigerating. The bread keeps 2 to 3 days refrigerated in plastic bags. Crisp 5 minutes or so on a pastry sheet in a preheated 400°F oven, turning the oven off as soon as the bread is in. Or use the microwave, but be very careful or you'll turn the loaf tough and dry.

Freezing. Freeze thoroughly cold loaves in plastic bags. It can happen

that thawed frozen bread separates—the crust or part of the outside portion works loose from the whole. I have asked several bakers about this and one likely theory is that there was a lack of gluten, and the dough did not have the force to stick together.

VARIATIONS

Forming Fat Round Loaves

One becomes so accustomed to the long loaf shape for French bread, one forgets that the very same dough can be formed in other shapes. Fat round loaves have a comfortable country look to them, and are just right for sandwiches or thick slices of toast. The master dough recipe (page 38) will make 1 big 12-inch loaf, or 2 loaves 7 to 8 inches in diameter.

Turn the risen dough onto a lightly floured surface and let it rest 5 minutes. (Cut it in half, if you wish, covering one half with a lightly floured towel while you form the other.) Lift one side of the dough

1. Lifting sides of dough to form a round loaf

with the palm of one hand and bring it almost over the other, as shown in illustration, step 1. Rotate the dough a quarter turn, and rapidly repeat the movement 8 to 10 times to make a smooth-bottomed cushion.

Turn the dough smooth side up, and rotate it rapidly between the sides of your hands, tucking a bit of dough under with your little fingers as you go, to make a smooth round loaf in a

2. Rotating ball of dough between sides of hands

dozen or so turns, step 2. These motions not only form the dough, but establish the surface tension, or gluten cloak, that holds the loaf in shape.

Turn the ball of dough over, smooth side down. Draw the edges of the former underside together by pinching them, step 3. Place the ball, pinched side up, on a lightly floured towel and cover loosely with a second lightly floured towel. Let rise 1 to 1½ hours, or to almost triple—I let mine rise in my turned-off slightly warm oven.

3. Pinching underside of dough to seal

4. The cross: Make 1 slash down the center, and a slash on each side

5. The cross-hatch: Make 4 slashes across the dough, then small slashes in between

6. The tree slash: Make 1 slash down the center, and 2 slanting slashes on each side

Flip the risen loaf, soft underside up, onto your sliding board or paddle. With quick, sure strokes of a razor held almost parallel to the surface, slash open the covering gluten cloak to make a decorative pattern. Illustrated here are the cross, photo 4, the cross-hatch, 5, and the tree slash, 6. Finished loaves are shown in the full-page photograph introducing this chapter.

Baking. As described in the preceding master recipe for French bread, immediately slide the loaf or loaves onto the baking stone in the preheated 450°F oven, throw in the ½ cup of water, and close the oven door. Check the bread in 20 minutes, when it should have puffed and browned. If the bottom is darkening, slip an oven rack under it. Continue baking 10 to 15 minutes or longer at 450°F, then turn oven down to 400°F (eventually even down to 375°F for a very large loaf), until the bread feels light, and the interior temperature is at 200°F.

Forming Round Rolls

Dough for the long French loaf also makes the perfect individual hard roll, the quintessential sop for those last lovely bits of sauce that you can't bear to leave on your plate. The master recipe will make 12 rolls.

Form the dough into an even long rope; cut it in half across the middle; cut the halves in half, then in thirds to make pieces all of one size. Fold each piece in half, as illustrated, step 1, and rotate under the palm of your hand to make a ball. Place each as formed, smooth side down, on a lightly floured towel, and pinch the

1. Rotating ball of dough under palm of hand

Forming Round Rolls (*continued*)

edges together, as for the large round loaf. When all are in place, cover with a lightly floured towel and let rise to almost triple.

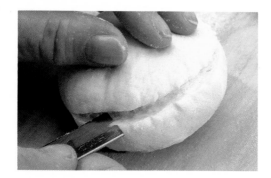

2. Slashing side of dough with razor

Arrange 3 or 4 risen rolls smooth side up on your sliding board, and slash with a razor, making 1 circular cut as shown, step 2, a straight slash, or a cross. Slide them into the oven, rapidly proceed with the rest, then toss in the ½ cup of water. Close the door, and bake 15 to 20 minutes. Leave 10 minutes more in the turned-off oven.

French Bread Dough Baked in a Loaf Pan

The French bread dough here produces fine sandwich bread and toast when baked in a loaf pan. Although made and risen in exactly the same way, this loaf has a completely different character. Follow the directions on the next page.

WHOLE WHEAT, RYE, AND WALNUT BREADS

Delicious as French bread is, the world was not built upon this loaf alone, though I find that the general mechanics of French bread work very well for all types of bread. Those include the preliminary mixing and kneading in the food processor, the final kneading by hand, the risings and the deflatings, and the forming of the loaves. There are slight variations, of course, but when you are used to the general system you will be creating your own formulae. Here are three ideas to start you off. Since the amounts and types of flour differ from the master recipe, here also are some hints.

● MASTER RECIPE

Whole Wheat Country Bread

Made with a yeast starter

For a rustic loaf with body and character, this formula makes wonderful buttered bread as well as equally good toast and sandwiches. Rather than a plain yeast dough, I have suggested a starter, or sponge—yeast, flour, and water fermented together for several hours or overnight. (Leave it for 2 to 3 days and it becomes a sourdough.) A starter, which you may also use in the same way for the French bread dough, gives the loaf not only a pleasantly moist texture but superior keeping qualities as well.

FLOUR-MEASURING NOTE: *To avoid trouble, always measure your flour by the scoop-and-level system described and illustrated on page 380.*

For 2 round loaves 9 to 10 inches in diameter

The yeast starter—2 to 3 hours or overnight
1 package dry-active yeast
1 cup water (not over 110°F)
1 cup unbleached all-purpose flour
⅛ tsp sugar

Additions to the yeast starter
1 cup cold milk, plus more as needed

The main ingredients
2½ cups whole wheat flour
2½ cups unbleached all-purpose flour
1 cup high gluten flour
4 tsp salt
4 ounces (1 stick) butter, cut into ¼-inch slices, optional, for tenderness

SPECIAL EQUIPMENT SUGGESTED: *A 4-cup measure for the yeast starter; a food processor preferably with plastic blade, but the steel blade will do; a fairly straight-sided 4-quart bowl for rising the dough; the baking equipment suggested for French bread (page 37)*

The yeast starter—several hours or overnight. Whisk together the yeast, water, flour, and sugar in the 4-cup measure; when smoothly blended, scrape down the sides of the cup with a rubber spatula. Cover the cup with

3. Kneading dough by hand

Knead by hand 20 vigorous strokes, step 3, turn it into a bowl, cover, and let rise to 1½ times its volume—40 minutes or so. Ideal rising temperature is 72°F to 75°F; if it is too warm the butter will begin to ooze out of the dough.

4. Flattening dough into a rectangle

To deflate the dough for its second rise, pat and push it out firmly into a 12-inch rectangle, step 4.

5. Folding dough into 3 layers

Fold the dough into 3 layers from one of the ends, step 5. Pat it out again and repeat the folding. Return the dough to the bowl, and cover with plastic wrap.

6. Risen dough at right: more than double in volume

Let the dough rise again, this time to more than double, step 6.

Ahead-of-time note: After this second rise the dough may be refrigerated: cover with plastic wrap, and push it down several times in the refrigerator until chilled, at which time its own congealed butter will hold it down. Refrigerated, the dough will keep nicely 2 to 3 days; let it come to almost-room temperature before proceeding.

Brioche Bread

Brioche bread is ideal for fancy sandwiches of smoked salmon or foie gras and makes delicious toast. Follow the directions for sandwich bread on page 47, and, if you want a regular loaf rather than the covered rectangular loaf described, fill the bread pan by two-thirds, and let the dough rise to the rim of the pan; bake it uncovered.

A Coffee Cake Ring

Your own spiced brioche dough makes the best conceivable coffee cake served for Sunday breakfast, brunch, or with afternoon tea.

Ingredients for a 12- to 14-inch ring

For the filling
1 cup chopped walnut meats
¾ cup dark brown sugar
1 tsp cinnamon
½ tsp mace
⅛ tsp salt
1½ cups mixed raisins (black and golden), chopped with 1 Tbs flour
1 Tbs corn syrup

Half the preceding spiced brioche dough

SPECIAL EQUIPMENT SUGGESTED: *A 12- by 17-inch baking sheet or tray; heavy-duty foil; a buttered pizza pan 16 inches in diameter*

(continued)

A Coffee Cake Ring (*continued*)

Preliminaries. Toss the filling ingredients in a mixing bowl and set aside.
Lightly flour the dough, pat it out
into a 10- by 14-inch rectangle, and
transfer it to the baking sheet. Cover
loosely, and chill 10 minutes or
more.

Forming the ring. Roll the dough into
an even rectangle 18½ inches long.
Cut ½ inch off one of the short ends
and reserve—to patch the seam after
forming the ring. Transfer the rectangle of dough to a sheet of lightly
floured foil. Lightly press the filling
into the dough.

Roll the dough up lengthwise to
make a trim log shape, using the foil
to help you, as illustrated, step 1.

1. Rolling up the dough

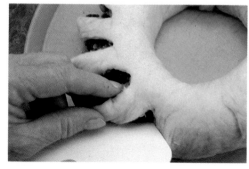

2. Turning a slash outward

Turn the log seam side down and
form into a ring, dampening the two
ends to seal them. Transfer to the
buttered pizza pan. Dampen one side
of the reserved dough strip, and
press it neatly over the seam.

With either large sharp kitchen
shears or a knife, slash the outside of
the ring all around at 1½-inch intervals to open it. Turn each slash outward to expose the filling, step 2.

Final rise—1 hour or more. Cover
loosely and let rise an hour or more,
until well puffed. Preheat the oven to
350°F.

Baking—45 minutes at 350°F. Set in
the middle level of the preheated
oven and bake until nicely browned
and crisp.

*Ahead-of-time note: When the baked
ring is thoroughly cold, you may
wrap it airtight and refrigerate for 2
days, or freeze it.

VARIATION

Sticky Buns

Cut this same filled and rolled-up log of dough into crosswise pieces, and you will have sweet spicy buns, as sticky as your heart desires.

For 8 to 10 buns

**Ingredients for the preceding filled
   coffee cake**

Sticky syrup
½ cup sugar
3 Tbs water
4 ounces (1 stick) butter

SPECIAL EQUIPMENT SUGGESTED:
*Buttered muffin tins or a buttered 8-inch
cake pan, no-stick recommended but not
essential*

Preliminaries. After preparing the dough and filling for the preceding recipe to the point of rolling it into a log shape, make the syrup as follows. Simmer the sugar and water in a small saucepan, swirling the pan by its handle for a minute or two, until the sugar has dissolved completely and the liquid is perfectly clear. Cut the butter into pieces, add to the syrup, and boil for several minutes, until the last drops to fall from the spoon are thick and sticky. Warm briefly before using, if necessary.

Dribbling syrup over a panful of baked sticky buns

Forming the buns. Slice the log of dough crosswise into 8 to 10 portions.

Either: in Muffin Tins. Drop a tablespoon of sticky syrup in the bottom of each buttered muffin cup, and plop in a slice of the dough, as illustrated.

Or: in a Round Cake Pan. Arrange the slices loosely together in a buttered cake pan.

Rising—60 minutes or more. Let rise an hour or more, until well puffed.

Baking—45 minutes at 350°F. Bake in the middle level of the preheated oven until nicely browned.

The sticky syrup. The muffin-tin buns have their sticky glaze baked on, but may need a few droplets more.

Unmold the cake-pan buns onto a rack, and dribble syrup over the top, as illustrated.

Using a muffin tin for sticky buns

The Provençal Beehive Cake
Le Nid d'Abeilles

I first saw this handsome cake a number of years ago at Chez Félix, a chic
small restaurant on the chic shopping
street La Croisette, bordering the
Mediterranean in Cannes. That is, I
saw it being paraded around and
served, but when our time came to
order a piece every crumb had been
gobbled up. Next time, our waiter
advised, we should order ours the
moment we came into the restaurant.
And a week or so later, we did. No
wonder it goes so fast—spiced
brioche dough, dome shaped, baked
with a honey and walnut topping,
split in half, anointed with liqueur
syrup, and filled with buttercream.
That takes the brioche about as far as
it can go—and what a great dessert
for a party!

*For a cake 14 inches across and 3 inches
high, serving 20 to 24*

**The cake dough: double the master
recipe for spiced brioche dough
(page 48)**

The beehive topping
**Egg wash (1 "large" egg beaten in a
1-cup measure with 1 tsp cold
water)**
½ cup slightly warmed honey
1 cup chopped walnut meats

Cake filling
**½ cup rum syrup (2 Tbs sugar
dissolved in ¼ cup hot water;
2 Tbs dark rum stirred in)**
**3 cups of either the rum-flavored
butter cream (page 468); or the
St. Honoré custard-cream filling
(page 400), flavored with a little
rum**

Accompaniments
**A bowl of fresh strawberries,
raspberries, or diced fresh
pineapple chunks, sweetened and
flavored with a tablespoon or two
of rum**
**1 cup heavy cream, whipped, folded
with 1 cup of the preceding cake
filling**

SPECIAL EQUIPMENT SUGGESTED:
*A food processor; a buttered pizza pan
16 inches in diameter; a pastry brush*

Forming the dough. Unless you have a
mammoth food processor, you'll be
preparing the double recipe of dough
in 2 or more parts, and uniting them
for the final kneading. When fully
risen, shape the dough into a round

loaf as described and illustrated for
French bread on page 43. Cover it
loosely with plastic wrap and let it
rest 5 minutes, then roll and pat it
out into a fat disk 12 inches in diameter; transfer it smooth side up to the
buttered pizza tray.

Final rise and beehive topping. Cover
loosely with floured plastic again, and
let the dough rise about 1 hour, until
it looks puffed and feels light to
gentle pressure—it will reach a
height of only about 2½ inches. (Just
before you think the rise is complete,
preheat the oven to 375°F.) Gently
brush a coating of egg wash over the
top of the dough, and let set for 2
minutes. Then brush with a coating
of tepid honey, and sprinkle the
chopped walnuts over the surface—
that gives the presumed "beehive"
effect.

Baking—about 30 minutes at 375°F.
At once set the cake in the middle
level of the preheated oven. Bake until the center has puffed up and the
top and sides have browned and
crisped—if the top browns too much
during baking, cover loosely with
foil. Cool on a rack.

*Ahead-of-time note: When thoroughly cool, wrap airtight and either
refrigerate for a day or two, or
freeze.

Filling. When the cake has thoroughly cooled, slice it in half horizontally. Turn the top half cut side
up, and sprinkle both halves with the
rum syrup. Spread 2 cups of the filling over the bottom half, re-form the
cake, and set it on a serving platter.

*Ahead-of-time note: May be completed a day ahead to this point; cover
and refrigerate, but let sit 20 minutes
or more at room temperature before
serving.

Serving. To serve such a large cake
attractively, cut a circle in the center
so that you can cut fat wedges from
the circumference to the circle's outer
edge, as shown. Then cut the final
circle into wedges, as for an ordinary
cake. Serve with a helping of fruit,
and pass the cream separately.

PIZZA AND CALZONE

One of the appeals of the pizza
is a crisp yet tender crust,
and here are four choices. The first is
a classic dough, but an especially fine
one developed by my colleague and
pizza queen, Rosemary Manell. The
second is a combination of white flour
and cornmeal, one of my favorites
because of its crisp texture. A third
choice is the flour tortilla, and a
fourth, the pita bread—both easily
available and always successful.

MASTER RECIPE

Rosemary's Classic Pizza Dough

One of the best white flour pizza
dough formulae I know, for a crisp
but tender crust.

For two 16-inch disks

The yeast mixture
1 package dry-active yeast
½ cup tepid water (not over 110°F)
⅛ tsp sugar

Additions to the yeast mixture
**¾ cup cold milk, plus more, if
  needed**
2 Tbs olive oil

The dry ingredients
**3 cups all-purpose flour (measure by
  scooping and leveling, page 380)**
1½ tsp salt

Rosemary's Classic Pizza Dough (*continued*)

SPECIAL EQUIPMENT SUGGESTED:
A food processor

Mixing the dough. Whisk the yeast ingredients in a measure and let bubble up 5 minutes or so to proof. Measure the dry ingredients into the bowl of the processor. Blend the ¾ cup of milk into the ready yeast mixture.

1. Dough softly massed on blade of processor

Turn on the machine and process in the yeast, then the oil, and droplets more milk, if needed, just until the dough masses on the blade of the processor, as shown, step 1.

The dough will be very soft. Let it rest 5 minutes, and it will develop enough body to be processed 2 seconds more in the machine. Then turn it out onto your lightly floured work surface.

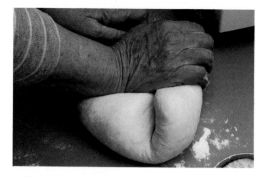

2. Final hand kneading

Knead 50 strokes by hand, give a 2-minute rest, and knead 20 strokes more to make a soft, smooth dough, step 2.

Rising—about 1½ hours. Let the dough rise in a covered bowl until doubled in bulk. Turn it out onto your work surface, and it is ready to cut and form as your recipe directs.

*Ahead-of-time note: If you are not ready to bake, punch the dough down and set the covered bowl in a cooler place, where it will keep safely for an hour or more. You can chill or even freeze it, but then it must be brought to room temperature and start to rise again before you form and bake it.

3. Forming dough into balls

Form dough gently with your hands into smooth balls, step 3. Cover loosely and let rest 10 minutes before making pizza or calzone, as described farther on.

Cornmeal Pizza Dough

A small proportion of cornmeal in a pizza dough gives a pleasantly crisp texture, and I find this formula particularly successful for the home pizza oven.

For a disk 12 to 14 inches across and about ¼ inch thick

The yeast mixture
1 package dry-active yeast
¼ cup tepid water (not over 110°F)
⅛ tsp sugar

The dry ingredients
1 cup all-purpose flour (measure by scooping and leveling, page 380)
⅓ cup cornmeal
1 tsp salt

Additions to the yeast mixture
¼ cup milk, plus more later, if needed
2 Tbs olive oil

SPECIAL EQUIPMENT SUGGESTED:
A food processor

Mixing and kneading the dough. Following the detailed directions for French bread dough on page 38, whisk the yeast mixture in a measure and let proof. Meanwhile measure the dry ingredients into the bowl of the processor. When the yeast is ready, whisk into it the ¼ cup of milk and the oil. Turn on the machine, and process in the liquid, adding droplets more milk if necessary—you won't need much, if any, so don't overdo. When the dough balls on the blade, let it rotate 8 to 10 times under the cover. Give a 5-minute rest, process 30 more revolutions, and turn the dough out onto your work surface. After a 2-minute rest, knead 30 strokes by hand.

Rising. Let the dough rise to 1½ times its volume in a covered bowl—40 to 60 minutes; deflate by patting it into a rectangle, folding into 3 layers, and repeating the process. Let rise again, this time to more than double, and the dough is ready to form.

*Ahead-of-time note: See notes at the end of the preceding classic dough recipe.

VARIATIONS

Tortilla Pizzas

Use large flour tortillas, the thinnest you can find. Top with any of the following suggestions, and bake them as usual but only long enough to cook the topping and crisp the tortilla base.

Pita Bread Pizzas

Use large white-flour pita breads, split in half. Treat them like the preceding tortillas.

TO TOP AND BAKE A PIZZA

From the pizza extravaganzas of famed Wolfgang Puck to the boutique pizzas of equally famed Alice Waters, that once humble pie has become a truly creative base. It is especially suited to the home cook, who can be fast and simple or infinitely elaborate. We start with basic tomato and cheese—always easy to assemble and always a favorite—and follow with more elaborate suggestions.

Baking Equipment Note:

Pizzas are at their peak when you have the right baking equipment—a pizza stone that heats up in the oven onto which you slide the pizza from a paddle or baker's peel. These are described and illustrated in the recipe for French bread (page 38). *Note:* If your pizza stone is porous, form the pizza on lightweight oiled foil set on your paddle or you'll have a smoke-filled oven. You can bake on a pastry sheet or pizza pan, but it is never as good—the crust is never quite as crusty as it should be.

Tomato Note:

For all pizzas specifying tomato sauce, your own (page 358) is always preferable, but you can make do with fresh tomato pulp (page 358) or a mixture of fresh and canned tomatoes, livened with seasonings, olive oil, garlic, and herbs. Or you can fix up a bottled sauce in the same manner.

Cheese Note:

A mixture of cheeses gives added interest, such as grated mozzarella or soft Jack, a hard cheese like Parmesan, aged Jack or Asiago, and for contrast thin finger-shaped slices of a third cheese like Swiss, Cheddar, or fontina. Reserve Roquefort, other blue cheeses, Camembert, Brie, etc., for your own unique boutique creations.

Tomato Pizza with Three Cheeses

Of course you can use one type of cheese only, but if one's good, three's better.

For a 14- to 16-inch pizza

Fully risen pizza dough, either the classic recipe or the cornmeal
¼ cup fruity olive oil
1½ to 2 cups cheeses: finely grated hard cheese, coarsely grated mozzarella, and thin-sliced fingers of Swiss (see preceding notes)
2 cups fresh tomato sauce (or see preceding notes)
Herbs to taste: thyme, oregano, sage, or Italian or Provençal herb mixture
Salt and freshly ground pepper, as needed

SPECIAL EQUIPMENT SUGGESTED:
A baking stone and pizza paddle (page 41); a sheet of foil oiled on top, if needed; a soft pastry brush for flour; a pastry brush for oil

Preliminaries. Place the pizza stone in the middle level, and preheat the oven to 450°F. If you are using foil, place it oiled side up on the paddle; if not, lightly flour the paddle.

Forming the pizza disk. Form the dough into a 14- to 16-inch disk about ¼ inch thick by rolling it out and stretching, or tossing in your hands as shown, step 1—a nice professional touch that takes not too much practice.

1. Tossing and stretching the dough over the tops of your hands

2. Spreading on the topping

Press it in shape as necessary with your fingers. Lightly flour the top, fold into quarters, and transfer it to the far end of the paddle, again pressing it into shape as needed.

The topping. Brush off excess flour, and brush on a light coating of olive oil. Dust with 2 tablespoons of grated hard cheese, and spread on the tomato. Drizzle on a little olive oil, spread on the mozzarella, interspersing it with the cheese slivers, and a sprinkling of herbs, salt, and pepper, step 2. Drizzle on a little more oil, and finish with the remaining grated hard cheese.

Baking—7 to 10 minutes. At once slide the pizza onto the hot baking stone in the oven. Bake until the edges have puffed, the cheese is bubbling, and when you lift up the edges you can see that the bottom has crisped—it should be a patchy brown.

Serving. Slide the pizza onto a serving board, and cut into wedges.

*Ahead-of-time note: A pizza is always at its best when freshly cooked; however, you can refrigerate leftovers and reheat on a baking sheet in the oven, or in the microwave.

ADDITIONS AND VARIATIONS

Using the same general ingredients of tomatoes, cheese, and a bowl of fresh herbs as a base, vary the proportions as you wish. Here are some of many possible additions, a number of which come from my friend Rosemary.

Italian Sausage

Steam several sweet or hot Italian sausages 5 minutes. Peel off and discard the covering skin casing, chop roughly, then sauté a few minutes, mashing and crumbling them. Sprinkle over the tomatoes before adding the cheese.

Finished pizza

Onion and Anchovy Pizza: the Pissaladière

This is one of my favorites, a specialty of Nice. Be sure the onions are perfectly cooked and tender since their sojourn in the oven is short, and be sure your anchovies are fresh and fine.

A 2-ounce can of flat anchovy fillets packed in oil
1 large clove of garlic, puréed
Ingredients for Tomato Pizza with Three Cheeses (page 56), minus the tomatoes and half the cheese
Salt, freshly ground pepper, and sage
4 cups sliced onions cooked until very tender in ¼ cup olive oil, cooled
A handful of Niçoise type small black olives

Mash 3 anchovy fillets with the puréed garlic and 1 tablespoon of olive oil; brush this paste over the disk of pizza dough. Sprinkle on 2 tablespoons of the grated hard cheese. Season the onions and spread them on. Place the remaining anchovies like the spokes of a wheel over the onions, and scatter the olives in between. Spread on a decent amount of cheese, and drizzle over the remaining olive oil.

Mushrooms

Slice a handful of trimmed fresh mushrooms, and toss with a little lemon juice, salt, and olive oil. Scatter them over the tomatoes before adding the cheese.

Clams

Chop a cup of fresh baby clams or use canned minced clams, and scatter them over the tomatoes along with ¼ cup of minced scallions and droplets of lemon juice. Then spread on the cheese and drizzle with oil.

Broccoli or Artichokes

Steam broccoli flowerettes until almost tender, or use quartered and marinated artichoke hearts—about 1½ cups. Arrange them over the tomatoes and sprinkle on a little lemon juice and ¼ cup of minced scallions; finish with the cheese and a drizzle of olive oil.

SPECIAL NOTE

About Anchovies

I think one reason some people hate anchovies is that they've been served stale ones that have been sitting around in an open can—they go off quickly. In other words, buy small cans (I've had best luck with Portuguese anchovies packed in olive oil), and use them all.

1. Folding half of dough over filling

2. Painting top of dough with remaining garlic oil

3. To serve, cut the calzone crosswise into 2 or 3 pieces.

Rosemary's Calzone

Italian sausage is given lightness and special flavor with fresh fennel, leeks, and red and green bell peppers. This is fine picnic fare, since it is good either hot or cold.

MANUFACTURING NOTE: *If you are cooking several calzone—one will amply serve 2 people—form them on sheets of oiled foil so that they may be slid in pairs from your pizza paddle onto your hot baking stone. The average pizza stone will hold 2, possibly 3, while 4 to 6 will go onto a tile-lined oven rack. Although you can bake them on a pastry sheet, the hot oven surface produces the best crust.*

For 1 calzone, serving 2

The fully risen classic pizza dough (page 53), which will make 3 calzone

Rosemary's filling

1 fresh sweet Italian sausage
1 large fennel bulb
1 large leek, white part only, or 1 onion
1 medium red or green bell pepper
Garlic oil (1 large clove of garlic puréed and blended into 3 Tbs fruity olive oil)
Salt
¼ cup finely grated Parmesan or other hard cheese
⅓ cup coarsely grated Swiss cheese
Herbs: 2 Tbs minced fresh parsley and your choice of others, fresh or dried
Drops of freshly squeezed lemon juice
1 ounce soft Jack or Cheddar, cut into 4 strips
Optional topping: a sprinkling of coarse salt

SPECIAL EQUIPMENT SUGGESTED: *A vegetable steamer; a pizza stone or quarry tiles and a pizza paddle (page 41)*

Preparing the filling and other preliminaries. As the dough is rising, prick the sausage and set to steam in a covered pan. Meanwhile slice the fennel and leek or onion thinly lengthwise and add to the steamer, not covering the sausage. Halve and seed the pepper; slice crosswise, and add to steam with the other vegetables for 2 minutes. Remove the steamer to let the vegetables drain. Cut the sausage into thin crosswise slices. Preheat the oven to 450°F with the baking stone a good 20 minutes before you plan to bake the calzone.

*Ahead-of-time note: The filling may be prepared in advance.

Forming. After the dough has been divided and given its 10-minute rest as described in the master recipe, form a ball of dough into a pizza-like disk 12 inches across, and place it on the edge of your lightly floured paddle or on oiled foil. Rapidly, so the dough will not rise, proceed to the filling as follows.

Filling. Leaving a free ½ inch all around, paint the surface of the disk with a coating of garlic oil. You are now to fill half the disk; the other half will be folded over to cover it. Salt the to-be-filled half lightly. Spread on half the grated hard cheese, half the Swiss cheese, then a mixture of the steamed sausage, vegetables, and herbs. Drizzle on drops of lemon juice, spread on the rest of the grated Swiss cheese, arrange the cheese strips on top, drizzle over half the remaining garlic oil, and sprinkle on the rest of the grated hard cheese.

Bring the top half of the dough over to cover the filling, and press the edges firmly together with your fingers to seal them, as illustrated, step 1.

Paint the top of the dough with the remaining garlic oil, step 2, and sprinkle lightly with the optional coarse salt.

Baking—about 10 minutes at 450°F. Slide the calzone onto the hot baking stone (or proceed rapidly to the next if you are baking several). The calzone is done when lightly puffed and browned, and when the bottom has crisped and colored nicely.

Other Fillings Adapt any of the pizza toppings to calzone, adding crumbled sausage, diced ham, or chicken, or an eggplant mixture such as ratatouille (page 317), or moussaka (page 319)—good use for leftovers!

Buttermilk Corn Sticks

Definitely dressier than cornbread baked in the traditional square pan (for which I usually use the recipe on the Quaker cornmeal box), cornsticks are so shapely you can well serve them not only at breakfast but at lunch, at dinner, or at high tea.

For 14 sticks 3½ inches long

⅓ cup fresh peanut oil, plus a little
     more to oil the molds
1¼ cups yellow cornmeal
½ cup white all-purpose flour
2 Tbs sugar
1½ tsp fresh and active double-
     acting baking powder
½ tsp baking soda
½ tsp salt
1 cup buttermilk
1 egg, lightly beaten

SPECIAL EQUIPMENT SUGGESTED:
Cast-iron cornstick molds—or baking sheets for free-form rounds

Preliminaries. Preheat the oven to 425°F. Brush the molds (or baking sheets) generously with peanut oil and heat in the oven 5 to 10 minutes before baking.

The batter. Mix the cornmeal, flour, sugar, baking powder, baking soda, and salt in a big bowl. When the molds or baking sheets are hot, vigorously and rapidly beat the buttermilk into the cornmeal mixture, then the egg, and finally the ⅓ cup of oil.

Forming. Plan to work fast at this point—and remember that the metals are hot!

Using either a large spoon or a pastry bag with a ¾-inch tube opening, fill the molds roundly full as fast as you can and pop them back into the oven. (Or rapidly form 2-inch rounds on the hot baking sheets with a spoon.)

Baking. Bake 15 to 20 minutes, until lightly puffed and brown—they will come easily out of the molds or off the baking sheets. Turn them over rapidly and return to the oven 2 to 3 minutes to brown on the other side.

**Ahead-of-time note:* These are best served hot and fresh, but I've reheated them, and also frozen them, with good results.

VARIATION

Boston Brown Bread

Boston Brown Bread, steamed in the traditional coffee can, is where it should be—with Boston Baked Beans on page 335.

Eggs

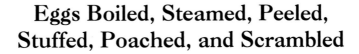

Eggs Boiled, Steamed, Peeled, Stuffed, Poached, and Scrambled

Eggs in Omelettes and Timbales

Eggs in Cheese, Vanilla, and Chocolate Soufflés

The egg, that perfect, pristine, primal object—we may not gobble it up as profusely now as we used to, but every mouthful should be memorable. The hard-boiled egg must be perfectly done and smoothly peeled, the scrambled eggs tender and creamy, the poached egg beautifully shaped, the omelette a dream, the timbale custard subtly flavored, and the soufflé proudly puffed. This chapter is a short reminder of the way to cook eggs, with a master recipe and an example or two in each category.

Eggs, of course, appear throughout cookery. We need them not only for their puffing abilities in soufflés, but also in cakes where perfectly beaten egg whites give air and lightness. We need them for their thickening abilities not only in the tender caramel custards and timbales described here, but in sauces like hollandaise and mayonnaise. We want them as binders in stuffings and meat mixtures. Thus the egg is not only a delicacy by itself, but one of the most useful staples in the culinary hierarchy.

WARNING. Be sure that your eggs come from a certified and carefully inspected source—and make every effort to see that poultry inspection and sanitary regulations are strictly enforced in your area. If we, the public, are alert and demanding, our elected officials have no choice but to follow.

Use Grade AA or Grade A eggs, and never buy or use cracked or dirty eggs since broken or contaminated shells may have allowed harmful bacteria to penetrate. Keep raw eggs and egg dishes refrigerated, serve cooked egg dishes as soon as they are done; wash hands, utensils, and work surfaces in hot soapy whenever raw eggs are involved in a recipe.

HARD-BOILED EGGS

The perfect HB egg has a tender white, and a yolk properly set. And the perfect HB egg shows not the faintest darkening of yolk where the white encircles it—a most unappetizing chemical reaction, shown at right in the photograph, caused by too much heat. Furthermore, the perfect HB egg can be peeled neatly.

The system described here, developed some years ago by the Georgia Egg Board, takes a bit of fussing, but it does produce the perfect HB egg—and what a blessing that is when you've several dozen to do.

SPECIAL NOTE

Help for Recalcitrant Peelers

If you have eggs boiled by another system and find them hard to peel, try the chill and 10-second boil—it can help just by expanding the shell.

At left, the perfect HB egg. At right, the dolefully discolored, badly cooked yolk.

●MASTER RECIPE

To Hard-Boil and Peel Eggs

Here the eggs are not boiled; rather they are brought to the boil, then sit in the hot water until cooked through. That's coddling—for a nonrubbery white and just-cooked-through yolk.

MANUFACTURING NOTES:

Pricking. There is a bubble of air in the large end of the egg, which expands when the egg is heated and can crack the shell. To let that air escape, always prick the large end with an egg pricker or a pin, going in a good ¼ inch.

How much water? That depends on how many eggs you have. The water should cover the eggs by 1 inch, so use a tall pan, and I would hesitate, under home conditions, to do more than 2 dozen eggs at once.

For 1 to 4 eggs...2 quarts of water
For 12 eggs ......3½ quarts of water
For 24 eggs ......6 quarts of water

SPECIAL EQUIPMENT SUGGESTED:
An egg pricker or drafting pin; a high rather than wide saucepan with cover; a bowl of sufficient size with ice cubes and water to cover eggs

The cooking. Lay the eggs in the pan and add the amount of cold water specified. Set over high heat and bring just to the boil; remove from heat, cover the pan, and let sit exactly 17 minutes.

The 2-minute chill. When the time is up, transfer the eggs to the bowl of ice cubes and water. Chill for 2 minutes while bringing the cooking water to the boil again. The 2-minute chilling shrinks the body of the egg from the shell.

The 10-second boil. Transfer the eggs (6 at a time only) to the boiling water, bring to the boil again, and let boil for 10 seconds—which in turn expands the shell from the egg. Return the eggs to the ice water, cracking the shells gently in several places.

Preventing that dark line around the yolk. Chilling the eggs promptly prevents that dark line from forming, and, if you have time, leave the eggs in the ice water (adding more ice if needed) for 15 to 20 minutes before peeling. Chilled eggs are easier to peel, too. Or peel them, as described in the next paragraph, and ice them at once.

Peeling. Crack an egg all over by gently tapping it against the sink. Then, starting at the large end, and holding the egg either under a thin stream of cold water or in the bowl of ice water, start peeling. As soon as you have peeled it, return the egg to the ice water so that it will continue to chill.

Storing the HB eggs. They will keep perfectly in the refrigerator, submerged in water in an *uncovered* container, for 2 to 3 days.

WARNING! Eggs and Salmonella

Eggs—about 1 in every 10,000 at this writing—may contain salmonella bacteria. The bacteria multiplies at room temperature, but is quiescent when chilled. It is killed when the egg is heated over 140°F, or is hard-boiled, and it is also killed by a fairly strong dose of acid—lemon juice or vinegar.

A healthy human immune system is built to handle a certain number of harmful bacteria, but infants, the ill, and the elderly should beware of raw and undercooked eggs.

As for me, I love eggs in any form, and I happily eat boiled, scrambled, soft-boiled, and poached eggs as well as soufflés and mayonnaise *at home* because I know my eggs have been handled in the USDA-

approved manner, and that they have been under refrigeration practically from hen to table. Away from home, I am wary and usually abstemious.

Some Egg Rules

1. Know your egg sources.
2. Never buy unrefrigerated eggs.
3. Never buy cracked eggs.
4. Never leave eggs sitting about in the kitchen—warmth allows bacteria to multiply—keep them always in the refrigerator. If they need to be at room temperature, place them in a bowl of hot water for several minutes, then use at once.
5. Always wash all bowls, utensils, work surfaces, and hands in hot soapy water after handling raw eggs.

Recipes for cooked egg mayonnaise and hollandaise are on page 377.

Perforated oval metal egg cups for perfect poached eggs every time

POACHED EGGS

The perfect poached egg is a graceful free-form egg-shaped oval; the yolk, which is softly liquid, is completely enrobed by the white. Really fresh eggs are easy indeed to poach—crack them one by one into barely simmering water and they form themselves perfectly. That is because the white of a really fresh egg clings closely around the yolk. However, as the days go by the white begins to relax, until in extreme old age it trails off in the water leaving the yolk almost naked—not a pretty sight.

Few of us have really fresh eggs available, but the following system works for reasonably fresh store-bought eggs.

● MASTER RECIPE

To Poach an Egg

Three Aids to Perfectly Poached Eggs:

A 10-second boil in the shell. Prick the large end of the eggs with an egg pricker or drafting pin, going down ¼ inch, so that the pocket of air in the shell may escape. Lower the eggs, no more than 4 at a time, into boiling water, submerging them completely, for exactly 10 seconds. This slightly coagulates a film of white around the body of the egg, and helps keep a reasonably fresh egg in shape.

The oval perforated egg cup. The oval perforated egg-poacher cup is the key to success. Arrange the egg cups in the pan of simmering water to cover them by ½ inch. After the pricking and the 10-second boil, rapidly break the eggs into the cups. Poach at the bare simmer 4 minutes.

Vinegar in extremis. If you must have poached eggs and have only store-bought eggs but no egg poachers, add 2½ tablespoons of white vinegar per quart of poaching water. After the pricking and the 10-second boil, drop the eggs in, breaking the shell as close to the surface of the water as possible, and poach 4 minutes. Although vinegar causes a faintly perceptible thickening to form around the outside of the egg, it most definitely does help the egg to coagulate.

The poached egg itself, the cups, the aspic, the ham, and the chilled decorations

Ahead-of-time note: Remove the eggs from the poaching water and submerge in a bowl of cold water (or iced water), and store in the refrigerator uncovered, where they will keep nicely 2 to 3 days.

To Serve Poached Eggs Hot: If chilled, lower them into almost simmering lightly salted water and leave 1 minute. Remove the eggs, one at a time, with a slotted spoon and roll each one over a clean towel to blot up excess moisture.

Poached Eggs with Mushrooms: A Hot Suggestion

For an elegant first course or luncheon dish, prepare the large Stuffed Mushroom Caps on page 313, top each with a hot poached egg, a spoonful of cheese sauce, and a sprinkling of cheese; run briefly under the broiler to brown.

To Serve Poached Eggs Cold. Place them in ice water for 2 to 3 minutes. Drain one by one in a slotted spoon and roll the egg over a clean towel.

Poached Eggs in Aspic: A Cold Suggestion

Poached eggs in fancy dress, nestled in wine-flavored aspic—they are easy to do, budget priced, and lovely objects to serve your guests at a summer luncheon.

For 6 chilled poached eggs

4 cups Port wine aspic (page 16)
Chilled decorations (such as those pictured here): pimiento and cooked carrot shapes; blanched green scallion tops; sliced stuffed olives; black olives; rounds of thinly sliced boiled ham for final layer

SPECIAL EQUIPMENT SUGGESTED:
6 chilled custard cups of 2/3-cup capacity on a tray; a small saucepan for chilling aspic; a bowl with ice cubes and water to cover; a fork and skewer for arranging decorations

First layer of aspic. Pour a ¼-inch layer of aspic into the bottoms of the custard cups and refrigerate for 10 minutes, or until set.

The decorations. Pour a cup of the aspic into the small pan, set over the ice, and, when cold but not set, dip each decoration into it so that the decoration will adhere as you arrange it over the aspic layer. (Rewarm and rechill the pan of aspic as necessary.)

In go the eggs. One by one drain the chilled eggs, roll them dry on a clean towel, and place best side down over the decorations. Spoon cold and almost-set aspic around each egg to come a third of the way up, and chill 10 minutes or until set—to anchor the eggs and decorations.

The elegant poached egg in aspic

Filling to the brim. Fill the cups with more cold, almost-set aspic and cover with the rounds of ham. Chill an hour before unmolding.

*Ahead-of-time note: May be made a day or two in advance; refrigerate, covered with plastic.

Unmolding and serving. One by one, dip the cups in very hot water just to loosen the aspic, run the blade of a thin knife around the inside edge if necessary, and unmold onto chilled plates or a platter.

Other Aspics: See also the Chicken in Aspic, both simple and fancy, on page 145, and the Mediterranean Fish Aspic on page 26.

SCRAMBLED EGGS

Perfect scrambled eggs are tender and creamy, really a kind of broken custard. The only secret is to do them slowly over low heat, so that the eggs coagulate into soft curds. You don't want the eggs too deep in the pan or they will take too long to cook, and if there is too shallow a layer they will cook too quickly—a one-inch layer is easy to handle, and a no-stick pan is certainly my choice: the 10-inch size does nicely for 6 to 8 eggs. Plain scrambled eggs are lovely for breakfast, but chopped green herbs are always an attractive addition, especially chopped fresh parsley, chives, or tarragon—add them along with the seasonings as you beat the eggs before scrambling them.

● MASTER RECIPE

To Scramble Eggs

For 8 eggs, serving 4 to 6

8 eggs
Salt and freshly ground pepper
1 Tbs or more butter
1 Tbs or more heavy cream, optional
Optional minced fresh herbs: 3 or 4
  Tbs minced parsley, or parsley
  and chives, chervil, tarragon, or
  dill

SPECIAL EQUIPMENT SUGGESTED:
A mixing bowl and fork; a 10-inch no-stick frying pan, and a straight-edged wooden or plastic spatula; warm plates

Cooking the eggs. Break the eggs into the bowl, adding salt and pepper to taste, and beat just to blend yolks and whites. Set the frying pan over moderately low heat and add enough butter to film the bottom and sides; pour in all but 2 tablespoons of the beaten eggs. Slowly scrape the bottom of the pan from the edges toward the center with the spatula, continuing slowly as the eggs gradually coagulate—it will take them a minute or so to start thickening—don't rush them. In 2 to 3 minutes or so the eggs will have thickened into a softly lumpy custard—cook them a few seconds longer if they are too soft for your taste. Fold in the 2 tablespoons of beaten egg, to cream the scramble. Carefully correct seasoning and, if you wish, fold in a tablespoon or so additional butter and/or cream, and the optional herbs.

Serving. Serve at once on warm (not hot) plates. Accompany with, for instance, bacon or sausage or ham, broiled tomatoes, and buttered toast wedges.

VARIATION

Dilled Scrambled Eggs: A Cold Suggestion

I first had these in Norway, with my first dilled salmon, gravlaks. Season the scrambled eggs with chopped fresh dill, and serve them forth with the salmon—a happy accompaniment. The Norwegians also include potatoes creamed in a dill-flavored sauce, and the combination of salmon, potatoes, and eggs is a winning luncheon or supper dish.

Egg Burritos: A Hot Suggestion

Scrambled eggs enclosed in egg tortillas—serve them for breakfast, brunch, lunch, or supper. And the good news here is that you can get them all ready for heating and serving well in advance.

For 8 burritos

12 eggs
Seasonings: salt, freshly ground
  pepper, and hot pepper sauce
1 to 2 Tbs butter
½ cup cottage cheese
Herbs: ¼ cup chopped fresh parsley
  and ¼ tsp fresh or dried thyme
2 cups fine tomato sauce (page 358)
¼ cup grated Cheddar cheese

SPECIAL EQUIPMENT SUGGESTED:
A small no-stick pan, 6-inch bottom diameter; a cover of some sort for the pan; a stack of eight 6-inch-square pieces of wax paper; a lightly buttered baking and serving dish

Making the burrito skins. Whisk the eggs in a bowl with the seasonings to taste. Set the frying pan over moderately high heat and brush lightly with butter; pour in 1½ tablespoons of egg and tilt the pan in all directions to film the bottom. Cover the pan for a few seconds until the egg has set, then slide it out onto wax paper, step 1. Repeat, making 8 in all.

The scrambled egg filling. Following the preceding master recipe, softly scramble the remaining egg mixture. Blend with the cottage cheese and herbs, and adjust seasonings to taste.

Forming the burritos. Roll up a portion of scrambled egg in each burrito skin, as shown, step 2.

Ready for the oven. Turn the tomato sauce into the baking dish, and arrange the burritos on top. Sprinkle on the grated cheese.

Ahead-of-time note: May be prepared in advance; cover and refrigerate.

Heating and serving—about 7 to 10 minutes at 450°F. Preheat the oven to 450°F. Shortly before serving, bake in the upper third level of the preheated oven just until the sauce bubbles and the cheese has melted. Do not overheat!

1. Covering pan while burrito cooks; finished skins at left

2. Rolling up with the filling

Egg burritos, filled, and ready for the oven

OMELETTES

Omelettes are such fun to make when you toss them off, as shown here. A fresh green salad, a glass of white wine, and an omelette make a lunch worth waiting the 30 seconds it takes to make one, and I say fie to those oenophilic spoilsports who insist that wine goes with neither eggs nor salads. Wine is essential with anything! Particularly omelettes for lunch.

Manufacturing Notes:

The omelette pan. In the days before no-stick pans, to find the right omelette pan was a real problem.

Fabled Dione Lucas, one of the great early cooking teachers and omelette practitioners, had a special heavy aluminum pan that no one was ever allowed to touch. And there were the black French steel pans 1/16 inch thick that needed special curing and very special care. Some cooks insist to this day that only the French iron pan gives the right color and consistency to an omelette. Wonderful pans they are, but try to find one for sale in this country. The pan to look for is the Wearever professional pan made of professional-quality aluminum, with heavy-duty no-stick interior.

It has a 10-inch top diameter, a 7½-inch bottom diameter, and the sides, with the slightest curve, are 2 inches high. It is not only an omelette pan, but the pan you will use most—of all your frying pans—for general cooking. Don't bother with the rubber

sleeves sold with some of these pans—they're almost impossible to get off when you want to put the pan in the oven for one reason or another. Get used to wearing a towel hung at your waist, as chefs do, and grab the handle with that.

The 2- to 3-egg omelette. Unless you are a whiz with a restaurant stove and heat source, I don't recommend more than the 2-egg omelette, 3 at most, since the eggs should be soft and tender inside, enclosed by a cloak of lightly browned coagulated egg. Too many eggs and you risk a second-class result. Besides, at 20 to 30 seconds per omelette, you can serve a goodly number of people in just a few minutes.

1. Beaten eggs poured into middle of hot pan

2. Shaking and swirling pan by its handle

3. Jerking pan toward you

4. Push any stray egg into mass with spatula.

5. Banging on pan handle with fist

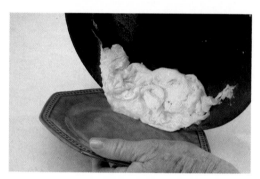

6. Turning the omelette onto the plate

● MASTER RECIPE

The Tossed Omelette

Remember that a tossed omelette goes very fast—really in 20 seconds—far, far less time than it takes to read all the directions here. Give a dry run or two before you actually cook your first omelette so that you are fully familiar with the movements. Plan to make 5 or more omelettes one after the other for friends or family, daring to be fast and rough and confident (whatever happens!). Then you will quickly master the technique of the jerk, a straight rough pull of the pan toward you by its handle—not a toss.

For a 1-serving omelette

2 "large" eggs
1 tsp water
Salt and freshly ground pepper
1 to 1½ Tbs butter
Optional serving suggestions: 1 tsp
  soft butter; parsley sprigs

SPECIAL EQUIPMENT SUGGESTED:
The no-stick 10-inch frying pan previously described; warm plates

The eggs. Break the eggs into a bowl, add the teaspoon of water, and salt and pepper to taste. Whisk with a fork just to blend yolks and whites.

Heating the pan. Set the pan over highest heat, add the butter, and as it melts tilt the pan in all directions to film the bottom and sides. Watch the butter carefully—when the foam begins to subside and the butter just

7. Shoring up the edges for a neat presentation

begins to color, pour the eggs into the middle of the pan, step 1—they should hiss gently as they go in, indicating also that the pan is hot enough.

Coagulating the bottom. At once shake and swirl the pan by its handle to distribute the eggs over the surface, step 2; then hold it still over heat for 2 to 3 seconds, to form a film of coagulated egg on the bottom of the pan.

8. The finished omelette

The omelette forms in the pan. Now, holding the pan by its handle, start jerking it toward you—thus throwing the egg mass against the far edge of the pan, step 3. Keep jerking roughly, gradually tilting the far edge of the pan over the heat as the omelette begins to roll over on itself. Push any stray egg into the mass with a spatula, if necessary, step 4. When nicely formed at the far edge, bang on the handle close to the near edge with your left fist and the omelette will begin to curl at its far edge, step 5. It is done.

Omelette onto plate. Turn the pan handle to your right, grab the underside of the handle with your right hand palm up and thumb on top, hold a warm plate in your left hand,

and tilt the two toward each other, step 6. Then reverse the pan over the plate to dislodge the omelette upon it. If it is not turned out neatly, shore up the edges with a spatula, step 7.

Serving. If you wish, rub the butter over the top of the omelette and decorate with parsley, step 8. Serve at once.

VARIATIONS

Serving a Crowd

Have a big bowl or pitcher for your whisked and seasoned eggs, a whisk to beat them lightly before each omelette, and a long-handled ladle that holds a scant ½ cup—2 "large" eggs measure 6 to 7 tablespoons, or a little less than ½ cup. Then with your butter measured out, and a stack of warm plates, you are ready to perform with speed and grace.

VARIATIONS

Fillings
Fresh Herbs: Omelette aux Fines Herbes

Whisk a tablespoon of fresh minced herbs into the eggs before making the omelette—parsley alone, or parsley and chives, chervil, or tarragon. Sprinkle a good pinch on top of the omelette before serving.

Cheese Omelette

After the eggs have coagulated on the bottom of the pan and before jerking the omelette to form it, rapidly spread 2 tablespoons of grated Swiss cheese over the eggs, then proceed.

Potato Omelette

Follow the preceding cheese omelette, but spread on ½ cup or so of diced potatoes that have been sautéed with herbs and shallots (page 327).

Other Fillings. A few more of the many possibilities:

Sautéed mushrooms or *chicken livers* or *diced ham*, or

Pipérade —green and red bell peppers sautéed with onions and garlic (page 90)—or

Broccoli florets (page 269), cooked chopped spinach (page 278), or *asparagus tips,* warmed first in butter and seasonings, or

Lobster, shrimp, or *crab,* warmed first in butter and seasonings.

TIMBALES: MOLDED CUSTARDS

They are very French, timbales—very much home cooking—carefully flavored chopped or puréed cooked vegetables or chicken livers or ham, baked with eggs and seasonings in a deep dish like a charlotte mold, then unmolded for serving. A vegetable timbale is an attractive accompaniment to roasts or grilled meats, and any of them make the main course for a luncheon or supper.

● MASTER RECIPE

Individual Timbales of Fresh Corn

This is one of my favorites in the timbale category, and the good news is that you can make it any time of the year—out-of-season corn is fine as long as it is fresh.

For 12 individual molds

3 cups grated fresh corn (about a dozen ears)
6 "large" eggs
⅔ cup lightly pressed down crumbs from fresh crustless homemade type white bread
3 Tbs grated onion
¼ cup lightly pressed down, minced fresh parsley
⅔ cup lightly pressed down, grated Swiss and/or Cheddar and/or mozzarella cheese

1 cup toasted and buttered bread crumbs, optional
⅔ cup heavy cream or milk
Seasonings: 1 tsp salt, 8 grinds of fresh white peppercorns, 8 drops of hot pepper sauce
A kettle of boiling water

Accompaniments:
See serving notes, at end of recipe

SPECIAL EQUIPMENT SUGGESTED: *A corn grater is most useful here; 12 buttered custard cups ⅔- to ¾-cup size (5 to 6 ounces); a roasting pan to hold the cups*

The timbale mixture. Scrape or grate the corn into a big mixing bowl, then beat in the eggs and the rest of the ingredients listed. Taste for seasoning. Pour into the custard cups, filling them by no more than five eighths. Arrange them in the roasting pan.

Baking—about 30 minutes at 350°F and 325°F. Preheat the oven to 350°F. Set the pan in the middle level of the preheated oven, and pour enough boiling water around the cups to come halfway up their outsides. Bake 5 minutes at 350°F, lower the thermostat to 325°F, and bake 25 minutes more, regulating oven heat so the water in the pan barely bubbles, never actually boils.

When are they done? When a skewer plunged down through the center comes out almost clean. Remove the pan from the oven and let the timbales settle for 10 minutes.

*Ahead-of-time note: You may leave them in the pan of water in the turned-off oven, its door ajar, for a good 30 minutes before serving.

Serving notes:

As a main-course accompaniment. If the timbales are to accompany a main course, such as a roast of beef or turkey, serve them as is or topped with buttered crumbs.

As a main course. Here you will need a sauce—fresh tomato sauce (page 358), or a light béchamel (page 272) with chopped fresh herbs—or a fresh green vegetable accompaniment.

Leftovers may be reheated in a water bath, or eaten cold.

Quiche Note:

The quiches starting on page 384, both those baked in crusts and the crustless quiches, are close relatives of the timbale.

VARIATIONS

A Large Corn Timbale

For drama, you may bake the timbale in one 2-quart fairly straight-sided dish about 3½ inches high—like a charlotte mold. Set it in a water bath coming halfway up the outside of the dish, but count on 1¼ to 1½ hours of oven time. Regulate the oven so the water never comes to more than the slow bubble. If it actually boils, the timbale will overcook and look grainy.

Timbale with toasted and buttered bread crumbs

SPECIAL NOTE

Cream of Mushroom Sauce

2 cups medium béchamel sauce (page 272)
½ cup mushroom duxelles (page 314)
Salt and freshly ground pepper
Optional enrichments: dollops of sour cream or spoonfuls of butter

Simmer the béchamel and mushrooms together for several minutes to blend flavors. Carefully correct seasoning. Just before serving, if you wish, stir in several tablespoons of heavy cream or, off heat and by spoonfuls, 2 to 3 tablespoons of butter.

Spinach, Broccoli, or Asparagus Timbale

Substitute 3 cups of beautifully cooked, carefully flavored, and finely chopped fresh spinach (page 278), broccoli florets (page 269), or asparagus tips for the corn.

Ham Timbale

Substitute 3 cups of puréed cooked ham for the corn, adding a tablespoon or so of tomato paste for color. The Cream of Mushroom Sauce (see Special Note) is a fine accompaniment here.

Chicken Liver Timbale

Substitute chicken livers and raw chicken breast for the corn as follows: Sauté 2½ cups of chicken livers in butter and minced shallots until barely springy to the touch, and still rosy inside. Purée in a blender or processor with 1 cup of raw chicken breast and the eggs and cream or milk called for in the recipe. Then proceed as directed. As a finishing touch, a little Béarnaise sauce (page 87) would glorify each serving.

SOUFFLÉS

The soufflé is undoubtedly the egg at its most magnificent, the egg in all its puffing power. How impressive is the chocolate or cheese soufflé, its head rising dramatically out of its dish, and swaying ever so slightly as it is borne to the table.

Fortunately, a reasonably well-assembled soufflé can be an automatic happenstance: a flavor base into which stiffly beaten egg whites are incorporated. When the mixture is baked, the heat of the oven expands the air bubbles in the egg whites and the whole mass rises. It stays puffed the few minutes needed to serve it; then, as it cools, the air bubbles deflate and the soufflé collapses. Soufflés are not difficult when you have mastered the beating of egg whites and the folding of them into the soufflé base.

The egg whites. They are beaten into stiff shining peaks, as described and illustrated on pages 461–62.

Folding—combining the egg whites and the soufflé base. For maximum puff, the beautifully beaten egg whites must retain their volume when they are incorporated. To help retain it, a quarter of the whites are stirred into the base to lighten it so that the remainder may be folded in easily. Folding is described and illustrated on page 463.

When is it done? A soufflé baked in a dish should puff 2 to 3 inches over the rim, and the top should be nicely browned. The puff should hold up when you release the collar just a little bit to check—if the puff sags, rapidly refasten the collar and bake a few minutes more. If you want the puff to hold and the soufflé to stand a reasonable time, test it by plunging a skewer down into the side of the puff: if wet particles cling to it the soufflé will be creamy inside and will not hold as long as if the skewer comes out almost clean. The fateful decision is up to you.

SPECIAL NOTE

For drama, you choose a dish that's a little too small, so that the soufflé puffs into a collar. When the collar is removed the puff holds itself 2 to 3 inches over the rim of the dish. Use a double thickness of buttered foil that will rise 3 inches over the top of the dish; secure the collar by inserting a straight pin head down—for easy removal.

Attaching the collar

Removing the collar

● MASTER RECIPE

Cheese Soufflé

For soufflés baked in a dish, soufflé toppings, and soufflé roulades

The basic cheese soufflé is a white sauce—béchamel—enriched with egg yolks and cheese, into which beaten egg whites are folded.

TIMING: *You will undoubtedly feel safer hovering over your oven during your first soufflé experiences. After two or three you'll have the confidence to set the timer and take yourself off until it summons you back into the kitchen.*

For a 1-quart baking dish 8 inches across, serving 4

2 Tbs finely grated Parmesan or
   other hard cheese
2½ Tbs butter
3 Tbs flour
1 cup hot milk
Seasonings: ½ tsp paprika, speck of
   nutmeg, ½ tsp salt, and 3 grinds
   of white pepper
4 egg yolks

5 egg whites (⅔ cup)
1 cup (3½ ounces) coarsely grated
  Swiss cheese

SPECIAL EQUIPMENT SUGGESTED:
*A buttered baking dish 7½ to 8 inches
top diameter, 3 inches deep; aluminum
foil; a heavy-bottomed 2½-quart saucepan; a wire whisk, wooden spoon, and
large rubber spatula; egg-white beating
equipment (pages 461–62)*

Preliminaries. Roll the grated cheese
in the buttered baking dish to cover
the bottom and side, and fasten on
the aluminum collar (see Special
Note). Preheat the oven to 400°F,
and set the rack in the lower third
level. Measure out all the ingredients
listed.

The white sauce—béchamel. Following
the detailed directions on page 272,
stir and cook the butter and flour together in the saucepan over moderate
heat for 2 minutes without coloring.
Remove from heat, let cool a moment, then pour in all the hot milk
and whisk vigorously to blend. Return to heat, stirring with a wooden
spoon, and boil slowly 3 minutes.
The sauce will be very thick. Whisk
in the seasonings, and remove from
heat.

Finishing the sauce base. One by one,
whisk the egg yolks into the hot
sauce.

The egg whites. In a clean separate
bowl with clean beaters, beat the egg
whites to stiff shining peaks as described on page 461.

Finishing the soufflé mixture. Scoop a
quarter of the egg whites on top of
the sauce and stir them in with a
wooden spoon. Turn the rest of the
egg whites on top; rapidly and deli-

cately fold them in, alternating
scoops of the spatula with sprinkles
of the coarsely grated cheese—adding the cheese now makes for a light
soufflé.

Ahead-of-time note: You may complete the soufflé to this point ½ hour
or so in advance; cover loosely with a
sheet of foil and set away from drafts.

Baking—25 to 30 minutes at 400°F
and 375°F. Set in the preheated oven,
turn the thermostat down to 375°F,
and bake until the soufflé has puffed 2
to 3 inches over the rim of the baking dish into the collar, and the top
has browned nicely (see "When is it
done?" notes preceding this section).

Serving. As soon as it is done, remove the collar, then bring the soufflé to the table. To keep the puff
standing, hold your serving spoon
and fork upright and back to back;
plunge them into the crust and tear it
apart.

Serving the soufflé

OTHER FLAVORS

Spinach or Broccoli Soufflé

After completing the white sauce, stir
in ¼ to ⅓ cup of cooked chopped
fresh spinach (page 278) or broccoli
(page 269) that you have warmed in
butter, shallots, and seasonings. Cut
down on the grated Swiss cheese—⅓
to ½ cup should be enough.

Crab, Lobster, or Shrimp Soufflé

Substitute chopped or finely diced
shellfish for the vegetables in the preceding suggestion. A hollandaise
sauce or the white butter sauce with
tomato fondue on page 91 would be
attractive accompaniments.

Salmon Soufflé
or Other Cooked Fish

Stir flaked cooked salmon or other
fish, or canned salmon, into the finished white sauce. Two or three tablespoons of shallots sautéed in butter
are often helpful for fish other than
salmon, as well as a spoonful or two
of minced fresh dill or parsley. In
some instances you may wish to accompany the soufflé with a lightly
cooked fresh tomato sauce, such as
that on page 358, or a colorful pipérade (sautéed onions with strips of red
and green peppers; see the rolled
soufflé variations farther on).

Soufflé on a Platter

A soufflé does not have to be baked in a dish. Try baking it on a platter instead. Arrange mounds of creamed lobster (page 107), or crab, or poached eggs on butter-sautéed croutons, on a buttered baking and serving platter. Divide the cheese soufflé mixture in mounds over each, top with a sprinkling of grated Swiss cheese, and bake 15 minutes or so in a 425°F oven. The mounded soufflés will puff to double and brown on top.

The Rolled Soufflé
Soufflé roulade

The rolled soufflé makes a particularly attractive luncheon dish, and you have an almost infinite choice of fillings, from the luxury of lobster to the gutsy penury of broccoli. Here it's a pipérade, with its colorful red and green pepper strips.

MANUFACTURING NOTE: *You want a 6-egg soufflé here to fill a jelly-roll pan—in other words, approximately half again the ingredients for the 4-egg master cheese soufflé. In the recipe illustrated here, I've made extra béchamel sauce, part for the soufflé itself, part to go into the filling, and the rest to accompany the roulade.*

For a 10- by 16-inch soufflé, serving 6

1½ cups of filling (see suggestions at end of recipe)

The béchamel sauce (for 5 cups)
4 ounces (1 stick) butter
¾ cup flour
4½ cups hot milk, plus droplets more, if needed

1 tsp salt and several grinds of white pepper

The soufflé mixture
3 cups of the preceding béchamel sauce
Seasonings: ¾ tsp paprika, pinch of nutmeg, ¾ tsp salt, 5 grinds of white pepper
6 egg yolks
6 egg whites, stiffly beaten
1 cup coarsely grated Swiss cheese

For unmolding the soufflé:
½ cup fresh white bread crumbs, toasted and tossed in 2 Tbs melted butter
Heavy cream
Grated Swiss cheese
Droplets of milk, if needed

SPECIAL EQUIPMENT SUGGESTED:
A lightly buttered jelly-roll pan lined with buttered wax paper that extends 2 inches beyond the 2 short sides; a baking sheet for unmolding the soufflé

Preliminaries. Prepare the pan, preheat the oven to 425°F, measure out all the ingredients listed, and prepare the filling.

The béchamel sauce. Following the master soufflé recipe, make the béchamel sauce. Remove and reserve 2 cups for later.

The soufflé mixture. Whisk the seasonings into the remaining 3 cups of sauce and beat in the egg yolks. Stir in a quarter of the beaten egg whites, and delicately fold in the rest, alternating with sprinklings of cheese.

Into the jelly-roll pan. Spread the soufflé mixture over the wax paper in the prepared pan, see illustration, step 1.

Baking—12 to 15 minutes at 425°F. Immediately set in the upper middle level of the preheated oven and bake

1. Spreading the soufflé over the wax paper

2. Before unmolding, cover with wax paper and upside-down baking sheet.

3. Spreading on the filling

4. Rolling it up

just until well set—do not overcook or it will break when rolled up.

Unmolding. Remove from the oven and sprinkle with three quarters of the toasted crumbs. Cover with a sheet of wax paper and lay the baking sheet on top, step 2; reverse the two and let cool 5 minutes. Remove the jelly-roll pan (now on top), using the wax paper overhang to help you. Carefully peel off the wax paper. Trim ¼ inch off the brittle edges of the soufflé all around to prevent it from cracking when rolled up.

*Ahead-of-time note: If you are not ready to serve, cover the soufflé loosely with wax paper and set over a pan of barely simmering water.

The reserved 2 cups of béchamel. Reheat the reserved 2 cups of béchamel sauce, and spread half of it over the soufflé. The remainder will surround the roulade; stir in a little cream and several tablespoons of grated cheese, thin out with droplets more milk if necessary, and season very carefully to taste—it should be light and delicious.

Filling and serving. Spread three quarters of whatever filling you have chosen over the sauce on the soufflé, step 3. Roll up the soufflé starting at one of the long sides, using the wax paper to help you, step 4. Transfer to a hot serving platter, and strew on the remaining crumbs and the reserved filling. Surround with the sauce, and serve.

SAUCES

A little sauce is really needed, since the soufflé is not moist. You may prefer a fresh tomato sauce (page 358).

FILLINGS

All kinds of fillings can go into these rolled soufflés, really the same ideas used for the soufflés cooked in a baking dish—cooked broccoli or spinach warmed in butter and seasonings, or such luxuries as lobster, shrimp, or crab. The Pipérade green and red pepper filling pictured here is on page 90, and following is one with ham and mushrooms.

Ham and Mushroom Filling
Another good filling.

3 cups quartered fresh mushrooms
2 Tbs butter
1 Tbs minced shallots or scallions
About 1 cup diced cooked ham
The reserved 1 cup béchamel sauce

Sauté the mushrooms rapidly in the butter, adding shallots or scallions and ham at the last moment. Season to taste. Spread a ⅛-inch layer of the béchamel sauce over the soufflé, then cover with ham mixture. Complete as in the preceding recipe.

DESSERT SOUFFLÉS

Soufflé for dessert—it invariably brings excitement and always pleasure. You can make a dessert soufflé using the usual béchamel white-sauce base, or a pastry cream *crème pâtissière* base, but I prefer the following bouillie, which I think makes a lighter soufflé.

● MASTER RECIPE

Vanilla Soufflé

Like vanilla ice cream, vanilla soufflé is always attractive since, good as it is by itself, you can add to your pleasure by accompanying it with fruits or a marvelous sauce as suggested in the Special Note on page 77.

For a 6-cup dish, serving 4

A little soft butter and granulated sugar for the dish

The bouillie sauce base
3 Tbs flour
¼ cup milk
⅓ cup granulated sugar
4 egg yolks
2 Tbs soft butter, optional

5 egg whites beaten to soft peaks
Pinch of salt
2 Tbs granulated sugar
2 Tbs pure vanilla extract
Confectioners sugar in a fine-meshed sieve

SPECIAL EQUIPMENT SUGGESTED:
A 6-cup baking dish such as a charlotte mold 3½ inches deep; aluminum foil; a 2½-quart stainless saucepan; a whisk, a wooden spoon, and a rubber spatula; egg-white beating equipment (page 461)

Preliminaries. Butter the baking dish, roll the sugar around in it to cover the bottom and sides, and pin on an aluminum foil collar (see Special Note, page 72). Preheat the oven to 400°F, and set the rack in the lower third level. Measure out all the ingredients listed.

The bouillie sauce base. Whisk the flour and half of the milk in the saucepan to blend; beat in the rest of the milk and the sugar. Stir with a wooden spoon over moderately high heat until the sauce thickens, then whisk as the sauce comes to the boil; continue boiling and whisking for 30 seconds. The sauce will be very thick; let cool for a moment, then beat the egg yolks one by one into the warm sauce. Beat in the optional butter.

The egg whites. In a clean separate bowl with clean beaters, beat the egg whites until foaming; add the salt and beat to soft peaks. Sprinkle in the sugar, and beat to stiff shining peaks, as described on page 461.

Finishing the soufflé. Whisk the vanilla into the sauce base, and stir in a quarter of the egg whites to lighten it. Delicately and rapidly fold in the rest of the egg whites and turn the soufflé into the prepared mold.

*Ahead-of-time note: The soufflé may be completed to this point ½ hour or more ahead; cover loosely with a sheet of foil and set away from drafts.

Baking—30 to 35 minutes at 400°F and 375°F. Set in the lower third of the preheated oven, turn the thermostat down to 375°F, and bake until the soufflé has begun to puff and brown—about 20 minutes.

The confectioners sugar, and finish. Slide the rack out gently; quickly dust the top of the soufflé with sifted confectioners sugar, and continue baking until the soufflé has puffed 2 to 3 inches over the rim of the baking dish into the collar, and the top has browned nicely under the sugar coating—see "When is it done?" notes on page 72.

Serving. As soon as it is done, bring the soufflé to the table. To keep the puff standing, hold your serving spoon and fork upright and back to back; plunge them into the crust and tear it apart.

SPECIAL NOTE

Vanilla Beans

Vanilla beans have lost their savor for me and I have sadly given them up. However, if you are lucky enough to find good ones, you can, for instance, slit 2 of them in half and bury them several days in a jar with a pound of granulated sugar, or warm a whole bean for 20 minutes in a covered saucepan with the milk you are using for the soufflé.

OTHER FLAVORS

Orange Soufflé Grand Marnier

Follow the directions for the master recipe but make a fresh orange flavoring by puréeing in a blender or food processor the zest (orange part of the peel) of 1 large orange with the sugar called for in the sauce base. After completing the sauce base, beat in 3 tablespoons of orange liqueur but only 2 teaspoons of vanilla. Proceed with the recipe. You might accompany the soufflé with prettily prepared and arranged fresh skinless orange segments flavored with a little sugar and orange liqueur.

SPECIAL NOTE

Fresh strawberry or raspberry sauce (page 419) is attractive with the soufflé, or fresh berries, or sliced fruits such as mangoes or peaches tossed with sugar and lemon. Chocolate sauce (page 422), Zabaione sauce (page 453), and caramel sauce (page 420) are other ideas.

Chocolate Soufflé

This is the best formula for chocolate soufflé I have run into so far—it has a fine chocolate flavor, a subtle texture, and it holds up well for serving. The secret is in the egg whites, which are beaten into a meringue—6 egg whites held up with ½ cup of sugar. The formula is slightly different from the preceding master recipe, but the technique is the same.

For a 2- to 2½-quart baking dish, 7½ to 8 inches in diameter, serving 8

7 ounces sweet baking chocolate smoothly melted with ⅓ cup strong coffee (pages 463–64)

The sauce base
⅓ cup flour
2 cups milk
3 Tbs butter, optional
A big pinch of salt
1 Tbs pure vanilla extract
4 egg yolks

6 egg whites (¾ cup)
½ cup granulated sugar
Confectioners sugar in a fine-meshed sieve
Optional accompaniment: lightly whipped cream flavored with confectioners sugar and pure vanilla extract (page 440)

Preliminaries. Melt the chocolate, measure out all the other ingredients listed, butter the soufflé dish, surround it with a foil collar (see Special Note, page 72), and preheat the oven to 425°F.

The soufflé base. Following directions in the master recipe, whisk the flour and milk together and boil slowly, this time for 2 minutes, whisking. Off heat, whisk in the optional butter, the salt, and the vanilla, then the egg yolks, and finally the smoothly melted chocolate.

The egg whites. In a clean separate bowl with clean beaters, beat the egg whites to soft peaks, gradually sprinkle in the ½ cup sugar, and beat to stiff shining peaks, as described on page 461.

Combining ingredients. Ladle the chocolate sauce base down the side of the egg-white bowl, rapidly fold the two mixtures together, and turn the soufflé into the prepared baking dish.

Baking—50 to 60 minutes at 425°F and 375°F. Set the soufflé in the lower level of the preheated oven and turn the thermostat down to 375°F.

Confectioners sugar, finishing, and serving. In 35 to 40 minutes the soufflé will have puffed and risen an inch or so over the rim of the dish. Following directions in the preceding master recipe, rapidly sprinkle the top with confectioners sugar, then finish the baking, and serve as directed; pass the optional whipped cream separately.

Fin Fish & Shellfish

**Fish Steaks, Fish Fillets,
and Whole Fish**

**Broiled, Roasted, Poached,
and Sautéed Fish**

**Ways with Lobsters,
Shrimp, Scallops, Oysters,
and Mussels**

**Mousses and Marinades;
Plain and Fancy Sauces**

Fish has become more and more popular as a delicious, low-fat, protein-rich alternative to meat, especially since fast cross-country transportation in refrigerated trucks and planes can make it possible to buy fish as fresh in Minneapolis, Omaha, and Phoenix as it is in Boston or Seattle. And fish fits in well with today's life styles, since there are so many ways to cook it quickly and easily.

When you are looking for speed and simplicity, for example, bake fish steaks practically as is in the oven. Or season a handful of fish fillets, dust lightly with flour, and sauté them rapidly in olive oil or butter. Or for a fast fat-free presentation, poach fish steaks or fillets in a pan of seasoned liquid on top of the stove and serve them with lemon and parsley. On the other hand, when you choose to be elaborate, you can present your fish in a bewildering array of sauces and garnitures.

Following the theme of this book, you'll find related items grouped by method—most fish steaks and fillets, as an example, are part of the baking, broiling, or poaching-in-wine categories. Shellfish, however, since each is so different from the other, are in categories of their own in most cases. To make it easy to locate the capabilities of a particular fish, a complete list of them by name and cooking method is in the index.

BUYING AND STORING FRESH FISH

The popular and well-known species of fish—salmon, trout, halibut, swordfish, gray sole, to name a few—are becoming more and more expensive, and when we are obliged to pay dearly for our fish, we most certainly want every penny of our money's worth.

Freshness is the key to the perfect enjoyment of fresh fish, but all depends on your market and how it handles its precious and highly perishable treasure. Your nose is the best judge of that. When you buy fish, open the package just outside the checkout counter (they rarely let you sniff before you choose it) and take a very careful, unhurried whiff. The fish should have a fresh, natural, appetizing aroma. If it smells "fishy" or chemical or not right in any way, take it immediately to the store manager, give him a whiff, and get your money back. He wants satisfied customers, and he wants to know if anything is wrong. How would he, if you didn't tell him? All of us should encourage our markets to supply good fish—and if we speak loudly enough we may get it.

When you know you are shopping for fish, take along a plastic cooler and a bag of ice to keep things chilled. As soon as you are home, place the chilled fish in a plastic bag, enclose that in another plastic bag, set them in a bowl with ice cubes, and place in the refrigerator. Very fresh fish will keep for a day or two this way, if you renew the ice as necessary.

FROZEN FISH

Frozen fish can be of excellent quality, again if it is handled correctly by fishermen, processor, and market. When buying it, you really have to depend on the reliability of your market, since it takes an expert to judge quality by looking at the package. In any case, the fish should have a pleasant smell, and there should be no indication in the package of loose frozen liquid, a sure sign that the fish has been thawed and refrozen.

Ideally, frozen fish has been bled, gutted, iced, and then frozen right on the boat at a temperature of minus 30°F or minus 40°F. It should remain at minus 20°F until you buy it, and if you are to hold it for more than a few days in your freezer, keep it at minus 10°F. Then, to prevent the ice crystals from cutting into the flesh and making it mushy, thaw the fish slowly in a bed of ice in the refrigerator. This is particularly important for whole fish and thick fish steaks.

In other words, frozen fish can be fine but it really needs all the TLC it can get.

Fish frames

1. Scoring milky side of fish fillets

2. Flattening a fish fillet

SOME FISH TERMS

Fish frame. The bone structure of the fish (minus gills, guts, and skin) after the fillets have been removed, plus the head. Essential for making your own fish stock, but hard to find unless you live near a fish processing plant.

Fillets—the "skin side" and the "best side." The skin side is rather milky-looking and sometimes has brownish areas; the "best" side was next to the bone, is better-looking, and is therefore the serving side.

To score the skin side of a fillet. To help prevent thin fillets from curling up when cooked, make diagonal cuts 1 inch apart and less than $\frac{1}{16}$ inch deep in the skin side, see illustration, step 1. Lay the flat of your big knife on the fillet and give one firm punch with your fist to flatten it, step 2.

Fish stock (page 23). Made like chicken stock, from bones and trimmings of fresh fish simply simmered for 30 minutes in lightly salted water to cover.

Fish stock substitutes. I used to suggest bottled clam juice, but I often find that to be too salty, too strong, and/or off in flavor. I now often prefer a light or diluted chicken stock, which gives the needed but subtle boost of flavor.

Court bouillon. Seasoned liquid in which to poach whole fish or fish fillets. It can be only salted water with perhaps a little wine vinegar for full-flavored fish like salmon. For mild-flavored fish or special effects it may contain white wine and aromatic vegetables.

FISH IN THE OVEN

BROILING, BRAISING, ROASTING, AND POACHING IN WINE

Whether to broil, braise, or roast your fish depends not only on its size and thickness but also on the effect you want. Thin fillets are so easy to broil, needing as they do only to be seasoned with salt, pepper, and perhaps an herb, then brushed with oil or butter before being set close under the broiler to brown 2 to 3 minutes and cook through—so simple that I need say no more about them here. Thick fillets and steaks want different treatment and offer more culinary possibilities in the way of saucings and flavorings. Large whole fish are delectable when simply roasted whole as is, but they also do beautifully in a winey aromatic braise, while the possibilities for fish fillets poached in wine are almost endless.

BROILING, BROIL-ROASTING, AND BRAISING

When you grill or barbecue, with heat coming from underneath, you must turn your fish to cook it on both sides. When you broil, however, there is no need to turn it because who will see its underneath? You can therefore concentrate all your skills on giving it a beautiful brown surface. In order for the fish to cook through yet remain moist, you place it in a pan that will just hold it comfortably and pour a little wine around the fish to steam the bottom while browning the top.

When is it done? These signs apply to almost all cooking methods. The first indication is when you begin to smell cooked fish, meaning that the juices have swelled in the flesh and are ready to escape. The flesh has turned from translucent to opaque, and is lightly springy to the touch. Above all, that flesh is still juicy, and can just be nudged cleanly but juicily from the bone. I don't know who invented the utterly erroneous term "cook until the fish flakes easily": if it flakes easily—indeed if it flakes at all—it has been woefully (willfully and wrongfully!) overcooked.

Timing. The theory of timing fish 10 minutes per inch at the thickest portion appears to work in some instances, but timing depends so much on the quality of the fish— whether it is light, or dense like shark or tuna. Oven timing depends also on how long it takes the cooking dish to heat up. A braised salmon fillet ½ inch thick takes 12 to 15 minutes, a thicker fillet wants a few minutes more, and a 1½- to 2-inch

cod fillet may take ½ hour or more. Always, if you have any doubts, cut into the fish to check; it is a shame to overcook it. But it is equally disappointing to find a partially raw, supposedly cooked fish on your plate.

A note on tough fish. When I complained about some tough shark steaks, my official fisherman source in Santa Barbara suggested that they may have come from a very large shark, and that often the larger the fish the tougher the flesh. This does not apply to salmon, however. If you catch your own, the fish will be tough if it is still in the rigor mortis (stiff) state—as I know from eating a bluefish too freshly caught off the coast of Maine.

SPECIAL NOTE

Fish for broiling. The universal favorite is swordfish, but its price is daunting. Thresher and mako shark, fresh tuna (ahi or yellowfin and albacore), and mahi-mahi (dolphin-fish) are other choices, as well as thick fillets of bluefish and salmon. Although you may certainly broil lean fish like cod, halibut, and bass, I think they need an additional boost of flavor and suggest the braising technique on page 84.

🐟◀ MASTER RECIPE

Broiled Fish Steaks

For 6 servings

2 pounds fish steaks or fillets ¾ inch thick, (see Special Note for suggestions—for thicker steaks, see broil-roasting notes at the end of the recipe)
Salt
Olive oil or peanut oil
½ to ¾ cup dry white French vermouth
1½ to 2 Tbs soft butter, optional

SPECIAL EQUIPMENT SUGGESTED:
A lightly oiled baking dish 1½ inches deep and just roomy enough to hold the fish easily in one layer

Preparing the fish. Cut off any surrounding skin, which is tough and inedible. I also cut out any brownish flesh, which, while edible, is both ugly and, I think, unduly oily, particularly with swordfish. Either leave the steaks whole for serving on a platter at the table, or cut them into serving portions. Keep the fish iced until just before cooking, then dry it in paper towels.

Preparations for broiling. Fifteen minutes or so before you plan to serve, preheat the broiler to high, and set the oven rack so the surface of the fish will be about 2 inches from the heat element. Season both sides of the fish lightly with salt, and rub with oil. Arrange in the dish and pour ⅛ inch of the vermouth around the fish.

Broiling. Broil for a minute or two, then rapidly spread the optional butter over the surface and continue broiling about 5 minutes more. The fish is done when lightly springy to the touch—cut into it and check if you are not sure. It should be cooked through and still juicy.

VARIATION

Broiled Fish Steaks au Naturel

To serve as is, arrange the fish on a hot platter or plates, spoon on the cooking juices; decorate with lemon wedges and parsley sprigs.

Lemon-Butter Sauce for Broiled Fish Steaks

**The juice of ½ lemon
4 or more Tbs cold unsalted butter,
    cut into tablespoon-size pieces
Salt and freshly ground pepper
3 Tbs minced fresh parsley**

Remove the fish to a platter or plates and keep warm in the turned-off oven, its door ajar. Swish the lemon juice in the baking dish, scraping into it any coagulated juices, then scrape the juices into a small saucepan. Rapidly boil them down until syrupy. Then, while still boiling, whisk in a piece of the butter, adding a new piece (with your fingers for quick action) as each has been almost incorporated. As soon as the last piece has been almost absorbed, remove the pan from the heat. Taste, season if necessary, blend in the op-

tional parsley, spoon the sauce over the fish, and serve.

Broiled Fish Steaks with Herbal Tomato Sauce

Follow the directions for oven-baked fish steaks (page 84).

Broil-Roasting for Thick Fish Steaks or Fillets

When steaks are more than ¾ inch thick, use the broil-roast method so that the fish will cook evenly—that is, brown the top nicely under the broiler and finish by baking at 375°F in the upper third level of the oven, basting occasionally with the juices in the dish.

Ahead-of-time note. You can brown the top, set the fish aside, and finish cooking somewhat later.

Broiled fish steak au naturel

BRAISING: OVEN BAKING

When there is no need for browning the top, braising fish steaks and fillets in wine and other flavorings is a simple and savory method. (Baking and braising are interchangeable terms for me in this case, but braising suggests a certain sophistication of treatment.)

◀ MASTER RECIPE

Fish Steaks Braised in Wine with Herbal Fresh Tomato Sauce

This is especially recommended for lean fish of the cod and pollack type.

For 6 servings

2 pounds fish steaks or fillets 1½ to 2 inches thick, such as cod, scrod, striped bass, cusk, eastern or Alaskan halibut, and ocean pollack
1 to 2 Tbs melted butter or peanut oil
Salt and freshly ground pepper
1 imported bay leaf
1 cup dry white French vermouth
1 cup fish stock or a light chicken broth
2 Tbs minced shallots or scallions
1½ cups diced fresh tomato pulp (tomatoes peeled, seeded, juiced, and diced, page 357), or half fresh tomatoes and half canned Italian plum tomatoes
3 or more Tbs butter, optional

SPECIAL EQUIPMENT SUGGESTED: *A lightly oiled flameproof baking dish just large enough to hold the fish comfortably in one layer; a bulb baster*

Preparing the fish. Remove any skin and bones from the fish, brush lightly with melted butter or oil, and dust with salt and pepper. Arrange the fish in the dish; add the bay leaf, and pour the liquids around the fish. If you are not cooking it immediately, cover and refrigerate. Preheat the oven to 350°F before proceeding.

Baking—about 20 minutes at 350°F. Bring just to the simmer on top of the stove, then place uncovered in the middle level of the preheated oven. Bake for 15 to 20 minutes, basting the fish 2 or 3 times with the cooking liquid. The fish is done when just springy to the touch—cut into it if you are not sure. Remove the fish to a hot platter, cover, and keep warm the few minutes required for making the sauce.

The sauce. Set the dish over moderately high heat, add the minced shallots or scallions, and boil down rapidly until the liquid is almost syrupy. Fold in the tomatoes and boil a few moments more, until lightly thickened. Correct seasoning. Remove from heat, and fold in the optional butter. Spoon the sauce over the fish, and serve.

VARIATION

Fish Steaks Baked with Onions

Any fish, lean or fat, does well baked in a cloak of wine and onions, and this is especially recommended for swordfish, and mako and thresher shark steaks. Start by sautéing 4 cups of sliced onions in butter and oil until tender and translucent; season nicely, adding a little oregano or thyme, and set aside. Then season the fish steaks, dredge in flour, and brown in the same pan for a minute or two on each side. Arrange the fish in a baking dish, cover with the onions, and strew on a handful of fresh white bread crumbs mixed with chopped parsley. Pour ⅔ cup of dry white wine around the fish and bake about 25 minutes, basting occasionally, until the top has browned lightly.

FISH STEAKS OR FILLETS BRAISED IN WINE AND AROMATIC VEGETABLES

Salmon is heavenly done this way, as are thick steaks or fillets of such fish as cod, pollack, whitefish, weakfish, halibut, and monkfish. For dieters, serve your fish just as is, and offer a sumptuous sauce on the side for those lucky ones who are fashionably thin.

◀ MASTER RECIPE

Braised Whole Fillet of Salmon in Wine and Aromatic Vegetables

For 6 to 8 servings

1 each large carrot and onion cut
 into neat ¼-inch dice
2 or 3 tender celery stalks, neatly
 diced
2 Tbs unsalted butter
Seasonings: salt, freshly ground
 pepper, and dried tarragon
A 2-pound skinless fillet of salmon
 about ½ inch thick
About 1½ cups dry white French
 vermouth

SPECIAL EQUIPMENT SUGGESTED:
A no-stick frying pan for the diced vegetables; tweezers or pliers to remove bones; a lightly buttered baking dish that will just hold the fish comfortably (or an ovenproof baking and serving platter, or, lacking either, cut the fish in half crosswise, and reassemble it after cooking—the vegetables will mask the surgery); buttered wax paper to cover fish

The aromatic vegetables. Cook the diced vegetables slowly in the butter until quite tender but not browned— about 10 minutes. Season lightly with salt, pepper, and a big pinch of dried tarragon.

Preparing the fish. Go over the salmon carefully with your fingers to detect any little bones; pull them out with tweezers or pliers. Score the skin side of the fish. Dust with salt and pepper, and place best side up in the baking dish.

Assembling. Spread the cooked diced vegetables over the fish, and pour ½ inch of vermouth around it. Cover the fish with the wax paper, buttered side down.

*Ahead-of-time note: May be assembled an hour or more ahead to this point; cover and refrigerate.

Baking—12 to 15 minutes at 350°F. Preheat the oven to 350°F. Set the fish in the lower middle level, and, when beginning to bubble lightly, baste the surface with the liquid in the dish, basting several times again until the flesh feels lightly springy to the touch.

Remove from the oven, and, holding the fish in place with a pot cover, drain the cooking juices into a saucepan. Slide the fish onto a hot platter; cover and keep warm while making the sauce.

VARIATIONS

Au Naturel: Braised Salmon Served in Its Own Juices

Rapidly boil down the cooking juices in the saucepan until almost syrupy. Pour them over the fish and vegetables, and serve.

Braised Salmon in Aromatic White Butter Sauce

The usual and lovely butter sauce of modern cookery can be as rich and buttery as you wish—from 3 or 4 tablespoons to half a pound. Using the preceding boiled-down juices as a base, proceed to beat in the butter as in the lemon-butter sauce for the broiled fish on page 83.

Braised Salmon in Winey Cream Sauce

A reasonable and equally delectable compromise is a light velouté sauce made with the cooking juices, then boiled down with cream, as follows. Cook together 2½ Tbs butter and 3 Tbs flour 2 minutes without coloring; off heat whisk in the hot braising juices and 1 cup heavy cream. Boil slowly until reduced to 1½ cups; season carefully. (Full details for velouté sauce are on page 272.) Either serve the fish cloaked in its vegetables and accompany with the sauce, or fold the vegetables into the sauce and spoon over the fish.

Fillet of Salmon Braised with a Mousseline of Scallops

To take the master recipe a step farther, you arrange it under its cloak of aromatic vegetables and top it with a tender mousse of scallops. Then, after braising it, you coat it with a little hollandaise and glaze it under the broiler. This chic presentation is a steal from the Haeberlin brothers, at whose three-star restaurant at Illhausern in Alsace I first had it years ago. Some years later I tried out my version on our students at the Robert Mondavi cooking classes in the Napa Valley. More recently Marian Morash and I (she was then executive chef for the Straight Wharf Restaurant in Nantucket) worked it out for the restaurant; her customers greeted it with such enthusiasm that it remained on the menu the whole season.

TIMING NOTE: *You may prepare the fish for the oven several hours ahead; after baking, the dish and sauce base can wait ½ hour or so. Once glazed, however, it should be served immediately.*

Serving 8 to 10 as a first course; 6 to 8 as a luncheon dish

Ingredients for the master recipe Braised Whole Fillet of Salmon (page 85)
For the mousseline of scallops—ingredients for the mousse of trout with scallops (page 126; you may substitute sole for trout)
1¼ to 1½ cups hollandaise sauce (see Special Note next page)
½ cup heavy cream, whipped

SPECIAL EQUIPMENT SUGGESTED: *A lightly buttered ovenproof baking and serving platter for braising the salmon*

Assembling for baking. Arrange the salmon on the baking platter, and spread the cooked aromatic vegetables over the fish. Then spread the mousse over both fish and vegetables. Cover with buttered wax paper cut to fit the platter.

Baking—20 to 25 minutes at 350°F. Preheat the oven to 350°F. Just before baking, pour enough of the vermouth around the fish to come almost ⅛ inch up its sides. Replace the wax paper, and bake in the lower third level of the preheated oven. The fish is done when you begin to smell its enticing aroma; both fish and mousseline will feel lightly springy. Pour the cooking juices into a small stainless pan and reserve for the sauce. Cover the fish and keep it warm while making the hollandaise.

Completing the sauce. (Preheat the broiler.) Add any accumulated fish-cooking juices to the pan of reserved juices, set over high heat and rapidly boil down to a syrup; beat them into the hollandaise sauce. Fold in the whipped cream.

Finishing the dish. Spread the sauce generously over the fish. Set the platter 2 inches from the hot broiler element, and, watching carefully, let the top brown lightly for a minute or so. Serve at once.

Variation: Individual Servings. For ease of serving at the table, rather than baking the fillet whole cut the raw salmon into portions before arranging on the platter, and build them individually. Or, for individual servings, bake each portion in a separate dish.

Hollandaise Sauce

Certainly one of the great sauces of the Western world, hollandaise has nevertheless given over some of its former popularity to the white butter sauces. But when you want a superior sauce that can cover an egg Benedict, or one that can both cover and gratiné under the broiler, as for our preceding salmon dish, you want a hollandaise.

For about 1 cup

3 egg yolks
1½ Tbs freshly squeezed lemon juice, plus more later as needed
4 Tbs cold unsalted butter, half at first and half later
5 ounces (1¼ sticks) melted unsalted butter
Salt and freshly ground white pepper

SPECIAL EQUIPMENT SUGGESTED:
A 6-cup fairly heavy-bottomed stainless saucepan and a wire whisk; a pan and a small ladle for the melted butter

Preliminaries. Vigorously whisk the egg yolks in the saucepan for a good minute or so, until they are thick and pale yellow, then whisk in the lemon juice. Add 2 of the tablespoons of cold butter, which while melting slowly will act as a kind of anti-curdling insurance.

The egg-yolk sauce base. Set the pan over low heat, whisking at a moderate pace and watching carefully until in a minute or more the egg yolks have thickened and you can see the bottom of the pan between strokes. At once remove from heat and beat in

the remaining cold butter a tablespoon at a time to stop the cooking.

Adding the butter. By driblets, beat in the warm melted butter to make a thick sauce. Whisk in the seasonings, adding a little more lemon juice if you feel it is needed.

*Ahead-of-time note: You can keep hollandaise for a certain amount of time over the faint heat of a pilot light, or near a stove-top burner. If it is kept too warm the egg yolks will start to scramble and force the butter out of suspension—the sauce will turn, in other words. However, since egg yolks are a fine breeding ground for bacteria, the safest advance plan is to cook the sauce base, and chill it. Just before serving, whisk over very low heat or hot water to loosen it, and then beat in the hot melted butter.

First Aid for Turned Sauce. If your sauce refuses to thicken or thins out after you've made it, or looks curdled, here's how to fix it—unless the eggs have actually scrambled because of overheating.

Whisk up the sauce and dip out a tablespoon into a mixing bowl. Whisk it with a tablespoon of lemon juice for a moment until it creams and thickens; gradually whisk in little dribbles of the sauce, letting each addition cream and thicken before adding more.

Cooked Egg Hollandaise. If you are wary of undercooked eggs, see the cooked egg alternative on page 377.

Additions

You may add other flavors to the finished hollandaise. In the preceding braised salmon dish, where you whisk in reduced fish-braising juices, you have officially produced a white wine sauce, *sauce vin blanc*. The addition of whipped cream makes it a *sauce mousseline*, and you have a *sauce mousseuse* if, instead of whipped cream, you fold in beaten egg whites—a lighter hollandaise to serve with soufflés or vegetables. It's useful to know the official names since you may run into them on traditional restaurant menus.

Béarnaise Sauce
For steaks, broiled fish, poached eggs

Béarnaise is hollandaise with a pronounced flavor of vinegar, shallots, tarragon, and pepper. It goes beautifully with tenderloin steaks, you could serve it with the crumbed salmon on page 100, and it gives interest to mild foods like poached eggs. For about 1 cup of sauce, boil down ¼ cup each of good wine vinegar and dry white vermouth with 1 tablespoon of minced shallots, ½ teaspoon of dried tarragon, and ¼ teaspoon each of salt and freshly ground pepper. When reduced to about 2 tablespoons, strain into another saucepan. Substitute this fragrant essence for the lemon juice in the hollandaise recipe and proceed with the egg yolks and butter, but add only 1 to 1¼ sticks of butter in all—to make an authoritative sauce.

FISH FILLETS POACHED IN WINE

The French cuisine introduced it, I do believe, that lovely method of laying fillets of sole in a buttered baking dish with shallots and wine, poaching them gently in the oven, then making a perfectly simple or madly elaborate sauce with the subtly flavored cooking juices. In any case the French shorthand recipe guide *Le Répertoire de la Cuisine* lists dozens and dozens of variations on sole in white wine, with such fanciful titles as Filets de sole Sarah Bernhardt, or George Sand, or Dieppoise, or Belles de Nuit. The names vary with the sauce—butter sauce, cream sauce, velouté—and with the garniture, from minced fresh herbs, to chopped tomato, medallions of lobster, spinach leaves, grated cheese, oysters, mushrooms, mussels, and mousses. Fish and sauces are interchangeable in almost all cases. Take the first variation, "au naturel," as an example. Here the pan juices are a simple reduction, but when you whip in butter and herbs or spread chopped tomatoes or mushrooms over the fish, you have a whole new recipe. Thus I shall go into the fundamentals with enough sauce and garniture suggestions to get you started on later frills of your own.

SPECIAL NOTE

Fish fillets to poach in white wine. Lean fish fillets ¼ to ⅜ inch thick are called for here. Imported sole, turbot, and John Dory (St. Peter fish) are born for poaching but are expensive indeed, not only because they are imported but because of their delicate flavor and desirable texture—their skinless and boneless fillets hold together perfectly when moved from baking dish to platter. Among the alternatives are gray sole, petrale sole, and trout. Silver hake (whiting) and baby halibut are also desirable but hard to find in our retail markets. Catfish fillets, orange roughy, and tilapia are other choices. Fish with less solid textures, such as flounder and red snapper, and sliced fillets of cod, hake, and halibut tend to break apart when moved; they do best when cooked and served in the same dish.

Just for convenience I shall call everything sole in the following recipes—but do experiment with fish other than those listed here. You may find perfection in the daily catch.

Amounts. In all of the following recipes 1 pound of skinless and boneless fish is considered sufficient for 3 normal servings; 2 fillets 8 to 9 inches long, 2 inches wide, and ¼ inch thick make a single serving. It is wise to buy by eye, however, and in recipes of this type remember that utterly exact measurements are not called for—it is the final result that counts.

Sauces. Among the variations here, you have examples of the principal sauce categories: pan juices, au naturel, a simple reduction of the cooking liquids; white butter sauce, much in vogue these days, delectable, easy indeed to make, but butter is butter; and the velouté, the traditional, light, flour-based white-wine fish sauce that is excellent when properly made, and especially useful for dishes assembled in advance.

*Ahead-of-time note: The gratinés at the end of this section are designed for ahead-of-time preparation; however, you can adapt the technique to any of the following ideas.

◄ MASTER RECIPE

Fillets of Sole Poached in White Wine

Here is the master poaching method, which is the base for all the following variations—and countless others.

For 6 servings

2 pounds skinless and boneless sole fillets (or other suggestions from the Special Note on this page)
Salt and freshly ground white pepper
2 Tbs finely minced shallots or scallions
1 cup liquid: ⅔ cup dry white French vermouth or full-bodied dry white wine mixed with ⅓ cup fish stock, chicken broth, or water, plus more if needed
Freshly squeezed lemon juice
Minced fresh parsley

1. Large fish fillets folded in half

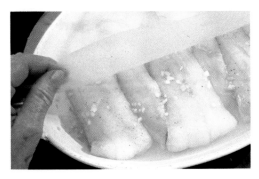

2. Covering fish with buttered wax paper before poaching

Sole with white butter sauce and herbs

3. Draining out the poaching liquid

SPECIAL EQUIPMENT SUGGESTED:
A lightly buttered flameproof baking-serving dish that will just hold the fish in one slightly overlapping layer— about 9 by 12 inches (or a 12-inch stainless frying pan); a sheet of buttered wax paper cut to fit into the dish; a flat pot cover to hold the fish in place while draining out cooking juices; an 8-cup stainless saucepan to hold them

Preparing the fish. (Preheat the oven to 350°F in time for the oven poaching, last step.) Pat the fish dry in paper towels; go over it carefully with your fingers to remove any remaining bones. Score the skin sides (page 81). Season lightly with salt and pepper.

Assembling the dish. Sprinkle half the shallots in the bottom of the buttered baking dish and lay in the fish, skin side down and with the pieces slightly overlapping. If the fillets are very large, fold them in half, as in the illustration, step 1. Sprinkle the remaining shallots over the top of the fish. Pour in enough liquid to come two thirds of the way up the fillets, and lay over them the wax paper, buttered side down, step 2.

*Ahead-of-time note: Refrigerate if you are not proceeding almost immediately.

Oven poaching—5 to 7 minutes at 350°F. Set the dish over moderate heat just until the liquid starts to bubble, then place in the lower third level of the preheated oven, where it should start to bubble slowly in a minute or so. The fish is done when its translucent flesh has turned to opaque, or milky white—folded fillets will take a few minutes more. (See also the "When is it done?" notes on page 82.)

Out of the oven. Remove from the oven. Set the cover over the wax paper and drain the cooking juices into the saucepan, step 3. Rapidly boil down the juices until almost syrupy; whisk in droplets of lemon juice and a sprinkling of minced fresh parsley. Spoon the juices over the fish.

Pipérade
Sliced red and green peppers in garlic and olive oil

This colorful vegetable sauté, of Basque origin, is a wonderfully useful condiment, either hot or cold. Use it on open-faced omelettes, for instance, or pizzas, and for various simmerings such as fillets of fish or breast of chicken.

For about 1½ cups

1 medium onion, sliced
2 Tbs olive oil
1 medium green bell pepper, sliced
1 medium red bell pepper, sliced
1 large clove of garlic, puréed
Salt and freshly ground pepper
Pinch of mixed dried herbs

The pipérade. Sauté the onion slowly 5 minutes in a frying pan with the oil. When tender and translucent, add the peppers along with the garlic, tossing with a sprinkling of salt, pepper, and herbs. Sauté uncovered, tossing several times, for 2 to 3 minutes, until the peppers are nearly tender.

*Ahead-of-time note: May be refrigerated 2 to 3 days; may be frozen.

VARIATION

Sole en Pipérade
Sauced with the pan juices
Sole with Sliced Peppers, Onions, and Garlic

This is a light and colorful dish with lots of good flavor that may be served either hot with rice or pasta, or cold with a salad.

For 6 servings

Ingredients for the preceding master recipe for 2 pounds of fish fillets poached in white wine
1 cup pipérade (cooked sliced red and green peppers with garlic; see Special Note at left)
2 to 3 Tbs tomato sauce or canned tomato purée

Assembling. (Preheat the oven to 350°F in time for oven poaching.) Prepare the fish and arrange it in the baking dish as directed in the master recipe. Scrape the pipérade over the fish, and pour in the liquid. Cover with the wax paper.

Oven poaching. Bring to the simmer on top of the stove, and poach 6 to 8 minutes in the preheated oven as directed.

Sauce and serving. Drain the cooking juices into a stainless pan and boil down rapidly with the tomato until lightly thickened. Correct seasoning, spoon over the fish, and serve.

To serve cold. Separate the fish fillets from each other while still warm; otherwise they will stick together as they chill.

Sole with White Butter Sauce and Fresh Herbs

The following recipes are for more dressy occasions, starting with an easy, delicious, and nicely calorific butter sauce, the same one used for the broiled fish steaks with lemon butter sauce on page 83. Boil the cooking liquid down to a syrup, adding droplets of lemon juice. Piece by piece, and still boiling slowly, beat in 4 to 8 tablespoons of butter. Whisk in 2 tablespoons of minced fresh herbs such as parsley and chives, chervil, or tarragon, and spoon over the fish for serving, see illustration.

Sole Duglére

*OTHER VARIATIONS ON THE MASTER
OVEN-POACHING METHOD*

Fillets of Sole Dugléré
Sole poached with wine and tomatoes
with a tomato-butter sauce

Here, and in the next recipe with
mushrooms, the garniture is poached
right on the fish, giving it additional
flavor. Prepare the fish for the oven
as described in the master recipe, and
spread 2½ cups of lightly seasoned
fresh tomato pulp (tomatoes peeled,
seeded, juiced, diced; page 357) over
the fillets. Poach and drain the fish as
described, boil down the liquid to 2
tablespoons, and whisk in from 2 to
8 tablespoons of butter, as for the
preceding butter sauce. Rearrange
the fish and tomatoes nicely in the
dish or on hot plates, spoon the sauce
over, and serve.

Sole Bonne Femme garnished with fluted mushrooms

Assembling the dish

Sole Bonne Femme
Sole Poached in White Wine and
Mushrooms
True Cream Sauce

Bonne femme is another classic combination, the "good wife's" special fillets of sole sandwiched between a
layer of sliced mushrooms. This recipe, rather than using a butter sauce,
calls for the fish-poaching juices to be
reduced with heavy cream—delicious

indeed. Simmer 2 cups of sliced
mushrooms in seasonings and a little
butter and lemon juice (page 312),
and sandwich them between the sole
fillets.

Poach them in the oven, as for the
master recipe, but for 10 to 12 minutes; drain their juices into a saucepan. Rapidly boil down the juices
over high heat until reduced to a
light syrup, stir in the cream, and
continue boiling a moment or two
more, until the sauce coats a spoon
lightly. Taste carefully, adding more
salt, freshly ground pepper, drops of
lemon juice, and a tablespoon or so of
fresh minced tarragon. Spoon the
sauce over the fish and decorate, if
you wish, with cooked fluted mushrooms (page 313).

Mousse-Stuffed Fillets of Sole gratinéed with mushrooms

Folding fillets over mousse stuffing

Mousse-Stuffed Fillets of Sole

Gratinéed with mushrooms in
a light velouté sauce

Another recipe with mushrooms, but
this time the fillets are folded over a
fish mousse and surrounded with
sliced mushrooms. A recipe like this
used to be considered very haute cuisine because a mousse took hours to
make. Now, with a food processor,
it's a matter of minutes—see the discussion on fish mousses, page 123.
To accompany it, we have the traditional velouté sauce, useful indeed for
dishes that are assembled in advance
and then reheated.

For 6 servings

**Ingredients for 2 pounds fish fillets
    poached in white wine (page 88)**
**1½ cups fish mousse, using 1 cup
    puréed fish, 1 egg white, and ⅓
    cup heavy cream (page 124)**
**2½ cups (½ pound) sliced fresh
    mushrooms**

For about 1½ cups of velouté sauce
1½ Tbs butter
2 Tbs flour
½ to ⅔ cup heavy cream

3 Tbs grated Swiss cheese

TWO EXAMPLES THAT
CAN BE COOKED AHEAD
AND REHEATED

So often you want a dish that can be
cooked ahead and reheated, which
works out well for fish fillets—with
two problems to be avoided. Exercise
great care in the reheating that you
do not overcook them, and be aware
that the fish exudes a certain quantity
of juice as it reheats, and that juice
thins out the sauce. If cooking a dish
ahead, therefore, I think it best to
complete fish and sauce separately,
and to combine them for the final
phase just before serving—then you
have control.

Assembling. Trim, score, and flatten the fish fillets for cooking as directed.

Lay them skin side up, divide the fish mousse into 6 portions, spreading one on the bottom length of each fillet. Fold in half to enclose the filling, see illustration. Sprinkle half the shallots and half the sliced mushrooms in the bottom of the buttered baking dish. Lay the folded fillets over them; spread on the remaining shallots and mushrooms. Pour around the fish enough liquid to reach halfway up; cover with the buttered wax paper. Poach in a 350°F oven as directed in the master recipe, but for 10 to 12 minutes.

Sauce and final touches. Meanwhile, in a 2-quart stainless saucepan, make a roux: cook the butter and flour together until they foam and froth for 2 minutes without coloring more than a buttery yellow. Set aside. When the fish is done, drain the cooking juices into another stainless saucepan and rapidly boil them down to 1 cup; whisk the hot juices into the roux. Beat in ½ cup of the cream, and bring to the boil. Simmer, stirring, for 2 minutes to make a sauce that will coat the spoon lightly—whisking in more cream if necessary. Taste very carefully and correct seasoning.

Gratinéing. Drain any accumulated fish juices into the sauce (boil down rapidly if the sauce thins out), and spoon the sauce over the fish. Sprinkle on the grated cheese, set under a hot broiler for a moment to brown the top of the sauce lightly, and serve.

*Ahead-of-time note: Poach the fish. Make the sauce, then clean off the sides of the saucepan and press a sheet of plastic wrap onto the surface to prevent a skin from forming. Cover and chill sauce and fish. Shortly before serving, cover the fish with its wax paper and warm in a 350°F oven, being very careful not to overcook it. Reheat the sauce. Drain the fish again, spoon the sauce over, and gratiné as described.

Fillets of Sole Florentine
Fillets of sole gratinéed on a bed of spinach
Mornay sauce—velouté with cheese

Fish and fresh spinach make a happy combination, and the nicely flavored light cheese sauce here gives it special attraction.

For 6 servings

3 packages or bunches of fresh spinach, blanched, chopped, squeezed dry, and warmed in butter (page 278)
Ingredients for 2 pounds of fish fillets poached in white wine (master recipe, page 88)
The sauce: double the amount in the preceding recipe (3 Tbs butter, ¼ cup flour, 2 cups hot liquid—fish poaching juices plus ⅓ to ½ cup milk and/or cream)
½ to ⅔ cup grated Swiss cheese (half for the topping)

Preliminaries. Cook the spinach as directed. Poach the fish fillets, and after draining out the cooking liquid, gently separate the fillets to prevent their sticking together as they cool.

The sauce. Make the velouté sauce as described in the preceding recipe,

Sauce going over poached fillets on a bed of braised spinach

but using the proportions given here. Whisk half the cheese into the sauce, then stir ⅔ cup of the sauce into the warm spinach.

Assembling. Spread the spinach in the buttered baking dish, and arrange the poached fillets on top. (Never mind if they break; the sauce will cover all.) Spoon the remaining sauce over the fish, see illustration. Sprinkle on the remaining cheese.

Gratinéing. Set the dish so its surface is 2 inches from a hot broiler element for 2 to 3 minutes, just until the sauce is bubbling hot and lightly browned on top.

*Ahead-of-time note: Here it seems best to cook spinach, sauce, and fish separately, and to combine for reheating as suggested in the preceding recipe.

WHOLE FISH

Someone may offer you a freshly caught whole large fish, like a salmon or a striped bass. Don't panic—take it! You can braise or roast almost any kind of a whole fish as long as it will fit into your pot or your oven—that goes for mackerel, trout, cod, weakfish, and bluefish as well as bass and salmon. We'll start with braising—actually steaming—with an inch or so of aromatic liquid in the bottom of a fish poacher or covered roaster. Then we'll move on to oven-roasted fish using a small fish as an example, but a large fish will roast the same way.

LARGE WHOLE FISH BRAISED IN WINE

Braising is far easier to do than poaching, where the whole fish must be submerged in simmering water; in addition, the aromatic braising juices become the basis for a splendid sauce.

Fish to use. The following recipe is for salmon, but bass, cod, or other large fish will do as well.

Frozen fish. Notes on frozen fish and defrosting are on page 80.

Half a fish. If you do not have or cannot borrow a large enough pan to hold a whole fish, you can cut it in half, cook it in two pans, and reassemble it for serving. Or, in the case of large salmon, you may wish to buy just a center cut, or the tail end.

Heads on. The well-dressed fish when presented whole should always look like a whole fish, meaning that it appears at the table with its head in place.

Timing. Since a braised or steamed fish may wait a considerable time before serving, give yourself ample leeway—a partially raw, supposedly braised fish is a failure.

SPECIAL NOTE

Equipment for Poaching a Whole Fish

The fish poacher at left has a removable perforated rack, which makes it easy to lift up the fish and slide it onto a platter. But you can use a large turkey roaster, set a rack in the bottom, and curve the fish to fit.

◀ MASTER RECIPE

Whole Salmon Braised in Wine
Or a large piece of salmon

For 10 to 12 servings

2 cups thinly sliced onions
1 cup thinly sliced carrots
1 cup thinly sliced celery stalks
6 Tbs unsalted butter
A 5- to 6-pound salmon, scaled and eviscerated (or a tail or center-cut section)
Tasteless salad oil
Salt and freshly ground pepper
A medium herb bouquet with tarragon instead of thyme, page 336
4 cups dry white wine or 3 cups dry white French vermouth
4 or more cups fresh fish stock or diluted chicken broth
1 cup heavy cream
4 Tbs unsalted butter, optional
Minced fresh green herbs, such as a mixture of parsley and tarragon

SPECIAL EQUIPMENT SUGGESTED:
A large piece of washed cheesecloth in which to wrap the fish; a large covered roaster or fish poacher with rack; a bulb baster; a serving platter or tray of sufficient size

Preliminaries. Sauté the vegetables slowly in the butter for 10 minutes or so, until tender but not browned. Meanwhile, wash and dry the fish, brush the outside with oil, and sprinkle ½ teaspoon of salt and several grinds of pepper inside the cavity. Oil the rack. Lay the cheesecloth

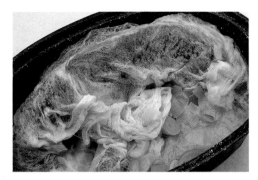

1. This weird object is the poached fish, ready for removal.

2. Skinning and trimming the fish

Fully dressed poached fish ready for serving

on your work surface. Center the rack upon it, then place the oiled fish on the rack. Wrap the cheesecloth around both the rack and the fish and place in the pan.

Sprinkle over it ½ teaspoon of salt. Season the cooked vegetables lightly with salt and pepper and strew them around the fish along with the herb packet. Pour in the wine and enough stock, plus water if needed, to a depth of 1 inch.

Ahead-of-time note: If you are not ready to proceed, cover and refrigerate. If you are using the oven, preheat it to 350°F before proceeding.

Braising—about 45 minutes, but the fish can wait an hour before being served. Set the pan on top of the stove over moderately high heat and bring the liquid barely to the simmer.

Cover the pan tightly (if necessary spread heavy foil over the top, then set on the cover and several weights of some sort for a snug fit). Either braise in the lower level of the preheated 350°F oven, or continue on top of the stove; regulate heat so liquid simmers very slowly throughout the cooking—too strong heat will cause the skin to burst and the flesh to flake. Baste several times during cooking with the liquid in the pan.

When is it done? The fish is done at a meat-thermometer reading of around 150°F, and when there is no raw red color near the bone when you unfold the cheesecloth and peer into the cavity. When you cut into the flesh from the edge of the back the fin ends pull out easily. Do not overcook—the fish should remain intact and the flesh juicy.

Ahead-of-time note: You may keep the fish warm and prepare the sauce, as follows, an hour before serving.

Keeping the fish warm. Brush any vegetables off the cheesecloth, lift the fish on its rack out of the pan using the cloth to help you. Strain the braising liquid into a large saucepan, pressing the juices out of the vegetables. Return the cheesecloth-wrapped fish to the pan, cover it, and set it over a kettle of hot but not simmering water to keep warm—it should stay warm but must not continue to cook.

The sauce. Bring the braising liquid to the rapid boil over high heat, and let it reduce to about 1 cup of almost syrupy liquid. Pour in the heavy cream and boil a moment or two more until lightly thickened. Set

Whole Salmon Braised in Wine (*continued*)

aside. Bring to the simmer just before serving; off heat, swish in the optional butter a tablespoon at a time, and the herbs.

Serving. Remove the fish from its pan, step 1, unfold the cheesecloth, and slide the fish onto the serving platter. Rapidly peel the skin off the top of the fish, scrape off and discard any brownish sections of flesh, and pull the remains of fins out of the ridge of the back, step 2. Spoon a coating of sauce over the fish; decorate with whatever you have chosen. Pour the rest of the sauce into a warm bowl, and bring the dinner to the table.

To serve a whole fish. The main bone of a salmon-shaped fish, lying flat for serving, runs horizontally, with two fillets on either side of the main bone on top, and two underneath the bone. Using a large serving fork and a serving spatula, cut straight down the central length of the top fillet until you reach the main bone; lift off serving portions from each side. (If the fish has been cooked upright, as in a roaster, the main bone will, of course, be vertical and the fillets will be on the right and left sides of the bone.) Then, either at the table or in the kitchen, lift up the bone from the tail end and remove it, to expose the bottom fillet for serving.

Suggested accompaniments. There's nothing wrong with the traditional small boiled or steamed potatoes and fresh green peas, and, for wine, a mellow white Burgundy or chardonnay.

SPECIAL NOTE

How to Serve and Eat a Whole Trout-Shaped Fish

To be able to serve and to eat a whole fish, especially a trout, is part of civilized dining. This applies particularly to the young, who should take to it as soon as they can handle knife and fork; this is a fine way for them to begin taking pride in themselves and their abilities.

Loosening flesh from bone. Set the fish so its tail faces you, and its back is to your right. Starting at the neck on the right side, slit through the skin of the back down to the tail, step 1. The main bone is running horizontally, branching out at the chest to encircle the visceral cavity. Starting at the back of the neck end, find the upper side of the bone with your knife; slide it across the bone from back side to belly side, then down to the lower third of the fish and to the tail, thus freeing the flesh of the top fillet from the bone, step 2.

Opening up the trout. Starting at the back or right side, flip the top fillet of flesh off the bone to the right, or belly side—if it won't come off smartly in a piece, do it as neatly as you can in sections.

Removing the bones. Gently lift up the central bone from the tail end, forking off the flesh underneath it as you go, step 3. You will note some feathery side bones branching out into the chest meat; these usually pull out with the main bone. Remove any left in the flesh, along with any small bones on the belly section of each fillet and along the back in the fin area.

Serving. The fish is now ready to serve. Sprinkle the flesh lightly with salt and freshly ground pepper, and spoon on a little melted butter, step 4, sauce, and/or lemon juice. The crisp skin makes fine eating, too.

1. Slitting down backbone

2. Flipping over top fillet

3. Removing central bone

4. Spooning on melted butter

Oven roasted large trout

WHOLE FISH, OVEN ROASTED

Clean and scale your fish, tuck a little seasoning in its cavity, brush it with butter or oil, and it's ready for roasting. It couldn't be a simpler way to cook a whole fish, and it could hardly be more delicious, the crisp skin holding in all its natural juices.

◀ MASTER RECIPE

Whole Roasted Fish: Trout Meunière

Large or small, whole fish are all roasted the same way, and, rather than a large salmon, we'll use a good-size trout in the 1-pound category.

MANUFACTURING NOTE: *The trout, because of its rather delicate skin, is dredged lightly in flour, which not only crisps its skin but keeps it intact as well as discouraging it from sticking to the roasting pan. Meunière, by the way, means the miller's wife, referring perhaps to her ever-floury hands.*

For 4 servings

2 trout (or other whole fish), about 1 pound each
Salt and freshly ground pepper

½ cup flour on a sheet of wax paper, for dredging
½ cup, more or less, clarified butter (page 139), melted
Parsley sprigs
Lemon wedges
Melted butter, or lemon-butter sauce (page 83)

SPECIAL EQUIPMENT SUGGESTED: *An ovenproof baking and serving platter is useful*

Preparing the fish. Leave the heads on the trout. Remove the gills and viscera; with shears, cut off the fins close to the body, and trim off a bit from the tails. Sprinkle a little salt and pepper inside each cavity.

*Ahead-of-time note: Cover and refrigerate if you are not proceeding shortly.

Roasting—15 to 20 minutes at 450°F. Preheat the oven to 450°F. Just before roasting, season the fish cavities lightly with salt and pepper, roll the fish in the flour and shake off excess. Brush melted clarified butter over the roasting platter or pan, lay the fish in place, and spoon over them a dribble of the butter. Set in the upper middle level of the preheated oven. In 8 minutes rapidly baste again with a spoonful or 2 of butter.

When is the fish done? When you begin to smell the buttery aroma of cooking fish, and you notice that juices are just beginning to appear in the platter. Test by pulling a small section of fin end out of the flesh at the ridge of the back—it should come fairly easily. Gently lift the belly flaps and peer into the cavity—there should be no bloody tinge way inside at the backbone. Do not overcook—the flesh should remain juicy.

Serving. Remove from the oven, and decorate with parsley sprigs—tucking a little into the eye sockets and the cavity. Serve as soon as possible, passing lemon and melted butter or butter sauce separately.

VARIATION

Oven Roasting Large Fish like Bass and Salmon

Roast larger fish in exactly the same way, except they need no dredging in flour. A 3-pound fish will take about 45 minutes, and, again, you can tell it is almost done when you smell it cooking, when juices just begin to appear in the pan, and when the back fins pull out fairly easily.

SPECIAL NOTE

Approximate Timings for Various Sizes of Salmon-Shaped Fish. Timing varies with the thickness of the fish. The Canadian formula of 10 minutes of cooking per inch of thickness is at least a guide, but the various indications noted in the preceding recipe are the sure signs.

Pounds	Total Minutes
2 to 4	20 to 25
4 to 6	25 to 30
6 to 8	35 to 45
8 to 10	45 to 60
10 to 12	60 to 75

STOVE-TOP COOKERY

THE SAUTÉS

A fresh fillet of sole, flounder, or red snapper quickly sautéed in the best butter, served with a sprinkling of lemon juice and parsley—it's quick, easy, and fish at its simple best. Of course you can elaborate, and add bread crumbs for a crisp crusty exterior—crumbs help a lot when you've a fish of no particular distinction. Pan frying is certainly the most direct way of cooking fish, and not only fillets but small fish, too, as well as shrimp, scallops, and lobster, each in its own special way.

FISH FILLETS SAUTÉED MEUNIÈRE

The fillets are scored on the skin side, seasoned with salt and pepper, and just before sautéing they are lightly floured; then you pop them into a frying pan of sizzling butter—a minute or two on each side is all the cooking they need. Here are a few tips before we begin.

Fish to use. Real European Dover sole is the dream fish here: its texture is firm enough to hold yet delicate to the tooth, it has its own natural flavor, and its size is perfect for sautéing. The only points against Dover sole are its expense and its scarcity in our retail markets. However, you may choose any fish with flesh that is not so flaky it will fall apart, and with fillets that are not too thick. The limit is about ¾ inch, while fillets ⅜ inch thick are ideal. If too thick they tend to overcook on the outside before they are done on the inside.

SPECIAL NOTE

Some fish choices for sautéing. Best examples are imported Dover sole, gray sole, flounder, whiting, and trout. Among other possibilities, although of a quite different taste and texture, are coho salmon, snapper, and bluefish.

Dredging in flour. A light coating of flour gently crisps the outside of the fish while helping it keep its shape as it browns in the pan. To dredge, spread ½ cup or more of flour in a plate (I keep a stack of 9-inch aluminum pie tins handy). The moment before sautéing, drop in a seasoned fillet to coat one side with flour, turn it to coat the other, and shake off excess flour, leaving just a dusting. Do only the number of fillets you are about to sauté. If you dredge more than a minute or so in advance, the flour gets wet, lumpy, and gummy—a doleful mess you certainly don't want on your fine fresh fish.

Clarified butter. Clarified butter (page 139) is by far the most satisfactory sauté medium to my mind: it browns well, smells wonderful as it cooks, and gives food that unbeatable taste of butter. Sautéing is obviously not for dieters—but stove-top poaching is, in the section following the sautés.

◄ MASTER RECIPE

Fillets of Sole Meunière

Fillets of sole (or other fish) sautéed in butter

For 6 servings

6 skinless and boneless sole or other thin fish fillets (see the Special Note on this page), all of a size, 4 to 6 ounces each and ⅜ inch thick
Salt and freshly ground white pepper
½ cup or so flour in a plate
About 4 Tbs clarified butter (page 139)
3 Tbs minced fresh parsley
4 to 6 Tbs unsalted butter
1 lemon, cut into wedges

SPECIAL EQUIPMENT SUGGESTED:
2 heavy no-stick frying pans would be useful, to hold all the fish at once; hot plates or a hot platter; a wide plastic spatula

Preparing the fish. Following the directions on page 81, dry the fish, remove any bones, score, trim, and flatten it. Lay it out on a sheet of wax paper.

Ahead-of-time note: If you are not proceeding, slip a pastry sheet under the fish, cover, and refrigerate.

Sautéing. Dust the fillets lightly on each side with salt and pepper. The moment before sautéing, rapidly drop each into the flour to coat both sides, and shake off the excess. Set the frying pans or pan over high heat and film with 1/16 inch of clarified butter. When the butter is very hot but not browning, rapidly lay in as many fillets as will fit easily, leaving a little space between each. Sauté a minute or two on one side, turn carefully so as not to break the fillet, and sauté a minute or two on the other side. The fish is done when just springy rather than squashy to the touch of your finger. Immediately remove from the pan to warm plates or a platter. (Or, if you are sautéing in 2 batches, keep the first warm for the few minutes necessary in a 200°F oven.)

Sauce and serving. Sprinkle each fillet with parsley. Wipe the frying pan clean, set over high heat, and add the fresh butter; heat until bubbling and pour over the fillets—the parsley will bubble up nicely. Decorate with lemon wedges, and serve at once.

TROUBLESHOOTING:

The fish didn't brown. You may have crowded too many fillets in the pan, and there was no room for browning—the fish steamed.

Or perhaps the butter was not hot enough.

Or your pan was too light in weight; it did not conduct and spread the heat.

Or the pan might have been too big for the heat source. A 12-inch frying pan cannot heat up all over on an 8-inch burner.

VARIATIONS

Sole Grenobloise
With brown butter and capers

The sharp taste of capers in browned butter does wonders, especially for fish of no distinctive individual fla-vor, like snapper and flounder. After sautéing the fish, as in the preceding recipe, remove them to hot plates, and brown the butter. Stir in 3 tablespoons of drained capers, heat a moment, and spoon over the fish. Decorate with parsley sprigs and serve.

Trout Meunière
and other whole small fish

Whole ½-pound trout are especially suitable for pan frying in butter, but any other small fish will do very well. Four should fit nicely into a 12-inch frying pan. Dry them, and season the cavities with salt and freshly ground pepper; just before sautéing, roll them in flour and shake off the excess. Sauté them slowly in clarified butter, counting about 5 minutes to a side. They are done when you can just separate flesh from bone at the ridge of the back, and there is no rosy red color near the bone when you peer deep inside the cavities. To serve, sprinkle with freshly chopped parsley and pour hot browned butter over them to make the parsley sizzle.

How to eat a whole trout with verve and confidence. See the illustrated directions on page 96.

SPECIAL NOTE

To Coat Food in Bread Crumbs
Paner à l'anglaise

A coating of fresh white bread crumbs and a sauté in real butter make a delicious salmon steak or chicken breast, or can give a bland fish or meat an interesting new dimension. In addition, crumbing gives more solidity to fish otherwise too flimsy or foods otherwise too soft for a regular sauté. This is also the coating for deep-fried foods. If you are unenthusiastic about breaded foods because you have always had them coated in stale or store-bought crumbs, and sautéed in butter substitutes or fried in smelly old fat, do give this classic method another chance. Fresh crumbs and real butter make all the difference!

For 6 pieces

6 pieces of fish fillets, sweetbreads, or chicken breast halves
Salt and freshly ground white pepper
1 cup flour in a plate
2 eggs, 2 tsp oil, and ⅛ tsp salt whisked together in a 9-inch pie plate
2½ cups moderately fine crumbs from fresh crustless homemade type white bread with body, in a 9-inch pie plate

Crumbing the food. Dry the food and season lightly on both sides with salt and pepper. One at a time, dip first in flour and shake off excess, then in beaten egg and shake off excess. Set in the crumbs, tossing them over the food and patting them in place. Lay each piece as done on a baking sheet covered with wax paper; when all are crumbed, cover and refrigerate 20 minutes or longer, so the crumbs will set.

SPECIAL NOTE

Tartar Sauce

For about 2 cups

1½ cups mayonnaise (page 363)
2 to 3 Tbs capers
1 smallish sour dill pickle
2 hard-boiled eggs
3 Tbs minced fresh herbs such as
    parsley, tarragon, and chives
Seasonings: Salt, freshly ground
    white pepper, lemon juice, Dijon-
    type prepared mustard

The mixture. Turn the mayonnaise
into a mixing bowl. Mince the capers
and pickle; twist them into a ball in
the corner of a towel to squeeze out
and discard their juices before adding
them to the bowl. Halve the eggs;
sieve the yolks and add to the bowl.
Chop and add the egg whites. Add
the herbs, blend all ingredients together, and season carefully to taste.

*Ahead-of-time note: Refrigerate in a
covered bowl.

VARIATION

Fish Fillets or Thin Fish Steaks Sautéed in Fresh Bread Crumbs

This makes a marvelous salmon
steak, coated in fresh crumbs and
sautéed in clarified butter. Dry the
steaks, season lightly with salt and
freshly ground pepper, and dip them
first in flour, then beaten egg, then in
the fresh crumbs as described in the
Special Note on page 99. After a 20-
minute chill to set the crumbs, sauté
them slowly in clarified butter for a
minute or more on each side, to crisp
the crumbs and brown them nicely.
The fish is done when lightly springy
to the touch, in contrast to its squashy
raw state. Serve at once with lemon
or the tartar sauce that also appears in
a Special Note on this page.

SPECIAL NOTE

Fish for Stove-Top Poaching

In addition to salmon, striped bass,
imported turbot, and John Dory, try
eastern and Alaskan halibut, monkfish, tilefish, and swordfish. Shark
steaks do well here, too—thresher
and mako—or try ahi, yellowfin, or
albacore. Even rather thin fillets may
be poached this way as long as they
are from the kind of fish that will
hold its shape—imported Dover
sole, as well as catfish, gray sole, petrale sole, and trout.

POACHING

Drop half a dozen chunky 6-ounce
fillets of salmon or bass into a large
saucepan of simmering salted water,
and in 8 minutes they are perfectly
and beautifully done. That's the best
kind of diet food—plain fish with
plenty of flavor. It's also the best kind
to show off butter sauces and hollandaise, since you have nothing to in-
trude on the marriage of fish and
sauce. But it is not only salmon or
bass that takes to this easy system; it
is any fish fillet or steak, fat or lean,
that has the inner strength to hold
together.

Top-quality frozen fillets and steaks
do well here too, taken directly from
freezer to pan. In the few minutes
needed to defrost in the poaching
water, they are practically cooked
through.

Julia buying fish in Santa Barbara Harbor

feels lightly springy. It should still be juicy. Fish that is resistant and flaky is overdone—too bad!

Ahead-of-time note: If you are not serving at once, remove the pan from heat and the fish may remain in its water 15 minutes or longer.

Serving. One at a time, remove the fillets with the slotted spatula and roll gently over the clean towel to blot up excess moisture. To serve simply, sprinkle on a little parsley, decorate with lemon wedges, and pass melted butter or hollandaise sauce (page 87) separately. Other suggestions follow.

Rolling poached fillets over a clean towel before arranging on the platter

◄ MASTER RECIPE

Stove-Top Poaching

For 6 servings

Salt
Wine vinegar
6 fish steaks or fillets 6 to 8 ounces each, such as one of the examples in the Special Note on the preceding page or the shark pictured at the opening of the chapter (skin and bones may be removed from your fish either before or after poaching)

SPECIAL EQUIPMENT SUGGESTED:
A roomy wide saucepan, chicken fryer, or electric skillet; a wide slotted spatula; a clean towel; warm plates or a platter

Cooking. Measure 3 inches of water into the pan. Add 1½ teaspoons of salt and 3 tablespoons wine vinegar for each quart of water, and bring to the boil. Slide in the fish. Bring to just below the simmer, and maintain the water below the simmer throughout the cooking—that is, the water is shivering and almost but not quite bubbling. (If the water actually boils the fish may break apart.)

Timing. Two to 3 minutes for sole or trout, 3 to 4 for shark, 8 for salmon or other fillets ½ inch thick.

When is it done? Fish is done when the flesh has turned from translucent to opaque and, rather than feeling squashy to the touch like raw fish, it

VARIATIONS

Lemon-Butter Sauce

This lightly lemony, deliciously buttery sauce is particularly attractive with salmon and trout, as well as such elegant lean fish as sole, turbot, and John Dory.

For about ¾ cup, serving 6

The grated rind of ½ lemon
2 Tbs freshly squeezed lemon juice
¼ cup fish stock or chicken broth
Salt and freshly ground white pepper
5 ounces (10 Tbs) unsalted butter, cut into ¼-inch slices
Minced fresh green herbs such as parsley, dill, and/or chives, optional

The flavor base. Bring the lemon rind, lemon juice, and the stock or broth to the boil in a 6-cup saucepan with ¼ teaspoon of salt and a few grinds of pepper. Boil slowly for several minutes, until reduced to a syrup—you should have almost 3 tablespoons.

*Ahead-of-time note: May be completed in advance to this point.

Finishing the sauce. Shortly before serving, bring the flavor base to the boil over moderately high heat. While boiling slowly, start whisking in the butter piece by piece, adding a new piece as each previous one is almost absorbed. Remove from heat as soon as the last piece of butter is almost incorporated, and whisk in the optional herbs. Correct seasoning and serve at once, since the sauce risks thinning out when you attempt to reheat it.

Ingredients for Provençal butter sauce

Provençal Butter Sauce
With garlic, rosemary, and tomato

Recommended for robust fish like shark steaks and red snapper, and such firm-fleshed but mild-flavored characters as monkfish.

For about 1¼ cups

Ingredients for the preceding lemon-butter sauce
1 large clove of garlic, puréed
⅛ tsp or so ground rosemary
2 ripe red tomatoes, peeled, seeded, juiced, and finely diced (about ⅔ cup)
2 to 3 Tbs fresh minced parsley

Add the garlic and rosemary to the saucepan of lemon flavor base in the preceding recipe. Gently toss the tomatoes with a sprinkling of salt and

Spooning Provençal butter sauce over poached fish fillets

pepper and turn into a sieve, letting the juices drain into the saucepan for several minutes. Remove the sieve, and boil down the juices to a syrup. Proceed with the recipe as described. Fold the drained tomatoes into the completed sauce, and correct seasoning. Spoon the sauce over the fish.

Poached salmon with cucumber sauce

Salmon or Bass with Cucumber Sauce

For a cool and delicious summer meal, serve this either hot or cold.

For 6 servings

1 cucumber
¼ tsp each salt, sugar, and wine
  vinegar
1 cup sour cream (or part yogurt
  and part sour cream)
2 to 3 Tbs minced fresh dill or
  watercress leaves
6 salmon or bass fillets 6 to 8 ounces
  each, poached as directed in the
  master recipe (page 101)

Neatly dicing the cucumber. Peel the cucumber and halve it lengthwise; scoop out the seeds with a teaspoon. Cut the halves into quarters and the quarters into crosswise pieces 2 inches long. Finally cut the quarters into matchstick julienne, stack the julienne, and cut into dice.

The sauce. Toss the cucumber in a bowl with the salt, sugar, and vinegar. Let stand 5 minutes or so, then fold in the sour cream. Season carefully to taste, and fold in the dill or watercress.

*Ahead-of-time note: May be completed hours in advance; cover and refrigerate.

The fish. Poach the fish as directed.

To serve hot. Remove and drain the fillets; arrange on hot plates or a platter. Either decorate with sprigs of fresh dill or parsley and pass the sauce separately, or spoon the cucumber sauce decoratively over the fish.

To serve cold. Let the fish remain in its poaching liquid at least 20 minutes, to pick up flavor. Remove, drain, and chill. Serve on a bed of greens, and decorate with the sauce as shown.

VARIATIONS

Pipérade

A colorful garnish of sliced onions, green and red peppers, and garlic sautéed in olive oil (page 90). Cook the pipérade a few minutes longer than directed, until tender, then spread over the hot fish. Serve the fish either hot or cold.

Florentine

Fish fillets gratinéed on a bed of spinach, useful for advance preparation. Substitute stove-top poached fillets for the oven-poached fillets on page 88.

FEASTING ON THE REMAINS

Coquilles of Poached Salmon, Bass, or Other Fish

Here is an easy way to make a nice little appetizer course or luncheon dish out of cooked or canned fish.

For 6 servings, you'll want about 2 cups of fish—canned salmon is especially good here, but other fish such as cooked halibut, cod, or snapper, or canned tuna, are also candidates. First you make a well-flavored white sauce, starting with a cup of minced onions sautéed in 4 tablespoons of butter; when tender and translucent, stir in the flour for your béchamel sauce—¼ cup. Proceed with the sauce, as directed on page 272, adding 1½ cups of milk and ½ cup of dry white French vermouth. Season nicely, fold in a little fresh minced dill, ⅓ cup of grated Swiss cheese, and the boned and flaked fish.

Turn the mixture into a buttered baking dish or individual shells, and sprinkle the top with a little grated cheese. All of this may be done ahead and refrigerated; you have but to pop the fish in the upper third of a preheated 400°F oven 10 to 15 minutes before serving.

Fisherman's salad

Fisherman's Salad

You can do so many attractive things with cold fish that it's worthwhile buying a little extra when you are at it, so you'll have leftovers to play with. For instance, you can turn that fish into a splendid cold salad, and serve it as a first course or have it as a main-course luncheon dish. All you need are a few extras, and you're ready to go.

For 6 people, you'll want 2 to 3 cups of cooked fish or canned salmon or tuna, turned into a bowl and smartly flavored with lemon juice, salt and freshly ground pepper, good oil, minced scallions or shallots, minced parsley, and fresh herbs such as dill.

Drain if juices accumulate, and fold with just enough mayonnaise to enrobe the fish.

For the attractive arrangement pictured here, start by lining the bottom of a large platter with curly endive greens that have been tossed with salt, pepper, and a little oil. Mound the fish in the center, and decorate with red pepper or pimiento. Ring the fish with shrimp, and place olives, halved hard-boiled eggs, tomato quarters, red bell pepper strips, and parsley sprigs at strategic intervals, embracing the decor with a duet of slim scallions.

THE GREAT AMERICAN LOBSTER

It's the glory of our North Atlantic coast—the American lobster, with its incomparable flavor. You now find them swimming about in supermarket glass tanks all over the country. They are alive and well and available to all of us—at a price. But almost all of the lobster can be used, including the shells.

Choosing lobsters: Live lobsters should be thoroughly alive, flapping their tails against their chests and waving their claws. Beware of buying a ready-cooked lobster: unless its tail is tightly folded against its chest, chances are the lobster was dead or dying before cooking. (Please read the Special Note on fish and shellfish safety, page 80.)

Storing live lobsters: Refrigerate them in a perforated brown paper bag, or in a perforated carton with fresh seaweed.

SPECIAL NOTE

Timing for Steamed Lobsters

Pounds	Minutes
1¼	12
1½	15
2	18
2½	20
3–5	21–25

SPECIAL NOTE

Male or female? You can always tell a female: the two tiny swimmerets underneath the tail where it joins the chest are fringed with hair, while male swimmerets are clean and pointed. Females are the most desirable for lobster stew and sauces, because the roe, or coral, turns everything a lovely salmon-coral pink.

Tomalley and roe (coral). The creamy green-gray substance in the chest cavity of a cooked lobster is known as tomalley. The female also contains the pink roe that nestles along the tail meat as shown; it is black when the lobster is undercooked or raw. These are prized parts of the lobster, giving flavor and color to sauces and stews.

Amount of meat per lobster. 1 pound of whole lobster should yield ⅓ to ½ cup (3 to 4 ounces) of cooked meat.

◄ MASTER RECIPE

The Best Way to Cook Lobsters: Steaming

People usually speak of cooked lobsters as being boiled, and if you run a fish restaurant with an immense caldron just for lobsters, that's certainly the way to do it. But steaming is far easier for the home cook. The number you can steam at once, however, depends on the equipment at your disposal.

For 6 lobsters, 2 pounds each

SPECIAL EQUIPMENT SUGGESTED:
A kettle 16 to 18 inches in diameter and 12 or more inches deep (or a large covered turkey roaster), and a rack or colander to fit inside; a tight-fitting cover; a weight to hold down the cover; a kitchen timer

Set the rack or colander in the kettle, pour in 1½ inches of water, and bring to the furious boil. Add the lobsters. Weight down the cover to keep in the steam, and, as it starts to escape, lower the heat and set your timer:

When are they done? Pull off one of the little legs, and suck out the meat—if it's done, the lobster's done. (If you are not making the stock described farther on, declare that all little legs are the cook's to eat.)

Lobster Shell Broth

The shells have fine lobster flavor, and when you chop them up and simmer them with aromatic flavorings you will have a wonderful base to store in your freezer for lobstery soups and sauces.

For 4 to 5 cups

2 Tbs fresh peanut oil
The chopped shells from 2 cooked lobsters
½ cup chopped onions
¼ cup chopped carrots
¼ cup chopped celery stalks
6 cups liquid: fish stock, or 3 to 4 cups chicken stock plus water
1 cup dry white French vermouth or dry white wine
1 cup chopped fresh tomatoes, or ½ cup canned Italian plum tomatoes
1 imported bay leaf
A pinch of tarragon
Salt

SPECIAL EQUIPMENT SUGGESTED:
A heavy-bottomed 3- to 4-quart saucepan

Heat the oil in the saucepan, add the chopped shells, onions, carrots, and celery; sauté 5 minutes over high heat, stirring. Add the liquid, vermouth or wine, tomatoes, and herbs; bring to the simmer, and season lightly with salt. Cover partially and simmer 40 minutes. Strain. Use as a base for sauces and fish soups.

*Ahead-of-time note: Cover and refrigerate when cool, or freeze.

VARIATION

Red Lobster Sauce à l'Américaine

That wonderful lobster sauce which goes with the famous lobster à l'américaine starts out in the same way as the preceding broth. Serve the sauce with fish dishes, and especially with any of the mousses starting on page 124.

For 1½ to 2 cups sauce

The chopped shells, including if possible the little legs, from 2 lobsters, 1½ to 2 pounds each
¼ cup each chopped carrots and celery stalks
½ cup chopped onions
2 Tbs fresh peanut oil
¼ cup Cognac or good brandy
1 cup fish stock or chicken broth
½ cup beef broth
¾ cup dry white French vermouth
3 ripe red tomatoes, unpeeled, washed, cored, and chopped (or 1 cup drained canned Italian plum tomatoes)
½ tsp dried tarragon
1 large clove of unpeeled garlic, crushed
Salt, freshly ground pepper, and hot pepper sauce
2 Tbs each flour and butter, creamed into a paste
A little tomato paste, if needed

Making the sauce base. Sauté the lobster shells and chopped vegetables in the oil for 5 minutes. Pour in the Cognac or brandy and ignite; let burn 15 seconds, shaking the pan, then extinguish with the stock and/or broth(s) and the vermouth. Add the rest of the ingredients except for the flour-butter paste and tomato paste,

and simmer 30 minutes. Strain into another saucepan, pressing juices out of ingredients. Boil down rapidly if necessary, to make about 2 cups of fragrant juices. Remove from heat, and whisk in the flour-butter paste; bring to the simmer, stirring, for 2 minutes. Whisk in a little tomato paste if you think it needed for depth of flavor and color; taste, and correct seasoning.

*Ahead-of-time note: Chill until cold, then cover and refrigerate or freeze.

Lobster à l'Américaine

When you have saved the shells for a sauce, and have on hand, or have bought, a little lobster meat, here's a beautiful way to serve it.

For about 2 cups

2 Tbs butter
The meat from 2 cooked lobsters (2 cups or so)
1 Tbs minced shallots
Salt and freshly ground pepper
¼ cup dry white French vermouth
⅓ cup heavy cream
⅔ cup of the preceding lobster sauce
If available: the coral and tomalley from the lobsters forced through a sieve with 2 Tbs butter
2 to 3 Tbs minced fresh parsley and/or tarragon or chervil

SPECIAL EQUIPMENT SUGGESTED:
A 10-inch no-stick frying pan

The lobster. Heat the butter to bubbling in the frying pan, add the lobster meat and shallots; sauté over moderate heat for 2 minutes. Season lightly with salt and pepper, add the vermouth, and boil down rapidly until liquid has almost evaporated. Fold in the cream and the lobster sauce; boil down a moment until lightly thickened. Correct seasoning. Remove from heat; fold in the optional coral and tomalley. Just before serving, fold over moderate heat to rewarm the lobster, but do not bring to the simmer.

Serving suggestions. Serve as a separate course over toast points or boiled rice, with a sprinkling of fresh herbs. Or serve it in puff pastry cases (page 391). Or use it as a filling and sauce for the fish mousse in a ring mold (page 126). When you have this lovely sauce or lobster mixture on hand, you'll find many an excuse for bringing it out.

Sauté of Lobster in Wine and Cream

This simple recipe, sautéing the tomalley and roe along with the lobster meat, brings out the very essence of lobster. It is a useful technique to have in your repertoire since you can serve the lobster as a first course with little fleurons of puff pastry or toast points. Or toss it with pasta, fold it into crêpes, use it as a base for soufflés or as a sauce for fish or fish mousses. Or, finally, make it the base for the fine lobster stew farther on.

MANUFACTURING NOTE: *The only way to achieve the natural lobstery pink color is to have female lobsters with roe. But if you can find only males, or only cooked lobster meat, stir in little dribbles of tomato paste until you get just the right subtle color.*

For 6 servings

2 cooked 2-pound lobsters, females if possible, with their tomalley and roe (about 2 cups lobster meat)
6 Tbs butter
1½ Tbs minced shallots or scallions
Salt and freshly ground white pepper
A big pinch of tarragon
2 to 3 Tbs dry (Sercial) Madeira, or ¼ cup dry white French vermouth
½ to ⅔ cup or more heavy cream
1 tsp or so tomato paste, if needed

SPECIAL EQUIPMENT SUGGESTED:
A fine-meshed sieve; a 10-inch no-stick frying pan

The lobsters. Shell the lobsters, cut the meat into bite-size pieces, and set aside. Push the roe, if you have it, and the tomalley through a sieve, and reserve.

The tomalley-roe sauté. Melt 4 tablespoons of the butter in the frying pan, stir in the sieved tomalley and roe, and sauté slowly over moderately low heat for 5 minutes—it will turn a beige-pink; beige only if you have no roe.

Adding the lobster meat. Fold in the lobster meat and shallots or scallions, season lightly with salt, pepper, and tarragon, and fold in the remaining 2

tablespoons of butter. Continue the slow sauté another 5 minutes or so, gently folding the lobster in the butter as the roe gradually turns the meat a salmony pink.

The wine and cream finish. Add the Madeira or vermouth, simmer a moment, then fold in the cream, which will turn pink and beautiful if you had lobster roe—otherwise mix in a little tomato paste as needed. Boil slowly several minutes, gently folding lobster and sauce together, until the sauce has thickened lightly. Taste, correct seasoning, and the lobster is ready to serve.

*Ahead-of-time note: May be cooked ahead and reheated.

Pasta with lobster sauce. You might serve this with angel-hair pasta, cooked at the last minute, drained, and tossed with a little butter and light virgin olive oil. Pile the pasta onto warm plates, then quickly fashion a well in the center and spoon in servings of lobster. Decorate with parsley or fresh tarragon, and serve.

VARIATION

Lobster Stew

To get the best out of a lobster stew, plan to make it a day or even two days before serving, since it takes time for the lobster flavor to insinuate itself throughout the cream. And it is cream here—milk just does not carry that uniquely lobster flavor through-out the stew. Furthermore, the but-ter, which also distributes the flavor, tends to separate from milk, while it homogenizes with cream, turning it a beautiful lobstery pink. Again, it's females you want here; otherwise you will have to achieve pinkness through tomato paste.

For about 2 quarts

**Ingredients for the preceding lobster
    sauté**
**5½ cups half-and-half or light cream
    (in addition to the cream in the
    sauté recipe)**
1 Tbs or so tomato paste, if needed
6 slices of chilled butter ⅜ inch thick
**Hot buttered white toast, or toasted
    and buttered English muffins**

The lobsters. Remove the meat from the lobsters. Cut 6 thin slices of tail or claw meat and refrigerate in a cov-ered bowl for final decoration. Pro-ceed to sauté the roe, tomalley, and lobster meat as directed. Let cool to tepid.

Adding the cream. Meanwhile, heat the cream to tepid—the same tem-perature as the lobster meat. Then,

by small dribbles, as though making mayonnaise, begin ladling the cream into the lobster meat, folding gently and continually while the cream ab-sorbs the butter and takes on a pale lobster hue, see illustration. (You would blend in a little tomato paste midway through here, if needed.) Season nicely with salt and pepper, let cool, then cover and refrigerate.

*Ahead-of-time note: It is best to make the stew 1 to 2 days ahead.

Serving. Folding gently, bring the stew slowly to below the simmer for 2 to 3 minutes. (Meanwhile gently warm the reserved pieces of lobster tail or claw in butter and seasonings.) Taste the stew again for seasoning, and ladle the stew into hot soup cups or plates. Rapidly float on each serv-ing a slice of chilled butter on which you place a piece of lobster tail or claw. Accompany with the warm toast or muffins.

Very slowly blending in the cream

ADDITIONAL LOBSTER RECIPES:

French Crêpes Gratinéed with Lobster (page 406) and variations (page 407)

Lobster Quiche (page 387)

Lobster Soufflé (pages 73 and 75)

Cold Lobster and Lobster Salad (pages 365 and 375)

SHRIMP

Shrimp seems to be the universal favorite seafood; even those who say they hate fish will dig into a bowl-ful with gusto. However, shrimp have become increasingly expensive, and they are exceptionally perishable. Because of this, many packers use a chemical called tripolyphosphate to keep shrimp firm and white. But when they use too much, the shrimp take on an unpleasant cleaning-fluid odor and taste. Read the package la-bel, if there is one, and know your market!

Buying and Storing Shrimp.
When buying frozen shrimp (and I
think you get better quality buying
them raw in the shell—any
preserving chemicals seem less
noticeable), rush them home on ice if
possible. Keep them solidly frozen at
0°F or lower until you plan to use
them; just before cooking, thaw them
in a basin of cold water. If your
market has thawed the shrimp, give
your purchase a serious sniff before
leaving the premises; store them on
ice, and use them at once. Top-
quality frozen shrimp (and they can
be excellent) should not only smell
sweet and fresh, but also be
beautifully tender when cooked.

SPECIAL NOTE

Shrimp Sizes. Shrimp are
classified in almost a dozen categories
according to the number of shrimp
per pound—headless shrimp-in-the-
shell, that is. The classes start with
"tiny" at over 70 per pound, going
through "large" at 31 to 35, "jumbo"
at 21 to 25, "colossal" at 10 to 15,
and "extra colossal" at under 10
shrimp per pound. Their cost
increases with size, extra colossals
being the quickest to shell and
topping the price list.

Peeling Shrimp. I have yet to find
a quick way to peel shrimp, and have
never found peeling gadgets
satisfactory. If I don't want any shell
on the tail, I squeeze off the shell at
that end, which sometimes loosens
the whole shrimp. Then, after
peeling off a round or two of the
shell at the underside of the large
end, I can usually pull the body out
of the rest of the shell.

Deveining. The intestinal vein is
the dark spot you usually see in the
flesh at the large end; it runs close
under the outside curve of the
shrimp. Rather than cutting the flesh
open along the back, you can usually
draw the vein out gently with your
fingers and the help of a paper towel.
Although it may be left in, that dark
line ruins the beauty of the shrimp.

SKEWERED, BARBECUED, AND SAUTÉED SHRIMP

The following recipes are akin, since
in each the shrimp have a flavoring
marinade, and a marinade is especially desirable for frozen shrimp.
With any of the three, serve a white
wine like Chablis, Sancerre, or a
light sauvignon blanc.

◀ MASTER RECIPE

Peeled Skewered Shrimp

These are attractive as appetizers, or
as a first course or luncheon dish.

Serving 6 to 8 as a first course

**30 to 32 raw "large" shrimp in the
shell (about 1 pound)**

*Marinade suggestions—any or all of
the following*

**3 to 4 Tbs fine fresh olive oil or
peanut oil**

**3 to 4 Tbs dry white French
vermouth or lemon juice**

Salt and freshly ground pepper

**Optional flavorings: hot pepper
sauce, soy sauce, dark sesame oil,
puréed garlic, and grated fresh
ginger**

½ tsp thyme, dill, or tarragon

**15 strips thick-sliced bacon, halved
crosswise**

Skewering the shrimp and bacon

Cutting down curved side of shell to open the shrimp

Skewering several shrimp together

Peeled Skewered Shrimp (*continued*)

SPECIAL EQUIPMENT SUGGESTED:
30 to 32 pointed wooden skewers 7 to 8 inches long; an oiled broiling pan, if needed

Preliminaries. Before peeling and deveining the shrimp, set the skewers to soak in cold water to keep them from burning. Beat the marinade ingredients in a bowl, gently fold in the shrimp, and let them steep 20 minutes. Drop the bacon into a saucepan with 2 quarts of water and blanch (boil slowly) for 5 minutes; drain, rinse, and pat dry in paper towels.

Skewering. Push the sharp end of a skewer through one end of a piece of bacon, then the large end of a shrimp, the middle part of a bacon strip, finally the tail of the shrimp and the bacon end, see illustration.

*Ahead-of-time note: Refrigerate in a plastic bag and set over ice until cooking time.

Grilling or broiling. Either grill a minute or so on each side, bacon side down at first, or set bacon side up close under a hot broiler element and broil a minute or so, then turn and broil on the other side. Serve at once.

Colossal Butterflied Shrimp

This is for giant shrimp in the shell—split open, bathed in heady flavors, and broiled or grilled on the barbecue. "Colossal" and "extra colossal" are the largest of the shrimp categories, but you could use whatever of the large sizes you can find— and afford.

For 24 shrimp, 2 or 3 per person

24 giant shrimp in their shells (6 to 8 headless shrimp per pound, if possible)
The marinade suggestions listed in the master recipe
¼ cup or so olive oil or peanut oil for basting

SPECIAL EQUIPMENT NEEDED:
48 long sharp-pointed wooden skewers, soaked an hour in cold water; a basting brush; a lightly oiled broiling pan, if needed

Butterflying the shrimp. To butterfly giant shrimp, arm yourself with small sharp-pointed scissors, and start cutting at the large end of the outside curve of the shell; cut through the length of the shell down to the beginning of the tail, see illustration. Then, with a knife, cut through the length of the flesh just to

but not through the underside of the shell. Remove the intestinal vein.

The marinade. Whisk the marinade ingredients in a large mixing bowl; fold in the shrimp. Cover and refrigerate for an hour or two, basting the shrimp with the marinade several times.

Broiling or barbecuing. Drain the shrimp and wipe them off with paper towels. (Reserve the marinade in a small bowl, beating in a little extra oil.) Open the shrimp flesh side up; push one skewer through the large ends to hold them open, and another near the tail end if needed. Or you can use a longer skewer for several shrimp, see illustration.

To broil: Set flesh side down close under the red-hot broiler element for 1½ minutes; turn, brush with marinade, and broil flesh side up another 1 to 2 minutes or so, depending on size, basting once or twice.

To barbecue or grill: Start flesh side down; turn, baste, and finish flesh side up, basting once or twice.

Jumbo Shrimp Sautéed in Wine and Spices

Sautéing shrimp is easier and faster than broiling them and this is a particularly successful free-form recipe in which you add the flavors you wish. You will note that the shrimp are sautéed in the shell and peeled afterward—which can, of course, be done at the table when you are serving informally. Or serve them as an hors d'oeuvre, on toothpicks.

For 24 "jumbo" shrimp

24 "jumbo" shrimp in their shells
The marinade suggestions in the master recipe
Fresh olive oil, freshly squeezed lemon juice, and fresh parsley, as needed

SPECIAL EQUIPMENT SUGGESTED:
A 12-inch no-stick frying pan

Sautéing. Heat the oil in a large frying pan until very hot but not smoking; toss in the shrimp. Add, for instance, droplets of sesame oil and soy, a clove of puréed garlic, a little grated ginger, salt, freshly ground pepper, and a good pinch of thyme. Sauté, shaking and swirling the pan by its handle, just until the shrimp begin to turn pink. Pour in the wine (you may want a little more than suggested) and continue cooking a moment or two more, tossing and turning, and basting the shrimp with the liquid. Cook them only until they are lightly springy rather than squashy to the touch, 2 or 3 minutes in all.

Finishing. Pour the shrimp and their cooking liquid into a bowl and let cool for 20 minutes, turning and basting the shrimp with their juices frequently.

Finishing the shrimp. If you plan to peel them, do so while they are still tepid. Meanwhile pour the cooking liquid back into the pan and boil it down until lightly syrupy. Stir in a little fresh oil, lemon juice, and salt and pepper to taste. Toss the shrimp in this liquid and decorate with parsley, if you wish. Serve tepid or chilled.

SAUCED SHRIMP

The following are more formal ideas, for shrimp to be served over rice, or in a croustade or patty shell, needing only a fresh green vegetable or a salad to complete the main course. You can adapt the same method for scallops, crabmeat, and lobster—or chicken breasts.

Curried Shrimp with Mushrooms

For this recipe you make a curried sauce with onions, mushrooms, and herbs, and fold in raw peeled shrimp at the end for their brief simmer. A chardonnay or white Burgundy wine would go here.

For 6 servings, 5 shrimp per person

The curried mushroom sauce
½ pound fresh mushrooms, trimmed, washed, dried, and quartered

2 or more Tbs olive oil or fresh peanut oil
2 Tbs minced shallots or scallions
½ cup finely minced onions
1 large clove garlic, puréed
2 tsp fragrant curry powder (more if you wish)
1½ Tbs flour
½ cup dry white wine or dry white French vermouth
1 cup chicken stock
¼ tsp dried thyme
Salt and freshly ground pepper

30 "large" raw shrimp (about 1 pound in the shell), peeled and deveined
Drops of freshly squeezed lemon juice as needed
½ cup, more or less, sour cream
Decoration: parsley sprigs and/or 6 whole shrimp sautéed in butter

SPECIAL EQUIPMENT SUGGESTED:
A 10-inch no-stick frying pan

The curried mushroom sauce. Sauté the mushrooms briefly in the frying pan with a tablespoon of the oil; toss in the shallots or scallions the last minute of cooking, then scrape the mushrooms into a side dish. Add the remaining oil to the pan, stir in the onions and garlic, and cook slowly for 7 to 8 minutes, or until tender and translucent. Stir in the curry and flour, and cook slowly, stirring, for 2 minutes. Remove from heat, and blend in the wine, stock, and thyme. Simmer 5 minutes, correct seasoning, and fold in the sautéed mushrooms. Simmer 3 minutes; taste and season nicely with salt and pepper.

(continued)

Curried Shrimp with Mushrooms (*continued*)

Adding the shrimp. Fold in the shrimp and simmer a minute or two only, just until they have curled and are barely firm when pressed. (If by chance the sauce is too liquid—it should enrobe the shrimp—drain it out into a saucepan and boil down rapidly until thickened, then return it to the frying pan over the shrimp.) Taste carefully and correct seasoning, adding drops of lemon juice as needed.

*Ahead-of-time note: If you are not continuing shortly, let cool, cover, and refrigerate. Reheat to just the simmer before serving.

Finishing the dish. Remove from heat, and fold in the sour cream by spoonfuls, only enough of it to enrich and thicken the sauce. Serve over rice, in a rice ring, or on buttered toast, or in toasted bread cases or patty shells. Top with parsley and/or a whole shrimp.

VARIATIONS

Curried Scallops or Chicken Breasts with Mushrooms

Substitute ¾ pound of fresh raw scallops or boneless skinless chicken breast for the shrimp. Cut the large sea scallops or chicken breasts into ½-inch dice; calico and bay scallops may stay as they are.

Curried Crab or Lobster with Mushrooms

Fold 1½ cups of cooked crab or lobster meat into the finished curried mushroom sauce, simmer 2 minutes, then complete the recipe. If you have any whole claw meat or little legs, save them out to decorate each serving.

Tabletop Shrimp Sauté

Quick-cooking shrimp lend themselves easily to tabletop cooking. Here are several versions, starting with a cream and mustard sauce that could be served over rice or on buttered toast, and with variations including mushrooms, or tomatoes, or a persillade of garlic and parsley. A sauvignon blanc should go well with any of these.

MANUFACTURING NOTE: *Be sure you have a proper heat source for your antics; see the notes for Crêpes Suzette on page 410.*

For 6 servings

36 "medium large" shrimp (about 1 pound in the shell), peeled
4 Tbs unsalted butter (or ¼ cup clarified butter)
Salt and freshly ground pepper
¼ to ⅓ cup Cognac
⅓ cup dry white French vermouth
2 Tbs minced shallots or scallions
A handful of fresh parsley, minced
Sprigs of fresh dill or tarragon, minced
⅔ cup heavy cream blended with 2 tsp cornstarch and 1½ Tbs Dijon-type mustard
1 lemon, halved

SPECIAL EQUIPMENT SUGGESTED: *A chafing dish set-up (page 410); a long-handled serving spoon and fork; a ladle for pouring in the Cognac*

Kitchen preliminaries. Shell and devein the shrimp, place in a leakproof plastic bag, and refrigerate in a bowl of ice until the moment of cooking. Arrange the rest of the ingredients in attractive containers on a tray, along with your cooking utensils. Bring hot plates, the wine, and other accompaniments to the table just before you begin—a helper would be welcome.

The cooking.

The Shrimp Go In. Set the chafing dish pan over high heat, and add the shrimp. Toss and turn for about a minute, twirling and shaking the pan by its handle to evaporate moisture. Add the butter, and when it has coated the shrimp toss with a sprinkling of salt and pepper. Continue cooking and tossing for a moment, until the shrimp turn pink.

Flaming in Cognac. Pour the Cognac first into a ladle (to prevent an explosion in the bottle!), then over the shrimp; tilt the hot pan into the flame to ignite (or light with a match).

The Finish. In a few seconds, douse the flame by pouring in the vermouth, toss with the shallots and herbs, then stir in the cream mixture. Spoon it over the shrimp for a minute or two as it bubbles and cooks. Taste for seasoning, adding more salt and pepper, if needed. Pierce the lemon with a fork and squeeze in drops of its juice from on high. Toss and baste a few seconds more, and serve.

VARIATIONS

With Mushrooms

Bring along to the table 2 cups of quartered fresh mushrooms, previously sautéed in butter; toss them in just before you add the cream/mustard mixture. This could be a main course, served over rice with a salad or fresh green vegetable.

With Tomatoes

Or omit the cream, and along with the herbs toss in a cup of diced fresh tomato pulp (tomatoes peeled, seeded, and juiced, page 357). This could be a first course, served with croûtes of French bread (page 24).

Persillade

Or omit the wine, Cognac, and the cream mixture. After tossing the shrimp with the butter and seasoning them with salt and pepper, toss with the shallots and a large clove of very finely minced garlic, then with a handful of fresh white bread crumbs, and finally ½ cup or so of chopped fresh parsley. You might serve this as a first course, with baked cherry tomatoes and garlic bread or toasted pita wedges (page 33).

Small and large sea scallops

SCALLOPS

Coquilles St. Jacques is the French name—France's St. Jacques being our St. James the Apostle. Among legends surrounding the name, my favorite is that medieval knights were bearing the remains of the saint to his final resting place in Spain. Nearing the end of their long journey, they crossed through an inlet of the sea, and when they emerged from the water live scallops were clinging to their horses' trappings and to their own clothing. This was taken to be such a good and holy omen that even today pilgrims traveling back from the apostle's tomb in Santiago de Compostela proudly wear the cockle shell of St. Jacques to show where they've been.

Many of us have never seen a whole sea scallop in its fan-shaped shell because most of ours are caught way off the New England coast and then shucked at sea. The only part of the scallop retained is the fat short white edible cylinder, the adductor muscle, that opens and closes the shells. Alas, another edible third of the scallop, the delicate and delicious pink roe, is thrown overboard. Perhaps one day fishermen will see fit to keep it, considering the price scallops bring.

Varieties. The most common scallop in our markets is the large sea scallop. The small, tender, and always more expensive bay scallop is seasonal and rarer (see illustration of the two). Recent entries into the market are Icelandic scallops, a little smaller and less expensive than sea scallops but cooked in the same way,

Scallops (*continued*)

and the much smaller and even less expensive calico scallops from Florida. Since the cooking method and timings are not the same for all varieties, the following master recipes are for sea scallops, with notes for bay and calico scallops.

Buying and Storing Scallops. Be sure to smell them on the premises, since scallops are perishable. They should have a sweet mild fresh odor; a strong-smelling scallop is a stale one. Refrigerate them in a leak-proof plastic bag in a bowl of ice, and cook them as soon as possible.

Scallop Roe. If you are so fortunate as to gather scallops yourself or to find them whole, the roe is the pink tongue attached to the muscle. Remove it delicately from the muscle, cook it separately since it is tenderer than the muscle, then either add it to the cooked dish or use it as a decoration.

Amounts. I shall specify 1 pound (2 cups) of scallops for 6 people as a first course, and 1½ pounds (3 cups) for 6 people as a main course.

Frozen scallops. Outside of the eastern seaboard, and certainly in the Far West, one usually finds frozen sea scallops in the markets. According to Susan Faria's *Northeast Seafood Book,* a fine source book (Massachusetts Division of Marine Fisheries, Boston 02202, 1984), shucked scallops, even when fresh, are often plumped by soaking in water, and frozen scallops can be plumped in a phosphate solution to whiten the meat and improve its texture. This finally explains to me why so often when sautéing scallops, everything is going along just fine when suddenly a burst of juice appears in the pan. For a solution to this problem, see the sauté recipe farther on.

Preparation for cooking. Look over each large sea scallop and pull off the hard little nubbin fastened to the side of the cylinder (it's tough when cooked but can be reserved and added to a fish stock). With the small scallops, especially calicos, I am less meticulous, removing only obvious nubbins. After de-nubbining, swish the scallops briefly, with your hands, in a bowl of cold water to rid them of any sand. Lift them out, again with your hands, into a sieve to drain. If you are using large sea scallops you may wish to cut them into slices ¼ inch thick across the grain, or cut them vertically into quarters or thirds. Keep scallops refrigerated on ice until the moment of cooking.

SAUTÉED SEA SCALLOPS

Sautéing is certainly one of the most direct and fundamental ways of cooking scallops. You may sauté them very simply indeed with just a bit of garlic and parsley, or you may add trimmings as in the variation following the master recipe. Serve the scallops as a first course with toasted French bread, or have them as a main course with green vegetables or salad. You'll want a dry white wine with a certain amount of character, like a Chablis, Sancerre, Alsatian riesling, or sauvignon blanc.

The juice problem. What to do when the juices escape, as they often do when one sautés scallops, remained a continuing problem to me until the day I was discussing squid cookery with my fish merchant in the south of France. Squid can exude juice, too. Start them in a dry pan over moderately low heat, he advised; let the juices come out, raise the heat to evaporate the liquid, and proceed with the cooking. It works for squid—and wild chanterelle mushrooms, too. Since one never knows with scallops, and they cook so quickly, I now test out 2 or 3 in a dry pan and if juices exude in the few seconds they take to warm through, I have two choices. Either change to another cooking method, or sauté them in batches in a dry pan, drain and dry them, and then begin the recipe but shorten the cooking time. So far it is the only solution I know for juice-exuding (probably water-plumped) scallops.

◀ MASTER RECIPE

Scallops Sautéed with Garlic and Herbs

Fast and simple, this is one of the tastiest ways with scallops.

MANUFACTURING NOTE: *It is essential here to have a high heat source and a heavy, heat-conducting frying pan that is not too large for your burner; sauté in two batches if necessary since if you crowd the pan the scallops will steam rather than brown.*

For 6 servings

1½ pounds (3 cups) sea scallops
  prepared for cooking as
  previously described, and cut into
  thirds or quarters if large
Salt and freshly ground pepper
½ cup flour for dredging
¼ cup, more or less, clarified butter
  (page 139) or olive oil
1 large clove of garlic, minced
1½ Tbs minced shallots or scallions
A handful of fresh parsley, minced

SPECIAL EQUIPMENT SUGGESTED:
A sheet of wax paper and a sieve for dredging; a heavy 10- to 12-inch frying pan, no-stick recommended (see preceding manufacturing note)

Dredging the scallops. Dry the scallops and spread on a piece of wax paper. Toss with a sprinkling of salt and pepper. The moment before sautéing, toss them in the flour, turn them into a sieve, and shake off excess flour.

Sautéing. Set the frying pan over high heat, add the clarified butter or the oil, and when thoroughly hot turn in the scallops. Let sit for 10 seconds, toss briefly, let sit 4 to 5 seconds more, and continue tossing slowly, swirling the pan by its handle, while the scallops begin to brown lightly. Then toss with the garlic and the shallots or scallions. Give several tosses to cook the trimmings; finally add and toss with the parsley. The scallops should just feel lightly springy to the touch, and the whole operation should take no more than 3 minutes. (If you are doing 2 batches, turn the sauté into a side dish and keep warm in a 150°F oven while doing the second group.)

Serving. Serve at once, either in individual shells or on hot plates.

For New England Bay Scallops Follow the preceding recipe, but leave the scallops whole.

For Calico Scallops Leave calicos whole and neither season nor flour them. Sauté a cupful at a time in a dry no-stick pan until the juices exude, and set aside. Wipe out the pan, then heat the butter or oil in it, add the garlic and shallots, sauté a moment, then add all the scallops, toss with salt and pepper, and then with the parsley. Sauté a moment more, and serve them.

Scallops Provençale being readied for the broiler

VARIATION

Gratiné of Sautéed Scallops Provençale

The scallops are sautéed with herbs and diced tomatoes, then turned into serving shells and gratinéed with cheese just before serving. These are attractive as a first course or luncheon dish.

For 8 servings, as a first course

**Ingredients for the preceding sautéed
  sea scallops, but cut them into
  slices ¼ inch thick**
2½ cups ripe red tomatoes, peeled,
  seeded, juiced, and diced (page
  357); and/or canned Italian plum
  tomatoes, drained, seeded, and
  diced
⅔ cup dry white French vermouth
¼ cup each grated Parmesan or
  Swiss cheese and fresh white
  bread crumbs mixed together
2 additional Tbs butter or olive oil

Gratiné of Sautéed Scallops Provençale
(*continued*)

SPECIAL EQUIPMENT SUGGESTED:
Equipment for the master recipe plus 8 lightly oiled serving shells (or an oiled baking dish)

Sautéing. Proceed with the master recipe, and just as the scallops begin to brown very lightly, after about 1 minute, toss with the garlic and shallots, then add the tomatoes and vermouth. Boil over high heat for a moment, tossing and folding until the juices have thickened enough to enrobe the scallops; fold in the parsley. Taste and correct seasoning.

Final assembly. Turn the scallops into the shells (or baking dish). Sprinkle with cheese and bread crumbs and drizzle a little butter or oil over the top.

*Ahead-of-time note: May be completed in advance to this point. Cover and refrigerate.

Gratinéing. Just before serving, heat slowly under a hot broiler for a minute or two, only until bubbling and lightly browned.

For New England Bay Scallops Proceed as for the recipe above, but leave the scallops whole.

For Calico Scallops Leave calicos whole and neither season nor flour them. Sauté 1 minute, a cupful at a time, in a dry no-stick pan and set aside. Heat the butter or oil in the pan, add and sauté the garlic and shallot briefly, stir in the flour, and cook slowly for 2 minutes without browning. Remove from heat and let cool several minutes before blending in the wine by dribbles. Fold in the

tomatoes and a sprinkling of salt and pepper. Simmer over moderate heat, stirring, for 2 to 3 minutes. Taste, and correct seasoning. Fold in the scallops.

Turn into buttered or oiled shells or a baking dish, spread with cheese and bread crumbs, and gratiné under the broiler as in the preceding recipe.

POACHED SCALLOPS

When you want to serve scallops in a sauce, poaching is often the best way to go. They cook in a minute or so, and the poaching liquid makes a perfectly flavored sauce base.

◀ MASTER RECIPE

Scallops Poached in White Wine

Here is the master method, with a number of sauce and serving suggestions. Scallops cook so quickly you must watch them closely—they should be tender and juicy; overcooking toughens them.

For 8 to 10 as a first course; 6 as a main course

1½ **Tbs minced shallots or scallions**
⅔ **cup dry white French vermouth**
½ **cup water, plus more if needed**
1 **smallish imported bay leaf**
½ **tsp salt**
3 **cups (1½ pounds) scallops, prepared for cooking as previously described; left whole if small, quartered or sliced if large**

SPECIAL EQUIPMENT SUGGESTED:
A 2-quart stainless saucepan with cover

The poaching base. Simmer the shallots or scallions slowly in the covered pan with the vermouth, water, bay leaf, and salt for 3 minutes. Add the scallops and a little water, if needed: the liquid should almost but not quite cover the scallops. Bring just to the simmer, and time as follows.

Timing.

For Whole Sea Scallops: Cover the pan and simmer slowly 1½ to 2 minutes, just until the scallops are lightly springy rather than squashy to the touch.

For Quartered Sea Scallops and New England Bay Scallops: Simmer just a few seconds, until lightly springy.

For Calicos: Bring just to the simmer.

Finishing. Let the scallops cool in the liquid 10 minutes or more, to pick up its flavor.

Serving suggestions. Sauce and serving suggestions are essentially the same as for fillets of sole poached in white wine, starting on page 88. Here are some examples.

VARIATION

Au Naturel
Sauced with the pan juices

When you omit the optional butter enrichment here, you have the ideal dieter's scallop, and non-dieters will never know.

For 6 people as a main course

**Ingredients for the preceding
    scallops in white wine
Minced fresh herbs, such as parsley
    and/or basil
Salt, freshly ground pepper, and
    drops of freshly squeezed lemon
    juice**

After poaching the scallops as described, remove them, using a slotted spoon, to a bowl. Boil down the poaching liquid over high heat until almost syrupy. Blend in the fresh herbs, correct seasoning, and fold in the poached scallops.

With Tomato

After boiling down the poaching liquid, stir in 1½ cups of peeled, seeded, and juiced tomatoes. Cover and simmer 2 to 3 minutes, for the tomatoes to render their juices, then uncover and boil several minutes to evaporate liquid and thicken the sauce. Season, and fold in the scallops.

To serve hot. Fold over moderate heat for a minute or so to warm the scallops but not to recook them. Serve over boiled rice, or with fresh peas and French bread.

To serve cold. This is particularly recommended if you have used the tomatoes in the preceding variation. After folding in the herbs, seasonings, and scallops, fold in a little olive oil, if you wish. Let cool. Serve on a bed of cold cooked pasta (page 367). Or arrange them on a bed of seasoned salad greens, and garnish, if you wish, with fresh green beans in vinaigrette, cucumbers, and black olives.

Scallops in White Butter Sauce and Herbs

Use exactly the same system for scallops as for the sole on page 90, where the poaching liquid is boiled down to a simmering syrup while a whole stick of butter is beaten in piece by piece—a most divine sauce for non-dieters.

Scallops in Cream

Another non-dieters' delight: after boiling down the poaching liquid, boil it again with 1 cup or more of heavy cream until lusciously thickened; season, and fold in the scallops.

Scallops and Mushrooms in Cream

If you wish to add mushrooms, simmer them in the poaching liquid after removing the poached scallops. Then boil down this now even more delicious liquid, and add the cream as described.

Scallops Gratinéed in Their Shells
"Coquilles St. Jacques"

This recipe and its following variation are useful for ahead-of-time preparation. The scallops are poached as usual, and then enrobed in a deliciously winey cream sauce made from their cooking liquid. It is a classic French treatment, and makes a most attractive first course or luncheon dish.

For 8 people as a first course or luncheon dish

**The master recipe for scallops
    poached in wine (page 116)
3 Tbs butter
3 Tbs flour
¾ cup or so heavy cream
Salt, freshly ground white pepper,
    and drops of freshly squeezed
    lemon juice
Milk, as needed
¼ cup grated Swiss cheese**

SPECIAL EQUIPMENT SUGGESTED: *8 buttered scallop shells or individual ovenproof serving shells or dishes*

The scallops. After poaching the scallops in white wine, remove them to a bowl. Boil down the poaching liquid to 1 cup.

Velouté sauce. Cook the butter and flour together 2 minutes without coloring; off heat beat in the hot poaching liquid and cream. Season and simmer 3 minutes, adding droplets of milk if the sauce is too thick. (Full details are on page 272.)

Assembling. Fold enough of the sauce into the scallops to enrobe them, di-

Scallops Gratinéed in Their Shells (*continued*)

vide them among the shells and top
each with ½ tablespoon of grated
cheese. Arrange the shells on a baking sheet (the sheet lined with
crumpled foil if they are unsteady).

*Ahead-of-time note: May be prepared
to this point in advance; cover and
refrigerate.

Serving. Shortly before serving, set
about 4 inches from a hot broiler element just until bubbling hot and the
cheese topping has browned nicely.

Accompaniments to Coquilles St. Jacques

As a first course, just French bread.
As a luncheon dish, a tossed salad or
fresh green vegetable could follow. A
chardonnay or white Burgundy
would be my wine of choice here.

Gratiné of Scallops Florentine

Fold a spoonful or so of the sauce
into 2 cups of beautifully flavored
cooked fresh spinach, and layer that
into a baking dish or individual
shells. Spread sauced scallops on top,
sprinkle on the cheese, and brown
under the broiler. This follows the
general directions for the sole Flor-
entine on page 93.

OYSTERS AND MUSSELS

Oysters and mussels make
great first courses, and both,
especially oysters, are becoming increasingly available, not only at specialty fish purveyors, but in our
everyday supermarkets.

---

*Buying and storing oysters in
the shell.* Make sure that the
oysters come from areas approved by
the health services. Oysters should be
displayed on ice, and if your market
is serious they will be placed so that
the curved sides of their shells are
down—meaning the oysters are
resting in their juices. If they are
packaged in plastic, you will have to
rely on your market, but it's always
best if you can choose them yourself.
Pick only those that feel heavy in
their shells, that are tightly closed,
and, for easy opening, those with a
gap in the hinge. When you bring
them home, scrub each under
running cold water with a vegetable
brush, drain, and pile curved side
down in a bowl, its bottom lined with
crumpled aluminum foil. Cover with
2 thicknesses of dampened paper
towels, and a loose topping of
aluminum foil. Refrigerate them,
and they will keep perfectly for a
week or more.

(Please see Special Note on fish and
shellfish safety, page 80.)

SPECIAL NOTE

*To open an oyster the
easiest way*

It is wise, when opening oysters, to
smell each one as you do so; it should
have a fresh, sweet, and appetizing
odor. When the oysters have a slight
gap at the closed hinge, you can make
quick work of them either with a
beer-can opener or a stout oyster
knife.

Place an oyster, curved side down, on
your work surface; the small or hinge
end of the oyster should be facing
you.

The beer-can opener. This is the easiest
opener. Turn it upside down, insert
the pointed end into the gap at the
hinge, press down on the handle
while holding the oyster firmly with
your other hand—the hinge pops
open.

Or the oyster knife. Work the point of
an oyster knife into the hinge with an
up-and-down pushing motion until
the hinge pops.

Removing the top shell. With the
hinge open and still facing you, insert a small knife inside the top shell
at the east-northeast corner section
where the muscle is attached; scrape
through the muscle to release it. Lift
up the front of the top shell and bend
the shell toward the hinge to snap it
free, and that's all there is to it.

Inserting beer-can opener into hinge of oyster

Bearding mussels with a knife

Shucked oysters bought in bulk.
I have tried several sources of
shucked oysters and I find they have a
quite strong off taste—almost of
iodine, probably from preserving
chemicals. I don't like them and do
not use them.

Preparing mussels for cooking.
Be sure your mussels come from
approved sources. Mussels are far
more perishable than the hardy
oyster, and cultivated mussels are
cleaner and easier to handle than wild
ones. Be sure the shells are tightly
closed, keep them well iced, and plan
to use them as soon as possible.
Before cooking, carefully look over

each mussel. It should have a sweet
fresh smell; scrape off the beards (the
hairy tuft protruding from one side
of the shells). Cultivated mussels
rarely have sand in the shells and now
usually come ready to cook.

Clams. Directions for choosing,
storing, scrubbing, and de-salting
clams are on page 22.

OYSTERS AND MUSSELS SERVED IN THEIR SHELLS

There's no problem what to serve for
a first course when you have oysters
and mussels at hand. They are the solution, and, seeing the price of oysters, even just two or three per
person will do.

SPECIAL NOTE

Cleaning wild mussels. If you
have wild mussels, scrub them under
cold water with a stiff brush and
scrape with a knife to remove
seaweed and so forth. Then, to rid
them of sand, drop the mussels into a
basin of lightly salted cold water (⅓
cup salt per 4 quarts water, says my
seafood manual, mentioned on page
114); knock them together with your
hands, and let them sit 10 minutes.
Remove them with your hands to a
colander and if more than a few
grains of sand remain in the basin,
repeat. Wild mussels often need
several soakings.

Preparing the oysters

◆◀ MASTER RECIPE

Oysters Broiled in Garlic Butter

A very simple method, and one of
the best—although I've given versions before, here's another in case
you missed them.

*For 18 oysters, serving 6 as a first
course*

18 oysters
6 Tbs butter in a small frying pan
1½ Tbs minced shallots or scallions
1 large clove of garlic, puréed
2 Tbs freshly squeezed lemon juice
Salt and freshly ground pepper
⅔ cup fine crumbs from fresh homemade type white bread
3 Tbs minced fresh parsley

SPECIAL EQUIPMENT SUGGESTED:
A broiling pan lined with crumpled foil

Assembling. Open the oysters. Drain
out the juices and save for fish stock.
Loosen the meat from the lower
(curved) shell and leave it in the
shell. Melt the butter, stir in the
shallots or scallions and garlic; sauté
1 minute, until translucent. Stir in

(continued)

the lemon juice, a big pinch of salt, and several grinds of pepper. Blend the bread crumbs with the parsley and spread over the oysters. Drizzle over each a tablespoon of the butter mixture.

Ahead-of-time note: May be prepared several hours in advance. Cover and refrigerate.

Broiling. Just before serving, set about 3 inches from a hot broiler element and, watching closely, let the crumbs brown lightly while the oysters warm through. Serve at once.

VARIATION

Mussels or Clams Broiled in Garlic Butter

Follow exactly the same system for mussels or clams, opening them raw, placing them on a broiling pan lined with crumpled foil, and spreading on the topping. Half a dozen large mussels or medium clams are sufficient per person.

◀ MASTER RECIPE

Mussels Steamed in White Wine
Moules marinière

Here is the classic way to serve fresh mussels. Steam them in minced onions, parsley, and white wine just until they open, and serve them mounded in great bowls. Use a pair of the hinged shells to pluck out the mussel meat, and when all are eaten, drink the fragrant liquor.

NUTRITIONAL NOTE: *For a fat-free marinière, simmer the onions in the wine rather than sautéing them in butter as described in the following recipe.*

For 6 servings

4 Tbs butter
1 cup minced onions
1 large clove of garlic, puréed, optional
A large handful of chopped fresh parsley
4 quarts fine fresh mussels, prepared for cooking as previously described
2 cups dry white French vermouth or dry white wine

SPECIAL EQUIPMENT SUGGESTED: *A 6- to 8-quart kettle with tight-fitting cover; big soup bowls*

Steaming the mussels. Melt the butter in the kettle, stir in the onions and optional garlic, and cook slowly for several minutes, until limp. Then add the parsley and the mussels, cover the kettle, and shake once to mix all the ingredients. Pour in the vermouth or wine and shake once again. Turn heat to high, cover tightly, and let steam for 3 to 4 minutes (without shaking again in case of sand), just until the mussels have opened.

Serving. Dip the mussels out, shells and all, into the soup bowls. Tip the kettle and ladle the fragrant cooking liquor into each serving, being careful not to include any sand at the bottom of the kettle.

Suggested accompaniments. Chilled dry white wine like an Alsatian riesling, and French bread.

Mussels steamed open

VARIATIONS

"Soup! Soup! Beautiful Soup!"

Start out with mussels steamed in wine, add a handful of aromatic vegetables simmered in butter, the winey mussel juices, and you do indeed create a beautiful soup. Not for mussels only, since the idea goes for other things, too, like oysters and chicken breasts. Here are two versions, one a little more elaborate and classical than the other.

MANUFACTURING NOTE: *These are cream soups, meaning you have a liaison of some sort that thickens the liquid and retains a certain amount of the ingredients in suspension. To make a liaison you need a thickening element. The richest and most beautiful, which I shall only mention here, is simply a goodly number of egg yolks and cream; it's the yolks that do the thickening. The more traditional approach is a velouté, meaning a butter and flour roux, and a modest egg-yolk and cream enrichment; this makes a splendid soup when lightly and carefully done. Lastly, rather than the butter and flour roux, there is a liaison of starch, like the cornstarch version in this group, or the purée of cooked rice on page 5; here you have no butter. In both cases the egg-yolk and cream enrichment is yours to contract, expand, or eliminate.*

Mussel Soup
With a julienne of vegetables

The aromatic base here is so good it makes a delicious soup all by itself. Although concocted in a different form, this is essentially the same sophisticated flavoring system as for the Waterzooi of chicken on page 147, and Waterzooi started out as a Belgian fish dish in the first place. Thus we gradually come full circle, starting with mussels.

For 2½ quarts, serving 6 to 8

4 quarts mussels steamed in wine, the preceding recipe

The vegetables
2 Tbs unsalted butter
The following vegetables cut into fine julienne (matchstick size): 3 or 4 medium carrots (2 cups); 2 medium onions, white of leek, tender celery stalks, and cucumbers (1 cup of each)
4 cups liquid: mussel steaming juices and/or fish stock or light chicken broth
1 large imported bay leaf

The roux base
2½ Tbs unsalted butter
2 tsp curry powder, optional
3 Tbs flour
2 cups hot milk

Salt and pepper

SPECIAL EQUIPMENT SUGGESTED: *A heavy-bottomed 3-quart stainless saucepan with cover for the vegetables and soup; a 6-cup stainless pan for the roux base*

The mussels. After steaming the mussels as described in the master recipe, discard the shells and reserve the meat in a bowl. Carefully pour the cooking liquid into a stainless saucepan, adding also as much of the parsley and onion as you safely can without including any sand that may be at the bottom of the kettle.

All-purpose soup base.

The vegetables. Melt the butter in the 3-quart saucepan, turn in all the vegetables except for the cucumbers, and toss several times to coat them with the butter; then pour in the 4 cups of liquid, add the bay leaf, and bring to the simmer. Cover partially and simmer 15 minutes, or until the vegetables are tender. Add the cucumbers the last 2 to 3 minutes of cooking.

The velouté sauce. Cook the butter, optional curry powder, and flour slowly together for 2 minutes; off heat beat in the hot milk; season and simmer 3 minutes—full details on page 272.

Finishing the soup. Pour the velouté into the vegetables and their liquid. Simmer 2 to 3 minutes, taste, and correct seasoning. Fold in the steamed mussels.

*Ahead-of-time note: May be completed in advance to this point. Float a film of milk on the surface to prevent a skin from forming. When cool, cover and refrigerate.

Serving.

To serve as is. Fold the soup over moderate heat and bring to just below the simmer; correct seasoning again. Top each serving with a dollop of sour cream and a good pinch of chopped fresh parsley or chervil, and place 2 or 3 mussels in their shells in each bowl.

A cream and egg-yolk enrichment. Blend 3 egg yolks in a bowl with ½

Mussel Soup (*continued*)

to ⅔ cup of sour cream or heavy cream; by driblets, whisk in 2 cups of the hot soup liquid. Gradually blend back into the soup. Add 3 to 4 tablespoons of minced fresh parsley or chervil and fold the soup over moderate heat as it rethickens lightly and comes to just below the simmer. Carefully correct seasoning again, and serve, adding mussels in their shells to each, if you wish.

VARIATION

Oyster Bisque

Using the same system of white wine, a broth of some sort, and an aromatic vegetable base, you are set for all kinds of delicious soups, such as this oyster bisque.

For 2½ quarts, serving 8

32 or more large fresh oysters
Ingredients for the base in the preceding mussel soup including the strained oyster juices and 1 cup or so of white wine or vermouth in the 4 cups of liquid called for

Drain the oysters and place in a stainless frying pan with 1 cup of the liquid; bring to the simmer for a minute or two, just until the oysters plump and swell. Set aside, and fold into the finished soup base.

Variations with Fish or Chicken. Substitute thin strips of fish, such as sole or flounder, or of chicken breast for the mussels or oysters in the preceding recipes, simmering them for just a moment in the soup base.

Monterey Bay Sole Food Stew

This is the same idea as the preceding recipes, but a simpler version I once did for a stand-up demonstration in Monterey. You could use this system, too, for oysters or mussels.

For 6 servings

2 each: medium carrots, whites of leeks, tender celery stalks, and onions, all thinly sliced
2 to 3 Tbs butter
Seasonings: salt, freshly ground white pepper, and tarragon
2½ cups dry white wine (such as a young Monterey chardonnay)
2½ cups fish stock or light chicken broth
1 Tbs cornstarch blended with 2 Tbs white wine
1½ cups diced tomato pulp, page 357
1½ pounds (3 cups) Monterey or other sole fillets, cut into thin slanting slices, like smoked salmon
2 egg yolks blended with 1 cup sour cream
Chopped fresh parsley or chervil

The vegetable base. Sauté the sliced vegetables slowly in the butter in a covered saucepan about 10 minutes, until tender. Add the seasonings to taste, wine, and stock or broth. Simmer 5 minutes, and remove from heat.

Finishing the soup. Blend dribbles of the soup liquid into the cornstarch and wine, and after about a cup has gone in, blend the mixture back into the rest of the hot soup. Simmer 2 minutes, then fold in the diced tomatoes and the fish. Bring just to the

Oyster Bisque

simmer. Carefully taste and correct seasoning. Blend a cup of hot soup by dribbles into the egg yolks and cream; fold this into the soup, and remove from heat.

Ahead-of-time note: May be prepared in advance to this point; refrigerate, and cover when chilled.

Serving. At serving time, reheat to below the simmer, folding gently with several tablespoons of chopped parsley or chervil. Taste again and correct seasoning. Turn into a warm tureen or warm soup bowls.

Chicken Breast Bisque

For a superior chicken soup, substitute thin slices of raw chicken breast and chicken broth for the fish and stock in the preceding recipe.

FISH MOUSSES

In the old days a fish mousse took several hours of hand labor, and was strictly in the realm of the professional kitchen and *haute cuisine.* Because of that wonderful machine, the food processor, there is so little fuss to making a mousse that it is now part of plain everyday cooking. But not such plain cooking that you cannot perform remarkably attractive, even lightning-speed acrobatics with it. Mousses are fun to fool around with, and as soon as you have made one or two and see the possibilities, you will be creating your own presentations. First, a short discussion on fish.

MOUSSE FISH

A fish mousse is a purée of high-quality fish into which you beat as much heavy cream as it will take and still hold its shape, either to be poached in butter or in liquid, or to be baked in a mold. Its texture is infinitely finer than fish cake or dumpling because of the cream, and the more cream it takes unto itself, the lighter and more delicious it will be. However, this is obviously not a dish for dieters, who had best stick to the simple fish cake. Flimsy fish like flounder and California halibut are hopeless mousse candidates, while fish with a certain gelatinous quality, like Eastern halibut, gray sole, petrale sole, salmon, and trout, are just what you want. Shrimp and scallops are a special case. Because of their firm and gelatinous texture a mousse of scallops alone, for instance, can be rubbery unless combined with a lighter fish like flounder, or with

bread crumbs. But shrimp or scallops are useful additions to bolster a mixture that otherwise lacks texture.

In other words, there is really no rule of thumb, but you can't lose out if you are on an experimental spree because if the mousse is too soft to form by hand, try dropping it from a spoon into simmering water. If it's too loose for that, bake it in a mold. If all else fails, turn it into a delectable creamy fish soup simply by simmering it with milk or fish stock.

Some desirable choices of fish for mousses: Eastern halibut, freshwater trout, gray sole, imported Dover sole, John Dory (St. Peter fish), Pacific petrale sole, salmon, scallops, shrimp, imported turbot, whiting (silver hake).

Manufacturing Notes:

Egg vs. panade vs. bread crumbs. The classic fish mousse includes a panade, a simple pâte-à-choux pastry cream, to act as a binder and liaison. Fresh bread crumbs are an easy alternative, and useful for quick action. Or, if you have very gelatinous fish or shellfish, you can use only egg whites and cream. The three methods are interchangeable.

Keep everything chilled. A chilled fish will absorb more cream, and will hold better when formed for poaching.

1. Scallops going into processor with fish

2. Process the fish until perfectly smooth.

If to be dropped from a spoon, it can be a little looser; you might cook a sample as a test.

If to be baked in a mold. It can be looser still but should hold its shape softly. Process in bread crumbs to give it body, or cream to loosen it.

Final seasoning. Process in a teaspoon or so of brandy, if you wish. Taste very carefully, and correct seasoning.

**Ahead-of-time note:* May be done several hours in advance; pack into a covered container and refrigerate in a bowl of ice. You may freeze the mousse.

◣◀ MASTER RECIPE

All-Purpose Fish Mousse

For about 4 cups

1 pound (2 cups) best-quality chilled skinless and boneless fish from the preceding list (if your fish is light in texture like flounder, include 4 ounces or ½ cup of raw shrimp or scallops)
1 "large" egg, chilled
½ to 1 cup (or more) heavy cream, chilled
Seasonings: 1 tsp salt, freshly ground white pepper, and a small pinch of nutmeg
If needed: up to 1 cup lightly pressed down crumbs from fresh homemade-type crustless white bread with body
1 tsp brandy, optional

SPECIAL EQUIPMENT SUGGESTED: *A food processor.*
You may use the plastic blade here if you have tender fish; some cooks feel it makes a more tender mousse.

The mousse. Cut the fish into 1-inch pieces. (If you are using shrimp chop them roughly; wash scallops, remove the small tough muscle attached to one side, and chop roughly if they are the large sea scallops.) Drop the fish, see illustration, step 1, into the bowl of the food processor along with the egg, ½ cup of the cream, and the seasonings to taste. Process, using half a dozen 1-second spurts; process several seconds continuously, then start checking. The mousse should be perfectly smooth, step 2; scrape down the bowl and process a few seconds more if necessary.

Consistency test.

If to be molded by hand for sautéing or poaching. It should hold a definite shape in a spoon, its peaks and valleys quite well defined. If it seems loose and lacking in body, process in bread crumbs by ¼ cupfuls (or you could add ¼ cup or more raw shrimp or scallops). On the other hand, if too stiff, process in more cream by small dollops.

VARIATION

Choux Pastry Mousse

See the Timbales of Sole, page 128, for an example.

1. Flouring the galettes

2. Sautéing the other side

Fish Galettes—Fish Burgers—Fish Cakes

These are quick to make, almost as quick as a hamburger. They're elegant morsels to serve just as they are with a parsley butter sauce and fresh spinach or green peas. Or be more elaborate with something like the lobster sauce à l'américaine on page 106.

For 6 to 8 galettes

The master recipe for All-Purpose Fish Mousse, chilled—make it firm enough to hold its shape
3 to 4 Tbs unsalted butter
1 cup flour on a sheet of wax paper

SPECIAL EQUIPMENT SUGGESTED:
A bowl of cold water beside you; 1 or 2 no-stick frying pans

Forming and sautéing. Divide the mousse into the number of galettes you are making. Just before sautéing, film the pan or pans with a 1/16-inch layer of butter and set over low heat. Fish cakes are far less solid than hamburgers to form. The following system works for me: dip your hands in the cold water, form a cake, turn lightly in the flour, see illustration,

step 1, and set it in the warm frying pan. Continue rapidly with the rest. (Note: If too soft to form into cakes, you may drop portions into the hot butter from a spoon.) Sauté slowly 2 to 3 minutes (while you wash your hands!), turn, and sauté on the other side, step 2.

When are they done? When just springy rather than squashy to the touch, and they should barely color.

Serving and sauce suggestions: Adapt any of the sauces listed for poached fish fillets starting on page 88, such as a white butter sauce with herbs and/or tomato, cream sauce, curry with mushrooms, lobster sauce, and there's always hollandaise. One of the easiest and most attractive suggestions is the following black butter sauce.

VARIATION

Galettes with Black Butter Sauce

For about 3/4 cup, serving 6 to 8

3 Tbs minced fresh parsley
6 ounces (1½ sticks) unsalted butter, cut into slices
3 Tbs capers

After removing the galettes to hot plates or a platter, sprinkle the parsley over them. Toss the sliced butter into the hot pan and increase heat to high. Swirling the pan by its handle, swish the butter around as the bubbles subside, and in a few seconds the butter will begin to turn a walnut brown (not black!). Pour the hot butter over the galettes—the parsley will sizzle. Drop the capers into the pan, heat them briefly until they bubble, and spread them over the galettes. Serve at once.

QUENELLES
(Delicate fish dumplings)

For quenelles, you either roll portions of the mousse lightly in flour to form sausage shapes and drop them into simmering salted water, or you nudge them into the water from a spoon. Here is the latter system, which is easy and pleasantly freeform. While sausage-shaped quenelles need a reasonably firm mousse, those dropped from a spoon can be softer. In any case, make a small test run to be sure they will hold their shape.

Shrimp Quenelles in a Tomato Sauce

For 6 to 8 quenelles

Salt
The master recipe for all-purpose
fish mousse, made with 1½ cups
raw shrimp meat and ¾ cup sole
or flounder—well chilled
3 Tbs butter
⅓ cup dry white French vermouth
1 cup fresh tomato sauce (page 358)

SPECIAL EQUIPMENT SUGGESTED:
A saucepan or electric skillet 10 to 12
inches in diameter and just over 2
inches deep; 2 soup spoons and a rubber
spatula in a pitcher of cold water; a
rack covered with paper towels; a 12-
inch no-stick frying pan with cover

Poaching the quenelles. Pour 2 inches
of water into the saucepan and add
1½ teaspoons of salt per quart of
water. Bring to the simmer. Dip a
wet soup spoon into the chilled
mousse and bring up a rounded gob;
shape the top neatly by inverting the
bowl of the second wet spoon over it,
see illustration, step 1. Nudge it into
the water with the rubber spatula,
step 2. Rapidly continue with the rest
of the mousse. Maintain the water at
just below the simmer for 6 to 8
minutes—if the water simmers or
boils, the quenelles may disintegrate.

When are they done? The quenelles
are done when they roll over easily.
Remove them with a slotted spoon to
the rack.

*Ahead-of-time note: May be poached
in advance; cover and refrigerate.
May be frozen.

2. Poaching the quenelles

1. Forming quenelles with two wet spoons

3. Poached quenelles in tomato sauce

Sauce and serving. Melt the butter in
the frying pan, arrange in it the quenelles and baste with the butter. Mix
the vermouth with the tomato sauce
and pour over and around the quenelles, step 3. Cover and simmer
slowly for several minutes, basting
once or twice with the sauce, until
well heated through. Serve on hot
plates or a hot platter.

Suggested accompaniments for galettes and quenelles

A fresh green vegetable such as green
peas, broccoli florets, beans, or
asparagus tips. French bread, and a
dry white wine with body, such as a
chardonnay, pinot blanc, or white
Burgundy.

Crown Mousse of Trout
to be served hot or cold

Here is an elaborate presentation for
that special occasion such as a luncheon or summer dinner—a handsome treat whatever the weather,
since it can be served either hot or
cold.

MANUFACTURING NOTE: *It's useful to*
know that trout is one of the best choices
for a mousse, since trout are almost al-
ways to be had throughout the country
while other desirable fish are not. As an
added attraction here, the mousse is
crowned with salmon fillets. Because
this creation is for a party, the propor-
tions are for 12 rather than 6, but the
mousse-making procedure is the same.

For 6-cup ring mold, serving 12

2½ cups skinless and boneless trout
fillets (4 fish, 1 pound each)
½ cup (4 ounces) scallops
2 cups lightly pressed down crumbs
from crustless fresh white home-
made type bread
2 cups combined sour cream and
heavy cream, plus more if needed
¼ cup freshly squeezed lemon juice
Seasonings: salt, freshly ground
white pepper, and nutmeg to taste
½ pound salmon fillet (all brown
flesh removed)

Pounding salmon fillets

Filling the mold

Cover going over buttered wax paper

SPECIAL EQUIPMENT SUGGESTED:
A heavily buttered 6-cup ring mold and a roasting pan that will hold it in the oven; an appropriate serving platter

The mousse mixture. Chop the trout fillets and scallops roughly. Place in the food processor with all of the mousse ingredients except the salmon. Process 15 seconds, or until the purée holds its shape softly; add more cream by spoonfuls if it seems too stiff; taste carefully and correct seasoning.

The salmon, which is to line the mold. Cut the salmon fillet into crosswise slices about ⅓ inch thick and 1 inch wide. Pound one at a time between sheets of wax paper to expand and widen them. If you are short of salmon don't worry; just space them out decoratively in the next step.

Lining and filling the mold. Lightly salt and pepper the salmon and press the pieces into the sides and bottom of the buttered ring mold. Scoop the mousse into the mold without disturbing the salmon. Bang the mold firmly but gently on your work surface to collapse any air bubbles.

**Ahead-of-time note:* May be prepared a few hours ahead to this point. Cover with plastic wrap, set in a pan of ice, and refrigerate.

Baking—about 1 hour at 350°F. Cover the mold with buttered wax paper and a lid, as shown. Set it in the roasting pan in the lower third level of the oven, and pour simmering water around the mold to come halfway up its outside. Bake for about 1 hour (add more water, if needed).

When is it done? When slightly risen, the top feels lightly springy, and it shows a very faint line of shrinkage from the sides of the mold. Let it settle for 10 minutes before unmolding onto a hot buttered platter.

Sautéed Chicken (*continued*)

Serving Suggestions for Ring Molds

To serve hot. Fill the center of the ring with vegetables, such as the peas and onions in the photograph and the following recipe. Or fill it with the Broccoli-Sauced Broccoli on page 270. A light hollandaise sauce (page 87) or the sour-cream sauce following here could both enrobe the mousse and be passed separately.

To serve cold. You fill the ring with watercress, or with cress and the sliced cucumbers in sour cream on page 356, or with a fish or a lobster salad (pages 104 and 375).

VARIATIONS

Sour Cream Sauce for Hot or Cold Mousse

For about 2 cups

1¾ cups sour cream
Seasonings: freshly squeezed lemon juice, prepared horseradish, Dijon-type mustard, salt, freshly ground white pepper
Minced fresh dill or parsley

Mix into the cream all the ingredients listed and season carefully to taste; refrigerate in a covered bowl until serving.

Fresh Green Pea and Onion Filling for the Mousse

Cook 3 cups of fresh green peas and 1½ cups of small white onions and let cool. Shortly before serving, toss them with a dressing, such as the oil and lemon recipe on page 350, and turn them into the center of the ring.

SPECIAL NOTE

To Fillet a Trout

First free the fillets from each side of the backbone, as indicated at left—don't worry about the tiny (calcium rich!) hairlike bones in the meat itself, which will be ground up with the flesh in the processor. Remove the skin by pulling the small end of the fish skin in one hand while sliding your knife against it, almost parallel to your work surface, as shown at right.

Timbales of Sole with Mussels

Individual mousselines of sole filled with mussels

A fish mousse can line a mold, and the mold can then be filled with a deliciously sauced something like lobster or scallops, or, as in this case, mussels in a winey cream. Formed in individual molds, these make a dressy first course or luncheon dish.

MANUFACTURING NOTE: *Here, for a change, is the classic mousse with panade; however, you may substitute the all-purpose bread-crumb formula if you wish.*

For 6 servings

3 pounds fresh mussels steamed in white wine (page 120)
Choux pastry made with ½ cup water, ½ tsp salt, 2 Tbs butter, ½ cup flour, and 2 "large" eggs (page 396)
The master recipe for all-purpose fish mousse, made with 1¼ cups sole and ¼ cup raw scallops or shrimp, and the choux pastry rather than bread crumbs

For the sauce

3 Tbs butter
¼ cup flour
2 cups mussel-cooking liquid, heated
A small pinch of saffron, or ¼ tsp curry powder
½ cup heavy cream

SPECIAL EQUIPMENT SUGGESTED: *A food processor; individual molds of ¾-cup capacity (such as Pyrex custard cups), heavily buttered; a roasting pan to hold the molds in the oven*

Assembling the timbales

Preliminaries. Prepare the mussels and reserve their juices. Prepare the choux pastry, then prepare and chill the mousse.

The velouté sauce. Cook the butter and flour together for 2 minutes without coloring. Off heat, whisk in the mussel-cooking liquid and the saffron or curry powder. Simmer 3 minutes, thinning the sauce with dribbles of cream—it should be fairly thick. Carefully correct seasoning. Let cool, stirring frequently to prevent a skin from forming on the surface.

Assembling the timbales. Spread ½ cup of the mousse evenly around the bottom and sides of each mold. Spoon in 1½ tablespoons of the cold sauce, then 2 tablespoons of mussels, adding another tablespoon or so of sauce to fill the cups to within ¼ inch of the top. Spread a covering of mousse over, see illustration.

*Ahead-of-time note: May be prepared several hours ahead; refrigerate in a pan of ice.

Baking—about 40 minutes at 350°F. Preheat oven to 350°F. Arrange the molds in a roasting pan, pour in simmering water to come halfway up the outsides of the molds, and bake uncovered in the middle level of the preheated oven.

When are they done? When slightly puffed, when the tops are softly springy, and when they show a very faint line of shrinkage from the sides of the molds. Remove and let settle 10 minutes.

Serving. Unmold onto hot plates. Meanwhile turn the remaining mussels into the rest of the sauce, reheat just to the simmer, then spoon the sauce and mussels over and around the mousselines.

Serving Suggestions for the Timbales

These should be served as a separate course, accompanied only with French bread or the puff pastry fleurons on page 395. And here is an opportunity to bring out one of your finest chardonnays, white Burgundies, or Graves.

HOME-CURED FISH

Dilled Salmon: Gravlaks
A fast cure in slices

Fresh raw salmon cured in a macera-
tion of salt, dill, and Cognac—it's
more delicate in taste than smoked
salmon, and it is easy to make yourself. The traditional gravlaks is done
with whole sides of salmon and takes
5 or 6 days, but when you cure it in
slices it is ready within a few hours.
Serve gravlaks with buttered pumpernickel or white sandwich bread as
a fine first course or cocktail appetizer, or present it for lunch or as a
snack, with scrambled eggs.

For a 2½- to 3-pound salmon fillet

**2½- to 3-pound fillet of fresh salmon,
    skin on**
**1¼ Tbs salt and ¾ Tbs sugar mixed
    in a small bowl**
2 tsp fragrant dried dill
2 to 3 Tbs Cognac or good brandy
**Optional final decoration: sprigs of
    fresh dill**

SPECIAL EQUIPMENT SUGGESTED:
*Tweezers or small pliers for removing
bones; a very sharp long slicing knife; 2
pastry sheets to hold the salmon slices*

Preparing the salmon for its cure. Rub
your finger over the fillet, especially
at the heavy portion of the large end,
to locate small bones buried in the
flesh; pull them out with tweezers.
Trim off all jagged or too-thin edges.

Slicing the salmon. Starting at the
large end, and going almost parallel
to the salmon, cut long neat slices less
than ⅛ inch thick, as though slicing
smoked salmon. Arrange them in one
layer on the pastry sheets.

Applying the cure. Sprinkle a good
pinch of the salt-sugar mix over each
of the salmon slices, then a dusting of
dill; finally rub in a few drops of Cognac or brandy. Turn the slices over
(dry your fingers well so the salt
won't stick to them), and repeat on
the other side. Season the flesh side of
the salmon skin in the same fashion.
Rearrange the salmon slices over the
skin, and slip it onto a serving platter. Cover with the optional fresh
dill, then with plastic wrap. Refrigerate for several hours and the fish is
ready to eat, although with another
day of cure it will be even better.

*Ahead-of-time note: Keeps 7 to 10
days in the refrigerator.

Serving suggestion. As a first course,
make a mustard-horseradish butter
(recipe follows). For each serving
spread the butter on large, very thin
slices of rye or pumpernickel bread.
Cover with a large slice of salmon
and decorate with a sprig of fresh
dill—or slice of cucumber. You
could serve a few slices of cucumber
on the side, and iced aquavit or a
crisp, very dry white wine like a
Sancerre or Muscadet.

SPECIAL NOTE

Mustard-Horseradish Butter

For gravlaks, beef tartare, carpaccio,
broiled meats

For ⅔ cup, serving 8 to 12

**4 ounces (1 stick) soft unsalted
    butter**
**1 Tbs or more Dijon-type prepared
    mustard**
1 tsp or more prepared horseradish
**Seasonings: salt, freshly ground
    white pepper, and drops of hot
    pepper sauce**

Cream the butter in a 2-quart bowl
with a wooden spoon; when light and
fluffy, beat in mustard, horseradish,
and seasonings to taste. For fish, the
butter should have a certain authority,
but not be overpowering.

OTHER FISH

Other fish take nicely to the cure,
too. I've used tuna, swordfish, trout,
eastern bluefish, and striped bass with
great success.

SALT COD

New England Codfish Balls with Egg Sauce

Salted cod, mashed potatoes, and egg, formed golf-ball size and dropped into bubbling hot fresh fat until golden brown—it's a crisp and fragrant treat. I grew up on this because my New England mother had freshly made codfish balls almost every other Sunday for breakfast even though we lived in California. She served them with bacon or sausage, and a creamy egg sauce. They're an idea, too, for Sunday night suppers, accompanied perhaps with fresh spinach and buttered beets. But what dinner wine goes with codfish balls? My good books do not say. Why not champagne!

My mother's recipe was passed down in the family, so they say, from our great-great-great Duxbury aunt, Priscilla. It produces remarkably light codfish balls because the long soaking takes out the preserving salt, leaving tender cod that is almost like fresh fish.

MANUFACTURING NOTE: *If you don't want New England codfish balls, a Provençal alternative follows on the next page.*

For 4 cups codfish mixture, making 2 to 3 dozen 1½- to 2-inch balls

1-pound piece of salt cod
1 smallish onion, thinly sliced
4 peppercorns
1 imported bay leaf
2 cups firm plain warm mashed potatoes (dehydrated potatoes are permissible here)

2 "large" eggs beaten with a pinch of salt
Salt and freshly ground white pepper
1½ to 2 quarts very fresh frying oil

SPECIAL EQUIPMENT SUGGESTED:
A 2½-quart saucepan for soaking and poaching; a mixing fork for beating; a deep-fat fryer or 3-quart saucepan; a frying thermometer is useful; a wire skimmer

Soaking the codfish—24 to 48 hours. Sufficient soaking is crucial here for best taste and texture; if the unsoaked fish is very dry and hard, you'll probably need 48 hours at least. Cut or chop it into ½-inch slices; wash the codfish in cold water, and set on a rack in a large bowl of cold water— slicing the fish makes it soak faster, and the rack lifts it out of the salt that sinks to the bottom of the bowl. Refrigerate the bowl, changing the water several times; soak until the fish feels fresh, and tastes hardly of salt.

*Ahead-of-time note: May be soaked in advance; drain and refrigerate for a day—or you may freeze it. As soon as it is de-salted, by the way, the cod is as perishable as fresh fish.

Poaching the codfish. Simmer the sliced onion, peppercorns, and bay leaf for 10 minutes in 2 cups of water, then add 2 more cups of water and the soaked fish, pouring in a little more water if necessary to cover it. Bring to the simmer, cover the pan, and remove from heat; let stand for 10 minutes, or until you are ready to use it. (Simmering or boiling toughens salt cod.)

The codfish mixture. Drain the codfish, and flake it into a mixing bowl. (Reserve the poaching water for the

egg sauce following, or for the chowder on page 20.) Vigorously beat in the warm mashed potatoes, using the mixing fork to shred the fish so that it will make whiskers later. Beat in three quarters of the egg, adding driblets more if the mixture is very stiff—it must be firm enough to form. Beat in salt and pepper to taste. Let stand at room temperature for ½ hour or so; it will firm up as it cools, and make for easier forming.

*Ahead-of-time note: May be made in advance. Cover and refrigerate when cool; beat up briefly before using.

Frying the codfish balls—shortly before serving. Heat the frying oil to 375°F; preheat the oven to 200°F. Line a pizza tray or jelly-roll pan with several thicknesses of paper towels. Now scoop up rounded lumps of the codfish mixture with a soup spoon; dislodge into the hot fat with a rubber spatula, making somewhat roughly shaped balls—the shape and the protruding whisker shreds of codfish make for lightness and a crisp coating. Fry 4 or 5 at a time for 2 to 3 minutes, or until nicely browned. Remove with the skimmer to the paper-lined tray, and keep warm in the oven while continuing with the rest. Plan to serve as soon as possible, with the following egg sauce.

Frying codfish balls

VARIATION

New England Egg Sauce

For about 2½ cups

4 Tbs butter
¼ cup flour
1 cup strained codfish-poaching
water heated with 1 cup milk
2 hard-boiled eggs, chopped
Salt and freshly ground pepper
1 to 2 Tbs additional butter or heavy
cream, optional

The sauce base. Melt the 4 tablespoons of butter in a heavy-bottomed saucepan, blend in the flour, and cook, stirring, over moderately low heat until flour and butter foam and froth together for 2 minutes without turning more than a buttery yellow. Remove from heat, and when bubbling has stopped, pour in three quarters of the hot liquid, whisking vigorously to blend. Return over moderately high heat and simmer, stirring, 2 minutes, thinning out the sauce as necessary with driblets more liquid. Fold in the chopped eggs, and salt and pepper to taste.

*Ahead-of-time note: If not to be used shortly, clean off the sides of the pan with a rubber spatula, and film the surface with a little milk, cream, or butter.

Serving. Just before serving, reheat the sauce, remove from heat, and fold in the optional butter or cream.

Brandade de Morue: A Multiuse Extra
Provençal purée of salt cod with potatoes, garlic, and olive oil

If you decide you have more of the codfish mixture than you need, or you would like to switch gears into a brandade anyway, here is how to make this fragrant mixture. Serve it as an hors d'oeuvre or first course with the hard-toasted rounds of French bread on page 24.

For an indeterminate amount

Ingredients for the preceding codfish
balls minus the eggs
1 or more large cloves of garlic
Salt
Fruity olive oil
A little *crème fraîche* (page 7),
heavy cream, or sour cream
Freshly ground white pepper

Place the warm codfish and mashed potatoes in an electric mixer or food processor. Purée the garlic onto a board; using the flat of a knife, stroke back and forth with a little salt to make a fine paste. Add the garlic to the machine. Start beating or processing, adding dribbles of olive oil to make a thick smooth purée. Incorporate a little of the cream at the end, and season carefully to achieve a smooth, tender, creamy, warm, authoritatively garlicky and subtly fishy ambrosia.

New England Brandade Balls

Add the eggs called for in the codfish-ball recipe, but go easy on the olive oil and cream so as to keep the mixture stiff enough to form. Shape into smaller balls and deep-fry, for splendid cocktail appetizers. Serve them on toothpicks alone or with a tomato-sauce dip.

Poultry

**Chickens, Turkeys,
Poussins, Game Hens, Geese,
Ducks, and Rabbits**

**Sautés, Ragouts, Fricassees,
Stews, Blanquettes,
Roasts, Broilings and Broil-Roastings,
Bonings, Debreastings, and
Re-assemblings**

Since all birds roast in about the same manner, and simmer, sauté, and stew in almost the same way, you'll find them grouped together that way here, for the most part. It makes more sense, it seems to me; then you have the theory and practice for each technique, whatever your bird happens to be. Actually it would make even more sense to group the beasts along with the birds—since beef bourguignon in red wine is a true cousin to coq au vin, that noted chicken stew in red wine, but I have resisted carrying logic that far.

Preparation for Cooking— and a Solemn Warning

Why be careful? Preparation details are taken up in each section, but we must all be very careful indeed with raw poultry, especially chicken, because of harmful bacteria. Bacteria, including salmonella, are killed at a temperature of 140°F—when the chicken is still almost raw. Thus there is no worry about cooked chicken as long as careful precautions are taken during its preparation.

How to proceed. Before you begin, set a cutting board—dishwasher-safe plastic recommended—on an ample spread of newspapers. Get out all the knives, string, seasonings, and other utensils you will be needing, including a dozen or more sheets of paper towels. Then unwrap the chicken at the sink, let hot water run over it inside and out, washing the giblets as well. Dry it in paper towels, set it on the cutting board, and go to work. If you want to touch anything else but your chicken and its utensils, wash your hands first. When you are through, place cutting board and all utensils in the sink, wrap the newspaper in a plastic bag, and dump it. Wash everything to do with the chicken thoroughly, including yourself, in hot soapy water. Don't forget the kitchen towels—put them in the wash while you are cleaning up the chickenry, or you'll forget them.

SAUTÉS, FRICASSEES, AND STEWS

SAUTÉS

Among the quickest, easiest, and most attractive ways to do chicken is to sauté it—meaning to brown it in a frying pan, then to season it, cover the pan, let it cook slowly 20 to 25 minutes, and it's done. It will have produced some nice brown juices in the pan, which, literally in a flash and with a dollop of wine, you turn into a perfect little sauce. That's primal cooking of the very best sort, and you'll be using the same system or one of its variants for veal and pork chops, turkey wings, and March hares, to name a few examples. Before getting into the actual cooking, here are some hints on preparing the chicken.

Buying and preparing the chicken for sautéing

How wonderfully convenient that we can buy what we want in the way of chicken parts—all breasts, all wings, all thighs, or the whole chicken cut into pieces for a little of each. Buying by eye and guessing at appetite capacity seems the best rule for amounts, and I shall arbitrarily count on 2½ to 3 pounds of assorted chicken parts for 4 people. A minute of simple surgery on some of the parts, as in the following illustrations, will make for easier cooking and eating.

1. Separating wing with strip of breast

2. Cutting through ball joint at thigh and drumstick

3. Left: 2 breast halves and 2 wing/breast servings Right: 2 drumsticks and 2 thighs

BONE-IN BREAST WITH WING AT-TACHED *If you buy the whole breast half with wing attached, you can make two servings when you cut off the wing to include the lower third of the breast as illustrated, step 1. Then trim off the bony section of the lower rib cage with scissors. Finally, to make a neat chic serving of the wing, snip off the bony nubbin protruding from the elbow, which shows clearly in the photograph, and fold the wing akimbo by tucking the wing end under the shoulder.*

DRUMSTICKS AND THIGHS *If the legs and thighs are attached together, separate them—wiggle the drumstick to feel where they join at the knee, then cut through the ball joint, step 2. You may wish to whack off the protruding ball joint at the end of the drumstick; this will make it lie flatter for more even browning. Take a good look and feel of the thigh; if there is still some backbone attached to one end, scrape it free—the thigh will then be easier to eat; it also has a protruding bone end which you may wish to chop off. The thigh, by the way, is one of your best buys—fine tender meat and little bone. You will now have 8 pieces, see step 3.*

WASHING *Wash the chicken briefly under the hot water faucet; dry it thoroughly in paper towels. Wash all boards, knives, and your hands in hot soapy water.*

SPECIAL NOTE

Simple Chicken Stock

Chicken stock is always useful to have on hand for use in a quick sauce or for soups. Why buy it when you can make your own for free, and know exactly what's in it? You may wish to freeze raw bones and scraps, then boil them up when you have collected a worthwhile group.

To make the stock, roughly chop all bones and scraps—either cooked or raw or a combination of both—and simmer for an hour in lightly salted water to cover. Strain, degrease, and refrigerate uncovered; cover when chilled. The stock will keep 2 to 3 days under refrigeration, or may be frozen.

 MASTER RECIPE

Sautéed Chicken

All sautés start out this way, and following the master recipe are a number of variations and additions to start you on your own course.

For 4 servings

2½ to 3 pounds frying chicken parts, as previously described
2 to 3 Tbs clarified butter (see Special Note), or olive oil, or 2 Tbs butter and 1 Tbs oil
Salt and freshly ground pepper
A big pinch of tarragon or thyme, optional

Optional deglazing sauce
1 Tbs minced shallots or scallions
½ cup chicken stock (see Special Note)
½ cup dry white wine or dry white French vermouth
1 or 2 Tbs butter for final sauce, optional
2 Tbs minced fresh parsley, chives, or tarragon, optional

SPECIAL EQUIPMENT SUGGESTED: *A heavy-bottomed 12-inch frying pan or casserole about 2 inches deep with a tight-fitting cover; a wooden or plastic spoon and fork for turning the chicken*

Browning the chicken—about 5 minutes. Be sure the chicken is well dried or it will not brown properly. Set the frying pan over moderately high heat; add the oil and/or butter. When it is very hot but not smoking, lay in the chicken pieces skin side down. (Do not crowd the pan: there should be a little air space between each piece for proper browning; do the chicken in 2 batches if necessary.) Turn the chicken every 20 seconds or so, allowing it to color a fairly even

Turning the chicken to brown the other side

Basting

Pouring the sauce over

walnut brown on all sides (see illustration). If you've a mixture of white meat (breasts and wings) and dark (legs and thighs), remove the white meat to a side dish after browning: it takes a little less time to cook than dark meat.

Finishing the cooking. Cover the pan, lower the heat to moderate, and if you've removed the white meat, cook the dark meat slowly (it should sizzle gently) about 6 minutes, turning

Sautéed Chicken (*continued*)

once. Then return the white meat to the pan. Baste the chicken pieces with the accumulated fat and juices in the pan; season the chicken lightly with salt, pepper, and optional herbs. Cover the pan again and cook another 6 minutes. Turn the chicken, baste again, and continue cooking 7 to 8 minutes more, basting once again.

When is it done? The chicken is done when the thickest parts of the drumsticks and thighs are tender when pressed, and when the juices of any piece of chicken pricked with a fork run clear yellow with no trace of pink—it should still be juicy.

Deglazing sauce—3 to 4 minutes. Remove the chicken pieces to hot plates or a platter. Rapidly spoon all but a tablespoon of fat out of the sauté pan. Stir in the tablespoon of minced shallots or scallions and cook for a few seconds over high heat, stirring. Pour in the ½ cups of chicken stock and of wine, and boil, scraping up coagulated juices from the bottom of the pan; continue boiling and swirling the pan for a moment until the liquid has boiled down to the almost syrupy stage. Remove the pan from heat and, if you wish, swirl in a tablespoon or two of butter by spoonfuls—to smooth out and enrich the sauce. Pour the sauce over the chicken, strew on the optional herbs, and serve as soon as possible.

*Ahead-of-time note: Sautéed chicken is at its best when served almost at once. It may be browned in advance, but if you allow it to cool and then reheat, it will always taste like reheated precooked chicken. Sautéed chicken is delicious cold, however.

Dieting notes. Sautéed chicken is not designed for dieters, although thoroughly degreasing the final juices and removing the chicken skin after sautéing will dispense with a number of calories. See the fat-free Chicken Simmered in White Wine (page 144).

VARIATIONS

Sautéed Chicken Pipérade
With sliced green and red bell peppers

The colorful way to dress up the simple sauté is to finish it off with that fragrant shower of sautéed sliced green and red bell peppers with onions, known as the pipérade (page 90). It's quick to make on the spot, or have it on hand in your freezer.

Sauté the chicken as described, and when it has 7 or 8 minutes left to cook in its covered pan, spoon out the fat (but not the juices) and strew on the pipérade. Cover and finish cooking, basting 2 or 3 times with the accumulated juices.

Cold Pipérade of Chicken

Peel the skin off the cooked chicken pieces, and let cool surrounded by the pipérade. To serve, you might toss cooked pasta with seasonings and a little olive oil (page 367), and top with the chicken pipérade. This makes a delightful summer meal, accompanied by a tossed green salad and French bread.

Sautéed Chicken Pipérade

Sautéed Chicken with Braised Onions and Diced Potatoes

Add potatoes and onions to finish cooking with sautéed chicken and, besides giving all three a boost of flavor, your main course is complete except for an accompanying fresh green vegetable or a salad.

When the chicken in the master recipe has 7 or 8 minutes to finish cooking in its covered pan, spoon out cooking fat (but not juices), and add a dozen small white-braised onions and their cooking liquid (page 286) to the pan along with 2 to 3 cups of sautéed diced potatoes (page 327). Baste with the pan juices, cover, and finish cooking the chicken, basting several times with accumulated juices. After removing chicken and accompaniments, rapidly boil down the juices and, if you wish, swish in the enrichment butter as described in the master recipe. Decorate the platter or each serving with a sprinkling of minced fresh parsley and/or chives.

Sautéed Chicken Provençale
With tomatoes, garlic, and herbs

Provençale always means "with tomatoes, garlic, and olive oil," and often olives and other typical ingredients from that sunny clime.

Sauté the chicken in olive oil, as in the master recipe, remove it to a side dish and spoon the fat but not the juices out of the pan. Stir in 2 cups of ripe red tomato pulp (page 357), a sprinkling of mixed Provençal herbs, and a couple of puréed garlic cloves. Boil several minutes to thicken the sauce, correct seasoning, stir in several tablespoons of dry white French vermouth, and return the chicken to the pan. Baste it with the sauce, cover, and simmer several minutes to warm through, basting again 2 or 3 times.

SPECIAL NOTE

Accompaniments to Sautéed Chicken

For the simple sauté, you might serve sautéed potatoes or the potato galettes on page 324, plus a fresh green vegetable or the stuffed tomatoes Provençale on page 306. The sauté with potatoes and onions would need only a green vegetable or salad, while a rice or pasta dish, or just French bread, would go with the Pipérade. A light red wine like a pinot noir, zinfandel, or Beaujolais goes with sautéed chicken, or a rather fruity white such as a sauvignon blanc or chardonnay.

SPECIAL NOTE

Clarified Butter

There is no substitute for the taste of butter in good cooking, especially when you are sautéing delicate foods like chicken breasts, or fillets of sole, or when you are making croutons. Plain butter will burn and speckle rapidly because of the milky residue it contains, but when you clarify the butter you rid it of that residue.

The simple system is to melt the butter and pour the clear yellow liquid off the residue.

The more thorough professional system is to cut the butter into smallish pieces for quick melting. Bring it to the slow boil in a fairly roomy saucepan, listening and watching for several minutes until its crackling and bubbling almost cease, indicating the milky liquid has evaporated and the clarification is complete. (At this point watch that the butter does not burn and darken.) Pour the clear yellow butter through a tea strainer into a preserving jar. It will turn a yellowish white when cold and congealed, and will keep for months in the refrigerator or freezer.

VARIATIONS

Cold Chicken Provençale

Peel the skin off the cooked chicken, and let it cool bathed in its sauce. You might serve it surrounded with fresh green beans, cooked, chilled, and tossed with a vinaigrette dressing, and decorate the chicken platter with black Mediterranean olives.

Chicken Marengo

This is Napoleon's amusing and legendary dish, created especially for him, so they say, after the famous battle. My favorite version is chicken in its Provençal tomato sauce surrounded by deep-fried eggs on croutons, écrevisses or shrimp cooked in the shell, black olives, and decorative sprigs of parsley—it's a quite marvelous combination.

To deep-fry croutons, eggs, and shrimp. While the chicken is cooking, heat 1 cup of olive oil in a small frying pan until very hot but not smoking. Lightly brown four ¾-inch rounds of French bread in the hot oil; set them aside on a paper-towel-lined baking sheet. One at a time, fry 4 very fresh eggs in the oil, and set them aside next to the bread croutons. Then add 4 large shrimp to the hot oil and fry just a minute or two, until they curl up; sprinkle lightly with salt and pepper, and add to the eggs and croutons. Before assembling the dish and serving, set for 3 to 4 minutes in a 250°F oven to warm through.

Assembling the dish. Place the eggs on the croutons and arrange around the chicken, interspersing them with the shrimp and a scattering of black Niçoise olives.

Sautéed Chicken with Mushrooms and Cream

Mushrooms and cream go naturally with chicken, just as they do with fillets of sole. Thus it must be true that mushrooms contain their own MSG,

Chicken Marengo with its French fried eggs

which accentuates the chicken flavor while also imparting their subtle aroma to the cream.

While the chicken is cooking, sauté in butter 2 cups of trimmed and quartered fresh mushrooms (morel mushrooms are heavenly here!); season lightly and set aside. After sautéing the chicken and making the deglazing sauce, add the mushrooms and cream to the pan. Boil down rapidly for a minute or two, until the sauce thickens lightly, then add the chicken and baste with the sauce and mushrooms. Cover and simmer 2 to 3 minutes to warm the chicken through, basting several times. Taste carefully and correct seasoning, adding a little freshly squeezed lemon juice if you feel it needed.

RAGOUTS, FRICASSEES, AND STEWS

Ragouts, fricassees, and stews simmer in liquid, and that means you can complete the cooking in advance without worrying about the telltale taste of precooked and reheated chicken, duck, or whatever your bird happens to be. The section starts with an uncomplicated and hearty ragout of chicken and onions in red wine— I like the rather stylish sound of ragout, and shall use the term instead of fricassee since there is no serious technical distinction between the two in my book. With a few additions, as you'll see in its following variation, the basic ragout turns itself into the famous coq au vin.

🐔 MASTER RECIPE

Ragout of Chicken and Onions in Red Wine

For 4 servings

2½ to 3 pounds frying-chicken parts
  (pages 136–7)
2 Tbs butter
1 Tbs olive oil or good cooking oil
3 cups sliced onion
Salt and freshly ground pepper
1 or 2 large cloves of garlic, puréed
1 imported bay leaf
¼ tsp or so thyme
1 large ripe red unpeeled tomato,
  chopped, or ⅓ cup canned Italian
  plum tomatoes
3 cups young red wine (zinfandel,
  Mâcon, or Chianti type)
1 or more cups chicken stock
Beurre manié for the sauce (1½ Tbs
  each flour and softened butter
  blended to a paste)
Fresh parsley sprigs, or chopped
  parsley

SPECIAL EQUIPMENT SUGGESTED:
*A heavy-bottomed 12-inch frying pan
or casserole 2 inches deep, and a cover
for the pan (or an electric frying pan)*

Browning the chicken—about 5 minutes. Dry the chicken parts thoroughly, and brown in hot butter and oil, as described in detail for sautéed chicken on page 137. Remove to a side dish, leaving the fat in the pan.

The onions. Stir the onions into the pan and sauté over moderate heat until fairly tender, then raise heat and

Ragout of Chicken and Onions in Red Wine

brown lightly. Drain in a sieve set over a bowl to remove excess fat.

Simmering the chicken. Season the chicken lightly with salt and pepper; return it to the pan. Add the browned onions, and the garlic, bay, thyme, and tomato. Pour in the wine and enough stock barely to cover the ingredients. Bring to the simmer; cover, and simmer slowly 20 minutes, or until the chicken is tender when pressed.

Finishing the chicken—the sauce. Remove the chicken to a side dish, and spoon surface fat off the cooking juices. Pour the juices (and onions) into a saucepan and taste very carefully for strength and seasoning. Boil down rapidly if it needs strength, adding more of the seasonings if you think them necessary.

Off heat, whisk the beurre manié to make a lightly thickened sauce (see Special Note, page 143). Bring briefly to the simmer—the sauce should be just thick enough to coat a spoon lightly. Wash out the casserole; return the chicken to it, basting with the sauce and onions.

*Ahead-of-time note: If you are not serving shortly, set aside uncovered. Or, for later serving, refrigerate uncovered. Cover when chilled.

Serving. Before serving, reheat, basting the chicken with the sauce; simmer a few minutes to rewarm nicely but not to overcook. Decorate with parsley and serve. See the Special Note on the next page for suggested accompaniments.

VARIATIONS

Coq au Vin
Chicken in red wine with small braised onions, mushrooms, and lardons of pork

An elaboration on the far more elementary preceding ragout, *coq au vin* involves more hand work since you have lardons of bacon to prepare for the special flavor they give to the sauce. Then there is the traditional garnish of small braised onions and sautéed mushrooms. The combination makes a wonderfully satisfying dish, and a fine one for company.

For 4 servings

½ cup (4 ounces) lardons—1- by ¼-inch strips of blanched slab bacon or salt pork (see Special Note)
Ingredients for the Ragout of Chicken and Onions in Red Wine (preceding page), minus the sliced onions
⅓ cup good brandy, optional
12 to 16 small brown-braised white onions (page 287)
3 cups fresh mushrooms, trimmed, quartered, and sautéed (page 313)

Browning and simmering the chicken. Before browning the chicken, sauté the blanched bacon or salt pork and remove to a side dish, leaving the fat in the pan. Brown the chicken in the pork fat, adding a little olive oil, if needed. Flame the chicken with the brandy, if you wish (see Special Note, page 411)—it does give its own special flavor, besides being fun to do. Then proceed to simmer the chicken in the wine, stock, tomatoes, and seasoning as directed in the master recipe.

Finishing the dish. Strain, degrease, and finish the sauce, also as described. Strew the braised onions and sautéed mushrooms over the chicken, baste with the sauce, and simmer a few minutes, basting, to rewarm the chicken and to blend flavors.

SPECIAL NOTE

Suggested accompaniments for a ragout of chicken

Either arrange the chicken on a hot platter and decorate with small steamed potatoes and parsley, or mound it on a bed of rice or noodles. You could also serve a fresh green vegetable, or follow the chicken with a tossed green salad and cheese. A light young red wine is recommended here, presumably the same one you used in the dish itself.

SPECIAL NOTE

To blanch bacon or salt pork

When you use bacon or salt pork in cooking, you want to remove its salt as well as its smoky flavor, which would permeate the rest of the food. To do so, you blanch it, meaning you drop it into a saucepan of cold water to cover it by 2 to 3 inches, bring it to the boil, and simmer 5 to 8 minutes; then drain, refresh in cold water, and pat dry in paper towels.

Turkey Wing Ragout
With garlic and kidney beans

When you see the need for a hearty budget meal of the finger-food variety, turkey wings are a good buy and make remarkably good eating when served this way.

For 6 servings

Ingredients for the master recipe Ragout of Chicken and Onions in Red Wine, but substitute for the chicken 6 to 9 whole turkey wings (containing both the lower part and the meaty upper wing—1 per person may be enough)
1 whole head of large garlic cloves
2 cups home-cooked or canned red kidney beans and ½ cup of their juices
A handful of fresh parsley, chopped

SPECIAL EQUIPMENT SUGGESTED:
A broiling pan for browning; a large frying pan or casserole that will hold all the wings comfortably in 1 layer for the simmering; a cover for the pan

Browning the turkey wings. Cut off and discard the wing nubbins at the elbows. Wash the wings rapidly under the hot water faucet and dry thoroughly; if they are not too recalcitrant, fold them akimbo by tucking the wing ends in back of the upper arms. Brush with oil, and arrange in a single layer in the broiling pan. Brown under the broiler, turning to color both sides nicely.

The garlic. Separate the garlic cloves, drop them for 30 seconds in a saucepan of boiling water, drain and peel them, and set aside.

Simmering the wings. Simmer the wings with browned onions, stock, wine, and tomato as described for the ragout of chicken, adding also the peeled garlic cloves. Simmering time will be about 40 minutes, until the wings are tender when pierced with a fork.

Adding the beans and finishing the dish. Fold in the beans and ½ cup of their juices; simmer 5 minutes or so, basting beans and turkey with the sauce in the pan. Taste carefully and correct seasoning; the bean juices will have thickened the sauce nicely. Serve sprinkled with chopped parsley.

*Ahead-of-time note: Like the master ragout of chicken, this dish may be cooked ahead and reheated.

Rabbit Ragout— Rabbit Stew

March hare in herbs and wine

Rabbit tastes much like chicken, but it is a little meatier. In fact, most recipes for chicken work well with rabbit, and vice versa, although the rabbit may need a little longer cooking. In this dish, the rabbit is marinated, which gives the meat added flavor and tenderness; however, you may omit this step and add the marinade ingredients to simmer with the rabbit. As a variation in technique and to make an automatic sauce thickener, the rabbit pieces are floured before being browned.

A cut-up rabbit

For 4 to 6 servings

A 3½-pound roaster rabbit

For the marinade
⅓ cup olive oil
1 tsp mixed dried herbs (such as Italian seasoning)
3 large cloves of garlic, puréed
1½ Tbs soy sauce
The minced zest (yellow part of peel) and strained juice of 1 lemon
10 grinds of fresh pepper
½ cup finely minced onion
⅓ cup finely sliced carrot

Salt and freshly ground pepper
1 cup flour in a plate
Olive oil for browning the rabbit
1 cup sliced onions
2 cups dry white French vermouth or dry white wine
2 fairly large ripe red tomatoes, peeled, seeded, and juiced (page 357), or a 1½-cup mixture of fresh tomato pulp and strained canned Italian plum tomatoes
1 cup or so chicken broth

SPECIAL EQUIPMENT SUGGESTED: *A large bowl or enameled casserole for marinating the rabbit; a rack for draining it; a roomy chicken fryer or casserole 2½ to 3 inches deep with cover (or an electric frying pan) for the cooking*

SPECIAL NOTE

Beurre Manié

Flour-butter paste: a quick sauce thickener

Beurre manié—meaning literally butter and flour worked to a paste with your impeccably clean fingers—is the traditional sauce thickener for informal stews such as our chicken and onions in red wine, and its variation, coq au vin, as well as its cousin, boeuf bourguignon.

After the sauce has been degreased, reduced, and seasoned, it becomes obvious to you that it needs thickening so that it will enrobe the ingredients it accompanies.

Proceed as follows: for each cup of sauce, mash 1 tablespoon of butter to a smooth paste with 1 tablespoon of flour, using a rubber spatula if you wish. Remove the sauce from heat, whisk in the butter-flour paste, and when thoroughly absorbed, bring briefly to the boil and the sauce will thicken—if not thick enough, repeat the process with, say, ½ tablespoon each of flour and butter.

Rabbit Ragout (*continued*)

Preparing the rabbit. Store-bought ready-cut rabbit may look like this— or you can cut it yourself this way. At the lower left are the leg-thighs, which you can separate at the knee joint. In the center is the loin, which you may chop crosswise into 2 pieces. At the upper right are the forelegs with ribs—the pieces with the most bone and the least meat.

The marinade. Whisk the marinade ingredients together in a large bowl, and turn the rabbit pieces in it. Cover and refrigerate for 24 to 48 hours, basting and turning the rabbit 3 or 4 times a day. When you are ready to proceed, drain the rabbit on a rack, scraping off and saving the marinade. Dry the rabbit in paper towels.

Browning. The moment before browning them, dredge the rabbit pieces in flour. Film the frying pan or casserole with 1/16 inch of oil, and, when very hot but not smoking, brown the rabbit nicely on all sides and remove to a side dish. Drain the vegetables out of the marinade, and sauté them along with the sliced onions for 5 minutes or so in the oil left in the pan. Pour in the vermouth or wine and swish about, to incorporate any rabbit-browning bits into the liquid. Arrange the rabbit pieces in the pan, add the tomatoes, the marinade liquid, and enough chicken broth almost to cover the rabbit.

Final cooking—about 1 hour. Bring to the simmer on top of the stove, cover, and simmer slowly, basting occasionally with the cooking liquid, until the rabbit pieces are tender

when pierced with the sharp prongs of a kitchen fork. The sauce will be lightly thickened; taste it carefully and correct seasoning.

*Ahead-of-time note: May be simmered ahead and reheated, as described for the master ragout of chicken on page 141.

Serving and accompaniments for Rabbit Ragout. Serve the rabbit from its casserole, or arrange it on a hot platter. Noodles or rice would go nicely, fresh peas or broccoli, and a light red wine like a pinot noir, or a white sauvignon or chardonnay.

STEWS

A chicken in every pot—in the days of yore that meant stewed chicken, a whole stewed chicken, certainly the easiest way of all to cook anything. But how infinitely easier and faster it is for us today, when, rather than buying a whole chicken for the pot, we can stew just its chosen parts.

The following is my all-time favorite. It's quick, uncomplicated, and, with its wine and aromatic flavorings, it makes such delicious eating you cannot believe that this heaven-sent dish is bona-fide strict diet food. In its master recipe, it is certainly that. However, its variations, which include turkey as well, run the gamut from aspic, to pot pie, Belgian waterzooi, and even blanquettes of both chicken and turkey.

 MASTER RECIPE

Chicken Simmered in White Wine
With aromatic vegetables

For 4 to 6 servings

The vegetables, cut into 1½-inch julienne

2 medium carrots, trimmed and peeled
The tender part of 2 medium leeks, cleaned and washed
4 to 6 tender celery stalks, trimmed and washed

Seasonings: salt and freshly ground pepper, ¼ tsp dried tarragon, 1 imported bay leaf
3½ pounds cut-up frying chicken (1 or 2 pieces per serving, as described on page 136)
1½ cups dry white French vermouth or dry white wine
About 1½ cups clear chicken broth

SPECIAL EQUIPMENT SUGGESTED: *A covered flameproof casserole, chicken fryer, or electric frying pan that will hold the chicken and vegetables comfortably*

Cooking the chicken. Toss the vegetables with salt, pepper, tarragon, and bay leaf; strew a third of them in the bottom of the casserole. Season the chicken pieces with salt and pepper, and bury them in layers with the rest of the vegetables. Pour in the wine and enough chicken broth barely to cover the chicken. Bring to the simmer, cover, and simmer slowly for 25 to 30 minutes, or until the chicken is done (the legs and thighs are tender when pressed, and

Assembling chicken with aromatic vegetables

their juices run clear with no trace of rosy color). Let the chicken steep in its cooking liquid for 10 to 15 minutes before proceeding—it will pick up flavor. Degrease the liquid, remove the bay leaf, and you may wish to peel the skin off the chicken pieces.

Ahead-of-time note: May be cooked even a day in advance, and reheated.

Accompaniments—the dieters' delight. Serve the chicken and vegetable julienne over a bed of steamed rice basted with the chicken juices. You might accompany this with fresh green beans or asparagus tips. A light white wine like a dry riesling would go nicely.

Jellied chicken, home-style version

A Simple Chicken in Aspic
Jellied chicken

In this home-style arrangement, the chicken pieces are arranged in a deep serving bowl, the aromatic cooking liquid is thoroughly degreased, mixed with gelatin, cooled, and poured over the chicken. It is chilled until set, and served directly from the bowl.

For 4 to 6 servings

The preceding chicken simmered in wine
Unflavored gelatin (1 Tbs per each 2 cups of cooking liquid)
¼ to ⅓ cup of dry French vermouth or dry white wine

SPECIAL EQUIPMENT SUGGESTED:
A serving bowl or casserole deep enough to submerge the chicken pieces in their jelly

The chicken. After the chicken has steeped in its cooking liquid, pour the contents through a large sieve set over a 2-quart saucepan. Peel off and discard the chicken skin. Arrange the pieces closely together in the serving bowl, decorate with the vegetable julienne, cover, and refrigerate.

The aspic jelly. Let the gelatin soften in a small bowl with the wine—5 minutes or so. Thoroughly degrease the cooking liquid. (You'll want 2½ to 3 cups—add a little chicken stock, if needed.) Taste it carefully and correct seasoning. Blend in the softened gelatin and heat, stirring, to dissolve the gelatin completely. Pour through a tea strainer into another saucepan to clarify it somewhat. When the chicken has chilled, stir the aspic over a bowl of ice cubes and water for several minutes until cold and almost syrupy. Pour it over the chicken. Cover and chill several hours, or until serving time.

Dressy chicken in aspic surrounding chicken liver mousse

Spooning aspic over chilled pieces

VARIATION

A More Formal Presentation
A dressy chicken in aspic

For an elegant presentation, clarify the wine-flavored cooking stock—meaning that you turn it clear and sparkling, and add gelatin, as described on page 15. Then you spoon it over the chicken, affixing colorful decorations as you go. If you enjoy fussing and decorating, aspics are fun to make—all you need is room in the refrigerator, and time for the successive coatings of aspic to set.

AMOUNTS. *I inevitably find that I want twice as much aspic as I thought I needed, and for 1 chicken 6 to 8 cups should be more than ample. You can freeze leftover aspic, anyway.*

The chicken. Peel the skin off the wine-poached chicken parts, trim them neatly, if needed, arrange them on a rack over a tray, and chill in the refrigerator.

The first aspic coatings. Have the main quantity of aspic in a saucepan. Pour a cup of it into a small pan and set in a bowl of ice cubes and water to chill until the aspic is cold and almost set. Spoon a coat or two of almost-set aspic over the chicken parts (the tray catches dribbles); chill 10 minutes, and repeat with another coating or two—rewarming and rechilling the aspic in the small pan as necessary.

The decorations. Decorations may be anything you choose—here we have black olives and red pimiento while the blanched green of scallions makes the swirling lines. Chill the decorations on a plate. Skewer each piece

and, before placing it on the chicken, dip it in almost-set aspic so that it will adhere. Chill 10 minutes. Spoon a coating of aspic over the decorations, chill, and repeat with 2 or 3 more coatings.

Serving suggestion. Pour ½ inch of aspic into a pan and chill 20 minutes, or until set. You may then cut it into shapes. Or, as shown in the illustration here, chop it to line a chilled platter. Here decorated pieces of boneless chicken breast surround a chicken liver mousse—for which the recipe follows.

Chicken Liver Mousse

Chicken liver mousse goes nicely with chicken in aspic, and this is a fine example. Sautéed chicken livers and onions are puréed with wine, seasonings, aspic, butter, and cottage cheese—you'll think you're eating foie gras!

For about 4 cups

1 Tbs unflavored gelatin
¾ cup rich chicken stock (page 4)
¼ cup minced onion
6 ounces (1½ sticks) unsalted butter
3 cups (1½ pounds) chicken livers

Seasonings: salt, freshly ground
pepper, and a pinch of dried
tarragon
⅓ cup Sercial Madeira or dry Port
wine
1 cup cottage cheese

SPECIAL EQUIPMENT SUGGESTED:
*A 10-inch no-stick frying pan; a food
processor or electric blender*

Preliminary. Blend the gelatin into
the chicken stock and let soften while
sautéing the chicken livers.

The chicken livers. Sauté the onion
slowly 8 to 10 minutes in 4 tablespoons of the butter until tender and
translucent. Add the chicken livers,
raise heat, and sauté 2 minutes more,
tossing the pan by its handle, until
they are lightly springy when
pressed—they should remain rosy inside. Season with salt, pepper, and
tarragon; pour in the wine and boil
30 seconds. Turn the livers into a
bowl, leaving the liquid in the pan.

The gelatined flavor base. Boil down
the cooking liquid by half, pour in
the gelatined chicken stock, and simmer a moment to dissolve the gelatin
completely, then add the remaining
butter, cut into smallish pieces, to
melt.

Puréeing the livers. Purée the cottage
cheese in the processor or blender
with the gelatined flavor base, then
add and purée the sautéed livers and
onion. Taste carefully and correct
seasoning. If you wish a very smooth
mixture, force the purée through a
sieve.

Serving. Either turn it into a decorative bowl and pass as an hors

d'oeuvre with toast or crackers; or
line a bowl with plastic wrap, pack in
the mousse, and chill several hours
(or until set), then unmold, remove
the plastic, and decorate the surface
as shown.

Waterzooi of Chicken

This traditional Belgian dish is our
same chicken simmered in white
wine with a julienne of vegetables,
but its aromatic broth is turned into a
delicate sauce. To make it a true waterzooi, serve it in deep soup plates.

For 4 to 6 servings

**The master recipe for Chicken
Simmered in White Wine**

6 egg yolks
½ cup heavy cream
**½ Tbs cornstarch, optional anti-
curdling insurance**
3 Tbs minced fresh parsley

The chicken is cooked, the skin removed, and the broth has been
strained and degreased. For the
sauce, whisk the yolks and cream in a
mixing bowl with the optional cornstarch to blend; gradually whisk in
the hot cooking broth. Pour it over
the chicken.

Serving. A few minutes before serving, set the casserole over moderate
heat and swirl slowly until the sauce
heats through and thickens—do not
rush things, and do not let it come to
the simmer or you will curdle the
egg yolks. Ladle chicken, sauce, and
vegetables into large soup plates,
sprinkling each serving with parsley.
Serve with boiled potatoes, good
French bread, or the gnocchi on page
403.

Blanquette of Chicken in White Wine Sauce

Blanquette is simply a dressy term
meaning a creamed something, the
most famous being a blanquette of
veal, which is done the same way as
the following chicken.

For 4 to 6 servings

**The master recipe for Chicken
Simmered in White Wine (page
144)**
4 Tbs butter
5 Tbs flour
½ cup, more or less, heavy cream
Salt and freshly ground white pepper
**Drops of freshly squeezed lemon
juice**

The white wine sauce. The chicken is
cooked, the chicken pieces are peeled,
and the cooking liquid has been
strained and thoroughly degreased.
Cook the butter and flour together in
a 2½-quart saucepan for 2 minutes
without coloring; off heat, whisk in
the hot cooking liquid; season and
simmer 3 minutes—full details on
page 272. Thin out the sauce with
dribbles of cream—it should be thick
enough to coat a spoon nicely. Taste
very carefully and correct seasoning,
adding drops of lemon juice as you
think them needed. Pour the sauce
over the chicken and its julienne of
vegetables.

**Ahead-of-time note:* May be com-
pleted in advance to this point.

Finishing the blanquette. Cover and
bring to the simmer for several minutes, basting frequently, to reheat and
blend flavors.

(continued)

Blanquette of Chicken (*continued*)

Accompaniments to a blanquette of chicken. Serve the chicken on a bed of rice or noodles, and accompany with a fresh green vegetable like broccoli florets or asparagus tips. A fine white wine like a chardonnay or Burgundy is the choice here.

VARIATIONS

Turkey Blanquette

Turkey meat is fine in a stew; its texture is more solid than chicken, so that it holds up nicely when simmered. However, since the pieces are so much larger than chicken, a julienne of vegetables would be lost; I suggest instead a garnish of mushrooms, whole small onions, and carrots that finish with the blanquette.

For 8 servings

5 to 6 pounds bone-in raw turkey breast and/or thighs
3 cups dry white wine or French vermouth
3 cups turkey stock or chicken broth
Salt and freshly ground white pepper
Drops of freshly squeezed lemon juice

The vegetable garnish:

16 smallish carrots, trimmed and peeled
24 small white onions about 1 inch in diameter, peeled
1 quart (10 ounces or so) fresh mushrooms, trimmed and quartered

3 to 4 cups white wine blanquette sauce, made following the directions for the preceding chicken blanquette
Decoration: fresh parsley

SPECIAL EQUIPMENT SUGGESTED:
A 4-quart pan or casserole for simmering the turkey; a vegetable steamer set in a covered pan

Preliminaries. Peel off and discard the turkey skin. If you are using a whole breast, remove the meat from the breast bones (use the bones for your stock, page 4), and cut the meat into large serving pieces.

Simmering the turkey. Place the turkey meat in the casserole, then pour in the wine and enough stock or broth barely to cover the turkey. Bring to the simmer, and skim off gray scum that will continue to rise for 5 minutes or so. Salt lightly as necessary, cover partially, and simmer 1¼ to 1½ hours, until the turkey is tender—eat a bit as a test.

The vegetable garnish. While the turkey is cooking, steam the carrots for 10 to 15 minutes, or until just tender. Pierce a cross in the root ends of the onions, and simmer in a covered pan in an inch of the turkey-cooking liquid 25 minutes or so, until the onions are tender but still hold their shape; add the mushrooms to the onions the last 2 to 3 minutes of cooking.

Assembling turkey and vegetables. Drain the turkey- and onion-cooking liquids into a saucepan. Arrange the turkey in the casserole along with the vegetables. Make the white wine sauce using the cooking liquids, and spoon it over the turkey and vegetables.

Serving. Shortly before serving, cover and simmer several minutes over moderate heat, basting frequently with the sauce. Decorate with parsley sprigs.

Chicken Pot Pie

Chicken or Turkey Pot Pies

Use the recipe for either chicken or turkey blanquette, making the sauce fairly thick. Arrange the blanquette in individual baking dishes about 2½ inches deep and 5 inches across; and let cool. Cut disks of pastry dough (page 381) or of puff pastry (page 389) ¼ inch thick and ½ inch larger around than the rims of the dishes. Brush the rims with cold water and press on the disks. Pierce a ¼-inch vent hole in the top of each pastry, paint with water, and affix decorative cut-outs.

Just before baking, paint with egg glaze (1 egg beaten with 1 teaspoon of water). Bake in the middle level of a preheated 375°F oven 35 to 40 minutes, or until the filling is bubbling up into the vent holes.

CHICKEN BREASTS

I t's hard to believe that chicken breasts used to be such a supreme luxury that they were served under a glass bell only to the very rich indeed. Now, while breasts are the most expensive of the chicken parts, they are hardly out of sight, particularly when you need a quick main course for special occasions.

PREPARING CHICKEN BREASTS FOR COOKING

In the following recipes, you'll find breasts with skin and wings attached as well as boned and skinned breast halves, the latter of which you can, of course, buy ready to cook. You'll save considerable money, however, if you do them yourself—it's about the easiest boning job there is.

SPECIAL NOTE

Crumbed chicken breasts sautéed in slices—*goujons*

For a quick snack of a meal, and for a change, cut the chicken breasts into slices crosswise, give them a crisp coating of fresh bread crumbs, and sauté them in clarified butter. See the directions for crumbing and sautéing on page 99. They get their name because at first glance they might be those tiny whole deep-fried fish we know as whitebait and the French call *goujons*.

1. Scraping meat off sides of breastbone

Boning. Whether you have bone-in breast halves or whole breasts, start by pulling off the covering skin. For whole breasts, cut down each side of the ridge of the breastbone. Then, for either whole or half breasts, scrape your knife down the side of the breastbone and/or the rib cage to remove meat from bone (see illustration, step 1). If the wing is attached, cut through its ball joint to remove it from the shoulder, and to detach it from the meat.

2. Pulling out white tendon

The white tendon. The breast meat is composed of two long flaps. On the underside of the smaller flap is a white tendon running two-thirds its length; you should remove it because it tends to draw the meat out of shape during cooking, step 2. Cut ½ inch along two sides of its exposed end, grab the end with a towel and pull the tendon out, scraping it free against your knife.

3. Flattening the breast meat

Trimming. Cut any bits of fat and jagged edges off the meat. Placing it flat on your work surface, lay the side of a large knife on it and pound with your fist to flatten the breast slightly, step 3.

The breasts are now ready to cook. Wrap and refrigerate them if you are not proceeding shortly.

1. Dredging in flour

2. Brown butter going over chicken breasts

Chicken Breasts Meunière: Sautéed in Butter

Fast and delicious, and one of the best ways to do chicken breasts—be prepared to work quickly for this one.

For 4 servings

4 boneless and skinless breast halves from frying chickens prepared as previously described
Salt and freshly ground pepper
1 cup flour in a plate
2 to 3 Tbs clarified butter (page 139)

Optional lemon-butter sauce
2 Tbs butter
½ lemon
2 Tbs minced fresh parsley

SPECIAL EQUIPMENT SUGGESTED:
A heavy 10-inch frying pan, no-stick recommended; hot plates or a platter

Season the breasts lightly with salt and pepper. The moment before sautéing, dredge them in flour, step 1, and shake off excess. Set the frying pan over high heat, add the

clarified butter, and, when very hot but not burning, lay in the chicken breasts. Sauté 1 minute on one side, turn, and sauté on the other side—the meat is done when just springy to the touch. Remove it to hot plates.·

Optional sauce. Swish the fresh butter in the pan, and heat a moment until it turns a light brown. Squeeze drops of lemon juice over the chicken, pour on the hot butter, step 2, sprinkle with parsley, and serve at once.

To accompany Chicken Breasts Meunière. Try baked tomatoes and fresh buttered spinach or broccoli; the sautéed potatoes on page 327 would also be welcome, as would a light red wine like a pinot noir or Beaujolais.

Chicken Breasts Poached in Butter

Here is a lovely longer method, where the chicken breasts poach slowly in butter in a covered casserole. Do them this way when you want a sauce with your chicken.

For 4 servings

4 boneless and skinless breast halves from frying chickens, prepared as previously described
Salt and freshly ground pepper
Drops of freshly squeezed lemon juice
A pinch of tarragon
4 Tbs butter
Chopped fresh parsley

SPECIAL EQUIPMENT SUGGESTED:
A heavy covered flameproof casserole just large enough to hold the breasts comfortably in one layer; a round of wax paper to cover the breasts

Poaching the breasts. Preheat the oven to 400°F. Season the breasts lightly with salt, pepper, lemon juice, and tarragon. Heat the butter to bubbling in the casserole on top of the stove; roll the breasts in the butter and lay the wax paper over them. Cover the hot casserole and set in the middle level of the preheated oven for 6 to 8 minutes, or until the meat is lightly springy when pressed with your finger. Remove them to a side dish.

Serving. You may serve them simply, pouring the butter sauce over the breasts, and decorating with a sprinkle of parsley. See also the two following variations, just to give yourself an idea of what else you can do.

VARIATIONS

Mushrooms and Cream

Remove the poached chicken breasts from the casserole to a hot plate and cover them. Stir a tablespoon of minced shallots into the poaching butter and set over moderately high heat. When bubbling, toss in a cup or so of sliced fresh mushrooms and sauté 2 minutes. Pour in ½ cup of heavy cream and boil, folding cream and mushrooms together, until the sauce has thickened lightly. Taste carefully for seasoning, and add a few drops of freshly squeezed lemon juice. Fold in a tablespoon of minced fresh parsley and/or chives or tarragon; spoon the sauce and mushrooms over the chicken.

To accompany chicken breasts in mushrooms and cream. Lay the chicken breasts over a bed of noodles or steamed rice, and accompany with a fresh green vegetable like asparagus tips, spinach, or broccoli flowerettes. A great white wine, chardonnay or Burgundy, would be a perfect choice.

Chicken Breasts Chasseur
With tomatoes and mushrooms

After removing the poached breasts from the casserole, set it over moderately high heat and add 2 cups of quartered fresh mushrooms. Sauté for 1 minute, tossing, then drain and scrape over the chicken breasts, leaving the butter in the casserole. Stir ¼ cup of thinly sliced onions, a big pinch of thyme, and 1 large clove of puréed garlic into the casserole, and

Upper right: Stuffed chicken legs and breasts; Lower right: Winged Victory; Left: Chicken Breasts Chasseur

sauté 5 to 6 minutes, until the onions are tender. Then add 1½ cups of fresh tomato pulp (page 357) and stir over high heat for a minute or two to evaporate juices and thicken slightly. Taste and correct seasoning. Fold in the chicken and mushrooms, basting and simmering a moment just to reheat the chicken but not to overcook it.

Suggested accompaniments to chicken breasts chasseur. Steamed rice would go nicely here, or just French bread, plus a fresh green vegetable and either a young red wine or a strong white like a sauvignon.

STUFFED CHICKEN BREASTS

Kiev with its famous spurt of butter is not the only stuffed chicken breast; here are others.

Chicken breast ready for stuffing

Stuffed chicken breasts ready for baking

Winged Victory

An aromatic stuffing under the skin

For 6 servings

The stuffing

2 Tbs butter
⅓ cup each: finely diced carrots, onions, and celery
⅓ cup finely diced boiled ham

6 bone-in chicken breast halves, wings attached
Seasonings: salt, pepper, tarragon
2 to 3 Tbs butter (1 Tbs or so melted butter for basting, 1 Tbs or so for sauce enrichment)

SPECIAL EQUIPMENT SUGGESTED:
A small sharp knife for boning; a buttered baking dish (or 2 dishes) that will hold the breasts comfortably in one layer

The stuffing. Heat the butter in a small saucepan, stir in the vegetables and ham, and sauté about 10 minutes, stirring and adding seasonings to taste. The vegetables should be perfectly tender but not browned. Set aside to cool.

Preparing the breasts. Each breast half consists of all or part of the breastbone and the rib cage on which the breast meat rests, plus the wing, which is attached to the shoulder. Being careful to keep the skin whole, scrape and pull it from the breast meat, but leave it attached to the shoulder. Now scrape the breast meat from the breastbone and ribs, cutting through the ball joint of the wing but keeping the wing attached to the breast. (This is far easier than it sounds, as you will see.)

Here is the boned breast loosened from its skin, but still attached to the wing. Lightly dust the meat with salt and pepper, and it is ready for stuffing.

Lay the breast skin side down, lift up the meat, and spoon a portion of the stuffing on the skin, as shown. Fold the meat down onto the stuffing, and fold the skin around to enclose it partially.

Arrange the breasts skin side up in a buttered dish, as you see them here. Brush on melted butter, and season lightly with salt and pepper.

Ahead-of-time note: May be prepared in advance to this point; cover and refrigerate.

Baking—30 to 40 minutes at 375°F. Bake in the upper third level of the preheated oven, basting with accumulated juices once or twice.

When is it done? The chicken is done when the meat is lightly springy to the touch and the juices run clear.

Remove to a hot platter or side dish, cover, and keep warm the few minutes it takes to make the sauce.

Sauce and serving. Skim fat off cooking juices and pour the juices into a small pan; boil rapidly for a few minutes, until reduced almost to a syrup. Swirl in a tablespoon or two of butter to give a light liaison, and pour over the chicken breasts.

Suggested accompaniments: potato galettes, roasted tomatoes, and a smooth white wine—a chardonnay.

Chicken Breast Ballottines
Stuffed whole chicken breasts

In this recipe you remove the bones from each side of the breast but leave the breast halves attached under the skin, which is folded around to enclose meat and stuffing. The neat sausage shapes are then baked and sliced for serving— making an attractive dish either hot or cold.

For 6 to 8 servings

3 whole chicken breasts, minus wings
About 1 cup sweet Italian sausage stuffing (see Special Note, page 155)
1 to 2 Tbs melted butter

SPECIAL EQUIPMENT SUGGESTED:
3-inch steel turkey skewers, white string

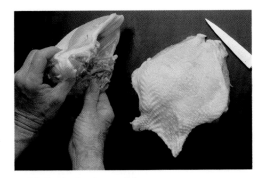

1. Whole wingless breast, left
Boned whole breast, right

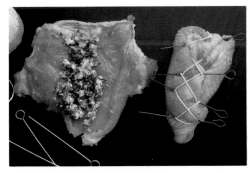

2. Left: Stuffing on flesh side of breast
Right: Skin skewered over stuffed breast

3. Removing skewers before arranging breasts on platter

Top: Boned and stuffed breasts and legs; Bottom: Sliced, boned, and stuffed breast

Preparing the breasts. The whole wingless breast and the boned whole breast are illustrated, step 1. Aim to keep the skin intact during the following operations. Scrape flesh from the bone on one side of the breast, going up to but *not over* the ridge of the breastbone. Repeat on the other side. Then lift up the carcass and scrape close against the ridge of the breastbone to release the carcass. You now have the two breast halves attached to the skin, as shown at right in the photograph.

Stuffing and trussing. Step 2 shows the boned double breast, at left; it is spread out skin side down, with 3 to 4 tablespoons of stuffing placed down the center. Skewer it closed, winding cotton string around the skewers, as you see here on the right.

Ahead-of-time note: The recipe may be completed to this point a day in advance; cover and refrigerate.

Baking and serving—about 1 hour at 350°F. Bake the chicken and make the sauce as described for the preceding Winged Victory. Remove the skewers and arrange on a platter, step 3. To serve, cut the chicken into ½-inch slices, like a sausage.

VARIATION

Stuffed Chicken Legs

Chicken legs may also be boned and
stuffed, and if you include the thigh,
you have more of a serving. Scrape
flesh from bone starting at the hip
end of the thigh and coming three
quarters of the way down the length
of the drumstick. Chop off the bone
there, leaving about 1 inch of the
drumstick end, so the leg will look
like a leg. Push the stuffing down
into the drumstick, spread more into
the thigh, then truss the meat closed.
Bake and serve as described for the
chicken breasts.

Boning the leg-thigh

BROILING, BROIL-ROASTING, AND BUTTERFLYING

Next to stewing, broiling is
certainly the simplest way to
cook poultry, and one of the most satisfactory because of its appetizing
aroma, its crisp brown skin, and its
juicy meat. It beats roasting, too, in
many ways—not the least of them
being that a chicken will broil in half
the time it takes to roast. This applies
not only to poussins, game hens, and
young broiling chickens but to large
roasters and even to turkeys. In the
case of the larger birds, you use a
combination of broiling to brown the
two sides and seal in the juices, and
roasting to finish it.

MASTER RECIPE

Broiled Butterflied Chicken

Of course you can broil a half
chicken or chicken in parts, but when
you want a handsome presentation at
the table, butterflying is the way to
go.

To butterfly a chicken. First remove
the backbone by cutting down close
to it on each side with a heavy knife
or sturdy shears. Spread the chicken
skin side up on your work surface
and bang the breast with your fist to
break the collarbones and some of the
ribs; this flattens the chicken. Cut off
the little nubbins at the wing elbows,
and fold the wings akimbo by tucking the wing ends behind the shoulders. Then make a slit in the skin at
either side of the breast tip, see illustration. Push the knee of the drum-

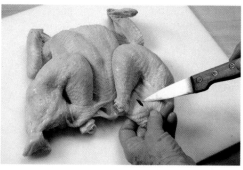

Slitting skin to insert drumstick

stick firmly up under the armpit to
loosen the joint; then pull it down
and insert the tip of the drumstick
through the skin slit. The leg will be
held in place as shown at the left in
the photo.

For 4 servings

**A 3-pound broiler-fryer chicken,
butterflied as described in the
preceding paragraph**
**2 Tbs melted butter mixed with 1 tsp
olive oil or cooking oil**
Salt and freshly ground pepper
**A pinch of thyme, tarragon, or
mixed herbs, optional**

Optional deglazing sauce
**1 Tbs finely minced shallot or
scallion**
**½ cup chicken stock and/or dry
white wine or French vermouth**
**1 to 2 Tbs butter for enrichment,
optional**

SPECIAL EQUIPMENT SUGGESTED:
*A stout knife and/or shears for prepar-
ing the chicken; a basting brush; a baking dish about 1 inch deep (without
rack) that will just hold the butterflied
chicken easily*

Broiling—25 to 30 minutes. Preheat
the broiler. Brush the chicken all
over with some of the butter and oil.
Arrange it skin side down in the bak-

ing dish, and set it so the surface of the flesh is about 5 inches from the hot broiler element. After 5 minutes, brush the flesh, which should just be starting to brown, with the butter and oil. Baste again in 5 minutes—use the juices in the pan when the butter mixture is gone. Broil another 5 minutes, then sprinkle lightly with salt, pepper, and optional herbs. Turn the chicken skin side up. Broil and baste 15 minutes or so more.

When is it done? The chicken is nearly done when brown juices begin to appear in the pan. It is definitely done when the drumsticks feel tender, and, when the thickest part is pricked with the sharp tines of a kitchen fork, the juices run clear yellow. Do not overcook.

Sauce. Remove the chicken to a hot platter; cover to keep warm the few minutes required for the optional sauce. Skim fat off the cooking juices, stir in the chopped shallot or scallion, and sauté a moment on top of the stove. Add the liquid and boil rapidly, scraping into it any coagulated cooking juices. When reduced almost to a syrup, swirl in the butter. Pour the sauce over the chicken.

Serving. To carve, cut straight down one side of the breastbone to separate the chicken in two lengthwise. Grab under one of the knees with your fork to lift it up, slit the skin front and back, and bend the knee back at right angles to break open the joint at the small of the back. Then cut through the ball joint to separate the thigh from the carcass. Separate drumsticks from thighs at the knee joints. Remove the wings along with a lengthwise strip of meat from the lower third of the breast, to make meaningful servings. You now have 2

drumsticks, 2 thighs, 2 wings with a breast strip, and 2 breast sections—everyone has a little selection of both dark and light.

Suggested accompaniment to broiled chicken: You could serve broiled tomatoes, sautéed potatoes, and a green vegetable, or be more elaborate with an eggplant dish such as the soufflé on page 292, or the ratatouille on page 317. Another idea is the hot corn salad on page 376. For wine, either a sturdy white wine like a chardonnay or sauvignon, or a light red such as a pinot noir or Beaujolais.

SPECIAL NOTE

Sweet Italian Sausage, Parsley, and Crumb Stuffing

For about 1 cup of stuffing (used for 3 stuffed boned whole chicken breasts)

1 sweet Italian sausage
1 Tbs butter
½ cup minced onion
1 cup crumbs from fresh homemade type white bread
½ cup minced fresh parsley
¼ cup sour cream
Salt and freshly ground pepper

Prick the sausage in several places with a pin, place in a small covered frying pan with ¼ inch of water, and steam 5 minutes. Drain. Peel off the skin, chop the sausage, and sauté several minutes in the tablespoon of butter to brown lightly. Scoop into a mixing bowl, leaving the fat in the pan. In it sauté the onion slowly for 6 to 8 minutes. When tender, add to the sausage. Blend in the remaining ingredients and season carefully to taste.

Assembling game hens on wild rice croutons

SPECIAL NOTE

Croutons of Wild Rice

Serve these by themselves to garnish a platter, or use them as a base for small roast or broiled birds.

For 6 servings

6 slices of homemade type white bread
1 egg
⅓ to 1 cup grated Swiss cheese
2 cups braised wild rice (page 330)

Trim the bread into ovals about the size of the game hen halves; sauté to brown lightly in clarified butter (these are now, officially, croutons). Beat the egg and ⅓ cup of the cheese into the wild rice, and mound the rice on the croutons.

If these are to be served as a separate garnish, sprinkle the tops with the remaining grated cheese and brown lightly under the broiler before serving.

Deviled Chicken: With Mustard Coating

The chicken is broiled until almost done, then coated with mustard, herbs, and fresh bread crumbs for a crisp brown finish.

For 8 servings

2 butterflied chickens

The mustard and herb coating
The cooking juices from the chicken
6 Tbs Dijon-style prepared mustard
3½ Tbs finely minced shallot or scallion
½ tsp tarragon or mixed herbs
4 drops of hot pepper sauce
2 cups crumbs from fresh home-made type white bread

The chickens. Follow the preceding recipe, but broil the 2 chickens only 10 rather than 15 minutes on the second (skin) side.

Mustard and herb coating. Drain the fat and juices out of the broiling pan into a small bowl; skim off and discard all but 2 tablespoons of fat from the top of the juices. Blend the prepared mustard in another bowl with the minced shallot or scallion, herbs, and hot pepper sauce. Beat up the remaining juices; blend half of them into the mustard. Spread the mustard over the top (skin side) of the chickens (see illustration), then pat on a coating of crumbs. Baste with the remaining juices.

Ahead-of-time note: May be prepared somewhat ahead to this point; set aside at room temperature.

Deviled chicken ready for carving

Final cooking and serving. Roast in the upper third level of a 400°F oven for 10 to 12 minutes (20 minutes if cooking is delayed).

When is it done? The chicken is done when the drumsticks are tender if pressed, and the crumbs should brown nicely.

Grilling note. The crumb coating does not work for barbecuing since it will fall off and burn when you turn the chicken. However, you can use just the mustard and herb mixture, basted on during the last few minutes of cooking (beat a few tablespoons of oil into the mustard to take the place of chicken fat).

Spreading on the mustard coating

VARIATION

Deviled Rabbit

The preceding recipe is especially
successful with rabbit. Marinate the
rabbit pieces for several hours or
overnight, following directions for
the rabbit stew on page 143. Scrape
off the marinade, then brown the
rabbit for 10 minutes on each side
under the broiler. Paint the top sides
with the mustard and herb coating
described above, pat on the crumbs,
and roast 15 to 20 minutes in the upper third level of a preheated 350°F
oven.

When is it done? The rabbit is
done when the meat is tender if
pierced.

SPECIAL NOTE

A Special Sauce for Marinated Rabbit or Chicken

**The marinade juices and the
roasting juices**
**½ cup dry white wine or French
vermouth**
½ cup heavy cream

Pour the marinade juices into a
saucepan, and deglaze the roasting
pan with the wine, scraping the resulting liquid into the saucepan. Boil
rapidly until liquid has reduced and
thickened lightly, then whisk in the
cream and continue boiling until
again lightly thickened. Correct seasoning, and pass in a warm bowl,
with the rabbit or chicken.

Cornish Game Hens Split and Broiled with Cheese
Croutons of wild rice

For 6 servings

3 game hens
**About ½ cup clarified butter (page
139)**
Salt and freshly ground pepper
**6 wild rice croutons (see Special
Note, page 155)**
4½ Tbs grated Swiss cheese

Preparing the game hens. With heavy
shears, cut the backbones out of the
game hens, and split each in half
lengthwise by cutting down one side
of the breast. Slit the skin of each at
the lower side of the breast, and tuck
in the end of the drumstick (see illustration for Butterflied Chicken, page
154). Brush both sides of each bird
with clarified butter, season lightly
with salt and pepper, and arrange
skin side down in a roasting pan.

Preliminary cooking. Set 6 inches or
so under a hot broiler and brown
lightly 6 to 7 minutes on each side.
Remove to a side dish, and pour the
juices from the pan into a small
bowl.

Broiled game hen with caramelized onion quarters
and a sauté of zucchini with red peppers

Arrange the croutons of wild rice in
the broiling pan. Cover each with a
game hen half, pressed flesh side
down onto the rice. Spread 1½ tablespoons of grated cheese over each
game hen, and baste with the reserved broiling juices.

*Finishing the cooking—15 to 20 min-
utes.* About 20 minutes before you
are ready to serve, bake in a preheated 375°F oven.

When are they done? The birds are
done when the thighs are tender if
pressed.

Using a sturdy spatula, lift them off
with their wild rice croutons onto hot
plates or a serving platter.

*Suggested accompaniments to game hens
broiled with cheese.* A sauté of zucchini and red peppers (page 295) and
caramelized onion quarters (page
315) are attractive here. Serve a mature smooth red wine such as a cabernet or Bordeaux.

BROIL-ROASTING

When you have a 5- to 6-pound roasting chicken or a turkey, and you are not called upon to present the whole upstanding "festive bird," you will cook it in half the time if you butterfly and broil it—in a special way. You start out broiling, but if you continued broiling to the end you would burn and dry out the outside by the time the inside was cooked through. The solution is simple—start out broiling, but finish up roasting. You get that appealing broiled effect of crisply brown, well-basted flesh and skin, and you'll have a delicious juicy bird that is very easy to carve and serve.

Broil-roasting will suit all roasting chickens, and any size of turkey, but for most home cooks a 14- to 18-pound turkey is the size that will fit the usual home oven and roasting pan.

Preparing the bird. Either ask your market to cut out the backbone of the chicken or turkey with a buzz saw, and then to saw it in half close along one side of the ridge of the breastbone, or perform this simple surgery yourself with cleaver and mallet (as illustrated for the

re-assembled turkey on page 170). Reach in under the skin at the neck, locate the remains of the wishbone, and cut it out.

Broil-roast all or part. Particularly if you are dealing with a frozen turkey, you may want to roast one half only, and keep the other half in the freezer. Or, to serve a few more people, you may want one turkey half plus just the leg-thighs or just the breast of the other half. When you broil-roast, you have the choice.

Number of servings per turkey. Count on 1 pound of whole turkey per person if you want seconds and a reasonable amount of leftovers. Thus half a 16-pound turkey serves 8 generously, and if you add a breast half or an extra leg-thigh, you will feed 12.

Timing for butterflied chickens and turkeys. Roasting time is about half the estimate for whole roast birds; however, always add on a 20- to 30-minute buffer, just in case. Here are approximate roasting estimates:

Butterflied Chicken

5 to 6 pounds	1 to 1¼ hours

Butterflied Turkeys

8 to 12 pounds	1½ to 2 hours
12 to 16 pounds	1½ to 2 hours
16 to 20 pounds	2½ to 3½ hours.

 MASTER RECIPE

Broil-Roasted Turkey

For a 15-pound butterflied turkey (or half of it with or without a half breast or extra leg-thigh)

Timing—2½ hours to be on the safe side

A 15-pound turkey, butterflied (page 154)
⅓ cup melted butter or fresh cooking oil
1 cup each roughly chopped carrots and onions
Seasonings: salt, and sage or thyme
Ingredients for whatever gravy you have chosen (page 173)

SPECIAL EQUIPMENT SUGGESTED: *A roasting pan 2 inches deep that will hold the turkey easily in one layer; a basting brush; an instant meat thermometer*

Broiling start. Preheat the broiler. Brush the turkey all over with melted butter or oil and arrange skin side down in the roasting pan. Set so the surface of the flesh is 7 to 8 inches from the red-hot broiler element. (You want it to brown slowly and evenly; adjust the broiler heat accordingly.)

Minute 6. Check on progress. Baste flesh with butter or oil. It is just beginning to brown.

Minute 12. Check and baste again.

Minute 16. The flesh side should be nicely browned; if not, give it a few minutes more. Salt the flesh side lightly, turn the turkey skin side up, baste the skin side, and continue.

Minute 22. Check on cooking and baste with the fat that has accumulated in the pan.

Minute 26 to 30. The skin side burns easily under the broiler—check and baste. The skin side should be lightly browned; if not, give it a few minutes more.

Roasting finish—minute 30 to the end. Now change to a preheated 325°F oven. Strew the chopped vegetables in the pan, basting them and dusting lightly with the herbs. Continue basting the turkey with accumulated fat every 20 minutes.

When is it done? The turkey is done when a meat thermometer inserted into the thickest portion of the breast near the armpit area shows a reading of 162°F to 165°F. The drumsticks should feel fairly tender when pressed.

Carving notes. For serving, the leg-thighs come off easily; carve them in the usual manner. For the breast, cut off the wing, then start slicing the breast from the front, angling your knife gradually parallel to the ridge area of the breastbone. You may wish to carve in the kitchen, and arrange the pieces attractively on a hot platter.

VARIATION

Broil-Roasted Chicken or Capon

Use exactly the same system as for the preceding turkey.

Laid-Back Turkey
Semi-boned, butterflied, and broil-roasted

The turkey is completely boned except for the wings and drumsticks, which are left on to give it that unmistakable turkey look. It is broiled on the flesh side to seal in juices, then laid flesh side down on the stuffing for roasting. The meat takes on flavor from the stuffing, and vice versa, while carving is, of course, a breeze. It's an amusing as well as practical presentation, especially recommended to the home butcher.

For a 12- to 14-pound turkey, serving 12 to 16

Timing: 1½ to 1¾ hours

A 12- to 14-pound turkey
⅓ cup melted butter
Seasonings: salt, freshly ground pepper, and thyme or sage
5 to 6 cups of turkey stuffing—the mushroom duxelles (see Special Note, page 160) is especially recommended
1 cup each: roughly chopped carrots, onions, and celery stalks, to flavor the roasting juices
Ingredients for whatever gravy you have chosen (page 173)

SPECIAL EQUIPMENT SUGGESTED:
A stout boning knife; 2 skewers about 10 inches long; a food processor for the stuffing; a pastry sheet with one flat end that will fit into the roasting pan on several thicknesses of heavy foil (for sliding off turkey-with-stuffing after roasting); an instant meat thermometer

Boning the turkey. From inside the neck area, cut out the wishbone. Next, slice through skin and flesh down the middle of the backbone from neck to tail. Then, always

1. Boned turkey ready for skewering

scraping against the bone and not slitting the skin, bone one side of the turkey at a time up to but *not over* the ridge of the breastbone, cutting through the ball joints of the wings and thighs as you come to them. When you have boned the second side, lift up the carcass; being careful because the skin is thin, scrape close against the ridge of the breastbone to release the carcass.

Turn the turkey skin side down. Locate the two thigh bones (their ball joints protrude from the flesh on either side of the lower section); cut and scrape flesh from bone, then cut through the knee joint to remove the thigh bones on each side. Cut off the wing nubbins at the elbows. (See illustration of boned turkey, step 1.) Secure the wings to the carcass with one skewer, and the legs with another. Paint the turkey all over with melted butter.

Make a turkey stock with the carcass and bones (directions are on page 173).

Ahead-of-time note: The turkey may be boned a day in advance; wrap and refrigerate it. You may also complete

(continued)

2. Its underside browned, boned turkey now goes over stuffing.

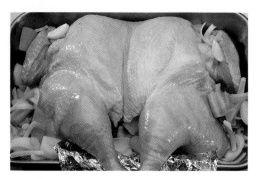

3. Turkey ready for the oven

Laid-Back Turkey (*continued*)

the turkey stock, and whatever stuffing you have chosen.

Browning the turkey. Lay the turkey skin side down in the roasting pan and brown the flesh side under the broiler, as for the preceding butterflied turkey. Dust with salt, pepper, and thyme or sage.

**Ahead-of-time note:* You may brown the turkey an hour or so ahead.

Roasting—1½ to 1¾ hours at 350°F. Butter the baking sheet or foil, set it in the roasting pan, and mound the stuffing upon it. Turn the turkey flesh side down over the stuffing; remove the skewers, and arrange the turkey so that it encloses the stuffing completely, step 2. If the legs hang over the pan, tuck a double thickness of foil under them, as shown here.

4. Laid-back turkey roasted and resting before being carved

Strew the chopped vegetables around the turkey, step 3, and roast in the middle level of the preheated oven, basting every 20 minutes first with butter and then with accumulated juices.

When is it done? The turkey is done when a meat thermometer, plunged into the thickest part of the breast near the wing-shoulder area, registers 162°F to 165°F; the legs should feel fairly tender when pressed.

Gravy, carving, and serving. Remove the turkey-with-stuffing on its baking sheet or foil, and slide it off onto a carving board or hot platter. Let it rest 10 minutes or so before carving, while you finish whatever gravy you have chosen. To carve, slice the turkey in half, right down through the center where the breastbone used to be; serve slices of white meat and stuffing. (By the way, those who claim they eat only dark meat will be delighted with their unusually savory white meat this time.) The dark meat will be, of course, the drumsticks, plus the easy-to-slice thigh meat on the lower sides of the turkey.

SPECIAL NOTE

Mushroom Duxelles Poultry Stuffing

For 5 to 6 cups

2 cups diced onions
4 Tbs butter
2 quarts (1¼ pounds) minced fresh mushrooms (chop roughly and mince a handful at a time in the food processor, then squeeze dry; add juices to your sauce)
Salt and freshly ground pepper
¼ tsp thyme
3 to 4 Tbs dry Port wine
4 boneless and skinless chicken breast halves
2 egg whites
½ cup sour cream

The onions and mushrooms. Sauté the minced onions in a 10-inch no-stick frying pan with the butter for 6 to 8 minutes, until tender but not browned. Stir in the minced and squeezed mushrooms and continue sautéing for several minutes over moderately high heat until the mushroom pieces begin to separate from each other. Season nicely with salt, pepper, and the thyme, and pour in the Port wine. Boil several minutes to evaporate liquid.

Finishing the stuffing. Purée the chicken breasts in a food processor with the egg whites and sour cream; when smooth, scrape in the mushroom duxelles and pulse off-on 2 or 3 times just to blend. Taste carefully and correct seasoning.

ROASTING THE WHOLE BIRD

Bring to the table an ample, beautifully browned, fragrantly just-roasted chicken, and it's a party. There's just something special about a whole bird, even a small one. And since from 8-ounce squabs to 25-pound turkeys the technique is much the same, I shall group them together, starting with chickens.

WHOLE ROAST CHICKEN

From tiny poussins to hefty capons, all chickens roast in essentially the same way. The most common size is the 3- to 3½-pound fryer, but for a real treat look for a 5- to 6-pound roaster or a capon. Not all markets carry large roasting chickens, and sometimes those that do will stock roasters only on weekends. But these large chickens are worth looking out for (or ordering in advance) because you get more meat per pound, bigger servings, and the bird has reached a stage of maturity that gives you fine old-fashioned chicken flavor. In spite of its affluent look, however, a large chicken is a relatively economical party treat because a 5½-pound roaster, which costs only a dollar or so a pound, will feed 6 or even 8 people. But whether you have a real roaster or a 3½-pound fryer, here's how to truss it.

SPECIAL NOTE

To Stuff or Not to Stuff

A stuffed bird, particularly a small one, takes a little longer to roast than an unstuffed one. Stuffing does add some flavor to the meat, but you can achieve much the same effect by flavoring the cavity itself with salt, pepper, herbs, celery leaves and/or a handful of chopped carrots and onions previously sautéed in butter.

Although you may prepare any of the stuffings starting on page 184 in advance, do not stuff the bird itself until shortly before roasting because the stuffing could start to spoil in the cavity, and thus spoil the whole uncooked bird. For the same reason, remove to a separate container any stuffing left in the bird after serving.

To Truss a Chicken

To truss means to hold in place, and when you want a chicken to look its best, you truss it to keep the legs and wings close to the body. But trussing is not only for looks. It also makes for more even roasting. Untrussed drumsticks will stick up and dry out; untrussed legs can gape away from the body and even fall off.

Some of our roasting chickens come with a wire insert that holds drumstick ends to the vent but leaves the knees free to gape. Far better to truss your own. Besides a trussing needle, you'll want some white cotton string, the kind butchers use to tie up corned beef. Then go to it, following the directions here.

WASHING THE CHICKEN. *Please see Preparation for Cooking—and a Solemn Warning, on page 136.*

THE WELL-TRUSSED CHICKEN. *Its drumsticks rest nicely in place against the tip of the breastbone; the wing tips are folded back beneath the shoulders. All is made neat and chic for its roasting and its grand entrance. Proceed as described and illustrated on the next pages.*

To Truss a Chicken

The Wishbone. Remove the giblets and fat from inside the cavity, then wash and dry both chicken and giblets (I use hot water!). Now, to make for easier carving of the breast meat, cut out the wishbone from inside the neck cavity, as shown (see illustration, step 1). Thread your needle and begin trussing. (You'll note that in all the instructions for beasts and birds I speak of knees, armpits, elbows, etc., since I find it easier to understand the parts when one realizes they are built essentially just like us, with rib cages, backbones, necks, and so forth.)

First Thrust. Lift up the drumstick ends, then push the knees under the armpits at the shoulder end. While one hand holds the legs up, push the needle through the flesh under one knee and through carcass, step 2; draw the needle out under the opposite knee. (Leave a 5-inch length of string at your point of entry under the first knee.)

Turn the chicken breast down. Fold the wings akimbo, tucking the wing ends under the shoulders as shown here. Then, on the same side of the chicken where you came out from the second knee, poke the needle through the upper arm of the wing, catch the neck skin, if there, and pin it to the backbone, and come out through the second wing, step 3.

Tie #1. You now have two string ends on the same side of the chicken: the loose end you left behind when you first went under the first knee and the end where you come out at the wing. Turn the chicken on its back, pull the two ends tight, and tie, step 4.

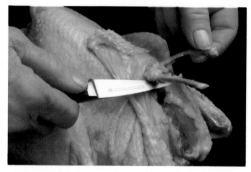
1. Removing the wishbone

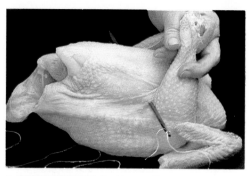
2. FIRST THRUST. Pushing needle through carcass under the knee

3. CONTINUATION. Going through wings

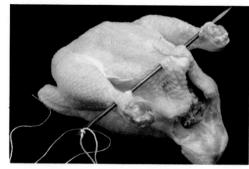
4. TIE #1

5. In goes the stuffing.

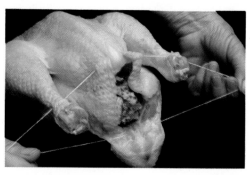
6. Going through drumstick ends and tip of breastbone

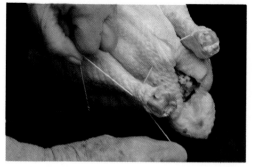
7. The string has gone through tailpiece.

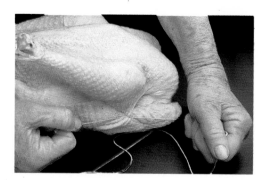
8. Final tie to close cavity

5. Leg-thighs in pan ready to roast

6. Trussing wings to breast

7. Mounding the breast on the stuffing

8. Breast ready for the oven

Ready to roast. Preheat the oven to 325°F. Surround the turkey stuffing with a double strip of oiled foil, step 8, at lower left.

Roasting the dis-assembled turkey. Roast the breast and the legs as you would a whole turkey (page 168), basting with oil, then accumulated juices, every 20 to 30 minutes; the last hour, surround the breast with a cup each of chopped carrots and onions to flavor the juices. The breast of this 14-pound turkey will take 1¾ to 2 hours to reach 165°F on your meat thermometer; the legs about 1¼ hours. See the box on page 168 for comments on timing.

Re-assembling and presentation. To present the bird, slide the turkey breast, on its bed of stuffing, onto the platter or carving board. Remove all skewers and strings, and arrange the legs in their rightful place, step 9.

Slicing the thigh. Simply pick up one of the legs, and start slicing the thigh (second joint) crosswise like a sausage, making medallions about ¼ inch thick, step 10. Slice the drumstick lengthwise, in the usual awkward way. (If the turkey people would remove those drumstick tendons—and they easily could—the drumstick would come into its own.)

Removing the wing. Protecting your fingers with a napkin, grab the wing by its elbow. Cut around it where it joins the shoulder; then, bending it forward to loosen it, cut through the ball joint at the shoulder to remove the wing, step 11.

Slicing the breast. Now start slicing the breast from the front end, gradually angling your knife parallel to the breastbone as you proceed, step 12.

9. Re-assembling and presentation

10. Carving the boned thigh

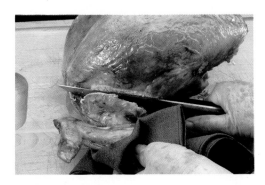

11. Removing a wing

12. Slicing the breast

1. Removing lobe of meat on other side of breastbone

2. Arranging lobes of meat on turkey skin

3. Spooning stuffing over the meat

4. Sewing up the bundle

Boned Stuffed and Roasted Turkey Breast

You don't need a whole bird if you're serving a small group, and our markets abound in fine turkey breasts. Most of the year they are frozen, so buy from a market with a fast turnover. It's always best to let the breast defrost quietly for 2 to 3 days in its original plastic, in the refrigerator. For a legless but whole turkey look, you slice the two massive raw lobes of breast off the bone, as described here, then nestle them back on the turkey skin and re-form the now boneless breast. Roast it to brown and beautiful, and it couldn't be easier to carve nor more delicious to eat.

For a 10-pound bone-in turkey breast, serving 10 to 12

A 10-pound bone-in turkey breast
½ cup or so melted butter
Salt and freshly ground pepper
2½ cups stuffing (recipes start on page 184)
½ cup each chopped carrots and onions
For the gravy: see the recipes starting on page 173

SPECIAL EQUIPMENT SUGGESTED: *A jelly-roll pan; a 24-inch square of washed cheesecloth; a trussing or darning needle and white cotton string*

Boning the turkey breast. Carefully pull and cut the skin off the breast, keeping it whole. Slicing down one side the length of the breastbone, remove the lobe of meat on that side of the carcass, then the other, as shown in step 1. Cut extra bits of turkey flesh from the carcass and skin; reserve them for your stuffing, and make a turkey stock out of the bones (see next page).

Assembling. Dip the piece of cheesecloth in the melted butter and spread it out on a baking pan. Paint melted butter over the turkey skin; spread it, outer side down, on the cheesecloth. Season the turkey lobes with salt and pepper, paint them with melted butter and arrange the meat smooth-side down on the turkey skin, step 2.

Stuffing goes on. Spoon ⅓ to ½ of the stuffing over the meat, step 3, then bring the cheesecloth up over to enclose it completely. Tie the 2 ends of the bundle securely, and cut off excess cheesecloth.

Sewing up the bundle. Sew the edges of cheesecloth together over the top of the bundle, step 4. Turn the turkey over, skin side up. Strew the chopped vegetables in the pan, and the turkey is ready to roast. (Spoon extra stuffing into a buttered casserole, set in a pan of boiling water, and bake with the turkey.) Preheat the oven to 325°F.

Roasting—about 2 hours at 325°F. Place the turkey in the lower middle level of the preheated oven, and roast to a meat-thermometer reading of 162°F to 165°F, basting occasionally with melted butter, then with the fat in the pan—the skin will brown nicely under the cheesecloth.

Onto the platter. When done, remove the turkey to a platter and let it rest 20 minutes. Meanwhile deglaze the roasting pan and complete the gravy. After its reconstituting rest, cut the cheesecloth at the lower part of one side and carefully pull it off the skin; turn the turkey over and remove the cloth from the other side. Finally turn the turkey right side up, and it is ready to serve.

Carving and serving. Starting at the large end, carve the meat into bias slices on one side, then on the other. Serve stuffing from the casserole until the stuffing in the turkey is revealed.

Turkey gravies

A good turkey gravy starts out with a good turkey stock. You may make a simple turkey stock by simmering the neck and trimmings in lightly salted water as described for the chicken stock on page 137, or produce the more elaborate version here, which is particularly recommended when you have a good amount of raw turkey bones and scraps.

 MASTER RECIPE

Brown Turkey Stock

Its agreeable dark color comes from browning the bones and vegetables before the simmering starts. The resulting amount of stock depends, of course, on the quantity of bones and scraps you have.

The neck, and any other raw turkey bones such as from the breast or the backbone
2 to 3 Tbs clear turkey-roasting fat, or fresh oil
½ to 1½ cups each chopped carrots and onions (depending on how many bones you have)
½ to 1 cup dry white French vermouth or dry white wine
2 to 4 cups liquid (water and/or chicken stock or broth)
1 or 2 celery stalks with tender leaves
Seasonings: salt, freshly ground pepper, 1 bay leaf, and thyme

Chop the bones into pieces of reasonable size and, in a large frying pan, brown them in hot fat or oil, adding the carrots and onions about halfway through. Transfer to a heavy saucepan, leaving the fat in the frying pan. Pour out the fat, and deglaze the frying pan with the wine (pour it in and bring to the boil, scraping up coagulated browning juices). Scrape the wine into the saucepan, adding enough liquid to cover the ingredients by an inch. Add the celery and simmer, skimming fat and scum off the surface, for 30 minutes. Salt and pepper lightly, adding the bay leaf and thyme. Simmer partially covered for 1½ hours; strain and degrease.

*Ahead-of-time note: Refrigerate uncovered; cover when chilled, will keep several days; may be frozen.

> *SPECIAL NOTE*
>
> ## Gravy Basics
>
> The gravy base is made while the turkey is roasting. After the turkey has been removed to its platter, the fat is skimmed off the vegetables and juices in the roasting pan and the pan is deglazed—meaning you pour in a cup or so of wine or stock and simmer briefly as you scrape the pan with a wooden spoon to gather into the liquid all the coagulated roasting bits. Pour this flavorful brown liquid mixture into a saucepan and simmer for several minutes, skimming off fat, and finally you pour it through a sieve set over your gravy base, pressing the juices out of the roasting vegetables. Now finish the gravy as directed in the recipe.

Old-Fashioned Brown Gravy

For 2½ to 3 cups, giving 3 to 4 tablespoons of gravy to each of 12 to 14 people

3 Tbs clear turkey roasting fat, skimmed from the pan
¼ cup flour
3 cups hot turkey stock (see recipe preceding)
1 cup dry white French vermouth or dry white wine (or more stock), for deglazing the roasting pan
The degreased turkey-roasting juices
Salt and freshly ground pepper
2 to 3 Tbs butter, optional

SPECIAL EQUIPMENT SUGGESTED:
A wooden spoon and a wire whisk; a heavy-bottomed 2½-quart saucepan; a sieve set over a smaller saucepan

The gravy base. Make a brown roux by blending the turkey fat and flour in the saucepan with the wooden spoon; stir slowly over moderate heat for several minutes while the roux colors a walnut brown. Remove from heat, stirring for a moment until the bubbling stops. Vigorously whisk in the hot turkey stock; simmer, stirring occasionally, for 10 minutes.

*Ahead-of-time note: May be prepared well in advance and refrigerated.

Completing the gravy. Deglaze the roasting pan with the wine, and degrease it as described in the Special Note; pour the liquid into the gravy base and simmer several minutes, skimming off any surface fat, while the sauce reduces and concentrates in flavor. Carefully correct seasoning. Just before serving, if you wish, whisk in the butter by tablespoons.

VARIATIONS

Cream Gravy

Complete the gravy as described, but omit the optional butter at the end. Instead, whisk in ½ cup or so of heavy cream, and simmer to reduce and re-thicken the sauce.

Giblet Gravy

Simmer the turkey gizzard in a little turkey stock until tender—about 40 minutes, adding the heart to simmer 10 minutes, and the liver to simmer 5 minutes. Peel the gizzard, mince it along with the heart and liver, and sauté for a moment in a tablespoon of butter. Reserve them in their cooking stock, and add to the turkey gravy base along with the deglazing liquid.

Port Wine Gravy
A faster, starch-thickened gravy

Thickening with cornstarch rather than the flour-butter roux makes for a quick and fat-free gravy, but a less stable one—in other words, the sauce may thin out on occasion, but you can always thicken it again with more cornstarch. Deglaze the degreased roasting pan with 3 cups of turkey stock. Blend 3 tablespoons of cornstarch in a bowl with 3 tablespoons of Port wine. After simmering, skimming, and straining the stock, whisk dribbles of it into the cornstarch. Return the cornstarch mixture to the pan and simmer 3 minutes. Correct seasoning.

WHOLE ROAST GOOSE

There's nothing quite like goose, with its crisp brown skin and its wonderfully flavored all-dark meat. It's grand on a platter, and when you perform a little trick surgery on the joints before roasting, it's amazingly easy to carve.

Goose is not a tender bird like chicken: it has a certain texture and chewiness, and its own special flavor. And goose has a fat problem. The best way to deal with that, in my experience, is to steam it first for about an hour on top of the stove. This renders out a great deal of fat. Then you braise it in a covered roaster with aromatic flavorings for an hour or so more, which renders out more fat. Finally you uncover it to let the skin brown and crisp. This system renders out the most fat and gives the most succulent flesh of any cooking technique I've tried, and it also works well with duck, as described on page 176.

Steam-Roasted Goose

For 8 to 10 servings

Cooking time: 2¼ to 3 hours

A 9½- to 11-pound young roasting goose
Juice of 1 lemon
Salt
Stuffing, optional—see notes in recipe
The neck, wing ends, heart, and gizzard
1 each: large carrot, onion, and celery stalk, roughly chopped
2 to 3 cups of red wine, white wine, or water
½ cup of Port wine blended with 1½ Tbs cornstarch

SPECIAL EQUIPMENT SUGGESTED: *A deep roasting pan just large enough to hold the goose comfortably; a rack and a tight-fitting cover for the roaster*

Preparing the goose for cooking.

Surgery. Pull all loose fat out from the cavity at the rear of the goose. Chop off the wings at just below the elbow. To make carving much easier, cut out the wishbone from inside the neck of the goose, as illustrated for chicken (page 162). For even easier carving, you can loosen the wings and legs as follows.

For the wings, wiggle the upper arm of a wing to locate where it is attached inside (at the shoulder end), just below the outside edge of the shoulder blade (this will take some poking about); cut through the ball joint from inside the neck cavity, and you will feel that the wing is free.

Steam-Roasted Goose

For the legs, from outside, at the small of the back, locate (by wiggling it) where the second joint joins the back; thrust the point of your knife into the joints on each side to cut the tendons and loosen the thighs. Then sew or skewer the skin slits closed.

Seasoning. Rub the goose inside and out with lemon juice; lightly salt the inside of the cavity.

Trussing. Push a long skewer through the carcass at the shoulder end, to secure the wings. Run another through at the hips to secure the legs. Tie the drumstick ends in place against the tailpiece. To help in rendering out fat, prick the skin with a sharp-pointed skewer or darning needle in numerous places (but not so deep as to reach the flesh) around the lower breast and thighs.

*Ahead-of-time note: The goose may be prepared to this point a day in advance; cover and refrigerate.

Preliminary cooking—steaming (¾ to 1 hour). Place the goose, breast up, on the rack in the roasting pan. Add an inch or two of water; bring to the boil on top of the stove, and cover the pan tightly. Reduce heat and steam for ¾ to 1 hour, depending on the size of the goose. Check on the water level occasionally, adding a little more if it has boiled off.

Stuffing options. Stuffing is not necessary; simply season the cavity with salt and pepper and a sprinkling of thyme or sage. Or use an aromatic flavoring: a chopped carrot and onion sautéed until tender in goose fat or butter; stuff that into the cavity along with a small handful of chopped celery leaves and a sprinkling of thyme or sage. Or pick one of the stuffings beginning on page 184—the prune and liver pâté (page 185) is especially recommended.

Goose stock. Chop up the neck and wing ends. Simmer 2 hours in lightly salted water to cover, with the heart and gizzard. Strain, degrease, and refrigerate. You should have about 2 cups.

Final cooking—braising—1½ to 2 hours at 325°F. Remove the steamed goose from the roaster and let it cool 20 minutes or so. Pour the liquid out of the roaster (you will have several cups of pure goose fat, which will rise to the surface: save the fat for sautéing potatoes or other uses; use the liquid in stocks or soups). Remove the hip skewer and insert whatever flavoring or stuffing you have chosen; replace the skewer. Place a double sheet of foil over the rack and lay in the goose, breast down. Strew the chopped vegetables in the pan around the goose and pour in a cup or so of wine or goose-steaming liquid—renew during cooking, as needed. Cover tightly and braise 1 to 1½ hours, depending on the size of your bird; check occasionally to see all is well, and baste with accumulated juices.

When is it done? The steaming is done when the legs feel almost tender if pressed.

Browning—about 30 minutes. Turn the goose breast-up, and baste it with the juices in the pan. If the bird is already brown, set the cover slightly askew. If it needs browning, remove the cover.

(*continued*)

Steam-Roasted Goose (*continued*)

When is it done? Continue roasting another ½ hour or more, basting once or twice, until the drumsticks feel quite tender when pressed.

Remove the goose to a carving board or platter and set it in the turned-off oven, leaving the door ajar.

Gravy. Degrease the roasting pan; pour in the goose stock and Port-cornstarch mixture. Simmer a moment, scraping up any coagulated roasting juices. Strain into a saucepan, pressing juices out of the vegetables that cooked with the goose.

Carving the goose

Simmer several minutes, skimming fat off the surface. Carefully correct seasoning. Pour into a hot gravy boat.

Carving and serving. Remove the leg on the side nearest you—it will come off quite easily if you've disjointed it. Remove the wings, and save for second helpings. Then, cutting down your side of the length of the breastbone, remove the whole breast-half in one piece (see illustration). Cut it on the slant, like a sausage, to make nice medallions about ¼ inch thick.

Repeat on the other side. Slice the drumsticks and second joints lengthwise, in the usual manner. Give each customer a selection of each, and moisten the meat with a big spoonful of gravy.

WHOLE ROAST DUCK

Steam-roasting solves the three-fold problem we supermarket shoppers have in cooking our 4½- to 5½-pound ducks: all that fat under the skin, tough leg-thighs, but tender breast. Roasting the regular way can't give you perfect breast meat and tender legs plus crisp skin, but with the steam-roast you can have all three. The other solutions are to separate the duck, as described starting on the next page; this works beautifully, but it's labor-intensive. Steam-roasting is a relatively simple procedure, and it gives savory results. Except for timing, it's the same method as for steam-roasting a goose, and here are the brief details.

Steam-Roasted Duck

For 4 servings

A 5-pound duckling
1 lemon
Salt
Sage or thyme, optional
½ cup each: chopped onion, carrot, and celery
1½ cups red wine, white wine, or water

SPECIAL EQUIPMENT SUGGESTED: *A covered roaster or casserole with rack, just large enough to hold the duck comfortably; a shallow roasting pan with rack for final cooking*

Preparing the duck for roasting. Pull all loose fat out of the cavity of the duck, remove the wishbone for easier carving of the breast, and, for even easier carving, cut through the ball joints of the wings and thighs (as described for the goose, page 174). Chop off the wings at the elbows; save them, as well as the neck and giblets, for duck stock. Wipe the duck dry, and rub all over the outside and inside the cavity with cut lemon. Salt the inside of the cavity lightly and add, if you wish, a sprinkling of thyme or sage.

Preliminary steaming—30 minutes. Place the duck breast up on the rack in the casserole, add 1 inch of water, and bring to the boil on top of the stove. Cover the casserole tightly, reduce heat, and let it steam 30 minutes.

Braising—30 minutes at 325°F. Remove the steamed duck from the casserole, pour out the liquid (which you can degrease and use for your duck stock), and drain the duck. Place a double thickness of foil over the rack, and return the duck, breast down. Strew the vegetables around, and pour in the wine or water. Bring to the simmer on top of the stove, cover the casserole, and braise in the preheated oven for 30 minutes.

Final roasting—30 to 40 minutes at 375°F. Remove the duck to the rack in the shallow roasting pan. Roast uncovered to brown and crisp the skin—the duck is done when the legs feel reasonably tender.

Sauce. Meanwhile skim the fat off the cooking liquid in the covered casserole, and simmer the liquid, mashing in the vegetables. Then boil it down until it is almost syrupy. Strain, pressing the juices out of the vegetables—you will have just enough delicious liquid to moisten each serving.

Prune and Apple Garnish

A faintly sweet-and-sour yet meaty fruit garnish goes nicely indeed with roast duck, goose, or a suckling pig, and makes an attractive picture when you surround roasted apple quarters with a heap of spiced prunes.

For 10 to 12 servings

The prunes
A 2-pound package of pitted "tenderized" prunes
¾ cup dry white wine or French vermouth
1 cup beef, chicken, or duck broth
3 Tbs butter, optional
Seasonings: ½ tsp sage or thyme, a big pinch of allspice, salt and freshly ground pepper

The apples
8 to 10 Golden Delicious or Granny Smith apples
4 to 6 Tbs melted butter
Seasonings: ⅓ cup sugar, ½ tsp allspice, and ⅛ tsp salt, blended in a bowl

SPECIAL EQUIPMENT SUGGESTED:
A 2½-quart saucepan with cover, for the prunes; 2 buttered jelly-roll pans, no-stick recommended, for the apples

The prunes. Simmer the prunes in the covered pan with the wine or vermouth, broth, optional butter, and seasonings. When the prunes are tender but still hold their shape, uncover and boil to evaporate most of the liquid.

The roasted apples. Quarter, core, and peel the apples; arrange them in one layer on the jelly-roll pans. Brush with the melted butter and sprinkle with the seasonings. Bake about 20 minutes in the middle level of a preheated 400°F oven, until tender—they may puff up, but will sink down as they cool.

Serving. Arrange the prunes and apples attractively together on a platter or around the roast. Serve warm or cold.

Cranberry Chutney

You can make chutney out of almost anything, it seems—mangoes, peaches, apricots—and it all has a kindred sweet-and-sour taste whatever the ingredients. (See also the Cranberry Relish, page 165.)

For about 1 quart

1 cup sliced onions
1 cup water
¾ cup dark brown sugar
½ cup granulated sugar
¾ cup cider vinegar
2 Granny Smith apples, peeled, seeded, and diced
Seasonings: ½ tsp salt, 1 tsp grated fresh ginger, ½ tsp each mace and curry powder
The grated zest of 2 oranges
1 quart cranberries, picked over and washed
½ cup currants (small black raisins)
The strained juice of the 2 oranges

Simmer the onions for 30 minutes with the water and sugars. Stir in the vinegar, apples, seasonings, and orange zest. Boil slowly 30 minutes longer, then stir in the cranberries, currants, and orange juice. Boil slowly about 10 minutes, or until the cranberries burst. Correct seasoning, adding a little more sugar if too sour—but it is a relish, and should not be too sweet.

SPECIAL DUCK RECIPES

Only a very young duckling can be successfully roasted whole, a bird so juvenile and tender it has not developed its leg muscles by swimming about. That's not the kind we the public see in our markets. We find the more mature, 4½- to 5-pound ducklings. They are still young, but when we roast them as is and want rosy breast meat we get tough legs; if we want tender legs and a crisp skin, we must settle for an overdone breast. One solution for whole roast duck is the preceding steam-roast system. Another is the separated duck described here, in which the breast cooks one way, the legs another, and the skin is turned into crisp cracklings. Admittedly, this makes far more work for the cook, but it is time well spent indeed for anyone who adores duck dinners.

Number of servings per duck. A 4½- to 5½-pound duck is too much for two people, usually too little for four, and does not always divide up conveniently for three. In many instances you'll want one duck for two, and count on delicious leftovers for a cold lunch the next day.

Designer Duck
Roasted whole, separated, the legs crumbed

If you had a duck press, this would most resemble the classic treatment. The duck is roasted whole just until the breast meat is rare and firm enough for slicing and warming in Port wine and shallots. The legs,

which need more cooking, are removed and finished off in the oven with a mustard and crumb coating, while the skin is turned into savory brown cracklings. This is a dish sure to turn any neophyte into a lifelong duck buff.

For 4 to 6 servings

Two 4½- to 5½-pound roaster ducklings
Salt
Thyme or sage
2 imported bay leaves
1 Tbs cooking oil
Freshly ground pepper and allspice, for cracklings

Final seasoning of breast slices

1 Tbs minced shallot or scallion
Salt and freshly ground pepper
¼ to ⅓ cup Port or Madeira wine
⅔ cup strong brown duck stock (adapt Turkey Stock, page 173)

For crumbing the legs

½ cup Dijon-type prepared mustard
1 cup lightly pressed down fresh crumbs from homemade type bread with body
2 Tbs duck-roasting fat or butter

SPECIAL EQUIPMENT SUGGESTED: *A cleaver; 2 roasting pans, one large enough for 2 ducks, and one to hold the crumbed legs; a 12-inch no-stick or enameled frying pan, for breast slices*

Preparing the ducks. Chop the duck wings off at the elbows and reserve for the duck stock; remove the wishbone from inside the neck cavity. Inside each cavity sprinkle a big pinch of salt, a pinch of thyme or sage, and tuck in a bay leaf. Prick the skin all over on the back and sides where you see yellow fat showing through—use a skewer or sharp-pronged fork but

do not go down into the flesh or juices will seep out and stain the skin during roasting. Truss the ducks (adapt the needle-and-string system for chicken on page 162).

Preliminary roasting—30 to 35 minutes at 350°F. Lightly oil the ducks, place breast-up in the pan and roast in the middle level of the oven until the breast meat is just springy rather than squashy to the touch—meaning the meat is rosy and will be easy to carve; the legs and thighs (which will cook more later) are still firm and very rare.

Skinning the ducks; leg and wing removal. While the ducks are still warm, peel off the skin as follows: First cut a slit down the length of the breast, then peel it down the sides of the breast and the thighs. Remove the leg-thigh sections along with the oysters of meat lodged at the small of the

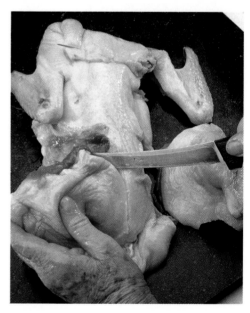

1. Removing duck leg-thigh section

back and at the side of the tailpiece (see illustration, step 1). Remove the wings also, being careful to disturb the breast meat as little as possible; wings have little meat, and could be roasted with the legs, or saved for duck stock. Peel off any remaining skin from the legs and back, and all visible fat.

Preparing the breast meat. Film the frying pan with duck fat or butter; sprinkle in half the minced shallot or scallion. Remove the breast meat on each side in one piece, and carve on a slant into neat thin slices, step 2; arrange them slightly overlapping in the pan. Season lightly with salt and pepper, and sprinkle with the remaining shallot or scallion. Pour in the Port or Madeira and the duck stock. Cover and set aside.

2. Carving breast meat

Crumbing the leg-thighs. Cut through the knee joints to separate legs from thighs. Paint both with a thin coating of mustard, roll them in the bread crumbs, step 3, and arrange them in a baking dish. Sprinkle lightly with duck fat or melted butter, and set aside.

3. Crumbing legs and wings

Ahead-of-time note: All of the foregoing may be completed several hours in advance.

Finishing the ducks.

Roasting the legs—25 minutes at 400°F. Half an hour before you plan to serve, set the crumbed legs and thighs in the upper third level of the oven. Roast until just tender when pressed. Keep them warm in the turned-off oven, its door ajar.

Designer Duck: lower left—cracklings; middle—rosy slices of breast meat; upper right—roasted legs and wings

The breast slices. Just before serving, bring the frying pan with the duck-breast slices almost to the simmer, to poach the meat but keep it rare and rosy. Arrange the slices on a hot platter and rapidly boil down the cooking juices until syrupy while you arrange the legs and skin cracklings on the platter. Pour the pan juices over the breast meat and serve at once.

Suggested accompaniments to roast duck: Sautéed potatoes, or the sliced potato galettes on page 324, and the angel-hair julienne of carrots and turnips on page 294 would complement the duck nicely, as would a fine red Burgundy or pinot noir.

Turning Duck Skin into Cracklings

Cut the duck skin and fat into strips ¼ inch wide. Arrange them in a baking dish and set in a 350°F oven, tossing occasionally, for about 30 minutes. The cracklings should be nicely browned, and their rendered fat a clear yellow. Drain the cracklings on a dish lined with paper towels, and toss with a sprinkling of salt, pepper, and allspice. Reheat briefly in the oven before serving.

Ahead-of-time note: They keep several days, covered, in the refrigerator and may be reheated. You may wish to chop them for sprinkling on salads, over scrambled eggs, etc.

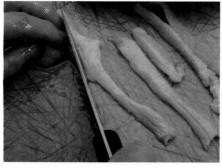

Cutting skin into strips for cracklings

Rendered Duck Fat

Strain the clear yellow fat from the cracklings into a jar, where it will keep for weeks in the refrigerator— save for such operations as sautéing potatoes, basting roast poultry, or for the confit in the following variation recipe.

VARIATIONS

You can vary the general theme of the preceding recipe in a number of ways, of which here are a few ideas. Since these make chic little main courses for four, you may decide that your two ducks will do for two meals: the breasts one evening, and the legs another day.

A DIFFERENT BREAST

Duck Breasts Sautéed: Magrets de Canard

Rather than roasting and slicing the breast meat, you can remove it as a boneless and skinless morsel, and sauté it. If you have traveled in France the last few years, you will have found *magret* in even quite modest restaurants, since now anyone can buy packaged breasts from foie-gras ducks in the *super-marchés*— they are almost always large and rather tough. The smaller and tenderer breasts from roaster ducklings are far superior, and make a beautiful main course for four.

For 4 servings

4 skinless and boneless duck breasts
**Seasonings: salt, freshly ground
    pepper, and allspice**
**2 to 3 Tbs duck fat or clarified butter
    (page 139)**
**Several spoonfuls of sauce (see
    Special Note, page 182)**
½ Tbs chopped green peppercorns

Preparing the duck breasts. Cut close against the length of the breastbone on each side of the duck, and remove the breast-wings. Cut off the wing, and scrape the breast meat from the skin. Flatten each breast slightly by pounding briefly between sheets of wax paper with a rubber hammer or pestle. Dust the meat with salt, pepper, and allspice, rub with a little duck fat or butter; wrap and refrigerate until you are almost ready to serve.

Sautéing and serving. Heat the duck fat or butter in a 10-inch pan until very hot but not browning. Sauté the duck breasts a minute or two on each side, only until the meat is lightly springy when pressed, in contrast to its squashy raw state. Pour in the sauce, and bring just to the simmer. Arrange the breasts on hot plates, give the sauce a quick boil with the chopped green peppercorns, and spoon it over the duck breasts.

Suggested accompaniments to sautéed duck breasts. Any of the accompaniments suggested in this section, including fresh green peas, your own home-made beautifully buttered mashed potatoes, and a fine red Bordeaux or cabernet.

VARIATIONS ON THE LEG-THIGH THEME

The Confit

Rather than roasting the leg-thighs, simmer them in duck fat—this is in fact an old-world method for goose and duck that is easy, delicious, and renders out excess fat while crisping the skin. (If you have made duck cracklings, or if you have steam-roasted a duck or a goose, you may have plenty of fine clear fat for a confit.)

Season 4 duck leg-thighs with salt, pepper, and allspice, cover, and let steep for an hour or more. Heat in a saucepan with duck fat and/or fresh oil to cover by ½ inch, and maintain the fat temperature at 275°F to 300°F for 30 to 40 minutes, until the meat is tender when pressed—the skin should color slowly and evenly but the fat should never turn more than a deep yellow. Drain on paper towels and keep warm until serving time.

Steam-Roasted Leg-Thighs

In this method the leg-thighs are steamed ½ hour to melt out most of the excess fat, then roasted until the flesh is tender and the skin crisp. Follow the recipe for steam-roasted whole duck, and since this also manufactures its own sauce, adjust the master recipe accordingly.

Ragout with a Fondue of Onions

After steaming the leg-thighs as in the preceding recipe, brown them in a frying pan. Then add 4 cups of sliced onions, cover the pan, and cook slowly for 20 to 30 minutes, until tender. Deglaze with dry white French vermouth and duck stock, seasoning with a few drops of red wine vinegar and Port wine. Tender and tasty, and especially recommended when you are serving legs only but want something informal to go with beans or rice. An attractive salad to go with this would be the hearts of curly endive with garlic dressing and a sprinkling of duck cracklings described on page 180.

Crisp Parcels of Duck

Crisp Parcels of Duck

In this ingenious roasting system the leg-thighs and wing-breasts are partially boned, skewered, and slow-roasted to render out fat before being crisped under the broiler.

For 4 servings

A 4½- to 5-pound roaster duckling
Seasonings: salt, freshly ground
   pepper, thyme, and allspice
1 each medium onion and carrot,
   roughly chopped
1 cup duck stock
⅓ cup Port or Madeira wine

SPECIAL EQUIPMENT SUGGESTED:
A stout boning knife; small steel skewers (aluminum skewers are no good: they bend); white cotton string; a roasting pan that will hold the duck easily, and a shallow pan for broiling

Boning the duck. Slit the duck skin down the back from neck to tail. From inside the neck cavity remove the wishbone. Disjoint the leg-thighs

from the carcass; keeping the leg-thighs attached, remove the thigh bones. Cut along the length of the breastbone on each side; disjoint the wing from the shoulder as you remove the breast meat from the carcass.

1. Scraping fat off duck skin

Removing excess fat. You want the skin to remain whole so you can form the packets in the next step. Leaving the flesh attached to the drumsticks, pull and scrape it up from its skin, step 1. Do the same for the breast meat, freeing it from its skin but leaving it attached to the wing. Scrape excess fat from inside the skin, particularly around the thighs and knees.

2. Skewering the parcels

Seasoning and trussing. Season the duck flesh with a sprinkling of salt, pepper, thyme, and allspice. Leaving the leg and wing bones free, bring the skin around to enclose the flesh, step 2. Skewer and tie in place to make a neat parcel of each.

Crisp Parcels of Duck (*continued*)

Slow roasting—about 1¾ hours at 275°F. Arrange the duck parcels skewered side up in a roasting pan and surround with the chopped vegetables. Roast in the upper middle level, basting several times with accumulated fat. Occasionally remove excess fat from the pan with a bulb baster. After 1¼ hours, remove the breast-wing pieces, and continue with the leg-thighs for another 30 minutes, or until tender when pressed. Arrange the duck pieces skewered side up in a shallow pan, remove trussing paraphernalia, and set the duck aside.

The sauce. Strain the roasting liquid into a saucepan, pressing juices out of the vegetables. Degrease thoroughly, then add the duck stock and wine; boil down until well reduced and full of flavor.

*Ahead-of-time note: May be completed somewhat ahead; set duck aside at room temperature.

Finishing the duck. Just before serving, brown and crisp both sides of the duck briefly under the broiler. Arrange the pieces best side up on a hot platter; cover and keep warm while you skim fat out of the roasting pan and pour in the sauce. Boil it rapidly, scraping up and mixing in coagulated juices as the sauce reduces and thickens slightly. Pour it into a hot sauce bowl, and serve.

Suggested accompaniments: fresh asparagus tips or broccoli florets and potatoes scalloped in cream (page 323) go beautifully with roast duck or the crisp parcels of duck, as would a robust zinfandel.

VARIATION

Duck-Leg Mousse
Cuisses de Caneton en Côtelettes

The final leg-thigh solution sounds more elegant in French, or you could be utterly non-elitist and call them duckburgers.

Bone out the leg-thighs and purée the meat in a food processor with 1 cup of cooked sliced onions and dollops of cream—the purée should just hold its shape in a spoon. Season with salt, pepper, allspice, and thyme. Form into pear-shaped patties about ⅝ inch thick, dredge in flour, and sauté 4 to 5 minutes each side in rendered duck fat or clarified butter. Serve with a deglazing sauce made from the pan juices—a little finely minced chutney goes nicely in the sauce here.

Suggested accompaniments: golden purée (carrots and potatoes, page 285) or one of the scalloped potato dishes starting on page 322, buttered fresh green beans, and a mellow red wine, such as a merlot.

SPECIAL NOTE

A Little Sauce for Duck
Sauce Ragout

Chop up the gizzard and carcass of a boned duck and brown in a frying pan with a little rendered duck fat or oil, adding a sliced carrot and onion.

Transfer with a slotted spoon to a saucepan, toss with 1½ tablespoons of flour, and brown lightly over moderately high heat, tossing frequently for 2 to 3 minutes. Remove from heat. Pour cooking fat out of the frying pan in which you browned the duck carcass, pour in 1 cup of chicken stock, and simmer, scraping the brown residue into the liquid; stir the liquid into the saucepan, blending smoothly with the browned flour. Add ½ cup of dry white French vermouth, a small crushed clove of unpeeled garlic, a small chopped unpeeled tomato, and water to cover ingredients by ½ inch.

Bring to the simmer, skimming off gray scum that will continue to rise for a few minutes; cover loosely and simmer 1½ hours. Strain, pressing juices out of ingredients, degrease, and correct seasoning.

You should have about 1 cup of fine, strong, lightly thickened sauce. When cool, cover and refrigerate; lift any congealed fat from the surface of the sauce before serving.

FRESH FOIE GRAS

Sautéed Scallops of Fresh Duck Foie Gras
With hearts of curly endive and cracklings

Fresh duck foie gras, those very special pale large duck livers so famous in Europe, are now available in this country—at a hefty price, as is the case with this great delicacy, wherever you buy it (see illustration). The following recipe makes a small but most elegant first course, which you could serve with a glass of Port wine, or a fine Sauternes, or an excellent merlot or pinot noir.

WHERE TO BUY FOIE GRAS. *If your specialty market, great restaurant, or the poultry section of the yellow pages cannot help you, here is one producer that supplies most of the country at this writing:*
Commonwealth Enterprises,Ltd.
P.O. Box 49, Mongaup Valley, NY 12762
Telephone: (914) 583-6630

A BOOK ON FOIE GRAS. *The only English-language book I know of on Foie Gras, and a fully authoritative treatise it is, is written by an expert from that region, and I highly recommend it now that we have our own production:* Foie Gras, Magret, and Other Good Food from Gascony, *by André Daguin and Anne de Ravel (New York: Random House, 1988).*

Fresh American duck foie gras

For 12 servings, 2 sautéed slices per person

1 whole fresh "Number 1 quality" fresh duck foie gras (1¼ to 1½ pounds)
Seasonings: 1 tsp salt, ⅛ tsp freshly ground white pepper, and a medium pinch of allspice, blended in a bowl
Droplets of Port wine
Triangles of toasted white sandwich bread, 2 per person
The tender leaves near the heart of curly endive, tossed just before serving in light olive oil, salt, pepper, and droplets of raspberry vinegar—a handful per person
1 cup duck cracklings (page 180), optional
Rendered duck fat (page 180) or clarified butter

SPECIAL EQUIPMENT SUGGESTED: *1 or 2 cast-iron or heavy cast-aluminum frying pans for sautéing the foie gras*

Preparing the foie gras. Soak the foie gras in a bowl of lightly salted water for ½ hour or so, until it has softened enough so that you can gently pull the 2 lobes apart. Carefully pull out the bits of fat and red veins lodged between the lobes. (It is difficult to get all the veins out; do not worry because they hardly show when the liver is sautéed.) Chill the liver for ease in slicing, next step.

Slicing the liver. With a sharp knife, dipped in boiling water for each slice, cut the chilled liver into 24 fairly even slices about 1 by 2 inches and ¼ inch thick. Lay them on an oiled baking sheet. Dust lightly with the seasonings and droplets of Port wine on one side; turn (dry your fingers!) and season the other side. Cover and chill at least 20 minutes, or until cooking time. (The liver is chilled so a minimum of fat will exude during cooking.)

Sautéing the foie gras—2 to 3 minutes. Your guests are at the table. Have your plates warm but not hot, your toast in place upon them, and your salad dressed and sprinkled with the optional cracklings. Film the frying pan or pans with a ¹⁄₁₆-inch layer of duck fat or clarified butter and heat to very hot but not burning. Rapidly sauté the foie gras slices less than a minute on each side, just to brown them around the edges. Arrange them as done at the edge of the salads, and serve with all possible speed.

STUFFINGS FOR POULTRY AND VEGETABLES

Most of the stuffings here may be used for vegetables as well as poultry, and for goose and duck as well as turkey and chicken.

ESPECIALLY FOR TURKEY AND ROASTING CHICKENS

Cornbread, Sage, and Sausage Stuffing

For 2 to 2½ quarts, enough for a 14- to 16-pound turkey

1 pound sausage meat
2 cups chopped onions
1½ cups chopped celery stalks
5 cups crumbled yellow cornbread (a box-label recipe is fine here or see page 344)
1 cup lightly packed crumbs from fresh homemade type white bread
2 eggs, lightly beaten
Salt and freshly ground pepper
1 Tbs sage, or to taste
4 ounces (1 stick) melted butter

Break up the sausage meat and sauté in a frying pan for several minutes, until the color changes from reddish to gray. Scrape into a large mixing bowl, leaving the fat in the frying pan. In it sauté the onions until tender—5 to 6 minutes; add the celery and sauté 2 minutes more. Blend the onions and celery with the sausage meat, adding the crumbled cornbread, white crumbs, and eggs. Season nicely to taste, and fold in the melted butter.

Savory Sausage and Crouton Stuffing

For about 2½ quarts, enough for a 12- to 14-pound turkey

2 quarts diced homemade type white bread
1 pound sausage meat
4 or more Tbs butter, as needed
3 cups diced onions
3 cups diced celery
2 eggs, lightly beaten
Seasonings: salt, freshly ground pepper, and sage

To make croutons, spread the bread cubes in a large baking pan and toast 20 to 30 minutes in a 350°F oven, tossing occasionally, until lightly browned. Meanwhile, break up the sausage meat and sauté several minutes in a frying pan, until the color changes from reddish to gray. Drain, return the fat to the pan, and turn the sausage into a large mixing bowl, breaking it up again into small bits. Add enough butter to the frying pan to make about ½ cup combined with the sausage fat. In it sauté the onions until tender and translucent, then add the celery and sauté 2 to 3 minutes more. Turn into the bowl, blend in the eggs, and toss in the croutons. Season carefully to taste.

VARIATION

When stuffing a turkey or chicken with either of the two preceding formulae, purée any raw scraps of the meat in a food processor or blender with the 2 eggs listed, and fold into the bowl with the rest of the ingredients. The raw meat lightly binds the stuffing together.

Mushroom Duxelles Stuffing

Minced mushrooms with onions, chicken breasts, and sour cream. The recipe is in the Special Note on page 160, where it is suggested for boned turkey, and would do well also for chicken, or veal, and for stuffed onions.

Ham and Bread Crumb Stuffing

To be braised in a whole cabbage or cabbage leaves.

For about 4 cups

1 medium onion, roughly chopped
A 1½-inch cube of Swiss or Cheddar cheese, roughly diced
2 cups or so scraps or pieces of ham, trimmed of fat
2 eggs
1 large clove of garlic, puréed
1½ cups crumbs from fresh homemade type white bread
Seasonings: salt, freshly ground pepper, and thyme or sage

Drop the onion into the food processor and chop into ¼-inch pieces with several on-off pulses. Add the cheese and the ham to the onion, and chop them with 5 or 6 pulses; pulse in the eggs and garlic, then the crumbs. Season nicely to taste.

Rice and Giblet Stuffing

For about 8 cups

4 cups diced onions
1 turkey or chicken gizzard, peeled and chopped
4 Tbs butter
3 cups diced celery
1 turkey heart or 2 chicken hearts, minced
1 whole turkey liver or 2 chicken livers
5 cups cooked rice
2 eggs
1½ cups chopped fresh parsley
Seasonings: salt, freshly ground pepper, and sage

Cook the onions and gizzard in the butter 10 minutes, or until the onions are tender. Stir in the celery, minced heart(s) and whole liver(s). Sauté, tossing, for 2 to 3 minutes, until the liver feels lightly springy. Remove the liver, chop it, and toss it in a bowl with the other sautéed ingredients. Blend in the rice, eggs, and parsley; season carefully to taste.

ESPECIALLY FOR GOOSE

Prune and Apple Stuffing with Sausage

For about 12 cups, enough for a 10- to 12-pound goose

1 pound sausage meat
4 cups chopped onions
A little butter—if needed for onion sauté
3 cups chopped celery
2 Granny Smith apples, peeled, cored, and chopped
3 cups pitted "tenderized" prunes
½ cup dry white French vermouth
3 cups toasted crumbs from homemade type white bread
3 eggs, lightly beaten
Seasonings: salt, freshly ground pepper, and about 1 tsp ground sage

Preliminary sauté. Break up the sausage meat and brown lightly in the frying pan, continuing to break it up as it cooks. Remove with a slotted spoon to a large mixing bowl. Sauté the onions in the sausage fat, adding butter if needed, and when tender fold in the celery; sauté slowly 4 minutes, folding, then turn in the apples and sauté 4 minutes more. Turn into the mixing bowl.

The prunes. While the onions, etc., are cooking, quarter the prunes, and simmer slowly in a saucepan with the vermouth, tossing and turning frequently until the liquid is absorbed— about 5 minutes. Add to the mixing bowl.

Finishing the stuffing. Fold the crumbs and eggs into the stuffing, turning

and tossing to blend. Taste very carefully, adding salt, pepper, and sage, to make a perfectly seasoned dressing.

*Ahead-of-time note: If you are making the dressing ahead, the apples and crumbs won't stand up: omit them until later. Just before stuffing, sauté the apples in a little butter, and add them to the stuffing along with the toasted crumbs.

Prune and Liver Pâté Stuffing, to Accompany Goose or Duck

Enough to accompany a 10-pound goose

The goose or duck liver, finely minced
2 Tbs minced shallots
2 Tbs goose or duck fat, or butter
½ cup Port wine
4 ounces (½ cup) canned foie gras or best-quality liver pâté
¼ cup fine crumbs from fresh homemade type white bread
Seasonings: about a pinch each of allspice, thyme, salt, and freshly ground pepper
50 large pitted "tenderized" prunes

Sauté the liver and shallots in fat or butter for 1 minute. Scrape into a mixing bowl. Pour the wine into the sauté pan and boil down rapidly to 1 tablespoon; scrape into the liver. Beat in the foie gras or pâté and bread crumbs. Season carefully. Spoon ½ teaspoon into each prune.

OTHER STUFFINGS

Sweet Italian Sausage, Parsley, and Crumbs

Sweet Italian sausage and sautéed onions blended with bread crumbs, parsley, and sour cream—this is used on page 155 to stuff chicken breasts, or would be an excellent stuffing for onions, tomatoes, zucchini, and other vegetables.

Bulgur and Mushroom Vegetarian Stuffing
Also for stuffed cabbage

2 cups bulgur (cracked wheat— available in health food stores)
2 quarts hot water
1½ cups mirepoix (1 cup each: diced carrots, onions, and celery, cooked in 4 Tbs butter, see Special Note, page 297)
½ to 1 cup mushroom duxelles, page 314 (finely diced mushrooms sautéed with shallots and seasonings)
1 cup chopped raisins
1 egg
½ cup ricotta or cream cheese
Flavorings: salt, freshly ground pepper, freshly squeezed lemon juice, and mint or thyme

Soak the bulgur in the hot water 5 minutes, or until barely tender. Drain, squeeze dry, and toss with the rest of the ingredients. Season carefully to taste.

A carnivorous variation. Add 1 cup of chopped boiled ham.

Ground Beef with Ham, Olives, and Pine Nuts

This stuffing was designed for the flank steak on page 246, and is also good for stuffed cabbage leaves or onions. For about 2 cups of stuffing, mix 1½ cups of hamburger with 3 tablespoons each of chopped boiled ham, black olives, chopped pine nuts or almonds, and grated hard cheese, plus 1 egg, a large clove of puréed garlic, 1 teaspoon of salt, several grinds of pepper, and ¼ teaspoon of ground rosemary or thyme.

Duck-Leg Mousse

In this recipe on page 182, the mousse is sautéed as patties, but it could well be used to stuff vegetables.

Rice and Onions with Cheese

For the onion-stuffed braised onions on page 303, but it could stuff other vegetables as well, such as zucchini or tomatoes.

Sausage and Swiss Chard Stuffing

This colorful green stuffing (page 250) is used for the braised Stuffed Breast of Veal on page 248. Although spinach may replace chard, chard leaves are really better since they hold their color more effectively. You could also use it to stuff a whole head of cabbage (page 304), or for Braised Flank Steak (page 246).

Meat

Sautés and Pan-Fries

Roasts, Braises, Stews, and Ragouts

**Steaks, Chops, Burgers,
Butterflied Legs,
and Marvelous Miscellaneous
Mixtures**

The meat chapter, perhaps more than any other in this book, best illustrates the way to cook, the way to learn, and the way to think about cooking.

Veal chops and pork chops are sautéed like first cousins, a butterflied loin of pork and a butterflied leg of lamb roast almost alike, hamburgers and lamburgers pan fry like sisters, and an American meat loaf is for all the world a French pâté minus the wine and truffles.

Thus, meat fits the pattern of theme and variations wonderfully well, and with that attitude in mind, meat cookery makes sense. Of course, a leg of lamb is prepared for roasting in a different way from roast ribs of beef because one is a leg and the other a rib, but the general principles are the same, and if you can roast one, you can roast the other.

Thus all items that cook alike stay together—as far as feasible and sensible. The idea, as usual in this book, is to make method make sense: a roast is a roast is a roast, in other words, whether it be pork, ham, or beef. However, everything is listed by specific beast in the index.

A NOTE ON MEAT TERMINOLOGY

It would certainly help us nationwide if every state legislature passed and enforced a law saying that all meat markets, butchers, wholesalers, and so forth must adopt the standard nomenclatures for meat cuts that have been agreed upon by a national group of packers, processors, and markets under the auspices of the National Live Stock and Meat Board in Chicago.

At this writing the Meat Board tells me that 9 states are considering such a law, that in 10 states the standard nomenclature is voluntary, and that 11 states have actually passed a law. However, it is not always enforced, and one of the most serious lawbreakers is the great State of New York—especially serious because New York City is the center of the food magazine and cookbook publishing industry.

Even the presumably careful *New York Times,* for example, recently instructed its readers to buy "1 pound of veal shoulder fillet"—and what could that possibly be? The "mock tender" lodged atop one side of the shoulder blade? The shoulder end of the rib eye? Who indeed knows, except perhaps a neighborhood New York City butcher? On the other hand what, for instance, is a "lifter steak" or a "puff roast"?

You would know, and everybody in the nation would know, if it carried its official name on its label: "Beef Chuck: Top Blade Roast." Its fanciful puff roast alias could be listed under the official name, but there could be no mistaking that this is that triangular piece of meat on top of the shoulder blade, opposite the mock tender.

We Americans are a mobile lot, and a Chicagoan is lost in a New York meat market, as would a New Yorker be in Massachusetts, Illinois, or California. We must all urge our state legislators, newspapers, food writers, and purveyors to adopt—and enforce—this uniform system. Otherwise it is impossible to communicate nationally, and we shall continue to be one mighty nation—divisible by its meat cuts.

TWO USEFUL BOOKS FOR YOUR BUTCHER AND YOU

Uniform Retail Meat Identity Standards. This is the fully illustrated official industrywide cooperative meat identification handbook, published by the National Live Stock and Meat Board.

The Meat Board Guide to Identifying Meat Cuts. A fine pocket-size pamphlet for the home cook. Illustrated with color photographs, it names and pictures all of the standard cuts, along with descriptions and basic cooking methods. (Under $2.00)

Both of these are available through:

The Department of Merchandizing
The National Live Stock and Meat
 Board
36 South Wabash Avenue
Chicago, Illinois 60603

The fat-free cooking of meats on cast-iron grills

Cast-iron stove-top grill

A cast-iron meat grill is an alternative to sautéing and broiling. They come in various styles, but all are essentially heavy rectangles with a washboard surface of raised iron ridges. The grill fits over either an electric or a gas burner. You heat up the grill, lightly oil the surface of your meat, and you have an indoor barbecue right on top of the stove. All the cooking fat falls between the iron ridges, and you have practically fat-free cooking of your steak, chop, or hamburger. You'll find these grills in many of the cookware catalogues and gourmet shops.

Timing and sauce notes. Timing is the same as for pan frying. If you want extra flavoring, anoint the grilled steaks with one of the flavored butters described on page 193, or rub the surface with salt, freshly ground pepper, butter, and perhaps a sprinkling of thyme or Provençal seasoning.

SAUTÉS AND PAN-FRIES

Sautéing or pan frying, whichever you wish to call the process, is certainly the quickest and easiest way to cook a steak or a chop, and it has the happy advantage of practically making its own simple and delicious sauce from the juices left in the pan. Here we have beef steaks, pork and veal chops, veal scallops, ham steaks, calf's liver, and the all-American hamburger.

The best beefsteaks

HOW TO BUY A GOOD PIECE OF MEAT. *Although the days of the personal butcher who cuts up his own whole beef carcass are fast disappearing, you can still get personal service at the supermarket. Introduce yourself to the head butcher and ask his—or her—advice. Butchers like to be recognized and consulted, if you don't take up too much of their time. It's a wise idea to learn all you can about meat cuts, too, so that you will know whereof they speak.*

Quality. The color of the meat should be a healthy, deep red with firm, creamy yellow fat. A certain amount of marbling—creamy yellow streaks of fat in the flesh—very . much enhances its flavor, but raises the fat content. Personally I do not go in for diet meat on those gala occasions when I have a steak: either it's the best and most beautiful, or it's no steak at all for me.

Steak types. Assuming that you are planning on the best, pick a boneless steak no more than 1½ inches thick—1 inch is ideal—from the rib, loin, sirloin, or tenderloin. Steaks from the chuck and round can also be excellent, but it takes a knowledgeable professional or home butcher to choose them. Bone-in steaks are for broiling, like the T-bone, porterhouse, rib, and wedgebone steaks.

Steak cuts: Porterhouse steak

Steak cuts: T-bone steak

Steak cuts. Not counting the tenderloin, which follows later in its own category, my favorite steak for sautéing is the top loin; that is, the larger side of the T-bone and the

porterhouse. Or cut the eye of meat out of the rib steak and you have a rib-eye or Delmonico steak. Or use the tenderloin butt portion of the sirloin.

Steak cuts: Bone-in rib steak

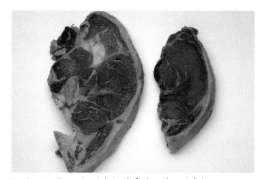

Steak cuts: Bone-in sirloin, left; boneless sirloin, right

Top-loin steak: untrimmed, right; trimmed, center; trimmings, left

Frozen steaks

Frozen steaks are frowned upon by some purists, but I always keep a couple on hand in my freezer and haven't had a raised eyebrow yet at the table. The secrets are not to keep them too long—4 weeks maximum is my limit—and to maintain the freezer temperature at minus 5°F or lower. Let them defrost slowly but only partially in the refrigerator (or in the microwave, watching closely). Then, to prevent juice loss, plan to cook them when the outside has softened somewhat, and the inside has softened just enough to bend a little.

PREPARING A STEAK FOR COOKING. *Trim off all excess fat, including, if you wish, the strip of fat around the circumference. Top loins have a line of gristle between fat and meat (upper right-hand section in the T-bone and porterhouse illustrations); either trim it off or cut through it vertically at ½-inch intervals. The gristle is tough, and, if left on, it will curl a thin steak out of shape during cooking. Dry the steaks in paper towels. Then I like to brush each side with a film of light olive oil; I feel it seals in the juices, as well as preventing the steak from sticking to the pan.*

*Ahead-of-Time Note: May be prepared a day in advance; wrap in plastic and refrigerate. Dry off again before cooking.

🍖 MASTER RECIPE

Sautéed Beefsteaks

For 6 servings

2 Tbs or so butter
2 tsp or so light olive oil or peanut oil
6 beefsteaks 1 inch thick, top loin suggested but any other steak cut will do, prepared as described
Salt and freshly ground pepper

SPECIAL EQUIPMENT SUGGESTED: *2 frying pans for the steaks (I like no-stick here, as usual)*

Film the pans with ¹⁄₁₆ inch of butter and oil, then set over high heat, swirling the pans to distribute the butter over the surface until its foam begins to subside. Lay in the steaks, which should fit in one layer with ¼ to ½ inch between each. Sauté 1½ minutes, turn, and sauté about 1½ minutes on the other side.

When are they done? Test a steak by pressing the meat (see illustration). They are red rare, *saignant,* when barely springy to the touch, in contrast to their squashy raw state. They are medium rare, *à point,* a few seconds later, when a pearling of red juice just begins to appear on the surface. Season lightly with salt and freshly ground pepper, and remove at once to hot plates or a hot platter. Either degrease the sauté juices and pour over the steaks, giving but a delicious dribble per serving, or make the following quick and classic deglazing sauce.

Testing doneness by pressing meat

Deglazing Sauce with Red or White Wine

This is the very fast finish to any sauté from fish to fowl to good red meat, and always deliciously in character with the specific dish of the moment.

For 6 steaks, a spoonful of sauce for each

2 Tbs minced shallots or scallions
1 cup dry white wine, French vermouth, or red wine
¼ cup beef or chicken stock, optional
2 to 3 Tbs butter
2 Tbs minced fresh parsley, optional

After removing the sautéed meat from the pan, pour out most of the sauté fat, leaving a good teaspoon for flavor. Turn the minced shallots or scallions into the pan and stir over moderate heat for a moment. Then pour in the wine and optional stock, and scrape about to loosen coagulated sauté juice. Boil down over high heat for a minute or so, until the liquid is almost syrupy. Remove from heat and add a tablespoon of the butter, swirling the pan until the butter is absorbed before adding another tablespoon, step 1. Sprinkle in the optional parsley, pour over the steaks, step 2, and serve.

1. Swirling in the butter

2. Pouring sauce over steak

Flavored Butter Toppings

For steaks, chops, hamburgers, broiled fish, pastas, and to beat into sauces

Simple to make, and especially recommended for steaks on the barbecue or the stove-top grill, flavored butters consist of soft butter into which you beat anything you wish, such as the classic combination of lemon juice, shallots, and parsley—which is always delicious on a steak. Or you might switch to mustard and puréed garlic, or include whatever items are in fashion at the moment, such as chili pepper, puréed pimiento, ginger, exotic herbs, and so forth. Flavored butter can also be beaten into a deglazing sauce instead of plain butter.

SPECIAL NOTE

To Cream Butter

If the butter is at room temperature, beat it vigorously in a roomy bowl with a wooden spoon until it is soft and fluffy. (You can use a hand-held mixer, but it's such a nuisance to scrape the butter out of the blades!) If you need only a small amount and the butter is chilled, melt it, then beat it over a bowl of ice and water, where it will quite rapidly congeal and become soft and creamy. Ice is a good solution, too, for butter you have softened too much. For a large amount, cut the butter into ½-inch slices and whiz it in the food processor, adding the required flavorings as you go.

Maître d'Hôtel Butter

For about ½ cup, enough for 6 to 8 steaks

4 ounces (1 stick) butter, creamed
1 Tbs freshly squeezed lemon juice
2 to 3 Tbs minced fresh parsley
1 Tbs very finely minced shallot or scallion
Salt and freshly ground white pepper

SPECIAL EQUIPMENT SUGGESTED:
A 2-quart mixing bowl and wooden spoon; a rubber spatula

The mixture. Beat the butter in the bowl, adding the lemon juice ¼ teaspoon at a time. Beat in the parsley, shallot or scallion, and salt and pepper to taste.

Serving. Either spread the butter over each steak, or plop on a lump, or pass the butter separately. Or form it into a log or a rectangle, chill, then cut into serving-size disks or slices.

*Ahead-of-time note: May be covered and refrigerated; may be frozen.

VARIATIONS: ALTERNATE FLAVORINGS

Mustard Butter. Substitute 1 tablespoon or so of prepared Dijon-type mustard for the lemon juice in the preceding recipe.

Garlic Butter. Purée 1 or 2 large cloves of garlic into the mixing bowl and mash to a fine paste with ¼ teaspoon of salt. Beat in the butter, lemon juice, and herbs.

Other herbs can be added, such as 1 tablespoon or so of tarragon, or chervil, or ground rosemary, or chives, plus the lemon juice, shallots, and seasonings.

Red- or White-Wine Butter. Boil ½ cup of wine with the minced shallots and an imported bay leaf until reduced to 1 tablespoon; let cool. Beat it into the butter, along with salt, pepper, and herbs to taste.

TENDERLOIN STEAKS

Although tenderloins sauté the same way as other steaks, they are in their own luxury category and deserve special consideration. The tenderloin is the left-hand side of the porterhouse in our illustration on page 191; you'll note how much smaller it is in the T-bone. The smallest tenderloins are called filet mignons, the T-bone size here is a fillet steak, while the largest porterhouse size is the Châteaubriand, the heart of the tenderloin. For best taste and texture, look for lightly marbled meat from prime and choice cuts of beef—if you are going to spend all that money, pick a butcher who caters to the carriage trade.

Sautéed Beef Tenderloin Steaks

For 6 servings

6 ready-to-cook tenderloin steaks about ½ pound each and 1¼ to 1½ inches thick
2 to 3 Tbs clarified butter (page 139), or 2 Tbs butter and 1 Tbs peanut oil
Salt and freshly ground pepper

SPECIAL EQUIPMENT SUGGESTED:
A heavy frying pan that will just hold the steaks comfortably, no-stick recommended

Sautéing the steaks. Dry the steaks in paper towels. Set the pan over high heat and film with ¹⁄₁₆ inch of the butter (or butter and oil). When very hot but not browning, lay in the steaks. Sauté for 2 minutes on one side, turn, salt lightly, and sauté on the other side, adjusting heat so the steaks are not browning too much.

When are they done? Tenderloins are harder to judge than other steaks because they are so much more tender, and an extra few seconds can overcook them. For rosy rare they will have taken on a little texture and spring when pressed with your finger; if you have any doubts, cut into one. As soon as they are done, remove them to hot plates or a hot platter.

Sauce and serving suggestions. Sauce them with any of the preceding suggestions for beefsteaks, or be rich and elegant with the Béarnaise sauce on page 87, which you could spoon into individual artichoke bottoms (page 281) or scooped-out tomato halves. The potato galettes on page 324 and a green vegetable like asparagus tips or broccoli would go well, as would a mature red wine like a cabernet sauvignon or Bordeaux-St. Emilion.

A Fast Sauté of Beef for Two

With small onions, mushrooms, and sautéed potatoes

This is an almost complete main course with a certain jazzy style, something to keep in mind for a rather important and intimate occasion when you are in a hurry but want a good meal. If you had time beforehand you could trim the meat and ready the vegetables. But when you are an informal twosome, why not prepare the whole meal while having meaningful conversations and apéritifs together in the kitchen?

MANUFACTURING NOTE. *You can do everything in one 10-inch frying pan if you're cramped for space, but a reasonably fast well-equipped cook starting from scratch and juggling all pans at once can complete this dish in less than ½ hour. With a few minutes to spare, one cook can finish off the whole meal, but a friendly hand is always welcome.*

A menu for 2 people

The onions

6 to 8 small white onions about 1 inch in diameter
½ cup chicken stock
A pinch of tarragon or mixed herbs

The potatoes

3 or 4 medium "boiling" potatoes
A pinch of tarragon or mixed herbs
3 Tbs minced fresh parsley

The mushrooms

6 to 8 large fresh mushrooms
1 Tbs minced shallot or scallion

The meat

2 center-cut beef tenderloin steaks 1½ inches thick, or the equivalent cut from a piece of tenderloin

The sauce

2 Tbs minced shallots or scallions
⅓ cup dry French vermouth
⅓ cup beef or chicken stock
⅓ cup heavy cream (or ½ cup stock blended with ½ Tbs cornstarch)

Other ingredients

Salt and freshly ground pepper
Butter and light olive oil or peanut oil

SPECIAL EQUIPMENT SUGGESTED:
2 frying pans, 10-inch size, no-stick recommended; a 2-quart covered saucepan; a side dish

The onions. Drop the onions into boiling water for 1 minute. Drain. Shave skin from the tip and root ends, then slip off the remaining skins. Pierce a cross ¼ inch deep in the root ends, for even cooking, step 1. Simmer slowly in the covered saucepan with the stock, herbs, and a little salt until tender—about 20 minutes. Meanwhile, continue with the rest of the items.

The potatoes. Peel the potatoes and cut into ¾-inch slices; cut the slices into ¾-inch strips, and cut the strips into cubes as illustrated, step 2. Dry the potatoes. Set one of the frying pans over high heat, add 1 tablespoon each of butter and oil, and when the butter foam has almost subsided, add the potatoes. Sauté without disturbing for 1 minute, swirl the pan by its handle to toss them, and leave for another minute—to sear them. Season lightly with salt and pepper, and sauté over moderate heat, tossing fairly frequently, for about 15 minutes. When lightly browned and tender, keep them just warm, uncovered, over a pan of barely simmering water.

1. Piercing cross in root end of an onion

2. Dicing the potatoes

3. Preparing the mushrooms

The mushrooms. Trim ¼ inch off the stems of the mushrooms and either wipe the caps clean with a towel or wash them rapidly, if dirty, and dry them. Quarter them as shown, step 3. Sauté several minutes in hot butter in your second frying pan, adding the shallots or scallions at the end, just as the absorbed butter reappears on their surface and they begin to brown.

4. Trimming and cubing the tenderloin, upper left, and the steak, lower right

5. Turning out sautéed mushrooms into a side dish

6. Sautéing the beef

7. Wine and stock go into pan.

8. Basting

9. Adding potatoes—the finale

A Fast Sauté of Beef for Two (*continued*)

The meat. Whether you are using steaks or a piece of tenderloin, both of which are shown in this succulent display, step 4, cut off outside fat and slice the meat into 1½-inch chunks. Dry them well before sautéing.

Midway point. Everything is cooking at once except for the meat, which is lying in wait. The onions are simmering away in their saucepan; the potatoes are sautéing. When the mushrooms are done, turn them into a side dish, step 5.

Sautéing the meat. Set the mushroom sauté pan over moderately high heat, adding a little butter and oil. When very hot, almost smoking, add the meat. Brown, tossing frequently for

several minutes, step 6, until barely springy when pressed—the beef must be very rare because it gets a little more cooking later. Toss it with a sprinkling of salt, and scrape it into the dish with the mushrooms.

The sauce. Spoon all but a tablespoon of fat out of the pan, stir in the minced shallots or scallions, and sauté a moment; then pour in the wine, the stock, and any juices from the onions, step 7. Boil rapidly and let reduce almost to a syrup before adding the optional cream (or the stock/cornstarch).

Final simmering. Scrape the beef, onions, and mushrooms into the pan and bring to the simmer, basting with the sauce, step 8—just to warm the beef through without overcooking; it should be rosy rare. Taste the sauce carefully and correct seasoning.

*Ahead-of-time note: You may finish the dish in advance to this point. When you're about ready to eat, reheat the meat, basting—be careful not to overcook.

Serving. Toss the potatoes over high heat to crisp, adding a tablespoon of butter, the herbs, and parsley. Strew the potatoes over the meat, step 9, and serve.

VARIATION

Sauté of Pork Tenderloin

Substitute pork tenderloin for beef, and follow the same directions; you'll save a little money and have a first-rate main course. Now that perfectly trimmed whole pork tenderloins come in separate packages, this is a particularly appealing recipe.

HAMBURGERS AND OTHERS

Hamburger is the great American favorite, and rightly so since it is easy to cook and you can serve it elegantly or simply, in the dining room or on a picnic barbecue. And it's hamburger that makes meat departments tick, because so much of their business is in ground beef. In fact markets that do their own meat cutting couldn't afford to carry their expensive pieces of beef without hamburger, which takes care of their meat scraps and unsalable or less tender morsels.

Buying the best

The cut. The meat industry tells us that lean ground beef is lean ground beef, wherever it comes from. They are telling us, in other words, that whether it's from the arm or the leg or the flank its source on the animal makes no difference in its quality. We, the public, however, have different ideas. Some of us prefer the ground sirloin, perhaps reading special quality into a luxury name, others always choose ground round, and some insist that chuck is the choicest because chuck is shoulder, shoulder gets exercise, and exercise means flavor. I am of the chuck and neck

Chuck steak

group, particularly since it is less expensive—but I do want my beef trimmed of all gristle, tendons, and stringy bits. I am paying for good meat, not ground et cetera!

The fat content. Fat adds to the flavor and juiciness of ground meat. The round is 10 percent fat, while the chuck can average 30 percent, depending upon how the meat is trimmed. It is interesting to note that markets and industry people like to speak of ground beef as being 80 percent lean rather than 20 percent fat—emphasis on lean looks and reads better. Most hamburger buffs, including me, opt for 20 to 25 percent fat, but I do not consider a good hamburger to be diet meat.

Amounts. Opinions vary about size, from 4 ounces to the mammoth ¾-pounder. I like a 5-ounce burger 3 inches across, ¾ inch thick, and just the right size for a bun.

To grind your own hamburger meat

The grinder. Unless your meat is perfectly trimmed of gristle, a food processor will give you chopped meat and chopped gristle. A meat grinder is more trouble, but it does the best job for hamburger because the gristle, etc., won't go through the screen, which, by the way, should be a number 10 with ³⁄₁₆-inch holes.

The meat. You often see packages of unidentified stew meat, or meat for brochettes—they're fine for hamburger when well trimmed. Or buy something more reasonably priced,

Hamburger dinner. Gratin of hominy, lower left, the hamburgers with sautéed mushrooms, right, and your own hamburger buns

like the chuck steak pictured at left, and cut it yourself. If you want to raise the fat content of lean meat like the round, consider that it has a residual 10 percent fat. According to my pocket calculator, then, ½ pound of it makes 1 cup or 16 tablespoons, of which about 1½ tablespoons are fat—add to it 1½ tablespoons (¾ ounce) of beef suet, beef marrow, or butter as you are grinding, and you will have your 80 percent lean hamburger—with 20 percent fat.

To grind the meat. Chill the meat to minimize juice drip. Trim off all gristle, and as much visible fat as you deem fit. Cut the meat into strips about 1½ inches across, and alternate lean and fat to keep the fat moving through the machine. When the grinder slows down or clogs, remove the grinding mechanism, clean off stringy bits from screw and blade, run hot water through the screen, and you're ready to go again—the less gristle in the meat, the less often you will have to go through this.

Steak Tartar

While on the technique of grinding, let us not forget steak tartar—chopped raw beef that each guest garnishes to taste with onions, capers, anchovies, egg, and other good things. It's the perfect cold carnivorous lunch. But to be at its best the beef must be impeccably freshly ground—preferably home-ground a few minutes before serving. And it must be the beef with the right texture and the most flavor—I vote for the round, only the tenderest cuts of it, nearest the rump.

Steak tartar as a luncheon dish

Per serving

6 to 8 ounces of freshly ground lean beef trimmed of all visible fat, from the first cuts of the round nearest the rump

To be served on the plate with the beef
1 fresh egg yolk in the half-shell
2 Tbs finely minced red onion
1 Tbs Dijon-style prepared mustard
2 best-quality anchovies packed in oil, from a freshly opened can
2 Tbs capers
2 Tbs chopped fresh parsley

Steak Tartar

To be passed separately
Worcestershire sauce
Prepared horseradish
Hot pepper sauce
Salt
A pepper grinder

The arrangement. Mound the beef on a plate, topping it with the egg yolk cupped in its half-shell. Surround with the minced onion, mustard, anchovies, capers, and chopped parsley.

Pass Worcestershire sauce, horseradish, hot pepper sauce, salt, and a pepper grinder. Everyone mixes his own.

As a crowd-pleasing appetizer. For anyone who enjoys performing in public, it is often appealing for guests to see the house special mixed before their eyes.

Use the same ingredients and proportions as suggested above, but furnish the performer with a big fine chopping board, two large chef's knives or Chinese cleavers for blending and seasoning, and a handsome serving bowl.

With great flourish and the flashing of blades, mix in salt, pepper, egg yolks, anchovies, mustard, and so forth. Again with flourish, taste the mixture, and dramatically add a smidgen of something, then expertly gather the meat into the bowl. Guests spoon on their own minced onions and capers as they heap their savory portions onto squares of buttered rye or pumpernickel bread.

🐷 MASTER RECIPE

Sautéed or Pan-Fried Hamburgers

The advantage of pan frying, besides its ease and directness, is that you can make a sauce with the sauté juices. The following is for plain hamburger meat, but see also the flavored hamburger at the end of this section, since it is particularly recommended for dressy hamburgers served on a platter.

For 4 servings

1¼ pounds hamburger formed into 4
   patties ¾ inch thick
2 to 3 Tbs clarified butter (page 139),
   or 2 Tbs butter and 1 Tbs fresh
   olive oil or peanut oil
Salt and freshly ground pepper

SPECIAL EQUIPMENT SUGGESTED:
*A heavy 10-inch frying pan, no-stick
recommended*

Sautéing. Set the frying pan over moderately high heat, add the clarified butter or butter and oil, and, when very hot but not burning, add the hamburgers. Sauté 2 to 3 minutes on one side, until nicely browned. Turn, season lightly with salt and pepper, and brown on the other side.

When are they done? If you are a practiced hamburger cooker, you can tell how it is just by pressing the top of the meat with your finger. If still squashy, they are blue rare inside; if barely springy, they will be rare to medium, but if they are the consistency of a rubber ball, they are very well done. The surest way to tell is to cut one open—but rapidly, since they can overcook in a few seconds.

HAMBURGERS ON A PLATTER: SAUCES

Deglazing Sauce

The accumulated juices from pan-fried hamburgers give you the base for the classic deglazing sauce used for steaks and described on page 192. Moreover, rather than the plain butter in that recipe, swish in 1 or 2 tablespoons of one of the flavored butters with herbs, or mustard, or garlic, as described on page 194.

Mushrooms

After sautéing the hamburgers and removing them to a hot platter, make the deglazing sauce. Fold a cup or so of sautéed mushrooms (page 313) into the sauce and simmer a moment; remove from heat, and, if you wish, swirl in a tablespoon or two of butter. Mound the mushrooms in the center of your platter and spoon the sauce over the hamburgers.

Tomato

Use the same system with a cup of diced fresh tomato pulp.

Peppers

Or sauté strips of green and red bell pepper in oil or butter, and perhaps a bit of minced garlic; swirl them into the deglazing sauce, give them a quick simmer, and spoon them over the hamburger.

Suggested Accompaniments to Hamburgers on a Platter

Giant baked onions (page 314) and a gratin of hominy (page 340) make a great combination, or any of the suggestions for beefsteaks on page 194. You'll want an uncomplicated wine like zinfandel, Beaujolais, or a good jug red.

(continued)

SPECIAL NOTE

Salsa

Fresh tomato and onion sauce with
Mexican overtones

For 2½ cups

**2 cups tomato pulp (2 to 3 firm ripe
   red tomatoes, peeled, seeded,
   juiced, and diced; page 357); or a
   mixture of fresh tomatoes and
   seeded canned Italian plum
   tomatoes**

**¼ cup finely minced sweet onion or
   scallions**

**1 medium cucumber, peeled, seeded,
   and finely diced**

**½ mild green chili pepper (Anaheim
   type) or bell pepper, seeded and
   diced**

**Fresh herbs to taste: such as
   cilantro, parsley, chives, and/or
   basil**

**Seasonings to taste: salt, freshly
   ground pepper, a pinch of sugar,
   wine vinegar, hot pepper sauce,
   and droplets of olive oil**

**1 small ripe avocado, peeled, seeded,
   and diced**

The mixture. Fold the tomato in a
bowl with the onion, cucumber, pepper, herbs, and seasonings, tasting
carefully and adding more of whatever you think necessary. Fold in the
diced avocado. Cover with plastic
wrap and refrigerate until serving
time. (If too juicy, drain out excess
liquid before turning the salsa into a
serving bowl.)

1. Forming hamburger patties

Suggested Accompaniments to Hamburger on a Bun

The best hamburger deserves the best
bun, one that has texture, one that
won't go soggy—the one you'll find
in the bread section, on page 47.
Rather than ketchup and mustard,
you might try the sprightly Salsa in
the Special Note on this page.

VARIATIONS

Flavored Hamburger

To give more flavor and interest to
plain hamburgers that you plan to
serve on a platter, blend 1¼ pounds
of ground beef lightly in a large mixing bowl with 2 tablespoons each of
grated raw onion and sour cream,
plus salt, freshly ground pepper, and
thyme, and 2 to 3 tablespoons of
beaten egg, to make a somewhat soft
but not loose mass. Taste, and correct
seasoning. Form somewhat loosely
into 4 patties (see illustration, step
1). Dredge lightly in flour, step 2, if
you wish, the moment before
sautéing.

2. Optional dredging in flour

Broiled Hamburgers

Broiling is wonderful for hamburgers, but only when you have a broiling element that efficiently and
quickly browns the meat when set
about 1 inch under the red-hot element for 1½ minutes or so on each
side. Otherwise you are better off
with the following stove-top grill.

Hamburgers on the Stove-Top Grill

This recipe refers to the ridged cast-
iron grill described on page 190,
which sits on top of a burner. It does
an easy and beautiful job with 2 to 4
hamburgers and is, I think, easier
than broiling because you can see
what is going on. Preheat the grill,
brush it lightly with peanut oil or
non-stick spray, and cook the hamburgers 2 to 3 minutes on each side.

Hamburgers on the Barbecue

Prepare a bed of hot coals that have turned ashen gray, but do not place the grill too close to the coals or you will make burn marks in the meat. I like to brush the burgers with oil before barbecuing, to prevent them from sticking. Cooking will probably take a bit longer than sautéing or stove-top grilling—3 to 4 minutes per side for ¾-inch burgers.

VARIATION:

Lamburgers

These are best when you grind the lamb yourself, because then you can first remove all visible fat. Lamb shoulder is the cut to ask for here, or use scraps from the boning-out of a rack or the butterflying of a leg.

For 4 large patties 3½ inches across and 1¼ inches thick; or for 6 smaller patties

⅓ cup rice simmered until very
 tender in ⅔ cup chicken stock
1 cup minced onions sautéed and
 lightly browned in 2 Tbs butter
1 egg
1 clove of garlic, puréed, optional
1 pound (2 cups) lean ground lamb
Seasonings: salt, freshly ground
 pepper, and ground rosemary or
 thyme

Clarified butter (page 139) or olive
 oil, for sautéing

Optional sauce
⅓ cup dry white French vermouth
⅔ cup fresh tomato sauce (page 358)

SPECIAL EQUIPMENT SUGGESTED:
A 10-inch no-stick frying pan for onions and patties; a food processor or blender for puréeing rice; a meat grinder

The lamb mixture. Purée the cooked rice, onions, egg, and optional garlic in the food processor or blender. Scrape into a bowl and blend with the ground lamb, adding a teaspoon of salt, several grinds of pepper, and a good pinch of rosemary or thyme. Form into patties and arrange on wax paper—they will be rather soft.

**Ahead-of-time note:* May be prepared several hours or a day in advance; cover and refrigerate.

Sautéing. Film the frying pan with butter or oil and set over moderately high heat. When hot, scoop in the patties with a pancake turner and sauté a minute or so on each side— watch that they do not brown too much. They are done to medium rare when just springy rather than squashy to the touch of your finger. Remove to hot plates or a hot platter.

The optional sauce. Pour excess fat out of the pan, and pour in the wine and tomato sauce, stirring with a wooden spoon for the few minutes it takes the sauce to boil up and thicken. Spoon the sauce over the patties, and serve.

Suggested accompaniments. Something fresh and green, like broccoli, peas, or spinach. Or something red like the eggplant pizzas on page 318, or eggplant ratatouille (page 317). Or homemade mashed potatoes, or the Gratin Dauphinoise on page 322, and a green salad.

OTHER BURGERS

Adapt any of the preceding suggestions to create veal, pork, or turkey burgers. I've even tried out abalone burgers with great success.

SAUTÉED PORK OR VEAL CHOPS

Pork and veal chops are relatively lean. Unless cooked with special care they can be dry, and pork, which is a close-textured meat, can be tough as well. Slow cooking over moderate heat is the secret.

The perfect pork chop

The meat is a pale grayish pink, firm, smooth, silky to the touch. The fat is firm and white, and thin strands of fat are embedded in the flesh. Pictured here is the rib chop, corresponding to the rib steak in our beef illustration on page 191. Loin chops have the same large lobe of meat plus a smaller lobe, the tenderloin, on the other side of the bone; it is the same cut as the T-bone and porterhouse steaks in the beef illustration. Loin and rib chops are the most desirable and therefore the most expensive; sirloin and blade-end

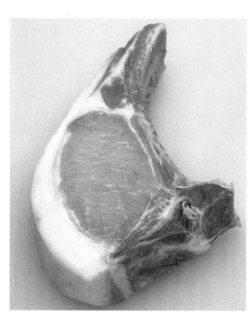

The perfect pork chop

Pork chop with braised red cabbage and steamed potatoes

chops are neither as handsome nor as tender, being a mixture of muscles.

Thickness of Chops. Because pork chops should be cooked slowly, a thin chop is easily subject to overcooking—¾ inch is a minimum thickness, in my experience. Chops over 1 inch thick can overcook on the outside before the inside is done; they do best, after their initial browning, simmering slowly in a covered pan to finish their cooking.

Bone-in vs. Boneless Chops. Many markets now remove the whole loin from the bone and cut it into steaks—the same cut as in top loin beefsteaks. These are usually called boneless pork loin chops, and although they do not have the generous look of the conventional chop, their size is convenient for a sauté because they take up less room in the frying pan. Use either boneless or bone-in chops in the following recipes.

PREPARING PORK CHOPS FOR COOKING. *Trim off excess fat, which includes most (or all) of the surrounding fat from the handsome rib chop illustrated here. You may wish to hack off ½ inch or so of the protruding rib bone piece, lower right.*

Sautéed Pork Chops

For 4 pork chops

4 pork rib or loin chops ¾ to 1 inch thick (for thicker chops, see the note following this recipe)

Optional spice marinade
½ tsp Spice Marinade (see Special Note on next page)
½ tsp salt

1 to 2 Tbs light olive oil or peanut oil, for sautéing
⅔ cup dry white French vermouth or chicken stock

SPECIAL EQUIPMENT SUGGESTED:
A heavy frying pan just roomy enough to hold the chops in 1 layer

Preparing the chops. Trim and defat the chops as described. If you wish to marinate them, mix the ingredients in a bowl, rub into the meat of the chops on both sides, cover, and refrigerate an hour if possible, or overnight. Dry the chops in paper towels before proceeding.

Cooking the chops. Film the frying pan with oil and set over moderately high heat. When hot, arrange the chops in the pan, turn heat to moderate, and brown them slowly 4 to 5 minutes on one side. If you have not marinated them, season lightly with salt and pepper. Turn the chops, season them if necessary, and brown lightly on the other side.

When are they done? Pork should not be overcooked or it will be dry and tough. The chops are done when the flesh feels fairly firm to the touch; it should be still juicy, and a faint pink when you cut into the flesh near the bone.

Sauce and serving. Remove the chops to hot plates or a hot platter. Spoon out the sauté fat, pour in the vermouth or stock, and boil it down rapidly until almost syrupy. Spoon the juices over the chops, and serve.

A note on thick pork chops. For chops 1¼ to 1½ inches thick, brown them slowly 4 to 5 minutes on each side, as described, then pour the wine into the pan, and cover it. Simmer slowly 4 to 5 minutes on one side, turn the chops and simmer 4 to 5 minutes on the other side. Remove the chops, boil the juices down to a syrup, spoon them over the chops, and serve.

Pork Chops with Cream and Mushrooms

After removing the chops from the pan and rapidly boiling down the juices, pour in ½ cup of heavy cream, boil rapidly for a moment to thicken lightly, then fold in a good handful of sliced sautéed mushrooms (page 313). Boil briefly, again to thicken lightly; correct seasoning, adding drops of freshly squeezed lemon juice, if needed. Fold in 2 to 3 tablespoons of minced fresh parsley, spoon the sauce and mushrooms over the chops, and serve.

Suggested Accompaniments to Pork Chops

For a hearty winter combination, serve pork chops with steamed potatoes and the braised red cabbage on page 289. Pork chops also go happily with such simple accompaniments as fresh spinach and mashed potatoes, or the golden purée of potatoes and carrots on page 285, or the purée of parsnips (page 286). Beets, turnips, or winter squash are other ideas, as are stuffed onions. Beans, lentils, or one of the hominy recipes starting on page 340 are good with plain pork

chops, as would be the prune and apple garnish on page 177. Or add the chops to finish cooking with braised sauerkraut as in the following recipe.

Wine with pork. Try one of the dry Alsatian rieslings, and/or a sauvignon blanc, or a light red such as a Beaujolais or a young pinot noir.

SPECIAL NOTE

Spice Marinade for Pork, Pâtés, and Sausages As Well As for Goose and Duck

A sojourn of several hours or overnight in the following spice mixture gives pork chops, roasts, and sausage meat an exceptionally fine flavor; a jar of it in your spice rack is useful to have on hand. (I have reserved a small, cheap, electric coffee grinder just for herbs and spices.)

For about 1¼ cups

2 Tbs each ground: imported bay leaf, clove, mace, nutmeg, paprika, and thyme
1 Tbs each ground: allspice, cinnamon, and savory
5 Tbs white peppercorns, ground

To make it. Blend all the ingredients together and store in a screw-top jar.

Proportions to use. Up to ½ teaspoon per pound of meat.

Homemade sausage is the star of this sauerkraut dinner, which begins with broiled oysters and ends with pears in custard.

it, and if the sauerkraut seems dry pour in a little of the wine or stock.

*Ahead-of-time note: May be prepared a day in advance to this point; refrigerate until chilled, then cover.

Braising—about 45 minutes at 400°F and 350°F. Bring to the simmer on top of the stove, cover the casserole, and set in the lower third level of the preheated 400°F oven. As soon as the contents are bubbling slowly, in about 10 minutes, reduce heat to 350°F and bake for another 20 to 30 minutes, until the chops test done as described in the pork chop recipe.

Serving. Serve directly from the casserole; or make a lavish arrangement on a large hot platter with the optional additions, as shown in the illustration.

Choucroute Garnie

Old-fashioned braised sauerkraut with pork chops and sausages

The luxurious platter in this photograph takes a sauerkraut dinner about as far as it can go, but you may be less opulent with a parsimonious single chop per person—and perhaps a single slice of sausage just for fun.

For 8 servings

Ingredients for the 2 pounds braised sauerkraut (page 290)
16 pork breakfast sausages; your own (page 257) or store-bought
8 pork rib chops 1 inch thick
Spice Marinade (Special Note, page 203), optional
4 bratwursts
4 weisswursts
½ cup or so dry white French vermouth or chicken broth

Optional additions

8 thin slices of boiled ham
Steamed potatoes
A handful of chopped fresh parsley

SPECIAL EQUIPMENT SUGGESTED:
A roomy covered casserole to hold all the above ingredients

The sauerkraut. Prepare the sauerkraut as described on page 290.

The pork chops and sausages. While the sauerkraut is simmering, prick the breakfast sausages with a pin in several places and brown lightly in a frying pan. Remove to a side dish, leave the fat in the pan, and brown the pork chops lightly. Prick the bratwursts and weisswursts in several places.

Combining. When the sauerkraut is done, bury the chops and sausages in

SPECIAL NOTE

Menu for a Sauerkraut Dinner

Oysters on the half-shell
Braised sauerkraut with all the trimmings
   French bread
Pear and Custard Tart: Clafouti
(page 442)
   Wines
     An Alsatian riesling or light sauvignon blanc with both oysters and sauerkraut
     A Sauternes or gewürztraminer with the tart, or a sweetish sparkling wine like a Vouvray

VEAL CHOPS

Beautiful big thick pale pink veal chops are never easy to find in retail markets, and when you are so fortunate as to see any, grab them. (Veal freezes well!) Here is one excellent way to cook them.

Veal Chops Sautéed with Wine and Tarragon

2 to 3 Tbs clarified butter (page 139), or 2 Tbs butter and 1 Tbs light olive oil or peanut oil
4 veal loin or rib chops 1 inch thick (see note for thick veal chops following this recipe)
Salt and freshly ground pepper
½ tsp or so dried tarragon (or sprigs of fresh tarragon)
⅔ cup dry white French vermouth
2 to 3 Tbs butter, for the sauce, optional

SPECIAL EQUIPMENT SUGGESTED:
A heavy frying pan that will just hold the chops in one layer without crowding, no-stick recommended

Cooking the chops. Film the frying pan with ¹⁄₁₆ inch of clarified butter or butter and oil, and set over moderately high heat. When hot, arrange the chops in the pan, turn heat to moderate, and brown the chops slowly and lightly for 5 minutes on one side. Turn them, season lightly with salt and pepper, and brown lightly on the other side. Pour out the sauté fat, turn and season the chops again, and sprinkle (or lay) on the tarragon. Pour in the vermouth, cover the pan, and simmer 1 or 2 minutes more on each side.

When are they done? I like veal cooked to "medium," with the flesh faintly pink when you cut close to the bone.

Sauce and serving. Remove the chops to hot plates or a hot platter. Rapidly boil down the juices to a syrup, off heat swish in the optional butter a tablespoon at a time, pour over the chops, and serve.

A note on thick veal chops. For veal chops 1½ inches thick or more, choose a frying pan that will go into the oven. Brown them first on top of the stove as described. Season them, add the tarragon, and set the hot pan in the upper third level of a 375°F oven. Roast 5 to 6 minutes. Then (watch that hot pan handle!) turn the chops, baste with the accumulated juices, season them, and roast another 5 to 6 minutes, or until done. Remove the chops to a hot plate or platter, add the vermouth, and boil down the juices to a syrup. Swish in the optional butter, spoon over the chops, and serve.

Suggested accompaniments. Anything you would serve with chicken goes with veal: risotto or one of the scalloped potato dishes beginning on page 322, or a gratin of cauliflower, or broccoli hashed in cream. Stuffed onions or stuffed mushrooms, braised celery, endives, or leeks, or asparagus, green peas, or artichoke bottoms are additional possibilities.

Wine. You might serve a mature but light red wine with plain veal chops, such as a pinot noir, cabernet, merlot, or Bordeaux. Full white wines also go with veal—chardonnays or Burgundies.

VARIATIONS

Veal Chops with Tarragon, Mushrooms, and Cream

Ingredients for the preceding veal chops
The cream and mushroom variation for pork chops (page 203)

Sauté the veal chops as described, and finish the sauce as for the pork chops.

OTHER SAUCE VARIATIONS

See the variations for sautéed chicken (pages 139–40), such as the garnish of braised onions and sautéed potatoes, the pipérade with sliced green and red peppers, and the Provençal, with tomatoes. Any of these can be adapted verbatim to veal chops.

HAM STEAKS

Here are some fast and fancy ways to
treat those big fat slices of packaged
ready-to-cook ham you buy at the supermarket. When you douse them
with a bit of wine and make a fragrant little sauce, they make easy and
attractive main courses.

 MASTER RECIPE

Sautéed Ham Steaks Simmered in Wine

This is the basic recipe which you can
serve as is, or elaborate with mushrooms, cream, and so forth.

For 4 servings

1½ to 2 pounds cooked ham in a
    slice about ⅜ inch thick
2 Tbs unsalted butter
1 Tbs light olive oil or peanut oil
2 Tbs finely minced shallots or
    scallions
⅓ cup dry Port or Madeira wine, or
    dry white French vermouth
⅓ cup ham, beef, or chicken stock

SPECIAL EQUIPMENT SUGGESTED:
*A frying pan large enough to hold the
ham slices comfortably, no-stick recommended; a cover for the pan*

Sautéing the ham. Trim off any excess
fat, and cut the ham into serving
pieces following the natural muscle
separations if possible; dry in paper
towels. Heat the butter and oil in the
frying pan, and when the butter
foam begins to subside, brown the
ham lightly for a minute or two on
each side. Add the shallots or scallions, wine, and stock; cover the pan
and simmer 5 minutes.

Simple deglazing sauce. Remove the
ham to hot plates or a hot platter,
rapidly boil down the juices to a
syrup, spoon and scrape them over
the ham, and serve.

Suggested accompaniments. Fresh
braised or buttered spinach and
home-made mashed potatoes or one
of the potato gratins starting on page
322 are natural accompaniments
here—and a light red wine such as a
pinot noir or Beaujolais, or a full
white like a chardonnay.

VARIATIONS

Ham Steaks with Cream and Mushrooms

This is a marvelous combination,
similar to one served by the great
chef André Surmain at his 3-star restaurant in Saulieu. Complete the recipe as directed, but add a good
handful of sautéed sliced mushrooms
(page 313) to simmer with the ham
and cream. You may wish to fold in a
little chopped fresh parsley before
spooning the sauce over the ham.

Ham Steaks with Madeira Cream Sauce

Sautéing. Brown the ham, simmer it
with the shallots, Madeira wine, and
stock, and remove it from the pan as
described. After boiling down the
cooking liquid, blend 2 tablespoons
of mustard with 1 tablespoon of tomato paste in a bowl with ½ to ¾
cup of heavy cream. Pour it into the
sauté pan, simmer for a moment to
blend flavors, and return the ham to
the pan, basting it with the sauce.
Bring to the simmer for several minutes, basting the ham as the sauce
thickens around it. Taste, and correct
seasoning. Remove the ham to hot
plates or a hot platter, spoon the sauce
over it, decorate with parsley, and
serve.

Sautéed Ham Steaks with Fresh Green Peas and a Border of Mashed Potatoes

You may wish to leave the ham slice
whole, and, after simmering it in its
Madeira cream sauce, remove it to a
hot lightly buttered platter. Spoon a
little of the sauce over the ham, and
turn 2 cups of cooked fresh green
peas into the pan to simmer a moment in the sauce. Pipe warm
mashed potatoes around the edge of
the platter, spoon the peas and sauce
around the ham, and serve.

SAUTÉED VEAL SCALLOPS

Fast, fabulous, and, as top-quality veal always is—expensive. Grab up any prime veal scallops you see because you won't find them often in the supermarket.

The color of prime veal

Pick veal by its color—pale creamy pink, about the shade of a raw chicken thigh. Some cuts of the dark pink or reddish so-called free-range veal may be tender, but in my opinion it neither looks nor tastes like veal. It should be called calf.

Veal cuts. Top, veal chop; bottom, the round

Cuts of meat for scallops. Veal scallops are bought ⅜ inch thick and are pounded down to ¼-inch thickness: pounding breaks down the tissues, making the meat lie flat during its sauté. You therefore want a cut of veal with no muscle separations, which will stay in one piece when pounded. The ideal cut is the trimmed top or bottom round, but you can bone out a veal chop (see illustration).

Pounding veal scallops

To pound veal scallops. Trim any fat and gristle off the circumference of the scallops. Lay one between 2 sheets of plastic wrap and pound firmly but not roughly back and forth and up and down using the smooth side of a meat tenderizer, or a plumber's rubber hammer, or a rolling pin—or even the side of a bottle. The scallop will spread out to almost double, and should be a quite even ¼ inch thick all over. Wrap and refrigerate the scallops until you are ready to sauté.

Sautéed Veal Scallops

For 6 servings

12 veal scallops 2 to 3 ounces each and ⅜ inch thick, prepared for cooking and pounded as described
¼ cup clarified butter (page 139)
Salt and freshly ground pepper

SPECIAL EQUIPMENT SUGGESTED:
A heavy 12-inch frying pan; a hot platter; a cover for the platter

Sautéing. Dry the scallops in paper towels. Set the frying pan over high heat and film with 1/16 inch of clarified butter. When very hot but not smoking, rapidly lay in half the scallops—they should fit in one comfortable layer. Sauté 1 minute on each side. Remove them to the platter, season rapidly and lightly with salt and pepper, and cover to keep warm. Add more butter to the pan as needed, sauté the remaining scallops, and arrange them also on the platter. Serve them as is, or sauce them with one of the following choices.

SAUCE SUGGESTIONS

Deglazing Sauce with Lemon and Parsley

After removing the preceding sautéed scallops to the platter, make the classic deglazing sauce on page 192—sautéing a tablespoon or so of shallots, deglazing the pan with wine and chicken stock, adding a little lemon juice and parsley, swirling in a bit of butter if you wish, and pouring the sauce over the scallops.

(*continued*)

Tarragon Sauce

Make the preceding classic deglazing sauce and add ½ teaspoon of fragrant dried tarragon, or leaves of fresh tarragon, to the wine and stock as you are boiling it down. Garnish with fresh tarragon leaves if you have them, or with chopped fresh parsley.

Tarragon Cream Sauce

Complete the preceding tarragon sauce, and when it has boiled down to a syrup, pour in 1 cup of heavy cream. Return the veal scallops to the pan, basting them with the sauce, and simmering for a moment until well heated through. Taste carefully for seasoning, adding drops of lemon juice, if needed. Garnish with fresh tarragon leaves or parsley.

OTHER SAUCE SUGGESTIONS

The cream and mushroom sauce for pork chops (page 203) is an attractive possibility, as is the Provençal treatment with tomatoes and herbs for sautéed chicken on page 139 and the black butter sauce with capers for the fish galettes on page 125.

Wines and Vegetables to Serve with Veal Scallops

All the vegetables and wines suggested for veal chops on page 205 also go nicely with veal scallops.

CALF'S LIVER

Liver may be a mature taste, an acquired taste, and, if your family members are not yet liver lovers, they may well become so when you bring out a dish of liver and onions.

Buying liver. Look for color—a rather deep terra-cotta rather than purplish brown—then you will have the liver with the best taste and tenderest texture. For the following sautés it should be sliced ⅜ inch thick, and the slices should contain a minimum of tubes and gristly pieces buried in the meat. The membrane surrounding the outside circumference should be removed, or it will pull the slices out of shape as they sauté.

Storing. Liver is perishable; it should be kept under refrigeration, and be used within a day or two of purchase. I have had success freezing raw liver at 0°F for a week or two, and letting it thaw slowly in the refrigerator. Would anyone know the difference? I'm not sure I would.

⬤ MASTER RECIPE

Sautéed Calf's Liver

Here is the master recipe for a simple sauté of calf's liver, which cooks hardly more than a minute on each side. Overcooked liver is gray, dry, and disappointing—perfectly sautéed, it is a rosy pink when you cut into it.

For 4 servings

4 slices or about 1 pound top-quality calf's liver sliced ½ inch thick
Salt and freshly ground pepper
½ cup or so flour in a plate
3 Tbs clarified butter (page 139), or butter and light olive oil or peanut oil

SPECIAL EQUIPMENT SUGGESTED: *A heavy 10-inch frying pan, no-stick recommended*

Sautéing. The moment before sautéing, season the liver on both sides with a sprinkling of salt and pepper, and dredge in the flour, shaking off excess. Set the frying pan over high heat and film with ¹⁄₁₆ inch of clarified butter or butter and oil. When very hot, lay in the liver and sauté 1 minute on each side.

When is it done? It should be barely springy when pressed with your finger, and a deep pinky red when you cut into a piece. Serve as is, or try one of the suggestions that follow.

Calf's Liver and Bacon

Cook 2 slices of bacon per person and keep warm on a plate lined with paper towels. Pour the bacon fat into a small bowl, wipe the pan clean, and spoon in clear bacon fat. Use that rather than butter for sautéing, to give the liver a special flavor. Serve the bacon with the liver.

Sautéed Calf's Liver with Wine and Mustard Sauce

For 4 servings

1 Tbs Dijon-type prepared mustard
¼ cup beef or chicken stock
¼ cup dry white French vermouth
Ingredients for Sautéed Calf's Liver
1 Tbs butter
1 Tbs minced shallot or scallion
2 Tbs minced fresh parsley

Whisk the mustard, stock, and vermouth in a small bowl. Sauté the liver and remove to hot plates or a hot platter. Wipe out the pan with a paper towel, add the tablespoon of butter, and sauté the shallot or scallion in the pan for a moment; blend in the mustard mixture and simmer a moment or two, until the sauce has thickened lightly. Swirl in the parsley, spoon the sauce over the liver, and serve.

OTHER SAUCES OR TOPPINGS FOR
SAUTÉED LIVER

Flavored Butter Topping

Rather than making a sauce, top each slice with a tablespoon of mustard butter (page 194), or of Maître d'Hôtel Butter (page 193) with its parsley and lemon, or the red or white wine butter. These are convenient and fast because they can be made ahead and stored in the refrigerator.

Black Butter Sauce with Capers

This is described on page 125, and is particularly successful with liver, the capers giving it an agreeably tart overtone.

Liver and Onions

Liver and onions—and beautifully browned tender sliced onions they must be—are an unbeatable combination.

For 4 servings

Ingredients for the master recipe for sautéed liver
½ cup tenderly browned sliced onions (see Special Note on this page)
¼ cup dry white French vermouth
⅓ cup beef or chicken stock
2 to 3 Tbs minced fresh parsley, optional

The liver. Season, dredge in flour, and sauté as described in the master recipe, but keep it rarer than usual.

Finishing the dish. Scrape the onions over the liver, pour in the vermouth and stock, raise heat, and boil rapidly, basting the liver with the sauce as it thickens lightly. Remove the liver to hot plates or a hot platter, spoon the sauce over, and decorate with the optional parsley.

Suggested accompaniments. Your own home-made mashed potatoes would be lovely here, broiled or baked tomatoes, and perhaps a lightly dressed salad of young spinach leaves. You'll want a fairly hearty red wine, like zinfandel or Beaujolais.

SPECIAL NOTE

Tenderly Browned Sliced Onions—"Marmelade"
To serve with steaks, hamburgers, sautéed liver

This is for about ½ cup of browned sliced onions, enough for the garnishing of 4 to 6 servings. Slowly sauté 3 cups of sliced onions in 2 to 3 tablespoons of butter or oil in a covered pan, stirring frequently, until the onions are very tender—15 minutes or so. Uncover the pan, salt lightly, raise the heat to moderately high, and let the onions brown nicely, stirring frequently—5 minutes or more.

Ahead-of-time note: The onions may be browned even a day in advance, or may be frozen and thawed. (Blissful idea: have medium-size packets of browned onions in the freezer, ready to be thawed in the microwave.)

VARIATIONS

Calf's Liver and Onions, alla Veneziana

Reminiscent of Harry's Bar in Venice. Cut the liver into strips about 2½ inches long. When the onions are done and out of the pan, and just before serving, season the liver, toss with the flour, and shake in a sieve to remove excess flour. Sauté and sauce as described in the preceding recipe.

Chicken Livers alla Veneziana

Chicken livers are a fine substitute for calf's liver, and the terra-cotta rather than purplish color is most desirable if you can pick them out one by one. Follow the preceding recipe, substituting chicken livers for the strips of calf's liver.

BROIL-ROASTING

By the time a broiled or pan-fried thick steak is cooked through, the inside is dandy but the outside is too often blackened, tough, and dry. The solution is to brown it on both sides under the broiler and to finish it off in the oven. This works nicely not only for 2-inch steaks, but for other pieces of meat not thick enough to require actual roasting but too thick for successful broiling. Butterflied pork loin and butterflied leg of lamb are other examples; broil-roasting is also fast and fine for butterflied chickens and turkeys, beginning on page 154.

MASTER RECIPE

Broil-Roasted Sirloin Steak

BEEF CUTS TO CHOOSE. *Referring to our beef chart on page 492, prime choices for thick steaks are the porterhouse, T-bone, rib steak, and sirloin. The sirloin is my choice when serving more than 4 people, but they all cook as in the following directions.*

For 6 to 8 servings

A 3-pound boneless sirloin steak 2 inches thick (or 2 T-bone, porterhouse, or rib steaks)
1 Tbs fresh oil
Salt and freshly ground pepper
¼ tsp thyme or herb blend
⅓ cup dry white French vermouth
⅓ cup beef stock
1 to 2 Tbs butter, optional

SPECIAL EQUIPMENT SUGGESTED:
A frying pan or shallow flameproof roasting pan that will just hold the steak comfortably; a bulb baster and pastry brush are useful; an instant meat thermometer

Preparing the steak. Dry the steak, trim off excess fat, and rub both sides lightly with oil. Arrange the steak in the pan.

Preliminary broiling. Preheat broiler to high, and set the steak so its surface is close under the heat element. Rapidly brown the top—about 2 minutes. Remove cooking fat with a bulb baster or spoon (so it will not catch fire in the pan). Season lightly with salt and pepper, turn, and brown briefly on the other side. Season this side lightly, baste with the fat in the pan, sprinkle on the herbs.

*Ahead-of-time note: May be prepared in advance to this point.

Finishing in the oven. Turn the oven thermostat to 375°F, and set the steak in the upper third level to finish cooking for 15 to 20 minutes, turning and basting once. It will be done to a rosy rare at 125°F on your meat thermometer. Remove the steak to a warm platter and let it rest 5 minutes or so before carving, so that the juices will retreat back into the flesh.

*Ahead-of-time note: After its rest you can then hold it at 120°F or less for a good hour before serving.

Sauce and serving. Meanwhile, spoon the cooking fat out of the baking dish, pour in the wine and stock, and boil over high heat on top of the stove, scraping up coagulated juices. In a few seconds, remove from heat, swirl in the optional butter, pour over the steak, and serve.

Suggested accompaniments. There's nothing wrong with baked potatoes, or homemade mashed potatoes, or one of the potato gratins on page 322. Or you might choose an eggplant dish such as the soufflé on page 292, the eggplant and tomato ratatouille on page 317, or eggplant pizzas (page 318). And/or fresh green peas, or beans, or—I shall not go on since almost anything goes with steak. Certainly a red wine, a fine Bordeaux or cabernet, or a Burgundy or pinot noir.

OTHER SAUCE AND SERVING SUGGESTIONS

See the red wine sauce for sautéed beefsteaks, as well as the Béarnaise sauce and the flavored butters, all of which go nicely with broil-roasted steaks.

How to slice and serve the steak

Butterflied Loin of Pork

A loin of pork roasts in half the usual time when it is butterflied, and that means simply to untie the boned loin that you bought at the supermarket. Spread it out, slash the thick portions to even it out, and there is your butterfly. Rather than a broil-roast it's the other way around—start it in the oven and finish it under the broiler.

For 8 servings

A 3- to 3½-pound boned pork loin roast
1½ tsp salt
1½ tsp of the Spice Marinade (see Special Note, page 203), or a mixture of ground allspice, sage or thyme, and freshly ground pepper
1 Tbs light oil
1 Tbs coarse (Kosher) salt, optional

SPECIAL EQUIPMENT SUGGESTED: *A shallow roasting pan that will just hold the pork comfortably; an instant meat thermometer*

Preparing the pork. Trim off excess fat, leaving, however, a ⅛-inch layer on the outside. Set fat side down, and make several lengthwise slashes in the thick sections of the meat, to even it out. Rub the spices over the meat, then rub with the oil. Set flesh side up in the roasting pan; cover and refrigerate several hours or overnight.

*Ahead-of-time note: May be completed 2 days in advance.

Preliminary roasting—1 hour at 375°F. Preheat the oven to 375°F. Roast in the middle level for about 1 hour, or to an internal meat thermometer reading of 140°F, basting with accumulated fat every 20 minutes. Turn fat side up, and make decorative shallow cross-hatch slashes 1 inch apart in the fat; gently rub in the optional coarse salt.

*Ahead-of-time note: May be completed somewhat in advance to this point; remove from the oven, cover loosely, and set at room temperature.

Final broiling—20 minutes. Set the meat so its surface is 3 inches from the hot broiler element as it slowly browns; the internal meat temperature should be 162°F to 165°F. The meat should be firm but juicy, and a faint pink when you cut into it. Let rest 10 minutes before carving.

*Ahead-of-time note: After roasting and its 10-minute rest, you can then hold it at 120°F for a good hour before serving.

Serving. Carve into slanting slices, spooning a little pan juice over each.

Suggested accompaniments. A roast of pork is an opportunity to bring out some of the wonderful-tasting earthy vegetables, like braised butternut squash, or the rutabaga and parsnip dishes starting on page 285, or the grated beets on page 293, or the stuffed winter squash on page 307. Any of the suggestions for pork chops on page 202 go with roast pork, too. You'll want a full white wine of the chardonnay type, or a light red—a merlot or a Bordeaux.

1. After trimming off fat, remove the hip bone.

2. The knee cap

3. Removing the leg bones

4. Making lengthwise slashes in meat

Butterflied Leg of Lamb with stuffed tomatoes

VARIATION

Butterflied Leg of Lamb

A butterflied leg of lamb cooks in a third the usual time, and is a breeze to carve. If your butcher does not go in for butterflying, it is easy enough to do yourself.

To butterfly a leg of lamb. Trim off the outside fat. Then turn the lamb skin side down, the small (shank) end facing you. Note the cut end of the hip-bone protruding slightly near the large end, step 1. It is attached to the main leg by a ball joint. Cut under hip bone to separate it from the joint, then around its convoluted structure to release it, along with the tail assembly, from the meat. The ball end of the bone that fits into the hip joint belongs to the main leg bone; make a straight cut down through the meat

from the ball end to the knee, scraping the meat away from the bone all around. At its outside angle, against the skin, is lodged a moon-shaped white chip that is the knee cap, step 2. Remove it. Cut around the flesh of the shank bone to detach its lower part; then cut around the knee to free the two leg bones in one piece, step 3. (The flesh of the shank contains white tendons that make this meat less tender than the rest. Cut it off if you wish, and save it for the lamburgers on page 201; or cut out the tendons one by one and use the meat for the kabobs at the end of the butterflied lamb recipe.) Spread the meat skin side down; cut out visible fat. To make the meat more even in thickness, cut lengthwise slashes, step 4. (A 6½-pound leg serves 10 to 12 people easily; if you are having fewer guests, cut off a nice lobe of meat and save it for another meal.)

Finishing the job. Run two long skewers crosswise through the meat to keep it in place. Paint the meat with oil. Or paint both sides with the following mustard coating, and refrigerate the meat for at least an hour if possible—overnight is better.

Broil-roasting. If you are using it, reserve 2 tablespoons of the mustard coating for the final cooking. Brown the lamb slowly under the broiler for 10 minutes on each side, basting several times with oil.

*Ahead-of-time note: After browning, you may let it sit at room temperature for up to an hour.

Finishing the lamb—about 20 minutes at 375°F. When you are ready to finish it off, set the lamb skin side up and paint with the reserved mustard coating. Roast for 15 to 20 minutes in the upper third of the preheated oven.

When is it done? The lamb is done when the flesh has just achieved a springy texture to the pressure of your finger, in contrast to its squashy feel when raw. Red rare will be 125°F on your meat thermometer; medium pinky rare, 130°F. Remove the meat from the oven and let it sit 10 to 15 minutes before carving so the juices can retreat back into the tissues.

*Ahead-of-time note: After roasting, and letting the meat rest at room temperature for 10 minutes, you can hold it at 120°F for a good hour without fear of overcooking.

Serving. To carve, cut into slanting slices across the grain—not as neat as for a bone-in leg, but carving is easy. Moisten each serving with accumulated pan juices.

Suggested accompaniments. As for vegetables, eggplant is a natural with lamb, and so easy to do when you steam it (page 291). White beans go beautifully, too, and are fast to cook when you use the quick-soak system on page 332. Two other suggestions: green beans, cooked the French way so they retain their bright color and texture (page 276), and tomatoes Provençale, baked with fresh bread crumbs and herbs (page 306).

BARBECUING NOTE. *You may cook the butterflied leg entirely on the barbecue grill, turning and basting it with oil in the usual manner.*

SPECIAL NOTE

Mustard Coating and Marinade for Roast and Broiled Lamb and Kabobs

2 large cloves of garlic
½ tsp salt
2 Tbs Dijon-style prepared mustard
1 Tbs soy sauce
1½ tsp fragrant ground rosemary, thyme, or oregano
2 Tbs freshly squeezed lemon juice
¼ cup olive oil or peanut oil

Purée the garlic into a small bowl and mash to a paste with the salt. Whisk in the mustard, soy, herbs, lemon juice, and then the oil, to make a mayonnaise-like cream.

Basting kabobs with Mustard Marinade

VARIATION

Lamb Kabobs: Skewered Lamb

Colorful skewered fantasies of meat with pineapple, green peppers, mushrooms, little onions, and cherry tomatoes look so pretty when raw, but just try to cook one successfully! If the meat gets done properly, the peppers and onions will be raw, the mushrooms and tomatoes will fall off, and only the pineapple may survive. Better to use meat alone, and save the trimmings for accompaniment.

For an unspecified number

Chunks of tender roasting-quality lamb, such as unused lobes of meat from a butterflied leg
The mustard marinade (see Special Note), or a mixture such as olive oil, lemon juice, drops of soy sauce, and ground rosemary
Strips of thick-sliced bacon cut into 2-inch crosswise pieces, optional
Imported bay leaves

SPECIAL EQUIPMENT SUGGESTED: *A hinged double-sided barbecue rack that will fit over a roaster; or a roaster with rack to fit on top to hold the skewers, as illustrated*

Lamb Kebobs: Skewered Lamb (*continued*)

Preparing the lamb. Remove fat and gristle, and cut the lamb, as well as you can, into 2-inch chunks. Toss in a bowl with the marinade ingredients and let steep an hour if possible, or overnight. Drop the bacon into a saucepan of boiling water and blanch (boil slowly) 5 minutes; drain, rinse in cold water, and pat dry in paper towels. Thread the lamb onto skewers, reserving the marinade, interspersing the pieces with either the optional bacon or a piece of bay leaf.

*Ahead-of-time note: May be prepared even a day in advance; cover and refrigerate.

Broiling. Baste the kabobs again with the reserved marinade. Set close under a hot broiling element for 2 minutes, turn, and broil another 2 minutes, or until the meat has just taken on a light springiness in contrast to its squashy raw state. (Cut into a piece if you have doubts.) Baste the kabobs with any juices that have fallen into the pan, and serve.

BARBECUE NOTE. *If you are kabobing on a barbecue, you'll find it helpful to enclose the skewered meat in a hinged rack, where they are easy to turn and baste.*

FEASTING ON THE REMAINS

Wonderful things can be done with leftover lamb, raw or cooked. For example, ground roast lamb makes the splendid moussaka on page 319, or it could go into the stuffed cabbage on page 304, and there are always lamburgers (page 201). Here are two other ideas.

Syrian Salad Platter

Cold roast lamb is delicious in itself, but it's also good dressed in Syrian robes, as in the following suggestion.

For 6 servings

A bulgur base
1 cup raw dry bulgur (cracked wheat) in a bowl
4 cups boiling water
1 small onion, grated
½ cup chopped fresh parsley
1 or more Tbs olive oil
Salt and freshly ground pepper
Freshly squeezed lemon juice

Garlic and anchovy sauce for lamb
2 large cloves of garlic
Salt and freshly ground pepper
1 lemon
6 anchovies packed in olive oil
Rosemary or thyme
Dijon-type prepared mustard
½ cup or more olive oil
2 Tbs capers, chopped
2 to 3 Tbs chopped fresh parsley
12 slices of cold roast leg of lamb
Decorative suggestions: quartered tomatoes or halved cherry tomatoes; cucumbers, peeled, halved lengthwise, seeded, and sliced; sliced green and/or red bell peppers; black olives; halved or quartered hard-boiled eggs

Syrian Salad Platter

The bulgur. While stirring the bulgur, pour on the boiling water; let soak 15 minutes or longer, until it is tender enough to chew pleasantly. Pour through a sieve to drain, rinse in cold water, and squeeze as dry as possible by twisting it by handfuls in the corner of a towel. Toss it in the bowl with the grated onion, parsley, and olive oil, adding salt, pepper, and lemon juice to taste.

Garlic and anchovy sauce for lamb. Purée the garlic into a small bowl and add a pinch of salt. Mince a 2-inch strip of peel from the lemon, add it to the garlic, and mash all together with a wooden spoon until a fairly smooth paste. Then mash in the anchovies along with ¼ teaspoon or so of rosemary or thyme. Blend in a tablespoon of lemon juice, another of Dijon mustard, and finally beat in the olive oil by driblets to make a lightly creamy sauce. Blend in the capers and parsley, and season to taste.

Saucing the lamb. Place the slices of lamb in a dish and baste with the sauce; let marinate, basting occasionally, for at least ½ hour.

*Ahead-of-time note: The lamb may be sauced a day ahead; cover and refrigerate.

Serving. Mound the bulgur in the center of a platter and arrange the slices of lamb attractively around it. Place whatever decorative suggestions you are using around the platter in bountiful profusion. (Flavor the cucumber, if you wish, with a teaspoon or so of wine vinegar, ¼ teaspoon of salt, and a pinch of sugar—toss to blend, and let macerate 10 minutes or so; pour the juices over the tomatoes.)

Scotch Broth: Barley Soup
Lentil or Bean Soup

The bones from a butterflied leg of lamb make a first-rate main-course soup, filled with good flavors and good things.

For 2 quarts or so, serving 6

Lamb stock

The uncooked bones and scraps from a boned leg of lamb
1 medium carrot, chopped
1 medium onion, chopped
Salt and freshly ground pepper
1 large celery stalk, chopped
2 large cloves of garlic, smashed
1 imported bay leaf
¼ tsp rosemary or thyme

The vegetable garnish

A little chicken stock or bean-cooking liquid, if needed
½ cup barley or lentils, or 1½ cups almost-cooked white beans, or 1½ cups canned beans
½ cup each: diced onions, turnips, and carrots
1 cup diced tomato pulp (fresh or canned)
2 to 3 Tbs chopped fresh parsley

SPECIAL EQUIPMENT SUGGESTED:
A roasting pan to brown the bones; a large saucepan or a kettle for the stock

Browning the bones. Chop or saw the lamb bones into convenient-size pieces, arrange in the roasting pan with the chopped carrot and onion, and brown 30 to 40 minutes in the upper third level of a 425°F oven, turning and basting with accumulated fat once or twice. Drain out fat and transfer the bones and vegetables to the saucepan or kettle. Pour a cup of water into the roasting pan and simmer on top of the stove a moment or two, scraping coagulated juices into the liquid; pour the liquid into the saucepan with the bones.

Simmering the stock. Add water to cover ingredients by an inch, and bring to the simmer. Skim off accumulated scum for several minutes, salt and pepper the stock lightly, and add the chopped celery, garlic, bay leaf, and rosemary or thyme. Cover loosely and simmer 3 to 4 hours, or until you feel you have gotten the best out of your bones—add water as needed to keep the ingredients covered. Strain and degrease; wash out the saucepan and return the stock to it.

Finishing the soup. Bring the degreased stock to the simmer—you should have almost 2 quarts; add a little chicken stock or bean liquid if needed. Add the barley, lentils, or beans, and the onions, turnips, and carrots; cover loosely and simmer until the vegetables are tender—15 minutes or so. Taste carefully and correct seasoning.

*Ahead-of-time note: May be completed a day in advance. When cool, cover and refrigerate.

Serving. Bring the soup to the simmer. Fold in the diced tomato and the parsley; simmer a moment more. Correct seasoning again, and the soup is ready to serve.

SPARE RIBS

 MASTER RECIPE

Broiled or Barbecued Spare Ribs

Spare ribs on the barbecue, all of a summer's night, or browning away under the broiler of a winter evening—spare ribs are a year-round treat, and these are especially good because of their preliminary spicing. It gives them extra flavor, as does frequent basting with the special house BBQ sauce.

For 6 servings

3 whole spare ribs, making 12 sets of 3-rib portions

Salt and spice marinade

Either 1½ Tbs salt and 1 tsp of your own Spice Marinade (Special Note, page 203)

Or 1½ Tbs salt, ½ tsp ground allspice, ½ tsp freshly ground pepper

Special house BBQ sauce

½ cup fresh peanut oil
½ cup soy sauce
½ cup honey
1 tsp thyme or sage
1 tsp paprika
¼ tsp cayenne pepper or chili powder, or to taste
2 Tbs vinegar

Barbecue dinner: the ribs, upper left; lentil salad, right; ratatouille, lower right

Trimming the ribs. Most ribs you buy in the supermarket are trimmed and ready to cook. If yours are not, cut the cartilage bone ends from the large side and remove any excess fat and gristle from the whole rib section. Slash between every 2 or 3 ribs at the large side to make for easy cutting into portions after cooking.

Preliminary salt and spice marinade. Mix the spices and salt in a small bowl; rub the mixture into both sides of the ribs (see illustration, step 1). Cover and refrigerate. Leave at least ½ hour, but overnight is more effective.

Special house BBQ sauce. Mix the ingredients for the sauce in a bowl, and paint a coating on both sides of the ribs. Set the ribs, curved side down, in a roasting pan or pans. Reserve the rest of the sauce.

1. Rubbing in dry marinade

2. Painting final marinade over partially cooked ribs

Ahead-of-time note: The recipe may be prepared a day in advance to this point. Cover ribs and sauce, and refrigerate them.

Pre-barbecue roasting—40 minutes at 375°F. Baste both sides lightly with another coat of sauce, step 2, and roast 20 minutes on each side in the preheated oven—this starts the cooking and eliminates some of the excess fat.

Ahead-of-time note: May be done somewhat in advance; let cool, then cover and refrigerate.

Final cooking.

Either on the barbecue. Have your coals just right—a hot gray, not a burning red. Basting the ribs with the sauce, turn them over the coals for 15 to 20 minutes, until a nice crusty brown.

Or under the broiler. Instead of finishing on the barbecue, turn the ribs under a moderate broiler for 15 to 20 minutes, basting frequently with the sauce.

Suggested accompaniments. An eggplant and tomato casserole, the famous ratatouille (page 317), would go beautifully, as would lentils (page 337), hot or cold, and a tossed green salad. Serve beer, cider, or a spicy sauvignon blanc.

Real spare ribs, top; country style, lower right; back ribs, lower left

VARIATION

Back ribs and country-style ribs

Use the same general system for these, but because country-style ribs are meatier and fattier, give them about an hour's preliminary roasting before their final browning. On the other hand, back ribs are thinner and leaner; omit the preliminary roasting and concentrate on a slow broil, or barbecue to cook and brown them under their basting sauce.

ROASTING

Roast beef usually means roast ribs of beef, and, like roast turkey, it is one of the easiest pieces of meat to deal with. Set it in the oven, baste it occasionally, and the only other attention it needs is that you check the timing and the meat thermometer. No worries about guests not arriving on time, either, because you can hold the roast perfectly for over an hour. Although other and less expensive cuts can be roasted successfully (and some of them are discussed on page 242), the ribs, and top loin, and the tenderloin are the great traditional roasting choices. You'll see them pictured on our beef carcass (page 492).

Cuts of beef for roasting. Left, trimmed rib roast; center, whole tenderloin; right, top loin roast

Rib roasts. Left, trimmed roast; right, untrimmed roast

Roast beef

BUYING AND TRIMMING. *There is a lot of waste to an untrimmed rib roast, whether or not it's the prime rib— prime meaning top-quality. This is particularly true if you buy the shoulder end of the rib section. For the beautifully prepared loin end roast on the left, all the "cap" meat (layers of meat and fat surrounding the "eye") has been removed except for a thin layer of covering fat. The rib bones have been shortened and "frenched" (trimmed of fat and gristle); the chine (backbone) is off; and butcher's twine is looped around the roast between each rib. Any good market will do this for you given a few days' notice, but it's a nice bit of work for the home butcher and when you slice the fat off the trimmings, you have the base for fine hamburgers or a beef stew.*

HOW MANY SERVINGS? *Some authorities figure 2 people per rib, but our 5 ribs served 16.*

ROASTING METHODS. *Although I have tried various fast and slow and on-again, off-again methods for roasting beef, I always return to the uncomplicated 325°F oven, where the cook has easy access and complete control.*

Roast beef dinner with all the trimmings

MASTER RECIPE

Roast Prime Ribs of Beef

Here is the recipe for a large top-quality 5-rib roast, for a big family dinner serving 12 to 16. Smaller roasts cook exactly the same way; it is only the timing that differs, as described in the preceding chart.

MANUFACTURING NOTE. *Roasting is so easy—put the meat into a 325°F oven and roast to a temperature of 120°F at the large end—2¼ to 2¾ hours, basting with accumulated fat every 30 minutes. The following is a full-scale treatment in case this is your first roast beef and you're nervous about having spent all that money for all that meat.*

TIMING. *Count on 3½ hours to be on the very safe side—a generous 2¾ hours for roasting, plus a ¾-hour leeway and rest before carving. Be sure your oven thermostat is correct! Check it with an accurate oven thermometer.*

For 12 to 16 servings

A fully trimmed 5-rib (approximately 12-pound) roast of beef from the loin end, ribs 8 through 12
2 Tbs fresh cooking oil
½ cup each chopped carrots and onions, to flavor the juices
½ tsp dried thyme
2 cups beef stock, preferably your own, which you can make from the rib ends and chine bones (page 14); or a combination of beef and chicken broths

SPECIAL EQUIPMENT SUGGESTED:
A shallow roasting pan just large enough to hold the beef comfortably; a pastry brush for basting; an instant meat thermometer

Preliminaries. Prepare the roast according to the preceding suggestions, and rub the exposed ends of meat with cooking oil. Arrange it fat side up in the roasting pan. If you plan to make your own beef stock, start it going well ahead—it can be refrigerated or frozen.

*Ahead-of-time note: May be prepared a day in advance; cover and refrigerate. A chilled roast may take a little longer to cook than the times indicated.

Roasting—2¼ to 2¾ hours at 325°F. Place the roast in the lower middle level of the preheated oven. In ½ hour check the oven to be sure all is going well; baste the ends of the meat with the fat accumulated in the pan. After 1 hour, strew the chopped carrots and onions around the beef; baste them with pan fat and sprinkle with the thyme. Baste again in another ½ hour, and, when 2 hours are up, begin taking its temperature. When it has reached 110°F, watch out—it rises quickly from now on.

When is it done? For rosy rare at the large end, the temperature should be 120°F; the small end will be 125°F—test rapidly but leave the thermometer in for a good 15 seconds. Test in several places if you have any doubts—a few minutes

---

SPECIAL NOTE

Timing for fully trimmed ready-to-roast ribs

Oven roasting temperature: 325°F

Meat thermometer reading:

Rare: 120°F at the large end, to give rosy rare at the large end and pinky rare at the small end

Medium rare: 125°F to 130°F

Medium: 140°F, a pinky gray color—note that this is the official "safe" temperature for cooked meats, where various bacteria are surely killed off.

Rest period after roasting: A rest is essential after roasting so that the juices will retreat back into the flesh. Allow 25 to 30 minutes for a 5-rib roast, and 10 to 15 minutes for a 2-rib roast.

Approximate minutes per pound: (6-pound roasts and on up—small roasts

take a little more time) 12 to 13 minutes per pound for rare; 14 to 16, for medium rare; 17 to 20, for medium

Roasting chart: Approximate timing for prime and choice grades roasted to 120°F at the large end, rest period not included. Always count on the longest time plus a 20-minute rest out of the oven, to be sure your roast will be done—you can keep it safely once cooked, as described at the end of the recipe.

A 5-rib roast (11 to 13 pounds)	2¼ to 2¾ hours
A 4-rib roast (9 to 10 pounds)	1¾ to 2¼ hours
A 3-rib roast (7 to 8½ pounds)	1½ to 1¾ hours
A 2-rib roast (4 to 5 pounds)	1 to 1¼ hours, which includes 15 minutes at 450°F and continuation at 325°F

---

more roasting will bring it up several degrees, to whatever stage of doneness you prefer.

Removing the roast. Remove the beef to a platter or carving board and discard trussing strings; let it rest at room temperature for 20 to 30 minutes, allowing the juices to retreat back into the meat. (You'll note that the temperature will go up about 10 degrees as the meat juices gradually circulate from the hot surface to the interior.)

*Ahead-of-time note: If the wait is longer, after its rest set the roast anywhere that it will stay warm enough but will not overcook—use a warming oven, but be sure the temperature cannot go over 120°F, or set the roast in a pan or on a platter, cover loosely, and place over a kettle of almost-simmering water. You may keep it warm for an hour or more.

(continued)

Vertical English carving method

Roast Prime Ribs of Beef (*continued*)

Carving. An easy and attractive way to carve the roast is in the vertical English manner (see illustration): cut a slice off one end, turn the roast up on that end, and slice straight across the top with a very sharp knife. The ham slicer shown here does an easy carving job.

Suggested accompaniments. Rather than the usual mashed potatoes (however welcome), you might accompany the beef with yellow squash cut into angel-hair julienne and sautéed in butter (page 294). Broccoli could be the green vegetable, and the following creamy horseradish sauce would go very well, as would a noble red Bordeaux or cabernet sauvignon.

SPECIAL NOTE

Horseradish Sauce

The quickest horseradish sauce is a simple stirring-up of bottled horseradish, Dijon-type mustard, salt, and white pepper into whipped cream or sour cream, using your taster as your guide. Here's a more elaborate version.

For 2 cups

4 to 5 Tbs bottled horseradish
2 Tbs or more Dijon-type prepared mustard
Droplets of white-wine vinegar
1½ cups white sauce (2½ Tbs butter and 3 Tbs flour cooked together without coloring; off heat 1½ cups hot milk blended in; season and simmer 3 minutes—page 272)
2 egg yolks
⅓ to ½ cup heavy cream
Salt and freshly ground white pepper

Stir horseradish, mustard, and vinegar to taste into the white sauce; whisk in the egg yolks. Whisk slowly over moderate heat to poach the yolks and thicken the sauce but do not bring it to the simmer. Whisk in the cream by driblets to make a sauce the consistency of mayonnaise. Taste and correct seasoning, adding more mustard, horseradish, or whatever you think needed. Serve warm or tepid.

**Ahead-of-time note:* May be made in advance and reheated, or kept for a short while over warm water.

VARIATION

Roast Top Loin of Beef

The top loin strip, also known as a New York strip, is the large lobe of meat on our porterhouse steak (page 191); it makes a beautiful roast. Being a boneless length of meat, it does not have the visual grandeur of the standing rib, but it is a cut preferred by many beef buffs because of its excellent flavor, and by cooks, too, because it is easy to roast, carve, and serve. It's expensive!

Number of servings. A 4½-pound boned and trimmed top loin of beef serves 8 to 10 people.

Preparations for roasting. All but a ⅛-inch layer of fat should be sliced off the top length of the roast, and the meat should be tied around its circumference at 1½-inch intervals. Rub the exposed parts of the meat with oil. Arrange the beef fat side up on an oiled rack in a shallow, rather narrow roasting pan.

Roasting—1¼ to 1½ hours at 425°F and 350°F. Roast in the upper third level of a preheated oven for 15 minutes, then turn the thermostat down to 350°F. Several times during roasting, baste the ends of the meat with the fat accumulated in the pan. After 45 minutes, slice a large onion and strew it in the pan, then salt the meat.

When is it done? The beef is done to a rosy rare at a meat thermometer reading of 120°F; 125°F, for medium rare.

Serving and sauce suggestions. While the roast is resting, skim the fat off the juices in the pan. If you are carving in the kitchen, turn each piece of beef in the pan juices before arranging it on a hot platter. If carving at the table, either make a deglazing sauce on page 192, and spoon a little over each serving; or pass a bowl of Béarnaise sauce with the beef juices beaten in. See also the Port or Madeira wine sauce on page 222.

Carving. Carve straight down, like a loaf of bread. If the slices are less than ⅛ inch thick, everyone may have 2 or 3 pieces for a generous look on the plate.

SPECIAL NOTE

TIMING NOTE FOR LOIN STRIPS AND TENDERLOINS. *Boneless lengths of meat such as the top loin and the tenderloin are timed according to their dimensions rather than their weight in pounds. A top loin 5½ to 6 inches wide and 3½ inches high, regardless of length and weight, will take 1¼ to 1½ hours, starting at 425°F and finishing at 350°F. A fully trimmed whole prime or choice tenderloin will take 35 to 45 minutes at 400°F.*

Tenderloin of beef

The tenderloin is the most tender as well as the most expensive of all the beef cuts, yet since it takes such a short time to roast—35 to 45 minutes—it is well worth considering when you must put on an important dinner fast. First a few facts to help you with the general techniques.

Description. The whole prime or choice tenderloin weighs in at 8 to 9 pounds but when trimmed of covering fat, membranes, and the long thin side muscle of meat attached to its length, it is down to a mere 4 pounds or so. The small end of its long tapering shape begins in the loin, inside the small of the back at the end of the rib section. Its large end or butt is part of the sirloin or hip, and is sometimes not included—in this case you will be buying a "short tenderloin."

NUMBER OF SERVINGS. *A fully trimmed 4-pound tenderloin will serve 6 to 8 people.*

To trim a tenderloin of beef. The side that was next to the backbone has ridges with fatty streaks. The other side is covered with rather loose surface fat; remove this loose fat and the membrane covering the meat. Cut and pull loose the side muscle of meat, which you might reserve for the beef tenderloin sauté on page 194. If you have the whole tenderloin with butt, you now want to make the roast an even circumference from one end to the other. First, separate and cut off the flap of meat at the butt end; it will make a nice steak for two another day. Next, if you don't want the whole roast, cut off several inches of the small end, the filet mignon, and reserve for a sauté or kabobs. Or to even the roast, fold those several inches under the membrane side. Tie the circumference of the roast with white butcher's twine at 1½-inch intervals.

IF YOU CANNOT FIND WHOLE TENDERLOIN. *By the way, use 2 short ones, cutting off the small ends if you wish; two will roast in approximately the same time as one.*

SPECIAL NOTE

An "Au Jus" sauce for Beef Roasts

While the roast is resting, skim excess fat from the roasting pan, pour in a cup or so of homemade beef stock and bring to the boil, mashing the roasting vegetables into the liquid and scraping up coagulated juices. Pour into a saucepan and simmer several minutes, skimming off additional fat; correct seasoning. Just before serving, strain into a warm sauce bowl, pressing juices out of the vegetables and adding any juices from the roast. There will be just a small delicious spoonful to moisten each serving of beef.

Roast Tenderloin of Beef

Roasting—35 to 45 minutes at 400°F.
Brush the roast all over with melted
clarified butter and set it fattier
(ridged) side up in a roasting pan just
long and wide enough to hold it easily. Place it in the upper third level
of the preheated oven. In 6 to 8 minutes, rapidly turn it and baste with
clarified butter. Turn twice more during roasting, basting with butter,
then with accumulated pan juices.
When 30 minutes are up, salt the
meat and start testing.

When is it done? It will begin to take
on a slight springiness when pressed,
and it is done to rosy rare at an internal thermometer reading of 120°F.
(See Special Note for timing details.)

Resting before carving. Remove from
the oven and let rest 10 to 15 minutes
before carving. Spoon the roasting
fat out of the pan, leaving the juices.

*Ahead-of-time note: See the notes for
roast beef (page 219).

Carving. Remove trussing strings.
Carve the meat into slices from ½ to
1 inch thick. If you are carving in
the kitchen, turn each slice in the pan
juices before arranging on hot plates
or a hot platter.

Suggested accompaniments. You might
serve the platter of sliced tenderloin
garnished with bouquets of beautifully cooked fresh vegetables, such as
green beans and a julienne of carrots
and zucchini interspersed with the
potato galettes on page 324. Or consider the lush gratin of potatoes
baked in cream on page 323, or the
broccoli-sauced broccoli on page 270.
As for wine, pick your best red Bordeaux or cabernet.

---

*OTHER SAUCE AND SERVING
SUGGESTIONS*

Béarnaise Sauce

Béarnaise Sauce (page 87) is always
delicious with beef tenderloin. You
might serve the sauce in large individual broiled mushroom caps or in
artichoke bottoms, and garnish the
platter with broiled cherry tomatoes
and watercress.

Madeira or Port Wine Sauce

Madeira or Port wine sauce made in
the classic manner is marvelous but
takes 4 to 5 hours of simmering; this
is a more informal version. Your own
beef stock is always preferable because it does not taste of the can, but
a respectable can will certainly do if
there is no alternative.

For about 2 cups

2 Tbs clarified butter (page 139)

**Aromatic flavoring: 3 Tbs each
finely chopped onion and celery; 2
Tbs chopped carrot; 1 small garlic
clove, chopped (you may do these
together in a food processor)**
1 Tbs lean chopped boiled ham
**Seasonings: 1 imported bay leaf, a
big pinch of thyme, 8 parsley
stems, 1 allspice berry**
**½ cup dry white French vermouth
or white wine**
**3 cups or so homemade beef stock
(page 14), or a combination of
beef and chicken broths**
**1 small ripe red tomato, chopped; or
1 tsp tomato paste**
Salt and freshly ground pepper

Final touches

**1½ Tbs cornstarch blended in a
small bowl with ¼ cup dry
Madeira or Port wine**
1 to 2 Tbs butter, optional

The sauce base. Heat the butter in a
smallish heavy-bottomed saucepan,
stir in the chopped vegetables, and
sauté over moderately low heat for 7
to 8 minutes, or until tender; raise
heat slightly and brown lightly, stirring, for several minutes. Stir in the
ham, herbs, wine, 3 cups of stock,
and the tomato. Cover loosely and
simmer 1 hour. Correct seasoning,
and strain into a clean pan, pressing
juices out of the vegetables with the
back of a spoon. Skim off surface fat.
You should have about 2 cups of fragrant, beautifully flavored brown
liquid.

*Ahead-of-time note: May be completed in advance; when cool, cover
and refrigerate or freeze.

Final touches. Beat ½ cup of the base into the wine-cornstarch mixture, and pour that back into the base. Bring to the simmer, and simmer slowly 2 minutes. The sauce should be lightly thickened; if too thick, stir in dribbles of additional stock.

*Ahead-of-time note: May be completed in advance.

Deglazing the roasting pan. Pour a little of the sauce into the degreased roasting pan, and simmer a moment, scraping up coagulated juices. Pour this back into the saucepan.

Serving. Just before serving, bring the sauce to the simmer. Remove from heat, and swirl in the optional butter.

Madeira or Port Wine Sauce with Truffles

Drain a 1-ounce can of truffles (pieces or peelings may be used here), and add the juice to the sauce base in the sauce recipe. Finely dice the truffles, and stir them into the wine-cornstarch mixture. Proceed to prepare the sauce, adding the wine-cornstarch mixture with truffles at the end, as described in the recipe.

ROAST LEG OF LAMB

Like a great roast of beef, a whole leg of lamb is a welcome sight on the family dinner table. And carving is dramatic when you hold up the leg by its shank as you make long, wide, thin, stylish slices down its length. Pink juicy lamb is marvelous eaten hot, the leftovers are delicious with a salad of tomatoes or in sandwiches, ground lamb makes a moussaka or stuffs a cabbage, and lamb bones produce one of the great soups—Scotch broth.

Choosing the lamb. For lengthwise carving you will want the lower leg bone intact, not bent at the knee—you need that lower leg as a handle for your elegant slices.

Untrimmed whole leg of lamb

Leg of lamb comes in several ways: the short leg, which does not include the sirloin (the hip and tail section), the sirloin section, which is difficult to carve, or the whole leg illustrated here. Ask that the hip bone and tail be removed to make carving easier; or remove them yourself as illustrated for the butterflied leg of lamb on page 212. Save the bones for making the lamb sauce on page 225.

Preparing the leg for the oven. At home, cut off all excess fat, especially at the side of the large end and the hip. Leave a thin layer of fat over the main body of the meat, and leave on the fell (membrane also covering the meat). You'll note the loose flaps of meat at the large end where the hip and tail were removed; skewer and lace them against the large end. Either rub the exposed flesh of the lamb with olive oil or fresh peanut oil, or paint it with the mustard coating described in the Special Note on page 213.

*AHEAD-OF-TIME NOTE: The lamb may be prepared to this point a day in advance. Cover and refrigerate.

The trimmed and skewered leg, hip bone removed and at upper right

Temperatures for Lamb

Always take the temperature of the meat at the oven with an instant meat thermometer, leaving it in the meat 15 seconds so that it can register— when the lamb is finally out of the oven, the temperature will rise some 10 degrees as the hot juices from the exterior circulate into the interior of the meat. (The following are in-oven temperatures.)

120°F	Very rare
125°F	Rosy rare
130°F	Medium rare—pink
140°F	Medium—pinky gray, the official "safe" temperature where all harmful bacteria are killed

Timing. Because of its bulging shape, *any leg* from 5 to 8 pounds will take 1¼ to 1½ hours of roasting to reach an internal meat thermometer reading of 125°F. Legs weighing 9 to 10 pounds may take 10 to 15 minutes longer.

A boned and rolled leg takes a good 2 to 2¼ hours.

The shank end half should take about 1 hour.

The sirloin half, as well as *the Frenched or short leg* (minus sirloin or hip), needs about 1¼ hours.

◉ MASTER RECIPE

Roast Leg of Lamb

Whether it is a whole large leg, a boned and stuffed leg, the shank or sirloin half, or the short leg, they all roast the same way regardless of timing.

For 8 to 10 servings

A 7- to 8-pound whole leg of lamb, prepared as previously described (hip and tail bones removed; shank intact; knee not bent)
1 Tbs olive oil, or mustard coating (see Special Note, page 213)
1 onion, roughly chopped
3 large cloves of unpeeled garlic, smashed
½ tsp rosemary or thyme

SPECIAL EQUIPMENT SUGGESTED:
A shallow roasting pan long enough to contain the lamb (you may need to place foil under the ends); a rack for the pan; an instant meat thermometer; a very sharp carving knife and a napkin for holding the lamb shank

Roasting—1¼ to 1½ hours at 350°F. Place the lamb fat side up on the rack in the roasting pan—if the ends of meat overhang, make extensions under them with double folds of aluminum foil. Set in the middle level of the preheated oven. No basting is necessary if you have used the mustard coating, otherwise baste several times with accumulated pan fat. When 45 minutes are up, strew the onion and garlic in the pan, sprinkle over them the rosemary or thyme, and baste with accumulated pan fat. After 1 hour, start testing for doneness by taking the meat's temperature, doing so quickly so the oven doesn't cool off.

When is it done? The indications are the same as for the roast beef on page 219: the meat begins to take on a slight springiness when pressed, and after a reading of 110°F the temperature rises rapidly. Plunge the point of the thermometer into the center of the bulge at the large end and wait 10 to 15 seconds, until the needle stops moving. 120°F for very rare, 125°F for rosy rare, 130°F for pinky rare, and at 130°F juices will begin to appear in the pan. At 140°F for medium, there will be quite a bit of juice.

Removing the roast. As soon as the lamb is done, remove it from the oven and place on a board or a platter; discard trussing strings. As for roast beef, the lamb should rest 15 to 20 minutes out of the oven before carving so that its juices can retreat back into the meat.

*Ahead-of-time note: Again, as for roast beef, if the wait is longer after its rest, set the lamb anywhere that it will stay warm enough but will not overcook—use a warming oven but be sure the temperature cannot go over 120°F, or set the roast in a pan or on a platter, cover loosely, and place over a kettle of almost simmering water. You may keep it warm for an hour or more.

Sauce. Either follow the directions for the "au jus" sauce in the Special Note on page 221, or, for a larger quantity, see the lamb sauce at the end of this recipe.

Carving the leg

Carving. Holding it with a napkin in your left hand, raise the shank end of the leg at an angle. With the knife almost parallel to the surface of the meat, start at the bulge midway between the shank and the large end, cutting a long thin flat first slice. Lift it off, arrange it on a hot plate or platter, and start the next slice at a slight angle right or left. Continue, angling your knife to either side as you come to the main leg bone; finally turn the leg over to carve the underside.

Suggested accompaniments. Homemade mashed potatoes, fresh green peas, and broiled tomatoes are traditional American accompaniments, and always good with lamb. A favorite French one is a combination of fresh green beans and dried beans—"haricots panachés"—and often Tomatoes Provençale (page 306), broiled with bread crumbs and herbs. Another idea is the eggplant and tomato casserole, ratatouille, on page 317, accompanied by sautéed potatoes. You'll want a red wine here, such as a merlot or pinot noir, or one of the Bordeaux.

Leftovers. See Feasting on the Remains following the lamb kabobs, on page 214.

A Little Sauce for Roast Lamb

You want to make sure in making a sauce for lamb that it does not adulterate the special flavor of the lamb itself—the sauce should be an extension of tastes, in other words. That means no other predominant flavors, like tomatoes, carrots, or beef stock. Onions, garlic, a whiff of celery, parsley, and a little bay leaf, rosemary, or thyme are enhancers, and chicken stock is neutral but gives body. The following sauce has a slight liaison, and gives a little more per serving than a deglazing sauce.

For 1½ to 2 cups

3 cups or so chopped raw lamb bones, such as the hip, and any miscellaneous bones like neck or shoulder
2 Tbs fresh peanut oil
1 medium onion, chopped
2 Tbs flour
2½ to 3 cups chicken broth
½ cup dry white French vermouth or dry white wine
1 medium celery rib, chopped
3 large cloves of garlic, smashed
A medium pinch of rosemary leaves
A small handful of parsley stems
Salt and freshly ground pepper

SPECIAL EQUIPMENT SUGGESTED:
A heavy-bottomed 2½- to 3-quart saucepan

Browning the bones. Dry the bones in paper towels. Set the saucepan over moderately high heat with the oil, and brown the bones, tossing and turning fairly frequently. After 2 to 3 minutes, toss in the onion and continue sautéing several minutes more until bones and onion are lightly colored. Stir in the flour; toss and turn over moderate heat for 2 minutes, to brown. Remove from heat and let cool several minutes.

Simmering. Slowly blend in the chicken stock to mix well with the flour. Add the wine, celery, and garlic. Bring to the simmer, and skim for a few minutes, until scum ceases to rise. Blend in the herbs, cover loosely, and simmer 1½ to 2 hours, or until you feel you have gotten their all out of the bones—add a little water to keep ingredients covered if necessary. Strain, pressing juices out of vegetables, and degrease. Correct seasoning.

*Ahead-of-time note: May be made in advance. When cool, cover and refrigerate or freeze.

To use. After degreasing the roasting pan, deglaze with a little wine or stock. Pour in the sauce and simmer a moment, mashing the roasting vegetables into it as you scrape up coagulated roasting juices. Strain into a saucepan, pressing juices out of ingredients with the back of a spoon. Bring to the simmer, skimming off surface fat. Season carefully to taste.

VARIATIONS

Shoulder of Lamb

Shoulder of lamb is usually a third less expensive than the leg, but it does need boning because of its complicated structure. And unless it comes from a young spring lamb—hard to find outside of specialty markets—it is less tender than the leg. The easy way here is to buy a boned rolled shoulder of whatever weight you want, untie it, cut out visible fat, slather the interior with an herbal flavoring (a big handful of chopped parsley, 2 or 3 chopped shallots or scallions, 1 or 2 large cloves of garlic, puréed, ¼ teaspoon or so of ground rosemary, and salt and freshly ground pepper). Tie it up again, and brush with the mustard coating in the Special Note on page 213. Roast it as in the master recipe for leg of lamb, counting on 2½ hours to be on the safe side.

Left, trimmed rack of lamb; right, untrimmed

Rack of Lamb

The rack makes an easy-to-roast and elegant main course when neatly trimmed, and there is serious trimming to do—a 3½-pound rack carries some 2 pounds of fat and scrap meat (see illustration of the trimmed and untrimmed). The rack is the whole rib-chop section on one side of the animal—7 chops bound together; 2 racks will serve 4 to 5 people; you should really count on 3 racks to serve 6.

Preparing a rack of lamb for cooking. A practiced butcher should be able to do this for you but, as always, it is useful to know how yourself.

The backbone. The backbone is removed to make carving easy. With meat saw and knife, very carefully detach the backbone from the tops of the ribs, starting at the rib side and continuing around the lobe of meat to the fatty top of the rack.

Frenching the ribs. From the fat-covered top side, trace a line across the ribs halfway from the bone ends to the meat; cut down through it to the rib bones. Remove the fatty lower layer to expose the lower part of the ribs. Cut and scrape the meat from around the rib bones.

Removing cap meat. Starting at the heavier end of the rack, cut and lift off the fatty layer, leaving but a thin covering over the eye of meat.

The remains. Save the bones for the lamb sauce on the preceding page. When you remove the fat from the between-rib and cap meat (a labor of love), you can use the meat for the lamburgers on page 201 or the moussaka on page 319.

The rack is now trimmed and ready for the oven.

*Ahead-of-time note: May be prepared in advance; cover and refrigerate.

Roast Racks of Lamb

An intimate dinner for four? Roast 2 racks of lamb, served rib ends up and interlocked on your heirloom silver platter. You can roast them as is, but an herb and mustard coating gives a subtle added flavor, and the crumb topping an attractive finish.

For 2 racks of lamb, serving 4 or 5

2 racks of lamb—7 ribs and about 3½ pounds each, untrimmed weight (1½ pounds fully trimmed)
The mustard coating (Special Note, page 213), minus the soy sauce and garlic
½ cup crumbs from fresh crustless homemade type white bread
2 Tbs melted butter

SPECIAL EQUIPMENT SUGGESTED:
A jelly-roll pan for roasting

Preparations for roasting. Score the fat side of the racks lightly (make shallow crisscross knife marks). Leaving the rib ends free, paint the mustard mixture over the tops and sides of the racks. Fold a double strip of foil over the rib ends so they won't burn.

Ahead-of-time note: May be prepared a day in advance; refrigerate covered.

Roasting—about 30 minutes at 500°F and 400°F. Preheat the oven and set the rack in the upper middle level. Roast the lamb for 10 minutes at 500°F to sear. Reduce the thermostat to 400°F, rapidly spread the bread crumbs over the top fat, drizzle on the butter, and return to the oven. Roast another 20 minutes, to rosy rare—125°F; the meat will be just lightly springy when pressed.

Rest before carving. Remove from the oven and let rest 5 minutes.

Serving. If you are presenting the racks and carving at the table, arrange the two of them on the platter rib ends up and intertwined. You might tuck watercress under the rib space, and place a vegetable garnish at the two ends. Cut into 1-rib portions, serving 2 to 3 per person.

Suggested accompaniments. Although a sauce is not necessary, you could pass a bowl of the lamb sauce on page 225. Choose any of the vegetables suggested for the butterflied lamb on page 212, or the preceding roast leg of lamb. You'll want a fine red wine—a merlot, cabernet, or Bordeaux.

ROAST PORK: THE LEG AND THE LOIN

When entertaining a crowd, give them something different—like a splendid roast leg of fresh pork that will serve two dozen hungry guests. Except for its outside layer of protective fat, fresh ham, as it is also called, is the leanest of meats, and such wonderful flavor it has after a couple of days in a spice marinade. The same is happily true for a loin of pork, particularly the double loin, which is the perfect pork roast for a dozen guests. Both legs and loins are easy to cook, and when they are boneless, as they mostly are in today's markets, they're easy indeed to carve.

Spice marinade note. The spice marinade can be your own bottled mixture, described for the pork chops in the Special Note on page 203, or the combination in the recipe to follow. Although you may work it into the meat and roast at once, a serious sojourn will give real penetration of flavor—from 24 hours for a loin, to up to 2 or 3 days for a boneless leg. A spice marinade also makes for unusually fine cold roast pork.

Temperatures and timing for roast pork

Meat temperature reading. Trichinosis and harmful bacteria are taken care of at an internal meat temperature of 138°F, when pork is almost rare. To be officially safe, all portions of the pork should reach 140°F—when it is still almost rare. A reading of 150°F is safer still, and particularly advisable for microwave users, since studies have found that bone-in pork roasted in a microwave oven does not cook uniformly near the bone at lower temperatures. However, I think pork develops its best flavor at higher temperatures.

In the days before instant thermometers, when you roasted your meat with the thermometer in place, I used to prescribe an internal temperature of 180°F—tastes change with the times. Many authorities suggest 170°F—not the "in oven" temperature, but the temperature reached after the meat has rested. I now like an in-oven temperature of 155°F for a large rounded roast like the leg, and since the hot juices at the exterior circulate around to the interior, in 15 minutes or so the temperature will rise to about 165°F. For the less hefty loin, I roast to 160°F, which rises to around 165°F. In both cases the meat is a pinky gray. The texture of pork, while more compact than that of beef or lamb, should always have a certain juiciness and its own porky brand of tenderness.

TIMING. *Always count on the longest estimate, since you can hold the roast perfectly for an hour or more, and always allow at least 15 minutes extra so that the meat can rest before carving. If you want the full benefit of the spice marinade, start the proceedings at least a day or two before you plan to serve. Make the sauce while the meat is roasting, or complete it the day before.*

⬤ MASTER RECIPE

Roast Leg of Fresh Pork

Here's the great roast leg of fresh
pork, its meat subtly spiced. It has
been boned, and the meat is neatly
tied into its original shapely form so
that it will easily carve into beautiful
thin slices to serve a big party.

A NOTE ON BONE-IN LEGS. *You rarely
see an unboned fresh leg in local supermarkets, but you could probably order
one. The equivalent here would weigh
14 to 15 pounds and, at 22 to 25 minutes per pound, would take a good 5 or
more hours in the oven. Before roasting,
slice off the rind and all but a ¼-inch
layer of covering fat; spice it as described in the recipe following, and
marinate it 3 to 4 days. To serve, carve
it like the ham on page 232.*

For 20 to 24 servings

**A 7- to 8-pound boneless leg of fresh
pork (fresh ham)**

Salt and spice marinade
**Either ¼ cup salt and 2 tsp of your
own Spice Marinade (Special
Note, page 203)**
**Or ¼ cup salt, 1 tsp freshly ground
pepper, and ¼ tsp each of ground
allspice, imported bay leaf,
paprika, sage, and thyme**

2 to 3 Tbs fresh oil
**An 8- by 10-inch piece of fresh pork
fat; or 6 to 8 strips of thick-sliced
blanched bacon (Special Note,
page 142), to baste the meat as it
cooks**
**1 each large onion and carrot,
roughly chopped**
**5 large unpeeled cloves of garlic,
halved**
**3 cups Port wine sauce, optional but
recommended (see end of recipe)**

Roast pork dinner with rice and hashed broccoli, lower left; prune and apple garnish, upper right

SPECIAL EQUIPMENT SUGGESTED:
*White butcher's twine; a trussing needle
and/or skewers; a roasting pan with
rack; an instant meat thermometer*

Spicing the leg. Remove the strings or
netting from the leg. Go over the
outside, if necessary, slicing off all
but a ¼-inch layer of covering fat.
Open up the roast and cut out any interior fat. Mix the marinade ingredients in a bowl and rub them all over
the inside and outside of the pork. If
you are planning on the full 2-day
marinade, place the meat in a closed
plastic bag and refrigerate it.

Trussing the leg. Using white butcher's
twine and/or a trussing needle or
skewers, tie or sew the underside of
the meat. Lightly score the fat side
(make shallow cross-hatch cuts ½
inch apart), then loop string around

the roast to re-form it in approximately its original shape, as pictured
here.

*Roasting—3¼ to 3¾ hours at 425°F
and 350°F.* Preheat the oven to
425°F. Dry the meat thoroughly with
paper towels, brush it all over with
cooking oil, set on the rack in the
roasting pan, and place in the middle
level of the oven. Roast for 15 minutes, rapidly basting twice with cooking oil. Turn the oven down to

Tied fresh ham, ready for roasting

350°F, drape the pork fat or blanched bacon over the meat (discard it during the last ½ hour), and continue roasting, basting exposed flesh every 20 minutes or so with the fat accumulated in the pan. After about 2½ hours, add the chopped vegetables and garlic.

When is it done? The first indication is that meat juices begin to accumulate in the pan. Start testing with the thermometer shortly after 3 hours. It is done at a reading of 155°F—take readings in several areas to be sure. Let it rest 20 to 30 minutes out of the oven, then remove the trussing strings.

*Ahead-of-time note: After its rest, you may keep the roast warm for an hour at around 120°F. See the directions for roast beef on page 218.

Carving. Carve into thin slanting slices as shown.

Suggested accompaniments. Hashed Brussels sprouts (page 275), rice soubise (rice braised with onions, page 330), and the prune and apple garnish on page 177 are one suggestion. Or rather than rice, your choice of the potato gratins starting on page 322; and there is never anything wrong with fresh green peas and homemade mashed potatoes, especially the garlic-mashed on page 321. See also the suggestions for butterflied pork on page 211, and those for pork chops on page 202. Serve a full white wine of the chardonnay type, or a light red like a merlot or Bordeaux.

VARIATIONS

Port Wine Sauce for Roast Pork

All sauces of this type are essentially the same in technique; follow the general method and proportions for the lamb sauce on page 225, first browning the pork bones with chopped carrots and onions, then sautéing them with a little flour to make an eventual thickening. Finally simmer them 2½ to 3 hours in wine and chicken stock, adding a couple of chopped tomatoes, a stalk or two of chopped celery, and an herb bouquet. After deglazing the roasting pan with the sauce and degreasing it, simmer for a moment with a few tablespoons of Port, and it is ready to serve.

Roast Loin of Pork

When you buy a bone-in pork loin roast, usually part of the backbone has been removed and the rest is sectioned between the ribs so that it may be sliced into chops after roasting. Far more elegant and also easier to serve is the boneless loin roast, which may be cut into attractive thin slices by anyone with a sharp knife. If you are in a hurry, however, do see the broil-roast for pork loin on page 211, which cooks in half the time.

Pork tenderloin note. The pork tenderloin is a lovely long thin tender piece of meat, and does especially well when cut into serving pieces and sautéed, as in the beef tenderloin variation on page 195. See also the Pork Tenderloin Salad, page 371.

Buying the roast. The loin of pork runs the length of the pig from shoulder to hip; it includes the shoulder blade at one end, the hip and tenderloin at the other, and the ribs in the middle. While loin roasts do come bone-in, many markets now buy it already boned; they cut some of it into boneless chops, and tie the rest into loin roasts. The center cut is the one to look for since it is the leanest; it is often folded, then tied, making a double loin roast 5 to 5½ inches in diameter. The single boneless loin minus tenderloin, however, is best broil-roasted, like the butterflied loin on page 211.

To roast a boned double loin of pork. A 4-pound boneless center-cut boned-and-tied double loin roast makes a splendid dish for 8 to 12 people, and either of the spice marinades used in the master recipe does much to enhance its flavor, especially if you can allow 24 to 28 hours for it to accomplish its task.

Preparing and marinating the roast. Untie the roast. Slice off, if necessary, all but a ¼-inch layer of exterior fat, and remove any interior fat. Blend the marinade ingredients (see Special Note on page 203) in a small bowl, and rub them all over the pork. Lightly score (make shallow cross-hatch cuts ½ inch apart) the fat side of each loin, and reassemble them, fat sides out. The roast should be quite even in circumference from one end to the other: in other words, a thick end should be against a thin end—if it is a whole folded piece of loin, you may have to cut it in half to reassemble. Make neat ties around the circumference at 1-inch intervals with white butcher's twine.

Roasting—2¼ to 2½ hours at 350°F. Roast the meat fattiest side up in the

(continued)

Roast Loin of Pork (*continued*)

upper middle level of the preheated oven, basting every ½ hour with the fat accumulated in the pan. After 1½ hours, strew in the pan a chopped onion and carrot, and 2 large unpeeled smashed cloves of garlic. Continue occasional basting, and roast to a thermometer reading of 160°F. Deglaze the pan as for the "au jus" sauce in the Special Note on page 221, or the preceding Port wine sauce.

Carving. Carve straight down like a loaf of bread, into slices less than ¼ inch thick—they will separate in two as you serve them. Spoon a little sauce over each. Other suggestions for vegetables, and for wines, are in the preceding master recipe.

Roast ham

HAM AND SMOKED SHOULDER

About 90 percent of the hams in our markets today are labeled "fully cooked," and are convenient, too, because you don't have to buy the whole thing—only the shank half, the butt half, or the big slice—and you can buy it bone-in or bone-out. On the other hand, rather than ham you may prefer the smoked shoulder or "picnic," which also comes with or without the bone. It doesn't slice up as nicely as ham but it tastes just like it and usually costs a third less per pound.

Just because it is labeled fully cooked doesn't mean you cannot cook it again—you can. Roasting, or most particularly braising, actually enhances its flavor besides giving out some lovely juices to play with when you are serving it hot.

● MASTER RECIPE

Braised Whole Ham
In wine and aromatic vegetables

Nothing takes the place of the whole ham standing proud, but boneless hams and bone-in or boneless shoulders may be substituted for the whole ham herein described.

For 24 servings, as a main course

A 14-pound bone-in fully cooked ham
1 cup each: sliced carrots, onions, and celery
1 tsp each peppercorns and allspice berries
2 tsp sage or thyme
3 imported bay leaves
1 bottle dry white wine, or ¾ bottle dry white French vermouth or Port wine, optional but desirable
Chicken broth

2 cups or so crumbs from fresh crustless white homemade type bread

SPECIAL EQUIPMENT SUGGESTED:
A covered roaster just large enough to hold the ham comfortably; a rack for the pan; an instant meat thermometer; a long sharp carving knife

Preliminaries. Unwrap the ham; remove any strings or cloth coverings. Scrub with a vegetable brush under warm running water to remove any extraneous matter and/or preservatives. (If the ham is too large for your roasting pan, saw off the shank—although carving is easier with the shank on.) Place the ham on the rack in the roasting pan. Strew the vegetables around it, sprinkle the seasonings over them, and pour in the optional wine. Add enough chicken broth to make about 1 inch of liquid.

Ahead-of-time note: May be completed in advance; cover and refrigerate.

Braising—3½ to 4¼ hours at 400°F and 325°F. Preheat the oven to 400°F. Set the roasting pan on top of the stove and bring to the simmer; cover it and set in the lower third level of the oven. In about 10 minutes, when the liquid in the pan is simmering quietly again, turn the thermostat down to 325°F. Maintain the liquid at a gentle simmer throughout the cooking, regulating heat as necessary. Baste occasionally with the juices in the pan. It is done at an internal temperature of 130°F on your meat thermometer—it will eventually rise to 140°F when it is out of the oven. Remove the ham to a cutting board and proceed to the next steps while the meat is still warm.

Removing the rind. With a sharp knife, cut off the brown rind. The ham will look a mess after this step, which is normal (see illustration, step 1).

Removing the fat. There will probably be a thick layer of fat over much of the top and sides of the ham. Slice it off, leaving on a ¼-inch layer.

Trimming. Cut off any dark, tough, or ragged pieces of meat and save them for grinding or for making ham stock. On the underside at the large end is the hip or H-bone, which you can easily dig out to make carving easier, step 2.

Crumbing the ham, and browning in the oven. Preheat the oven to 500°F. Press the fresh bread crumbs onto the ham, place it in the roasting pan, and baste with a sprinkling of ham fat or butter. Brown for 15 minutes or so in the preheated oven. The ham is now ready to serve either warm or cold.

Ahead-of-time note: The ham will stay warm, loosely covered, for a good hour or more, and may be served tepid.

The braising juices. Strain the braising liquid from the pan, pressing juices out of the vegetables with the back of a spoon. Degrease the liquid and taste. If too salty, dilute with strong plain chicken stock. Serve the ham juices as they are, or according to one of the following suggestions.

1. Removing rind and fat

2. Removing hip bone

SPECIAL NOTE

Timetable for Braised or Roasted Ham

The timing is the same whether you roast the ham in a 325°F oven, or braise it. The in-oven meat thermometer reading should be just over 130°F, meaning that it will reach between 138°F and 140°F after the ham has rested and the hot surface juices have circulated into the center of the meat. (The following figures are from the National Live Stock and Meat Board in Chicago.)

WHOLE HAM, bone-in or boneless: 15 to 18 minutes per pound

HALF HAM, bone-in or boneless: 18 to 25 minutes per pound

SMOKED SHOULDER ("picnic"), bone-in or boneless: 25 to 30 minutes per pound

Timing chart for fresh pork roasts

For legs, boned and tied: 25 to 30 minutes per pound

For double loins, boned and tied: 2½ to 3½ hours for a 4- to 8-pound roast 5½ inches in diameter (timing depends more on diameter than weight)

SAUCE VARIATIONS

Cream Gravy

Boil the juices with an equal amount of heavy cream until very lightly thickened.

Clear Port Wine Sauce

After boiling up and seasoning 3 cups of the braising juices, blend ¼ cup of Port wine smoothly into 3 tablespoons of arrowroot. Remove the braising juices from heat, whisk in the Port mixture, and simmer 2 to 3 minutes.

Port Wine Sauce with Raisins

Follow the preceding recipe, but plump ½ to ⅔ cup of currants (small black raisins) in the Port wine for ½ hour before blending with the arrowroot.

Mustard Sauce

Blend together in a small bowl 3 tablespoons each of Dijon-type mustard, arrowroot or cornstarch, and dry white French vermouth. Whisk this into the ham juices, and simmer 2 minutes.

Storing the braising juices. If you are not planning on a sauce, pour the degreased juices into screw-top jars and refrigerate or freeze. Use to make the split pea soup that follows, or add a little to sauces, stews, and soups when a subtle ham flavor is just what you need to give your dish that certain something of glory.

Carving the ham

To Carve a Ham

SPECIAL EQUIPMENT SUGGESTED: *A really sharp knife (the long gently serrated "ham slicer" shown here is recommended); a napkin with which to hold the shank bone*

The best way to carve, I think, is to position the ham with the small (shank) end toward you and to make long horizontal slices starting on top midway between shank and large end. Cut toward you, holding your knife almost parallel to the surface. (The first slice will be almost all fat!) Start the next slice a little farther toward the large end and continue, gradually angling your knife to the left side and then to the right side. When you come to the bone, keep angling the knife around it. For elegant slices, use long smooth strokes the length of the blade.

FEASTING ON THE REMAINS OF A HAM

The largesse of leftover ham—the stuffed cabbage rolls simmered in tomato sauce on page 304, the hashed brown turnip cakes with ham and poached eggs on page 264, to say nothing of plain and toasted ham sandwiches. Here is split pea soup, and a main-dish ham and potato casserole.

Split Pea Soup

Split pea is certainly one of the great main-course soups, as well as being an easy one to make as long as you have the ham bones those peas always seem to demand. The ham stock cooks first; that can be done way ahead and even frozen. The split peas and aromatic vegetables then go into the stock, and in less than an hour of fuss-free simmering, your soup is ready for the table.

For about 2½ quarts, serving 6

The ham stock

2 quarts or so bones and scraps from a cooked ham and/or 1 or more well-washed and scrubbed ham hocks

3 quarts water, or water and leftover ham-braising juices or chicken stock

1 cup each peeled and chopped carrots and onions

1 large rib of celery with leaves, washed and chopped

Split Pea Soup

An herb bouquet: 3 imported bay leaves, 1 tsp thyme, and 5 cloves or allspice berries tied in washed cheesecloth

Salt

The Soup

3 Tbs butter

⅔ cup each diced celery and onions

½ cup each diced carrots and turnips or rutabaga

3 Tbs flour

2 quarts of the ham stock, heated in a saucepan

1½ cups green or yellow split peas

Salt and freshly ground pepper

Garnish: 1½ cups small toasted croutons (page 353), or ½ cup diced ham sautéed in butter

SPECIAL EQUIPMENT SUGGESTED:
A kettle, for the ham stock; a heavy-bottomed 3-quart saucepan, for the soup

The ham stock. Chop up the ham bones and put them in the kettle with the water to cover by 2 inches. Add the ham scraps, chopped vegetables, and herb bouquet. Simmer 3 to 4 hours with the kettle cover askew to allow for air circulation; salt lightly after an hour or so and skim occasionally. Strain and degrease.

*Ahead-of-time note: May be prepared in advance; cover and refrigerate or freeze.

The soup. Set the saucepan over moderately high heat, add the butter, and sauté the vegetables, stirring frequently, for 5 minutes. Blend in the flour (to make a liaison so the eventual pea purée will not sink to the bottom of the soup); cook, stirring, for 3 minutes. Remove from heat and let cool briefly; blend in the hot ham stock, then the split peas. Bring to the simmer, stirring. Cover loosely and simmer about 45 minutes, or until the peas are tender—salt and pepper lightly to taste after ½ hour of simmering.

Finishing the soup. For a rough peasanty texture, mash the peas and vegetables into the liquid with a mixing fork. Or purée the soup through a vegetable mill or food processor. For a very smooth texture, force it through a fairly fine sieve after puréeing. Taste carefully to correct seasoning, adding a little ham stock or chicken broth if the soup seems too thick.

*Ahead-of-time note: Chill uncovered. The soup may be refrigerated for a day or two, or frozen. Bring to the simmer before proceeding, and check seasoning.

Serving. Ladle the hot soup into bowls, and garnish with the croutons or sautéed ham.

Granny's Ham and Potato Gratin for a Crowd

Here is a great crowd pleaser, as well as a deliciously economical one that needs only a copious salad, a loaf of bread, and a jug of light red wine to make the meal.

For 18 to 24 servings

**10 pounds "boiling" potatoes
Salt**

Garlic and mustard sauce (about 8 cups)

**5 ounces (1¼ sticks) butter
1 cup all-purpose flour
6½ cups hot milk
Salt and freshly ground pepper
A pinch of nutmeg
2 large cloves of garlic, puréed
¼ cup Dijon-type prepared mustard
½ tsp thyme or sage**

**4 cups coarsely grated cheese—
    Swiss or a mixture such as Swiss,
    mozzarella, Jack, and/or Cheddar
1½ to 2 quarts cooked ham, diced,
    thinly sliced, or ground (to make
    6 to 8 cups)**

SPECIAL EQUIPMENT SUGGESTED:
A food processor is useful for slicing and grating; an 8-quart covered kettle; a heavy-bottomed 3-quart saucepan, for the sauce; a buttered 6-quart baking dish about 3 inches deep, for the final dish

The potatoes. Have ready the kettle, containing 4 cups of cold water. Peel the potatoes and slice them ¼ inch thick, dropping them into the cold water to cover as you do so. Cover the kettle, and bring to the boil. Uncover and boil slowly 3 to 4 minutes, until barely cooked through—eat

Granny's Ham and Potato Gratin

several slices to check. Drain, cover the kettle again for 3 to 4 minutes to firm up the potato slices, then uncover.

The garlic and mustard sauce. Make the classic white sauce described in detail on page 272: cook the butter and flour together in the saucepan until they foam and froth for 2 minutes without coloring; off heat pour in half of the hot milk; whisk vigorously to blend as you pour in the rest; simmer 3 minutes, stirring. Remove from heat and whisk in the seasonings; bring to the simmer again, taste carefully, and add additional seasonings to taste.

Assembling. Spoon a ¹⁄₁₆-inch layer of sauce on the bottom of the buttered baking dish. Set aside 3 cups of the sauce and 1 cup of the cheese for the topping. Now, to arrange everything in 4 layers, start with a quarter of the

potatoes, then a quarter of the ham, follow by a third of the sauce, and sprinkle on a third of the cheese. Continue in layers, finishing the final layer with the remaining potatoes and ham; spread on the reserved 3 cups of sauce to cover completely, then the last of the cheese.

*Ahead-of-time note: May be prepared a day in advance; cover when cool, and refrigerate.

Final baking—about 45 minutes at 375°F. An hour or so before you plan to serve, preheat the oven to 375°F. Bake in the upper third level just until the potatoes are bubbling hot and the top has browned nicely.

*Ahead-of-time note: May be kept warm uncovered on a hot tray but be sure not to overheat or the potatoes and ham will dry out.

STEWS AND RAGOUTS

Stews are easy on the cook: brown the meat while you're cooking tonight's dinner, for example, set it to simmer whenever you see a free couple of hours, put it aside in the refrigerator, and reheat it the next day—or the day after that. It will only be the better for a sojourn with its flavor elements.

Counterclockwise from upper left: Meat Loaf Maison, Zinfandel of Beef, Rabbit Stew, Turkey Blanquette, and an Apple Tarte Tatin for dessert

POT ROASTS, BRAISED MEATS, STEWS, AND RAGOUTS

These are the meats that simmer quietly in wine, and onions, and herbs, and other good things, filling the kitchen with mouth-watering aromas—the succulent dishes that are the soul of good home cooking. They're made with the cheaper cuts of meat—a pot roast of beef serving 8 is half the price of the top loin roast, for instance. They are often the cuts with the most fla-vor, too—the meats that require long, slow, moist cooking. Whether it is called pot roast, braised beef, lamb stew, or ragout of pork, and whether it comes as a whole roast or in bite sizes, each is made in essentially the same way: first the meat is browned, then it is simmered in a fragrant liquid. Again, as so often in cooking, if you've tried one you've tried almost all, give or take a technical trick or two. We shall start small, with that old favorite, beef stew, and end large with a stuffed and braised breast of veal.

● MASTER RECIPE

Zinfandel of Beef
Chunky stew of beef in red wine

This rich and hearty stew is the model and the master recipe for the rest. If you are out of zinfandel, use another good young red wine and call it simply Beef Stew in Red Wine.

TIMING NOTE. *Most beef stews take 2½ to 3 hours, but can take longer, depending on meat quality. It is wise to cook stews a good hour or more in advance of when you plan to serve, since a wait always improves flavor.*

SAUCE NOTES. *The traditional beurre-manié sauce is suggested here, but see the other possibilities in the Special Note on sauces on the next page.*

For 6 to 8 servings

3 to 4 pounds boneless beef stew
　　meat cut into cubes about 1½ to 2
　　inches (see preceding notes)
Cooking oil
2 cups sliced onions
⅔ cup sliced carrots
5 to 6 cups liquid (all red wine or a
　　mixture such as 1 bottle of wine
　　plus beef stock or broth)
2 or 3 large unpeeled cloves of garlic,
　　smashed
2 cups tomatoes (1 whole unpeeled
　　tomato, cored and chopped, plus
　　canned drained Italian plum
　　tomatoes)
1 imported bay leaf
1 tsp thyme
Salt
3 Tbs flour and 2 Tbs softened
　　butter blended to a paste, for the
　　beurre-manié sauce

SPECIAL EQUIPMENT SUGGESTED:
A heavy 12-inch frying pan; a covered 3-quart casserole or baking dish, flame-proof if possible—or an electric skillet

Browning the meat. Dry the meat thoroughly with paper towels—damp meat won't brown. Film the frying pan with 1/16 inch of oil and set over moderately high heat. When very hot but not smoking, brown as many pieces of meat as will fit in one layer without crowding. Turn frequently to brown on all sides—3 to 5 minutes; transfer the pieces as they are done to the casserole.

Assembling. Skim all but a spoonful of fat out of the frying pan (if burned, discard all and add fresh oil); turn in the sliced vegetables, stirring and tossing for 3 to 4 minutes to brown lightly before scraping them out over the beef. Pour a cup of the liquid into the frying pan, swishing and scraping up any coagulated juices, and pour into the casserole. Add the garlic and 4 more cups of liquid to the casserole; fold in the tomatoes, bay leaf, thyme, and salt to taste. You should have enough liquid almost to cover the beef; add more if needed.

*Ahead-of-time note: May be prepared a day in advance; cover when cool, and refrigerate.

Stewing the beef 2½ to 3 hours or more at 325°F. Bring to the simmer on top of the stove; cook at the slow simmer either on top of the stove or in the oven, turning and basting the meat several times until just fork-tender. (Note: if your casserole is not flame-proof, set it in a 425°F oven for 10 minutes or so, until the simmer is reached; then reduce to 350°F and start timing.)

Assembling the beef stew

Finishing the stew. Pour the contents of the casserole into a colander set over a saucepan; wash out the casserole and return the pieces of beef to it. Press juices out of the residue in the colander into the saucepan; degrease cooking liquid and taste very carefully for seasoning. You should have about 3 cups. Boil it down rapidly if its flavor needs concentrating; remove from heat.

Traditional beurre-manié sauce. This is the flour/butter paste beaten into the degreased stewing juices described in the Special Note on page 143.

*Ahead-of-time note: Let cool, cover, and refrigerate. Shortly before serving, bring to the simmer, gently folding for several minutes until well heated through.

Suggested accompaniments. The stew has so much flavor in itself, accompaniments should not clash with it. You'll want something to sop up the sauce—small boiled potatoes are traditional, or rice, or noodles, or mashed potatoes (see the garlic mashed following), or the golden purée of potatoes and carrots on page 285, or just your own good French bread. Broccoli or fresh green beans and/or baked or broiled tomatoes would go well, or lightly dressed salad greens. A sturdy red wine is called for here, especially a zinfandel, or more of the red wine used in the cooking, or a Mâcon or Beaujolais.

ADDITIONS AND VARIATIONS

Beef Stew in Red Wine with Braised Garlic

Garlic loses its fiery bite when thoroughly cooked but retains its wonderful flavor in a stew. Braise large garlic cloves as described in the Special Note on page 321: pour the braising juices into the stew, and bury the garlic cloves among the pieces of beef just before pouring on the finished sauce.

Beef Stew with a Bouquet of Winter Vegetables

Carrots, turnips, and potatoes are always good in a stew, whatever the season, and this makes a full main course. You may also wish to add the whole garlic cloves in the previous recipe.

Steaming the vegetables. While the stew is simmering, steam together, over 1 inch of water, 6 medium peeled carrots cut into wedges (page 285), and 6 medium round white peeled turnips cut into quarters. Set aside, reserving the steaming water. About 30 minutes before the stew is done, steam 6 medium peeled and quartered potatoes.

Finishing the dish. Fold the vegetables into the finished stew, basting with the sauce. Boil down the steaming liquid to less than ¼ cup, and pour into the stew. Simmer several minutes, basting the meat and vegetables with the sauce.

Beef Stew in Red Wine with Onions and Mushrooms
Boeuf Bourguignon

Onions and mushrooms are one of the great combinations with beef in red wine, as they are with chicken, in coq au vin.

Omit the sliced onions in the master recipe; otherwise complete it as described. Meanwhile, prepare 24 small brown-braised onions (page 287), and sauté 3 cups of quartered fresh mushrooms (page 313). When the stew is done, fold into it the sautéed mushrooms and the onions with their juices. Simmer 2 minutes to blend flavors, and the Boeuf Bourguignon is ready to serve.

SPECIAL NOTE

Sauces for stewed and braised meat

A stew or a braise needs a sauce, since if the meat is not glazed with something to hide its nakedness it looks dry and unappetizing. Fortunately you have a number of choices, including the traditional beurre manié flour-butter paste beaten into the final juices to give them a light liaison; the following Zinfandel of Beef is an example. An alternative is the sauce ragout, where the meat is floured before simmering; this allows the liquid to thicken as it simmers, and when the stew is done the sauce is done, too, as in the lamb stew (page 238). Another method is to simmer the meat in a classic brown sauce, as in the Paupiette of Beef Gargantua (page 245). Two fat-free alternatives, cornstarch and the flour slurry, are discussed on page 244. These five methods are interchangeable: substitute one for the other in any of the recipes to come. (A further discussion of sauces is in the pot roast section, Special Note, page 244.)

Lamb Stews

Lamb stews follow almost exactly the master recipe for beef stews. However, in this case we have a different sauce method—the ragout.

SPECIAL NOTE

On Ragout Sauces

In this useful method, the sauce makes itself as the stew simmers because the meat is floured before the simmering begins, and the flour gives the cooking liquid a light liaison. It is the same idea as the lamb sauce on page 225. You may use the ragout method with any of the stews and braises, including the preceding beef stews.

Technical flouring note. Whether to season and flour the meat before or after browning is a matter of choice. It is easier before, as suggested here, and I have not found any real difference in taste between the two methods. When you season and flour the meat after browning, it is then best to pop the casserole into a 450°F oven for 15 minutes, tossing several times to brown the flour evenly—when browned on top of the stove it colors unevenly and risks scorching.

Lamb Stew with Wine and Rosemary

For 6 servings

4 pounds bone-in lamb shoulder
1½ cups sliced onions
Light olive oil or peanut oil
Salt and freshly ground pepper
½ cup or so flour in a dish
1 cup dry white French vermouth
2 large unpeeled cloves of garlic, smashed
½ tsp rosemary
1 to 1½ cups chopped tomatoes (unpeeled ripe red tomatoes; or a combination of fresh tomatoes and drained canned Italian plum tomatoes) or 1 tablespoon or so tomato paste
2 to 3 cups lamb stock (page 215) or chicken broth

Ready-cut lamb stew

Preparing the lamb. Lamb shoulder is often packaged ready-cut for stew, as in the photograph; or you may buy lamb shoulder chops. Cut off excess fat and cut the meat into chunks, about 1 by 2 inches. Unless you have objections, leave the bones in—they give added flavor; some will work loose during cooking, and can then be discarded.

Flouring the lamb before browning

Browning the onions and lamb. Sauté the onions for 5 minutes in a large frying pan in a tablespoon or so of oil, letting them brown very lightly. Scrape them into your casserole. Just before browning them, set the lamb pieces on a sheet of wax paper and toss with a sprinkling of salt and pepper, then toss with the flour. A big handful at a time, toss them in a sieve to shake off excess flour. Brown the lamb pieces a few at a time in the frying pan, as for the beef stew; transfer to the casserole, and deglaze the pan with the wine, pouring it into the casserole. Add to the casserole the garlic, rosemary, tomato, and enough stock barely to cover the ingredients.

*Ahead-of-time note: May be prepared a day in advance; cover when cool and refrigerate.

Simmering—1 to 1½ hours. Simmer either on top of the stove or in a 325°F oven until the lamb is fork-tender.

Finishing the stew. As in the master recipe, pour the stew into a large sieve or colander set over a bowl, and remove the meat (minus loose bones) to a clean casserole. Press juices out of ingredients into the sauce, and degrease the sauce. Correct seasoning, and pour the sauce over the lamb. Reheat to the simmer before serving.

Preparing the vegetables. While the preceding lamb stew is simmering, trim (and "french" if necessary, page 276) 1½ pounds of fresh green beans; shell enough green peas to make about 1 cup. Blanch both beans and peas until almost tender (page 276), refresh in cold water, and set aside. Peel 6 medium carrots, turnips, and "boiling" potatoes and cut into wedges; set aside in a bowl of cold water. Peel 24 small white onions, pierce a cross ¼ inch deep in the root ends, and set aside.

Adding the root vegetables to the stew. After the stew has simmered 1 hour, drain it, remove loose bones, and degrease and season the cooking liquid. Return the sauce and the lamb to the casserole, bury the carrots, turnips, potatoes, and onions among the pieces of lamb. Cover and continue simmering another 25 to 30 minutes, basting occasionally, until lamb and vegetables are tender. Correct seasoning again.

*Ahead-of-time note: May be completed somewhat in advance to this point. Set aside, cover askew for air circulation.

Finishing the stew. Shortly before serving, bring to the simmer, and bury the peas and beans in the stew. Simmer several minutes to reheat, basting meat and vegetables with the sauce. (You may wish to add a handful of fresh snow peas at this point; tip and string them in advance, and sauté briefly in hot peanut oil just before adding to the stew.) Serve as soon as possible so that the green vegetables will retain their bright color.

Spring lamb stew with polenta

*Ahead-of-time note: May be completed in advance.

Suggested accompaniments. The same as for the beef stew, and in addition—dried beans, and speaking of them, see the lamb shank variation as well as the fine collection of vegetables farther on.

VARIATIONS

Lamb Stew Printanière
With a collection of spring vegetables

Fresh green peas and beans in the old days were the harbingers of spring, and that's the classic term for this lamb stew—the best there is, but only when all ingredients are fresh. There's busy vegetable work here, but all of their preparation may be accomplished in advance, and this dish makes a complete main course.

Ragout of Pork with a Bouquet of Vegetables

Chunks of pork shoulder make a nourishing family stew, and a complete main course as well. Do it almost exactly like the preceding lamb stew with its carrots, turnips, onions, potatoes, and the green vegetables, too, if you wish to use them.

Preparing and browning the pork. Cut 3 pounds of pork shoulder into thick, 2-inch slices, and trim off visible fat. After sautéing the sliced onions in a frying pan and removing them to a casserole, season, flour, and brown the meat in the frying pan, sprinkling it with 1½ tablespoons of fragrant curry powder the last minute or two.

Braising. Continue with the recipe, simmering the pork for 45 minutes in the casserole with the rest of the ingredients listed. After draining, degreasing, and seasoning the sauce, and returning pork and sauce to the casserole, bury the root vegetables among the pieces of meat. (You may wish to include a head of large peeled garlic cloves, page 283.) Simmer another 25 minutes, or until meat and vegetables are tender, then bury the blanched green vegetables in the stew and simmer a few minutes more to warm through.

VARIATION WITH VEAL SHANKS

Ossobucco: Braised Veal Shanks

This recipe, my favorite among numerous versions, is the usual brown stew made like the preceding lamb, but with a zesty finale of finely minced orange and lemon peel, garlic, and parsley.

Browning and braising the veal. For 6 veal hind shanks 2 pounds each sawed crosswise into pieces 1½ inches thick, follow the recipe for Lamb Stew with Wine and Rosemary, using 2 to 3 cups of veal stock or chicken broth rather than lamb stock. When the meat is tender, in about 1½ hours, drain out, degrease, and season the braising liquid; pour it back over the veal.

The final flavoring. While the stew is braising, zest 1 large fine orange and 2 lemons (remove colored part of peel only), and mince finely, adding 2 large cloves of smashed and peeled garlic and a large handful of fresh parsley. Just before bringing the dish to the table, strew the flavoring over the stew, then fold it in as you begin to serve.

Suggested accompaniments. Steamed rice and a green vegetable such as fresh peas would be attractive accompaniments, and a light red wine of the merlot or Beaujolais type.

SPECIAL NOTE

About veal shanks

Ossobuco is the hind shank of veal, the marrow-bone hind leg from below the knee to just above the ankle—a favorite Italian morsel either sawed into thick crosswise pieces, as in the ossobuco recipe, or braised whole as in the variation for lamb shanks on the following page.

You'll want 1 hind shank per person. But since they are not always to be had, you may substitute foreshanks; they are bonier and gristlier but have a good texture when braised, and their gelatinous quality makes a fine sauce. One prime foreshank including the knuckle will weigh around 4½ pounds and serves 2 people.

About lamb shanks

Buying lamb shanks. Foreshanks (from the shoulder end) are meatier, larger, and usually cheaper than the smaller, tenderer shanks from the leg. You really have to buy by eye: 1 or 2 whole small hind leg shanks per person, or 1 meaty foreshank sawed crosswise into pieces 2 inches thick.

Lamb Shanks and Beans

Lamb shanks braise in a winey aromatic stock and finish their cooking with white beans, which absorb that lovely flavor. This country-style dish, this minor cassoulet and variation of our master lamb stew, also takes well to ahead-of-time cooking and reheating.

Browning the lamb shanks and initial simmering. For this recipe the lamb shanks are not floured, since the beans will thicken the sauce. After sautéing the sliced onions called for in the first recipe for lamb stew, brown the lamb shanks, and continue with the recipe, simmering about 1¼ hours, until the meat is almost tender. Drain, degrease, and season the braising liquid, and return it to the casserole.

Finishing the dish. Fold into the sauce 1½ cups of peeled, seeded, and chopped tomatoes (or drained and seeded canned Italian plum tomatoes), and 4 cups of cooked white beans (page 332) or drained canned cannellini beans. Bury the lamb shanks among the beans and sauce, adding a little bean juice, if needed. Simmer 10 to 15 minutes more, until the meat is tender but still clings to the bone.

VARIATIONS

Braised Veal Shanks with Beans or Lentils

Follow the preceding lamb shank recipe exactly, but substitute whole veal hind shanks for lamb shanks, and use either beans, as directed, or cooked lentils (page 337).

Lamb Shanks and Beans

Lamb Chops Champvallon
Shoulder chops braised with potatoes and onions

While loin lamb chops are a luxury, shoulder chops are far more reasonable and make excellent eating when browned and then simmered with some interesting flavorings—they need a longer cooking anyway to bring out their succulence. Serve a salad or fresh green vegetable along with this dish, and you have your main course.

Preliminaries with onions and chops. Sauté and brown 1½ cups of sliced onions in a frying pan filmed with oil, as in the recipe for Lamb Stew with Wine and Rosemary. Meanwhile cut any visible fat off 6 lamb shoulder chops ¾ to 1 inch thick—8 to 10 ounces per chop—and trim so they will fit in one layer in a baking dish 2 inches deep.

Assembling. Season the chops with salt, freshly ground pepper, and a sprinkling of thyme; arrange them in the baking dish with 6 to 7 cups of thinly sliced "boiling" potatoes. Pour in ¾ cup of dry white French vermouth and 1½ cups of lamb stock (page 215) or chicken broth. Mince 3 large cloves of garlic and add. Chop enough fresh parsley to measure ⅔ cup (loosely packed), and scatter over the potatoes.

Braising—1 to 1¼ hours at 350°F. If your baking dish is flameproof, bring to the simmer on top of the stove (for quicker cooking). Top the dish with a sheet of heavy foil and a cover, and set in the middle level of the oven. With a bulb baster, occasionally dribble the pan liquid over the potatoes until the chops are tender when pierced with a fork.

Lamb Chops Champvallon (*continued*)

Final browning and serving. Raise oven heat to 425°F. Taste the cooking liquid and correct seasoning. Mix ¾ cup of fresh white crumbs (from nonsweet home-made type bread) in a bowl with ½ cup of finely grated Swiss cheese, and spread over the potatoes. Baste with the juices in the pan, and set in the upper third level of the oven. Baste several times while the juices boil down and thicken, and the topping browns nicely—10 to 15 minutes.

SPECIAL NOTE

To degrease soups, sauces, and braising liquids

The degreasing pitcher. This is the simple solution—a glass or plastic pitcher with spout starting at the bottom. Pour the clear liquid at the bottom into a saucepan; stop pouring when the fat layer at the top enters the spout. If you can't find one easily, look in specialty cookware shops and cookware catalogues. See photograph at right.

Chilling. An easy method when you have the time is to set the pan with the liquid in the refrigerator—or in a bowl of ice cubes and water, if you wish faster action. When chilled, the surface fat will congeal on top of the liquid and can be lifted or scraped off.

BRAISED BEEF: POT ROASTS

A pot roast is definitely home cooking, the leisurely fragrant long-simmering kind known affectionately in France as *la cuisine mijotée*—slow-simmered cooking. One rarely sees anything like it in a restaurant anymore. The two terms, braised meat and pot roast, by the way, are synonymous, meaning meat that is browned then simmered in a fragrant liquid—just like the preceding stews and ragouts. But a pot roast makes a more dramatic appearance than a stew. It looks important, it makes fine cold meat for the picnic sandwich, and its leftovers can make the dressy beef salad on page 250.

Degreasing pitcher

The Beef to Choose

The most attractive cuts are either the *top round* or the *bottom round* because they are solid pieces of meat with no muscle separations, meaning that they slice nicely. Other possibilities are the boneless *chuck shoulder* pot roast, and the *chuck eye* roast with its mixture of fat and lean. Both the good-looking *eye of the round* and the more modest middle-cut *brisket* can be stringy when braised, but may be used successfully if you cook them ahead so they will compact themselves before you reheat and carve them into slanting slices. Whichever cut you choose, the cooking method is the same.

SPECIAL NOTE

Timing for pot roasts

You'll usually need a good 3 to 4 hours for the actual cooking, but it's wise to allow at least 5 so that the meat may rest and firm itself up. Then it will carve nicely when reheated.

🏷 MASTER RECIPE

Pot Roast of Beef

Bottom round of beef braised in red wine

This is the master recipe for braising a whole piece of meat, especially beef. Lamb, pork, and veal are done in the same way but you would choose white wine for braising rather than red. Although it is a detailed recipe you will note that the technique is the same as that for the preceding ragouts—in other words, it's just another variation of Beef Stew in Red Wine.

For 10 to 12 servings

- **A 5-pound fully trimmed bottom round of beef, all but an ⅛-inch layer of top fat removed (see previous notes for other cuts to use)**
- **2 to 3 Tbs fresh olive oil or peanut oil**
- **2 to 3 cups young red wine such as zinfandel, a good jug red, or Mâcon, or Chianti**
- **1 cup each chopped carrots and onions**
- **Salt and freshly ground pepper**
- **2 to 3 cups beef stock, plus more if needed**
- **1½ cups chopped ripe red unpeeled tomatoes and/or sufficient fresh tomatoes and drained canned Italian plum tomatoes**
- **An herb bouquet: 6 parsley sprigs with stems; 6 peppercorns; 3 whole cloves; 4 allspice berries; 1 tsp thyme; 2 or 3 large cloves of garlic, smashed; 1 large imported bay leaf—tied together in washed cheesecloth**
- **Salt to taste**
- **2 Tbs cornstarch blended with 2 Tbs red wine or dry white vermouth, plus more if needed**

1. Tying the beef

2. Assembling the beef for braising

SPECIAL EQUIPMENT SUGGESTED: *White butcher's twine, if needed; a jelly-roll pan, for browning the meat; a covered casserole or roaster just large enough to hold the roast comfortably*

Browning the beef. Dry the meat in paper towels. If it has not been tied, secure loops of string around the circumference at 1½-inch intervals (see illustration, step 1). Paint the roast with oil, lay it in the jelly-roll pan, and place 2 to 3 inches from a hot broiler element; turn every several minutes to brown all sides nicely—10 to 15 minutes in all. (*Note:* If your broiler is not efficient, brown the beef in a large frying pan.) Arrange the meat in the casserole or roaster; deglaze the pan with a little of the wine and pour over the meat.

Assembling. Meanwhile, preheat the oven to 400°F. Sauté the chopped vegetables in a frying pan with a little oil to brown lightly, and turn them into the roaster with the browned beef. Pour in the rest of the wine and enough broth so the liquid comes a third of the way up the meat. Add the tomatoes and herb bouquet, step 2.

*Ahead-of-time note: May be prepared a day or two in advance; cover and refrigerate, turning the meat every several hours. This will give the beef added flavor, since it is in fact a wine marinade.

Braising—2½ to 3½ hours or more. Bring to the simmer on top of the stove, lay a sheet of aluminum foil over the beef, cover the roaster, and set on the lower rack of the oven. (Or, if your casserole is not flame-proof, set in a 425°F oven until the simmer is reached.) In 10 to 15 minutes, when the liquid in the casserole starts to bubble, reduce the thermostat to 325°F. Baste and turn the meat several times, salt lightly in an hour, and maintain the liquid at a slow simmer throughout the cooking.

When is it done? The beef is done when a sharp-pronged fork will go through it fairly easily—cut off and eat a piece to check: it will be somewhat chewy but reasonably tender.

Remove the meat to a board or tray. Strain the braising liquid into a saucepan, pressing juices out of the vegetables. Return the beef to the roaster.

Pot Roast of Beef (*continued*)

The cornstarch-thickened sauce. Thoroughly degrease the braising juices (see Special Note) and bring to the simmer, skimming off any additional fat that rises. Taste very carefully for strength and seasoning; if the liquid is weak in flavor, boil down rapidly to concentrate it. You should have 2 to 2½ cups of deliciously winey meat juices. Correct the seasoning, remove from heat, and whisk in the cornstarch mixture. When blended, return to heat and simmer 2 minutes. The sauce should just coat a spoon lightly, meaning it will coat the meat lightly—if too thin, thicken with another spoonful or so of cornstarch

and wine. Pour the sauce over and around the beef.

**Ahead-of-time note:* You may now cover the casserole loosely and keep it warm. Or let it cool, then cover and refrigerate it; reheat for a good ½ hour either on top of the stove or in a 325°F oven.

Serving. Remove the meat to a carving board or hot platter, and discard the trussing strings. Either carve it in the kitchen or bring it to the table for carving. In this case spoon a little sauce over the meat to glaze it, decorate the platter with parsley sprigs, watercress, or vegetables, and pass the sauce separately.

Suggested accompaniments. The simple earthy accompaniments are often those the most appreciated with braised beef—noodles, mashed potatoes, or the carrot and potato purée on page 285, for instance; these make an attractive bed for slices of meat and sauce. You'll also want a green vegetable, like beans, peas, broccoli, or Brussels sprouts. Or you could have a bouquet of such homey vegetables as steamed turnips, carrots, onions, and potatoes, as suggested for the beef stew on page 237, as well as other suggestions in that group. An uncomplicated young red wine, such as that used in the cooking, or a zinfandel or Beaujolais would be your best choice.

SPECIAL NOTE

Further Remarks on Sauces for Pot Roasts, Braises, and Stews

When meat is stewed or braised it is cooked so long that its juices have combined with and enriched the braising liquid—giving the braising liquid its wonderful flavor but leaving the meat dry. It most definitely wants a sauce cover of some sort. The same is true of the preceding stews; their sauces are the cooking juices thickened with a beurre-manié flour-butter paste, or the ragout type, where the meat was floured lightly before browning. You may use either of these two systems for any of the braised meats in this section, but here are three more ideas to fill you out on the complete sauce picture.

Thickening with cornstarch. This is the easiest and quickest of the sauce methods: the thickened juices look like a real sauce, and it has the advantage of being fat-free. The cornstarch method appears in the following recipe for pot roast of beef. The disadvantage is that cornstarch is at times less stable than flour, meaning it may once in a while break down during reheating, but you can always repeat the process with more cornstarch. *Proportions:* 1 tablespoon of cornstarch blended to a paste with 1 tablespoon of wine or stock per cup of sauce.

The slurry sauce —a flour and wine thickener. This old-fashioned method is not considered chic, but it has its place. I first ran into the slurry during one of the National Beef Cook-offs, where contestants made stews and braises that had to sit around for several hours on their platters, waiting for the decisions of

the judges. Unthickened cooking juices dried up, leaving the meat parched and naked. Roux-thickened and starch-thickened sauces coagulated on top of the meat, looking gluey and unappetizing. It was only the slurry sauces that retained an agreeably moist and fluid appearance throughout the long wait. The disadvantages are that flour slightly whitens the sauce, and that if you add too much the sauce tastes floury. Used like cornstarch but with great care, it produces a fine sauce.

The classic brown sauce. After browning the meat, you make a brown roux (flour and oil or fat slowly browned together in a saucepan), and combine the roux with the wine and stock for the braise. Your sauce is ready-made when the meat is done. The Paupiette Gargantua variation, after the pot roast, is an example.

Paupiette of Beef Gargantua

Bottom round of beef stuffed with mushrooms and braised in red wine

Here is a grand dish for a crowd, especially since you can get all the cooking done well in advance. The beef is slit open on one side, and about a third of the interior meat is removed to be ground and mixed with a mushroom duxelles, herbs, etc., then returned to stuff the meat before trussing and braising.

For 15 to 20 servings

A 10- to 12-pound fully trimmed bottom round of beef, covering fat removed but left in one piece (to be tied around the beef for braising)
Olive oil or fresh peanut oil
Salt and freshly ground pepper
Dried thyme or Italian herb mixture
Several large cloves of garlic
The mushroom duxelles stuffing (page 160), omitting the chicken breasts and sour cream and adding ground beef removed from the roast, ½ cup pork breakfast sausage meat, and ½ cup grated Swiss cheese
⅓ cup all-purpose flour
3 to 4 Tbs oil
Double the braising ingredients in the preceding master recipe (wine, stock, chopped carrots and onions, garlic, tomatoes, and herb bouquet)

SPECIAL EQUIPMENT SUGGESTED:
The equipment called for in the master recipe; a food processor is useful for mincing onions and chopping meat

Preparing the beef. Lay the beef lengthwise, top side up (the smoother of the two wide sides). With your sharp knife, make a lengthwise pocket in the beef, removing the middle third of the meat so as to leave a thick shell open at one small end and open at one long side. Rub inside and out with a light smearing of oil, sprinkle inside with salt and pepper, and a good pinch of herbs. Purée several cloves of garlic into a bowl, mash with ¼ teaspoon of salt, blend in a spoonful of oil; smear this inside the meat with a rubber spatula.

Stuffing and browning the beef. With a rubber spatula, spread the stuffing inside the beef, but do not cram it too full—you will have some left over, which will make first-rate hamburgers or stuffing for vegetables. Sew or skewer the meat to enclose the stuffing completely, and tie loops of string around the circumference at 2-inch intervals. Dry the beef thoroughly, paint with oil, lay it in an oiled jelly-roll pan, and brown slowly under the broiler, turning as necessary. Tie the reserved fat (cut from the top of the beef) over the top and sides of the roast, and transfer to the covered roaster. Deglaze the jelly-roll pan with a little of the wine and pour over the beef.

The braising sauce. Make a brown roux as described in the Special Note on this page with the ⅓ cup of flour and 3 to 4 tablespoons of oil. Whisk in 2 cups of the beef stock; when thoroughly blended pour it around the beef, adding the rest of the stock, and the wine, then stirring to blend. Add the remaining braising ingredients.

Ahead-of-time note: May be prepared in advance, as for the master recipe.

Braising—2½ to 3 hours or more. Braise the beef as described in the master recipe, but do not turn it— baste every ½ hour or so. When done, remove it to a board or tray. Strain the sauce into a saucepan, pressing juices out of the vegetables. Return the beef to the casserole; cover loosely with the foil and the pan cover.

Finishing the sauce. Thoroughly degrease the sauce, bring it to the simmer, skimming off any fat that rises for several minutes. Taste very carefully for strength and seasoning; if it is too thin, boil it down rapidly; if too thick, thin out with spoonfuls of beef stock.

Ahead-of-time note: Follow the directions in the master recipe.

SPECIAL NOTE

Brown roux and the classic brown sauce

It is a luxury to have a modest hoard of brown sauce on hand when you need a light liaison for a meat sauce—add a spoonful or so to the deglazing juices of a roast or a sauté, simmer a moment, and the sauce is made.

Brown Roux for the Classic Brown Sauce

For about 6 cups of sauce, blend ⅓ cup of flour in a small heavy saucepan with enough clarified butter or fresh peanut oil to make a loose paste. Stir over moderately low heat with a wooden spoon for 6 to 8 minutes, or until the roux slowly turns a nice medium brown. Remove from heat.

*Ahead-of-time note: You could double or quadruple the proportions here, and refrigerate the extra in a covered jar—a cooked roux will keep almost indefinitely.

An All-Purpose Brown Sauce

Let the roux cool 2 minutes; gradually whisk in 2 cups of warm beef stock, and when well blended whisk in a cup of red wine or dry white French vermouth and another 4 cups of stock. Blend in ½ cup of cooked mirepoix (diced aromatic vegetables, page 297), 2 tablespoons of tomato paste, and add an herb bouquet. Simmer very slowly, loosely covered, skimming off fat and scum as necessary, for 2 hours or more. Add a little more stock if liquid reduces too much—the sauce should be a lightly thickened, deeply flavored, rich dark brown.

*Ahead-of-time note: Chill uncovered. The sauce may be refrigerated for several days in a covered container or frozen—freeze it in small batches for quick thawing in the microwave.

VARIATIONS

Stuffed and Braised Flank Steak

A less elaborate presentation for an informal dinner is the stuffed flank steak, done almost exactly like the preceding paupiette.

Preparing the steak. To serve 6 people, slit a pocket in the side of a 2-pound flank steak, and season the interior lightly with salt and freshly ground pepper. Make 2 cups of stuffing from the selection on page 184— the Ground Beef with Olives and Pine Nuts is especially recommended. Spread the stuffing in the pocket. Skewer the pocket closed. Film a large frying pan with oil, and brown the steak on both sides.

Braising—about 2 hours. Prepare the braising ingredients as described in the master recipe, but using only about a third of the amount specified; simmer the steak either in the oven or on top of the stove, basting once or twice with the braising liquid.

Sauce and serving. Degrease the cooking liquid and make the cornstarch-thickened sauce as described in the master recipe, napping the steak with a little of the sauce before bringing it to the table. Pass the rest of the sauce separately. Carve the meat into slanting crosswise slices.

Breast of Veal

Every once in a while you'll see a sale on prime veal breasts—and if they're down to a reasonable price per pound, grab a couple because veal freezes well. When you make a pocket in the boned brisket (front section of the breast) and stuff it, and braise it, you have wonderful eating either hot or cold.

MANUFACTURING NOTE. *For this recipe you want the boned brisket, a little ground veal for the stuffing, and some bones to make a veal stock. You won't readily find all these items at hand, but if you do find the whole breast, put the home butcher to work as follows.*

The breast of veal. The whole breast from one side of a prime veal carcass weighs about 7 pounds. The front half (see illustration, step 1), the triangular left-hand piece in the photograph, is the brisket that is to be stuffed and braised; it weighs about 4 pounds. The right-hand side, with its 7 ribs, is the plate; part of its meat is saved for another meal, its meat scraps will go to stuff the brisket, while the bones, added to the brisket bones, will make a beautiful stock for the braising.

To bone the brisket. Counting the ribs from the small end, separate the breast between ribs 6 and 7. Cut around and under the rib bones of the brisket (the triangular 6-rib section); pull up and break each away from its cartilaginous attachment to the breastbone. Cut around the convolutions of the breastbone, and remove it. After boning out the brisket

Braised stuffed breast of veal

and slicing off excess fat, you will have the 2½-pound triangular piece of meat ready for stuffing at left in the photograph. The bones at right, chopped up, are waiting to create a veal stock.

To bone the plate. Slice off the skirt— the flap of meat covering part of the ribs in photograph 1, right side. Cut around and remove the ribs and the prolongation of the breastbone. Cut off the thick meaty part of the plate that contained the end of the breastbone; package it for stewing or grinding and another meal. Chop the bones and add to the stock pile, photograph 2.

Other usable meat. Scrape usable meat from the membranes covering the plate, skirt, and ribs; grind the meat, and use in the stuffing.

Cutting breast in two: left side is brisket to be stuffed

Brisket at left, bones for stock at right

Your Own Veal Stock

Veal stock is akin to chicken stock but has much more body because of the gelatinous quality of veal bones. Since prime veal is not available in many markets, a veal stock is somewhat of a rarity in home cooking nowadays. It freezes perfectly and is well worth having on hand for such events as a velouté sauce for a blanquette—veal stew, as adapted from the chicken blanquette on page 147—or another especially fine sauce.

For about 1 quart

2 or more pounds (2 quarts or so) veal bones chopped into 2-inch pieces
1 to 2 Tbs oil
1½ cups in all: chopped celery, onions, and carrots
Salt

Browning the bones. Toss the bones in a baking pan with the oil and vegetables. Brown lightly for 30 to 40 minutes in a 400°F oven, turning once or twice. Transfer to a saucepan, pour browning fat out of the baking pan, and deglaze the pan with a cup of water. Pour the deglazing water into the saucepan. Add additional water to cover the ingredients by 1 inch. Bring to the simmer, skim off scum for several minutes, and salt lightly. Simmer 3 to 4 hours, partially covered. Strain and degrease.

*Ahead-of-time note: Chill uncovered. Will keep several days in a covered container, or may be frozen.

Braised Stuffed Breast of Veal

The stuffing here is veal, pork, rice, and Swiss chard, the chard giving an attractive green speckle to the meat when it is carved. Other stuffing possibilities begin on page 184, of which the mushroom duxelles would be a worthy substitute.

For 6 servings

A 2½- to 3-pound boned prime brisket of veal (about 7 pounds bone-in, as previously described)
Sausage and Swiss Chard Stuffing (see Special Note, page 250)
2 to 3 cups olive oil or peanut oil
½ cup dry white French vermouth or white wine

Braising ingredients

1 large unpeeled tomato, chopped
2 large unpeeled cloves of garlic, smashed
1 big onion stuck with 2 cloves
An herb bouquet: 4 parsley sprigs, 1 imported bay leaf, ½ tsp thyme— tied together in washed cheesecloth

Either 3 to 4 cups of your own veal stock (see Special Note on this page) or chicken stock

2 Tbs each cornstarch and white vermouth or white wine, blended in a small bowl for the final sauce

SPECIAL EQUIPMENT SUGGESTED: *A baking pan and large saucepan for the stock; a 10-inch frying pan and mixing bowl for the stuffing; a casserole or covered roaster just large enough to hold the veal and vegetables*

Stuffing and browning the veal. Make a pocket in the veal by slicing from the large end toward the point, but not piercing the sides.

1. Spooning stuffing into pocket

The stuffing. Spoon the stuffing into the pocket, but don't fill it too full, step 1. Skewer the pocket to enclose the stuffing, step 2. Brush the veal with oil, and brown it on both sides in the frying pan.

Assembling. Transfer the meat to the casserole, deglaze the frying pan with a little of the vermouth or wine, and pour it over the veal. Surround with the braising ingredients, including enough stock to come two thirds the way up the ingredients, step 3.

*Ahead-of-time note: May be prepared a day in advance; refrigerate covered.

Braising—about 2½ hours at 325°F. Following directions in the master recipe (page 236), braise the meat, turning and basting twice, until tender.

Sauce and serving. Finish as in the preceding recipe.

2. Stuffed, skewered, and ready for braising

Smothered Brisket of Beef
Slow roasted with tomatoes and herbs

An extremely simple method for such braising cuts as beef brisket, and chuck or round steaks 2 inches thick. No browning, no tying, no stuffing, no fussing—and even no saucing. Cover the meat with chopped onions, tomatoes, and herbs, top it with foil, and set it in a 300°F oven, where it quietly simmers to tenderness, making its own delicious sauce. No matter that this is not a true braise since the meat is not browned; it makes prime eating.

TIMING NOTE. *You may assemble, cook, and serve the brisket with no delays, but both the 24-hour marinade and the final rest and reheating bring it to its optimum.*

For 6 to 8 servings

A 4-pound fresh brisket of beef (single brisket, center cut), or a chuck or round steak 2 inches thick
Salt
½ tsp thyme
1 or 2 large cloves of garlic, puréed into a small bowl
¼ cup fresh olive oil or salad oil
⅛ tsp freshly ground pepper
2 cups cored but unpeeled chopped fresh ripe tomatoes (or a combination of fresh tomatoes and canned Italian plum tomatoes)
1½ cups sliced onions

SPECIAL EQUIPMENT SUGGESTED: *A wide roasting pan large enough to hold the raw brisket easily; heavy-duty foil to cover the pan; if needed, a smaller pan for final cooking*

Smothered Brisket of Beef with vegetables

Assembling. Trim excess fat off the brisket, but leave an ⅛-inch layer on the fatty side. Mash ½ teaspoon of salt and the thyme into the garlic to make a paste; beat in the oil and pepper. Spread over both sides of the brisket. Place the meat fat side up in the roasting pan. Spread on the tomatoes and onions, and season lightly with salt. Cover tightly with foil.

3. Assembling

*Ahead-of-time note: The dish may be prepared to this point in advance, and will be even better if refrigerated for several hours or more.

Slow-roasting—3½ to 4 hours at 300°F. Set the dish in the middle level of the preheated oven. Check on progress and baste the meat with accumulated juices about every ½ hour. The brisket is done when a fork pierces it quite easily, but it should still hold its shape. (Note that brisket is never tender like steak, but it should be pleasantly chewable and will have a real beefy flavor.)

*Ahead-of-time note: Optional resting before serving—from 1 hour to 24

(continued)

Smothered Brisket of Beef (*continued*)

or more. Transfer the brisket with its vegetables to a smaller pan—it will have shrunk. Degrease the juices and pour them over the meat. Chill uncovered. May then be covered and kept under refrigeration for a day or two.

Sauce. Cover and reheat for 20 minutes or so in a 350°F oven, basting 2 or 3 times with the juices. Remove the meat with its vegetable topping to a carving board. Pour the juices into a saucepan, degrease them, and rapidly boil them down almost to a syrup. (Or, if you want more of a sauce, thicken the juices with 1½ Tbs cornstarch blended with 2 Tbs wine or stock, as described in the master recipe on page 244; serve in a sauceboat.)

Serving. Carve the meat across the grain into thin slanting slices, and accompany each serving with a spoonful or two of sauce and vegetables.

Suggested accompaniments. The steamed potatoes and carrots pictured here are a perfect accompaniment. A healthy young red wine is the best choice, like a zinfandel or Beaujolais.

SPECIAL NOTE

Sausage and Swiss Chard Stuffing
For veal, beef, and braised cabbage

1 cup minced onions
2 Tbs butter
6 to 8 large leaves of Swiss chard
½ cup (¼ pound) each sausage meat and ground veal
1 cup boiled rice
½ cup grated Swiss cheese
Seasonings: ½ tsp salt, ¼ tsp thyme, freshly ground pepper; more as needed

While sautéing the minced onions slowly in the butter, pull the white central rib out of the chard leaves. Drop the leaves into a pan of boiling water and boil 5 minutes; drain, refresh in cold water, squeeze dry, and chop. Stir 1 packed cup of the chard leaves into the onions and sauté 2 minutes; scrape onions and chard into a mixing bowl. Beat into them the sausage, ground veal, rice, cheese, and seasonings. Sauté a small spoonful; taste, and add whatever you think needed—it should be delicious, and slightly overseasoned if to be served cold.

*Ahead-of-time note: The stuffing may be prepared in advance and refrigerated; if you are stuffing meat in advance, be sure to let the stuffing cool beforehand.

FEASTING ON THE REMAINS

A Salad of Cold Roast or Braised Beef

Some of the best main-course salads are made out of cold roast or braised beef, like the suggestion here. See also the Syrian salad with cold roast lamb on page 214, which could be adapted for beef.

For 6 people, make about 1 cup of vinaigrette sauce, seasoned with shallots and a good dollop of Dijon mustard, page 351. You should have about a pound of cold beef carved into thin slices (about 2 generous cups). If it is brisket, cut the slices in half crosswise, then into thirds lengthwise. Marinate on a large pie plate or platter with a sprinkling of thyme and several tablespoons of the vinaigrette, basting several times— several hours of marinating are useful if you have the time.

Assembling. Line a serving platter with lettuce leaves tossed in a spoonful or so of the vinaigrette. Mound 2 to 3 cups of potato salad (French or American, page 362) in the middle. Arrange the brisket slices around the potatoes, and decorate the platter to your fancy with such items as tomatoes, hard-boiled eggs, black olives, rings of red onions, parsley, etc.

GROUND MEAT MIXTURES

MEAT LOAF, FRENCH PÂTÉS, CITY SCRAPPLE, AND YOUR OWN ITALIAN SAUSAGES

It is hard to think of a magnificent French pâté as having its origins in scraps—the otherwise unusable leftovers from the butcher's block. Happily, what on earth to do with tag ends and rejects has given rise over the centuries to some of our most lofty creations, as well as to such useful domestic favorites as meat loaf and scrapple.

A NOTE ON FAT. *Like hamburgers, ground meat mixtures need a certain amount of fat or they are dry in the mouth. A great deal of the fat cooks out, but a good meat loaf or pâté is not diet food. Carl Sontheimer, American father of the food processor, has done some experiments using cooked brown rice to replace fat; rice, brown or white, does indeed make for a moister low-fat pâté. An example is the turkey and rice alternate to pork in the master recipe.*

MEAT LOAF

You can make a great meat loaf out of raw meat, cooked meat, or a combination of raw and cooked, and you can make it out of beef alone, or pork, veal, turkey, lamb, or a combination. Your main concern is that it be carefully flavored, reasonably moist, that it hold together for slicing, and that it make wonderful eating hot or cold.

 MASTER RECIPE

A Beef and Pork Meat Loaf

For a 2-quart loaf, serving 12

2 cups minced onions
2 Tbs butter or oil
1 cup lightly pressed down crumbs
    from homemade type fresh white
    bread
2 pounds ground beef chuck
1 pound ground pork shoulder, or
    fresh sausage meat, or ground
    raw turkey plus 1 cup cooked rice
2 "large" eggs
½ cup beef bouillon
⅔ cup grated Cheddar cheese
1 to 2 cloves of garlic, puréed,
    optional
Seasonings: 2 tsp salt, ½ tsp pepper,
    2 tsp each thyme and paprika, 1
    tsp each allspice and oregano
3 imported bay leaves, for the top

SPECIAL EQUIPMENT SUGGESTED:
A frying pan for the onions; a large mixing bowl; for baking—a 2-quart loaf pan, or a jelly-roll pan for a free-form loaf; recommended—a thermometer that can remain in the meat as it cooks

Browning the onions. Sauté the onions in the butter or oil 5 minutes or so, until tender and translucent; raise heat and sauté a few minutes longer, until lightly browned. Scrape into the mixing bowl.

The mixture. Toss all the rest of the ingredients except for the bay leaves rather gently with the onions. Sauté a spoonful, and taste carefully—if you are to serve the meat loaf cold, exaggerate a bit on the seasoning. Either

(continued)

Free-form meat loaf

A Beef and Pork Meat Loaf (*continued*)

form into a loaf shape on a buttered jelly-roll pan, see illustration, or pack the meat into a buttered 8-cup loaf pan and bang on the table to deflate air bubbles. Top with the bay leaves.

Ahead-of-time note: May be prepared in advance; cover and refrigerate or freeze. *Note:* If you want to freeze a meat loaf, it is best frozen raw; defrost overnight or longer in the refrigerator before baking.

Baking—about 1½ hours at 350°F. Preheat the oven and set the meat loaf in the lower middle level.

When is it done? It is done when the juices run almost clear with a pale pink tinge, and the meat is lightly springy to the touch. A meat thermometer should read 155°F—do not remove the thermometer until the meat rests before serving time, or the juices will burst out.

Serving. Let cool for 30 minutes. Pour off fat and juices. Transfer the loaf to a board or platter. Serve hot with salsa (page 200), or tomato sauce (page 358). Or let cool, then wrap and refrigerate—the star of any picnic.

VARIATION

FEASTING ON THE REMAINS

Cooked meats may also make a marvelous meat loaf. Many of these mixtures, such as the following Meat Loaf Maison, make fine fillings for onions, cabbage leaves, and squash, as well as for turkey and other fillable foods. See also the selection of stuffings for poultry and meat beginning on page 184, any of which might well become all or part of a gorgeous meat loaf.

Meat Loaf Maison

This is the handsome solution to the leftovers of a braise, a stew, or a roast, and it can be made of meat or

Meat Loaf Maison

fowl—or even fish. A certain amount of raw meat—sausage meat, or raw chicken or turkey, for instance—added to the cooked meat gives moisture and also acts as a binder.

For a 6-cup loaf pan or baking dish, serving 8 to 10, start by sautéing 2½ cups of minced onions until tender in 3 tablespoons of oil or butter; when tender, pour in 1 cup of wine and/or leftover meat sauce or stock, and boil down until almost evaporated. Meanwhile purée 3 cups of cooked meat, poultry, rabbit, etc., in a food processor with 1 cup of cooked rice or pasta and 3 "large" eggs. Blend the purée in a bowl with the cooked onions, ½ to ⅔ cup of leftover braised vegetables if you have them, ½ pound (1 cup) of sausage meat, ½ cup of grated Swiss cheese, 1 or 2 large cloves of puréed garlic, salt and freshly ground pepper to taste, and ¼ teaspoon or so of thyme or mixed herbs. Sauté a spoonful and taste analytically for seasoning—overdoing a little if the dish is to be served cold.

Baking and serving. Follow directions for the preceding meat loaf.

FRENCH PÂTÉS AND TERRINES

The distinction between pâté and terrine has so blurred with time that they both mean the same thing—a winey spiced-up ground meat mixture that is baked and served cold. Terrine originally meant a comfortable earthenware baking dish, usually loaf shaped, in which the pâté was baked and served. A *pâté en croûte*, on the other hand, is the same mixture baked in a handsome highly decorated pastry crust. They are both French variations on the American meat loaf, as we chauvinists like to point out.

Country Pâté: Pâté de Campagne
Liver, onions, sausage, and chicken

This is an especially easy pâté to make—grind everything together, pack neatly in a buttered loaf pan, and it's ready for the oven. Make it more elaborate if you wish, since pâtés are built according to cook's mood-of-the-day. Layer strips of ham or chicken as you pack in the meat, for instance—a quarter pound would do. Or you might fold peeled pistachios into the mixture. Such touches as these make it your very own.

For a 6-cup baking dish

⅔ **cup minced onions cooked until translucent in 2 Tbs butter**
1¼ **pounds (2½ cups) pork sausage meat, your own (page 257) or store-bought**

Ingredients for a Country Pâté

¾ **pound (1½ cups) raw chicken breasts**
½ **pound (1 cup) pork or beef liver**
1 **cup lightly pressed down crumbs made from fresh homemade type white bread**
1 **"large" egg**
⅓ **cup cream cheese or goat cheese**
1 **medium clove of garlic, puréed**
2 **to 3 Tbs good brandy**
1 **Tbs salt**
¼ **tsp each ground allspice and thyme**
¼ **tsp ground imported bay leaf**
¼ **tsp freshly ground pepper**

The mixture. Purée all the ingredients together in a food processor; or put them through the fine blade of a meat grinder, then beat in a large mixing bowl to blend. To check seasoning, sauté a spoonful in a small frying pan, let cool, and taste it analytically; correct as necessary, exaggerating the flavors since pâtés are served cold.

Assembling and baking. Pack into a well-buttered loaf pan, cover with buttered wax paper, then with foil, allowing only 1 inch of overhang. Bake in a bain-marie (a pan of boiling water) in a 350°F oven as described for the preceding Meat Loaf Maison. It is done in 1¼ to 1½ hours at a meat thermometer reading of 162°F—when the meat is pressed, the juices are pale yellow with just a trace of rosy color.

Cooling. When done, let cool for an hour, then weight down with a twin pan or a board and a 5-pound weight (such as a canned good). When cool, cover and refrigerate—let the pâté mellow for a day or two before serving.

Serving. See directions at the end of the following Duck Pâté.

Duck Pâté Baked in Its Own Skin

A duck pâté baked in its own skin—sounds rather exotic for the average home cook. But when you find that boning a duck is not much of a trick, and you know that a pâté is a dressed-up meat loaf—why not give it a try?

For an 8-cup terrine or loaf pan

A 5-pound roaster duckling, including if possible its gizzard, heart, and liver
Seasonings: salt, freshly ground pepper, allspice, and thyme
¼ cup Cognac or good brandy
½ cup minced onions sautéed in 1 Tbs butter
1 pound (2 cups) ground pork shoulder
1 large clove of garlic, puréed
2 "large" eggs
½ cup peeled pistachio nuts, optional
3 imported bay leaves

SPECIAL EQUIPMENT SUGGESTED: *A food processor; an oiled 8-cup terrine or loaf pan, and a larger pan to hold it; an instant meat thermometer; a board or twin baking pan and weight for cooling*

To bone the duck.

First step—skin and flesh. You are to use the duck skin to line the terrine, and want to keep it intact except for the opening slit. Bone the duck as described for turkey on page 159—slitting it down the back from neck to tail, and cutting through the ball joints to separate the legs and wings from the carcass as you scrape meat from bone on each side.

Duck Pâté

The wings. With the carcass removed, you have the skin with legs and wings attached. From the skin side, chop each wing off above the elbow; from the flesh side scrape the meat from the remaining upper bone as you pull the skin sleeve inside.

The legs. From the skin side, chop off the ball joints of the drumstick ends. See illustration, step 1: from inside, scrape the meat off the second joints and drumsticks and pull the skin sleeves inside.

1. Removing meat from duck skin

2. Pan lined with duck skin

3. Final layer of duck strips and pistachios

4. Skin folded over

Removing breast meat from skin. Carefully pull and scrape the breast meat halves from the skin; cut it into long strips and toss in a bowl with a sprinkling of salt, pepper, allspice, thyme, and the Cognac or brandy.

The leg and wing meat. Remove as much of the leg and wing meat as you safely can, and reserve for grinding. Cut out and discard any easily removable fat.

The filling (or meat loaf mixture). In the food processor or meat grinder, chop the duck leg and wing meat with the duck gizzard (peeled) and heart, and the sautéed onions. Scrape into a large mixing bowl, and beat in the ground pork, 2 teaspoons of salt, ½ teaspoon each of pepper and thyme, ¼ teaspoon of allspice, the puréed garlic, and the eggs. Sauté a spoonful and taste very carefully for seasoning—it should seem oversalted and overspiced, since the seasoning will be muted when the pâté is served cold. Beat in the liquid from the breast strips.

Forming the pâté. Arrange the duck skin flesh side up in the oiled terrine, step 2. Spread over it a third of the filling, lay half the breast strips over the filling alternating with half the duck liver (cut into strips), and a double row of the optional pistachio nuts.

Cover with half the remaining filling, the rest of the breast strips, liver, and pistachios, step 3, then the last of the filling. Bang the dish on the table to flatten any air pockets. Lay 3 bay leaves over the top and fold the skin over, step 4. The pâté is ready for baking after you have covered it with a sheet of buttered foil and a lid of some sort.

Ahead-of-time note: May be prepared in advance; cover and refrigerate or freeze. If frozen, thaw in the refrigerator before baking. Note that this is the best time to freeze, since a baked pâté does not freeze well—it has a watery texture when thawed.

Baking—1½ to 2 hours at 350°F. Bake in a bain-marie (a pan of boiling water) to a meat thermometer reading of 160°F. Let cool for an hour, then weight down with a twin pan or a board, and a 5-pound weight (like canned goods). When cold, cover and refrigerate for a day or two before serving, to allow the pâté to develop its full flavor.

Serving. Set the terrine over heat for a few seconds to loosen the pâté; pour out fat and juices, and unmold the pâté onto a platter. Scrape and wipe off the surface. Decorate the top with parsley, pimiento strips, or whatever seems appropriate. (Note: Before decorating, you may wish to brush the surface with a coat or two of glistening aspic—⅔ cup of the degreased cooking juices dissolved with 1 teaspoon of gelatin; aspic directions are on page 16.)

Uncle Hans's City Scrapple
Pennsylvania Dutch Pork Loaf

Scrapple—slice it, sauté it, and serve with your breakfast eggs, or as part of a family supper. Traditional farm scrapple is made from pork scraps and bones that are boiled up for several hours with herbs and vegetables. The meat is then scraped from the bones and chopped, the broth is strained and boiled up with cornmeal, then the two are combined and baked into a loaf. Following is a simple city version that is far easier than the original, and every bit as tasty—perhaps even tastier—than scrapple from scraps.

For an 8-cup loaf pan

2 pounds best-quality pork sausage
    meat
1¼ cups store-bought boxed yellow
    cornmeal
4½ cups well-flavored meat or
    poultry stock
Seasonings: salt, freshly ground
    pepper, and sage
2 "large" eggs
For sautéing: more cornmeal, and
    sausage fat or butter

SPECIAL EQUIPMENT SUGGESTED:
A large frying pan for the sausage; a 3-quart saucepan for the cornmeal and a larger pan with simmering water to hold it; an 8-cup loaf pan, well greased with pork fat or butter; greased aluminum foil

The sausage meat. Break up the sausage meat and sauté in a large frying pan over moderate heat, breaking it up and stirring it occasionally until it has lost its pink color—about 10 minutes.

Uncle Hans's City Scrapple

The cornmeal. Place the cornmeal in the saucepan and, by dribbles at first, whisk in the stock. Bring to the simmer, stirring, and simmer 5 minutes, or until a quite thick mush. Cover and set in the larger pan of simmering water; cook 40 minutes, stirring occasionally. Uncover, and stir over moderately high heat until very thick, and the mush holds its shape quite solidly in a spoon.

Combining sausage and cornmeal

Combining sausage and cornmeal.
Combine the two, blending thoroughly (see illustration). Stirring over moderately low heat, season well with salt, pepper, and sage—exaggerate a bit on the sage. Remove from heat, stirring to cool slightly; beat in the eggs one at a time.

Molding and baking. Preheat the oven to 350°F. Pack the scrapple mixture into the baking pan, banging on the table to remove air pockets. Cover with foil (greased side down), and bake in the middle level for about an hour, until the scrapple has swelled up ½ inch or more.

Cooling, storing, and unmolding. Let cool for an hour, cover, and weight down until cold; refrigerate until well chilled.

To serve. Scrape off surface fat. Set the pan over heat to loosen the scrapple loaf; run a knife around the sides, and unmold onto a board. Slice the scrapple into crosswise pieces about ¾ inch thick. Dredge in cornmeal, and sauté in sausage fat or butter and oil to brown lightly on each side.

Accompaniments. Serve either as a breakfast dish or as a main-course lunch or supper dish. You might accompany the scrapple with fried or scrambled eggs, and broiled tomatoes. Sautéed apple slices and coleslaw or a salad are another idea, or the grated beets on page 293. For dinner, would a glass of light red wine go with scrapple? Cider or beer would perhaps be better.

SAUSAGES

Sausage links and patties are easy to make at home, and when you grind and season your own, you know exactly what you've got—good fresh meat.

● MASTER RECIPE

Pork Sausage Meat

This is the all-purpose formula for sausage cakes, sausage links, and any recipe calling for pork sausage meat.

For 2½ pounds—about 5 cups

2½ pounds fresh pork shoulder butt (you want approximately 2 parts lean to 1 part fat, which the butt should give)
1 Tbs salt
¾ tsp mixed ground herbs and spices (your own bottled mix, see Special Note, page 203; or allspice, thyme, imported bay leaf, paprika, and sage)
¼ tsp freshly ground pepper

SPECIAL EQUIPMENT SUGGESTED:
A meat grinder (the food processor is not recommended); a heavy-duty mixer with flat blade is useful

The mixture. Trim gristly bits, etc., from the pork, and cut the meat into strips 1 inch across. Put first through the coarse screen of the meat grinder, then through the fine screen. Beat either in the heavy-duty mixing machine or a big mixing bowl, adding the salt, herbs, spices, and pepper. Sauté a spoonful to cook through completely and taste it very carefully.

Correct seasoning. Cover and refrigerate for a day to allow the flavorings to penetrate the pork.

Ahead-of-time note: Sausage meat will keep 2 days or so under refrigeration; it will keep several weeks in the freezer but the flavor will gradually deteriorate.

Sausage Cakes or Patties

The preceding 2½ pounds of sausage meat makes 16 breakfast-size cakes 2½ ounces each. For uniform size, scoop out the meat with a ⅓-cup dry measure. Dipping your hands first in cold water, scoop the sausage meat out of the cup and roll into a ball between the palms of your hands, then flatten it into a cake and place on the tray. Sauté or broil in the usual manner.

Ahead-of-time note: May be prepared for cooking a day in advance; cover and refrigerate. If you are not cooking them at once, place between sheets of wax paper and refrigerate.

Electric meat grinder with sausage horn

State-of-the-art sausage stuffer

Sausage casings. Partially filled, left: empty casing, right

Making Link Sausages

You can use these sausages in so many ways. For instance, see the sauerkraut dinner, page 204.

EQUIPMENT. *Like so many things, sausages are easy to make when you have the right equipment. To find it, look in the yellow pages under either Sausages or Butcher's Supplies. Here is what you need:*

A good meat grinder.

Sausage casings. For Italian-style sausages, bratwursts, and large breakfast sausages you will want *small hog casings*, size 32–35mm; for small breakfast sausages about ½ inch in diameter, *sheep casings*. If your butcher cannot supply you with a few lengths of fresh natural casings, you will have to buy a whole hank from a supplier—and a hank is enough for 100–120 pounds of meat sausages! However, natural sausage casings

packed in salt will last indefinitely as long as they remain in the salt and under refrigeration.

A sausage stuffer. Shown here is a state-of-the-art hand sausage stuffer: the meat goes into the body of the machine, the casing on the nozzle, and the trigger moves the pusher plate against the meat to push it gradually into the casing. Also available is the old-fashioned but efficient cast-aluminum model—a long handle attached to a metal plate that pushes the sausage meat through the body of the machine and out into the casing attached to it. Another possibility is an electric meat grinder with sausage horn, which works fairly well.

Then there is the pastry bag with metal tubes—inefficient and maddening to use, but better than nothing. No directions given here—just muddle through.

Sausage horn or nozzle. Tapered metal tube that holds the casing; the tube is fastened onto the small end of the machine.

To prepare sausage casings. If you have a whole hank, unwind it—quite a job—cut it into lengths of 8 feet or so, and rewind each length; pack in coarse salt in a screw-top jar and

store in the refrigerator, where it will keep indefinitely. To prepare the casing for sausages, select the amount you need, unwind the lengths, and soak in a basin of cold water for an hour to soften—but not longer or they will soften too much. Cut the casing into convenient lengths—4 feet long for drama; a 2-foot length is probably wise if this is your first session.

Wash the sausage horn and insert its small end into one end of the casing. Push the large end of the tube against the cold-water faucet and slowly run water through the length of the casing to test for holes—if there are any, cut off the casing at that spot. Then, with the water running slowly, push the length of the casing up onto the horn, leaving 4 inches dangling free.

Either attach the horn to the sausage stuffer, or attach it to the meat grinder (fitted with large-holed screen and cutter knife).

Italian-Style Sweet Sausages with Fennel

For 1 dozen 5-inch sausages, 1¼-inch diameter

½ tsp ground fennel seeds
½ tsp coarsely ground pepper
¼ tsp nutmeg or coriander
5 cups all-purpose sausage meat
  (page 257)
⅓ cup ice water, if needed
10 feet or so small hog casings,
  unsalted, soaked, and tested as
  previously described

SPECIAL EQUIPMENT SUGGESTED:
The items previously listed

The mixture. Blend the fennel, pepper, and nutmeg or coriander into the sausage meat. If you are using a sausage stuffer, loosen the mixture by small additions of ice water; however, a mixture for the meat grinder should be fairly solid. Sauté a spoonful to check seasoning.

Using the sausage stuffer. Pack the sausage meat into the body of the machine. Attach the casing-filled horn to the nozzle. Force an inch or so of sausage out of the nozzle into the casing. Tie a knot in the casing to hold the meat. Gently but firmly force the meat into the casing and, if your mixture is just loose enough, the casing will fill with sausage meat. Squeeze excess sausage from the last 4 inches of casing, and return the meat to the machine. Tie a knot in the casing to enclose the open end.

Using the meat grinder. Follow the directions that come with the machine.

Forming the links. Twist the filled casings into 5-inch lengths, and tie into links with extra casing or string, to keep them in shape during cooking.

To cook link sausages. A preliminary steaming prevents home-made sausages from bursting later on, especially when broiled or barbecued—a safe and sensible precaution.

Preliminary steaming. The sausages will swell slightly as they cook, and to prevent them from bursting prick each in several places with a pin. Arrange in one layer in a frying pan with ⅓ inch of water. Bring to the simmer, cover, and cook at the barest simmer for 3 to 4 minutes; pour out the water. They are now ready for barbecuing, broiling, or for a sauerkraut dinner.

To brown in a frying pan. Film a frying pan with oil, and brown the sausages very slowly, turning them frequently. Pork sausages 1¼ inches in diameter will take about 10 minutes to cook through.

VARIATIONS

You can make wonderful sausages out of all manner of meats, poultry, and fish. The master recipe for fish mousse on page 124, for instance, makes perfect sausages. Fold in bits of the sautéed lobster meat on page 106, and you are right in there with the 3-star chefs, especially if you accompany your fancy fish dogs with the splendid lobster sauce on page 106. Or substitute ground turkey for fish, and you have turkey dogs.

HOME-CURED BEEF AND PORK

Why make corned beef when you can buy it at any market? No serious reason except for the pride of authorship; besides, it's easy to do, and you know exactly what's in it. The only requirements are a big piece of beef—or pork, since pork is done the same way— plus a sturdy plastic bag, seasonings, room in the refrigerator, and a chunk of time. Corning, or the preserving of meat in salt, was the age-old method of keeping food before the inventions of canning and freezing; meat preserved this way has its own very special flavor. By the way, don't worry about the use of salt since it is well soaked out before cooking.

🫓 MASTER RECIPE

To Corn Your Own Beef

Brisket is the traditional beef cut, but it's not the only one. Boneless chuck, such as the eye roast, which contains the continuation of the rib eye, is another choice. However, I really prefer either the top or bottom round because it slices up into neat chic pieces.

TIMING: *2 weeks minimum for the cure to take place.*

For a 12-pound piece of beef

A fully trimmed boneless 10- to 12-pound top or bottom round of beef (or the eye round, boneless chuck, or brisket)

The following seasonings mixed in a bowl

1⅓ cups coarse (Kosher) salt
1 Tbs cracked peppercorns (pound whole corns to crack them)
2 tsp each allspice and thyme
1 tsp each: paprika, sage, and ground or crumbled imported bay leaf

SPECIAL EQUIPMENT SUGGESTED:
A heavy-duty plastic bag roomy enough to hold the meat comfortably; a pan to hold it; a pan and weight to cover the meat

Salting and spicing the meat. Place the meat in the plastic bag and rub the seasonings all over it, see illustration. Press as much air as possible out of the bag, then tie it securely closed

Corned beef and vegetables

and set it in a pan or bowl. Place in the refrigerator, where the temperature should remain between 37°F and 38°F. For the first 2 days of the cure, keep it covered with the second pan and weight.

Rubbing seasonings into meat

A reminder

The cure. Within a few hours, red liquid will exude in the bag—the cure has begun. Once a day, without opening the bag, massage the meat with its juices and spices, and turn the bag over. I put a sign on my refrigerator to remind me. In 2 weeks the cure is done, and the special flavor has been achieved. The beef will now keep several months under refrigeration—but turn it every several days just to be sure all is well. If you've a large piece, you may want to cook only part of it and leave the rest in the cure.

De-salting—24 hours or longer. Before cooking the beef, wash off the salt cure and soak the meat in a large bowl of cold water, changing the water 2 or 3 times. As the salt leaves the flesh the meat softens and, when thoroughly de-salted, it will feel almost like fresh beef—cut off a snippet and taste it to be sure. De-salting may take 2 to 3 days if the meat has cured a number of weeks.

*Ahead-of-time note: As soon as the beef is de-salted, it is just as perishable as fresh meat—keep it refrigerated and cook it soon.

VARIATION

To Corn Pork

Use exactly the same system to corn fresh pork—the boneless shoulder is especially recommended here since the leg and loin tend to be dry when cooked in a boiled dinner.

To Cook Corned Beef

Corned beef goes beautifully as a substitute for fresh in the Smothered Beef Brisket recipe on page 249, where the meat is buried under a blanket of chopped tomatoes, onions, garlic, and herbs, then baked with no more ado, forming its own delicious juices. Corned beef and cabbage go wonderfully together, and the boiled dinner is an old standby.

Following is an expanded boiled dinner, including not only corned beef but pork, chicken, and sausage—the perfect main course for an informal crowd.

La Potée Normande
A boiled pork, beef, chicken, and sausage dinner

A sumptuous dinner for a dozen guests, where a variety of meats all cook together with aromatic liquid in a big kettle. This is a favorite of my French colleague Simca, born in Normandy, where the dish originated, who often serves it for Christmas Eve, after the midnight mass. Of course you don't have to add all the meats indicated—use only beef, or only pork, but here is the grand scheme.

PROCEDURE. *Various items are added to the kettle at different times according to how long each takes to cook, and are so listed with their directions in the recipe. If one part is done before the rest, remove it, adding it again to warm up before serving.*

TIMING. *Count on about 5 hours from start to finish, but the kettle needs only occasional attention as you go about your business elsewhere. When all is done, the boiled dinner will happily wait for an hour or more.*

For 12 to 16 servings

Starting off with the beef—3 to 4 hours of simmering

A boneless 4- to 6-pound piece of corned beef, such as top round or chuck eye, de-salted (or fresh beef)

2 each: medium celery ribs, carrots, and onions

1 pound beef-neck bones, plus some veal bones if available

A large herb bouquet: 8 parsley sprigs, 6 peppercorns, 4 whole cloves, 3 large cloves of garlic, 2 tsp thyme, 2 imported bay leaves—tied in washed cheesecloth

Cold water to cover ingredients

2 Tbs salt, or to taste

SPECIAL EQUIPMENT SUGGESTED: *White butcher's twine; a 10- to 12-quart kettle; several yards of cheesecloth*

(continued)

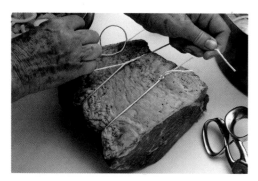

Tying the beef

La Potée Normande (*continued*)

Tie the beef with loops of string around its circumference as shown. Attach an 18-inch length of string to it, place the beef in the kettle, and tie the end of the string to the handle of the kettle—for easy removal later. Add the vegetables, bones, herb bouquet, and enough water to cover the ingredients by 6 inches. Bring to the simmer, skim off scum for several minutes, salt lightly, and prepare the rest of the ingredients as follows.

Adding a stuffed stewing hen—2½ to 3 hours. See list of stuffings on page 184—the cornbread and sage would be good here, or the ham and bread crumb. (*Note:* Stewing chickens are not always available—substitute a cut-up roaster; tie the pieces in cheesecloth and add the bundle along with the vegetables, later.)

Stuffing the chicken. Shortly before cooking it, stuff and truss the chicken (page 162), and tie a long string to it.

The chicken into the pot. After the beef has simmered for an hour, add the chicken to the kettle, tying the end of its string to the kettle handle. Bring the kettle rapidly back to the simmer, skimming as necessary.

Adding the pork (or veal)—2½ to 3 hours.

A fully trimmed boneless 4-pound shoulder of pork (fresh or corned), or boneless veal shoulder

Tie the meat to keep it in shape, as directed for the beef, leaving a length of string for the kettle handle. Following the chicken, add the pork or veal, also tying its string to the handle. Rapidly bring the kettle back to the simmer, skimming as necessary.

The vegetables and sausage, and completing the cooking

8 to 12 medium carrots and turnips, peeled and quartered
24 to 32 small white onions 1 inch in diameter, peeled and root ends pierced
12 to 14 leeks, cut 6 to 8 inches long, green part split lengthwise, thoroughly washed
1 or 2 whole Polish sausages, or individual sweet Italian sausages

Adding the vegetables—1 hour of simmering. Prepare the vegetables and tie each group in washed cheesecloth; add the bundles to the kettle 1 hour before the end of the estimated simmering time. (Include also the cut-up chicken, if you are using it.)

The sausage—½ hour of simmering. Prick the sausage or sausages in several places with a pin. If you are using Italian sausages, tie them in washed cheesecloth. Add the sausage or sausages ½ hour before the estimated end.

Finishing the potée. The meats and chicken are done when a fork pierces the flesh easily. Remove any that are done before the rest, and return them to the kettle at the end.

*Ahead-of-time note: The potée will stay warm or may be kept warm (at well below the simmer) for a good hour. *Note:* Never cover a warm dish airtight—you risk spoilage: always cover loosely to allow air circulation.

Serving. Drain the meats, discard trussing strings, carve into serving portions, and arrange them either on separate platters, or grouped together. Arrange the vegetables around the meats. Strain and degrease the cooking stock, basting the meat and vegetables with generous spoonfuls; pour additional stock into a large gravy bowl.

Suggested accompaniments. Boiled rice or potatoes and/or French bread. You may want to include steamed cabbage wedges (page 288). Besides the cooking broth, additional suggestions are fresh tomato sauce (page 358), horseradish sauce (page 220), plus capers, mustard, coarse salt, and sour pickles. A light red Bordeaux or merlot wine would go nicely here.

FEASTING ON THE REMAINS

Kitchen treasures, that's what the remains can be—we all hope—particularly such splendid offerings as those of a roast turkey, a ham, braised beef, roast lamb. We have a number on hand elsewhere in the ham, lamb, and beef sections. Here are four more general-purpose ideas, and you'll find the whole roster in the index listed under "Feasting."

Old-Fashioned Hash

For leftover ham, lamb, beef, and poultry

This is real hash, with a crusty outside and tender savory inside. Wonderful on its own, it's even better topped with a poached egg and side order of fresh tomato sauce.

MANUFACTURING NOTE. *The secret of a crusty hash is time—it needs slow cooking so that it will brown nicely on the bottom.*

For a 10-inch pan, serving 4

1½ to 2 cups boneless and skinless cooked meat or poultry
Salt and freshly ground pepper

Optional marinade

1 or more Tbs freshly squeezed lemon juice, white wine, Port, or Madeira
Minced fresh herbs, such as thyme and tarragon, or Italian herb mixture

1 to 2 Tbs light olive oil

1 cup diced onions
2 or more Tbs butter
2 Tbs flour
1½ cups hot liquid (milk, meat or poultry stock, and/or gravy or cream)
2 or 3 "boiling" potatoes
Optional: ¾ cup either diced cooked vegetables (such as peas, carrots, broccoli, turnips), or meat or poultry stuffing, or a mixture
⅔ cup lightly pressed down, grated cheese, such as Swiss, Cheddar, Monterey Jack, or mozzarella
3 to 4 Tbs chopped fresh parsley

Optional accompaniments

4 poached eggs (page 64)
Parsley sprigs
1 cup fresh tomato sauce (page 358)

SPECIAL EQUIPMENT SUGGESTED: *A food processor is useful; a heavy 10-inch frying pan (no-stick recommended); a cover of some sort for the pan*

The meat or poultry. Cut the meat into ¼-inch dice—if using a food processor, do only 1 cup at a time with on-off pulses. Toss in a bowl with a sprinkling of salt and pepper and such of the optional marinade ingredients as seem appropriate—lemon juice and tarragon with turkey or chicken, for instance; wine and Italian seasoning for beef.

The hash base. Sauté the onions slowly in the frying pan with the butter until tender; raise heat slightly and brown lightly—about 10 minutes. Blend in the flour; cook, stirring, for 3 minutes. Remove from heat, blend in 1 cup of the hot liquid; simmer, stirring, for 2 minutes. Season to taste with salt and pepper.

The potatoes. Meanwhile, peel and dice the potatoes—you should have about 2 cups. Drop them into a pan of lightly salted boiling water and simmer 5 minutes or so, until barely tender. Drain.

Assembling. Fold the potatoes into the hash base along with the meat and its marinade, the optional vegetables and/or stuffing, and the remaining liquid.

Cooking the hash—35 to 40 minutes in all. Cover the pan and simmer rather slowly for 10 to 15 minutes, until the hash begins to crust on the bottom. Uncover, stir the crust into the body of the hash, and if the mixture seems dry, pour in a little extra liquid. Taste and correct seasoning, adding more herbs if you feel them necessary. Cover and let crust on the bottom again for 10 to 15 minutes or so.

*Ahead-of-time note: May be completed somewhat ahead to this point; set aside uncovered, at room temperature.

Finishing the hash. Stir up again, blend in the cheese and parsley, cook 5 to 10 minutes more, uncovered this final time, until the bottom is nicely browned and well crusted.

Serving. Either flip the hash over in the pan and slide onto a warm serving platter, or unmold it onto the platter. Decorate, if you wish, with poached eggs and parsley, and surround with the tomato sauce.

VARIATION

Hashed Brown Turnip Cakes with Ham and Eggs

The glories of the leftover ham and the turnip are never more subtly displayed than in this crêpelike creation where turnips are grated and combined with grated potatoes, cream, and eggs. Baby cubes of the ham are scattered over each crustily sautéed cake, which is then topped with a poached egg. Serve them to a happy few for breakfast, brunch, lunch, or supper.

For 4 turnip cakes

The garnish

1⅓ cups diced cooked ham
2 Tbs butter
Seasonings: salt, freshly ground
 pepper, sage, thyme, and 1 tsp or
 so chutney or Hoisin sauce
4 poached eggs (page 64)

The turnip cakes

2 large white turnips
1 "baking" potato the size of one
 turnip
¼ cup sour cream
1 "large" egg
Salt and freshly ground pepper

2 or more Tbs clarified butter (page
 139), or fresh peanut oil
1 Tbs minced fresh parsley
½ cup fresh tomato sauce (page
 358), or hot ketchup

SPECIAL EQUIPMENT SUGGESTED:
A 6- to 7-inch frying pan, for the ham; a food processor with grating disk is useful; a large spatula and big mixing fork; a 10-inch frying pan, for the turnip cakes (no-stick recommended); a cover of some sort for the pan

The ham and the poached eggs. Sauté the ham briefly in the small frying

Serving of turnip cake with poached egg

pan with the butter, just to brown very lightly; set aside. Poach the eggs and set in cold water; just before serving, place them in a pan of lightly salted simmering water for 1 minute to reheat.

The turnip cakes.

The mixture. Shortly before sautéing them, grate the turnips and potato, then by handfuls twist in the corner of a stout clean towel to extract as much juice as you can—you should have about 3 cups after squeezing. At once, to prevent discoloration, blend them in a mixing bowl with the cream and egg. Season to taste.

Sautéing the cakes. Film the large pan with ¹⁄₁₆ inch of butter or oil, and set over moderately high heat. With the spatula and mixing fork, rapidly form 4 cakes about ⅜ inch thick in the hot pan. Lower heat to moderate, cover the pan, and cook slowly for about 5 minutes, or until lightly browned on the bottom. Turn

carefully—they are fragile—cover the pan, and cook 5 minutes more on the other side.

**Ahead-of-time note:* If you are not quite ready to serve, set the pan over very low heat, with the cover slightly askew.

Serving. Reheat the ham and the eggs. Serve the cakes on hot plates, each cake garnished with a spoonful of diced ham, topped with a poached egg, and a pinch of parsley. Spoon a dollop of tomato sauce or ketchup on the side.

Chinese Manicotti
Giant pasta tubes stuffed with leftover meat or poultry, baked in a Chinese sauce

Those fat tubes of pasta—manicotti—were made to be stuffed, and they are so much easier to fill with delectable mixtures than are sausage casings, crêpes, or green peppers. Boil the manicotti until limp, and push into them whatever delicious mixture comes to mind—or is in the stuffing list on page 184, and bake them in a pungent sauce. The following free-form internationally mixed recipe makes an especially fine Italo-Sino conversation piece, and unusually good eating.

For 4 to 6 servings

For the stuffing

⅔ cup sliced onions
2 Tbs butter
8 ounces (1 cup) leftover ground
 cooked meat or poultry, or
 sausage meat
3 Tbs chopped scallions
8 ounces (1 cup) raw peeled shrimp,
 or chicken breast

½ cup lightly pressed down crumbs from fresh white homemade type bread

1 large clove of garlic, puréed

1 "large" egg

2 Tbs cornstarch mixed in 2 Tbs sherry and 1½ Tbs soy sauce

½ Tbs grated fresh ginger

Seasonings: salt and freshly ground pepper

12 large manicotti, packed in plastic forms

For the baking sauce

¼ cup dried mushrooms (Chinese or other)

1 large clove of garlic, finely minced

2 Tbs peanut oil

1 Tbs Chinese fermented black beans

⅔ cup chicken broth

1 tsp dark sesame oil

1 tsp soy sauce

2 tsp cornstarch dissolved in ½ cup dry white French vermouth

⅔ cup grated Swiss cheese

SPECIAL EQUIPMENT SUGGESTED:
A 10-inch frying pan; a food processor; an oiled 9- by 12-inch baking dish; a pastry bag with ⅜-inch tube opening

The stuffing. Sauté the onions slowly in the frying pan with the butter until tender, then purée with the rest of the stuffing ingredients in the food processor. Sauté a spoonful; taste and correct seasoning.

The manicotti. Manicotti are packed in plastic forms to keep them safe and unbroken. Drop them carefully into a pan of boiling salted water (see illustration, step 1). Boil slowly 8 to 10 minutes, until softened but still at the slightly underdone *al dente* stage—they must hold their shape for stuffing and baking. Handle them with great care after boiling, so they

Serving of Chinese Manicotti

1. Boiling the manicotti shells

2. Filling boiled manicotti shells

won't split before stuffing. Drain; place on an oiled tray.

Filling the manicotti. Stuffing wet, slippery pasta tubes is difficult without a pastry bag. The one shown here

3. Pouring on the sauce

is of flexible vinyl, 12 to 14 inches long. Fill the pastry bag with the stuffing and insert it into the manicotti, arranging each piece in the oiled dish as you do so, step 2.

The baking sauce. Wash the mushrooms; discard tough stems. Chop the mushrooms, and soak 5 minutes in ½ cup of very hot water. Using the same frying pan, warm the garlic briefly in the oil, then add the mushrooms and their soaking liquid, plus all the remaining ingredients except the cheese. Simmer 3 minutes.

*Ahead-of-time note: The manicotti may be filled in advance, covered with oiled foil, and refrigerated, and the sauce completed.

Baking—about 40 minutes at 375°F. Set the covered manicotti dish in the oven to warm through—5 minutes or so. Discard the foil, and pour the sauce over the manicotti, step 3. Spread on half the cheese. Bake 20 minutes, until bubbling, spread on the rest of the cheese and bake 20 minutes more to brown lightly.

Serving. Serve the manicotti as a first course, or as a main-course luncheon or supper dish with a lightly dressed tossed salad. A white wine would go here, a sauvignon blanc or Mâcon.

Vegetables

Green Vegetables, Root Vegetables, Winter and Summer Vegetables

Boil-Steamed Vegetables

Grated, Braised, and Stuffed Vegetables

Vegetable Dishes That Make a Meal

New Ideas for Potatoes, Rice, Beans, and Lentils; Wheat Berries, Hominy, and Grits

From artichokes and asparagus to cabbage and zucchini, there is more interest in fresh vegetables now than ever before. Not only are more varieties available in our supermarkets, but specialty growers and specialty stores are catering to America's increasing demand for superior quality and freshness. In addition, the truth has dawned that fresh vegetables are not only good for you, they are wonderfully good to eat—when lovingly prepared.

This chapter follows the general system of grouping cook-alikes, as far as logic allows. Thus all stuffed vegetables are together in one section, braised vegetables together in another, grated in another, and so forth. This means, as an example, that the versatile onion is featured in three different areas, first among the braised vegetables, then in stuffed vegetables, and lastly in Other Vegetables, a miscellaneous catchall for methods that refuse to be catalogued.

A full listing of all the recipes for each vegetable appears under its own name in the index.

THE BIG FIVE—MOSTLY GREEN for Blanching and Steaming

Broccoli and cauliflower, Brussels sprouts, green beans, and spinach

BROCCOLI AND CAULIFLOWER

Broccoli and cauliflower, those culinary cousins, are blissfully in season throughout the year, and thank heaven for broccoli. Its welcome green color and its distinctive but not obtrusive taste make it a perfect companion to almost any first- or main-course dish, from scrambled eggs to braised beef and onions. Freshly cooked broccoli, too, is another vegetable that is perfect for dieters, since it can suffice with nothing more than a little seasoning and a wedge of lemon. However, it carries on very well with white butter sauces, hollandaise, and the like.

Broccoli cooks up infinitely faster, fresher, greener, and better in every way when you cut it into florets, peel the stems of the florets, and then cut and peel the main stem too. Cauliflower, as well, is infinitely more tender and delicious when peeled. The extra minutes thus spent, as is so often the case, are the hallmarks of fine and careful cooking, *la cuisine soignée*—and that is highest praise.

Broccoli

Buying and storing. Choose clean, firm, smooth-stemmed, crisp-feeling

Broccoli and cauliflower

and fresh-smelling heads with dark green or purple florets that are tightly closed. Old broccoli will have some yellowing in the floret area, some open buds, and a stale old-cabbage odor. To store, wrap the heads loosely in slightly dampened paper towels and refrigerate in a plastic bag.

Amounts to buy. One pound (or 2 medium heads) will serve 4 amply.

Preparation. Cut the floret from the central stalk, leaving the stem 2 inches long. Starting at the butt end of each, rapidly lift off the peel in strips with a small sharp knife, going almost up to the flower buds all around. Cut off the tough butt ends of the central stalks, peel the stalks down to the tender pale inside flesh; cut the stalks in half lengthwise, then into diagonal pieces.

Cauliflower

Buying and storing. Choose firm, fresh-looking and fresh-smelling heads, all white with no brown or discolored patches. The floret clusters should be closely packed together; the clusters of old or stale cauliflower begin to separate from each other. The freshest cauliflower heads still have some crisp green leaves attached to the base of the head.

Amount to buy. A 7-inch, 2-pound, or average medium head serves 4 to 6.

Preparation. Cut the central stem out of the cauliflower, going an inch or so up into the floret area. Peel the stem, going deep enough to reveal the tender inside flesh; halve or quarter; and cut into diagonal pieces. Snap off the florets and peel their stems, as for broccoli. Make a 1-inch slit through the stems of any fat pieces, for faster cooking.

Peeling broccoli stem

Peeling central stem

Peeling cauliflower stem

Ahead-of-time note: Both broccoli and cauliflower may be prepared even a day in advance; wrap in a slightly dampened towel and refrigerate in a plastic bag.

 MASTER RECIPE

Blanched Broccoli

When you cover a green vegetable while it's cooking, you risk losing its beautiful green color. Therefore,

SPECIAL NOTE

Blanching

To blanch means to drop food into boiling water either to boil it briefly so that it wilts or softens, as for boiling a whole head of cabbage, not until it is cooked, but only until the leaves come loose so that you can remove them. Or to drop a whole tomato into boiling water for 10 seconds so that its skin loosens for easy peeling. Or to blanch salt pork or bacon for 10 minutes to remove its salty or smoky flavor. On the other hand, you can blanch long enough to cook foods, such as green vegetables like green beans, spinach, or broccoli, when you boil them until they are just cooked through.

In the case of green vegetables, you use a very large quantity of rapidly boiling water so that it will come back to the boil as rapidly as possible after the vegetables go in, thus retaining their bright green color. The recipe for blanching broccoli is a perfect example, as is that for green beans.

Nutritional and dietary note. "But aren't you losing all the vitamins and nutrients, boiling them in that much water?" I have eaten, and even cooked, green vegetables prepared by the rules of nervous nutritional nellies, in which sprouts or green beans were boiled in a small covered pan—they have been invariably unappetizing, inedible, and a dull gray-green. One reason, I am sure, that many people hate vegetables is because they are cooked like medicine. But fresh vegetables are glorious food! And any fresh broccoli or Brussels sprout that looks as green and tastes as fresh as it does when cooked as described here can only be filled with nature's goodness. They are so good, in fact, that you can eat them as is, with perhaps only a sprinkling of salt and pepper.

while steaming is fine for cauliflower, it is risky for broccoli unless you are precooking and will finish it off later, such as in the brief sauté in olive oil and garlic described farther on.

For 4 servings

1 pound broccoli (2 medium heads), prepared as previously described
A large kettle of lightly salted, rapidly boiling water

SPECIAL EQUIPMENT SUGGESTED:
A large perforated scoop or Chinese wire skimmer, or a wire salad basket

Wash the peeled broccoli rapidly under cold water, drain, and plunge it into the boiling water. Boil slowly, uncovered, for 2 to 4 minutes, until just cooked through but with the slightest crunch. Taste a piece to be sure. Remove at once.

Ahead-of-time note: Peeled broccoli is so quick to cook, I see no reason for doing it in advance if it is to be simply served. However, if it must be done in advance, refresh the broccoli in cold water as for the green beans on page 276.

Steaming the cauliflower

 MASTER RECIPE

Steamed Cauliflower

You may blanch cauliflower, just as you blanch broccoli, but since you do not have the color problem, it is quicker and easier to steam it, especially when you have broken it into florets and peeled their stems.

For 4 to 6 servings

1 head of cauliflower 7 inches across, trimmed, stems peeled, as described at the beginning of this section

SPECIAL EQUIPMENT: *A steaming basket set in a covered saucepan*

Pour 1 inch of water in the saucepan, place the trimmed cauliflower in the basket, cover closely, and set over high heat. When steaming, lower heat to moderate, and steam 3 to 5 minutes, or until just cooked through but with the slightest crunch. Eat a piece to check.

*Ahead-of-time note: Since you have no green color to worry about, cauliflower may be cooked in advance and reheated. Remove the steaming basket and let the cauliflower cool before covering and refrigerating it.

SERVING SUGGESTIONS FOR BROCCOLI AND CAULIFLOWER

Buttered Broccoli or Cauliflower

Season lightly with salt and pepper, and spoon on melted butter. For cauliflower, a sprinkling of parsley is usually welcome.

Broccoli Bouquets

A burst of color, perhaps for Christmas broccoli. Decorate each serving with a bow of red pimiento—canned red pimiento cut into strips.

Broccoli Sautéed in Olive Oil and Garlic

A quick and easy accompaniment to steaks, chops, hamburgers, and broiled chicken or fish

Either blanch the broccoli until barely tender, as in the master recipe, or steam it as described for cauliflower, but stop it while still undercooked or its bright green will turn dull. Just before serving, film the frying pan with 1/16 inch of olive oil, and set over moderately high heat. Finely mince and stir in 1 or 2 large cloves of garlic and sauté a moment just to soften but not to brown it. Toss in the broccoli, season lightly with salt and freshly ground pepper, and toss, swirling the pan by its handle, to heat it through thoroughly and to finish the cooking. Toss with a dribble more oil, if you wish, and serve.

VARIATION

Cauliflower Sautéed in Oil, Garlic, and Parsley

Finish off steamed cauliflower florets in exactly the same way as the preceding broccoli, but when trimming and peeling, cut them a little smaller than usual. Sprinkle with fresh parsley before serving.

Broccoli-Sauced Broccoli

Here is an elegant broccoli presentation, in which a handful of the flower bud ends are cooked separately, and folded into a lemon-butter sauce before being spooned over the rest. This would be a highly suitable accompaniment to something rather special, like butter-poached chicken breasts, a roast of veal, veal scallops, or small roast birds. Although the main preliminaries may be completed ahead, the final cooking and saucing are done at the last minute.

For 6 servings

About 2 pounds broccoli
The grated rind of ½ lemon
2 Tbs freshly squeezed lemon juice
2 Tbs chicken broth
Salt and freshly ground pepper
5 to 6 Tbs unsalted butter
2 to 3 Tbs clarified butter (page 139)

SPECIAL EQUIPMENT SUGGESTED: *A 6-cup saucepan and whisk for the sauce; a 6-inch no-stick frying pan for the floret buds; a large kettle and either a steaming basket or large perforated scoop for the broccoli*

Preliminaries. Cut just the small flower buds off one head of broccoli, enough to give you 1 cup or so. Set aside. Cut and peel the remaining broccoli florets, leaving them 1½ inches long and, if you need more broccoli, also a portion of the stalks. Have lightly salted water in the kettle at the full boil 6 to 8 minutes before you expect to serve.

For the sauce. Boil the grated lemon rind, lemon juice, and chicken broth in the 6-cup saucepan with ¼ teaspoon of salt, a few grinds of pepper, and 1 tablespoon of butter until reduced to a syrupy 2 tablespoons. Set aside. Cut the remaining butter into tablespoon pieces and reserve on a plate.

The broccoli buds. Shortly before proceeding to the next step, heat the clarified butter in the 6-inch frying pan, add the broccoli buds, and sauté over moderate heat a minute or two, until just tender; set aside. (Clarified butter coats them to prevent discoloration when added to the sauce later.)

Cooking and serving. Shortly before serving, blanch the main part of the broccoli as described in the master recipe. Meanwhile set the sauce base over moderately high heat and, when it comes to the boil, start whisking in the butter piece by piece, adding a new piece as each previous one is almost absorbed. Remove from heat as soon as the last of the butter has gone in, and fold in the reserved broccoli

buds. Arrange the hot broccoli on a hot serving dish, spoon the sauce over, and serve.

VARIATION

Broccoli-Sauced Cauliflower

Rather than the usual parsley to decorate steamed cauliflower, anoint it with a sprinkle of broccoli-flower buds in lemon-butter sauce, as described in the preceding recipe.

Broccoli or Cauliflower with Browned Bread Crumbs

This is an attractive way to serve broccoli or cauliflower when you want to make it more important, such as a vegetable first course, or a main-course luncheon dish to go with something like poached or baked eggs.

Before cooking the broccoli, melt 2 to 3 tablespoons of butter in a 10-inch frying pan and when foaming stir in ¾ cup of fresh crumbs. Sauté over moderate heat, tossing and turning, for 2 to 3 minutes, until the crumbs are lightly browned. Toss with salt and freshly ground pepper to taste and set aside; reheat briefly just before serving.

When the broccoli or cauliflower is done, arrange it on hot plates or a platter, season lightly with salt, pepper, drops of lemon juice, and, if you wish, a little melted butter. Strew on the browned crumbs, and serve.

VARIATION

Broccoli or Cauliflower à la Polonaise

Push a hard-boiled egg through a coarse-meshed sieve, toss with a little salt and freshly ground pepper, then toss with the browned crumbs just before sprinkling over the vegetables—add a handful of chopped fresh parsley if it's cauliflower.

Hashed Broccoli

When you need to cook broccoli in advance, or you want hashed greenery as a garnish or as a filling for something like crêpes or a rolled soufflé, blanch the broccoli, then hash (chop it fine with a big knife) it; toss it in a frying pan with butter and seasonings just before serving. You may also substitute Brussels sprouts for broccoli in the two following variations.

VARIATIONS

Broccoli Hashed in Cream

This goes nicely with broiled chicken or fish, as well as with hamburgers and steaks. After tossing the broccoli in a little butter, and seasoning it, fold in ½ cup or so of heavy cream. Heat through to bubbling, correct seasoning, and serve.

THE CLASSIC WHITE SAUCES: BÉCHAMEL AND VELOUTÉ

These are the old standbys of home cooking, and you will use them countless times in one guise or another—for baked vegetables, for egg and fish dishes, in cream soups, and so forth. Flour-based sauces have a bad reputation because they are too often carelessly put together, but there is no excuse for grainy floury-tasting sauces when they are so very easy and quick to make. The essential, really, is the initial cooking together of the thickening element: the flour-butter paste—the white roux.

White Sauce—Cream Sauce—Béchamel Sauce

For 2 cups of medium-thick sauce

2½ Tbs butter
3½ Tbs flour
2 cups hot milk
½ tsp salt and several grinds of white pepper

SPECIAL EQUIPMENT SUGGESTED: *A heavy-bottomed 2½-quart stainless saucepan for the sauce; a wooden spatula or spoon; a small saucepan for the milk; a wire whisk*

The white roux. Melt the butter in the 2½-quart saucepan, then blend in the flour with a wooden spoon to make a smooth somewhat loose paste. Stir over moderate heat until the butter

and flour foam together for 2 minutes without coloring more than a buttery yellow. Remove from heat.

Adding the milk. When the bubbling stops, in a few seconds, pour in all but ½ cup of the hot milk at once, whisking vigorously to blend thoroughly. Then whisk rather slowly over moderately high heat, reaching all over the bottom and sides of the pan, until the sauce comes to the simmer; simmer 2 to 3 minutes, stirring with a wooden spoon and thinning out the sauce as necessary with dribbles of the milk. The sauce should be thick enough to coat a spoon nicely. Whisk in the salt and pepper, tasting very carefully and adding more as needed.

*Ahead-of-time note: To prevent a skin from forming over the surface of the sauce, (1) whisk it every few minutes until it has cooled, *or* (2) film the surface with milk—spread a tablespoon or so of it over the surface of the sauce with the back of a kitchen spoon—*or* (3) press a sheet of plastic wrap right down onto the surface. The sauce will keep 2 to 3 days under refrigeration or may be frozen.

For a thicker or thinner sauce.

Thin sauce, such as for cream soups: 1 Tbs flour and ¾ Tbs butter per cup of milk.

Thick sauce, such as for cheese soufflés: 2 Tbs flour and 1½ Tbs butter per cup of milk.

For a lighter or a richer sauce, use skim milk for the former, or, for a

rich sauce, use half-and-half or whisk several tablespoons of butter into the finished sauce.

First aid for a lumpy sauce. Push it through a fine-meshed sieve, then whirl it in an electric blender, and finally whisk it over heat until it simmers a moment.

Velouté Sauce

For vegetables, fish, and white meats

This is exactly the same as white sauce except that, rather than milk alone, you use vegetable, fish, or meat juices or stock, plus milk and/or cream if called for. A detailed recipe is on page 8.

Cheese Sauce: Mornay Sauce

Make either a white or a velouté sauce, and let it cool several minutes before whisking in grated cheese. Proportions are usually ¼ cup of cheese per cup of sauce, and the cheese is usually Swiss, although you may use any kind you wish. Usually, too, a speck of nutmeg is included.

First aid for stringy cheese sauce. When cheese is added to a very hot sauce the sauce can become stringy— Swiss cheese is often the culprit here. To remedy, bring it to the simmer whisking in drops of lemon juice or dry white wine—a tip from our late great American culinary authority James Beard—and it usually works.

Hashed Broccoli Mornay
Gratinéed in cheese sauce

This is a useful dish when you have a plain roast or sauté and need a somewhat substantial but not starchy vegetable to go with it.

Prepare the hashed broccoli and fold into it 1½ cups of cheese sauce, see the Special Note. Turn the broccoli into a buttered baking dish, spread on 2 more tablespoons of grated cheese. Twenty minutes before serving, bake in the upper third level of a preheated 425°F oven until the contents are bubbling and the cheese topping has browned lightly.

Cauliflower au Gratin

Even if the doleful dishes of steamtable institutional food have discouraged you from this one, it is an excellent preparation as well as a useful one when you need an ahead-of-time vegetable that can take the place of potatoes. The only secrets are: don't overcook and don't let it sit around on a steam table!

Assembling. For 4 to 6 people, lightly butter a 2-quart baking dish 2 inches deep, and spoon in a thin layer of cheese sauce (see Special Note). Arrange the steamed cauliflower florets, heads up, over the sauce. Season with a sprinkle of salt and freshly ground pepper, and a dusting of grated Swiss cheese. Spoon 1½ to 2 cups of cheese

sauce over the cauliflower to mask it completely. Spread on 2 to 3 tablespoons of grated cheese.

Baking. Fifteen to 20 minutes before serving, bake in the upper third level of a preheated 425°F oven just until hot through and the cheese topping has browned lightly.

VARIATION

Gratin of Cauliflower and Spinach, Mornay

Here is a dish for vegetable lovers: you could well serve it as the main course for a luncheon, or as the single vegetable to go with a roast or broiled fish.

Preliminaries. Prepare the ingredients for the preceding gratin. Meanwhile, in a 10-inch no-stick frying pan, sauté 2 tablespoons of minced shallots or scallions in 2 tablespoons of butter for a moment, then add 2 cups of blanched chopped fresh spinach (page 278), and sauté several minutes to evaporate excess moisture. Cover and cook slowly several minutes more until tender. Season carefully to taste with salt, freshly ground pepper, and nutmeg, and fold in 3 tablespoons of the cheese sauce.

Assembling and baking. Spread the spinach in the bottom of the buttered baking dish, and then continue with the steamed cauliflower and the sauce as described in the preceding recipe.

Piercing root end of a sprout

BRUSSELS SPROUTS

Fresh Brussels sprouts are with us in abundance from September through February. They begin to dwindle off in March, and are practically nonexistent from April through August. Thus one of our great winter vegetables is also a bright and hearty accompaniment to winter meals— turkey, pork, and roast and braised meats of all kinds.

Buying. Choose Brussels sprouts that are firm to the squeeze—and do squeeze them to be sure the heads are hard. If they are soft and the leaves are not tightly bunched, they will cook into a disappointing mush. Yellowing of the leaves indicates stale old sprouts: their color should be a fresh bright green.

Preparation. Trim off the stems close to the heads without detaching the leaves; pull off any loose or wilted leaves. For even cooking, pierce a cross ⅜ inch deep in the stem ends. Wash and drain them before cooking.

*Ahead-of-time note: If you are not to cook the Brussels sprouts shortly, wrap them in slightly dampened paper towels and refrigerate in a plastic bag.

MASTER RECIPE

Blanched Brussels Sprouts

Like all green vegetables, Brussels sprouts remain fresher and greener if blanched in a large open kettle of rapidly boiling water.

For 4 to 6 servings

1 to 1½ pounds or quarts Brussels sprouts, prepared as described at the beginning of this section
6 quarts or more rapidly boiling water
3 Tbs salt (1½ tsp per quart of water)

SPECIAL EQUIPMENT SUGGESTED: *An 8-quart kettle or pan with cover; a wire salad basket to hold and remove the vegetables, or a large perforated scoop or Chinese wire skimmer—for easy removal*

Plunge the sprouts into the rapidly boiling water, cover the pan only just until the water comes back to the boil, then boil slowly uncovered. In 4 minutes begin testing: dip out a Brussels sprout and pierce it with a small sharp-pointed knife—it is done when the knife goes in fairly easily. Cut one open and eat it, to be sure: it should just be cooked through but still have a slight crunch. Drain immediately.

For immediate serving—Buttered Brussels Sprouts. Turn them out onto a hot serving dish. Season lightly with salt and freshly ground pepper, and fold them in melted butter.

For later serving. Plunge the vegetables into a large basin of cold water with a tray or two of ice cubes, to stop the cooking and set the green color and texture. Drain when cold—in 2 to 3 minutes. Finish them off later in one of the ways following, which are useful indeed when you must prepare things in advance, or have a crowd of people to serve.

VARIATIONS

Brussels Sprouts in Brown Butter

Very lightly browned buttery Brussels sprouts have a wonderfully nut-brown taste, and a quite new character. These go well with steaks, chops, broiled chicken or fish, or with scrambled or fried eggs.

Halve or quarter the blanched Brussels sprouts lengthwise. Shortly before serving, set a 10-inch no-stick frying pan over moderately high heat, add 3 tablespoons of butter, and, when bubbling, add the sprouts. Season lightly with salt and pepper, and toss, swirling the pan by its handle, for several minutes while the sprouts heat through and begin to brown very lightly. Serve as soon as possible.

Brussels Sprouts with Chestnuts

Brussels Sprouts with Chestnuts

The meaty, rather muted taste of braised chestnuts needs the kind of hearty perking-up contrast of Brussels sprouts, and this dish calls out for roast turkey, goose, or suckling pig. Roll the hot blanched Brussels sprouts in butter or brown them lightly in butter as in the preceding recipe, then combine them with the braised chestnuts on page 311.

Brussels Sprouts Baked with Cheese

This one you can make as rich or as lean as you wish, with more or less butter and more or less cheese—again, these go with simple broiled or sautéed meats, fish, or chicken.

Assembling. Quarter the blanched sprouts lengthwise and, in a 1½-quart baking dish 1½ inches deep, toss with 2 to 3 tablespoons of melted butter and a sprinkling of salt and freshly ground pepper. Then toss with ½ cup of finely grated Swiss cheese. Spread 2 to 3 tablespoons of cheese over the top and drizzle over another spoonful of melted butter.

Baking—about 20 minutes at 425°F. Set uncovered in the upper third level of the preheated oven. Bake just until the cheese has melted and the top is starting to brown lightly.

VARIATION

Brussels Sprouts au Gratin

Quarter the cooked sprouts and fold them into 2 cups of cheese sauce, as for the Cauliflower au Gratin on page 273.

Hashed Brussels Sprouts

When you want loose greenery, hash blanched Brussels sprouts. To do so use a big knife, or chop them a bit at a time with pulses of the food processor. The French triple-threat half-moon cutter pictured here does a particularly good job.

Hashing blanched Brussels sprouts

VARIATION

Hashed Brussels Sprouts Sautéed in Butter

Once hashed, sauté them briefly in butter and seasonings, and serve them around a mound of rice, for instance, or as an accompaniment to broiled fish or meat.

VARIATIONS

See also the ideas for hashed broccoli starting on page 271.

FRESH GREEN BEANS

"Green beans," wrote Escoffier in his introduction to *haricots verts* in the *Guide Culinaire,* "are one of the most exquisite of vegetables, but they must be prepared with greatest care. They are best when a little firm to the tooth, but not with exaggeration." The great French chef penned those words at the beginning of this century, and they still hold. Preparation "with greatest care," however, does not mean with great difficulty, since green beans are among the easiest of vegetables. It just means: "Pay attention to what's cooking!"

Types of beans. The small thin green beans, usually called *haricots verts* in the few specialty shops that sell them, are less than ¼ inch thick. The eastern variety is the pencil-thick round bean, while the flat bean almost ½ inch wide is commonly found in the West.

Buying. Buy from a market that sells beans loose, and pick out each one, choosing beans that are smooth, a fresh green color, stringless, and crisp in texture. Snap and bite into several to check on texture, and whether strings run down their sides.

Amount to buy. 1½ pounds of round or flat beans will serve 6 people. For the tiny *haricots verts,* 1 pound should do.

Storing. If you are not serving soon, wrap in slightly dampened paper towels; refrigerate in a plastic bag.

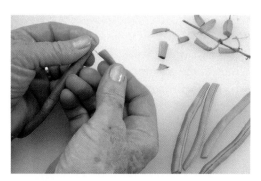

Snapping the ends off green beans

Frenched green beans

Preparation. This is the time-consuming part, but the only one. Wash and drain the beans. Snap off the stem and pull it down toward the tail on one side to remove a possible string. Repeat with the tail on the other side—unless the beans are fresh from the garden and the tails are very tender.

Frenching. Leave pencil-thin round beans as they are. Larger and flatter beans cook faster and look more elegant when you french them, meaning you slice them into 1½- to 2-inch slanting strips about 3/16 inch wide.

*Ahead-of-time note: Green beans may be prepared for cooking in advance: wrap in slightly dampened paper towels and refrigerate in a plastic bag.

MASTER RECIPE

Blanched Green Beans

The secret to cooking green beans so that they retain all their beautiful bright color and fine fresh texture is to blanch them in a very large amount of rapidly boiling water—the more water per bean the quicker the water will return to the boil, and the greener and fresher the cooked bean will be. Then, if you are not to serve at once, you refresh them in cold water—ice water if possible—to stop the cooking and to retain that color and texture. (A discussion of blanching with nutritional comments is in the Special Note on page 269.)

For 6 servings

1½ to 2 pounds fresh green beans, prepared as described
6 to 8 quarts rapidly boiling salted water (1½ tsp salt per quart of water)
2 to 3 trays of ice cubes, optional but effective

SPECIAL EQUIPMENT SUGGESTED:
An 8- to 10-quart kettle for boiling; a cover for the kettle; a large colander that will not quite fit down into the kettle

Blanching. Drop the prepared beans into the boiling salted water. Cover briefly, to bring the water quickly back to the boil, then immediately remove the cover. Boil uncovered until the beans are just cooked through but retain a slight crunch of texture—2 to 3 minutes for tiny beans or frenched beans; 4 to 5 for whole round beans. Test by eating several.

Draining the beans. Immediately the beans are done, bring the kettle to the sink; holding the colander in place over it, tip the kettle and drain out all the boiling water.

*Ahead-of-time note: Refreshing. If you are not serving at once, keep the colander in place and run cold water into the kettle. Drain again, add ice if you have enough on hand, and cover with more cold water. The faster you chill the beans the greener and fresher they will remain. As soon as they are chilled, in 3 to 4 minutes, drain again. If you are not to serve for several hours, wrap them in a clean dry towel, and refrigerate in a plastic bag.

Storage note. Thoroughly chilled cooked green beans keep well for a few hours, at least from noon to dinner time. But I think I can usually spot the telltale taste of a too-long-held cooked bean. Refrigerating them in a clean dry towel seems to help, however.

Serving suggestions for green beans. Carefully cooked fresh green beans are so good in themselves they need little else for enjoyment. Toasted shaved almonds—considered ultra chic in the 1930's—are still stylish, although I'd just as soon not have my beans interfered with. In another guise, cooked green beans are marvelous cold in a vinaigrette sauce, as described for the Salade Niçoise on page 365.

To reheat and serve. Just before serving, turn the beans into a large nostick frying pan and toss over moderately high heat for a moment to evaporate excess moisture. Then toss with a sprinkling of salt and freshly ground pepper, and several tablespoons of softened butter. (Or, for fat-free beans, toss with a tablespoon or two of water, plus seasonings.) Finish off, if you wish, with a sprinkling of chopped fresh parsley and a squeeze of lemon juice; serve immediately.

FRESH SPINACH

There is no avoiding the time it takes to wash and stem fresh spinach, but what a marvelous and versatile vegetable it is. Enjoy it by itself, its fresh green leaves steamed and served only with lemon, or relish chopped spinach simmered in cream accompanying a thick veal chop, or spinach braised in stock along with ham in Madeira sauce, or spinach omelettes and spinach soufflés, and spinach fillings in crêpes and roulades.

Buying

When spinach season comes in your area, buy it loose in bunches, choosing fresh leaves with no wilting, and no darkened or yellowed patches. If it is bagged in plastic, look carefully and avoid those with many broken or darkened leaves.

Stemming spinach leaves

Amount to buy. Two 10-ounce packages or 2 bunches serve 4 people;

1 package or 1 bunch of fresh spinach makes a generous ½ cup of cooked chopped spinach.

Storing

If you are not to prepare the spinach shortly, wrap loose bunches in slightly dampened paper towels and refrigerate in a plastic bag. Spinach bought in plastic bags will usually revive and even swell up when you turn the leaves into a sinkful of cold water and let them soak for ½ hour or so.

Preparation

The flavor of spinach is in the leaves, not at all in the stems; it therefore behooves the serious cook to remove the stems. Begin by dumping the spinach into a large bowl or sinkful of cold water; pump it up and down several times to loosen the dirt. Then, rapidly one at a time, grasp a leaf upside

down between the thumb and forefinger of one hand, its stem pointing toward your thumbnail; pull most of the stem out toward the tip of the leaf with your other hand. Discard the stem, and drop the leaf into a bowl of fresh cold water. When all leaves are stemmed, pump up and down again in the water, and lift them out with your hands (leaving any sand behind); if there are more than a few grains of dirt in the bottom of the bowl, wash again—and again, if need be. It would be a cruel waste of time to have gritty spinach after all that stemming!

*Ahead-of-time note: Spinach may be prepared for cooking in advance; wrap in slightly dampened paper towels and refrigerate in a plastic bag.

COOKING VERY YOUNG AND HOME-GROWN SPINACH. *When spinach is very fresh, young, and tender and you want to serve the leaves whole and simply, you need only pinch off and discard the stem, wash the leaves, drain them briefly, and toss for a few minutes in a stainless frying pan with butter, salt, and freshly ground pepper.*

COOKING OLDER SPINACH. *When the spinach is older and the leaves are to be served whole and simply, stem and wash it, then pile it into a vegetable steamer basket and steam it in a covered saucepan for several minutes. When tender, either season it with salt, freshly ground pepper, and drops of freshly squeezed lemon juice—perfect diet food—or toss it with seasonings and butter.*

⚏ MASTER RECIPE

Cooked Chopped Spinach

When your recipe calls for cooked chopped spinach, you will blanch it in the usual green-vegetable way, in a great pot of boiling water, then refresh it in cold water to stop the cooking and set the fine green color. Finally you squeeze out the excess water, chop the spinach, and you are ready to proceed.

Removing excess moisture. By handfuls, squeeze as much water as you can out of the spinach—save the last colorful drops as a tonic for the cook. Place the piles of spinach on your work surface.

Chopping the spinach. With a stainless knife (plain steel will leave a metallic taste), chop the spinach on your cutting board—a food processor can be risky unless you want puréed spinach.

*Ahead-of-time note: May be cooked in advance to this point. Store in a covered bowl in the refrigerator, where it will keep nicely for a day at least.

Braised Spinach

What to serve with ham slices sautéed in Madeira? Spinach braised in a nicely flavored meat stock. Chicken breasts poached in butter? Spinach braised in cream. Want to stuff crêpes or a soufflé roulade? Think braised spinach. Think braised spinach also for poached eggs, for broiled mackerel, for roast beef. Braised fresh spinach, in fact, goes just about anywhere.

Half an hour or so before you are ready to serve 4 to 6 people, melt 2 to 3 tablespoons softened butter in a heavy-bottomed stainless or no-stick frying pan. When bubbling, blend in 1 generous cup of cooked chopped spinach and stir over moderately high heat for a minute or so to evaporate remaining moisture. When the spinach begins to stick to the bottom of the pan, stir in ⅓ cup or so of beef or chicken bouillon or heavy cream. Lower heat, season lightly with salt, freshly ground pepper, and perhaps a speck of nutmeg, then cover the pan. Simmer slowly for 5 to 7 minutes, stirring frequently to prevent scorching, until the spinach is tender. Season carefully to taste. Just before serving, if you wish, blend in a tablespoon or so more butter.

VARIATION

Subrics: Spinach Packets

When you want to present spinach in an unusual way you save out some of the big fresh leaves, braise the rest, and flavor it beautifully. You then wrap the braised spinach in the big leaves to make individual spinach packets which you warm slowly in butter a few minutes before serving.

For 6 subrics 3 by 2½ inches, you will need 5 packages or bunches of fresh spinach. Save out a dozen of the largest leaves and cut off their stems at the base of the leaves; blanch them about a minute until wilted, refresh in cold water, and reserve. Sauté the rest in butter, as directed in the preceding recipe, adding a tablespoon of minced shallots. Before pouring in the stock or cream, blend in 2 tablespoons of flour and stir over moderate heat for 2 minutes to cook the flour. Remove from heat, blend in the liquid, and proceed with the recipe.

Assembling. Arrange the reserved leaves best side down to form 6 wrapping centers. Divide the cooked spinach into 6 portions, form oval-shaped cakes of spinach on each wrapping center, and fold the spinach leaves around to enclose them.

*Ahead-of-time note: Cover and refrigerate until 10 minutes before serving.

Final cooking. Sauté in butter over low heat for a minute or more on each side, to warm through thoroughly. Serve as soon as possible.

Butter-braised spinach packets and baked cherry tomatoes

OTHER GREEN VEGETABLES

ARTICHOKES

Artichokes have always been a luxury, from the time of the Romans and the Medicis on up to the present day. And what a pleasure to have with us something that is both a vegetable and a treasure. You can feature a handsome boiled artichoke all by itself to begin the meal, or serve it as a separate vegetable course in place of a salad, or present it as the main attraction for a luncheon. One artichoke aspect that endears it to the cook is that an artichoke can be served hot, tepid, or cold, and one that especially appeals to calorie counters is that it needs nothing in the way of a sauce—a wedge of lemon will do. In addition, like many high-priced items such as porterhouse steaks, beef tenderloins, and veal chops, artichokes are easy indeed to cook.

Buying. Artichokes are in season all year long, but are most plentiful and therefore least expensive in March, April, and May. Choose those that

Left: Whole artichoke
Top: Halved artichoke and quartered artichoke
First row: Whole artichoke bottom, quartered artichoke heart

feel heavy, and that have crisp fleshy leaves. Very fresh artichokes will talk to you when you squeeze the head—squeaky fresh, in other words. Don't worry about a few blisters and brown spots as long as the leaves feel full and fresh—growers insist these are frost spots, and that frost enhances flavor—and what else could they say?

Storing. If you are not going to cook artichokes almost at once, shave ¼ inch off the stems, and wrap them starting at the stem end in slightly dampened paper towels. Store in a plastic bag in the refrigerator, where they will keep perfectly for several days. Artichokes, like flowers, need moisture.

Preparation. You may cook artichokes just about as is, after spreading the leaves apart and running cold water into them to wash off any grit. However, if the leaves have prickly points that can needle the eater, slice off the top inch of the cone of leaves with a heavy knife. Then cut off the top ½ inch of the remaining leaves with kitchen shears—rubbing cut portions with half a lemon to prevent them from darkening. Cut off the stem of the artichoke even with the base, and pull off any small or withered bottom leaves—rubbing again with cut lemon. Plan to cook them at once.

 MASTER RECIPE

Steamed Artichokes

Cook artichokes either by boiling them in a large kettle of salted water, or by steaming. Steaming is certainly easier for the home cook, and I think steaming makes the leaves more tender toward the tip. Whether you boil or steam them, however, the artichokes will never remain bright green; they always turn a green-gray because they need long cooking. Therefore, if you see a cooked artichoke of a beautiful grass-green color, beware! It has been boiled with soda, which is a no-no because soda has a bad effect on vitamins.

For 4 servings

4 artichokes 2½ to 3 inches at their largest diameter
1 lemon

SPECIAL EQUIPMENT SUGGESTED: *A saucepan or kettle large enough to hold the artichokes, bottom up; a steaming basket to hold them; a tight-fitting cover*

Steaming the artichokes. Prepare the artichokes as previously described. Arrange them upside down (bottom up!) in one layer on the steaming basket; pour an inch of water into the pan or kettle, cover it closely, and turn on the heat. When steam starts to escape, maintain at the slow boil for 30 to 40 minutes, checking water level once or twice to be sure it has not boiled away. The artichokes are done when the bottoms are tender if pierced with a small knife, and the

(continued)

Steamed Artichokes (*continued*)

bottom half of a leaf is tender when the inside flesh is scraped off between your teeth.

Serving suggestions. Place each artichoke, bottom down, on a dessert plate. It is wise to serve sauces separately, since some will want only a large lemon wedge. Melted butter served in individual bowls is traditional with warm artichokes. Or pass a large bowl of hollandaise sauce, and each guest helps himself. Mayonnaise or vinaigrette goes with cold artichokes.

To eat an artichoke. Start with the leaves at the bottom of the artichoke. Remove one and, holding it by the top, dip the large bottom end into the sauce, then scrape off the tender flesh between your teeth. When you come to the tender cone of central leaves, pull off the cone, and eat the bottom portion. Where you removed the cone is a cluster of small leaves under which is a hairy growth, the choke, that covers the deliciously edible bottom of the artichoke. With knife and fork from now on, cut the bottom into wedges, cut off and discard the hairy portion, and dip each wedge into the sauce before popping it in your mouth.

Artichoke Bottoms

Artichoke bottoms are attractive first courses with a cold filling, such as a purée of artichoke leaves, as in the following recipe. Or you can use a crab or lobster salad, or a vegetable combination. On the other hand, artichoke bottoms are delicious hot, baked with a creamed filling of some sort and a cheese topping. Or to be more elegant fill a warm artichoke bottom with, for instance, a wine-flavored mushroom duxelles topped with a tenderly poached egg and Béarnaise sauce. Or fill it with poached oysters in a wine sauce, as described farther on. Another idea is to cut them in wedges, sauté them, and serve as part of a hot vegetable combination, as on page 315.

Steamed Stuffed Artichoke Bottoms

In this method, you use already-cooked artichokes, stuffing the bottoms with a cunningly flavored purée of the leaves. It is admittedly time-consuming to scrape the flesh off all those leaves, but worthwhile for 2 to 4, and possibly 6, servings as a first course, or as part of a main-course luncheon dish.

Filling artichoke bottoms

For 4 servings

**4 steamed artichokes 3 inches in
    diameter**
Salt and freshly ground pepper
1 lemon cut in half
A little olive oil
**2 Tbs finely minced shallots or
    scallions**
2 Tbs minced fresh parsley
2 to 3 Tbs mayonnaise
**Decoration: parsley sprigs, or
    medallions of lobster, or shrimp**

Preparing the steamed artichokes. Carefully remove the leaves from the artichokes, disturbing the bottom as little as possible. Scrape out the choke, and trim the sides to make a neat shape. Scrape the tender flesh from the leaves (group 2 or 3 together by their tips, and scrape off the flesh with a spoon). Purée the flesh through a vegetable mill or sieve into a bowl.

Seasoning and assembling. Season the artichoke bottoms with salt, pepper, lemon juice, and olive oil, and arrange on plates or a platter. Beat the minced shallots or scallions and parsley into the puréed flesh, adding mayonnaise and more lemon juice, salt, and pepper to taste. Fill the bottoms with the purée, and decorate with whatever you have chosen.

Raw Artichoke Bottoms

While preparing stuffed artichoke bottoms from cooked artichokes is one method, the neatest and most professional way is to start with raw artichokes. You bend the leaves until they snap, so that the tender part of their flesh remains attached to the bottom, giving you a bigger and meatier area to fill. After trimming the bottoms, you cook them in a *blanc*, a solution of flour, water, salt, and lemon juice, which prevents them from discoloring. Then, if you have made an extra artichoke bottom or two or if you boil up and scrape the leaves, you can turn the *blanc* into an artichoke soup (page 12)—two meals instead of one.

To Cook Artichoke Bottoms

For 6 servings

The *blanc* for cooking the bottoms
6 cups cold water
¼ cup flour in a 2-quart saucepan
½ tsp salt
¼ cup freshly squeezed lemon juice

6 very fresh large artichokes 3 to 3½ inches in diameter
1 lemon, cut in half, to use when trimming the bottoms

The blanc. Gradually beat 3 cups of the cold water into the flour in the pan, and bring to the boil; simmer a moment, whisking, to be sure the liquid is smooth and lump free. Whisk in the 3 remaining cups of water with the salt and lemon juice.

Preparing the artichokes. Prepare them one at a time. Break the stem off the base of an artichoke. Holding the artichoke bottom up, bend a lower leaf back on itself until it snaps, then peel it off toward the base, leaving the meat at the bottom of the leaf attached to the bottom of the artichoke. Continue all around as

1. Bending off leaves

2. Separating cone of leaves from artichoke bottom

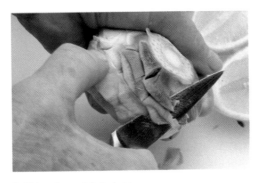

3. Trimming artichoke bottom

4. Scooping out the choke

shown, step 1, until you have gone beyond the curve where leaves fold inward over the top of the artichoke bottom. Cut off the remaining cone of leaves at this curve, step 2. Rub cut portions with lemon to prevent discoloration.

With a small sharp knife, step 3, and then with a vegetable peeler, trim off all bits of green to expose the tender whitish flesh around the bottom and at the leaf ends, frequently rubbing the cut surfaces with lemon. Drop the prepared bottom into the *blanc* and continue with the rest. (The choke is removed after cooking.)

Cooking the artichoke bottoms—30 to 40 minutes. Once all of the prepared artichoke bottoms are in the *blanc*, add a little more water if they are not completely submerged. Simmer 30 to 40 minutes, until the artichokes are perfectly tender when pierced with a knife. Let them cool, then refrigerate in the liquid until needed.

*Ahead-of-time note: They will keep perfectly in their cooking liquid for 2 or 3 days.

Scooping out the choke. Shortly before using them in whatever recipe you have chosen, wash them under cold water, and scoop out the choke with a teaspoon, step 4. Trim off any tough leaf ends, and they are ready to go. Save the *blanc* for artichoke soup, on page 12.

Fonds d'Artichauts Olympe
With oysters, in white wine sauce

When you want to be elegant—or are confronted with a situation where you have to be—this is the kind of dish that will serve you well. Use small oysters here if you can find them; little olympias from the Seattle area are ideal.

For 6 servings

6 large fine cooked artichoke
   bottoms 3 inches in diameter if
   possible—the preceding recipe
Salt and freshly ground white pepper
2 Tbs melted butter plus 2 or more
   Tbs additional butter
1 pint fresh shucked oysters (if
   unusually large, cut them in half
   after cooking)
1 Tbs minced shallots
½ cup or so dry white wine or dry
   white French vermouth
½ cup or so *blanc* (artichoke cooking
   liquid; see preceding recipe)
1 egg yolk blended in a bowl with ½
   cup heavy cream
2 Tbs minced fresh parsley

Warming the artichoke bottoms. Season the artichoke bottoms lightly with salt and pepper, and paint with the melted butter. Set in a covered pan.

About 15 minutes before serving, heat through either in a 300°F oven or over simmering water.

The oysters and their sauce. Drain the oysters in a sieve; reserve the juices. Sauté the shallots slowly in a heavy stainless saucepan with 2 tablespoons of butter; when shallots are limp, fold in the drained oysters. Sauté over moderate heat for a minute or so, until they plump up gently; remove to a bowl with a slotted spoon. Add the reserved juices, the wine, and ½ cup of the artichoke cooking liquid to the juices in the pan. Boil down rapidly until lightly thickened. Blend by driblets into the egg yolk and cream, and pour back into the pan. Stir over moderate heat, bringing the sauce just to the simmer. Carefully correct seasoning, and fold in the oysters.

*Ahead-of-time note: Set aside or refrigerate, the top filmed with a little cream; reheat to below the simmer before proceeding.

Serving. Arrange the hot artichoke bottoms, hollow side up, on a hot platter or plates. Fold a tablespoon or so of softened butter into the oysters if you wish, then divide the oysters among the artichoke bottoms and spoon the sauce over them. Decorate with a sprinkling of parsley, and you may wish to accompany the dish with fleurons of puff pastry (page 395), or toast canapés (heart-shaped cut-outs of white bread sautéed in clarified butter, page 139).

Artichoke Bottoms or Hearts
Braised with whole cloves of garlic

Artichoke hearts are the bottoms plus the tender part of their covering cone of leaves. If you are fortunate enough to gather very young artichokes in the spring, they'll be tender enough so that you can use all but the outer leaves; or you can pare down small artichokes, halve or quarter them, and cut out the choke as well as the tough upper part of the inner leaf cone. Whatever the artichoke, the following recipe is a particularly savory way to do them.

For 4 to 6 servings, or as part of a vegetable garnish

1 or 2 artichoke bottoms or
   artichoke hearts per person
2 or more Tbs fruity olive oil
Salt and freshly ground pepper
1 or more Tbs wine vinegar
2 cups sliced onions
2 heads of large garlic cloves, peeled
   (see Special Note next page)
Thyme, oregano, or rosemary
½ cup dry white wine or French
   vermouth, and/or chicken broth
2 to 3 Tbs chopped fresh parsley

SPECIAL EQUIPMENT SUGGESTED:
A heavy covered 10-inch chicken fryer or frying pan 2 inches deep

The artichokes. Prepare the artichoke bottoms as directed in the recipe on page 281, and cut into quarters or sixths; or prepare the hearts as described in the headnote to this recipe.

Braising. Film the chicken fryer with a 1/16-inch layer of olive oil, add the artichokes, and sauté over moderately low heat, tossing occasionally, until just beginning to color—3 to 4 minutes. Season lightly with salt and pepper, and toss with droplets of the vinegar. Sauté a moment longer, then add the onions and garlic; toss with a little more salt and pepper, and with whatever herb you have chosen. Cover the pan and cook slowly 5 minutes; add the wine or stock, cover, and simmer another 5 minutes, or until the artichokes are tender. Uncover and boil off excess moisture, tossing; correct seasoning.

Serving suggestions. Toss with the parsley and, if you wish, a little more olive oil. Serve as they are—with steaks, chops, broiled fish, or chicken. Or add them to finish cooking with an otherwise plain chicken sauté, such as the master recipe on page 137. Or fold them into sautéed potatoes or braised carrots.

Peeling and storing asparagus

ASPARAGUS

Like artichokes, asparagus is another beautiful luxury vegetable that can stand on its own as a separate course. Again like the artichoke, it's easy on the cook since it can be served hot, warm, or cold, and asparagus is perfect diet food because it is delicious eaten just as it is.

Buying. Buy firm spears that are completely closed at the bud end—serious markets keep asparagus standing on damp towels or in a shallow pan of water. Choose fresh, firm, smooth fat spears that are all the same size—fat spears are just as tender as thin ones and much easier to prepare.

Storing. At home, cut a finger width off the butts to reach the moist ends, wash the spears thoroughly, especially at the tip ends, and stand them upright in a container, their butts in 2 inches of cold water. Cover loosely with a plastic bag, and refrigerate. Treated this way, fresh asparagus will stay fresh and fine for 2 to 3 days.

Preparation. It is a cruel waste to bend asparagus until it breaks, and then to throw the rest—a good third of it—away! Carefully peeled, asparagus spears are tender from tip to butt, and long peeled spears are elegant to serve. In addition, peeled asparagus cooks in far less time than unpeeled asparagus, and also remains greener and fresher. To peel the spears with a small sharp knife, start at the butt end and, holding the spear butt up, cut down to the tender flesh, making the cut more shallow as you reach the tender area near the tip. Or lay the spear flat and use a vegetable peeler.

*Ahead-of-time note: If you are not cooking shortly, wrap peeled asparagus in damp towels and refrigerate.

SPECIAL NOTE

To Peel Garlic Cloves

Separating the cloves from the head. Shave the tops off the heads of garlic, then bang down on the tops with your fist to separate the cloves.

Peeling. To peel them easily, drop them into a pan of boiling water for 30 seconds, drain, run cold water over them, and slip off the skins with your fingers.

Plain Boiled Asparagus

Once peeled, asparagus is easy indeed to cook. None of that old-fashioned steaming-the-tips-and-boiling-the-butts business because the stalks are tender from end to end.

For 6 servings, 6 to 8 fat spears per person

36 to 48 fine fresh asparagus spears, all the same diameter, and all peeled
4 to 5 quarts rapidly boiling water in an oval casserole or large frying pan
1½ tsp salt per quart of water

Suggested accompaniments
For hot asparagus: melted butter; hollandaise sauce (page 87); lemon-butter sauce (page 83); and/or lemon wedges
For cold asparagus: vinaigrette dressing and its variations (page 351); mayonnaise (page 363); and/or lemon wedges

Lay the asparagus in the boiling salted water, cover the casserole or pan, and watch carefully until water comes back to the boil; immediately uncover it. Boil slowly for 4 to 5 minutes, just until asparagus spears start to bend a little when lifted. Test by eating the butt end of a spear. Asparagus should be just cooked through with a slight crunch. Immediately remove the asparagus from the water.

To serve hot. Arrange on a napkin-lined platter—to catch moisture; or drain briefly on a clean towel, then arrange in a hot platter or on hot plates.

To serve cold. Drain in one layer on a tray lined with a clean towel and rapidly cool, near an open window if possible. Then arrange on a platter or plates. If you are seasoning the asparagus with vinaigrette dressing, which should be added at the last minute to preserve the green asparagus color, you may then wish to decorate with strips of red pimiento, or spoon over the upper third a mixture of chopped hard-boiled eggs and parsley tossed with a sprinkle of salt and pepper.

VARIATION

Sautéed Asparagus Tips

When you want an attractive vegetable garnish to accompany an egg dish, a ragout of duck, or a sauté, think of asparagus tips. Peel the asparagus and boil as described in the preceding master recipe, but boil only until almost but not quite tender. Cut into slanting pieces about an inch long—if you have fat spears you may also want to halve them lengthwise. Just before serving, heat 2 tablespoons of butter in a large frying pan, over moderately high heat. When bubbling hot, turn in the asparagus. Season lightly with salt and freshly ground pepper, and, swirling the pan by its handle, toss the asparagus in the hot butter for the minute or two it takes to warm it through. Toss with an additional tablespoon or two of softened butter if you wish to glaze the asparagus. Serve immediately.

BOIL-STEAMING: BRAISING

WINTER SQUASH, RUTABAGA, CARROTS, TURNIPS, AND BEETS AS WELL AS GREEN PEAS AND ONIONS

Carrots, turnips, rutabaga, beets, onions, and winter squash are wonderfully sturdy characters, each with its own nourishing personality, but all may be cooked in much the same way.

The boil-steam or braise method is the general technique when you plan to serve the vegetable whole, like onions, or in nicely cut bite-size pieces, or when you are to purée it. The boil-steam works wonders for store-bought green peas as well.

Boil-Steamed Butternut Squash

For 6 servings

A 1½-pound butternut squash (or other hard yellow-fleshed squash)
Salt
2 Tbs butter, optional

The best way to halve a winter squash

SPECIAL EQUIPMENT SUGGESTED: *A mallet and heavy knife or cleaver if needed; a heavy-bottomed 2½-quart saucepan with tight-fitting cover*

Preparing the squash. Halve the squash (using mallet or cleaver if necessary), and scrape out all seeds and stringy parts. Cut off the hard outside peel. If you are to serve the squash simply as is, cut the flesh into neat ¾-inch chunks; otherwise, cut it into rough pieces.

Boil-steaming. Fill the saucepan with enough water to come halfway up the squash, bring to the boil, and add ½ teaspoon of salt and the optional butter. Toss up once or twice, cover the pan, and boil 8 to 10 minutes—adding more liquid if needed, until the squash is tender. If it is done and liquid remains, uncover and boil it off. (Cooked this way, no flavor escapes: it is all reabsorbed into the squash.)

*Ahead-of-time note: Set aside uncovered. To reheat, add a dribble of water, cover, and let steam a minute or two, watching it does not scorch.

Serving suggestions.

With herbs and butter. Just before serving, toss the squash gently with a little butter and chopped fresh chives or parsley.

Purée of yellow squash. Purée the cooked squash in a food processor or végetable mill. Stir several minutes over moderate heat in a heavy-bottomed pan to evaporate excess moisture. Then blend in as much butter and/or cream as you deem fitting. Season carefully to taste.

VARIATION

Golden Purées

These are alternatives to mashed squash or mashed potatoes, and go especially well with roast turkey or goose. After puréeing the cooked squash (or the carrots or rutabaga in the following recipes) and stirring over heat to evaporate moisture, blend in a cup of mashed potatoes, beating in butter or cream and seasonings.

OTHER VEGETABLES

BOIL-STEAMED CARROTS, TURNIPS, RUTABAGA, PARSNIPS, PEAS, AND ONIONS

Peel the vegetables, and leave them whole or cut them into neat pieces or chunks, depending on your final intentions. Boil-steam them in a covered pan with water, salt, and optional butter the same way as in the master recipe for butternut squash. Here are some special treatments.

The wedge cut for carrots

Carrots

Boil-steaming and braising are interchangeable cooking terms for vegetables, but for carrots one usually speaks of braising, although they are boil-steamed in the same way as the preceding examples. When braised carrots are served as a garniture, you may wish to use baby carrots—time-consuming as they are to peel; or cut large carrots into attractive pieces. Braising, or boil-steaming—where you lose none of the cooking liquid—gives carrots a particularly fine taste.

AMOUNTS. *A 7- to 8-inch carrot weighs 3½ to 4½ ounces; count on 1 to 1½ carrots per person.*

SPECIAL NOTE

The Long-Wedge Cut for Cooked Carrots

Choose fine crisp carrots 7 to 8 inches long and 1¼ inches across their stem end—if they have their green foliage attached, you know they are freshly harvested. Trim them with a knife, and peel them with a vegetable peeler. Cut in half lengthwise, then cut the halves crosswise into lengths of approximately 1½ inches. Leave the ends as is, but cut the other pieces lengthwise into halves, thirds, or quarters so that all pieces look nearly alike. In French cooking this is known as the bourgeois cut; the housewife or *ménagère* cut is in easy round slices. In the *haute cuisine*, however, you make the long wedge and then round all the edges *en gousse*—in the shape of large garlic cloves—très chic indeed, when you have the time.

Boil-Steamed Carrots
And braised and glazed carrots

For 6 servings

**6 to 9 carrots 8 inches long, peeled
    and cut into long wedges, as in
    Special Note, page 285
Salt**

For glazed carrots

**3 Tbs butter (2 for initial cooking, 1
    for glazing)
1½ tsp sugar**

Preliminary cooking. Boil-steam the
carrots in a covered saucepan with
water to come halfway up them, and
salt, as described in the master recipe; add 2 tablespoons of butter if
you are to glaze them. When tender,
and the liquid has evaporated, the
carrots will begin to sauté in the
residue of their juices. Correct
seasoning.

Glazing. Just before serving, add the
additional butter and the sugar. Toss
gently over moderately high heat to
glaze them with a buttery sheen.

Gratin of Rutabaga or
Winter Squash

This goes beautifully with roast turkey or a roast of pork. The squash
has its initial cooking in a steaming
basket, before undergoing a very
slow gratiné, where it acquires its
special flavor and texture.

For 6 servings

For the initial cooking

**1½ pounds rutabaga or winter
    squash, cut into ¾-inch dice—4 to
    5 cups
½ tsp grated fresh ginger
1 large clove of garlic, minced**

For the gratiné

**2 cups classic white sauce (3 Tbs
    butter, 3 Tbs flour, 2 cups milk;
    see Special Note, page 272)
3 Tbs fresh white bread crumbs
3 Tbs grated Swiss cheese**

SPECIAL EQUIPMENT SUGGESTED:
*A vegetable steamer in a tightly covered
saucepan; a 2½-quart pan for the
sauce; a buttered 6-cup baking dish
about 2 inches deep*

The initial steaming. Place the diced
rutabaga or squash in the steaming
basket with the ginger and garlic.
Cover and steam over 1 inch of water
for about 10 minutes, until almost
tender. Remove the steamer. Boil
down the steaming liquid to ¼ cup;
whisk into the sauce.

Assembling and baking. Preheat the
oven to 325°F. Fold the rutabaga or
squash into the white sauce, and turn
into the buttered baking dish. Spread
on the crumbs and cheese. Bake in
the middle level of the oven for 1½
hours; the top should be nicely and
lightly browned, and the sauce almost
completely absorbed.

VARIATION

Purée of Parsnips Mellowed
with Cream

A heavenly accompaniment to a
roasted goose or duck, the Thanksgiving turkey, or a loin of pork.
Purée a handful of boil-steamed parsnips. Blend them in the top of a
double boiler with a modest amount
of cream (½ to ⅔ cup for 4 cups of
parsnips), and season to taste. Cover
and cook, stirring occasionally, for
15 to 20 minutes—the purée will develop a new and delicious character
as it warms with the cream. Correct
seasoning again before serving.

Onions

White-Braised Onions

This is the same boil-steam system
used for squash, carrots, turnips, and
beets—where the cooking liquid is
almost entirely absorbed by the vegetable, and none of the essential flavor
is lost.

**12 to 16 onions 1 inch in diameter,
    peeled (see Special Note)
½ cup or so water or chicken broth
Salt
1 imported bay leaf, optional
1 Tbs butter, optional**

SPECIAL EQUIPMENT SUGGESTED:
*A covered saucepan or frying pan that
will hold the onions easily in one layer*

Piercing the root end of an onion

SPECIAL NOTE

To Peel Onions

When you have a lot of onions that need neat peeling, especially the small white ones used for creamed onions and a number of other dishes, here's the easy way.

Drop them into a pan of boiling water for exactly 1 minute; remove with a slotted spoon. Shave off the root and stem ends, keeping the onion layers attached at the root.

Slip off the skins, and pierce a cross ⅛ inch deep in the root ends to help prevent bursting.

Boil-steaming. Place the onions in the pan, add water or chicken stock to come halfway up the onions, and salt lightly; add the optional bay leaf and butter. Cover the pan and simmer slowly 25 to 30 minutes, until the onions are tender when pierced but still hold their shape—be careful to cook them slowly so they will not burst.

Serving suggestions. These are usually called for as part of another recipe. But to serve them as is, boil down

rapidly, uncovered, to evaporate any cooking juices; fold with a little butter and minced fresh parsley, and they make a fine accompaniment to almost any main-course dish.

*Ahead-of-time note: May be braised in advance, and reheated.

VARIATIONS

Creamed Onions

Creamed onions go beautifully with roast chicken or turkey, and this is a particularly succulent way to do them. When the preceding onions are just tender, fold in ⅔ to ¾ cup of heavy cream and simmer several minutes, until thickened, basting several times with the cream. Correct seasoning, and fold, if you wish, with minced parsley.

Brown-Braised Onions

These would go with braised beef, coq au vin, or in any dish where a white braised onion would look inappropriately stark.

In a pan just roomy enough to hold them in one layer, sauté the peeled onions in a little clarified butter or oil, swirling the pan to turn them; they will not brown evenly, but will take on a decent amount of color. Then add chicken broth (and, if you wish, a little red wine) to come halfway up. Season lightly with salt and perhaps a bay leaf or a pinch of dried herbs. Cover and simmer slowly 25 to 30 minutes, until the onions are tender when pierced but still hold their shape.

An unlikely candidate for the boil-steam system

Fresh Green Store-Bought Peas

Few of us are so lucky as to have tender fresh green peas just out of the garden, so sweet and young they hardly need warming through. However, and remarkably enough, the boil-steam system will allow you to cook up your store-bought peas deliciously green, sweet, and tender. This is the method of my old French chef and *maître* Max Bugnard, and I have always used it with great success.

For 4 to 6 servings

2 pounds fresh peas (about 3 cups shelled)
½ tsp salt
1 Tbs, more or less, sugar (see note at end of recipe)
¼ cup minced scallions (white part and tender green)
2 or more Tbs butter, optional but desirable
Water, as needed

Place the peas in a heavy-bottomed saucepan, add the salt, ½ tablespoon of the sugar, scallions, and optional butter. Mash the peas roughly with a rubber spatula to bruise them and work a bit of the other ingredients into their skins—you do not have to be rough, but you should bruise the peas slightly. Add water barely to cover the peas, put a lid on the pan, and bring to the full boil. Boil for 10 to 15 minutes, or more, until the peas are tender (adding driblets of water if necessary to prevent them

(continued)

Fresh Green Store-Bought Peas (*continued*)

from scorching)—taste one or two as a test. When the peas are done, all the water should have evaporated; if not, uncover and boil it off. Correct seasoning.

*Ahead-of-time note: If done somewhat in advance, set aside uncovered; toss over heat with several tablespoons more water until well heated.

Serving. Just before serving, if you wish, toss with a tablespoon or two of additional butter.

Note: The natural sweetness of peas diminishes almost as soon as they are picked, so the addition of a little sugar is needed—taste the peas as they cook, and add if you feel it necessary, being very careful not to overdo and exceed nature's own.

CABBAGE AND SAUERKRAUT

Cabbage and sauerkraut were the vegetable mainstays in the days of old-world cooking, when cabbage was the only winter greenery around in those long-ago pre-refrigerator times. They bring forth visions of fragrant soups and stews, steaming platters of pork and sausages, and the good simple life. It's a boon today, as well, to have a vegetable like cabbage at hand, since it keeps well under refrigeration, ready at once to become a salad, the perfect accompaniment to the perfect pork chop, or a quick vegetable to go with the ham or the boiled dinner. And speaking of boiled dinners, certainly the best way to cook the traditional cabbage is to steam it in wedges.

Steaming cabbage wedges

▓ MASTER RECIPE

Cabbage Steamed in Wedges

For 6 servings

A 2½-pound cabbage (a 7- to 8-inch head)
2 cups or so meat or chicken stock
Salt and freshly ground pepper
2 Tbs butter, optional
A handful of chopped fresh parsley, optional

SPECIAL EQUIPMENT SUGGESTED:
A wide and deep saucepan with cover; a steaming basket

Steaming. Halve the cabbage through the root; cut each half into 3 wedges. Being careful always to keep the leaves in their wedge shape, cut out the central cores. Pour 1½ inches of stock (plus water if needed) into the pan. Fit the steamer into the pan, and arrange the cabbage wedges in it, curved sides down. Baste the cabbage with a little of the stock, salt lightly, cover the pan, and steam about 15 minutes, or until just tender.

*Ahead-of-time note: May be cooked ahead, and set aside uncovered. Baste with the stock in the pan, cover, and steam to warm through just before serving.

Optional sauce: Remove the steamer and keep the cabbage warm while you rapidly boil down the steaming liquid until almost syrupy. Off heat, swirl in the butter a tablespoon at a time, correct seasoning, fold in the parsley, and anoint each wedge with a spoonful of sauce.

SPECIAL NOTE

To Shred (Finely Slice) Cabbage

By hand. Halve, then quarter and remove cores from the cabbage. Place a wedge of cabbage curved side down on your work surface. Holding it by its pointed wedge end, make very thin slices on the bias with a big sharp knife as illustrated.

In a food processor. Processor shredding remained a cook-stumper until Carl Sontheimer, the American father of that revolutionary machine, evolved this ingenious system. Slice off the cap (top) and the stem sections (bottom) of the cabbage, leaving yourself with a thick cylinder. Core out the cylinder's central stalk with a stout sharp knife, and cut the cylinder into wedges of a size to fit into your machine. Now you are ready to shred, wedge by wedge.

Shredding cabbage

MASTER RECIPE

Steamed Shredded Cabbage

This is very fast, taking only 5 to 7 minutes of cooking.

For 6 servings

A 2-pound head of cabbage,
   shredded (see Special Note)
½ cup beef or chicken stock, or
   water
Salt and freshly ground pepper
2 to 3 Tbs butter, or goose, duck, or
   pork fat, optional
A handful of chopped fresh parsley,
   optional

SPECIAL EQUIPMENT SUGGESTED:
A heavy stainless saucepan with cover

Place the cabbage in the saucepan with the stock or water, a little salt, and the optional butter or fat. Bring to the rapid boil, cover, and boil 5 minutes, tossing once or twice, until just tender. Taste, and correct seasoning. Toss with the optional parsley.

*Ahead-of-time note: May be cooked ahead. Set aside uncovered; cover and toss over heat just before adding the parsley and serving.

VARIATION

Creamed Cabbage

When the preceding cabbage is tender, fold in ½ cup or so of heavy cream and boil down rapidly until thickened.

Braised Shredded Red Cabbage

Red cabbage makes an especially attractive accompaniment to such homely delights as pork chops and sausages. It also goes well with turkey, goose, duck, and roast pork, and is surprisingly good with broiled swordfish steaks and mackerel. As usual with red vegetables, you need a little acid to retain the color—in this instance a sour apple, a little red wine, and a discreet dollop of red wine vinegar.

For 6 servings

3 Tbs butter or oil, or rendered
   goose, duck, or pork fat
1 large red onion, thinly sliced
2 large cloves of garlic, puréed
6 cups shredded red cabbage (half a
   6-inch head)
Seasonings: salt and freshly ground
   pepper, 2 tsp caraway seeds, and
   1 imported bay leaf
1 cooking apple, such as Granny
   Smith, grated
¾ cup chicken broth
¾ cup red wine
1 Tbs red wine vinegar
1 Tbs sugar
¼ cup chopped fresh parsley

SPECIAL EQUIPMENT SUGGESTED:
A heavy stainless 3-quart saucepan with cover; a big sharp knife for shredding, or a food processor (see Special Note)

Assembling. Set the saucepan over moderate heat with the butter, oil, or fat. When hot, stir in the onion and sauté several minutes, until limp. Add the garlic and cook a moment more. Then fold in the cabbage along with 1 teaspoon of salt, several grinds of pepper, the caraway seeds, bay leaf, the grated apple, chicken broth, red wine, vinegar, and sugar.

Cooking—10 to 15 minutes. Cover the saucepan and boil 10 to 15 minutes, tossing occasionally, until the cabbage is just tender—add a little more broth (or water) if the liquid evaporates before the cabbage is done. On the other hand, if the cabbage is tender and liquid remains, uncover the pan and boil it off, stirring and tossing to prevent scorching. Taste very carefully and correct seasoning. Toss with a handful of chopped fresh parsley, and the cabbage is ready to serve.

*Ahead-of-time note: If cooked in advance, set aside uncovered and toss over heat, adding parsley just before serving.

Braised Sauerkraut

Sauerkraut is shredded green cabbage that has been layered with salt and weighted down in a crock until it ferments—an ancient way of preserving before canning and freezing were known. Sauerkraut has its own distinctive and slightly sour quality that blends deliciously with pork, ham, and sausages. Look for it in bottles or packaged in plastic, in the refrigerated meat or deli case. Read the label—do not buy sweetened sauerkraut (usually Kosher); Dutch and German styles are generally nonsweet.

Unlike most recipes for sauerkraut, the following is fat-free. Serve as is or use it in the choucroute with pork chops and sausages on page 204.

For 8 servings

2 pounds sauerkraut
3 cups thinly sliced onions
1 cup dry white French vermouth or dry white wine
3 cups chicken broth
Seasonings: ½ tsp each caraway seeds and thyme, 2 imported bay leaves, salt, and freshly ground pepper

Soaking the sauerkraut. Drain the sauerkraut, and taste it. If you wish to remove some of the sour taste, soak it in a large bowl of cold water for 20 minutes. Drain, wash, and taste again to see how you like it. Soak again, and repeat several times

Braised sauerkraut and sausages

if necessary. Finally drain the sauerkraut and squeeze by handfuls to remove excess water; fluff up the strands, and you are ready to go.

Assembling. Meanwhile, in a heavy 5-quart covered saucepan, simmer the onions in the vermouth or wine for 8 to 10 minutes, or until tender. Blend the soaked and squeezed sauerkraut into the onions, folding in the chicken stock, caraway, thyme, bay leaves, a little salt, and several grinds of pepper.

Braising. Bring to the simmer on top of the stove, cover the pan, and boil slowly for about 30 minutes, stirring up occasionally, until the sauerkraut is tender. The liquid should have almost completely evaporated. If not, uncover the pan and boil rapidly, tossing, until it has reduced to nothing. Correct seasoning.

STEAMED EGGPLANT DISHES

Steaming is an easy way to cook whole eggplant, and you have perfect control over its cooking. When tender through and through halve and season it, then serve it just as is. Or turn it quickly into eggplant caviar, that habit-forming Middle Eastern purée. Or, to be elegant, turn it into a handsome soufflé.

Choosing and storing eggplant. Be choosy indeed, and pick only eggplant that is firm and shiny with taut skin and no bruises: if it is dull and even slightly soft it will have a bitter unpleasant taste. Since eggplants do not keep well, plan to cook it soon; but if you cannot, wrap it loosely in paper towels, slip it into a plastic bag and refrigerate.

⋮⋮⋮ MASTER RECIPE

Steamed Whole Eggplant

1 or several firm shiny eggplants

SPECIAL EQUIPMENT SUGGESTED:
*A steaming rack in a roomy covered
saucepan, or a rack in a covered roaster*

MICROWAVE NOTE: *You can use the
microwave oven for whole eggplant if
you fuss over it, turn it, and keep testing; I find steaming far easier.*

Wash the eggplant and place in the
steaming contraption. Add an inch or
so of water, cover tightly, and steam
20 to 30 minutes, depending on size.
The eggplant is done when it is soft
and somewhat shriveled: a skewer or
sharp-pronged fork will pierce
through it easily. Lay it on your work
surface; slice off the green cap, then
slice the eggplant in half lengthwise—the flesh should be tenderly
soft and white throughout, with the
seeds a light tan.

Steamed Eggplant with Parsley Sauce

Serve this quick-to-prepare eggplant
as a first course or in place of a salad,
or as a vegetable to accompany roast
lamb or broiled chicken or fish. It is,
by the way, the perfect dieter's dish,
since you may omit the olive oil in
the sauce, and still have lots of flavor.

While it is still warm, slice the
eggplant into quarters lengthwise,
and arrange on a platter. Slash the

Steamed Eggplant with Parsley Sauce

flesh in several places with cross-
hatch cuts ⅜ inch deep. Mash ¼ teaspoon salt with a large clove of puréed garlic to a paste in a small bowl.
By droplets, whisk in 1½ to 3 tablespoons of lemon juice and, if you
wish, several tablespoons of olive oil.
Spoon this sauce over the eggplant,
and spread on a generous topping of
chopped fresh parsley. Serve warm,
or let cool, basting several times with
the accumulated juices.

VARIATION

Steamed Eggplant with Salsa Garnish

Top the steamed eggplant with salsa
(page 200). That spicy Mexican relish, with its tomatoes, peppers, cucumbers, and herbs, makes steamed
eggplant a more elaborate dish. Serve
it on a buffet table or to accompany
cold cuts, meat loaf, or cold sliced
chicken or turkey.

Eggplant Caviar
Eggplant puréed with garlic, lemon, and
olive oil

This marvelous mixture to serve as a
vegetable or cocktail dip is described
on page 333.

Eggplant Sautéed with Onions and Parsley

A milder version of the preceding
eggplant caviar, and especially attractive as a vegetable to go with broiled
fish or chicken, roast meats, steaks,
chops, and hamburgers.

Steam the eggplants as directed in the
master recipe, and scoop out the
flesh. Meanwhile, set a frying pan
over moderate heat, add a little olive
oil, and sauté 1½ cups of minced onions until tender. Fold in 2 or 3 large
cloves of puréed garlic and sauté a
few seconds; blend in the eggplant
flesh. Season with salt and freshly
ground pepper, cover the pan, and
cook slowly 10 minutes, stirring occasionally, until the eggplant is thoroughly tender. Uncover, raise the
heat, and sauté for several minutes,
tossing, to brown very lightly. Fold
in a handful of chopped fresh parsley; taste and correct seasoning.

Noncollapsible Eggplant Soufflé

As you can see, eggplant makes a handsome molded soufflé, especially when decorated with shiny purple eggplant skin. And this one is, actually, noncollapsible, so you need have no worries. Serve it hot, warm, or cold with roast or barbecued meats or poultry, have it as a main course with a salad of sliced tomatoes, or even take it on a picnic.

For 8 servings

Two 1½-pound eggplants: the preceding sauté of eggplant, but save the skin as described here in the recipe
Olive oil

The soufflé base

3 egg yolks
1 cup thick white sauce (4 Tbs butter, 5 Tbs flour, and 1½ cups hot milk; see Special Note, page 272)
Salt and freshly ground pepper
½ cup coarsely grated Swiss cheese
5 stiffly beaten egg whites (page 461)

2 cups fresh tomato sauce (page 358), for serving

SPECIAL EQUIPMENT SUGGESTED:
A grapefruit knife for scooping flesh from skin; a 10-inch frying pan and a lid or pie plate to fit down into it, for eggplant skin; a round 2½-quart oiled baking dish; a 2½-quart saucepan for the soufflé base; a double-thickness strip of oiled aluminum foil and straight pins, as a collar for the dish; a roasting pan to hold the dish

Noncollapsible Eggplant Soufflé

The eggplant. Follow directions for steaming the eggplants, and, when done, quarter them lengthwise. Scoop off all but ⅛ inch of flesh, leaving the skin intact. Continue with the preceding sauté recipe, cooking the onions, and adding the eggplant flesh and seasonings.

The eggplant skin. Meanwhile, oil the frying pan and the eggplant skin. Lay the skin flesh-side down in the frying pan and set a lid or pie plate on top to flatten it as illustrated; cook slowly over low heat until the skin is tender but not browned—15 to 20 minutes. Cut the skin into strips and arrange skin side down in the baking dish, to make a decorative pattern.

Cooking the eggplant skin

The soufflé mixture. Beat the egg yolks into the white sauce, then fold in the eggplant, salt and pepper to taste, and the grated cheese.

**Ahead-of-time note:* The recipe may be completed in advance to this point.

Finishing the soufflé. Preheat the oven to 400°F and place a roasting pan with 1 inch of water on a rack in the lower middle level. Beat the egg whites. Stir a quarter of them into the eggplant mixture; delicately fold in the rest. Being careful not to disturb the eggplant skins, turn the soufflé mixture into the baking dish. Pin the oiled collar of foil around the top of the dish, letting it come 2 inches above the rim but no more than 1 inch below the rim—or it might syphon up the water in the pan.

Baking—1¼ hours at 400°F. Set the soufflé in the pan of water and bake in the preheated oven until it has puffed, and is browned lightly on top.

Serving. Remove the soufflé from the oven and let cool 15 minutes—it will sink an inch or so. Remove the collar, and turn a serving platter upside down over the dish; reverse the two to unmold the soufflé. You may wish to decorate the top with tomato cutouts and parsley, as shown. Pass the tomato sauce separately. Serve hot, tepid, or cold.

Ahead-of-time note: You may keep the unmolded soufflé warm for ½ hour or more: leave it in its pan of water, cover loosely, and let it remain in the turned-off oven, its door ajar.

GRATED SAUTÉED-STEAMED VEGETABLES

Most of our full-flavored root vegetables are long to cook in conventional ways, and are therefore too often neglected. But with the grated-sauté system you can serve, for instance, a ten-minute confetti of turnips to garnish the pork chop, or a fast and pretty nest of beets with your rapidly sautéed breast of duck. Zucchini, too, is easy, fast, and attractive when done this way.

BEETS

Cooked fresh beets have such fine flavor of their own, I am surprised they figure so rarely on vegetarian menus. And how beautifully they go in any form with duck, pork chops, and even a little sauté of fresh foie gras. They take well to garlic vinaigrettes, too, as well as to composed salads. If you bake, boil, or steam them whole, they need almost an hour. However, when you grate them, they are ready in under 15 minutes.

SPECIAL NOTE

Removing Beet Stains

Fresh beets are perhaps avoided by some of us because they do stain fingers and cutting boards a bright beet red. Remove stains from your hands by wetting them and rubbing with salt, then washing in soap and water. A little bleach will immediately remove stains from boards and utensils.

Grating beets in a food processor

MASTER RECIPE

Grated Sautéed-Steamed Beets

For 6 servings

2 pounds fresh beets, without tops
2 or more Tbs butter
Salt and freshly ground pepper
1 tsp red-wine vinegar or raspberry vinegar

SPECIAL EQUIPMENT SUGGESTED:
A food processor or vegetable mill with grating-disk holes of about ³/₁₆ inch; a 10-inch no-stick frying pan with cover

Peel and grate the beets—you will have about 4 cups. Melt the butter over moderate heat in the frying pan, add the beets, and toss about to coat with the butter. Toss with ½ teaspoon of salt, some pepper, and 1 teaspoon of vinegar, then add ¼ inch of water. Cover and cook about 10 minutes, tossing occasionally—careful not to mash or coagulate them—until the beets are tender and the liquid has evaporated (add droplets more water

(continued)

Grated Sautéed-Steamed Beets (*continued*)

if needed during cooking). Toss with more butter, if you wish, and adjust seasonings to taste.

Ahead-of-time note: May be cooked ahead and reheated.

Beet variations

Shallots or garlic. Sauté 2 to 3 tablespoons of minced shallots for a moment in the butter before adding the beets. Or purée a clove or two of garlic and toss with the beets before sautéing.

Herbs. And/or toss with a sprinkling of minced fresh parsley or chives before serving.

Grated beets in garlic vinaigrette. Use olive oil rather than butter for cooking the beets; purée a clove or two of garlic and toss with the beets before sautéing. After cooking, toss with a little more olive oil and droplets more vinegar; let cool, and toss again with seasonings before serving.

VARIATION

Grated Sautéed-Steamed Turnips, Rutabaga, or Carrots

Peel, grate, and sauté-steam turnips, rutabaga, or carrots the same way as for the preceding beets; however, they will take only about 5 minutes to cook.

SPECIAL NOTE

Angel-Hair Winter Squash, Turnips, or Carrots

Use the fine (#2) disk of the little Mouli Julienne machine pictured here, reasonably priced and available in most hardware and gourmet stores. These very finely grated vegetables cook in 3 or 4 minutes. You might flank a serving of duck or turkey, for instance, with angel-hair squash on one side, and white turnips on the other.

Grating squash in hand-crank Mouli Julienne machine

GRATED ZUCCHINI

Zucchini is so quick and easy to cook when grated and sautéed, and this cooking method gives it a real texture. You do have to squeeze grated zucchini before sautéing it, however, to rid it of its extra moisture. If you don't squeeze, it takes too long to cook and rather than textured zucchini you end up with mush.

MASTER RECIPE

Grated Sautéed Zucchini

Grated zucchini goes with almost everything—roast or sautéed chicken, broiled fish, steaks, and chops. The recipe here sautés in butter, but you might also look at the fat-free zucchini with onions and red peppers, and with spinach, farther along.

For 6 servings

2 pounds zucchini (6 to 8 zucchini, 8 inches long)
½ tsp salt
3 Tbs butter
2 Tbs chopped shallots or scallions

SPECIAL EQUIPMENT SUGGESTED: *A food processor or vegetable mill with medium grating disk; a colander; a towel, for squeezing; a 10-inch no-stick frying pan, or a wok*

Preparing the zucchini. Scrub the zucchini under cold running water; shave off the two ends but do not peel. Grate it, and toss with the salt in the colander. Let steep for a few minutes, then twist by handfuls in the corner of the towel to extract excess liquid—you will be surprised at the amount, which you can save for when you make the Gratin of Grated Zucchini #2, which follows later.

Sautéing. Heat the butter to foaming in the frying pan, toss in the shallots or scallions, then the zucchini. Toss over high heat several minutes, just until tender. Serve as is.

Ahead-of-time note: Zucchini cooked this way is at its best when served at once. But you can grate and squeeze it out well in advance.

OTHER SERVING SUGGESTIONS

The first three suggestions here are especially useful for ahead-of-time preparation.

Grated Zucchini Simmered in Cream

Sauté until the grated and squeezed zucchini is almost tender. A few minutes before serving, fold in ½ cup or so of heavy cream, and simmer several minutes, until the cream has thickened and is almost absorbed. Fold with a little chopped fresh parsley—or tarragon—and serve.

Gratin of Grated Zucchini #1

Turn the creamed zucchini into a shallow baking and serving dish, and sprinkle 3 to 4 tablespoons of grated Swiss cheese over the surface. Several minutes before serving, set 3 to 4 inches under a hot broiler element to warm through and brown the top lightly.

Gratin of Grated Zucchini #2

Velouté sauce. Save the squeezed-out juices from the zucchini. While the zucchini is sautéing, or afterward, make a pale green velouté sauce (see page 8), with the zucchini juices plus milk or cream as needed (2 tablespoons of butter, 3 tablespoons of flour, 1½ cups of hot liquid).

Assembling. Fold the sautéed grated zucchini into the sauce, taste, and correct seasoning. Turn it into a buttered baking and serving dish, and spread 3 to 4 tablespoons of grated Swiss cheese over the surface.

Baking—20 minutes at 400°F. About 20 minutes before serving, set in the upper third level of the preheated 400°F oven and bake until bubbling hot and the top has browned lightly.

OTHER VARIATIONS ON THE GRATED ZUCCHINI THEME

Grated Zucchini with Onions and Red Peppers

Zucchini, onions, and red peppers will go with just about any main course, and you will note this dish can be fat-free. See page 157 for illustration with game hens.

While the zucchini is steeping in salt, purée 2 large cloves of garlic and simmer them with 2 cups of sliced onions in ½ cup each of white wine and chicken broth. When tender, in about 10 minutes, fold in the grated and squeezed zucchini and 1 or 2

slices of red bell pepper or strips of bottled pimiento. Boil over high heat, uncovered, for a few minutes, until the zucchini is tender and the liquid has evaporated. Correct seasoning and fold in, if you wish, a little olive oil or butter.

Grated Zucchini and Spinach

Another slim-jim recipe, but you'd never realize it when eating this happy mixture. Simmer the zucchini in the vermouth and stock for several minutes, just until tender. Remove to a side dish, leaving the juices behind. Blend into the juices 2 packages or bunches of stemmed and washed spinach leaves (page 277) and boil several minutes, until just tender. Remove the pan from heat. Blend 1½ tablespoons of cornstarch in a small bowl with an equal amount of chicken stock; when smooth, blend it into the spinach and its cooking juices. Fold in the zucchini, and bring to the boil, folding the vegetables and liquid together for 2 minutes, to cook the starch and thicken the sauce. Correct seasoning.

Julienne of cucumbers

CUCUMBERS

Cucumbers, although we tend to think of them as salad material, make a delicious cooked vegetable with their tender flesh and subtle taste.

Sauté of Julienned Cucumbers

Sautéed cucumbers go with almost anything, from fish to fowl to good red meat. They are particularly attractive with veal dishes, or fish or chicken in cream or butter sauces, where you want a simple accompaniment.

For 4 servings, julienne and season 2 large cucumbers as described in the Special Note. Shortly before serving, so the cucumbers will retain their texture, heat 2 tablespoons of butter to bubbling in a 10-inch frying pan, add the cucumbers, and toss over moderately high heat for 2 to 3 minutes, just until tender but still with a slight crunch. Season to taste, toss with a little minced fresh dill and/or parsley, and serve as soon as possible.

VARIATIONS

Sauté of Spinach with Grated Cucumbers

Substitute cucumbers for zucchini in the preceding section.

Creamed Cucumbers

Serve these with plain broiled or roast chicken, poached fish, or with veal chops. Sauté the cucumbers briefly in 2 tablespoons of butter, fold in ½ cup of heavy cream, and boil over high heat until the cream has reduced and thickened, then fold in chopped fresh dill or parsley.

SPECIAL NOTE

Preparing Cucumbers for Cooking

Peel the cucumbers, halve them lengthwise, and scoop out the seeds with the end of your vegetable peeler or a teaspoon. Depending on how you want them to look, grate them or cut them into wedges. Or for julienne matchsticks, halve the seeded halves lengthwise, and then into crosswise pieces about 2 inches long. Finally, cut these pieces into matchstick-size julienne—excellent knife practice, and the faster and neater you can do it, the more professional you are. However you cut them, you may cook them the same way as in the upcoming recipe for julienned cucumbers.

To Season Cucumbers

If you wish to accentuate the cucumber taste before cooking, toss the cut cucumbers in a bowl with a sprinkle of salt and droplets of wine vinegar to taste; a pinch of sugar will also help bring out the cucumber flavor. Let them steep 10 minutes or so; drain before cooking.

BRAISED CELERY, LEEKS, AND ENDIVES

Serve them warm as a vegetable, or cold as an agreeable first course—braised celery, leeks, and endives are happy additions to any table.

SPECIAL NOTE

Mirepoix: Diced Aromatic Vegetables
For flavoring sauces, meats, and vegetables

The mirepoix is one of fine cooking's great inspirations, an all-purpose flavor-enhancer made of finely diced and sautéed carrots and onions, and often celery and ham. Used in sauces, with braised vegetables like celery, or with chicken breasts poached in butter, it imparts that real "je ne sais quoi" of sophistication to anything it is associated with. You may want to triple or quadruple the recipe, since a mirepoix keeps nicely in the freezer.

For ¼ to ⅓ cup

¼ cup each finely diced onions and carrots, and celery, too, if you wish
2 Tbs butter
⅛ tsp thyme
¼ cup diced boiled ham, optional

In a small covered saucepan, cook the diced vegetables slowly in the butter, adding the thyme and optional diced ham after 5 minutes; continue for another few minutes, until the vegetables are tender but not browned. Season lightly to taste, and set aside.

Dicing carrots and onions for mirepoix

Dicing onions

⫘ MASTER RECIPE

Braised Celery, Mirepoix

Simmering celery in broth and the classic aromatic vegetable mixture known as a mirepoix gives that otherwise mild vegetable a marvelous flavor. Once cooked, as you will see from the variations to come, you can then serve it hot with a sauce made from the cooking juices, or au gratin, or cold as a salad or hors d'oeuvre.

For 6 servings

¼ cup mirepoix (see Special Note)
Salt and freshly ground pepper
2 or 3 celery hearts—⅓ to ½ head per person, depending on size
1 cup or more chicken broth

Quartering celery heads

SPECIAL EQUIPMENT SUGGESTED:
A buttered rectangular or oval flameproof baking-serving dish 2 inches deep, and large enough to hold the celery in one crowded layer; buttered wax paper and foil to cover the celery while baking

Preparing the celery for cooking. Keeping the form of the heads intact, remove all tough outer stalks, leaving just those you judge will be tender when cooked—no tough strings to them, in other words. Cut off the tops to make the heads about 8 inches long; trim the roots, being careful not to detach the stalks. Slice the heads lengthwise into halves, thirds, or quarters (see illustration), depending on size.

Assembling the baking dish. Spread half the mirepoix vegetables in the baking dish, arrange the celery cut side up over them, salt lightly, and spread the rest of the mirepoix over the celery. Pour in enough stock to come ⅓ of the way up the celery, and lay over it the buttered wax paper.

Braising—30 to 40 minutes. Bring to the simmer on top of the stove, cover closely with foil, and cook either on

(*continued*)

Braised Celery, Mirepoix (*continued*)

top of the stove or in a 350°F oven for 30 to 40 minutes or longer, basting fairly frequently with the liquid in the dish. The celery is done when it is very tender but still holds its shape.

Optional for added flavor. Let the celery cool 20 to 30 minutes in the cooking liquid, basting frequently.

To serve cold. See the suggestions on page 300.

To serve hot. This would go with almost any main course, especially when you want something not too rich. Or it could well be a first course.

Bring the braised celery to the simmer in its dish, basting several times. Remove the celery to a hot platter and keep warm while rapidly boiling down the cooking liquid until it is almost syrupy. Correct seasoning and, if you wish, remove from heat and swirl in 2 to 3 tablespoons of butter, a tablespoon at a time. Spoon the liquid over the celery, sprinkle with chopped parsley, and serve.

Braised Leeks

Leeks have so much of their own wonderful flavor that you need no aromatic enhancers such as the mirepoix braised with the preceding celery. Serve leeks with steaks, chops, roasts—in fact with almost any main course where you want an uncomplicated accompaniment. You can also serve them au gratin, or cold, as suggested farther on.

Splitting leeks

For 6 servings

6 large or 12 small leeks (1 or 2 per person)
Water or chicken broth
Salt and freshly ground pepper
2 or more Tbs butter

Preparing the leeks for cooking. Trim the root ends of the leeks, being careful to keep the leaves attached. Remove any wilted leaves, and cut off the tops to leave the leeks 6 to 7 inches long. Slit each lengthwise down to where the white begins (see illustration); give the leek a quarter turn and slit again. Wash very thoroughly under cold running water, spreading each leaf apart to rinse off all dirt and grit. If the leeks are fat, cut them in half lengthwise.

Braising. Following the general procedure in the master recipe, arrange the leeks in a buttered baking dish (cut side down if they are halved). Pour in water or broth to come halfway up the leeks, salt lightly, and dot with a tablespoon or so of butter. Cover with buttered wax paper and foil, and either simmer 15 to 20 minutes on top of the stove, basting with the braising liquid several times, or bake 30 to 40 minutes in a 350°F oven.

To serve hot. Boil down the cooking juices and enrich with butter, if you wish, as described in the master recipe for braised celery.

Braised Endives

Cooked endives are far more interesting than raw endives in a salad. Their slight bitterness combined with a buttery braise makes them one of the great accompaniments to roast veal, chicken, and turkey. Now that we are raising our own in this country, let us hope they may become less of a luxury item.

Buying. Details on buying and storing endives are in the salad chapter on page 348.

Cooking. Give yourself plenty of time, since braised endives may be cooked even a day or two ahead, and they are a true braise—they are cooked not only until tender but, more important, until there has been a real exchange between the buttery lemony braising juices and the endives themselves. That is the point at which they are unique; and truly delicious.

For 6 servings

12 endives—fresh, firm, and fat, all the same size, all creamy white, and all neatly closed at the pointed tip end

¼ tsp salt, plus a little more, if needed

½ cup water

½ Tbs freshly squeezed lemon juice, plus a little more if needed

2 to 4 Tbs butter, cut into slices

2 to 3 Tbs chopped fresh parsley, optional

SPECIAL EQUIPMENT SUGGESTED:
A covered flameproof stain-resistant casserole or heavy saucepan just large enough to hold the endives in 2 layers

Braised endives

Preparing the endives for cooking. Trim the root ends of the endives, being careful that the leaves remain attached. Remove any wilted leaves and cut out any brown portions. Wash the endives under cold running water.

Braising—1½ to 2 hours. Arrange the endives in the casserole, adding the salt, water, lemon juice, and butter. Cover and boil slowly on top of the stove for about 20 minutes, or until the vegetables are fairly tender and the liquid has been reduced by half. (You can now, or later on, probably push the endives gently together into one layer.) Either cover and cook slowly on top of the stove; or lay buttered wax paper over the endives, cover, and bake in a 325°F oven. Taste and correct seasoning halfway through.

When are they done? When done, the vegetables should be a very tender

Endives ready for braising

pale golden color and almost all the liquid will have evaporated. Serve as is, sprinkled with parsley.

*Ahead-of-time note: May be cooked ahead and reheated.

ANOTHER SERVING SUGGESTION

Endives Sautéed in Butter

This is an especially attractive way to serve braised endives, although it does raise the calorie count to some extent.

The moment before serving the preceding braised endives, film a no-stick frying pan with 1/16 inch of clarified butter and heat to very hot but not browning. Lay in the endives and sauté a moment or so on each side to brown, turning carefully so as to disturb the leaves as little as possible. Serve with a sprinkling of parsley.

VARIATIONS

Braised Celery and Leeks Served Cold

To serve either braised leeks or braised celery cold, you can simply turn the braising juices into a vinaigrette, using the directions for the following Celery Victor, then pour the sauce over the vegetables, sprinkle with parsley, and serve. But here is that famous celery dish.

Celery Victor

Celery Victor

This celebrated celery was created by Chef Victor Hirtzler, of the St. Francis Hotel in San Francisco, way back in the early part of this century. As with most historic dishes, there are many versions. Here is my favorite, but see also the simpler cooking method and the green tapénade garnish in the variation that follows.

For 6 servings

The master recipe for braised celery (page 297)

Celery vinaigrette sauce
The celery braising juices
2 Tbs wine vinegar
1 Tbs Dijon-style prepared mustard
1 Tbs finely minced shallots or scallions
1/3 to 1/2 cup olive oil
Salt and freshly ground pepper

The garnish
2 Tbs chopped capers
3 Tbs chopped fresh parsley
1 hard-boiled egg, chopped
Salt and freshly ground pepper
12 strips of canned red pimiento
12 fine fresh flat anchovy fillets packed in olive oil

Preliminaries. Remove the celery itself to a platter, and drain the celery braising juices into a small pan. Gently squeeze out excess liquid from the celery and add it to the rest. Arrange the celery neatly in one layer, cut side up. Boil the cooking liquid down until almost syrupy.

The celery vinaigrette. Blend into the concentrated celery juices the wine vinegar, mustard, and shallots or scallions. Whisk in the oil by droplets. Season carefully with salt and pepper; spoon over the celery. Let macerate 10 minutes, then tip the platter and baste the celery with the sauce, repeating several times.

Ahead-of-time note: May be prepared several hours in advance. Cover and refrigerate, but bring to room temperature before proceeding, to decongeal the oil.

Garnishing and serving. Just before serving, toss together the chopped capers, parsley, and hard-boiled egg, seasoning to taste with salt and pepper. Strew this over the central portions of the celery, and decorate with crossed strips of red pimiento and anchovies.

VARIATION

A Green Tapénade of Celery Hearts

Celery hearts are poached in a lemon broth and topped with green tapénade—a purée of green-ripe olives, herbs, and garlic.

Poaching the celery. Prepare the celery hearts as described in the master recipe, but rather than braising them, simmer in lightly salted water to cover and the juice of 1 lemon—30 to 40 minutes, until perfectly tender. Let steep 20 minutes in the cooking liquid. Drain on a clean towel and gently press out excess liquid.

Assembly. Arrange the celery cut side up on a platter or individual plates.

Spoon tapénade down the central section of the stalks, leaving the ends exposed. Decorate attractively with such items as sieved hard-boiled eggs and chopped parsley, strips of red pimiento, and more green-ripe olives.

OTHER VARIATIONS FOR BRAISED VEGETABLES

Celery or Leeks au Gratin

For a substantial dish to go with, for instance, plain broiled or grilled meats, poultry, or fish, gratiné the preceding cooked celery hearts or the leeks on page 298 in a cheese sauce. Follow the gratin of cauliflower recipe on page 273, using a combination of celery- or leek-cooking juices and milk for the sauce.

Braised Endives au Gratin, with Ham

Endives gratinéed in cheese sauce with ham make a perfect little main course for a luncheon or supper. Accompany it with a green salad and a chilled white wine, like a French Chablis, or a sauvignon.

Make the cheese sauce as described, using all milk since there will be few if any endive braising juices. Spoon a thin layer of the sauce in the bottom of a shallow lightly buttered baking-serving dish. Wrap each endive in a slice of ham and arrange smooth side up in the dish. Spoon the rest of the sauce over, and sprinkle with the remaining cheese. Bake about 25 minutes in the upper third level of a preheated 425°F oven.

SPECIAL NOTE

Green Tapénade

The classic tapénade is made with black olives, and it's good to have a change with green. This pungent sauce is delicious with cold vegetables, especially braised celery, but can also be tossed with hot or cold pasta, or be a filling for hard-boiled eggs, or a spread for the hard-toasted rounds of French bread on page 353.

For about ⅔ cup

2 large cloves of garlic, puréed
1½ cups pitted green-ripe olives
6 fine fresh flat anchovy fillets packed in oil
2 Tbs capers
2 Tbs olive oil
¼ cup lightly pressed down parsley sprigs
Pinches of thyme and freshly ground pepper
½ Tbs brandy

Green tapénade. Purée the listed ingredients in a food processor or electric blender, and taste carefully for seasoning. Add more of any or all of the ingredients, as you see fit.

STUFFED VEGETABLES

Astuffing gives any vegetable more importance at the table. In fact, a stuffed vegetable may well serve as a first course, or even be the main course for a light meal. In most cases here, so that it will taste of itself, the vegetable is stuffed with its own trimmings, plus some additional flavorings, and a binder of some sort.

▓ MASTER RECIPE

Stuffed Onions

A fragrant big stuffed onion is a most edible object all by itself, and it is an attractive accompaniment to a plain roast chicken, veal, or turkey, as well as to chops, steaks, and hamburgers. The trick for success is to hollow the onions and blanch them before stuffing and baking them. Otherwise they take hours to cook and may well burst out of their shells before they are done.

For 6 large onions

6 large firm fresh perfect onions at least 3 inches in diameter
A saucepan of boiling water, for peeling
A large kettle of boiling salted water, for blanching
Melted butter and/or oil
Butter, for greasing the baking pan
Salt and freshly ground pepper
1½ to 2 cups stuffing (see recipe following, or see other suggestions starting on page 184)

Stuffed Onion

2 Tbs fresh crumbs from home-made style white bread
½ cup dry white French vermouth or dry white wine
½ to 1 cup beef stock or chicken broth

Peeling, coring, and blanching the onions. One at a time, shave off the pointed and root ends of the onions, being careful to keep the onion layers attached to the root. For easy peeling, drop them one or two at a time for exactly 1 minute into the saucepan of boiling water; carefully remove the skin. With a sharp knife, cut a cone-shaped core out of the top (not root) end of the onion, and reserve all cuttings. Then, being careful not to make the sides and bottom too thin—they should be about ⅜ inch thick—use a melon baller to dig circular sections out of the onion to form a cup of the interior. Drop the onion cups

Coring an onion

Stuffing the onion

into the kettle of boiling salted water and boil slowly 10 to 15 minutes; they should be just tender but they must still hold their shape. Drain upside down in a colander.

Stuffing the onions. Butter or oil the outside of the onion cups and arrange cup side up in a heavily buttered flameproof baking dish about 3 inches deep and just large enough to hold them in one layer. Season the inside of the cups lightly with salt and pepper, and fill with the stuffing, heaping it into a ½-inch dome. Top each with a teaspoon of bread crumbs and a drizzle of melted butter. Pour the wine around the onions, and enough broth to come a third of the way up.

Baking—about 1½ hours at 375°F. Bring to the simmer on top of the stove. Bake uncovered in the lower middle level of the preheated oven, maintaining the liquid at a slow simmer and basting the onions several times with the liquid in the dish. They are done when a knife pierces them easily, but they must keep their shape. (The outside layer will be slightly tough, but the insides deliciously tender.)

*Ahead-of-time note: The onions may be baked in advance, and reheated later; they are also good served cold.

An Onion Stuffing
For onions and other vegetables

The following is a combination of chopped onion, from their own interiors if it's for stuffed onions, plus a little cooked rice, cheese, cream, and herbs. If the stuffing is for other vegetables, like zucchini, add their chopped interiors and sauté with the onion.

For about 1½ cups

1 cup or so minced onions
Butter as needed
1 cup cooked rice
¼ cup heavy cream
3 to 4 Tbs grated Swiss cheese
2 to 4 Tbs fresh crumbs from nonsweet homemade type white bread
¼ cup minced fresh parsley
Fresh or dried tarragon, or fresh basil
Salt and freshly ground pepper

Cook the minced onions slowly in 2 tablespoons of butter in a covered pan until very tender; uncover pan and stir over moderately high heat to brown very lightly. Blend in the rice, cream, cheese, and 2 tablespoons of the bread crumbs, adding a few more crumbs if the mixture is too soft for easy stuffing. Stir in the parsley and other herb; season carefully to taste.

STUFFED CABBAGE, WHOLE AND IN PARTS

What to do with a lingering party ham? Put it to work in stuffed cabbage leaves, and braise them in a savory tomato sauce.

SPECIAL NOTE

To Remove the Leaves from a Hard-Headed Cabbage

You may core a whole head of cabbage and drop it into a large kettle of boiling water, then boil until the outside leaves loosen and can be nudged off, continuing to boil as they gradually loosen. Or here's an easier method.

Freeze it first. Cut out the core of the cabbage using a short stout knife, and making a cone-shaped cut about 2 inches deep. Place the cabbage in the freezer, as is, for 24 hours. The leaves will then be loose, but since they need blanching anyway, drop the whole cabbage directly from the freezer into a large kettle of boiling water. Separate the leaves from the head one by one with 2 long-handled spoons—they come off easily. Let the leaves boil a moment, then refresh them in a bowl of cold water. Drain on a towel, and they are ready to work with.

Braised Cabbage Rolls

![master recipe icon] MASTER RECIPE

Braised Cabbage Rolls

Since these make good eating either hot or cold, you may wish to make more than you need for one meal.

For 12 rolls, serving 6

The blanched leaves from an 8-inch head of cabbage (see Special Note on removing the leaves, page 303)
About 3 cups of stuffing (see suggestions on page 184; the Ham and Bread Crumb Stuffing is recommended)
2 Tbs butter
1 cup sliced onions
Salt and freshly ground pepper
3½ cups combined fresh tomatoes, peeled, seeded, and juiced, and strained canned Italian plum tomatoes
2 imported bay leaves

SPECIAL EQUIPMENT SUGGESTED: *A food processor; a chicken fryer or electric frying pan*

Filling the cabbage leaves. Remove the tough part of the central stem from the lower parts of the cabbage leaves, as necessary. Spread 1 leaf (or several small leaves combined) cupped side up on your work surface; divide the filling into 12 portions. Spread a cylinder of filling onto each leaf and roll up into a sausage shape, enclosing the filling completely.

Braising. Set the chicken fryer over moderate heat, with the butter, add the onions, and sauté for 5 to 6 minutes, until limp and translucent. Arrange the cabbage rolls best side up in a single layer over the onions. Season lightly with salt and pepper, pour the tomatoes over them, and bury the bay leaves in the pan. Bring to the simmer, cover, and simmer slowly,

basting occasionally, for about 30 minutes, or until the cabbage is tender. Taste and correct seasoning.

✻Ahead-of-time note: May be braised in advance, and reheated.

Suggested accompaniments: navy beans, rice, boiled potatoes, or just good French bread—and a simple red wine.

Stuffed Whole Braised Cabbage

There is always something quite splendid about a whole stuffed cabbage. Perhaps it is the incredulity of those who have never seen one before. Or it could be the enticing aroma, or the anticipation of what in the world they've put in the stuffing. For me, it is the enjoyment of looking at that handsome green cabbage, and knowing that it was taken apart leaf by leaf and cunningly re-formed with layers of stuffing; now it is just innocently sitting there, ready for eating.

You will note I have called for extra cabbage leaves here, since the original, after its long braising, needs perking up for its grand entrance.

For 6 to 8 servings

The blanched leaves of a 3-pound cabbage (see Special Note on page 303)
6 beautifully green large leaves from another cabbage, blanched until just tender, refreshed in cold water, drained, and reserved
6 cups of stuffing: either one or two

from the suggestions starting on page 184—the Bulgur Stuffing and the Mushroom Duxelles Stuffing minus the chicken would make a grand vegetarian meal

2 cups sliced onions
1 cup sliced carrots
2 Tbs butter
Seasonings: salt, freshly ground pepper, fresh lemon juice, and thyme
About 2 cups of liquid: chicken stock; or the soaking liquid from bulgur and/or mushrooms if you are using either, lightly salted
2 cups excellent tomato sauce (page 358), warmed

SPECIAL EQUIPMENT SUGGESTED: *A roundish-bottomed 3-quart stainless bowl with top diameter of about 8 inches; a round of buttered foil; a lid of some sort; an instant meat thermometer*

The braising base. Sauté the sliced onions and carrots 5 minutes in the butter. Season with salt, pepper, lemon juice, and thyme, and arrange them in the bottom of the 3-quart bowl.

Assembling the cabbage. Line the bottom and sides of the bowl with the largest leaves, stems up and curved sides against the bowl as illustrated, step 1. Spread on a layer of stuffing, and cover with a layer of leaves.

Spread on a thin layer of stuffing (the second stuffing if you are using two), and cover with another layer of leaves, step 2. Continue alternating stuffing and leaves, ending with a final layer of cabbage leaves. Pour the chicken stock or vegetable liquid over the cabbage, adding enough almost to cover it, step 3.

Braising—2½ hours at 400°F. Top with the round of foil and the lid, and set in the middle level of the preheated oven. The cabbage is done in about 2½ hours, at an internal temperature of 160°F.

Sauce and serving. Drain the cooking liquid out of the braising bowl into a saucepan, and boil down to about ⅓ cup. Pour in the tomato sauce and bring to the simmer. Unmold the cabbage onto a hot serving dish—it will be a fragrant gray-green. Cover with the reserved blanched green cabbage leaves, and surround with a spoonful or two of the tomato sauce,

Stuffed Whole Braised Cabbage

1. Lining bowl with blanched cabbage leaves

3. Adding the liquid

2. Layering-in stuffing and leaves

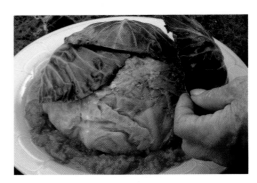

4. Decorating with blanched green leaves

step 4. Turn the rest of the sauce into a warm bowl. To serve, spoon a little sauce onto a hot dinner plate and arrange a wedge of cabbage over it.

Assembling Stuffed Tomatoes Provençale

Stuffed Tomatoes Provençale

The slight acidity of the tomato blends especially well with red meats, and especially with roast lamb. In addition, tomatoes Provençale are attractive with brunch dishes such as omelettes or scrambled eggs. For this easy recipe, stuff them in advance, and bake them just before serving.

For 8 tomato halves

4 large fine firm ripe tomatoes
Salt and freshly ground pepper
½ cup lightly pressed down crumbs
    from fresh homemade type white
    bread
2 Tbs minced shallots or scallions
1 large clove of garlic, puréed
¼ cup minced fresh parsley
3 to 4 Tbs olive oil

SPECIAL EQUIPMENT SUGGESTED:
A rack for draining the tomatoes; a lightly oiled baking dish that will hold them

Preparing the tomatoes for stuffing. Cut the tomatoes in half (not through the stem). Gently squeeze them to remove excess juice; dig out the seeds with your little finger. Salt and pepper the insides lightly and turn upside down on a rack to drain while you prepare the stuffing.

The stuffing. Toss the bread crumbs with the shallots or scallions, garlic, parsley, and salt and pepper to taste, blending in droplets of olive oil as you do so.

Stuffing. Divide the stuffing into 8 portions and mound into each tomato; arrange the tomatoes in the baking dish. Drizzle a little more oil over the crumbs, if you wish.

*Ahead-of-time note: May be prepared in advance to this point.

Baking. Preheat the oven to 400°F. About 20 minutes before serving, bake in the upper third level until the crumbs are lightly browned and the tomatoes are hot through but still hold their shape. Serve them soon, since they risk a collapse if kept warm.

VARIATION

Tomatoes Stuffed with Three Kernels

This unusual recipe for stuffed tomatoes—wheat berries, brown rice, barley, and cheese—is on page 339.

Feta Peppers

Bell or chili peppers baked with cheese

Halved or quartered fresh peppers are stuffed with a cheese filling, and baked to bubbling hot. Serve them as a garnish for salads, or with roasts, steaks, or chops.

For 6 servings

2 slender thin-skinned mild green
    chili peppers about 5 inches long,
    or 2 bell peppers

Feta Peppers

Ahead-of-time note: May be prepared in advance to this point.

Baking—about 15 minutes at 450°F. Bake in the upper third level of the preheated oven until slightly puffed and lightly browned. They may be kept warm for 15 to 20 minutes before serving, but the puff will deflate somewhat.

Stuffed and Baked Winter Squash

Is there never enough stuffing in the turkey? Make a large batch, then, and bake it in a beautiful big squash to give everyone plenty of stuffing plus another vegetable.

The squash and the cooking directions. This is the general idea, whatever the size of your winter squash: halve the squash and scrape out all seeds and stringy bits. Rub the inside with butter and seasonings. Bake in the lower third level of a preheated 400°F oven until the squash flesh is soft and edible but the squash still holds its shape—probably an hour or more, and you can do this well in advance. Reheat it again in the oven for 10 minutes or so, fill it with turkey stuffing or whatever else you choose (stuffings start on page 184), and bake again ½ hour or so (longer if the stuffing is chilled), basting 2 or 3 times with a spoonful of turkey (or any other) roasting juices, or with a little chicken stock and melted butter. Scoop up some of the tender squash flesh with each serving of stuffing.

The filling
¼ **pound (½ cup) feta cheese or goat**
   cheese
⅓ **cup sour cream**
1 egg yolk
Salt and freshly ground pepper
Worcestershire sauce
Hot pepper sauce

Preparing the peppers. Make boat shapes out of the peppers so that you can stuff them—depending on their size and shape, either halve or quarter them lengthwise; remove the seeds and ribs. Blend the filling ingredients with a mixing fork and season highly to taste. Divide it among the peppers, and lay them in an oiled pan.

Stuffed Pattypan Squash

Pattypans, those round, top-knotted green squashes, are available in many markets all year round; if yours does not carry them, make loud noises so that they do. Pattypans are much better for stuffing, I think, than zucchini, and the simple formula here goes nicely with fish or chicken, or as a first course, either hot or cold.

For 4 to 8 servings

**8 pattypans, about 3 inches in
    diameter**

The stuffing

1½ cups minced onions
**½ cup dry white French vermouth
    or dry white wine**
1 to 2 Tbs butter
1 "large" egg
**½ cup cream cheese, or ⅓ cup sour
    cream**
**½ cup lightly pressed down crumbs
    from fresh homemade type white
    bread**
Salt and freshly ground pepper
A pinch of thyme

¼ cup grated Swiss cheese
1 cup, more or less, chicken broth

SPECIAL EQUIPMENT SUGGESTED:
*A melon baller for scooping the squash;
a 10-inch frying pan for the stuffing; a
lightly buttered shallow baking dish to
hold the pattypans comfortably in 1
layer*

Preparing the squash. Drop the pattypans as is into a kettle of boiling salted water and blanch (boil) them 10 to 15 minutes, or until they just yield to pressure. Trim off and discard the stems at one end and the blossom buttons at the other. To make a cup for stuffing, cut a core

Stuffed Pattypan Squash

out of the blossom end with a small knife, leaving ¼ inch of flesh all around; scoop out the pulp with the melon baller.

The stuffing. Chop up the removed flesh with its skin. To remove and reserve excess juice, twist the flesh hard in the corner of a towel held over a bowl. Simmer the minced onions in the vermouth 7 to 8 minutes, until tender; add the butter and pattypan

flesh, and boil slowly to evaporate liquid almost completely. Let cool briefly; blend in the egg, cheese, and bread crumbs. Season to taste with salt, pepper, and thyme.

Stuffing the pattypans. Divide the stuffing into 8 portions, and mound it in the pattypans; top each with a pinch of grated cheese. Arrange them in one layer in the baking dish, and pour around them ¼ inch of chicken broth.

Ahead-of-time note: May be prepared ahead to this point.

Baking—about 15 minutes at 400°F. Bake in the upper third level of the preheated oven, basting several times with the liquid in the pan, until the squash are well heated through and the cheese has browned lightly—they may be kept warm for 15 to 20 minutes before serving.

Stuffed Zucchini Blossoms

If you are a gardener feeling guilty about your overabundant zucchini, catch them while still babies, 5 inches long and when the flowers are attached (see illustration). Trim them, stuff the flowers, and braise them in a light butter sauce. Incidentally, if you can't grow them, you may well find these flowering zucchini in one of the specialty vegetable markets during the season.

This is a pure and lovely dish, worth serving alone as a first course—no cream here, but a certain amount of butter.

For 4 to 6 servings

12 baby zucchini no longer than 5 inches, flowers attached
3 Tbs finely minced shallots or scallions
4 to 6 Tbs butter
⅓ cup lightly pressed down crumbs from fresh homemade type white bread
Salt and freshly ground pepper
A little water, as needed

Zucchini blossoms and blossoms attached to baby zucchini

1. Whittling the zucchini

2. Stuffing the blossoms

SPECIAL EQUIPMENT SUGGESTED:
A towel, for squeezing zucchini pieces; a smallish frying pan, for the stuffing; a 12-inch frying pan with cover, for final cooking

Preparing the zucchini. Cut off the zucchini 2 inches below the flower ends. Whittle down the remaining part to a fat point, step 1, leaving a collar of green at the flower end. Mince the remaining zucchini pieces very fine along with all shavings and

peelings; twist these in a corner of the towel held over a bowl to extract and reserve their juices.

The stuffing. Sauté the shallots or scallions briefly in 3 tablespoons of butter just until tender; add the minced and squeezed zucchini pieces and stir several minutes over high heat to cook them through and evaporate their moisture. Blend in several tablespoons of crumbs, just enough to make a mass that holds its shape lightly, for stuffing. Season carefully to taste with salt and pepper—you should have about 1½ cups, or 2 tablespoons per zucchini flower.

Stuffing the zucchini flowers. Divide the stuffing into 12 portions; slit the flowers down their sides, insert the stuffing with a teaspoon, step 2, and fold the flower around it. Smear a tablespoon of butter in the large frying pan, and arrange the zucchini in it, in a single, closely packed layer. Salt lightly, and pour in the reserved zucchini juices plus enough water to make ⅜ inch of liquid in the pan.

Ahead-of-time note: May be prepared in advance to this point.

Cooking and serving. Bring to the boil on top of the stove, cover, and boil slowly for several minutes, until the zucchini are barely tender when pierced with a small knife. Carefully transfer to a hot platter or plates; rapidly boil down the cooking juices until syrupy. Remove from heat, swirl in an additional tablespoon or two of butter, pour over the zucchini, and serve.

OTHER VEGETABLES

Chestnuts do not fit into a category: they have their own special ways, as do prune and apple garnishes, gnocchi, mushrooms, chutneys, and baked whole onions.

CHESTNUTS

Chestnuts, with their own subtle flavor and softly chewy texture, go beautifully with turkey, goose, and duck.

Buying and storing. Chestnut season is in the late fall and early winter. Buy shiny, heavy-feeling nuts, and if you are not cooking them soon, store them loosely in a cool, dry place. They will keep for several weeks, but use them while they still feel full and heavy.

Amounts. A pound (or 35 to 40 whole chestnuts) makes 2½ cups of peeled chestnuts.

SPECIAL NOTE

Preparing Chestnuts for Cooking Whole

Like many a treat, they do require time, especially when you want them to remain whole. First you must strip off the shiny brown outer shell, then peel, poke, and scrape off the thin brownish covering skin.

Removing the shells and inner skin. Cut a strip of shell off the outside curve of each chestnut, step 1. Cover with cold water in a saucepan and boil 1 minute. Set the pan aside.

Remove 3 at a time from the hot water; strip off the outer shells. Peel and scrape off the covering brown skin, step 2. Some nuts will refuse to peel; heat and try again.

1. Cutting off strip of shell

2. Peeling inner skin off blanched nuts

 MASTER RECIPE

Whole Cooked Chestnuts

For 48 chestnuts, serving 6 to 8

**48 peeled chestnuts (see Special
   Note on this page)
1 imported bay leaf
1 medium onion
1 large celery stalk, cut into several
   pieces
3 or more cups beef or chicken stock
Salt and freshly ground pepper**

Place the chestnuts in a saucepan with the bay leaf, onion, celery, and enough stock to cover them by ½ inch. Season lightly to taste, and bring to the simmer. Cover partially, and simmer slowly—watch that the liquid does not boil and disintegrate the chestnuts. Timing: about 40 minutes, or until the chestnuts are tender but hold their shape.

*Ahead-of-time note: May be cooked in advance. Refrigerate in their cooking liquid.

VARIATION

Chestnuts in Stuffings

Drain the chestnuts (reserve the liquid for sauce or soup) and use them as is in any stuffing recipe.

Braised Chestnuts

Serve these alone as a vegetable in place of potatoes or another starchy vegetable. I don't know why these are called "braised"; technically they are not, but the term is more appetizing than "buttered chestnuts."

Boil down the cooking liquid in a 10-inch frying pan until almost syrupy, add the preceding cooked chestnuts and reheat through, then fold and toss gently with several tablespoons of butter to glaze them.

VARIATION

Braised Chestnuts with Brussels Sprouts

One of the good ways to serve whole chestnuts is to contrast them with the distinctive taste and slight crunch of perfectly cooked fresh Brussels sprouts. Fold the preceding braised chestnuts with the buttered Brussels sprouts on page 274—3 or 4 of each would be enough per serving.

Chestnut Purée

A purée of chestnuts, with its wonderfully rich, almost sweet taste, goes beautifully with duck, goose, turkey, and pork—such as suckling pig. And a purée is much easier to make than whole chestnuts. You still have to peel them, and you will need more chestnuts for a purée, but you don't have to worry when they break apart.

For 6 servings, purée the cooked chestnuts in the master recipe—using a food processor or a vegetable mill and adding a little of their cooking juices as needed. Turn the purée into a saucepan and stir over moderately high heat to evaporate excess moisture—the purée should be thick enough to hold its shape softly in a spoon. Beat in butter and seasonings to taste.

MUSHROOMS

Here is a miscellaneous collection of techniques for cultivated mushrooms, so often called for in good cooking. It is said that mushrooms contain a natural MSG, or taste enhancer, which is undoubtedly why they are so often paired with chicken, veal, and fish dishes as a garnish or an accompaniment.

Buying and storing cultivated mushrooms. The caps should be firm and dry, and should look fresh with no bruised spots, the stems fresh and firm. Mushrooms will keep in the refrigerator a day or so, loosely packed in paper towels and stored in a plastic bag.

Trimming. Just before cooking, shave the ends off the stems to reach the clean flesh. If your recipe calls for mushroom caps, cut the stems off close to the bottom of the caps. Whatever their use, if there is a separation between cap and stem, break off the stem where it attaches inside the cap, so that you can wash out any grit lodged there.

> *SPECIAL NOTE*
>
> *Mushroom Amounts*
>
> 1 quart of whole mushrooms = ½ pound
> 1 quart of sliced or quartered mushrooms = 1⅓ to 1½ cups sautéed
> 1 quart of fresh mushrooms = ½ cup mushroom duxelles (sautéed diced mushrooms)

To wash or not to wash. If the mushrooms are clearly clean with no separation of cap from stem and no trace of sand, either dust them with a very soft brush or rub gently with a towel. But if there is the slightest doubt, wash them: drop them into a large bowl of cold water, swish them about for 4 to 5 seconds, then lift them out with your hands to a colander, leaving any sand behind. If more than a few grains of sand remain in the bowl, repeat the process. Pat them dry in a towel.

Cutting and Slicing Mushrooms

QUARTERED MUSHROOM CAPS. *Set a mushroom cap dome side up on your work surface. Cut it in half vertically; cut the half in half or into thirds, depending on the size you wish.*

SLICED MUSHROOM CAPS. *Set a mushroom cap dome side up on your work surface. Using your thumb as a pusher at one end, and your knuckles as a guide at the other, slice straight down, letting the side of the knife hit your knuckles as you push the mushroom forward after each slice. Practice every chance you get, in order to slice with speed and style.*

DICED OR CHOPPED MUSHROOMS. *You may use just the stems for this, and the food processor makes short work of it. Whether stems, caps, or whole, first chop them roughly by hand, then chop in the machine 2 cups at a time with half a dozen one-second on-off pulses.*

MUSHROOM STEMS. *Besides their use as chopped mushrooms, stems may also be combined with quartered mushroom caps simply by cutting the stems into wedges.*

Slicing and quartering mushrooms

Simmered Mushroom Caps

You may want these as the garnish, for instance, to a fish platter or an aspic, or to accompany other vegetables. They should cook with a little lemon juice to stay pale in color, but be sure not to add too much—the amount of lemon must be effective, but its taste should be hardly evident.

For 10 large mushroom caps, plain or fluted

10 mushroom caps 2½ inches across, trimmed and washed
¼ cup water
About 1 Tbs freshly squeezed lemon juice
A big pinch of salt
1 Tbs butter, optional

SPECIAL EQUIPMENT SUGGESTED:
A stainless saucepan with cover

Toss the mushroom caps in the saucepan with the water, lemon juice, and salt. Add the optional butter, bring to the simmer, cover, and simmer 2 to 3 minutes, just until softened. Keep the mushrooms in their cooking liquid until shortly before you are to serve them; include the liquid in whatever sauce you are making.

Broiled Mushroom Caps

Use these as a garnish for steaks or in a vegetable combination. You might fill the broiled caps with a Béarnaise sauce, for instance, to accompany roast tenderloin of beef in a glamorous way. These are definitely a last-minute affair if they are to remain fresh and keep their shape.

For 6 large mushroom caps

6 mushroom caps 2½ inches across, stemmed, washed, and dried
2 Tbs clarified butter (page 139), clear melted butter, or olive oil
Salt

SPECIAL EQUIPMENT SUGGESTED:
A pastry brush; a baking pan large enough to hold the mushrooms in one layer

Brush the mushroom caps inside and out with the butter or oil, and arrange them dome side up in the pan. Set them about 3 inches from the hot broiler element for 2 to 3 minutes, until the domes are bubbling lightly. Turn the mushrooms hollow side up, brush with a little more butter or oil, salt lightly, and broil 2 to 3 minutes more, until just tender when pierced with a knife. Their delicious juices will collect in their hollows.

Stuffed Mushroom Caps

Stuffed mushrooms could well be a first course—always difficult to think of something new and different for that. Or they could be part of an elegant vegetable garnish or vegetable platter. Although you may use any filling you wish, this is a sensible one since the chopped stems plus wine and seasonings fill the caps.

For 6 large mushrooms

½ cup mushroom duxelles made
  with the stems (see Special Note
  on page 314), or another stuffing
  of your choice
2 to 3 Tbs heavy cream
2 to 3 Tbs crumbs from fresh white
  bread
A big pinch of dried tarragon
Salt and freshly ground pepper
6 mushrooms 3½ inches across,
  stemmed
2 to 3 Tbs clarified butter (page 139)
  or clear melted butter
2 Tbs finely grated Swiss cheese

Assembling. Blend the duxelles in a bowl with the cream; add enough bread crumbs to make a mass that will hold its shape softly in a spoon. Season nicely to taste with tarragon, salt, and pepper. Brush the caps with butter, and spoon the stuffing into the cavities. Spread a pinch of grated cheese over the stuffing, and arrange the mushrooms in the baking dish.

*Ahead-of-time note: May be prepared in advance to this point.

Baking. About 20 minutes before serving, bake in the upper middle level of a preheated 400°F oven, just until the caps are tender when pierced with a small knife.

Sautéed Mushrooms

Sautéed mushrooms with omelettes, in chicken stews and beef ragouts— sautéed mushrooms go almost everywhere. An important point here is to sauté them so their juices do not exude, which is mostly a matter of high heat and not too many mushrooms in the pan at once.

For 2 to 2½ cups of sliced or quartered mushrooms

1 Tbs butter
1 tsp light olive oil or cooking oil
6 cups fresh mushrooms, trimmed,
  washed, dried, and quartered or
  sliced
½ Tbs chopped shallot or scallion
Salt and freshly ground pepper

SPECIAL EQUIPMENT SUGGESTED:
A 10-inch frying pan, preferably no-stick

Set the frying pan over high heat with the butter and oil. When the butter foam begins to subside, toss in the mushrooms. Toss frequently, swirling the pan by its handle, for several minutes, while the mushrooms absorb the butter. In a minute or two it reappears on their surface; toss with the chopped shallot or scallion a moment or two more if you wish them to brown lightly. Toss with a sprinkling of salt and grinds of fresh pepper. If they are to be part of a vegetable garnish, the sooner you serve them, the better.

VARIATION

Sautéed Mushrooms, Persillade
With bread crumbs, garlic, and parsley

When sautéed with garlic and parsley, mushrooms take on a distinctly new personality. Serve them with small roast or broiled birds, lamb chops, omelettes, or fried eggs.

Sauté the mushrooms as directed in the preceding master recipe. When they are done and almost beginning to brown, toss them with ½ cup of fresh white bread crumbs, sautéing for a good moment more. Then toss with a large clove of minced garlic and a handful of chopped parsley.

SPECIAL NOTE

Fluted Mushroom Caps

Hold a mushroom cap upright in your left hand. Grip a small, sharp knife tightly in your right hand with your right thumb resting on the cap, as illustrated. Rotate the mushroom *toward* you, starting at its crown; the mushroom cuts itself against the tightly held knife, making shallow grooves in the cap.

Fluting mushrooms

Mushroom Duxelles

Finely diced sautéed mushrooms

Duxelles is a concentrate of mushroom flavor, dry and compact—a
quick flavoring for sauces and stews,
also for stuffings and braises.

For about ½ cup

**4 cups fresh mushrooms or
    mushroom stems, diced
2 Tbs butter
2 Tbs minced shallots or scallions
Salt and freshly ground pepper
2 Tbs Port or Madeira, optional**

By handfuls, twist the mushrooms in
the corner of a towel to extract their
juices. Heat the butter to bubbling,
and sauté the mushrooms in hot butter over moderately high heat, stirring and tossing, until the pieces
begin to separate from each other—3
to 4 minutes. Add the shallots or
scallions and sauté a moment more;
season to taste. Add the optional
wine, letting it boil down rapidly to
nothing. For storage, pack into a
covered jar; refrigerate or freeze.

Whole baked onions

Big Baked Onions

Onions and hamburgers are a natural
combination, and a splendid way to
do them is to find yourself great big
ones, and to bake them whole, skin
and all.

*For each 3-inch ½-pound onion, 1 per
person*

1 Tbs or so butter or sour cream

Baking—1 hour or more. Preheat the
oven to 400°F, and place the onions
root side down (pick onions that will
stand up straight) on a baking sheet
lined with foil. Set them in the
middle level of the oven and bake
until they are definitely soft throughout when pressed and when pricked
deeply with a small knife or skewer.

Microwave baking: These do well
in the microwave one or two at a
time. I always prick them in several
places first, and count on 15 to 20
minutes—watch so that they do not
overcook.

Serving. Keep them warm until ready
to serve. At serving time, slit the
tops and place a pat of butter or a
spoonful of sour cream in each. To
eat them, scoop the warm flesh out of
the surrounding skin.

VARIATION

Baked Onions Gratinéed with Cheese

1 or 2 onion halves per person

The preceding baked whole onions
Salt and freshly ground pepper
2 Tbs butter per onion
3 Tbs grated Swiss or Parmesan
cheese per onion

When the onions are tender, cut them in half through the roots. Salt and pepper the flesh side of each half, spread on a tablespoon of butter and 1½ tablespoons of cheese. About 15 minutes before serving, set the halves flesh side up and return to the upper third level of a 400°F oven to reheat and to brown the cheese lightly.

Caramelized Onion Quarters

This attractive way to do onions is one suggested by my colleague Nancy Barr when we were doing our articles for *Parade* magazine. It takes more attention than big baked whole onions, but the results are unusual and delicious. Serve them with steaks, chops, broiled chicken, or fish (see illustration page 157).

For 6 servings, 2 onion quarters per person

3 big ½-pound onions 3 inches in
diameter
3 Tbs or more good olive oil
Salt
1 Tbs or so red-wine vinegar

Preparing the onions. Shave off the root and point ends of the onions, being careful to leave the onion layers attached together at the root. Quarter the onions lengthwise, but do not peel them.

Preliminary baking. Place them skin side down in an oiled pan, paint with olive oil, and sprinkle lightly with salt. Cover with foil and bake in the middle level of a 350°F oven for about 30 minutes, or until tender when pierced.

Final baking. Uncover, paint with more oil, and sprinkle each quarter with a few drops of red-wine vinegar. Continue baking 40 to 60 minutes more, turning the onions onto one side, then the other, as they brown lightly, and baste with the oil in the pan.

*Ahead-of-time note: May be baked in advance and reheated. The onions are also good cold, with cold meats and poultry.

VEGETABLE MIXTURES

BOTH A RAGOUT AND A
 BOUQUET OF STEAMED
 VEGETABLES,
TWO GREAT EGGPLANT
 DISHES,
A CRANBERRY CHUTNEY, AND
A PRUNE AND APPLE GARNISH

Here is a motley crew that defies the categories of the grand design, starting out with a versatile ragout of mixed vegetables.

A Vegetable Ragout

A Vegetable Ragout
Free-form sauté of mixed vegetables

When you are not in the mood for an elaborate dinner, this informal recipe encourages you to sauté or wok at will, all in one pan. For a meatless meal, as an example, omit the sausages suggested here, or, if you are in a carnivorous state, add bacon or ham or chicken livers. Count on one or two of each vegetable per person, and start with those that take the longest to cook. The following is just a suggestion.

(continued)

A Vegetable Ragout (*continued*)

For 6 servings

**6 to 9 pork breakfast sausages
1 head of garlic, with large cloves if
   possible
6 each: medium "boiling" potatoes,
   carrots, and turnips
Olive oil or fresh peanut oil, optional
Salt and freshly ground pepper
A good pinch of thyme or mixed
   dried herbs
1 cup or so chicken broth
8 to 10 fresh mushrooms
1 large green or red bell pepper, or
   half of each
A small handful of fresh parsley,
   chopped**

SPECIAL EQUIPMENT SUGGESTED:
*A 10-inch frying pan for the sausages; a
12-inch frying pan or chicken fryer, or
a wok, for the main cooking (no-stick
lining recommended)*

The sausages and garlic. Slice the sausages into ½-inch pieces, and sauté
them slowly in the pan, letting them
brown lightly but without burning
the fat. Smash the garlic with your
fist on your work surface to separate
the cloves; drop the cloves into a pan
of boiling water and boil 15 seconds.
Remove, and slip off the skins.

The vegetables. Start peeling the potatoes and cutting them into quarters or
sixths (all vegetables should be cut
about the same size). Film the large
pan with ¹⁄₁₆ inch of sausage fat and/
or oil, set over moderate heat, and
add the potatoes as they are prepared.
Continue with the carrots, adding
them to the pan and tossing frequently to prevent sticking. Peel,
cut, and add the turnips. Season

lightly with salt, pepper, and herbs;
toss in the garlic and the browned
sausage pieces.

Continuing the cooking. After the vegetables have cooked 10 minutes or so,
pour in a ¼-inch layer of chicken
broth. Season lightly, cover, and simmer slowly until the vegetables are
almost tender. Meanwhile, trim,
wash, and quarter the mushrooms;
quarter and seed the pepper, and slice
crosswise. Add them to the pan when
the simmering vegetables are ready.
Baste and turn the vegetables; cover
and cook another few minutes.

*Ahead-of-time note: May be completed somewhat in advance to this
point. Set aside uncovered; reheat before proceeding.

Finishing. Boil off any remaining liquid. Correct seasoning, and fold in
the parsley. Serve as is or as follows.

Other serving suggestions.

Cheese topping. Spread several
tablespoons of grated Swiss cheeseon
top, and run the pan under a hot
broiler until the cheese is bubbling
and lightly browned.

Egg topping #1. Top each serving
with a fried or poached egg.

Egg topping #2—the frittata. Beat
up 4 or 5 eggs with a sprinkling of
salt and freshly ground pepper, pour
them over the warm vegetables,
shaking the pan to distribute the
eggs. Strew grated cheese on top, and
run under the broiler to brown the
top briefly.

A Bouquet of Steamed Vegetables

A savory group to serve with a boiled
dinner

Here you boil-steam the leeks in
chicken broth, then use that aromatic
liquid to baste and steam first the cabbage, then the carrots. Shortly before
serving, they all warm up together in
their heady broth, while the potatoes
steam by themselves.

*For 6 servings, 1 or 2 of each vegetable
per person*

**6 medium leeks
Salt
3 to 4 cups chicken broth
1 large cabbage (about 2 pounds)
3 Tbs melted butter, optional
12 slim carrots (or larger carrots cut
   into wedges)
12 red-skinned "boiling" potatoes 1¾
   inches across**

SPECIAL EQUIPMENT SUGGESTED:
*A large skillet or flameproof casserole
for the leeks, a steaming basket and covered saucepan for the other vegetables; a
bulb baster; a baking dish and foil for
final warming-up*

Leeks. Trim and wash the leeks, and
cut into 8-inch lengths, as described
on page 298. Drop them into boiling
water and boil 2 minutes, refresh in
cold water, and drain (to set color).
Arrange the leeks in one or two layers, salt lightly, cover by 1 inch with
chicken broth, and simmer uncovered until just tender—10 minutes.
Arrange them in the baking dish,
leaving the liquid in the pan.

A Bouquet of Steamed Vegetables

Cabbage. Cut the cabbage into 6 wedges, remove the cores and set the wedges cut side up in the vegetable steamer. Salt lightly, dribble on the optional melted butter, and baste with the liquid from the leeks. Steam about 15 minutes, basting several times with the liquid in the pan. Arrange in the baking dish with the leeks.

Carrots. Trim and peel the carrots. Leave them whole if young and tender; otherwise, quarter or halve them. Arrange them in the steamer; cover and steam 10 minutes, or until tender. Arrange them with the other vegetables and pour the remaining steaming liquid over all.

*Ahead-of-time note: Leeks, cabbage, and carrots may be cooked ahead; to reheat, cover with foil and place in a

300°F oven while the potatoes steam. I think it is safer to do the potatoes at the last minute, since they can go off in taste otherwise.

Potatoes. Scrub the potatoes and shave a circle of skin off their midriffs. Arrange them in the steaming basket and add 2 inches of water to the pan. About 25 minutes before you plan to serve, cover the steamer, turn on the heat; steam them about 20 minutes, or until a small knife pierces them easily.

Serving. Arrange the vegetables around your meat, or upon a separate platter. Rapidly boil down their aromatic cooking juices until almost syrupy and either pour them over the leeks, cabbage, and carrots, or add them to whatever sauce you may be serving.

MASTER RECIPE

Ratatouille

Eggplant and zucchini casserole with tomatoes, peppers, garlic, and Mediterranean seasonings

Numerous recipes for this wonderful Provençal eggplant casserole exist, and I think the best of them direct that the vegetables cook separately, then finish with a short communal simmer. Thus each one, rather than entering into a mish-mash relationship, retains its own character.

Ratatouille is especially good with roast lamb or beef, as well as with egg dishes, steaks, chops, and broiled fish. Serve it cold as a salad or with cold meats, and it is fine on a picnic. For illustration of the finished dish, see page 216.

For 6 to 8 servings

1 pound fresh shiny firm eggplant
Salt, as needed
1 pound zucchini
¼ to ⅓ cup olive oil, as needed
Thyme, oregano, or a bottled herb blend
1 pound (3½ cups, sliced) onions
2 or 3 large green bell peppers (2 cups sliced)
3 large cloves of garlic, puréed
3 cups tomato pulp (fresh tomatoes peeled, seeded, juiced; or, out of season, half fresh tomatoes and half drained and seeded canned plum tomatoes)

SPECIAL EQUIPMENT SUGGESTED:
1 or 2 lightly oiled jelly-roll pans for baking eggplant; a 12-inch frying pan for sautéing; a lightly oiled 2½-to 3-quart covered casserole 2 inches deep for final cooking

(continued)

Ratatouille (continued)

Preliminaries. Remove green caps but do not peel the eggplant; cut it into lengthwise or crosswise slices ⅜ inch thick. Salt lightly on each side and spread on paper towels. Scrub the zucchini, shave off the stem and bud ends, but do not peel; cut lengthwise into 2-inch slices ⅜ inch thick. Salt the zucchini slices, as for the eggplant. Let both vegetables stand 20 minutes; pat dry in paper towels.

Baking the eggplant. Preheat the oven to 400°F. Arrange the eggplant in the jelly-roll pan or pans, paint lightly with oil, and sprinkle with herbs. Cover with aluminum foil and bake 15 to 20 minutes, until just tender, but do not overcook: the slices must hold their shape.

Arranging ratatouille elements

The rest of the vegetables. Film the frying pan with 1/16 inch of olive oil. Dry the zucchini slices, and brown lightly on each side; remove to paper towels. Adding a little more oil if necessary, sauté the onions until tender but not browned. Stir in the peppers and garlic; fold and toss over moderately high heat for several minutes, until fairly tender. Set aside ½ cup of the tomatoes. Fold the rest into the onions and peppers; toss, adding salt and herbs to taste, until

the tomatoes have rendered their juice; continue for several minutes until the juices have almost boiled off.

Finishing the ratatouille—about 30 minutes. Set aside 4 of the best-looking slices of eggplant for final decoration. Arrange the rest of the vegetables in several layers in the casserole, starting and ending with the onion-pepper-tomato mixture as illustrated. Arrange the reserved tomato and eggplant decoratively over the top. Cover and bring to the simmer over moderate heat, either on top of the stove or in a 325°F oven. When bubbling gently, uncover, tip the casserole, and baste with the juices rendered; repeat several times until the juices have almost evaporated.

Serving. Serve hot, warm, or cold.

Eggplant Parmigiano
Eggplant slices baked with Parmesan cheese

For 20 to 24 slices, serving 6 to 8

2 shiny firm perfect eggplants, about 9 by 3½ to 4 inches
Salt as needed
Olive oil or salad oil
A dried herb mixture such as Provençal or Italian herb seasoning
2 cups excellent home-made fresh tomato sauce (page 358)
About 1 cup grated Parmesan cheese

SPECIAL EQUIPMENT SUGGESTED:
1 or 2 jelly-roll pans; a lightly oiled shallow baking dish, such as an oval 9 by 12 by 2 inches

The eggplant. Cut, salt, oil, season, and bake the eggplant slices as described in the preceding ratatouille.

Final arrangement and baking. Arrange the slices overlapping in the baking dish, spreading each first with a spoonful of tomato sauce, then with a portion of grated cheese. Drizzle a little oil on top. Fifteen minutes or so before you wish to serve, bake in the upper third level of a preheated 400°F oven. Be careful not to overcook: the contents should be just bubbling hot and the exuding cheese should be browning lightly.

VARIATIONS

Miniature Eggplant Pizzas

These baked eggplant slices with pizza toppings are attractive in a vegetarian combination, or arrange them around a main event, be it an omelette, a steak, or a serving of roast lamb.

For about 24 slices, serving 6 to 8

Ingredients for the preceding eggplant Parmigiano

Cut the eggplant in crosswise slices ⅜-inch thick, and salt it as directed in the master recipe for ratatouille; oil, season, and bake them on jelly-roll pans as also described. When tender, spread on each a generous spoonful of the tomato sauce and an equally generous sprinkling of grated cheese; dribble on droplets of olive oil. Shortly before serving, run under a hot broiler for a minute or so to brown the cheese lightly.

An Untraditional Moussaka
Baked eggplant slices with lamb and a cheese topping

The perfect finale to a leg of lamb, or, seeing it is such a tasty dish, start from scratch with 1½ pounds of raw ground lamb—it is to be sautéed anyway. Serve moussaka hot with a green salad and a hearty red wine, like a zinfandel. Or take it along cold, on a picnic.

For 8 servings

**2 fine firm shiny eggplants 1½
    pounds each**
Salt
Olive oil
**Dried herbs such as rosemary or a
    mixture**

The lamb

**½ cup lightly pressed down parsley
    sprigs, washed and well dried**
**2 medium onions (to make about 1½
    cups, minced)**
2 large cloves of garlic, puréed
About 3 cups cooked lamb
**2 cups drained and strained canned
    Italian plum tomatoes**
**¾ cup red wine or dry white French
    vermouth**
⅛ tsp allspice
Salt and freshly ground pepper
**1 "large" egg, beaten to blend in a
    small bowl**

The topping

3 Tbs butter
¼ cup flour
2 cups hot milk
Salt and freshly ground white pepper
**1 cup grated mozzarella cheese or
    Swiss cheese**
A small pinch of nutmeg
**½ cup grated Swiss cheese, to top
    the topping**

An Untraditional Moussaka

SPECIAL EQUIPMENT SUGGESTED:
A 12-inch frying pan for the lamb mixture; baking pans and foil for the eggplant slices; a food processor; a 3-quart baking-serving dish 2½ to 3 inches deep

The eggplant. Cut into slices, salt, and then bake the eggplant as described for the preceding master recipe for ratatouille.

The lamb. Meanwhile, chop the parsley in the food processor; remove and reserve. Add the onions and chop with on-off pulses; remove and sauté them in the frying pan with 2 tablespoons of oil, adding the puréed garlic. While the onions cook, cut the lamb into 1-inch chunks and chop by cupfuls in the processor—it should not be too fine. When the onions are tender, in 6 to 8 minutes, add the lamb, raise heat to moderately high, and sauté several minutes

to brown very lightly. Then fold in the tomatoes, wine, parsley, and allspice, and a little salt and pepper as needed. Simmer over moderate heat, stirring frequently, for half an hour, or until the mixture is thick enough to hold its shape softly in a spoon. Taste analytically, and correct seasoning. Remove from heat and blend in the egg.

Into the baking dish. Lightly oil the baking dish. Line it with a layer of eggplant slices, pressing them down and together, spoon on half of the meat mixture, add another layer of eggplant, then the rest of the meat, and end with a layer of eggplant.

The topping. Make 2 cups of standard white sauce by cooking the butter and flour together for 2 minutes without coloring; off heat, blend in the hot

(continued)

An Untraditional Moussaka (*continued*)

milk; season, and simmer 3 minutes (full details are on page 272). Remove sauce from heat. Blend in the cup of mozzarella or Swiss cheese. Season nicely with salt, pepper, and a speck of nutmeg. Spoon the hot sauce over the top of the eggplant, shake the casserole to let some of the sauce sink down in, then spread over all the ½ cup of grated Swiss cheese.

*Ahead-of-time note: May be prepared even a day in advance to this point. Cover and refrigerate if the wait is longer than ½ hour.

The cooking. Bake for 45 minutes or so (longer if dish has been refrigerated) in the middle level of a preheated 350°F oven until bubbling hot and the top has browned lightly. Serve warm or tepid but not too hot. Good cold, too.

POTATOES

Man, it is said, could live on potatoes alone, with just a bit of fat now and then to keep the motor running smoothly. Potato recipes seem endless, so versatile and popular is this most valuable of vegetables. The French, to whom the potato came rather late in life, appear to have developed more potato recipes than any group. Their famous French culinary compendium *Larousse Gastronomique*, as an example, has 99 listings in the potato category; the equally famous *Répertoire de la Cuisine*, 118. Here I have only a dozen, but they are among my favorites.

Choose the Right Potato. Unless we grow our own potatoes, our supermarkets usually offer us only three varieties: bakers, boilers, and all-purpose. Bakers are floury, and with certain exceptions you want them for mashing; boilers have less starch, and are designed to hold their shape reasonably well when boiled or when sliced in casseroles and salads. For the recipes here in this book, "baking" potatoes mean russets—and all russets do *not* come from Idaho, much as the worthy growers from that great state would like us to believe. "Boiling" potatoes mean new potatoes, some of the yellow-fleshed potatoes like Yukon Gold, and those with red skins. You will find a detailed run-down on growing and cooking potatoes, by the way, in Marian Morash's splendid tome *The Victory Garden Cookbook* (New York: Knopf, 1982 and reprints).

MASHED POTATO DISHES

Boxed dehydrated mashed potatoes can be remarkably good when properly buttered up. But a dish of homemade mashed potatoes, freshly cooked and rich with milk and butter, smelling and tasting like real potato, is a soul-warming treat. Here they are pure and beautiful, both white and sweet potatoes, followed by a quick way to dress them *en duchesse*. See also the golden purées with other vegetables on page 285.

MASTER RECIPE

Homemade Mashed Potatoes

For 6 servings

4 or 5 large "baking" potatoes
Salt
½ cup or so milk and/or cream, heated in a saucepan
2 or more Tbs softened butter
Freshly ground white pepper

SPECIAL EQUIPMENT SUGGESTED: *A potato ricer, or an electric mixer*

Preliminary cooking. You may bake or steam the potatoes whole before mashing them, or boil them in pieces as suggested here. Wash and peel the potatoes and cut into quarters. Set in a saucepan with lightly salted water to cover (1½ teaspoons salt per quart of water). Bring to the boil, cover loosely, and boil 10 to 15 minutes or longer, until potatoes are tender when pierced with a knife. Cut a piece in half and eat a bit to be sure they are just done; undercooked potatoes will not mash properly. Drain the water out of the pan (you may wish to save it for soup making); toss the potatoes over moderate heat for a moment, until they begin to film the pan; this is to evaporate excess moisture.

Mashing. While still warm, either put the potatoes through a ricer (my preference) and return to the pan, or place in the large bowl of your electric mixer and, using the wire whip attachment and moderate speed; purée them with ¼ cup of the milk and/or cream.

Mashing note: Home-style mashed potatoes are becoming trendy in bistro-type restaurants at this writing, and they're careful to leave in some lumps so we'll presume they're not instant mashed—or perhaps they use instant plus one or two lumpily mashed fresh potatoes. Hmm!

Seasoning. Beat in driblets of hot milk and/or cream, alternating with ½ tablespoons of butter—careful not to make them too soft. Season with salt and pepper to taste. The sooner you can serve them, the better.

*_Ahead-of-time note:_ If you cannot serve at once, beat in only a minimum of milk, etc. (Turn the potatoes into a saucepan if you have used an electric mixer.) Set in another pan of hot but not simmering water, and cover the potatoes loosely—they must stay warm to retain their fresh quality, and they must have air circulation or they develop an off-taste. At serving time, bring the water to the simmer, beating the potatoes with a wooden spoon; then beat in more hot milk or cream and soft butter to your taste.

VARIATION

Garlic Mashed Potatoes

These are marvelous with almost anything, a subtle and fragrant but mellow touch of garlic in a rich mass of home-cooked mashed potatoes. After mashing the potatoes in the preceding master recipe, purée and blend in a head of garlic cloves simmered in cream (see Special Note on this page), then beat in more seasonings and cream and/or butter as you see fit.

SPECIAL NOTE

Braised Garlic Cloves

For use in vegetable mixtures or as a garnish

Select a head of large garlic cloves and peel them (see Special Note on page 283). Place in a small covered saucepan with 2 tablespoons of butter and cook over low heat 10 to 15 minutes, until very tender. They should not color more than a creamy yellow.

Braised Garlic Cloves Simmered in Cream

To be used as a garnish, or to be puréed and used in sauces or other purées

Pour ½ cup or so of heavy cream into the braised garlic, add a good pinch of salt and freshly ground white pepper, and simmer over low heat for 5 to 10 minutes, until meltingly tender.

Mashed Sweet Potatoes or Yams

More unusual is a purée of sweet potatoes or yams, which go so well with turkey, goose, duck, and pork. They are attractive, also, served in a dish with mashed white potatoes, to produce a Two Potato Purée. Or form them into little peaks in a baking dish as described in the variation following. The real yam, by the way, is a tropical vegetable we don't see in this country, although for an unknown reason we continue to use the term

yam for sweet potatoes that are dark-skinned and have dark orange flesh. I shall use both terms, but in the American sense.

For 6 servings

4 or 5 large sweet potatoes or yams (about 2 pounds)
4 or more Tbs softened butter (you can use milk and/or cream, but butter is better!)
½ tsp or so grated fresh ginger, optional
Salt and freshly ground white pepper

Scrub the potatoes under warm running water. Bake on a foil-lined pan in the middle level of a 425°F oven for an hour or more, until tender throughout when pierced with a knife. When done, cut in half and scoop the flesh into a heavy saucepan. Purée with a mixing fork or a potato masher. Set over low heat and beat in the butter (or warm milk and/or cream) by tablespoons, the optional ginger, and salt and pepper to taste.

*_Ahead-of-time note:_ If not served shortly, keep as suggested for the preceding mashed potatoes.

VARIATION

A Peaked Purée of Yams

Using a pastry bag with a ½-inch star tube, pipe the preceding finished purée into a buttered baking dish. Before serving, cover and reheat 10 minutes or so in a 325°F oven.

Duchess Potatoes

Duchess Potatoes

Fast and fancy mashed potato shapes—form them now, bake them later.

For about 2½ cups

3 egg yolks
2 cups plain firm warm mashed potatoes (omit the cream, butter, etc., in the master recipe)
3 Tbs butter
2 Tbs heavy cream
Salt and freshly ground white pepper
Freshly grated nutmeg
½ cup finely grated Swiss cheese

SPECIAL EQUIPMENT SUGGESTED:
A pastry bag with ½-inch star tube opening (see Special Note, page 460); 1 or 2 baking sheets, lightly buttered, dusted with flour, and excess knocked off

Beat the egg yolks one by one into the warm potatoes, then the butter and cream; season to taste. While still warm, pipe them onto the prepared baking sheets; sprinkle lightly with the cheese. Set aside at room temperature. Half an hour before serving, reheat and brown lightly in the upper third level of a 400°F oven.

SCALLOPED POTATO DISHES

Sliced potatoes baked in milk or broth or cream always go well with plain roast or broiled meats and poultry, and with steaks, chops, and hamburgers. They are good for a party, too, since you may bake the dish ahead and reheat it when the time comes.

MASTER RECIPE

Potatoes Dauphinoise
Scalloped potatoes baked in milk

This easy dish bakes quickly in a hot oven, or you may cook it on top of the stove as in the variation following. You may also make it fat-free, if you wish. The simple version here is without cheese, but you will find cheese in the variations, as well as in a version simmered luxuriously in heavy cream.

For 6 servings

2 to 2½ pounds "boiling" potatoes (6 to 7 cups, sliced)
1½ cups milk (use low-fat or skim milk, if you wish)
1 large clove of garlic, puréed
Salt and freshly ground white pepper
2 or more Tbs butter, optional

SPECIAL EQUIPMENT SUGGESTED:
A vegetable slicer or food processor is useful for even slices; a lightly buttered 8-cup baking dish 1½ to 2 inches deep, and flameproof if possible

Assembling. Preheat the oven to 425°F. Peel the potatoes, wash them, and cut into slices ⅛ inch thick.

Drop the slices, as you do them, into a bowl of cold water. Meanwhile, bring 1 cup of milk to the boil in the baking dish (or in a small saucepan if your dish is not flameproof; pour into the baking dish after adding the potatoes); add the puréed garlic, ¼ teaspoon of salt, and a few grinds of pepper. Drain the potatoes, spread them in the dish, adding a little more milk, if needed, to come three quarters of the way up the potatoes. Top with the optional butter, cut into bits.

Baking—about 25 minutes at 425°F. Bring again to the simmer, correct seasonings, and set in the upper third level of the preheated oven until nicely browned and the milk has been almost entirely absorbed—about 25 minutes; 10 minutes or so more if your dish is not flameproof.

*Ahead-of-time note: Bake the potatoes until barely tender. Set aside uncovered; when cool, cover and refrigerate. To finish cooking, preheat the oven to 425°F. Bring the potatoes to the simmer on top of the stove (or in the oven), adding a few spoonfuls of milk if needed, and finish cooking for about 10 minutes.

VARIATIONS

Scalloped Potatoes Savoyarde

The addition of onions, herbs, and cheese makes this a more assertive potato dish than the Dauphinoise. However, it is done the same way. Before you begin, sauté 3 cups of thinly sliced onions in 2 tablespoons of butter; provide yourself with 1½ cups of coarsely grated Swiss cheese, and 2 cups or so of chicken or beef stock blended with a good pinch of mixed dried herbs. Fill the baking dish with layers of onions, sliced potatoes, and cheese, ending with a layer of cheese. Pour in the stock to come halfway up, and bake about 40 minutes in the lower middle level of a preheated 425°F oven, sucking up juices with a bulb baster and spraying them over the potatoes several times.

Fat-free variation. If you are on a fat-free kick, you may omit the cheese as well as the butter—simmering the onions 5 minutes or so in the stock before adding the potatoes.

Stove-top variation: As an alternative to oven baking, you may turn the preceding fat-free version into a stove-top Savoyarde except for a light cheese topping. Follow the technique in the next recipe.

Stove-Top Dauphinoise

Bring 1 cup of the Dauphinoise milk to the boil on top of the stove in a no-stick frying pan, adding the garlic, sliced potatoes, seasonings, optional butter, and additional milk to come two thirds of the way up the potatoes. Cover and simmer 15 to 20 minutes (watch for boil-overs), or until the potatoes are tender and the milk has been almost absorbed. Uncover the pan. Shortly before serving, spread on ⅓ cup of grated Swiss cheese and set 4 to 5 inches below a hot broiler element to heat through and brown the top nicely.

Scalloped Potatoes Baked in Cream

Scalloped Potatoes Baked in Cream

Serve these heavenly potatoes with duck, chicken, steak, roasts, or just by themselves. They simmer in a combination of heavy cream and half-and-half, and an important plus is that you can complete the initial cooking hours in advance. I, for one, would far rather swoon over a small spoonful of this ambrosia than a large ladleful of instant mashed made with skim milk!

The first time I had these potatoes was when Catherine Brandel, who has cooked at Chez Panisse and at the Mondavi Vineyard, suggested them for one of our elaborate duck dishes in *Parade* magazine. Here is my version of that memorable experience.

For 6 servings

1½ to 2 cups each heavy cream and half-and-half cream
1 large clove of garlic, puréed
Salt and freshly ground white pepper
1 imported bay leaf
2 to 2½ pounds "boiling" potatoes (6 to 7 cups, sliced)
3 to 4 Tbs grated Swiss cheese

SPECIAL EQUIPMENT SUGGESTED:
A heavy-bottomed 3-quart stainless or enameled saucepan with cover; a buttered shallow baking and serving dish (or individual serving dishes) for the final baking

Assembling. Pour 1½ cups each of heavy and half-and-half cream into the saucepan. Stir in the garlic, ½ teaspoon of salt, several grinds of

(continued)

Assembling the potatoes

Grated potato galettes

Scalloped Potatoes Baked in Cream
(*continued*)

pepper, and the bay leaf. Slice the potatoes evenly ⅛ inch thick, dropping
them as sliced into the cream. When
all are in, add more cream if necessary, to cover the potatoes by ½ inch.

Preliminary cooking—1 to 1½ hours.
Bring to below the simmer and maintain at just below the simmer for an
hour or more, until the potatoes are
perfectly tender. Check frequently to
be sure they are not bubbling, since
that can cause the cream to curdle;
check also that the potatoes are not
sticking or scorching in the bottom of
the pan.

Into the baking dish. When tender,
correct seasoning and turn them into
the buttered baking and serving dish;
spread on the grated cheese.

*Ahead-of-time note: May be prepared
to this point several hours in advance. Cover when cool, and
refrigerate.

Final baking—20 minutes at 425°F.
About 20 minutes before serving, set
in the upper middle level of the preheated oven and bake until bubbling
hot and lightly browned on top: do
not overcook or the potatoes will be
dry rather than lush and creamy.

THREE POTATO GALETTES

It is useful at times to have a pan-
cake-type potato dish that you can put
such edibles upon as half a game hen,
a piece of duck, or even a fried egg.
Here are two stove-top models and
one for the oven.

Grated Potato Galettes

One of the crispest and most successful of potato pancakes, to my mind,
is made with grated cooked potatoes.
You may form and sauté them either
as thin and lacy as a crêpe, or pan-
cake-thick.

MANUFACTURING SECRET. *I had
these for the first time at Sally and John
Darr's New York restaurant, La Tu-
lipe, and thought they were remarkably
good. Sally's sous-chef at that time was*
*Sara Moulton. With Sally's kind per-
mission, Sara relayed the important information that "baking" potatoes are
required for this particular dish, that
they are boiled the previous day so they
will be cold for proper grating, and
that the trick is to keep them slightly
underdone. Then the potato pieces will
stick together enough in the sauté pan so
that you can flip them over to brown the
other side.*

EQUIPMENT NOTE. *For the grating itself, I prefer the old-fashioned 4-sided
hand grater; the food processor produces
too many small shards.*

For 6 galettes about 5 inches across

**2 or 3 large "baking" potatoes about
12 ounces each**
Salt and freshly ground pepper
**½ cup or so clarified butter (page
139) or olive oil**

SPECIAL EQUIPMENT SUGGESTED:
A hand grater, with its large holes ¼ inch across; a no-stick frying pan or seasoned iron crêpe pan, bottom diameter of 5 to 5½ inches

Cooking the potatoes—several hours or a day in advance. Scrub the potatoes under hot running water, then steam them for 12 to 15 minutes, until the potatoes are almost but not quite cooked. In other words, they should not be floury—after 12 minutes, pierce one with a sharp small knife, which should just penetrate. Cut one of the potatoes in half crosswise: if there is a raw central core, steam 2 or 3 minutes more. (If the central core is not cooked through it can discolor!) Let cool uncovered; the potatoes must be thoroughly cold before you grate them.

Unmolded Stove-Top Anna

Grating the almost-cooked cold potatoes

Grating. Peel the cold potatoes and rub through the large holes of the grater onto a baking sheet or tray, as illustrated. Toss lightly with a sprinkling of salt and pepper, leaving them loosely massed; set aside until you are ready to continue.

Sautéing. Film a frying pan with ⅛ inch of clarified butter or oil, and, when hot, spread in ½ to ⅔ cup of grated potato (the amount depends on how thick a galette you want). Sauté over moderate heat for 4 to 5 minutes, pressing the potatoes together lightly with a spatula, until the bottom has crusted and browned. Flip over, and sauté to brown the other side a few minutes more. Transfer to a baking sheet, and keep warm while finishing the rest.

*Ahead-of-time note: The galettes may be sautéed somewhat ahead. Set aside uncovered, at room temperature. Reheat briefly in a 425°F oven.

ANOTHER PRESENTATION

Make a large galette in a 10- or 12-inch pan, and if you don't have the courage to flip, brown the top under the broiler. After a light browning on the top, you could then sprinkle it with grated Swiss cheese, and brown again.

The Stove-Top Anna
Mold of sliced potatoes and cheese

This is a frying-pan take-off on the famous Potatoes Anna, in which a mold of sliced potatoes is baked in a hot oven and then unmolded like a cake. The classic Anna is a spectacular dish, a *tour de force.* The Stove-Top Anna, on the other hand, is not much of a trick provided you have

(continued)

Arranging the Stove-Top Anna

The Stove-Top Anna (*continued*)

the right frying pan. You will note here that you may include slices of Swiss cheese if you wish, and it could then be a luncheon or supper main course to serve with fried or poached eggs and/or a green salad.

For 6 servings

2½ pounds "boiling" potatoes (about 10 cups, sliced)
⅓ to ½ cup clarified butter (page 139) or olive oil
4 ounces Swiss cheese, cut into slices ⅛ inch thick and about 1 by 1½ inches across (to make 1 cup), optional
Salt and freshly ground pepper
Freshly grated nutmeg

SPECIAL EQUIPMENT SUGGESTED:
A heavy 10-inch no-stick frying pan, or a very well seasoned cast-iron pan; a cover for the pan

Preparing the potatoes. One at a time, peel the potatoes and cut into fairly neat round slices 1¼ inches in diameter and ¼ inch thick. Drop them, as you do so, into a bowl of cold water. When all are done, drain the slices, and dry in a towel.

Preliminary cooking. Pour ¼ inch of clarified butter or olive oil into the frying pan, set over moderate heat,

and rapidly arrange an overlapping layer of potato slices in the pan as illustrated, shaking it gently from time to time to prevent sticking. Baste with a sprinkling of butter or oil, arrange a second layer over the first, and over this arrange a layer of the optional cheese slices. Season a third layer of potatoes with salt, pepper, and a speck of nutmeg. Continue filling the pan with potatoes, optional cheese, seasonings, and end with a layer of potatoes. When filled, shake the pan gently again, and let cook 3 to 5 minutes over moderately high heat to be sure the bottom is crusting.

Finishing the cooking. Then cover the pan and set over low heat for 45 minutes, or until the potatoes are tender when pierced with a small knife. (Be sure the heat is regulated so that the potatoes do not burn on the bottom.) Run a spatula all around the edge of the pan and underneath the potatoes to loosen them; unmold onto a hot serving dish.

*Ahead-of-time note: If done somewhat in advance, cover the potatoes loosely and keep in a warming oven or over almost-simmering water—they must have air circulation, and they must stay warm to retain their freshly cooked taste.

Oven-Roasted Potato Galettes

Thinly sliced potatoes tossed in butter or olive oil and seasonings, then roasted in a thin layer in the oven—they are lightly brown and tenderly crisp. Form them as a large serving in a tart ring, or make individual portions.

For 6 servings

1¼ to 1½ pounds "boiling" potatoes (3 large ones)
2 to 3 Tbs melted butter, olive oil, or duck, goose, or chicken fat
Seasonings: salt, freshly ground pepper, and, if you wish, thyme or mixed herbs, and/or puréed garlic

SPECIAL EQUIPMENT SUGGESTED:
A slicing device is useful; a no-stick baking surface is essential; if you wish a neat form choose a tart or flan ring, or individual rings

Preparing the potatoes. Preheat the oven to 400°F. Peel and slice the potatoes, and drop as you do them into a bowl of cold water. Drain and dry them thoroughly, then dry the bowl and return the potatoes to it. Toss the slices to coat them with the butter, oil, or fat, and whatever seasonings you have chosen.

Baking—30 to 40 minutes. Arrange the slices neatly (especially the bottom layer) in or on whatever you have chosen. Bake in the upper middle level of the preheated oven for 20 minutes; rapidly press them down with a spatula. Bake 15 to 20 minutes more, until the potatoes are lightly browned. Turn them over (if you easily can), and bake a few minutes more to brown the carefully arranged underside.

*Ahead-of-time note: When done somewhat ahead, they will keep nicely if they remain uncovered at room temperature; reheat for a few moments in the oven just before serving.

A Fast Sauté of Diced Potatoes

Here is a quick and crusty garnish for hamburgers, chops, or a sauté of chicken or of beef tenderloin.

For 6 servings

4 or 5 medium "boiling" potatoes
2 to 3 Tbs clarified butter (page 139), or half butter and half olive oil
Salt and freshly ground pepper
A pinch of thyme or mixed herbs, optional
1 Tbs or so butter to finish, optional
A sprinkle of chopped fresh parsley or chives, optional

SPECIAL EQUIPMENT SUGGESTED:
A 10-inch no-stick frying pan

Preparing the potatoes. Peel the potatoes and cut into ¾-inch slices; cut the slices into ¾-inch strips, and the strips into ¾-inch dice.

Sautéing. Drain and dry the potatoes. Heat the butter or butter and oil in the frying pan until very hot but not browning. Toss in the potatoes, lower heat to moderate, and sauté, tossing frequently. When they begin to brown lightly, toss with a sprinkling of salt and pepper and optional dried herbs. Continue until nicely browned and tender—10 to 15 minutes in all. If you wish, toss with a little additional butter, and fresh parsley or chives.

*Ahead-of-time note: Set uncovered over very low heat or in a pan of barely simmering water. The potatoes will keep their fresh taste for ½ hour or so if they remain just warm and are left uncovered.

WHITE RICE AND WILD RICE

What is free of cholesterol, low in sodium, packed with all eight of the essential amino acids, reasonable in price, easy to cook, non-allergenic, readily digestible, and is also, in spite of all this, really good to eat? It's regular white RICE, and you can do so many things with it, from soups to salads to main courses to delicious desserts. Now that we are advised by the nutritional worthies to consume a little less meat and more carbohydrates, and since we all want to shrink our food bills, rice is well worth our serious culinary consideration. For a few useful facts, see the Special Note on page 329.

 MASTER RECIPE

Plain Boiled White Rice

For 3 cups cooked rice, serving 4 to 6

1 cup plain white rice, enriched or not, and either long-grain or short-grain
2 cups water
1 tsp salt
1 to 2 Tbs butter (or olive oil or other fat), optional

SPECIAL EQUIPMENT SUGGESTED:
A heavy-bottomed 2½-quart saucepan with cover; a wooden fork (or something like it, for fluffing the rice without breaking the grains)

Measure the rice into the saucepan and stir in the 2 cups of water (either hot or cold; it makes no difference). Add the salt and optional butter.

Steam holes

Bring to the boil over high heat, stir up once thoroughly, and reduce heat to the simmer—slight movement and slow bubbling. Cover the pan and set the timer for 12 minutes (8 minutes for Italian arborio rice).

After 12 minutes. Take a quick peek at the rice: 12 minutes is probably not enough, but it is wiser to be safe than eventually gummy. The cooked rice is done, or almost done, when the liquid has been absorbed, and you see steam holes, as illustrated. Fork up a few grains—but do *not* stir it, because stirring at this point could turn the grains sticky. Bite into it. The grains should be very slightly *al dente*—with the very faintest crunch at the center, but almost tender; cover the pan and set it away from heat, where the rice will finish cooking in another 2 or 3 minutes. (If it is definitely not done, and liquid remains at the bottom of the pan, cover and simmer a few minutes more.)

(continued)

Plain Boiled White Rice (*continued*)

Rice is overcooked when the grains are splayed out at the ends; they should remain slightly rounded. You can still enjoy it, of course, but the rice will have lost much of its desirable texture and flavor.

If the rice is done but the liquid has not been absorbed, uncover the pan and set over moderately low heat for a few minutes to evaporate excess liquid. Or drain the rice, put it back in the pan, and toss lightly with a wooden fork over moderate heat.

If the rice is not tender but the liquid has boiled off. Sprinkle on droplets of water, cover, and cook a few minutes more.

*Ahead-of-time note: Reheating cooked rice. Once the rice has cooked, allow it to cool, and you can refrigerate it for a day or two before reheating. To reheat, first fluff it lightly with a wooden fork. Then you have several choices:

The frying pan. Sauté the rice lightly in butter, tossing and turning and fluffing with a wooden fork as it warms.

Double boiler. Turn the rice into a covered pan and set that in a larger pan of simmering water; add droplets of water, and fluff as it heats.

Steaming. If you have cooked your rice without butter, oil, or other fat, fold it into a clean, damp towel and set in a sieve or colander. Cover it, and place over a pan of simmering water; steam several minutes, until well heated through.

Braised Rice: Risotto

To give rice more character so that it can stand on its own, sauté the grains briefly in butter, then simmer as usual, but with herbs and onions, and chicken stock or beef stock rather than water. Note that this is the French risotto, not the Italian method.

For 3 cups cooked rice

⅓ cup finely minced onions
2 Tbs butter
1 cup unwashed raw white rice (Carolina long-grain works well in a risotto)
¼ cup dry white French vermouth, optional
2 cups light chicken stock heated in a small saucepan
Salt and freshly ground pepper
1 medium imported bay leaf (or a small herb bouquet—1 small bay leaf, ⅛ tsp thyme, and 3 parsley sprigs tied in washed cheesecloth)

SPECIAL EQUIPMENT SUGGESTED: *A heavy-bottomed 6-cup saucepan with cover; a wooden fork*

Sautéing the rice. Sauté the onions slowly in the butter for several minutes until soft and translucent. Stir in the rice and sauté, slowly stirring, for several minutes more until the grains, which first become translucent, turn a milky white. This step cooks the starchy coating and prevents the grains from sticking.

Braising. If you are using vermouth, stir it in now and let it boil down for a moment. Blend in the chicken stock, correct seasoning, and add the bay leaf or herb bouquet. Bring to the simmer, stir once thoroughly, then cover tightly and proceed as for the master recipe—regulating heat so that the rice cooks at the slow simmer without stirring again for 12 to 15 minutes, until almost tender—faintly *al dente.* Cover the pan and set aside for several minutes, while the rice finishes cooking.

Finishing the rice. While still warm, remove the bay leaf or herb bouquet, fluff the rice with a fork, and correct seasoning.

Vegetarian note. Substitute water for chicken stock, and double the onions and herbs.

Serving suggestions. Serve the rice as it is to accompany simply sauced fish or chicken dishes, or you may wish to make a more important vegetable or main course of it by folding in cream and/or grated cheese, or mushroom duxelles (see Special Note, page 314), diced sautéed eggplant or ham, and so forth. See also suggestions for the rice salads on page 369.

VARIATIONS

Curried Rice

Following the preceding recipe, blend a teaspoon of fragrant curry powder into the butter and onions as they cook, then proceed.

Variations continue on page 330

Rice Facts

More than 40,000 varieties of rice are grown in the world today, says the Rice Council of America. But in the United States, only a few of them are cultivated commercially. These fall into four main categories, and I am speaking only of white rice:

Long-grain rice is four to five times as long as it is wide and cooks up the fluffiest—the grains are less inclined to stick together. It is recommended for boiled rice, pilaffs, and salads.

Medium-grain rice is a little shorter and tenderer than long-grain and is especially good for rice desserts like our Louisiana Bavarian on page 448.

Short-grain rice is even tenderer and more inclined to stickiness than medium-grain. It is used widely by Oriental and Caribbean cooks.

Glutenous rice is short, plump, chalky white, and really sticky—used mostly for commercial gravies and some Oriental preparations.

A Note on Imported Italian Rice

Italian arborio rice with its fat short grains is tender, relatively fast-cooking, and has wonderful flavor. Use it in Italian-style creamy risottos, but it boils up nicely, too, if not overcooked.

Wild Rice

Wild rice, which is not a member of the rice family at all and does not cook in the same way, is dealt with starting on the next page.

Parboiled Rice

This is rice treated by a special steam process designed to harden the grains so they will not stick together. You cook it like plain white rice, although it may take a few minutes longer and may require a little more liquid. The package label should say "parboiled." "Converted," by the way, is the pat-ented term for an avuncular brand of parboiled rice, and the manufacturer will sue anybody who uses the term as a generic.

Enriched Rice

An increasing number of states require by law that all rice, processed or not, be enriched. And it is quite possible that even if your state has no such law, the rice you buy has been enriched. The box label will tell you.

"Enriched" means that certain minerals and vitamins are added to replace those lost during milling—iron, niacin, and thiamine, plus, in some cases, vitamin D, riboflavin, and calcium.

Since the enrichment is on the surface of the grains, it is soluble. One therefore should not wash enriched rice before cooking nor rinse it afterward, nor, of course, cook it in a large amount of water and then drain it.

Enriched rice cooks a little faster than plain rice.

Saffron Rice

Steep a medium pinch of saffron threads in the chicken stock as you are sautéing the onions, then add the chicken stock to the rice as usual.

Rice Soubise
Braised rice and onions

A savory accompaniment to roasts, especially pork, as well as steaks, chops, chicken, and turkey, is this classic French combination known as *soubise*. Surrounding it as in the photo with hashed Brussels sprouts (page 275) adds to its appeal, and the fact that you can do the main cooking in advance makes it particularly useful for a crowd.

For 10 to 12 servings

4 cups minced onions
4 Tbs butter
2 cups raw white rice (long-grain or "parboiled")
4 cups liquid (water only, or water and chicken broth)
½ cup dry white French vermouth or white wine, optional
¾ to 1 tsp salt, or to taste
1 imported bay leaf
Freshly ground pepper
Optional final additions: several Tbs softened butter and/or sour cream, heavy cream, and grated Parmesan cheese

SPECIAL EQUIPMENT SUGGESTED:
A heavy-bottomed 4-quart saucepan with cover

Cook the minced onions slowly with the butter in the covered saucepan for 10 to 15 minutes, until almost tender but not browned. Uncover the pan and simmer several minutes to evaporate excess moisture, then fold in the rice and cook for several minutes, stirring, to coat the grains with the butter. Blend in the 4 cups of liquid, optional vermouth or wine, and the salt and bay leaf. Bring to the simmer. Stir up once, then cover and let cook at a moderate simmer, without stirring again, for 12 to 15 minutes—until the liquid is absorbed and the rice grains are almost tender. Eat a few to test. Cover the pan and set aside; the rice will finish cooking by itself.

*Ahead-of-time note: When cool, cover and refrigerate. To reheat, place the rice in its cooking pan in another and larger pan of simmering water; fluff the soubise gently with a wooden fork as it warms through.

To serve: Taste carefully and correct seasoning, fluffing in salt and pepper as needed, and the optional butter, sour cream, heavy cream and/or cheese.

OTHER RECIPES USING WHITE RICE

Rice is every bit as good as pasta for salads, and far less commonplace; see pages 369 and 370 for East Bay Hot Rice Salad and for the Emperor's Rice. On page 448 is a splendid dessert with caramel sauce, the Louisiana Bavarian.

WILD RICE

Wild rice, the seed of a special grass that is of a different species than regular rice, was formerly gathered uniquely by American Indians. Now that it is also being cultivated by growers in various parts of the country, it is more easily available, though never cheap. The pronounced flavor and pleasantly chewy texture of wild rice make it a welcome accompaniment to meats with personality, such as pork, duck, goose, and game, although it also has its role as a contrast to the milder flavors of chicken and game hens.

 MASTER RECIPE

Wild Rice Braised with Mirepoix

For about 4 cups of cooked rice, serving 6 to 8

1½ cups wild rice
¼ cup mirepoix (finely diced sautéed onions, carrots, celery, and boiled ham, Special Note on page 297)
⅓ cup dry white French vermouth or dry white wine
2 cups or so chicken stock or duck stock
Salt and freshly ground pepper
2 Tbs or so butter for final enrichment, optional

SPECIAL EQUIPMENT SUGGESTED:
A heavy-bottomed 2-quart saucepan

Preparing the rice for cooking. Wash and either blanch or soak the rice as described in the Special Note on the next page; drain and wash it.

Cooking the rice. Turn the rice into the pan with the mirepoix, add the optional vermouth, and boil a moment, until the liquid has almost evaporated. Pour in enough stock to cover the rice by about ¼ inch, season lightly to taste, and simmer covered for 15 minutes or more (soaked rather than blanched rice will probably take longer), adding a little more liquid if needed until the rice is the consistency you like—such as quite tender but still with a touch of chewiness. Uncover, and sauté, stirring with a wooden fork, to boil off any remaining liquid. You may then wish to add a tablespoon or so more butter, sautéing an additional minute or two to let the rice dry off and crisp lightly. Correct seasoning, and the rice is ready to serve.

Ahead-of-time note: May be cooked in advance and reheated, with about a tablespoon of stock or water.

VARIATIONS

Wild Rice Braised with Mushroom Duxelles

A mushroom flavoring is delicious with wild rice, and more subtle than the preceding mirepoix. Follow the directions for the preceding wild rice but rather than mirepoix, substitute the same amount of mushroom duxelles (finely diced sautéed mushroom, Special Note on page 314).

Wild Rice Croutons

Directions for making individual cakes of wild rice are on page 155, where they accompany split game hens broiled with cheese.

SPECIAL NOTE

Wild Rice Cooking Notes

Grit and dirt. Wild rice, particularly "wild" wild rice, contains sandy particles and needs careful washing. Wild rice can also take a very long time to cook unless it has a preliminary blanching or soaking. I've found this a satisfactory system: pour the rice into a close-meshed sieve and swish it in a bowl of water, rubbing it between your hands; if there are more than a few grains of sand in the bottom of the bowl, repeat with fresh water.

To tenderize the rice.

System #1, blanching. After washing the rice, simmer it for 10 to 15 minutes in twice its volume of water, until it has softened but still has a grain of hardness when you bite into it. Drain, and wash it again just to be sure all grit is out. Blanching will also remove some of its strong taste.

System #2, soaking. After washing the rice, turn it into a bowl and pour on twice its volume of boiling water. Cover and let soak for an hour or more, then drain and wash it.

DRIED VEGETABLES

BEANS, LENTILS, WHEAT BERRIES, HOMINY, AND CORNMEAL

DRIED BEANS AND LENTILS

Beans and lentils, and dried vegetables in general, are some of the world's oldest foods. Full of nature's bounty, they are a fine source of that life-supporting ingredient, the protein, yet they are one of the least expensive items on our grocery lists. In the old days great-grandmother used to soak them all night and boil them all day. Now, with the quick-soaking method, the otherwise 12-hour sojourn in water is reduced to an hour, and a pressure cooker reduces the otherwise 1½-hour cooking time to minutes.

All-Season Bean Salad, Boston Baked Beans, and Lamb Shanks and Beans all go well with Boston Brown Bread.

Amounts. 1 cup of dried beans produces 3 cups of cooked beans, serving 4 to 6.

To Quick-Soak Dried Beans

1 cup dried beans
3 cups of water (10 cups for
**   antiflatulence)**

Turn the beans into a sieve and pick them over carefully, removing any stones or other debris—worth doing because a tiny stone can be a tooth breaker. Wash thoroughly, and turn the beans and 3 cups of water either into the pan of a pressure cooker or into a saucepan. Bring to the boil and boil uncovered for exactly 2 minutes; cover the pan and set aside for exactly 1 hour. The beans are now ready to cook. (If you have used the antiflatulent 10 cups of water, drain and wash the beans; add 3 cups of fresh cold water.)

MASTER RECIPE

Pressure-Cooked Beans

Pea beans, navy beans, Great Northerns, black beans, soybeans, but not French flageolets

For 3 cups of cooked beans

1 cup of the preceding presoaked
**   ready-to-cook dried beans in their**
**   3 cups of fresh water**
Optional additions: 2 Tbs olive oil,
**   peanut oil, or butter, or a 2-inch**
**   square of blanched salt pork**
**   (page 142); 1 imported bay leaf or**
**   an herb bouquet**
¾ tsp salt

SPECIAL EQUIPMENT SUGGESTED:
A medium pressure cooker

To the soaked beans and their liquid in the pressure pan add the optional ingredients and salt; cover and bring to 15 pounds pressure. Pressure-cook exactly 3 minutes. Remove from heat, and let the pressure go down by itself—10 to 15 minutes. Uncover, eat a bean or two, and if not quite tender, simmer partially covered 5 to 10 minutes, adding a little boiling water if necessary. The beans are now ready for further flavoring, hot or cold.

MASTER RECIPE

Open-Pot Bean Cookery
For all beans

For 3 cups of cooked beans

Ingredients for the preceding
**   pressure-cooked beans**

Optional additions
An herb bouquet (page 336),
**   including a large clove of garlic**
**   and 2 cloves**
1 medium onion
1 small carrot
A 2-inch square of blanched salt
**   pork (page 142)**

SPECIAL EQUIPMENT SUGGESTED:
A heavy 3-quart saucepan with cover

Simmer the beans and optional additions, partially covered, for 1 to 1½ hours, or until tender.

*Ahead-of-time note: Cooked beans may be done a day or two ahead; let them cool in their cooking liquid, then cover and refrigerate.

Serving suggestions. Once cooked, the beans are ready to be turned into a hot vegetable, or to finish off with a stew, or to become salad. Or you may cook them up in the first place as a fragrant bean soup. Here are some suggestions, and you will note that home-cooked and canned beans are interchangeable.

NOTES ON BEAN-COOKING LIQUID.
It makes a fine base for meat-based or vegetable soups. You can store it in the freezer.

Canned beans. Canned black beans, pinto beans, cannellini beans, kidney beans—use any of these in any of the recipes calling for home-cooked beans. Before using canned beans I like to drain them into a sieve set over a bowl, then rinse the beans under the hot water faucet.

VARIATIONS

Beans Maître d'Hôtel
Beans tossed with garlic and herbs (For cooked or canned beans)

These go with roast lamb, pork, or rabbit stew, or with sausages or ham.

For 4 to 6 servings, purée 1 or 2 large cloves of garlic and sauté in 3 tablespoons of butter or olive oil. After a moment, fold in 3 cups of drained cooked or canned beans. Let heat through thoroughly, and fold in seasonings to taste, along with drops of freshly squeezed lemon juice. Just before serving, fold and toss with a handful of chopped fresh parsley or other fresh green herbs such as basil or oregano.

The rooti-ti-toots

Some diners find the flatulent after-effects of home-cooked dried beans too distressing to contemplate. A number of years ago, scientists at the Western Regional Research Center of the U.S. Department of Agriculture in Albany, California, discovered that dried beans do indeed contain elements some people find difficult to digest. To cope, the human intestines send out voluminous gases of protest and rebellion.

Fortunately, however, these same scientists found that about 80 percent of the offending elements are soluble in water. This means that you can soak the beans, pour out the soaking water, and down the drain go most of the undesirable gas producers. Then add fresh water, cook the beans, and goodbye troubles for most bean eaters.

"But doesn't this also drain the nutrients out of the beans?" ask some nutritionally anxious cooks. There is but a minimal loss, say the scientists. However, if you are prone to gastric distress and have had to avoid beans, what other choice is there? Besides, if there is some minimal loss of nutrients, simply eat a minimally larger serving.

Purée of Beans

As an alternative to mashed potatoes, puréed beans go especially well with roast pork, pork chops, and ham dishes.

For 6 servings, purée 3 cups of drained cooked or canned beans in a food processor or vegetable mill, adding a little of their liquid as needed. Purée 1 or 2 large cloves of garlic and sauté briefly in 2 tablespoons of butter or olive oil; stir in the puréed beans. Stir for several minutes over moderate heat to evaporate excess liquid, then beat in butter or cream, as you wish. Carefully correct seasoning. Decorate with optional fresh herbs, such as parsley, basil, or oregano.

VARIATIONS

Bean Brandade
Purée of beans with a Mediterranean accent

This wonderfully heady purée and the variations that follow are all much the same, whether made of beans, chick-peas, cooked eggplant, or salt cod. Serve them as a dip with chips or crackers, or as a filling for hard-boiled eggs, or as one element in a cold salad plate. They are definitely free-form, and this formula is only a suggestion.

For about 2½ cups

2 cups cooked or canned beans, drained
3 Tbs olive oil
2 Tbs tahini (sesame paste)
1 Tbs freshly squeezed lemon juice
1 or 2 large cloves of garlic, puréed and then mashed with ½ tsp salt
Seasonings: salt, pepper, hot pepper sauce, and sage

SPECIAL EQUIPMENT SUGGESTED:
A food processor or vegetable mill

Purée the beans, and, if you are using a food processor, pulse in the rest of the ingredients. Otherwise purée into a mixing bowl and beat them in. Season carefully to taste.

Hummus

Substitute chick-peas for beans.

Eggplant Caviar

Scoop out the flesh of steamed eggplant (page 291), and sauté in olive oil to evaporate excess moisture until it has enough body to hold its shape in a spoon. Substitute for beans.

Brandade de Morue
Provençal purée of salt cod and potatoes

The recipe for this marvelously pungent dish is in the fish chapter on page 132.

All-Season Bean Salad

All-Season Bean Salad

Beans take well to salad dressings, herbs, peppers, onions, and garlic, but be sure to warm the beans before dressing them so they will absorb these added flavors.

For 6 to 8 servings

3 cups of warm home-cooked beans, or canned beans such as cannellini
3 Tbs finely minced onions or scallions
1 large clove of garlic, puréed and then mashed with ¼ tsp salt
2 Tbs or so good olive oil or salad oil
Herbs, such as fresh or dried thyme, oregano, and sage
Salt and freshly ground pepper
Additional elements, such as one or a combination of: strips of red or green bell pepper or pimiento; hard-boiled eggs; rounds of red onion; sardines, tuna, and/or salami; spinach leaves or salad greens

Flavoring the beans. Toss the warm beans in a big bowl with the onions or scallions, garlic, several tablespoons of oil, herbs, salt, and pepper to taste. Let stand 30 minutes, tossing several times, and correcting the seasoning.

Serving. Build an elaborate composition with eggs, sardines, and so forth, or use a simple decoration of spinach leaves, strips of red pepper or pimiento, and onion rings.

Boston Baked Beans
And the brown bread to go with them

The Boston baked bean is a story in itself, cooked long and slow, so that the beans literally caramelize in their juices. This is my favorite carefree cooking system, and the only one I've used since the day it was suggested to me by a kind reader a number of years ago. No soaking, no fussing, just dump everything into the pot and away you go; come back the next morning and the beans are done.

For about 2 quarts of beans, serving 6 to 8

A 2-inch square of salt pork (6 to 8 ounces)
2 cups small white beans, well picked over and washed
5 cups water
1½ tsp salt
1 cup finely sliced onions
2 large cloves of garlic, minced
2 Tbs dark unsulfured molasses
2 Tbs Dijon-style prepared mustard
½ tsp thyme
2 imported bay leaves
½ Tbs grated fresh ginger
6 grinds of pepper

SPECIAL EQUIPMENT SUGGESTED:
A slow cooker, or a 3-quart bean pot or heavy casserole

Cut the salt pork into strips ⅜ inch thick (leave on the rind). While you are assembling the other ingredients in the pot, simmer the pork 10 minutes in 2 quarts of water; drain, rinse in cold water, and add to the pot.

Ingredients for Boston Baked Beans

When all is in, cover the pot, and bring to the simmer; cook with low heat (250°F to 275°F), either in the slow cooker or in the oven. The beans should barely bubble, and will take 12 to 14 hours. Look at them once in a while to be sure all is well—they may need a little bit of boiling water. They are not done until they have turned a dark reddish brown. Correct seasoning.

*Ahead-of-time note: May be baked a day or more ahead, and reheated.

Serving. Serve them, in the good old Boston tradition, on Saturday night with coleslaw (page 375), and Boston brown bread, the following recipe.

Boston Brown Bread

Brown bread is quick to mix, but has a long, almost unattended 3-hour steam. Its taste is all its own, slightly sweet because of its molasses and raisins, and definitely sturdy with its base of cornmeal, rye meal, and buttermilk. Besides being a perfect match for baked beans, it toasts and butters beautifully when served for tea, or for breakfast. The following recipe, an adaptation from that great American culinary bible *The Joy of Cooking,* is my favorite.

For 2 cylindrical loaves baked in 1-pound coffee tins

1 cup yellow cornmeal
1 cup each rye flour and whole wheat flour
2 tsp baking soda

Boston Brown Bread (*continued*)

1 tsp salt
2 cups buttermilk
¾ cup dark unsulfured molasses in a
    4-cup measure
1 cup black raisins, roughly chopped
2 Tbs softened butter, for greasing
    tins and foil

SPECIAL EQUIPMENT SUGGESTED:
*A large (6- to 8-quart) mixing bowl; a
stout wooden spoon; 2 well-buttered 1-
pound cylindrical coffee tins; two 6-inch
squares of aluminum foil; white cotton
string; a kettle with rack and tight-
fitting lid, for steaming*

The batter. Blend the cornmeal,
flours, soda, and salt in the large
mixing bowl. Gradually whisk the
buttermilk into the molasses, then
vigorously blend the liquids into the
flours with the wooden spoon. Beat in
the raisins. Pour the batter into the
coffee tins. Butter the squares of foil
and tie them securely over the tops of
the tins with the string.

Steaming. Place the tins on the rack
in the kettle, pour in 2 inches of
water, and bring to the boil. Cover
the kettle and weight it down for a
tight seal, using canned goods or
bricks. Reduce heat and let steam
slowly about 3 hours, adding more
water to the kettle as necessary. The
breads are done when risen almost to
fill the cans and the centers have
puffed slightly—if the centers remain unpuffed, cover and steam 15
minutes or so more. Let cool 20
minutes in the can before unmolding.

Serving. Serve hot, warm, cold, or
toasted. Cut like a sausage, into slices
½ inch thick, using a serrated bread
knife—Mrs. Joy of C. and Fannie
Farmer suggest cutting warm brown
bread with a piece of tough string.
Serve with regular or whipped butter, or, for a change, cream cheese.

Lamb Shanks and Beans

Lamb shanks braised in a winey herbal sauce, page 241, are finished off
with cooked or canned beans, which
absorb that heady flavor.

page 241

SPECIAL NOTE

Herb Bouquet
To flavor soups, sauces, braises

An herb bouquet is a combination of
herbs, the traditional being thyme,
parsley with its long stems attached,
and imported bay leaf. However, you
may also include garlic, or other
herbs such as savory or oregano, and
spices such as cloves or juniper
berries.

You tie them together so they will
stay in a bundle and be easy to remove after cooking. If the herbs are
fresh, fold the parsley around them
and tie with white string. If they are
loose like dried thyme or allspice berries, wrap them in washed cheesecloth before tying.

A small bouquet would include 4
parsley sprigs, a small bay leaf, and
¼ teaspoon of thyme.

A Note on Bay Leaves. I specify "imported" bay leaves because California
bay has, to me, a disagreeably strong
and oily flavor. Quite different is the
true culinary bay, *Laurus nobilis*; although it may be grown anywhere, it
is usually imported from the Mediterranean area. You'll find it described and illustrated in color, along
with hundreds of other herbs, in Les-
ley Bremness's handsome and wonderfully authoritative *The Complete
Book of Herbs* (New York: Viking
Studio Books, 1988).

LENTILS

Lentils, a little more subtle and subtly different in flavor than most beans, go wonderfully well with lamb, either roast or braised, and with sausages and ham. They are, in addition, pleasantly satisfying just by themselves or in combination with such other hearty vegetables as carrots, turnips, and onions. Lentils are quicker to cook than beans, and the modern lentils have been processed for relatively fast cooking. However, if I want them to remain whole, I am careful to keep them just below the simmer since they can disintegrate during an actual boil.

LENTIL VARIETIES. *Lentils not only come in colors such as brown, green, red, and orange, but there are many varieties of lentils, and new processes have appeared to make the lentil an almost instantly cooked vegetable. Since I am not writing a treatise on this nutritious and protein-rich subject, I shall consider only the common brown lentil and the smaller common green lentil, both of which take to the conventional methods described here.*

TO SOAK OR NOT TO SOAK. *On most contemporary lentil packages the directions say soaking is not necessary, and that is certainly true for soups and purées. However, I have had better luck, when I want them to remain whole, if I give them an hour's preliminary soak in cold water.*

MASTER RECIPE

Cooked Lentils

To serve whole as a vegetable or in salads

Lentils have so much flavor of their own, and other flavors will be added when they are served, that I do not include aromatic vegetables and herbs during their initial cooking. However, if you wish to add them, follow the suggestions for open-pot beans on page 332.

For about 4½ cups of cooked lentils

1½ cups brown lentils
6 cups cold water
1½ tsp salt

Washing and soaking. Turn the lentils into a sieve and pick them over thoroughly to remove any pebbles or other debris; run cold water over them. Turn them into a 3-quart saucepan, pour in the 6 cups of cold water, and let soak for 1 hour. They are ready to cook when you bite into a few and there is a crunch but no brittleness at the center.

Cooking—12 to 15 minutes. Add the salt, and bring the lentils to the simmer in their soaking water. Maintain uncovered at just below the actual simmer—a slight movement in barely bubbling water. Skim off surface scum which will accumulate shortly after the below-the-simmer is reached. The lentils are done when tender throughout but they still hold their shape. This takes fairly constant watching and tasting, but that's a small price for perfectly cooked whole lentils.

Ahead-of-time note: Lentils may be cooked in advance and kept 2 to 3 days in their cooking liquid; cover and refrigerate when cool. Note that the cooking liquid is particularly full of flavor, and is a fine base for meat, bean, or lentil soups.

SERVING SUGGESTIONS

Lentils Maître d'Hôtel

Lentils tossed in butter with garlic and herbs: follow the directions for Beans Maître d'Hôtel on page 332.

Lentil Purée

Follow the general directions for Purée of Beans on page 333.

Lentils with Braised Lamb Shanks

Substitute lentils for beans in the braised lamb shanks recipe on page 241.

Garlic vinaigrette for Lentil Salad

Lentil Salad

Although a first-rate potato salad is hard to beat on a picnic or barbecue, a great lentil salad is both faster and easier to make.

For 6 to 8 servings

¾ **cup Garlic Vinaigrette Sauce (page 351)**
4½ **cups warm cooked lentils, well drained (the master recipe)**
Salt and freshly ground pepper

Optional other additions, one or two, or all

Spinach leaves or salad greens
Hard-boiled eggs
½ **cup finely minced scallions or red onions**
Tuna, anchovies, and/or sardines
Strips of red pimiento
Green and/or black olives
Minced fresh parsley and/or other herbs

SPECIAL EQUIPMENT SUGGESTED:
A 3-quart mixing bowl for dressing the lentils; a salad bowl or platter

Dressing the lentils. Prepare the garlic vinaigrette sauce. Drain the warm lentils thoroughly, and fold them in the bowl with the sauce, tossing gently. Correct seasoning. Let cool, and correct seasoning again before serving.

*Ahead-of-time note: May be prepared ahead to this point; cover and refrigerate, but bring to room temperature (to decongeal salad oil) before proceeding.

Serving. Either turn the lentils directly into a salad bowl and decorate the top with herbs and strips of pimiento, or be more elaborate with green leaves, eggs, anchovies, and so forth.

Lentil Soup

Like split-pea soup, lentil soup couldn't be easier or more satisfying, and the lentils need no soaking.

For 2 quarts, serving 6

6 **cups lamb broth (page 215), or beef stock or ham stock**
½ **cup lentils, picked over and washed**
½ **cup each: diced onions, turnips, and carrots**
A **medium herb bouquet, page 336, plus a small handful of celery leaves and 2 large garlic cloves**
Salt and freshly ground pepper
1 **or 2 tomatoes, peeled, seeded, juiced, and diced**
Slices of lemon, or lemon wedges, optional
3 **Tbs chopped fresh parsley**

SPECIAL EQUIPMENT SUGGESTED:
A heavy-bottomed 3-quart saucepan with cover

Simmering the soup. Combine all the ingredients except the tomatoes, optional lemon, and parsley in a roomy saucepan or kettle, bring to the simmer, and skim off surface scum. Simmer partially covered for about 40 minutes, or until all vegetables are tender. Discard herb bouquet. Taste, and correct seasoning.

*Ahead-of-time note: May be cooked a day or two in advance to this point. Cover and refrigerate when cool.

Serving. Bring to the simmer, add the tomato pulp and simmer a moment more. Correct seasoning again. Ladle into hot wide soup plates; serve with the optional lemon and a sprinkling of parsley.

VARIATION

Purée of Lentil Soup

For 2 quarts

Ingredients for the preceding lentil soup

Complete the cooking and reserve, if you wish, 1 cup of the lentils and vegetables. Purée the rest of the soup in a food processor or vegetable mill. Bring the soup again to the simmer, add the reserved vegetables, and serve as for the preceding recipe.

THE THREE KERNELS

WHEAT BERRIES, BARLEY, AND BROWN RICE

This unusual whole-grain combination has an attractively earthy flavor and is pleasantly chewy but not too much so. It's healthy food, in other words, but it also makes good eating. Serve it as is, or with sausages, broiled chicken or rabbit, or pork chops.

Purchasing note. You should be able to buy these grains at any health food store.

Manufacturing note. I would not attempt this without my trusty pressure cooker, since open-pot boiling of wheat berries can be endless and sometimes futile.

 MASTER RECIPE

To Cook the Three Kernels

For about 5 cups, serving 6 to 8

1 cup wheat berries
3 cups water
½ cup barley grains
½ cup brown rice
1 cup chicken broth
Salt and freshly ground pepper

SPECIAL EQUIPMENT SUGGESTED:
A pressure cooker

The wheat berries. Turn the wheat berries into a sieve, pick them over carefully, and run cold water over them. Turn them into the pressure cooker with the 3 cups of water, and bring to 15 pounds pressure for exactly 3 minutes. Let the pressure go down by itself—10 minutes or so.

Finishing the cooking. Pick over and wash the barley and brown rice; add to the wheat berries along with the chicken broth. Simmer, partially covered, for 10 minutes; add 1 teaspoon of salt, and continue simmering 10 to 15 minutes, or until the kernels are the texture you like: they should have a reasonable chewiness, but be pleasantly edible. Uncover and boil off excess liquid. Season to taste.

*Ahead-of-time note: May be cooked a day or more in advance. When cool, cover and refrigerate.

SERVING SUGGESTIONS

Three Buttered Kernels

2 or more Tbs butter
The preceding three kernels, cooked and drained
Salt and freshly ground pepper

Heat the butter in a frying pan, fold in the cooked kernels, and sauté several minutes to evaporate excess moisture. Season again to taste, and serve.

Bacon and the Three Kernels

For 6 servings

4 or 5 strips of thick-sliced bacon
2 or more Tbs bacon fat or butter
The master recipe for the 3 kernels, cooked and drained
Salt and freshly ground pepper

Cut the strips of bacon into 3 lengthwise, then into crosswise dice. Sauté in a frying pan to brown and crisp lightly. Strain, then toss the bacon in paper towels. Heat 2 or more tablespoons of the bacon fat or butter in a frying pan, add the cooked and drained kernels, and sauté several minutes to evaporate excess moisture. Fold in the bacon, season to taste, and serve.

Tomatoes Stuffed with Three Kernels

For 6 servings

6 fairly large red ripe firm tomatoes
Salt and freshly ground pepper
¾ to 1 cup grated Jack or mozzarella cheese
The preceding recipe for Bacon and the Three Kernels
A little olive oil

SPECIAL EQUIPMENT SUGGESTED:
A melon baller or teaspoon for cleaning out tomatoes; an oiled baking dish to hold them

(continued)

Tomatoes Stuffed with Three Kernels
(*continued*)

Filling the tomatoes. Core a top out of
the stem end of the tomatoes, scrape
out the ribs and seeds, salt and pepper lightly, and let drain upside down
5 minutes or so. Meanwhile blend
the cheese into the 3 kernels (the
cheese holds the kernels together),
and correct seasoning. Brush the outside of the tomatoes with oil, and
mound the kernels into their cavities.
Arrange them in the baking dish,
and top each with a drizzle of olive
oil.

*Ahead-of-time note: May be prepared
in advance to this point.

Baking—20 minutes at 400°F. Bake
in the upper middle level of a preheated oven until the toppings have
browned lightly, and the stuffing has
heated through, but the tomatoes still
hold their shape. Serve reasonably
soon, since the tomatoes may overcook and collapse if kept too warm.

HOMINY AND GRITS

Those of us who did not grow up in
the South are inclined to forget about
hominy, or "samp," as it is sometimes
called. Hominy, with its own very
individual taste, is dried kernels of
corn treated in a special way, with the
seed-germ and outer skin removed.
You can buy either coarsely ground
dried hominy, known as grits, or
canned whole hominy, all plumped
up and ready to go. Either way, it is
an inexpensive, nourishing, and interesting change from the usual
starchy vegetables.

Two ideas for canned hominy

Hominy Sautéed with Butter and Herbs

This is about as easy as they come—
the quintessential hominy; serve it
with fried or broiled chicken, pork
chops, or ribs.

For 6 to 8 servings

**Two 1-pound 14-ounce cans of
white hominy**
2 or more Tbs butter
Salt and freshly ground pepper
**2 to 3 Tbs chopped fresh parsley,
basil, chives, or a combination**

Drain the hominy in a large sieve,
and run cold water over it to remove
the taste of the can. Shortly before
serving, heat the butter to bubbling
in a roomy pan, fold in the hominy,
and toss over moderately high heat to
warm through. Season to taste with
salt and pepper, toss with the herbs,
and serve.

Hominy au Gratin

When you want a more elaborate
presentation, bake the hominy in a
cheese sauce, and serve with your
best hamburgers.

For 6 to 8 servings

**Two 1-pound 14-ounce cans of
white hominy**

The cheese sauce

3 Tbs butter
¼ cup flour
2 cups hot milk

Salt and freshly ground white pepper
A speck of nutmeg
**½ cup lightly pressed down grated
Swiss or Cheddar cheese**

**¼ cup additional grated Swiss or
Cheddar cheese**

SPECIAL EQUIPMENT SUGGESTED:
*A shallow buttered baking and serving
dish, approximately 8 by 12 inches*

The hominy and sauce. Drain the
hominy and wash under cold water;
set aside. Meanwhile, make 2 cups of
standard cheese sauce (cook the butter
and flour together without coloring;
off heat blend in the hot milk, season, and simmer 3 minutes; let cool
for 2 minutes; fold in the cheese.
Full details on page 272).

Assembling. Spoon a thin film of the
sauce into the baking dish. Pour in
the hominy and cover with the remaining sauce, shaking the dish so it
will sink into the kernels. Spread
with more grated cheese.

*Ahead-of-time note: Set aside until
shortly before serving.

Baking. About 25 minutes before you
wish to serve, set in the upper third
level of a preheated 425°F oven and
bake until bubbling hot and the top
has browned nicely.

Ingredients for Hominy au Gratin

Hominy Grits

Grits au Gratin

It's the dried hominy this time, the grits. Although a cousin in taste of the preceding dish, this is somehow a little more elegant, and goes beautifully with a roast of lamb, for instance. Or it might be the mainstay of a vegetable dinner.

For 6 to 8 servings

For cooking the grits

2½ cups regular hominy grits (for "instant" grits, follow package directions)

10 cups cold water

1½ tsp salt

4 Tbs butter

1 cup light cream or sour cream

3 "large" eggs

1½ cups coarsely grated Cheddar cheese—1 cup into the grits; ½ cup for topping

SPECIAL EQUIPMENT SUGGESTED: *A heavy 4-quart saucepan with cover, for initial grits cooking; a larger pan to hold the first, for final cooking; a buttered baking and serving dish, such as a rectangular one 8 by 12 inches*

Cooking the grits. Place the grits in the 4-quart pan and whisk in the water. Bring to the boil over moderately high heat, stirring frequently with a wooden spoon to blend and to prevent scorching. Add the salt and butter, and stir over moderate heat for 5 minutes or more, until the grits have thickened and hold their shape softly in a spoon. Bring an inch or so of water to the simmer in the larger

pan, and set the grits pan in it. Cover, and cook ½ hour or more, stirring up occasionally until the grits form a thick mass and are tender but not mushy.

Seasoning and assembling. Remove the grits pan from its water bath and set over moderate heat. Season the grits carefully to taste. Beat in the cream and simmer, stirring, for several minutes to rethicken the hominy. Remove from heat and beat in the eggs one by one, then 1 cup of cheese. Correct seasoning again. Turn into the baking dish, and spread the remaining cheese over the top.

*Ahead-of-time note: Set aside until shortly before serving.

Baking—45 minutes at 425°F. Set in the middle level of the preheated oven and bake until bubbling hot and the top has browned lightly.

POLENTA AND CORNMEAL DISHES

Polenta has a gastronomic ring to it. But how about cornmeal mush? Polenta is, of course, cornmeal mush, but thought of and served in an adult manner. It is the perfect dunk for a fine meat sauce, like that in a lamb or beef stew, or a wonderful bed for small roast game birds and their juices. It is also good indeed by itself as a first course, poured hot onto a serving board, doused with butter and cheese, and cut into steaming wedges. As a main-course luncheon or supper dish you'd need only a big salad, then, and a simple red wine.

The polenta mystique

Old-school-tie Italian-grandmother polenta recipes call for drifting the cornmeal slowly into boiling water, taking as much as ½ hour for a lump-free mix, and stirring in one direction only—no fudging! Then you stir, and stir, and stir, and keep on stirring for 45 minutes. It is finally done when the spoon can be stood upright in the middle of the pan.

This is certainly one way of keeping grandmothers busy, and in the old days when all generations lived together under one roof, giving grandmother her special and sacred task was undoubtedly a clever move. Perhaps the continual stirring produces a tenderer, creamier polenta, as perhaps does the continual stirring of a risotto. But I do not have that fine an Italian palate to taste the difference. Stir and stir and stir if you wish, particularly if you love to stir for its own sake.

Cornmeal notes. If you cannot find an Italian source for polenta meal, try a health-food store, where you will find stone-ground yellow cornmeal; choose the coarse or medium grind for best texture and flavor. By the way and in my experience, "instant" polenta meal, even if "made in Italy," does not have the quality of the real thing.

Cooked Polenta

For about 6 cups, serving 6

2 cups yellow cornmeal (see
   preceding notes)
6 cups cold water, plus more if
   needed
2 tsp salt, or to taste

SPECIAL EQUIPMENT SUGGESTED:
*A heavy 3-quart saucepan with cover; a
wire whisk, a stout spatula or spoon; a
larger pan with 1 inch of simmering
water, to hold the polenta pan*

The initial cooking. Measure the cornmeal into the 3-quart saucepan and
gradually but vigorously whisk in the
water, being sure there are no lumps.
Add the salt and bring to the simmer,
whisking and then stirring with the
wooden spatula or spoon as the mixture thickens into a heavy mush.
Continue stirring over moderate heat
for 5 minutes.

Final cooking. Then cover the pan
and set it in the larger pan of simmering water for 45 minutes, stirring frequently and adding spoonfuls
more water only if the mixture becomes so thick you have difficulty
stirring. When the 45 minutes are
up—they are needed to cook the
cornmeal thoroughly and to give it
the correct consistency—the polenta
should be a very thick, almost gelatinous mass. If not, remove the polenta pan from its water bath and stir
over moderate heat until it is well
thickened. Serve according to one of
the following suggestions.

*Ahead-of-time note: For later serving, cover and keep over almost simmering water; stir frequently.

1. Pouring the steaming polenta onto a board

2. Butter and cheese go over the polenta before
serving.

SERVING SUGGESTIONS

Polenta Family-Style

This is a wonderfully informal and
undoubtedly the best way to serve
freshly cooked polenta.

For 6 servings

4 or more Tbs butter, cut into ½-
   inch dice
1 cup grated Parmesan cheese
The preceding just-cooked polenta

SPECIAL EQUIPMENT SUGGESTED:
*A serving board or platter about 16
inches in diameter; a large rubber spatula for spreading; a serving spatula or
a pie server*

Have the butter and cheese ready to
go. Pour the steaming polenta onto
the board or platter and spread it out
into a circle or oval with the spatula,
step 1. Rapidly make cross-hatchings
1 inch apart on the surface; dot with
the butter and spread on the cheese,
step 2. Cut into wedges, and serve at
once.

*Polenta with Cream Cheese,
Lorenzo*

The irresistible combination of warm
polenta and cool moist cream cheese
is a specialty of a proud Italian cook
we know from Santa Barbara.

For 6 servings

4 ounces cream cheese
½ cup sour cream
The master recipe for hot just-
   cooked polenta

Blend the cream cheese and sour
cream in a bowl. At serving time,
pour the steaming polenta out onto
the board, and, rather than spreading
it out, cut it into fat serving portions.
Rapidly make a wedge in the center
of each, and plop in a generous
spoonful or two of the cheese mixture. Serve at once.

Polenta Baked with Cheese

This is useful for ahead-of-time serving as well as for leftovers.

For 6 servings

**The recipe for Polenta Family-Style
Grated Parmesan cheese**

Let the polenta with its butter and cheese topping cool for an hour or more, until cold and firm. Cut it into wedges and arrange slightly overlapping in a buttered baking dish or on a buttered pizza pan; sprinkle on a little more cheese.

*Ahead-of-time note: May be prepared even a day in advance; cover and refrigerate.

Baking. Bake in the upper middle level of a preheated 400°F oven for 25 to 30 minutes, until the top has browned lightly.

VARIATION

Polenta au Gratin
Polenta baked with eggs, sour cream, and cheese

Substitute cooked polenta, the master recipe, for the grits in Grits au Gratin on page 341.

Sautéing polenta cakes

Polenta Galettes

In the form of cakes or other shapes, polenta makes a rather formal accompaniment on the dinner plate with roasts and ragouts. And, of course, with bacon and eggs for breakfast, we would call it fried mush. Again, since this is useful for leftover polenta, I am not giving exact proportions.

For 2 galettes 2½ inches across per serving

**The master recipe for cooked
    polenta (on the preceding page),
    or polenta leftovers**
**Clarified butter, cooking oil, or
    bacon fat**
Flour on a plate

Forming the galettes. Spread out the polenta ⅜ inch thick on your work surface, smoothing the top with a wet spatula. Let cool for an hour or more, to firm up. Cut into shapes such as rounds, triangles, and/or squares.

*Ahead-of-time note: May be formed a day or more in advance; cover and refrigerate.

Sautéing. Just before cooking, heat ¼ inch of butter, oil, or bacon fat in a frying pan, dredge the galettes in the flour, and sauté over moderate heat 4 to 6 minutes to a side, until lightly brown and crusty.

Rhode Island Jonnycakes

It would be a shame to leave out jonnycakes, a rustic version of the preceding galettes, crusty on the outside and moist inside. They are fast to make and go well with eggs, sausages, ham, and bacon. To make the best possible authentic cakes, according to the natives of that state, you must have Rhode Island stoneground white cornmeal—or at least it should be stone-ground. The following is adapted from the recipe given out by The Society for the Propagation of the Jonnycake (P.O. Box 4633, Rumford, Rhode Island 02916), which would, incidentally, be delighted to put you in touch with the proper cornmeal.

For 6 to 8 jonnycakes

1 cup white cornmeal, stone-ground, and from Rhode Island if possible
½ tsp salt
1 cup boiling water
3 to 4 Tbs milk or cream
1 tsp molasses, optional
2 Tbs or so bacon fat, ham fat, or cooking oil

SPECIAL EQUIPMENT SUGGESTED:
A 12-inch griddle or a heavy skillet

The batter. Blend the cornmeal and salt in a bowl with enough boiling water to make a very thick mush. Then beat in milk or cream and the optional molasses until the batter is the consistency of mashed potatoes.

Cooking. Film the skillet or griddle with the fat or oil, and set over moderately high heat. When very hot but not smoking, drop in spoonfuls of the batter to make rather rough ovals ½ inch thick and 2 by 3 inches across. Fry 4 to 6 minutes on each side, until brown and crusty. Serve as soon as possible.

Box-top Cornbread

Here is a good plain quick-to-make corn bread, typical of most box-top recipes. However, they invariably contain sugar, far too much in my opinion—for poultry stuffings, like that on page 184, omit the sugar.

Manufacturing note: For poultry stuffings use 1 egg and 1 cup each of cornmeal and flour; 2 eggs and 1¼ flour to ¾ cup cornmeal make a lighter bread, and I prefer to omit sugar entirely in all cases. Be sure your baking powder is active, by the way—throw it out if a teaspoon of it does not bubble up almost at once in half a cup of hot water.

1 or 2 "large" eggs (see manufacturing note above)
1 cup milk
1 tsp salt
2 cups mixed cornmeal and all-purpose flour (see manufacturing note above)
2 to 4 Tbs melted butter, good fresh cooking oil, or rendered fat—chicken, duck, goose, turkey, or pork or bacon fat

Optional, but not for stuffings: 2 to 4 Tbs sugar
1 Tbs fresh double-action baking powder (see manufacturing note above)

SPECIAL EQUIPMENT SUGGESTED:
A buttered or greased square 8-inch cake pan; a food processor is useful but not essential

The batter. Preheat the oven to 425°F. Whisk the egg, milk, and salt in a 4-cup measure to blend. Measure the flour, cornmeal, and baking powder into the processor, then briefly process in the liquid, adding the melted butter, oil, or fat at the end. (Or place the dry ingredients in a big mixing bowl; beat in the liquids and melted butter, oil, or fat.)

Baking—about 30 minutes at 425°F. Immediately turn the batter into the prepared pan, and bake in the middle level of the preheated oven.

When is it done? The top will be a pale brown, and the bread will show a faint line of separation from the sides of the pan. Turn out onto a rack.

OTHER RECIPES USING CORNMEAL

Cornbread, sage, and sausage stuffing for turkey, page 184

Corn Sticks (cob-shaped corn muffins), page 59

Cornmeal pizza dough, page 54

Cornmeal in bread. ½ cup or more cornmeal could certainly be added to the whole wheat and rye bread formulas on pages 44 and 46.

Cornmeal used for sliding risen loaves of French bread dough into the oven—pulverize dry cornmeal in the blender and store in a screw-topped jar, page 41.

Julia looking at a display of potato dishes, taken on the set in Santa Barbara where the videotapes *The Way to Cook* were shot

Salads

Green Salads, Salad Greens and Salad Dressings

Composed Salads and What Goes into Them

Pasta, Rice, and Bean Salads

Poultry, Meat, and Fish Salads

Cabbage, Celery, and Corn Salads

Salads can make a charming light beginning to a meal, a splendid main course, or a welcome interruption to a succession of courses.

Here we shall discuss how to wash and store the greens, how to deal with such fundamental ingredients as avocados, tomatoes, cucumbers, parsley, and watercress, plus

how to make the best French dressing and how to be at ease with homemade mayonnaise. Also included are such items as the best way to prepare duck for a warm duck salad, the key to the perfect chicken salad, the all-important pasta for those increasingly popular pasta salads, and such perennial favorites as coleslaw and the all-American potato salad.

My hope is that when you have to wing it with what's on hand, this chapter will provide you with the know-how to create a salad that's a whole meal, and that will taste even better than it looks. Let us start at the beginning, with salad greens.

SALAD GREENS AND GREEN SALADS

Red, green, and oak-leaf let-tuce, escarole, curly endive, romaine, butter lettuce, Boston let-tuce, radicchio—to say nothing of sorrel, borage, baby spinach leaves, arugula—I'm naming just a handful of salad possibilities without mention-ing such others as edible flowers or our stalwart old friend iceberg let-tuce. So many varieties and exotics are becoming available to us, even in our local supermarkets, that I shall detail only the basics.

To Buy, Wash, Dry, and Store Salad Greens

These directions are for the tender butter or Boston lettuce types with overlapping leaves, the loose-leaf let-tuces that bunch rather than head, and the long-leaf romaine varieties. Carefully inspect each head of lettuce you buy, choosing only specimens that are fresh and crisp. If you won't be preparing them at once, layer loosely in paper towels, very slightly dampened if the greens seem un-usually dry, and refrigerate in a re-frigerator drawer or a plastic bag.

A salad dryer

Washing. Cut the core or stem out of the head, separate the leaves, and drop them into a large bowl of cold water. Swish about gently so the water enters each crevice, then let the leaves rest a moment, allowing any grit to sink down. Remove the leaves one by one, tearing off any discolored or wilted areas, and, if you are serving shortly, tear the leaves into convenient size.

Drying and storing the leaves. Wet greens wilt when stored, and wet leaves dilute a salad dressing. The old-fashioned method for drying salad greens was to roll the leaves loosely between clean towels, or to swing them in a salad basket or pillowcase. If you don't already have one, get yourself a modern salad dryer, the kind with a salad basket that spins off the water inside a container. For short-term storage, wrap the dried leaves loosely in a clean towel and refrigerate in a plastic bag. For longer storage, arrange single layers of leaves between paper towels in a deep tray, and cover with plastic wrap; they'll keep nicely for a day or two.

Special Cases

Crisphead or iceberg lettuce. In spite of its doleful reputation, iceberg definitely has its place. The heads have staying power in the fridge, and when shredded into a fine chiffonade, iceberg makes a crisp base for other mixtures. Pick solid heads with green outer leaves. Remove any wilted leaves, wash and dry the head, wrap loosely in slightly dampened paper towels, and refrigerate in a plastic bag.

Belgian endives, those fat, neatly pointed, and expensive creamy white spears, come packed between sheets of blue paper. Pick heads that are definitely neatly shaped, and a fresh creamy white with hardly a trace of pale green. Pack them in slightly dampened paper towels, and refrigerate in a plastic bag—they will keep several days. To use them, shave off the discolored portion at the base, and wash the heads. Some cooks (but not me) core out a cone-shaped 1/4 inch at the base on the theory that this operation will reduce their slight natural bitterness—do so if you wish. To use endives in salads, either separate into leaves or slice them crosswise or into julienne. If you've never eaten cooked endives, by the way, try the buttery braised whole endives on page 299.

Watercress. Leave it bunched, and swish in a basin of cold water, then set it leafy head up in a plastic container. Add enough cold water to come 1½ inches up the base of the stems. Cover loosely with a plastic bag and refrigerate. The cress will keep for several days and even start to grow.

Parsley. Leave the parsley bunched, swish in a basin of cold water, and let soak a few minutes, allowing grit to sink down. Lift it out, and either spin it in a salad basket or shake it dry. Wrap loosely in paper towels and refrigerate in a plastic bag. Very fresh parsley will keep 4 to 5 days when treated this way. Be sure the leaves are thoroughly dry before chopping, or your parsley will lump and be unsprinkle-able.

Other green herbs. I have good luck storing basil-on-the-stem like watercress; other herbs I usually treat like parsley.

The best ingredients make the best dressings.

SALAD DRESSINGS

Often the plain and simple is the best, the formula that uses the best and freshest oil, the best vinegar, the freshest lemon. This is an especially self-evident truth when you are making a plain green salad, where every flavor stands on its own.

Salad Oils

Taste and smell your oil with great care to be sure it is fresh and fine, because oils can turn rancid. There is nothing worse, to my mind, than a restaurant salad made with cheap off-flavor oil, or a stale bottled dressing.

Olive oils. I am an olive oil buff, and prefer the light but fragrant French and Italian oils. When looking for a good oil, try out several brands to find the one you like, but read the label before you buy: "pure" is oil from olives all right, but it might well be the last of the line, extracted with a heated press. "Virgin" or "vièrge" indicates the oil came from the first cold pressing, while "extra virgin" is the first cold pressing from specially selected olives. Extra virgin is lovely for

plain green salads, and as a special flavoring, but it is a waste to use such expensive oil for sautéing and regular cooking.

Other oils. Peanut oil, walnut oil, avocado oil, neutral vegetable oils, and so forth—it's up to you, but be sure they are fresh, pure, and fine. Often your best choice of these will be in a health-food store. A few drops of walnut oil or dark sesame oil added to your other oil, for instance, might be appropriate at times, and for special effects.

Storing oil. I keep olive oil in closed cans or corked bottles in a cool dark place, and have had no difficulties storing them for a year or more. Because some of the special varieties like unprocessed fresh peanut, walnut, and avocado have gone off in taste when left out, I now refrigerate them.

Vinegars. With the exception of cider vinegar on the great American potato salad, imported plain French red wine vinegar (Dessaux Fils, Dijon, usually) is my exclusive choice—my touchstone for all wine vinegars. I have had some excellent California vinegars made by the better wineries, as well as some with strange and pungent flavors. Again, test them out yourself. A few drops of balsamic vinegar may be appropriate occasionally, but only the barest few to my mind, because its flavor is so pervasive.

Lemon. Lemon juice must always be fresh, and for more zing you can mince or purée the zest (yellow part of peel) into your sauce.

Shallots and scallions. Finely minced shallots or scallions are often a welcome addition in a vinaigrette—but serve it shortly since their flavors can go off after several hours.

Garlic. The same applies to garlic: use a garlic dressing soon to retain its fresh taste. To peel, mince, and purée garlic easily, see the Special Note on this page. You may want to include a strip or two of lemon zest while you are mincing and mashing the garlic.

Mustard. A teaspoon or so of the Dijon-type prepared mustard goes well in a vinaigrette, and if you want a creamy dressing, mustard helps homogenize the ingredients.

Proportions. Vinaigrettes, as dressings for green salads are usually called, are made with all vinegar, or all lemon juice, or a little of both. Although standard proportions appear to be 1 part vinegar or lemon to 3 of oil, I think this makes far too acid a mixture, especially when you are serving wine with the meal. I opt for the dry martini proportions, 1 to 5; but you must judge this yourself for each salad. You can always toss in a little more lemon or vinegar if needed, but it's hard to remove or disguise an excess.

SPECIAL NOTE

To Mince or Purée Garlic

Knife method: Removing the peel.
1. Smashing garlic clove to remove peel: Place the garlic clove on your work surface, lay the flat of your big knife on top, and smash it with your fist, as illustrated. This loosens the peel, which you then pick off and discard.

Mincing. Then mince the garlic.

Smashing garlic clove to remove peel

Puréeing. 2. Puréeing with the flat of the knife: Sprinkle a big pinch of salt over the minced garlic, and purée it by pressing and rubbing the flat of your knife back and forth over it. The garlic purées rapidly because the salt softens it and brings out its juices.

Garlic press method. To make a smooth paste of garlic, purée the unpeeled clove into a bowl. Mash and rub it with a big pinch of salt against the sides of the bowl with the back of a spoon until perfectly smooth.

Puréeing minced garlic with flat of knife

 MASTER RECIPE

Oil and Lemon Dressing

For about ⅔ cup, enough for 6 to 8 servings

2 strips of fresh lemon peel (1 by 2½ inches each)
¼ tsp salt, plus more, if needed
½ Tbs Dijon-type prepared mustard
1 to 2 Tbs freshly squeezed lemon juice
½ cup fine fresh oil
Freshly ground pepper

SPECIAL EQUIPMENT SUGGESTED:
A small mortar and pestle, or a heavy bowl and wooden spoon; a small portable beater or wire whisk

Mince the lemon peel very finely with the salt, scrape it into the mortar or bowl, and mash into a fine paste with the pestle or spoon. Beat in the mustard and 1 tablespoon of the lemon juice; when thoroughly blended start beating in the oil by droplets to make a homogeneous sauce—easier when done with a small electric mixer. Beat in droplets more lemon juice and salt and pepper to taste.

Emulsion note: Slow additions of oil and constant beating make the emulsion here, and if the sauce doesn't "take"—too bad—just beat it well before using. *Or* whisk in a spoonful of raw egg white, heavy cream, or condensed milk, which should bring it together; for security these could be added at the beginning, with the mustard.

OTHER METHODS OF MAKING THE DRESSING

The Screw-Top Jar

Shake all the ingredients together in a screw-top jar—easy, but it does not make a permanent emulsion without the previously described emulsion helpers.

Oil the Leaves First

Rather than making a dressing separately, start by tossing the greens in their serving bowl with the oil—which you can do well in advance. Make the flavoring in a small separate bowl and toss a good portion of it into the salad just before serving, then taste a dressed leaf analytically, and toss in more flavoring, salt, and pepper as needed. I like this system for a plain tossed salad.

VARIATION

Vinaigrette

Omit the lemon peel, if you wish, and substitute wine vinegar for all or part of the lemon juice.

Herb Vinaigrette

Except for basil, which I think best minced then mashed with salt at the beginning, stir other herbs like tarragon, parsley, and chives into the finished sauce.

ADDITIONS

Shallots or Scallions

Omit the lemon peel, if you wish, and stir a teaspoon or so of finely minced shallot or scallion with the salt and mustard. Proceed with the recipe.

Garlic Vinaigrette

Mash and mince the garlic, then either mash it to a purée with the lemon peel, or alone with the salt. Proceed with the recipe.

GREEN SALADS

 MASTER RECIPE

Tossed Green Salad

How much lettuce to use? Play it by eye and by known appetites. A large head of Boston lettuce will weigh up to ¾ pound and should serve 4 to 6, while a large head of romaine will weigh over 1 pound and serve 6 to 8. One of the loose-leaf varieties might weigh only ½ pound and serve only 2 or 3. Use all one kind, like Boston, but a mixture of leaves including

A special presentation

perhaps some watercress or arugula is attractive, and you'll certainly want to mix in some tender other leaves when you have such strong and slightly bitter greens as escarole or mature curly endive.

WOODEN SALAD BOWLS. *Wooden salad bowls are lovely to look at but unless properly cared for they can turn rancid, and that horrid taste permeates the whole salad. If you are using wood, be sure it has a waterproof interior finish that can be thoroughly washed out.*

For 6 servings

1 pound or so of salad greens, all one kind or a mixture, washed and dried as previously described
⅔ cup salad dressing, from one of the preceding formulae

SPECIAL EQUIPMENT SUGGESTED: *A large salad bowl that will give you room to toss; a long-handled spoon and fork*

(continued)

Tossed Green Salad (*continued*)

Shortly before serving, turn the greens into the salad bowl, pour on half of the well-blended dressing, and swoop up the leaves with the spoon and fork, turning them over and over several times, and adding a little more of the dressing as needed so all the leaves are lightly and uniformly coated. Taste a leaf analytically; toss in more salt, pepper, vinegar, and lemon juice, if needed. Serve at once.

VARIATIONS

The Re-Formed Head

In this attractive presentation, the washed and dried salad greens are loosely arranged in the bowl to look again like a large head of Boston lettuce; the dressing is dribbled over the leaves just before serving.

Salade Mimosa

Salade Mimosa

A very simple and agreeable way to dress up a plain green salad—sprinkle on chopped hard-boiled egg and chopped herbs as follows. The title is a poetic allusion to the yellow and green of a mimosa tree in bloom.

For 6 servings

2 hard-boiled eggs
A handful of fresh green herbs—parsley, or a mixture such as parsley and chives, tarragon, or chervil
Salt and freshly ground pepper
The master recipe for Tossed Green Salad

Chop the eggs into small neat dice; toss in a bowl with the chopped herbs and a sprinkling of salt and pepper. After dressing the salad, and just before serving, sprinkle the mimosa over the salad—but do not toss it in.

Caesar Salad
Romaine with egg dressing, Parmesan, and garlic croutons
The kitchen version

You don't have to make a production of this delicious salad, which makes an ample first course, or could be the main course for a luncheon preceding a soup, for instance. The antic table-top version, however, appears in another book—a dramatic public affair where baby whole leaves of romaine are first elaborately tossed with olive oil, then with seasonings; in go 2 eggs, Parmesan cheese, and garlic croutons for a flourishing finale.

ANCHOVY NOTE. *Caesar salad was created in the 1920's, by the way. According to Chef Caesar Cardini's daughter, with whom I talked at length before doing the recipe for our TV show some years ago, the original contained no anchovies. However, you may certainly add them if you wish, mashing them into a purée with a bit of the olive oil and tossing them in before adding the cheese.*

MANUFACTURING NOTE. *You will hardly be a Caesar enthusiast if you've dined only on restaurant varieties made with cheap oil, store-bought croutons, garlic powder, and old bottled cheese! But what a marvelous salad it is when prepared with fine fresh ingredients.*

For 6 servings

1 or 2 heads of fresh young romaine (1 pound or so)
2 large cloves of garlic
About ¾ cup extra virgin olive oil
Salt and freshly ground pepper
2 cups plain unseasoned homemade croutons ⅜-inch size (see Special Note on the next page)
2 eggs
Juice of 1 lemon

A few drops of Worcestershire sauce
¼ cup (1 ounce) best-quality
imported Parmesan cheese,
freshly grated

Preliminaries.

The lettuce. Wash and dry the romaine. Break small leaves into crosswise halves or thirds; separate large leaves from their central rib, discard the tough rib, and tear the leaf halves into halves or thirds. Place the romaine in your salad bowl, cover with slightly dampened paper towels, and refrigerate.

The garlic croutons. Mince and mash the garlic with ¼ teaspoon of salt, then with 3 tablespoons of the oil. Strain into a small frying pan, pressing the oil out of the garlic. Set over medium heat; when hot, turn in the toasted croutons, tossing and turning them for a minute or so to coat them with the oil. Drain on a plate lined with paper towels.

The eggs. Pierce the large ends of the eggs with an egg pricker or push-pin, and lower them into a pan of boiling water. Boil exactly 1 minute; remove them and set aside.

Ahead-of-time note: May be prepared several hours in advance to this point.

Finishing the salad. Pour 3 to 4 tablespoons of oil over the romaine and toss to coat the leaves nicely. Sprinkle on ¼ teaspoon of salt, several grinds of pepper, and toss again. Squeeze on the lemon juice, add 6 drops of Worcestershire, break in the eggs, and toss to blend. Taste a leaf, and correct seasoning. Toss briefly with the cheese, and finally with the croutons. Serve at once.

SPECIAL NOTE

Toasted Croutons
Small cubes of white bread, lightly toasted

It is most important to get the right kind of bread here, the homemade type with body, such as the white sandwich bread on page 47. Croutons from squashy limp bread disintegrate into slime when they come in contact with moisture—not a pretty sight!

For about 2 cups

1 loaf (4 by 4 by 12 inches) somewhat stale—for easy cutting—homemade type white bread with body, unsliced if possible

SPECIAL EQUIPMENT SUGGESTED:
A jelly-roll pan

Preheat the oven to 325°F. Slice the crusts off the bread; cut the bread into slices ½ inch thick. Cut the slices into strips ½ inch wide, and the strips into ½-inch cubes. Turn them into the jelly-roll pan, and set in the middle level of the oven for 20 to 30 minutes, checking and turning the cubes frequently, until they are crisp and an even pale brown.

Ahead-of-time note: May be prepared in advance. If not to be used shortly, store for a few hours in a warming oven, or freeze.

Curly Endive with Bacon and Garlic Dressing

This old favorite is coming back into vogue, I noticed the last time we were in France.

For 6 servings

2 heads of curly endive
3 or 4 strips of thick-sliced bacon
1 large clove of garlic
Salt and freshly ground pepper
1 Tbs virgin olive oil
2 Tbs wine vinegar

Preliminaries. Wash and dry the endive, using the more tender leaves near the center if you have enough to spare, and turn it into a salad bowl; cover with damp paper towels and refrigerate until assembly time. Sauté the bacon until lightly brown and crisp, crumble it into a small bowl,

and set aside. Pour the bacon fat into a small bowl, wipe out the frying pan, and return 1 tablespoon of clear bacon fat to it. Purée the garlic, mash to a fine paste with ¼ teaspoon of salt, and set aside.

Assembling and serving. Just before serving, pour the oil into the bacon fat, blend in the mashed garlic, and warm over moderate heat—but do not let the garlic brown. Pour in the wine vinegar, bring to the boil, and pour over the salad, turning and tossing to blend, and adding several grinds of pepper as you do so. Toss in half the crumbled bacon; sprinkle on the rest, and serve at once.

VARIATION

Curly Endive and Bacon with Poached Eggs

Serve the salad in individual bowls or on plates, and top each with a warm poached egg—which dribbles deliciously over the leaves as you break it up with your fork. This makes an attractive luncheon dish, served with French bread or toasted English muffins, perhaps a bit of cheese, and a cool white wine.

COMPOSED SALADS: MAIN-COURSE SALADS

This is a general introduction to the main-course salad, a freely constructed composition that may contain any edible object, hot, warm, or cold. In addition to the preceding greenery, here are other standard salad elements.

STANDARD SALAD COMPONENTS

AVOCADOS

Avocados of one variety or another are in season all year long. Some are thick-skinned and pear-shaped with dark green, pebble-surfaced skin; others are large, more rounded, and a shiny green. Like pears, avocados are picked when mature, but they are ripened off the tree. You can delay the ripening by storing them in the refrigerator, or hasten it by leaving them at room temperature. (Although it is said that avocados ripen more quickly in a paper bag, I have not found the bag at all effective.) An avocado is ripe when it yields to gentle pressure if cradled in your hand. Once ripe, it will keep nicely in the refrigerator for two or three days.

Nutrition note. The average-size half avocado contains an estimated 136 calories, or 17 calories per slice, plus 8 essential vitamins and 5 minerals, and *no cholesterol*. In fact avocados, and olive oil as well, are mono-unsaturated—therefore good for you.

Avocado Recipes

You will find avocados listed in the index where they appear in salads and appetizers. Though I have tried cooking avocados—for instance, beautifully arranged upon a quiche—I find the taste of cooked avocado musty and extremely unpleasant. I have therefore been happy to leave this delicious object in the cold category and offer my favorite guacamole recipe.

Guacamole

An avocado purée

You will find all sorts of reasons to serve guacamole—for instance as a cocktail dip, or spread on toast for breakfast or lunch, or as an accompaniment to egg dishes and as a side dish with hamburgers. And when you discover your avocados look a bit bruised or are not otherwise suitable for slicing because you forgot they were ripening on top of the refrigerator, remember the guacamole.

For about 2½ cups

2 medium ripe avocados
2 Tbs finely grated onion
1 or 2 cloves of garlic, puréed into a
 very smooth mash (page 350)
Salt and freshly ground pepper
Olive oil
Freshly squeezed lemon or lime
 juice
Optional: chopped jalapeño pepper,
 minced cilantro, chopped fresh
 tomato and/or tomatillos—or
 even bottled Tex-Mex chunky
 taco sauce

Seed and peel the avocados and place the flesh in a mixing bowl. Blend in the onion and garlic with a mixing fork (leave some texture—it should not be like smooth baby food), adding seasonings and other ingredients to your taste to make a spicy, deliciously flavored concoction. Cover closely with plastic and refrigerate until serving time.

*Ahead-of-time note: Guacamole will darken in color after a few hours—stirring it up helps the looks, however.

Salad of green beans, fresh tomato relish, and marinated onion rings

BEANS—GREEN BEANS

Preparing and cooking green beans are also given a thorough treatment in the vegetable chapter, starting on page 276. Lovely indeed is the cold, bright green, perfectly cooked bean in a salad, but don't toss it in until shortly before serving because too long a dressed wait will fade its beautiful color.

BEANS—DRIED BEANS

Cooked or canned dried beans of all colors and shapes make wonderful salads, especially if you dress them while warm so that they absorb all the good flavors. Directions for the quick cooking of dried beans start on page 332, and there is a splendid all-season bean salad on page 334, both to be found in the vegetable chapter.

CUCUMBERS

Thank heaven cucumbers are available all year round because it is hard to think of a salad mixture without them, and what a delight is a plain cucumber salad on a warm summer day. But cucumbers make a delicious cooked vegetable too, as described farther on, and in the vegetable chapter beginning on page 296. Cucumbers are also happy with fish, and vice versa—poached salmon with cucumber and sour cream sauce, for instance, on the following page.

Buying and storing cucumbers

Feel each cucumber all over carefully: it should be a fresh green color, firm to the touch; the skin should seem tight, and there should be no soft spots anywhere. To keep in the humidity, supermarket field-grown cucumbers more often than not are sprayed with a nontoxic wax, which means you'll want to peel them. Top-of-the-grade cucumbers are no more than 2¾ inches in diameter and 6 to 9 inches long. The long, thin, almost seedless unwaxed hot-house cucumbers, usually encased in plastic, are much milder (too mild for me!) in taste. Refrigerate cucumbers in a plastic bag, where they will keep 2 to 3 days—but they will stay healthy a little longer at a cool-room temperature of 45°F to 50°F.

Cucumbers don't agree with the digestions of all diners, and, if you are one of those people, you may wish to try one of these suggestions. They came to me from kind readers when I asked for help in a magazine article some years ago. One of these conflicting theories may work for you.

Cucumber skin. Leave on all or part of the green skin, since cucumber skin, some believe, contains a burp-discouraging enzyme. (But you will want to peel a waxed cucumber because waxing gives the skin a disagreeable texture.) On the other hand some theorists insist that you must peel off every part of green because it is the peel that makes the burp.

The naked rub. An unusual practice that is sworn to by one group is this: cut a slice off the vine end of the cucumber, and rub the cut part with the cut part of that end; then cut a slice off the other end of the cucumber and rub that with the original vine end.

Soaking solutions. Another school advocates soaking sliced cucumbers in salt, others advise salt and vinegar, still others suggest vinegar alone, and a lone few swear by a dressing strong with mustard.

Cooking. When cooked, however, there seems to be nary a burp for most diners who feast upon them.

Sliced cucumbers

Peel the cucumbers or not, as you wish. Either slice them as is crosswise, or halve lengthwise, scoop out the seeds with a teaspoon, then slice them. See also the julienned cucumbers at the end of this section.

To crisp cucumber slices. Refrigerate them for an hour or more in a bowl with ice and lightly salted water. Drain well before using.

Flavored Cucumber Slices

A little steeping in salt, vinegar, and a pinch of sugar brings out the cucumber flavor. A fine beginning to cucumber salads, and perfect diet food.

For 4 to 6 servings, about 3 cups

2 cucumbers 8 inches long

The flavoring
½ tsp salt, or to taste
2 tsp wine or cider vinegar, or to taste
A scant ¼ tsp sugar

1 Tbs chopped fresh dill or parsley, optional

Peel the cucumbers, if you wish, slice them, and toss in a bowl with the flavoring. Let steep for a moment, taste, and add a little more flavoring if you feel it needed. Drain before serving, and toss in the optional herb. You may wish to use the steeping juices in whatever sauce you are making.

VARIATIONS

Sliced Cucumbers in Sour Cream, Buttermilk, or Yogurt

Serve these as part of a salad combination, or as an accompaniment to broiled or poached fish steaks.

For 4 to 6 servings

The preceding recipe for flavored cucumbers
½ cup or so sour cream, buttermilk, or yogurt, stirred to remove lumps

After flavoring the cucumbers with salt, vinegar, and sugar, refrigerate them for 10 minutes or so. Drain them, saving the juices, and fold in just enough sour cream, buttermilk, or yogurt to enrobe them, adding droplets of the juices if the mixture is too stiff. Fold in the dill or parsley, if you wish.

Julienned Cucumbers

For a different look in cucumbers, peel, halve them lengthwise, and seed them; cut into lengthwise quarters, then cut the quarters into 1½-inch lengths. Cut these into matchstick-size julienne—great knife practice! They are now ready to flavor as described, and to serve in a salad or to sauté.

Salad of Cooked Cucumbers

Cucumbers with a difference—cooking softens them and subtly changes their taste. These are also a welcome solution for those who cannot stomach cucumbers in the raw state.

For about 2 cups, serving 4

2 cucumbers 8 inches long, and the flavoring ingredients in the master recipe
Light olive oil or other fresh cooking oil
¼ to ½ cup heavy cream, optional

Preparing the cucumbers. Peel the cucumbers and halve them lengthwise; scoop out the seeds with a teaspoon. Halve them again lengthwise, and cut them on the slant into 1-inch lengths. Toss them in a bowl with the flavorings and let steep 5 minutes or more; drain them well just before proceeding.

Cooking. Warm the oil in a frying pan, and add the cucumbers; toss and turn over moderately high heat for several minutes until the cucumber pieces are barely tender. Correct seasoning.

Serving.

   With herbs. Toss with the dill or parsley, and serve.

   Or simmered in cream. Simmer for a few minutes with several spoonfuls of cream, then toss with the minced fresh dill or parsley.

TOMATOES

Red, ripe, sweetly acid tomatoes are certainly one of the most prized of salad ingredients, and if we wanted to pay a large price, we could have perfect examples all year round. The sad fact is that tomatoes are permanently traumatized if they remain for more than a few hours at temperatures lower than 55°F, whether in the field or in storage. Afterward they may turn red, and their interstices may fill with jelly, but their flavor will never develop that real tomato taste. When fully ripe, tomatoes still do not like a cold climate; store them at 55°F or at cool room temperature, since they lose flavor when refrigerated.

In other words, the tomato is a persnickety being, and it is no wonder we can rarely buy a good one either in or out of season. In season the best solution is to grow your own or to know a friendly gardener nearby; greenhouse tomatoes are probably your best choice out of season—if you buy them yourself or can find a market that knows how to handle tomatoes.

Cherry tomatoes

Cherry tomatoes often have better flavor than regular tomatoes, and that is usually true out of season because they are greenhouse grown. Keep them at room temperature. Wash them before using, and when cut in half for serving they are certainly easier to eat.

To Peel Tomatoes

Blanch the whole tomatoes—meaning drop 2 or 3 at a time into a fairly large pan of rapidly boiling water, and boil exactly 10 seconds. Cut out the core, and peel the skin down from it.

*Ahead-of-time note: You may blanch tomatoes several hours in advance, and peel them later—they keep fresher when still in their skins.

To Seed and Juice Tomatoes

Many recipes call for tomato pulp, meaning you must seed and juice your tomatoes. To do so, halve the peeled tomato crosswise (not through the core). Then, holding the half over a sieve set in a bowl, gently squeeze to dislodge most of the jelly-like substance, juice, and seeds; finally, poke out the residue with your little finger. Press the juices out of the residue in the sieve and use in soups or sauce, or as a refreshing drink for the cook.

Seeding and juicing peeled tomato halves

To Chop or Dice Peeled Seeded Tomatoes
Tomates Concassées

When you need a neat effect for decoration or special sauces, you want diced tomato pulp. First, using a potato baller, scoop the ribs out of the inside of the peeled and juiced tomato half, and cut these into neat dice. Then place the tomato half cut side down on your work surface and slice into neat strips; cut the strips crosswise into neat dice.

Suggestions for using diced tomatoes

As a garnish for soups. Shortly before you intend to serve, fold the diced tomato into a finished soup, such as a consommé or the beef and vegetable soup on page 16; simmer a moment just to warm through.

As a garnish for sauces. Diced tomato is particularly attractive in white butter sauces and fish veloutés, giving them not only color but a welcome lightly acid overtone. An example is the butter sauce with the fish fillets Dugléré on page 91.

SPECIAL NOTE

Fresh Tomato Sauce

An excellent tomato sauce in or out of season is essential to any good cooking. In season, you will use ripe red tomatoes full of flavor; out of season, a mixture of fresh tomatoes and Italian plum tomatoes, as described on the following page.

For about 2½ cups

½ **cup minced onions**
2 **Tbs olive oil**
4 **cups tomato pulp (out of season: half fresh and half canned tomatoes)**
¼ **tsp thyme**
1 **imported bay leaf**
1 **or 2 large cloves of garlic, puréed**
Optional: big pinch of saffron threads
Optional: ¼ tsp dried orange peel
Salt
Freshly ground pepper

Cook the onions and oil in a 2-quart covered saucepan stirring occasionally, until tender but not brown—6 to 8 minutes. Stir in the tomatoes; cover and cook slowly several minutes. Stir in the herbs, garlic, optional saffron and orange peel; salt lightly to taste. Simmer slowly, partially covered, for 30 minutes, adding a little juice from the tomatoes if sauce becomes too thick. Taste carefully and correct seasoning.

*Ahead-of-time note: May be cooked in advance and refrigerated; may be frozen.

SHALLOTS, SCALLIONS, AND ONIONS

Finely minced shallots or scallions are almost a must in a dressing for green beans or lentils, as well as being agreeable in a salad of mixed greens. Do not let a dressing made with them sit around for long, however, or it and they will go off in taste. Diced onions go in potato salad and coleslaw, and red onion rings are decorative as well as tasty in many a composed salad.

To take the bite out of onions. Drop diced or sliced onions into boiling water for barely a second, drain, and rinse in cold water.

Onions without tears. It's the chemical propanethial S-oxide that's the tear-producing villain here, and onions are full of it. When that combines with the moisture of your eyes it produces sulfuric acid, and it's no wonder we cry. But S-oxide's power is soluble in water—therefore, peel onions under a running cold-water faucet. And its effect is slowed way down by cold—refrigerate your onions before slicing, if you've a lot of them to do.

Fresh Tomato Relish

Use this fresh and delicious combination with broiled fish, hamburgers, egg dishes, as a salad garnish—anywhere, in fact, that the fresh flavor of tomatoes would be a welcome accompaniment.

For about 1½ cups

4 ripe red tomatoes (see note on
    canned tomatoes following)
1 Tbs finely minced shallots or
    scallions
½ tsp or so red wine vinegar
1 Tbs virgin olive oil
Salt and freshly ground pepper
Fresh basil leaves, if available, and 2
    Tbs minced fresh parsley

SPECIAL EQUIPMENT SUGGESTED:
A stainless sieve set over a bowl

Assembling. Peel, seed, and juice the tomatoes as previously described, then fold them gently in a bowl with the shallots or scallions, vinegar, oil, and salt and pepper to taste. If you are using fresh basil leaves, fold them in also. Let steep for 10 minutes to blend flavors.

Finishing. Turn into the sieve to drain. Return to the bowl, correct seasoning (remove the basil, if you wish), and fold in the parsley.

*Ahead-of-time note: You may make the relish an hour or so ahead if need be, but the fresher it is the better.

ADDITIONS AND VARIATIONS

You may wish to fold in other ingredients like finely diced green bell pepper, chili peppers, avocado, and garlic—which will actually turn the relish into more of a salsa.

Fresh or Canned Italian Plum Tomatoes

Make the same general tomato relish using all or part fresh plum tomatoes, peeled and seeded; although they do not have the tender texture of regular tomatoes, they usually have more out-of-season flavor. And if your field or plum tomatoes lack taste, the mixing in of some canned plum tomatoes, although mushy, will help give more interest—drain them, halve them lengthwise, gently scrape out the seeds, and dice the pulp.

Marinated Onions

A little extra flavor is hardly amiss when you are using onion rings in a salad or for hamburgers.

For 1 cup or so of onion rings

1 large red or yellow onion, cut into
    thin rings
A scant ¼ tsp salt
Several grinds of white pepper
A scant ¼ tsp celery seeds
1 to 2 tsp wine vinegar

SPECIAL EQUIPMENT SUGGESTED:
A mandolin or hand slicer is useful here

Assembling. Toss the sliced onions in a bowl with the salt, pepper, celery seed, and vinegar. Taste analytically after a few minutes, and correct seasoning.

*Ahead-of-time note: Cover and refrigerate until you are ready to serve.

Serving. Correct seasoning again. You may wish to add the exuded juices to whatever sauce or salad you are including.

A colorful group of bell peppers

Cutting out the ribs for julienne

Slice off both ends of the pepper to make a cylinder. Halve the pepper lengthwise, and remove the seeds. Lay a pepper half, skin side down, on your work surface (halve it again if it is too wide to work with); slice off the ribs and any protruding flesh, making an even strip. Cut the strip into julienne.

BELL PEPPERS

Not so long ago it was only green peppers, and occasionally red peppers; one never saw or heard of them yellow, purple, brown, orange, or white. With such a proliferation of colors is there a striped variety in our future? Bell peppers are lovely in salads—diced, julienned, or cut into rings.

Buying and storing bell peppers. Look over each pepper carefully to be sure it has no pock marks or bad spots, and that it is glossy and firm all over. Refrigerate them in a plastic bag, and plan to use them within 2 or 3 days, since they do not keep well at temperatures under 45°F.

A Neat Julienne of Bell Peppers

A julienne of fresh peppers, especially a mixture of colors, can look elegant in a salad. I always had trouble cutting them into those long thin even matchsticks until caterer Karyn Scott of Tucson showed me this way, which she said she had learned from one of her chef associates.

1 fine fresh firm bell pepper

SPECIAL EQUIPMENT SUGGESTED:
A very sharp chef's knife with blade at least 7 inches long

To Peel a Peck of Peppers

The only way to peel peppers is to blister the skin so that it rises off the flesh and can then be stripped off. For just a pepper or two, you may spear them one at a time with a 2-pronged fork, and turn them over a gas flame—or around a portable blowtorch—until the skin blisters all over. Or roast them 3 or 4 at a time over a grill, turning another side to the coals as each part blisters, or set them under a broiler. While the rest of the peck are on or under the fire, rapidly cut the hot peppers in half, remove the stem and seeds, and peel off the skin—do not delay since a blackened skin can eventually blacken the flesh. (Although some practitioners close the warm peppers in a paper bag for 5 to 10 minutes before peeling, I have never found that to be necessary when the skins are well blistered.)

A Salad of Peeled and Roasted Peppers

Peppers, olive oil, salt, and garlic are all you need for this simple savory, which is something that will keep several days in the refrigerator. Serve the peppers as they are to garnish a salad or broiled fish, or combine them with tomatoes, hard-boiled eggs, and anchovies for a perfect bistro-type first course.

For 1½ to 2 cups

1 clove of garlic—large, medium, or small
¼ tsp salt
⅓ cup virgin olive oil
3 or 4 medium to large bell peppers, peeled as in the preceding directions, halved, and seeded

SPECIAL EQUIPMENT SUGGESTED:
A garlic press is useful; a small mortar and pestle or a medium bowl and wooden spoon

Assembling. Purée the garlic into the mortar or bowl, then mash into a perfectly smooth paste with the salt. Whisk in the oil. Cut the peppers into ⅜-inch strips and arrange in layers in an oval dish, spooning the dressing over each. Cover and let steep 20 minutes, tilting the dish and basting the peppers with their dressing several times. Correct seasoning.

*Ahead-of-time note: Cover airtight with plastic wrap and refrigerate, and the peppers will keep nicely for several days. Let warm at room temperature for ½ hour or so before serving, to decongeal the oil.

POTATOES

There's hardly a soul alive, especially including me, who doesn't love potato salad in one form or another. My all-time favorite is the versatile so-called French version, where warm potato slices are seasoned very simply with vinaigrette—to go with hot sliced sausages, cold sliced beef, mayonnaise, or as part of a combination like Salade Niçoise. And I adore old-fashioned American potato salad. Although both appear in other books, I cannot resist repeating the first because it is so useful, and the second because I love it so. They both start out the same way, with cooked potato slices.

🐷 MASTER RECIPE

Cooked Sliced Potatoes for Salad

The easiest way to achieve cooked sliced potatoes is to slice them first before simmering them. You will of course get criticisms from those worthies who say if you don't cook them whole you're throwing away the best parts, or you're losing nutrients, and/or you're wasting this or that, etc., none of which I believe.

For about 1 quart

1½ pounds "boiling" potatoes, all the same size and shape if possible
Salt—1 to 1½ tsp per quart of water

SPECIAL EQUIPMENT SUGGESTED:
A 3-quart saucepan with tight-fitting lid; a vegetable slicer is useful

Slicing the potatoes. Fill the saucepan half full with cold water. Wash the potatoes. One at a time peel a potato,

and if it's round and fat rather than long and thin, cut it in half lengthwise. Cut the potato into slices ¼ inch thick, and drop the slices into the pan of water, to prevent discoloration while you prepare the rest.

*Ahead-of-time note: It is best to cook them within ½ hour to prevent the possibility of their turning gray.

Cooking. Drain out the water, then add clean cold water to cover, and the salt. Bring to the simmer, and simmer 2 to 3 minutes, or until the potatoes are just tender—keep testing by eating a slice to be sure. Crunchily undercooked potatoes are dreadful, and overcooked potato slices will disintegrate.

Firming up. Drain out the cooking water (you may wish to use it for soup or save a bit for the following salad). At once cover the pan and set aside for 3 to 4 minutes (but no longer than 5), to allow the slices to firm up. Then uncover the potatoes and plan to season them while still warm.

TWO POTATO SALADS

In both of these the warm potatoes are first steeped a few minutes with seasonings and a little liquid, then the oil or dressing is added. This not only gives the potatoes a fine flavor, but prevents them from drinking up too much oil.

French Potato Salad

For about 1 quart, serving 6 in combination with other items

The preceding 1½ pounds warm sliced cooked potatoes
2 Tbs finely minced shallots or scallions
Salt and freshly ground white pepper
¼ cup chicken stock or potato-cooking water
1½ Tbs wine vinegar
2 to 3 Tbs chopped fresh parsley
2 to 3 Tbs light olive oil, optional

SPECIAL EQUIPMENT SUGGESTED:
A roomy bowl for gentle tossing

Turn the warm potatoes into the bowl and toss gently with the shallots or scallions, a sprinkling of salt and pepper, stock or cooking water, vinegar, and parsley. Let steep 10 minutes or so, tossing gently several times. Then correct seasoning, toss with the optional oil, and the potatoes are ready for serving.

*Ahead-of-time note: The potatoes will keep a day or two covered and under refrigeration. If they are made with oil, let sit for ½ hour at room temperature before serving.

French Potato Salad

American Potato Salad

Trying to come up with the best possible potato salad, we picked this to accompany a boned and stuffed Chicken Melon on one of our "Company" TV series. It is still my favorite.

For about 2 quarts, serving 6 to 8

Double the preceding master recipe for warm cooked sliced potatoes
⅔ cup liquid—3 Tbs cider vinegar plus chicken broth or potato-cooking water
1 cup finely diced mild yellow onions tossed with a big pinch of salt
⅔ cup finely diced tender celery stalks
¼ cup finely diced dill pickle

Salt and freshly ground white pepper
3 or 4 strips of crisply cooked bacon, crumbled
3 hard-boiled eggs, diced
½ cup canned red pimiento, diced
2 to 3 Tbs minced fresh parsley
¾ to 1 cup homemade mayonnaise (see recipe following)—½ cup or so to be folded into the salad; the rest reserved for final decoration
Decorative suggestions: crisp salad greens; sliced or quartered hard-boiled eggs; parsley sprigs; strips of red pimiento; green and/or black olives; quartered tomatoes or halved cherry tomatoes

SPECIAL EQUIPMENT SUGGESTED:
A large bowl for gentle tossing

Assembling. Turn the warm potato slices into the bowl and toss gently with the liquid, onions, celery, pickle, and seasonings to taste. Let steep for 10 minutes, tossing carefully 2 or 3 times. When cool, toss with the bacon, eggs, pimiento, parsley, and just enough mayonnaise to enrobe the potatoes lightly.

*Ahead-of-time note: Cover and refrigerate, and the salad will keep perfectly for 24 hours.

Serving. Check the salad for seasoning again. Line a serving bowl or platter with the greens and mound the potato salad upon them. Spread a thin layer of mayonnaise over the potatoes and decorate the salad nicely with eggs, parsley, and whatever else you have chosen.

MAYONNAISE

Handmade mayonnaise was one gastronomic delight that many home cooks were afraid to tackle until the appearance of the electric blender before World War II, and until Anne Seranne came up with the first fool-proof machine-made mayonnaise. Now we have the food processor, and mayonnaise is even easier to make by machine—though maybe no easier to scrape out! If you've not tried it in the processor you'll find, after a batch or two, that you will confidently whirl up half a quart or more of that thoroughly addictive sauce in under 5 minutes. Perhaps the following notes will tell you more than you wish to know, but it may build up your confidence to have some idea of how things work.

Adding the oil slowly at first. Mayonnaise is an emulsion, meaning that egg yolks are forced to absorb oil and to hold it in a thick creamy suspension. For the emulsion process to take place, you first process the yolks to thicken them, which prepares them for the oil to come. Then you process in the oil a little bit at a time at first, to get the emulsion going. When the mixture has begun to cream and thicken you have won; you can add the oil a little more rapidly and all is well as long as you do not exceed the limit that the egg yolks can absorb—⅔ cup per yolk. Another caution—do not stop the machine until the emulsion is well under way or the sauce may refuse to thicken.

Don't worry. If the mayonnaise refuses to thicken, or if it thins out, that's easy to fix—see notes at the end of the recipe.

The plastic vs. the metal blade. The metal blade is so efficient that it often makes too stiff a sauce, and you'll want to thin it out. The shorter dull-edged plastic blade, however, which is a little slower in action and takes a little longer to thicken the sauce, gives a more tender result—if you can call a sauce tender!

The oil to use. What is the mayonnaise to accompany? Cold lobster or crab, for instance, would want a light oil, neutral in taste, with perhaps just a driblet of olive oil for flavor. A salad strong with garlic and

onions, on the other hand, will take, and even need, more pronounced tastes. For an all-purpose sauce, as an example, I use half to two-thirds peanut oil and the rest is virgin olive oil.

 MASTER RECIPE

Machine-Made Mayonnaise
Using the food processor

The beauty of your own mayonnaise is that you know exactly what is in it, and you can use the best and freshest oil, lemon, and/or vinegar.

For 2 to 2¼ cups

1 "large" egg
2 egg yolks
1 tsp Dijon-type prepared mustard
½ tsp salt
2 tsp freshly squeezed lemon juice and/or wine vinegar
1½ to 2 cups best-quality oil— peanut, olive, or other oil—all one or a mixture
Freshly ground white pepper
More mustard, salt, lemon juice and/ or vinegar, as needed
Droplets of sour cream, sweet cream, or water—to lighten the finished sauce if it is too stiff

SPECIAL EQUIPMENT SUGGESTED: *A food processor (the plastic blade is recommended but not essential); a pouring funnel is useful*

The egg base. Place the whole egg, the yolks, and the teaspoon of mustard in the container of the processor; process 30 seconds with a plastic blade;

(continued)

Machine-Made Mayonnaise (*continued*)

15 with the steel blade. Add the salt and lemon juice and/or vinegar and process 15 seconds with the plastic blade; 7 or 8 with the steel blade.

Adding the oil. With the machine running, start adding the oil, pouring it in a thin stream of droplets—keep your eye on the stream to be sure it is going in very slowly. Keep the machine always running, and when you see that the sauce has thickened, you may add the oil a little faster. Stop the machine after 1½ cups or so of oil, and check on the sauce: if it seems very thick, add droplets of lemon or vinegar, and taste it for seasoning. (You do not need to use all the oil; if you like a yellower sauce, for instance, 1½ cups may be sufficient.) Continue with the oil if you plan to use all of it.

Final flavoring. Taste the sauce carefully for seasoning, briefly processing in more as necessary. If the sauce is too stiff or thick, process in droplets of cream or water.

Store-Bought and Cooked Egg Mayonnaise. If you do not want to use raw eggs because of possible bacterial contamination, use store-bought mayonnaise, which is perfectly safe (I prefer Best Foods, or Hellmann's), or the cooked egg mayonnaise on page 377.

Additions and Variations

To change the taste and the view, there are all kinds of garnishes to stir into a finished mayonnaise. Following are some examples.

SPECIAL NOTE

Storing Mayonnaise and Trouble Shooting

Storing mayonnaise. Scrape the mayonnaise into a screw-top jar, and put in the refrigerator, where it will keep safely 4 or 5 days. Although lemon juice and vinegar discourage bacteria, home-made egg sauces are prime breeding grounds for them unless kept well chilled. Don't take chances!

Trouble shooting. Suppose you happen to pour in the oil too quickly and the sauce won't thicken? Or suppose it thins out? Or it separates? The processor won't fix it, but a wire whisk or hand-held mixer will. Place ½ tablespoon of prepared mustard in a mixing bowl, stir up the turned sauce so that you will have both egg and oil, and add 1 tablespoon of the sauce to the mustard. Whisk them together vigorously a few seconds until they thicken into a cream. Whisk in successive dribbles of stirred-up turned sauce until you have a good cup of restored mayonnaise, then you may add the turned sauce a little faster. This always works, as long as you go slowly at first so that the emulsion gets going again and the sauce really starts to thicken.

Herbal Mayonnaise

Stir fresh green herbs into the finished sauce, such as finely minced parsley, chives, chervil, basil, tarragon—1 or 2 tablespoons per cup of mayonnaise.

Green Mayonnaise

You might serve a green mayonnaise with fish or eggs. To get that verdant effect, blanch (boil briefly) for a few seconds until limp 1 packed cup of well-washed tender greenery such as stemmed spinach and watercress, young sorrel, or chives and Italian parsley. Drain. Run cold water over the leaves to set the color. Drain again, and twist them hard in the corner of a clean towel to extract excess water. Purée the greens in a food processor with a tablespoon or two of mayonnaise; add the rest of the 1 to 1½ cups of mayonnaise and blend briefly with a pulse or two.

Pimiento Mayonnaise

It's mayonnaise of a pretty pink, with a subtle new taste. This could be served with cold poached eggs, hard-boiled eggs, cold poached fish, cold breast of chicken, and cold vegetables.

Drain ½ cup of the broiled and peeled red peppers on page 360, or bottled brine-cured red pimientos. Twist them in the corner of a clean towel to extract as much juice as possible, then purée in a food processor with a spoonful or two of mayonnaise. Add the rest of the 1½ cups of mayonnaise and, if you wish, 2 tablespoons of minced parsley and/or chives; blend briefly with 2 or 3 pulses of the machine.

Lobster or Crab Mayonnaise

Cold boiled lobsters and crabs provide you with a special treat—the tomalley or green matter, and the roe. Blend it into mayonnaise and that shellfish will be even more delicious to eat.

Lobster Note: Be sure that your lobsters come from a reputable dealer and that they were gathered in a pollution-free area.

For 1¼ to 1½ cups

2 to 4 Tbs tomalley or green matter, and the roe if you are so fortunate, from cooked lobster or crab (illustrated on page 105)
1 to 1½ cups mayonnaise
Optional additions: 2 to 3 Tbs minced fresh parsley; 1 Tbs finely minced shallot or scallion; 1 Tbs minced capers (squeezed dry); 1 hard-boiled egg, finely chopped

SPECIAL EQUIPMENT SUGGESTED: *A fine-meshed sieve and wooden spoon for puréeing the tomalley*

The mixture. Push the tomalley and roe through the sieve to remove tiny shell bits (the only way to get rid of them), and whisk the tomalley mixture into the mayonnaise. Fold in any or all of the optional additions.

Serving suggestions.

Whole or halved lobster or crab. Spoon the mayonnaise, with or without its optional additions, into the cavity of the shellfish, and you might decorate the top of the sauce with minced parsley and chopped hard-boiled egg.

Lobster or crab salad. Halve and hollow out hard-boiled eggs, fill with the sauce, and decorate with minced parsley and the chopped yolks. Or fill tomato shells with the sauce and decorate with parsley.

Or be stodgy, and pass the sauce in a bowl.

Salade Niçoise

Some combinations become famous just because the mixture was such a happy one that it has lived on and on, pleasing successive generations of palates. Salade Niçoise is certainly one of these, and so famous that arguments exist as to what is the real thing. Being a great fan of potatoes, beans, eggs, and tomatoes in a salad, I naturally opt for the Escoffier ingredients; I am a great fan of his too, and he was a Niçois, after all. This is a fine example, by the way, of how to combine a number of good things into a happy whole, as well as into a whole main course. Since Salade Niçoise contains most of the elements dealt with in the preceding recipes, I shall refer you back to them rather than repeating everything again.

MANUFACTURING NOTE. *A bountiful arrangement in bowl or platter is so handsome to behold that I think it a cruel shame to toss everything together into a big mess. A careful presentation means more work, but it's easily manageable when you ready each of the numerous ingredients separately, which you can do well ahead. Season each just before assembling and serving, and you will have the perfect Salade Niçoise.*

(continued)

Important elements in a Salade Niçoise

Salade Niçoise (continued)

For 6 to 8 servings

1 large head of Boston lettuce, washed and dried (page 348)
2 to 3 Tbs virgin olive oil
Salt and freshly ground pepper
1½ pounds fresh green beans, trimmed, blanched, refreshed in cold water, and dried (page 276)
⅔ to 1 cup salad dressing, such as the Oil and Lemon Dressing on page 350, or its garlic variation
3 or 4 fine ripe red tomatoes, peeled if you wish, and cored, quartered, and seasoned before serving
8 to 10 ounces oil-packed tuna, drained and flaked
1 quart French Potato Salad (page 362)
8 hard-boiled eggs, halved lengthwise
1 can flat anchovy fillets packed in oil, opened and drained just before serving
½ cup black Niçoise-type olives
3 or 4 Tbs capers
¼ cup minced fresh parsley

Assembling. Shortly before serving, line a handsome, large and wide salad bowl or a roomy platter with lettuce leaves, drizzle a little olive oil on them, and dust with a sprinkling of salt. Toss the beans in a mixing bowl with a little of the dressing, and correct seasoning. Drizzle a spoonful or two of the dressing over the tomatoes. Season the tuna lightly with a spoonful or two of dressing. Place the potatoes in the center of the bowl or platter; mound beans at strategic intervals, interspersing them with tomatoes and mounds of tuna. Ring the salad with the eggs, and curl an anchovy on top of each. Spoon a little more vinaigrette over all; scatter on olives, capers, and parsley. Serve as soon as possible.

Suggested accompaniments—a one-course luncheon menu. French bread and a fine soft-ripening cheese like a Brie or Camembert, and a dry white wine such as Alsatian riesling or a light sauvignon blanc. You might finish with chocolate truffles (page 485) and coffee.

VARIATION

Niçoise Salad Ring

For a special luncheon or buffet, mound a modified Niçoise salad in a giant cream puff shell. It makes a conversation piece, and an edible container as well. How to serve it? Cut the puff into portions with a serrated knife.

Niçoise Salad Ring

For 6 to 8 servings

As many of the preceding Niçoise ingredients as you wish, or as suggested in the recipe here
½ cup or so mayonnaise

A giant cream puff 15 or more inches in diameter (the recipe on page 398, minus the sugar)

This is a free-form construction dependent upon the cook's whim and store of ingredients. For instance you might turn the tuna into a salad, mixing into it 2 or 3 chopped hard-boiled eggs, minced parsley, a little of the dressing, and several spoonfuls of mayonnaise. Just before serving, arrange the greenery in the bottom of the shell. Make mounds for each serving starting with a group of potatoes topped with tuna; decorate with olives, capers, and strips of tomato, green beans, and anchovies.

SUBVARIATIONS

The salad ring idea lends itself to all manner of combinations. For instance you might line the bottom of the shell with shredded iceberg or romaine, and construct mounds of beautifully seasoned chicken, turkey, lobster, or crab salad. Or use the general outlines of the colorful Fisherman's salad on page 104.

Elegant Additions to Composed Salads

Tiny asparagus spears vinaigrette, artichoke bottoms sliced and steeped with oil and lemon, marinated raw mushrooms, vegetables à la Grecque, fresh green beans tossed with shallots and vinaigrette—and there are many others, too, that have nary a mention in these pages. I don't have room for everything, alas, and there are recipes for them in many a cookbook, including others of mine.

PASTA SALADS AND RICE SALADS

Pasta has outstripped potatoes as a salad base, undoubtedly because pasta is so easy to prepare. Rice is less usual than either, but turns itself into a salad in much the same way. In either case, think about tomorrow or the day after when you're cooking up pasta or rice for a hot dish, since the salad comes naturally afterward.

PASTA SALADS

Now that pasta is universal, we don't have to try to be Italian about it anymore, and I, for one, cook it according to my own ideas. However, I do often refer to Jack Denton Scott's *Complete Book of Pasta* (Morrow, 1968 and reprints) with its drawings of pasta shapes, and with its nostalgic photographs of Italy by the late great Samuel Chamberlain. I especially like Mr. Scott's well-informed Italian, but realistically American, approach to his subject.

Free-form composition with potatoes, eggs, tomato, cucumber, chick-peas, tuna, avocado, and olives

 MASTER RECIPE

Cooked Pasta for Salads

Just because pasta is easy to cook doesn't mean you don't have to go about it carefully. It is hopeless, for instance, to try mixing a salad when the cooked pasta has glued itself together into an unyielding mass, and it is horrid to be served a salad of dried-out, badly cooked pasta. I therefore suggest that it be tossed in oil and seasonings as soon as it is cooked, and a little garlic is often a happy addition, too.

CHOICE OF PASTA. *Little rings, pasta bows, corkscrew rotelle, rice-shaped orzo grains, noodles, spaghetti—these all work nicely in salads. Hollow shapes like macaroni and the shell shapes might entrap too much of the dressing to be satisfactory.*

For 6 servings

Cooking the pasta
8 quarts water in a 10- to 12-quart kettle
1 pound pasta
2 Tbs salt
1 Tbs olive oil

Initial flavoring
1 large, medium, or small clove of garlic, puréed, optional
Salt and freshly ground white pepper
1 Tbs or so virgin olive oil

SPECIAL EQUIPMENT SUGGESTED: *A pasta fork, or a wire skimmer-scoop, or a perforated spoon and mixing fork; a mixing bowl or salad bowl*

Cooking the pasta. When the water in the kettle is at a rolling boil, dump in the pasta, salt, and tablespoon of oil (which discourages the pot from boiling over). Boil uncovered at medium speed until the pasta tastes done—test frequently by biting a piece. It should have the slightest texture, but be definitely done—on no account should it be crunchily undercooked. While it is boiling, prepare for the next step.

Preliminary flavoring. If you are using the garlic, purée it into the bowl and mash to a fine paste with a big pinch of salt. Blend in a teaspoon of oil. When the pasta is done, remove it to the bowl by forkfuls or spoonfuls, draining each well—as Jack Denton points out, a little humidity on the pasta pieces helps prevent them from sticking together. Toss with the oil, adding droplets more, just to coat the pasta with a light film. Toss in salt and pepper to taste. This is now ready to be a pasta salad, or you may cover and reheat it over simmering water for a hot dish.

*Ahead-of-time note: May be done a day or two in advance; cover and refrigerate.

Pasta Salad Printanière
Pasta garnished with fresh vegetables

This is a lovely, fresh, and pretty salad to serve for a luncheon main course, and a blessing for all concerned when there's a vegetarian in the midst. Here is one idea, and following that are a number of other suggestions.

For 6 servings

1 pound pasta, such as rotelle— smallish corkscrew-shaped pasta—cooked as in the preceding master recipe
1 cup each of the following *cooked* **vegetables: small broccoli florets, fresh green peas, diced fresh green beans**
4 scallions, cut into ½-inch diagonals
½ cup coarsely chopped fresh parsley
¼ cup salad dressing, such as the Oil and Lemon Dressing (page 350) or one of its variations
Salt and freshly ground white pepper
Optional decoration: salad greens, black olives, quartered tomatoes, halved cherry tomatoes, and strips or triangles of pimiento

Assembling. Toss the vegetables into the pasta with the scallions, parsley, and small spoonfuls of the salad dressing. Taste carefully, and toss in seasonings as necessary.

Serving suggestion. Line a bowl or platter with salad greens, mound the pasta salad upon them, and decorate with any or all of the suggestions listed.

Pasta Salad with Fresh Tomato and Basil

Here is one of the most delightful of summer pastas. Serve when large fresh basil leaves are abundant, and fresh tomatoes are red, ripe, and full of flavor. This would go, for instance, with cold meats or chicken or with broiled or poached fish.

For 6 servings

The master recipe for 1 pound Cooked Pasta for Salads
¼ cup or so salad dressing, such as the vinaigrette on page 351
A dozen or so large fine fresh leaves of basil
The fresh tomato relish on page 359

Serving suggestions.

In a salad bowl. An attractive presentation here is to place the pasta in a salad bowl, tossing with several spoonfuls of the dressing. Make a large central nest in the pasta, line it with the basil leaves, and spoon the tomato relish in the center. Spoon on a little of the dressing. Either let guests serve themselves, or toss the salad gently at the table.

Individual bowls. Or make separate servings for each guest, each with an individual bowl.

Additions. You could well enlarge on this idea, adding a modest amount of cooked shrimp or lobster, strips of ham, or slivers of feta or goat cheese. However, too much elaboration takes away from the simple delight of ripe tomatoes, basil, and pasta.

Table-Top Spaghetti Marco Polo

This is one of my favorites, another version of which first appeared on our "French Chef" series, then in my *Kitchen* book, and again on television for "Mr. Rogers' Neighborhood." Tossed at the table, it pleases young and old, and is best eaten with chopsticks. French bread and a white wine such as sauvignon blanc would go well here.

For 6 servings as a main-course luncheon dish

1 pound spaghetti prepared as in the master recipe Cooked Pasta for Salads, in a large salad bowl
1 cup each: chopped walnuts, chopped black olives, and chopped bottled red pimiento, tossed together in an attractive bowl
½ cup chopped fresh parsley, in a small bowl
12 large leaves fresh basil, thinly sliced, in a small bowl
¼ cup garlic dressing (page 351), in a bowl or pitcher with mixing fork
Salt and white pepper, both in grinders
1½ cups loosely packed chilled crumbled cheese such as feta, goat cheese, Roquefort, or blue

SPECIAL EQUIPMENT SUGGESTED:
A long-handled spoon and fork for tossing and serving; a tasting fork; chopsticks for eating

Tossing the salad. Have all the ingredients at the table. With flourish and confidence, begin by elegantly folding into the spaghetti the chopped nuts and vegetables, along with the parsley and basil. Toss in spoonfuls of dressing, tasting for seasoning, and adding salt and pepper as needed.

Serving. Serve onto chilled plates, and sprinkle each salad with crumbled cheese.

RICE SALADS

Leftover cooked rice is a real kitchen treasure, particularly for salads. Use either the plain boiled white rice on page 327, or its risotto variation, and following are some salad ideas to whet your appetite and imagination.

The Emperor's Rice

A sumptuous main course

For 6 servings

2 to 3 cups cooked rice
Olive oil or excellent salad oil, as needed
Freshly squeezed lemon juice and/or wine vinegar
Salt and freshly ground pepper
A good handful of fresh parsley, chopped

Garnishing suggestions—any or all of the following

Diced cooked shrimp, lobster, crab, ham, chicken, pork, and/or sausage

Rice salad ringed with cooked broccoli spears

Diced red and/or green bell peppers
Minced mild onion, shallots, or scallions
Pine nuts, or chopped walnuts, pecans, hazelnuts, peanuts, and so forth
Minced fresh herbs such as basil, dill, tarragon, and chives
Cucumbers, peeled, seeded, diced, macerated in salt, and drained
Diced hard cheese such as Cheddar, Swiss, Parmesan; or diced feta

Other elements for decoration

Leaves of Boston lettuce, shredded romaine or green iceberg lettuce leaves, and/or watercress
Broccoli florets, blanched
Black or green olives
Capers
Quartered or chopped hard-boiled eggs
Cherry tomatoes or quartered tomatoes
Mayonnaise passed separately

SPECIAL EQUIPMENT SUGGESTED:
A wooden or plastic fork for tossing

Toss the rice in a bowl with a little oil, lemon or vinegar, salt and pepper, and parsley. When nicely flavored, toss in other flavors, as you have them, such as the shrimp, peppers, onion, nuts, and so forth. When you have completed your rice mixture, arrange a salad bowl or platter with a shallow bed of greens, and the rice mounded in the center. Then you might ring it with a garland of green broccoli as in the photograph. Decorate with olives, capers, eggs, tomatoes, or whatever else your sense of impeccable taste and originality dictates. Cover with plastic wrap and refrigerate until serving time. The only accompaniment you will need is a bowl of mayonnaise, a bottle of white wine, and a loaf of French bread.

East Bay Hot Rice Salad

VARIATION

East Bay Hot Rice Salad

An attractive informal luncheon idea is the preceding Emperor's Rice hot, served in a bowl. Here it is mostly vegetables—cut string beans, cherry tomatoes, diced peppers, pasta, diced cheese, and mushrooms—the perfect chopstick meal.

POULTRY, MEAT, AND FISH SALADS

Chicken, crab, and tuna salad are American staples, but I believe it was the French nouvelle cuisine chefs in the early 1970's who first went exotic. The French, who had scoffed for years at the barbaric American first-course salad, began offering that very thing themselves in such daring combinations as Michel Guérard's Salade Folle, hearts of frizzy lettuce with bits of warm foie gras. It was usually duck foie gras, but if you use those precious livers for salad you must do something with the rest of the duck.

Thus was born, I presume, the present restaurant main-course staple, breast of duck, magret de canard, sautéed or roasted whole—and what better way to serve the legs and thighs than to dress them in a salad? A warm salad. Why not? The idea caught, and it follows that we now find all kinds of warm things besides duck and foie gras in salads—little split and broiled quail, for example, or chunks of warm lobster meat, and so forth and so on. These are pleasant indeed as little first courses, and ideal for a light luncheon. I shall start out with a few, to give the general idea, then on to the more familiar fare.

Warm Duck Salad

Suppose you have done wonders with duck breasts for a dinner party, the carcass has made a first-rate duck stock, and now, for another day, you have the legs and thighs for a salad. Here is one way to go about it, and a special sweet-and-sour dressing that accompanies duck and game especially well.

A NOTE ON LEFTOVER COOKED DUCK. *Leftover cooked duck is best, I think, served cold either with a condiment such as chutney, or marinated for ½ hour in a dressing such as the one described here. Warmed-over cooked duck unfortunately always has a telltale warmed-over taste, to my mind. For the best warm duck salad, start from scratch with raw duck meat, and I like the fast stir-fry, as in the following recipe.*

For 6 to 8 servings

Sweet-and-sour dressing (about ¾ cup)
1½ Tbs finely minced shallots or scallions

2 Tbs freshly squeezed lemon juice
1 Tbs wine vinegar or raspberry vinegar
1 Tbs Dijon-type prepared mustard
1 Tbs sweet-and-sour sauce, such as Chinese plum sauce or hoisin, or minced chutney
½ cup light virgin olive oil
Droplets of dark sesame oil
Salt and freshly ground pepper

Sufficient tender frizzy lettuce leaves (curly endive), or romaine leaves cut crosswise into ½-inch slices
4 uncooked legs and thighs from 2 roaster ducklings
Salt and freshly ground pepper
¼ tsp allspice
A spoonful or two of light virgin olive oil
Warm duck cracklings (rendered skin bits; page 180), optional

SPECIAL EQUIPMENT SUGGESTED: *A rubber mallet or other pounding instrument; a wok or a no-stick 10-inch frying pan*

The dressing. In a small bowl with a wire whisk, blend the shallots or scallions, lemon juice, vinegar, mustard, and sauce or chutney. By droplets, to make an emulsion, beat in the olive oil. Season to taste with droplets of the sesame oil, and salt and pepper.

The salad greens. Wash and dry the salad greens and turn them into a large bowl.

Readying the duck meat. Peel the skin and any clinging fat off the duck legs and thighs. As neatly as possible, cut the meat from the bone. Arrange the pieces in a single layer between 2 pieces of plastic wrap and pound firmly but not violently, widening them almost double—to tenderize the meat. Slice it into lengthwise strips about ¼ inch wide. Dust lightly with salt, pepper, and allspice.

*Ahead-of-time note: May be prepared to this point well ahead. Cover the dressing and set aside; cover and refrigerate the greens and the duck meat.

Stir-frying the duck meat. Set the wok or frying pan over high heat, add enough oil for stir-frying in the wok, or to film the bottom of the frying pan. When very hot but not smoking, stir in the duck meat, tossing and turning almost constantly for 2 to 3 minutes, until the meat begins to brown lightly but remains barely springy to the touch—it should be a pinky rose inside. Remove from heat, at once stir up the dressing if necessary, and blend 3 to 4 tablespoons into the meat, enough to coat it nicely.

Arranging the salad. Toss the salad greens with the remaining dressing; eat a piece to check seasoning. Arrange the dressed greens on individual plates, then place the duck meat on top of each in a tasteful display. Sprinkle with the optional warm duck cracklings, and serve.

VARIATIONS

You will not always have uncooked duck legs on hand, but you can substitute other meats as suggested in the following ideas.

Chicken. Substitute skinless and boneless chicken breasts for the duck, but they need no pounding and no pre-seasoning before the sauté.

Pork. Pork tenderloin is perhaps at its very best here—trimmed, cut into 1-inch crosswise chunks, and pounded.

Pork link sausages. Pork breakfast sausages take well to this treatment; cut them into ½-inch pieces after browning them, then toss with the dressing as described.

Foie gras. There would be no complaints from me if generous portions of foie gras were substituted for duck. Sauté the foie gras in slices as described on page 183, and arrange them around the tossed and dressed greens.

Garnishes

You may want to toss other items in with the salad greens, like diced or sliced peppers of various hues, or cherry tomatoes. Or you might serve grated steamed beets on the side (page 293), or celeriac (page 375).

COLD VARIATIONS

Salad of Cold Roast Pheasant, Game Hens, or Chicken Breast

Pheasant is an almost unheard-of luxury in most houses, although you can buy it in specialty markets. If you are so lucky as to have a surfeit of roast birds, the following will make you a chic VIP lunch (otherwise use game hens or chicken breast).

For 6 servings

1 cup of the master recipe for sweet-and-sour dressing
18 to 24 slices of cold roast pheasant breast, game hen, or chicken breast
Salt and freshly ground pepper
Sufficient leaves of tender frizzy lettuce (or of romaine cut into ½-inch crosswise slices)
24 to 30 neatly cut orange segments
12 paper-thin rounds (whole slices) of red onions, separated
1 cup pine nuts, toasted and tossed for 10 minutes in a 350°F oven

Seasoning the pheasant. Spread a spoonful or two of the dressing in a plate, and arrange the slices of poultry meat upon it. Dust them lightly with salt and pepper, and baste with a little of the dressing. Cover and let steep 10 minutes or so (refrigerate if the wait is longer).

(continued)

Salad of Cold Roast Pheasant, Game Hens, or Chicken Breast (*continued*)

Assembling. Shortly before serving, toss the greens in a bowl with enough of the dressing to coat them; taste and correct seasoning. Arrange a handful on each salad plate, and lay the strips of pheasant over the greens; decorate with the orange segments, and a scattering of onion rounds and pine nuts. Spoon the remaining dressing over each, and serve.

Cold Duck Salad or Cold Pork Loin Salad

Substitute cold sliced roast duck or loin of pork for the breast of pheasant.

TACCHINO TONNATO THEME AND VARIATIONS

Anything veal can do turkey does better—or at least turkey (or *tacchino*) is far cheaper than veal (or *vitello*). Substituting for veal in the traditional Italian *vitello tonnato*, turkey breast is more tender and absorbs the garlic, lemon, and seasonings of the sauce deliciously.

Turkey Talk. This is one of the great solutions for the remains of the holiday turkey, but the tenderest and juiciest meat results from the poaching of a whole turkey breast in seasoned broth, as follows.

SPECIAL NOTE

Poached Turkey Breast

Poaching is an excellent way to cook turkey that is to be sliced and served hot in a sauce or cold in sandwiches or salads. You will have not only juicy meat for the meal but a handsomely flavored broth to store in your freezer.

Set a 6-pound bone-in breast of turkey breast up in a kettle just large enough to hold it comfortably; surround it with 1 cup each of chopped carrots, onions, and celery, and a large herb bouquet (page 336). Pour in 2 cups of chicken broth, 1 cup of dry white French vermouth or dry white wine, and enough water to cover the breast by ½ inch. Bring to the simmer on top of the stove; skim off gray scum, which will continue to rise for several minutes. Salt lightly, then cover the pot loosely and maintain at the bare simmer for 2 to 2½ hours, adding a little boiling water if the liquid evaporates to expose the turkey.

When is it done? The breast is done when a meat thermometer, pushed into the thickest part near the shoulder (but not touching bone), reads 162°F to 165°F. Let the turkey cool in its broth for at least 30 minutes.

*Ahead-of-time note: Refrigerate uncovered; when chilled, remove the turkey to a covered container. It will keep well in the refrigerator for a day or two.

Tacchino Tonnato
Cold sliced turkey in tuna and anchovy sauce

This dish should be assembled at least a day in advance so that the sauce and the turkey will blend flavors as they should.

For 8 or more servings

Tuna and anchovy sauce (about 3 cups)
A 7-ounce tin (1 cup) tuna packed in water, drained
A 2-ounce tin of flat fillets of anchovies packed in olive oil, drained
¼ cup capers, squeezed dry
The grated peel of ½ lemon
2 to 3 Tbs Dijon-type prepared mustard
1 large clove of garlic, puréed, then mashed to a very fine paste with ¼ tsp salt (page 350)
4 egg yolks
1 to 1½ cups or more virgin olive oil
Drops of lemon juice
Salt and freshly ground white pepper

A 6-pound poached turkey breast (see box), or 16 to 20 generous but thin slices of cooked turkey breast
Decorations: ⅓ cup capers, drained; a large handful of coarsely chopped fresh parsley; lemon wedges

SPECIAL EQUIPMENT SUGGESTED:
A food processor, or an electric blender

The sauce. Purée the tuna, anchovies, capers, lemon peel, mustard, and garlic paste in the machine, then add the egg yolks and purée several seconds, until the mixture has thickened. Finally, with the motor running, start adding the oil in a very thin stream of droplets, and continue without pause until ¾ cup of oil has gone in and the sauce has thickened into a heavy cream. It will not be as thick as mayonnaise, but should hold itself in creamy suspension—process in ½ cup or more of oil, depending on how thick a sauce you wish to have. Season carefully to taste with lemon juice, salt, and pepper—the sauce should have character, but should not be too strong in taste or it will kill off the turkey.

Slicing the turkey. If you are using a poached turkey breast, discard the skin. Carefully remove in one piece the whole side of each breast from the carcass. Cut the meat at a slant crosswise (across the grain), into elegant slices less than ⅛ inch thick.

Assembling. Spoon a layer of sauce in the bottom of a serving platter, and arrange the turkey on top, spreading each slice with a coating of sauce. Cover with plastic wrap and refrigerate for 24 to 48 hours before serving.

Serving. Let the platter sit at room temperature for 20 minutes to take off the chill. Meanwhile sprinkle on the capers and parsley, and decorate with the lemon.

VARIATIONS

Veal or Pork Tonnato

Substitute thinly sliced cold roast veal or pork loin for the turkey breast.

Broiled or Poached Fish Tonnato

Serve the sauce with broiled fish, such as swordfish, bluefish, mackerel, shark, or with cold poached fish.

Pasta Tonnato

Tuna and anchovy sauce is a bright idea for hot pasta. Toss in a dollop along with your olive oil, add salt and pepper to taste, parsley if you wish, and perhaps a handful of the diced fresh tomato on page 358. Proportions are up to the cook.

Tonnato Spread Using Leftovers

Leftovers of the preceding sauced meats or fish can make an attractive spread for appetizers or a filling for sandwiches, hard-boiled eggs, or tomato shells. Purée them and their sauce in a food processor, adding more lemon juice, olive oil, and seasonings as needed.

SPECIAL NOTE

A Different Sauce: Green Tapénade Sauce

Garlic, anchovies, green-ripe olives, and capers puréed with olive oil, parsley, and seasonings also makes a fine topping for cold sliced meats or fish, as well as a spread. That recipe is in the variation for Celery Victor, on page 300.

CHICKEN, LOBSTER, CRAB, AND SHRIMP SALADS

I make all of these in much the same way, in that I first marinate the elements briefly with the seasoning elements to blend flavors, then toss them with only enough mayonnaise to bind them together. This way you are getting splendid flavor and are not overdoing on the sauce. In fact, rather than mixing it in you may well pass the mayonnaise separately, and calorie watchers may slather it on at their own discretion.

Deluxe Chicken or Turkey Salad

Serving 6 to 8

6 cups cooked skinless and boneless chicken or turkey that has been cut into good-size bites, such as rectangles about 1 by 1½ inches and ¼ inch thick
Salt and freshly ground white pepper
1 to 2 Tbs light virgin olive oil
2 to 3 Tbs freshly squeezed lemon juice
½ cup chopped fresh parsley
1 tsp finely cut fresh tarragon leaves, or ¼ tsp fragrant dried tarragon
1 cup diced tender celery stalks
½ cup minced scallions or mild onion
1 cup chopped walnuts, optional
¾ cup or more mayonnaise, preferably homemade (page 363)
1 medium head of romaine, washed and dried

Wedge shapes of chopped parsley and egg yolks, a garland of chopped egg whites, and a pimiento top-knot

Decorative suggestions: 2 hard-boiled eggs, a large handful of fresh parsley, several strips of red pimiento

Preliminary seasoning. Toss the chicken or turkey in a big mixing bowl with the salt, pepper, and enough oil to enrobe the meat very lightly. Then toss with the lemon juice, and finally with the herbs, celery, onions, and optional walnuts. Taste analytically, and correct seasoning. Let steep 10 minutes, tossing several times.

Ahead-of-time note: May be completed a day in advance to this point; cover and refrigerate.

Final seasoning. Drain any accumulated liquid out of the salad, correct seasoning again, and fold in just enough mayonnaise to enrobe the ingredients.

Serving suggestions. Shred the lettuce and arrange in a bowl or on a platter and mound the salad over it; spread a light coating of mayonnaise on top.

Either decorate with sliced hard-boiled eggs, sprigs of parsley, and strips of pimiento; or try the more formal decor pictured here, in which you chop the whites and yolks of the eggs separately and toss with a sprinkle of salt and white pepper. Chop the parsley. Then fold a double strip of wax paper in two to make a long V-shape; holding that in place as a guide for each quarter, its point at the middle point of the salad mound, sprinkle two opposite quadrants with chopped yolk and the other two with parsley. Ring the mound with the chopped whites, and make a decorative crisscross of pimiento strips in the center.

VARIATION

Lobster, Crab, or Shrimp Salad

Substitute lobster, crab, or shrimp for the chicken or turkey. You will probably want to eliminate the walnuts, and you may wish to arrange a different presentation, such as mounding the salad in individual shells in the case of lobster or crab and using claw meat or shrimp as decoration. See also the Lobster or Crab Mayonnaise (page 365), which uses the tomalley and roe in a most delicious manner.

CABBAGE, CELERY, AND CORN SALADS

 MASTER RECIPE

Coleslaw

It is hard to say whether potato salad or coleslaw is America's favorite. Coleslaw goes so well with hamburgers, with boiled lobster, with broiled fish, on a picnic—it is certainly one of the great inventions. This is my favorite formula because if there are dieters at the table (including me!) the salad is delicious just with its preliminary flavorings, and you can pass the dressing on the side.

For 6 to 8 servings

1 fine fresh hard-headed cabbage weighing about 1½ pounds (making about 4 cups when sliced)

⅔ cup diced celery
½ cup grated carrot
¼ cup diced scallions or mild yellow onion
½ cup finely diced green bell pepper
1 small apple, peeled, cored, and finely diced
1 medium cucumber, peeled, halved lengthwise, seeded, and diced
3 to 4 Tbs chopped fresh parsley

The preliminary flavoring

½ Tbs Dijon-type prepared mustard
2 Tbs wine (or cider) vinegar
1 tsp salt
1 tsp sugar
¼ tsp caraway or cumin seeds
¼ tsp ground imported bay leaf (if available)
¼ tsp celery seeds
Several grinds of fresh pepper

⅓ cup sour cream mixed with ½ cup mayonnaise, plus more if needed

Preliminary flavoring. Remove any wilted outside leaves, wash the cabbage, and shred it—see notes on hand and processor shredding on page 288. Toss the cabbage in a large mixing bowl with the celery, carrot, scallions, green pepper, apple, cucumber, and parsley. Mix together the mustard, vinegar, salt, and sugar. Toss vegetables with the mustard mixture, caraway or cumin, and seasonings. Toss several times, tasting and adding a little more salt or vinegar if you think it needed. Let stand 20 to 30 minutes to let liquids exude. Toss again and drain.

*Ahead-of-time note: May be prepared ahead to this point; cover and refrigerate.

Serving. Drain again, and correct seasoning. Either toss with the mayonnaise or serve as is and pass the sauce separately.

VARIATION

Harlequin Cole Slaw

For a more colorful effect, use half finely shredded green cabbage and half red cabbage.

Celeriac Rémoulade
Celery root in mustard dressing

That big brown, knobby ugly vegetable known as celery root or celeriac is almost snowy white inside, and it makes a marvelous salad, or an accompaniment to smoked or broiled fish, or to cold cuts, or to a collection of other vegetables.

MANUFACTURING NOTE. *Celery root can be tough unless very finely shredded; you need a machine to do that for you.*

For about 1 quart, or 6 to 8 servings

A 1-pound celery root (3 to 3½ inches across)
1½ tsp salt
1½ tsp lemon juice

The dressing

¼ cup Dijon-type prepared mustard
3 Tbs boiling water
⅓ to ½ cup olive oil or salad oil
2 to 3 Tbs wine vinegar
Salt and freshly ground pepper

2 to 3 Tbs chopped fresh parsley, optional

SPECIAL EQUIPMENT SUGGESTED: *A food processor with fine shredding disk, or a hand-crank julienne mill; two 2- or 3-quart mixing bowls; a wire whisk*

(continued)

Celeriac Rémoulade (*continued*)

Preparing the celery root. To prevent the celery root from discoloring, work quickly. Peel the brown outside off the celery root with a short stout knife (don't try to get every bit of peel out of every crack!), cut into chunks, and shred in the machine. At once, toss it in one of the bowls with the salt and lemon juice. (If you are doing a lot, shred and season in batches in order to prevent it from yellowing.)

The dressing. Meanwhile, warm the other bowl in hot water and dry it. Add the mustard, and by dribbles whisk in the boiling water, then the oil; finally dribble and whisk in the vinegar to make a thick creamy sauce.

Assembling. Taste the celeriac: if it seems salty, rinse it in cold water, drain, and dry it. Fold it into the sauce, and correct seasoning. Fold with the optional parsley.

*Ahead-of-time note: The celery root is ready to serve now, but will be more tender if it steeps in the refrigerator several hours. It will keep several days, covered, in the refrigerator.

Hot Corn Salad

Hot Corn Salad

This free-form, colorful summer salad may of course be served either hot or cold, and, although frozen kernels will do, it is always best with fresh corn. Serve it with steaks, hamburgers, barbecued ribs, or take it on a picnic.

For 6 to 8 servings

6 to 8 ears of fresh corn (to make 3 cups of kernels)
1 large green bell pepper
1 large red bell pepper
1 bunch of scallions—the white and the tender part of the green
⅓ cup virgin olive oil
Salt and freshly ground pepper
3 large fine carrots

SPECIAL EQUIPMENT SUGGESTED:
A corn scraper is useful—usually available from country-store catalogues

A corn scraper or stripper

The corn. Either remove the corn kernels using a corn scraper, or cut them off in rows with a small sharp knife. The picky business now is separating the individual kernels from their place on the row. (How do the packagers do it?) Drop them into a saucepan of boiling lightly salted water; bring to the boil for several seconds, and drain in a large sieve. Run cold water over them to cool fast, and set aside.

The peppers and scallions. Dice the peppers. Trim and wash the scallions, discard the upper tougher green parts, and cut the scallions on the slant into ½-inch pieces. Film a large frying pan with olive oil and sauté the peppers and scallions for 2 to 3 minutes briefly over moderate heat. When barely tender, season with salt and pepper, and set aside.

The carrots. Peel the carrots; shave 3 strips from each side with a vegetable peeler and drop them into a bowl of ice and water so they will form curls. The remains of the carrots, flat and thin after their shaving, are seasoned with salt and pepper and slowly cooked in olive oil in a covered pan until just tender.

Serving. Shortly before serving, reheat the carrot pieces. Fold the corn kernels into the pepper mixture, add a little fresh oil and heat through. Correct seasoning and turn into a platter. Decorate with the carrot pieces, surround with the carrot curls, and serve.

Cooked Egg Mayonnaise— and Hollandaise

When you do not want to use raw eggs for homemade mayonnaise, use the following simple sauce base containing cooked whole egg and hard-boiled eggs. This produces a sauce that tastes just like the real thing, and is useful, too, in hot weather, since cooked eggs are more resistant to bacterial growth than raw ones.

The sauce base. Whisk ½ cup of water into 2 tablespoons of flour in a smallish saucepan. When thoroughly blended and lump free, bring to a simmer, whisking, for 5 seconds. Remove from heat and rapidly whisk in 1 whole raw egg; return over moderate heat and, whisking thoroughly, simmer 5 seconds more. Scrape into a food processor.

Finishing the sauce. Have measured out, then process in: 2 hard-boiled yolks, 1 tablespoon Dijon-type prepared mustard, ½ teaspoon salt, and 2½ teaspoons each of wine vinegar and fresh lemon juice. When thoroughly blended, very slowly, especially at first, dribble in 1 cup of excellent oil. Taste, and adjust seasonings.

For a larger quantity. Double the quantities here, for about 1 quart of sauce. However, I have had trouble trying to produce more than that.

For Hollandaise and Béarnaise

Make just the sauce base, using fish or chicken stock rather than water if you wish. Season with lemon, herbs, etc. (see page 87 for ideas). Off heat and just before serving, beat several spoonfuls of butter one at a time into the warm sauce. Less rich than the real thing, when carefully simmered and seasoned this nevertheless is a more than acceptable substitute.

LIST OF SALADS IN OTHER CHAPTERS

Pastry Doughs

The Dough for Pie Shells and Quiches

French Puff Pastry from Peekaboo Tarts to Pissaladière

Choux Pastry, Chocolate Éclairs, and Puffed Tidbits

Crêpes Both Sweet and Savory

The mastery of pie-crust dough and puff pastry really makes one feel like a cook. Thanks to the food processor and the heavy-duty mixer those once-feared accomplishments can—and should—be in anyone's repertoire. Admittedly, they do take a certain modicum of expertise, but when you follow the illustrated directions here and remember to keep everything chilled, you will find there's not too much to making them.

A very good reason for having these doughs, as well as cream puff pastry and crêpes, at your fingertips is that you can make all of them ahead and keep them in the freezer. Then when you suddenly have company, you can bring them out with ease and confidence.

Pastry doughs also give you a chance to feast on the remains—my euphemistic term for leftovers. Plan on a quiche for yesterday's cooked salmon, for instance, or save sautéed mushrooms or spinach for the tower of crêpes on page 407. Don't throw out good but dried-out cheese—grate it in your food processor, bag it, freeze it, and turn it into little cheese cocktail puffs or that giant puffed cheese ring, the gougères on page 403.

It's a marvelous help to know that you have a stack of frozen crêpes waiting for your command, or disks of dough for topping chicken pot pies. The way to learn is to start right in with fearless determination, and you will never regret your decision. Once the feeling is in your hands, you'll retain it thankfully forever more.

PASTRY DOUGH—PÂTE BRISÉE

B.T.F.P.—Before The Food Processor—it was only the practiced cook who produced decent pastry dough. And what a to-do it was: first the making of a fountain of flour on a clean board, the clearing of a space in its center for the butter and liquids, and the working of them together with cool, deft fingers—all done by that practiced cook with an infuriatingly calm smile of superiority. Now, in less than 5 minutes, that wonderful F.P. machine enables any one of us to make perfect pastry dough every time. We are thus, with our own triumphant smiles, instantly masters of the quiche, the tart, the turnover, countless hors d'oeuvre niblets, to say nothing of the chicken pot pie.

SPECIAL NOTE

To Measure Flour
The scoop-and-level system

The measuring of flour is a serious business, since if you have less or more than your recipe specifies you can produce a dry tough dough, or a damp dough, or a heavy cake, or a failed soufflé. Although professional bakers must use scales for their large quantities, I find the scoop-and-level system perfectly satisfactory for the small quantities called for in general home cooking.

Dip a dry-measure cup into the flour container.

Using the straight edge of a knife or spatula, sweep off excess flour even with the lip of the cup. If you are to sift the flour, sift *after* measuring.

Scoop flour into dry-measure cup and sweep off excess.

Measuring chart for all flours—from all-purpose, rye, and whole wheat to cake flour—giving near approximations.

1 cup flour, scooped and leveled	5 ounces	140–145 grams
⅔ cup flour	3½ ounces	100 grams
⅓ cup flour	1¾ ounces	50 grams
¼ cup flour	1¼ ounces	35 grams
3 Tbs flour	Scant ounce	25 grams
1 Tbs flour	¼ ounce	7½ grams
3½ cups flour	1 pound	464 grams
3¾ cups flour	1.1 pounds	500 grams

METRIC CONVERSIONS
Ounces into approximate grams: multiply ounces by 28.4
Grams into approximate ounces: multiply grams by 0.35

A Note on Flour and Tender Pastry Crusts

Low-gluten pastry flour, the kind you find in biscuit-making Southern states or in some health-food stores, makes tender pie crusts while plain all-purpose flour usually makes brittle crust. To tenderize all-purpose flour, I include some cake flour—approximately 1 part cake flour to 3 parts all-purpose, and as a further tenderizing agent, I use 1 part vegetable shortening to 3 parts butter.

Dietary Note

The most delicious, tender, buttery pastry doughs contain 4 parts butter to 5 parts flour. In other words, the following dough, which will make two 9-inch tarts serving 12 people, contains 14 tablespoons of butter, meaning that each serving will provide 1⅙ tablespoons of butter—not bad for a heavenly indulgence.

◄■■► MASTER RECIPE

To Make a Butter Dough for Pastries and Pie Crusts: Pâte Brisée Fine

For two 9-inch tart shells or a 14- by 4½-inch rectangular crust

1½ cups all-purpose flour, preferably unbleached (scooped and leveled)
½ cup plain bleached cake flour
1 tsp salt (or, for dessert tarts, ¼ tsp salt and 2 Tbs sugar)
6 ounces (1½ sticks) chilled unsalted butter, quartered lengthwise and diced

¼ cup (2 ounces) chilled vegetable shortening
½ cup ice water, plus droplets more, if needed

SPECIAL EQUIPMENT SUGGESTED:
A food processor with steel blade

Blending flour and butter. Have all the ingredients measured out and ready to use. Put the flour, salt (or salt and sugar), and diced butter in the container of the processor and pulse (on-off half-second clicks) 5 or 6 times to break up the butter roughly. Add the shortening, turn on the machine, and immediately pour in the ½ cup of ice water, then pulse 2 or 3 times. Remove the cover and feel the dough—it should look like a bunch of small lumps, and will just hold together in a mass when you press a handful together—see its texture in my left hand (illustration, step 1). (It's important not to overmix; it should not mass on the blade of the machine.) If too dry, pulse in droplets more water. From now on work rapidly to keep the dough cold and manageable.

Final Blending. Turn the dough out onto your work surface; press it into a rough mass. For the final blending, rapidly and roughly, with the heel (not the palm) of your hand, push egg-size clumps of dough out in front of you in a 6-inch smear (step 2).

Resting and Chilling. Form the dough into a cake (step 3)—it should be fairly smooth and pliable. Wrap in plastic, slide it into a plastic bag, as at upper left, and refrigerate. Freshly made dough should chill 2 hours at least, allowing the flour particles to absorb the liquid, as well as to firm the butter and relax the gluten.

Ahead-of-time note: The dough will keep 2 days in the refrigerator before its unbleached flour will start turning grayish, but it can be frozen for several months.

1. Feeling the dough

2. Smearing out dough with heel of hand

3. Forming dough into a cake

Forming Tart Shells

Of course you can bake a tart in a pie pan, but it is far more stylish to serve it in its own free-standing pastry shell. Here are four suggestions for the free-standing shell: the first, formed in an open quiche ring; the second, formed on an upside-down cake pan; the third, taking advantage of the store-bought pie shell; and, finally, the free-form shell.

To Form a Pastry Shell in a Quiche Ring

The quiche ring, pictured here, is wonderfully convenient for baking free-form shells. You'll usually find it in gourmet cookware stores and catalogues—but if you don't, you have the three alternatives that follow.

SPECIAL EQUIPMENT SUGGESTED:
A straight rolling pin 1¾ to 2 inches in diameter and 18 inches long, such as the one in the photographs, or an Italian pasta pin; a 9-inch quiche ring, interior buttered; a pastry sheet, lightly buttered; lightweight aluminum foil; 1 pound of dried beans or aluminum bits

Keep It Cold! (A Word About Marble) Because of its high butter content, the dough softens rapidly. Work fast, but if the dough does lose its chill and becomes difficult to handle, stop where you are; refrigerate everything for 20 to 30 minutes, then continue. A cool marble work surface is of tremendous help in pastry making; buy one cut to the size of your refrigerator shelf, chill it before your pastry session, and you'll never have dough softening. (Look under Marble in the yellow pages.)

1. Unrolling dough over quiche ring

Rapidly roll out the chilled dough ⅛ inch thick and about 1½ inches larger than the circumference of the ring; roll it up on your pin, and unroll it over the quiche ring (illustration, step 1).

Lightly press the dough in place; then, to make the sides sturdy, push ½ inch or so of the dough down the sides all around (step 2).

Roll your pin over the top of the ring to cut off the excess dough (step 3).

Now push the dough up the sides with your thumbs to form a rim standing ⅓ inch above the top of the ring (step 4). Patch any thin areas with raw dough. Prick the bottom of the dough at ¼-inch intervals with the tines of a table fork.

Using the dull edge of a table knife, press a decorative pattern on the rim of the shell (step 5). Cover the shell with plastic wrap and refrigerate 30 minutes or more, to relax the dough so it will bake evenly.

*Ahead-of-time note: The formed shell may be wrapped and frozen.

Soggy bottom problems. Unless you plan to bake your quiche or pie on a sheet of foil set on a hot baking stone (as for the pizzas on page 55), you'll

1. Unrolling dough over quiche ring

2. Pressing dough down sides to make them thicker

3. Rolling pin over top of ring to trim off excess dough

4. Pushing dough up sides of ring

5. Making a decorative edging

get the best and crispest crust if you prebake it. But to prevent the sides from collapsing and the bottom from bulging up in the oven, the dough needs weighting down as follows:

Cut a square of lightweight foil 4 inches larger than the diameter of your shell. Lightly butter the shiny side and make a pouch of it, shiny side down. Fill with a good handful or two of beans or aluminum bits, (step 6). Gently line the pastry shell with the foil, pressing it against the edges.

6. Pouch of foil and beans going in

Baking—about 15 minutes at 450°F. Bake in the lower middle level of the preheated oven. (Check in 5 minutes. If you find the edges have collapsed in places, push them up with a spatula or patch with raw dough and brace more beans against them.) Bake until the bottom of the pastry is set but still slightly soft. Remove the foil and beans, prick the bottom again with a fork, and bake a few minutes more, until the pastry is just beginning to color and to separate slightly from the edges of the ring. Let cool 10 minutes before unmolding onto a rack.

SPECIAL NOTE

Sweet Pastry Dough: Pâte Sablée

A very special dough for sweet tarts and cookies, much the same as the preceding one but with egg yolk and sugar, is in the cookie chapter (page 489).

To Form and Prebake an Upside-Down Shell

A useful alternative to the quiche ring is an upside-down pan, with which you can make the shell deeper than you could in a ring. Use a round cake pan as in the illustration, or you may want a square or a loaf pan shape—for instance, you could use the long angel-loaf pan for a coulibiac in a crust or a beef Wellington. The dough here needs an egg, which holds it in place—otherwise the sides slide off during baking.

For 2 shells baked on 8-inch cake pans

2½ cups all-purpose flour, preferably unbleached (scooped and leveled)
1 cup plain bleached cake flour
10 ounces (2¼ sticks) chilled unsalted butter
5 Tbs chilled vegetable shortening
2 tsp salt (or, for sweet crusts, ½ tsp salt and 3 Tbs sugar)
1 "large" egg blended with enough ice water to make ¾ cup, plus droplets more water, if needed

Make the dough as described in the master recipe; form it on the buttered outside of an upside-down cake pan. Prick it all over with the tines of a table fork, and chill 20 minutes. Preheat the oven to 450°F.

Placing buttered pan over upside-down shell

Butter the bottom of a second cake pan and place it on top of the pastry, as illustrated, to keep the dough from puffing up—remove the pan in 7 to 8 minutes, when the pastry is set and has started to brown. Continue baking 7 to 8 minutes more—until crisp and a fairly uniform light brown.

VARIATION

To Prebake Frozen Store-Bought Shells

Preheat the oven to 450°F. Prick the pie shell all over at ¼-inch intervals with the tines of a table fork.

Set a weighted twin pie plate in the shell—note the aluminum bits in the photograph—and prebake in the preheated oven. (Keep the shell in its aluminum plate when you fill and bake the tart later; ease it out of the aluminum for serving.)

Buttered twin pie plate with aluminum bits

Forming and Baking a Free-Form Shell

Illustrated directions for a rectangular shell are in the apple tart recipe on page 394. For a round shell, turn up the edges all around in the same way, and you may wish to turn them over once again in order to have a higher edge. Prick the interior of the disk with the tines of a table fork, and surround the shell with a double strip of buttered aluminum foil. After chilling the shell 20 minutes, line it with foil as previously described, and fill it with beans to brace the sides. Bake as directed in the master recipe.

FIVE EASY QUICHES

The quiche—pronounced *keesh*—that cheesy open-faced custard pie much in vogue starting in the mid-1960's, became so ubiquitous, and often so badly made, that its popularity waned. I vote it back in again because it is wonderfully good eating. And when you have ready-made dough in the freezer, or a ready-baked shell, it is fast to prepare as an easy first course or supper or luncheon dish.

Prebaked shell ready for filling

Dietary note. Perhaps one reason we see fewer quiches today is that people are afraid of their food—deathly afraid of eggs, and butter, and dairy products in general. However, healthy people are allowed a certain amount of each—and need a certain amount of each for a well-balanced diet. Why not enjoy every mouthful of our permitted ration? As an example, our first recipe, the shrimp quiche, is far from lethal. It contains, per person, about 1½ tablespoons butter in all—for the crust and for the shrimp sauté, plus 1½ teaspoons grated cheese, and half an egg. The milk or cream content is up to you, since you may use skimmed milk, regular milk, half-and-half, or heavy cream.

When your prebaked shell is standing beside you, assembly of the custard and filling is a matter of minutes—eggs, milk, plus almost anything that strikes your fancy—cheese, bacon, leeks, onions, canned pimiento, ready-cooked vegetables, tomato sauce, and so forth.

Manufacturing notes.

What it is. The quiche filling is a flavoring held together with a custard—that is, eggs and a liquid of some sort. The eggs slowly coagulate in the oven, holding the rest of the ingredients in creamy suspension. You don't want too much custard—a mistake made by some over-enthusiastic cooks—since the beauty of the quiche is the balance between its delicious, tenderly baked buttery crust and its filling.

Measurements. You can't be exact about total filling amounts, since

Bracing the filled shell with a strip of foil

shells vary in depth, but you can calculate the custard part by egg, adding more or less as needed. For each "large" egg, break 1 egg into a cup and add liquid to reach the ½-cup level.

Support for the shell. A free-standing shell needs support when filled for baking. Keep it in its quiche ring, or pin or clip an aluminum collar around its outside.

Shrimp Quiche

For a 9-inch quiche, serving 6

1 cup cooked shelled shrimp
2 Tbs butter
Seasonings: salt, freshly ground pepper, and a pinch of tarragon
¼ cup dry white French vermouth
A 9-inch prebaked shell (see master recipe for butter dough)
The custard: 3 "large" eggs blended with enough milk or cream to make 1½ cups
3 Tbs grated Swiss cheese

Preheat the oven to 375°F. Sauté the shrimp with the butter and seasonings for 1 minute. Add the vermouth and boil rapidly for 30 seconds. Strew the shrimp in the pastry shell. Pour in custard to within ⅛ inch of the rim, and sprinkle on the cheese.

Bake 30 to 35 minutes in the pre-heated oven, until puffed and browned.

Cheese and Bacon Quiche before baking

Cheese and Bacon Quiche

For a 9-inch quiche, serving 6

6 crisp strips of cooked bacon
A 9-inch prebaked shell (see master recipe for butter dough)
½ cup coarsely grated Swiss cheese
Seasonings: salt, freshly ground pepper, and nutmeg
The custard: 3 "large" eggs blended with enough milk or cream to make 1½ cups

Preheat the oven to 375°F. Break up the pieces of bacon and strew them in the bottom of the shell. Sprinkle on all but a spoonful of the cheese. Season the custard, and pour it to within ⅛ inch of the rim; sprinkle on the rest of the cheese. Bake 30 to 35 minutes in the preheated oven, until puffed and browned.

VARIATION

Quiche Lorraine

Quiche Lorraine, the most famous of all, is the mother quiche. Follow the preceding recipe but, rather than using plain milk as a base, substitute the best and fattest and richest cream, and bacon only as its special flavoring. No cheese. It's marvelous indeed. Try just a tiny sliver and see for yourself.

Spinach Quiche

For a 9-inch quiche, serving 6

2 Tbs minced shallots or scallions
2 Tbs butter
10 ounces (1 bunch or package) fresh spinach, stemmed, washed, blanched, and chopped (page 278)
Seasonings: salt, freshly ground pepper, and nutmeg
The custard: 3 "large" eggs blended with enough milk or cream to make 1½ cups
¼ cup lightly pressed down, grated Swiss cheese
A 9-inch prebaked shell (see master recipe for butter dough)

The spinach. Preheat the oven to 375°F. Sauté the shallots or scallions briefly in the butter, add the spinach;

Adding the spinach-custard

stir over heat until tender. Season, let cool, and blend into the custard.

Filling and baking the quiche. Reserving 2 tablespoons of the cheese, strew the rest in the shell. Pour in the spinach-custard up to ¼ inch of the rim. Sprinkle on the remaining cheese; bake 35 minutes until puffed and brown.

Arranging the sausage slices over the custard mixture and cheese

Sausage and Onion Quiche

For a 9-inch quiche, serving 6

2 cups minced onions
2 Tbs butter or olive oil
¼ cup dry white French vermouth
Seasonings: salt, freshly ground
    pepper, and sage
A 9-inch prebaked shell (see master
    recipe for butter dough)
2 Italian-style sausages, 5 inches
    long
The custard: 3 "large" eggs blended
    with enough milk or cream to
    make 1½ cups
¼ cup lightly pressed down, grated
    Swiss cheese

Onions and sausage. Preheat the oven to 375°F. In a frying pan sauté the onions with the butter or oil for 8 to 10 minutes, until perfectly tender; add the vermouth and boil down rapidly to evaporate the liquid. Season carefully and spread in the bottom of the shell. Meanwhile steam the sausages 10 minutes. Slice them on the slant to make large ovals ⅜ inch thick, and brown them lightly in the frying pan.

Filling and baking the quiche. Pour the custard mixture over the cooked onions, to within ⅛ inch of the rim. Spread the cheese over the custard and arrange the sausage slices on top, as illustrated. Bake 30 to 35 minutes in the preheated oven, until the custard is puffed and browned.

Provençal Tomato Quiche

It's a different formula here for tomatoes—no milk or cream needed or wanted, mostly for aesthetics (cream looks mottled when baked with tomatoes). This quiche is, of course, best at the height of the season, when the tomatoes are ripe and full of flavor.

For a 9-inch quiche, serving 6

2 cups sliced onions
¼ cup or so olive oil
1 large clove of garlic, puréed
5 medium fine fresh ripe tomatoes,
    peeled, seeded, juiced, and
    chopped (page 357)
Seasonings: salt, freshly ground
    pepper, oregano, and cayenne
    pepper; tomato paste, optional
1 egg plus 3 yolks, lightly beaten
    together
¼ cup lightly pressed down, chopped
    fresh parsley
8 anchovy fillets packed in oil,
    drained and mashed to a purée
    with 1 Tbs olive oil
A 9-inch prebaked shell (see master
    recipe for butter dough)
¼ cup grated Parmesan or other
    hard cheese
1 or 2 large fine ripe red tomatoes,
    sliced

The tomato base. Preheat the oven to 375°F. In a 10-inch frying pan, sauté the onions with 2 tablespoons of the oil for 8 to 10 minutes, until tender but not browned. Stir in the garlic,

Tomato mixture going into shell

Leftover Quiche

I've had good luck cutting leftover quiche into serving portions and refrigerating or even freezing it. About 15 minutes before serving I sprinkle the tops with a little more grated cheese and reheat, uncovered, in the upper middle level of a preheated 400°F oven. Convenient for unexpected cocktail guests.

Asparagus

Use the same system for asparagus as for broccoli—the spokes of a wheel idea is particularly attractive here.

Eggplant

Eggplant makes a marvelous quiche. Use the diced eggplant sautéed in olive oil, garlic, and parsley on page 291, then proceed as for the shrimp quiche.

Lobster and Crab

It's hard to beat the elegance of lobster or crab in a quiche, and it's just too bad, as with shrimp, that these shellfish are so expensive. Follow the system for the shrimp quiche.

then the chopped tomatoes, and simmer 10 minutes, stirring frequently, until a thick purée. Stir in seasonings to taste, including a little tomato paste if you think it needed; let cool to tepid. Then beat in the eggs and parsley.

Filling the shell and baking. Spread the anchovy purée in the shell and cover with the tomato base; strew on the cheese, arrange the tomato slices tastefully on top. Salt lightly, and drizzle over them a little olive oil. Bake 30 to 35 minutes in the preheated oven, until lightly puffed and an agreeable patchy brown.

Other ideas

The preceding five quiches give the general idea—they're all much the same but with little differences. Here are other suggestions.

Broccoli

Toss ⅔ cup or so of cooked chopped broccoli in a little hot butter and seasonings. Proceed as for the spinach quiche. Or you might place the broccoli florets like the spokes of a wheel around the edge of the shell, with the chopped sautéed stems in the middle; then pour on the custard.

Green and/or Red Bell Pepper or Canned Pimiento

Start out with a cup of sliced onions sautéed in oil, then add minced garlic, sliced peppers or canned pimiento, and seasonings—leftover pipérade (page 90) comes in handy here. Proceed as for the spinach quiche.

Leek and/or Onion Quiche

Sauté 2 or 3 cups of sliced onions and/or white of leek in butter or olive oil, then proceed as for the spinach quiche.

The Crustless Quiche

This is a handy system when you're in a hurry. Butter a shallow baking and serving dish and fill it with any of your quiche ideas. It bakes the same way. With a tossed salad and a bottle of wine, lunch is ready in 35 minutes. (See also the Timbales— vegetable custards—on page 70.)

There's many a quiche

Just about anything cooked or canned and ready to eat is quiche material, from sautéed mushrooms and/or chicken livers to shredded zucchini and onions; smoked, dilled, or canned salmon; and tuna. I've not yet tried sardines or canned beets, and I'm not sure I shall. But that's the intriguing part about the whole quiche story—it really has no ending.

FRENCH PUFF PASTRY: PÂTE FEUILLETÉE

For appetizers, first courses, cakes, and desserts

The opening photograph for this chapter looks the very picture of a pastry shop window— and you can produce wonders every bit as good as these. All you need is the dough to do it.

What it is. Puff pastry consists of literally hundreds of paper-thin layers of dough sandwiched between hundreds of paper-thin layers of butter—created by the special way you roll out the dough, fold it, and roll and fold it again. In the oven the separate layers of dough rise up between the layers of butter to make an airy, light, and tender puff. The classic method is to enclose a cake of butter in a package of dough, roll it into a rectangle, fold it in three, and continue, making 6 "turns," as a roll-and-fold is called. The entirely different method I describe here and which takes half the time, produces, I think, an equally first-class dough. The butter is broken into large flat pieces which are combined with the flour and water, and flatten more as the dough is rolled, folded into three, and rolled again, eventually making even layers by the fifth and sixth turns.

Puff pastry, like pastry dough and bread making, takes a certain amount of practice, but puff pastry is the dough that teaches you all the tricks—how to wield a rolling pin, how to cut and shape, and, in general, how to feel at home with

pastry dough. It's worth every minute you spend on it, and since you can freeze puff pastry for months, it is a treasure to have on hand since all of the items pictured here, and many more, can be assembled in a relatively short time—once you have the dough.

Manufacturing Notes.

I have gathered so many puff-pastry ifs, ands, buts, precautions, and miscellaneous hints through the years that I list the most meaningful of them here.

Flour. You will make the tenderest dough using 1 part plain bleached cake flour to 3 parts unbleached all-purpose flour. Measure by the scoop-and-level system described on page 380.

The hand vs. the machine. When making the dough itself, it is important that the butter be broken into big flakes. Form the dough either in an electric mixer with a flat beater or by hand, but when using the machine be careful not to overmix. The food processor is not at all recommended here since it breaks the butter into pieces that are too small, and the dough will not puff properly.

Keep it cold! Because of its large proportion of butter, puff pastry softens quickly and then becomes impossible to manipulate—keep it cold. If it warms up, refrigerate it immediately for 20 to 30 minutes. If you plan to do lots of pastry, buy yourself a cool marble slab to work on—see the remarks for butter pastry dough on page 382.

Roll evenly. Get yourself a long rolling pin like the one pictured— use a broom handle if you've nothing else. Keep the shape of your dough in a neat rectangle, all flaps meeting nicely and all edges straight. You are working to produce even layers for a uniform puff.

How thick to roll the dough. If you want a full rise, roll it ¼ to ⅜ inch thick; for a minimum rise but flaky effect, such as for a tart shell, roll it ⅛ inch thick.

Baking. The dough needs a hot start at 450°F on a slightly dampened baking sheet—to hold it down until it has puffed and browned, then a lower temperature, usually 400°F, to finish. Remember you have all those leaves of dough to cook through—730 of them at least, and a large piece takes a certain time to crisp.

Storing baked puff pastry. It is at its very best when freshly baked, but you can keep it for a certain amount of time in a warming oven.

Freezing.

Raw unshaped dough freezes perfectly. Thaw it in the refrigerator.

Shaped raw dough can usually be baked in its frozen state.

Baked pastries can also be frozen. To thaw, set in a preheated 450°F oven, and turn the oven off—but check small pieces in a few minutes to be sure all is well.

Puff pastry scraps. Directions on how to re-form and reuse them are in the Special Note on page 396. Keep your scraps flat on a pastry sheet.

◖▬▬◗ MASTER RECIPE

To Make French Puff Pastry Dough

For 2½ pounds of dough, making a ready-to-roll rectangle 18 by 12 by ¼ inches

1 pound, 10 ounces (6½ sticks) chilled unsalted butter, quartered lengthwise and diced
1½ tsp salt
3 cups all-purpose flour, preferably unbleached (scooped and leveled), plus more for sprinkling
1 cup plain bleached cake flour
1 cup, more or less, ice water

SPECIAL EQUIPMENT SUGGESTED: *Essential:* a straight rolling pin 16 to 18 inches long; a pastry scraper; a baking sheet with at least 1 straight edge (for turning pastry, step 5). *Useful:* a heavy-duty electric mixer with flat beater; a marble slab to work on (page 382)

1. Chilled diced butter to be tossed with flour

2. Rapidly flattening chilled butter pieces between tips of fingers

Step 1. The butter and flour. Toss the chilled diced butter, salt, and the flours together either in the bowl of a heavy-duty mixer with flat beater, or on your work surface (illustration, step 1).

Step 2. Flattening the butter. Mixing it rapidly with the flour, flatten the chilled butter to ⅞ by ½-inch ovals—the size of flattish fordhook lima beans—either briefly in the mixer with the flat beater, or squeezing it rapidly between the balls of your fingers, as shown in illustration, step 2. It is important that the butter remain cold—if it has softened, re-frigerate the mixture for 20 to 30 minutes.

To Make French Puff Pastry Dough
(*continued*)

Step 3. Adding the ice water. If you
are using a mixer, blend in ¾ cup of
the ice water at slow speed, blending
in droplets more water just until the
dough will mass; then turn it out
onto your work surface. By hand,
blend and turn with a pastry scraper
(illustration, step 3), until the dough
holds together when massed. It will
look an impossible mess.

Step 4. Forming the rectangle. Flouring the top lightly as necessary, rapidly push, pat, and roll the dough
into a rough rectangle (illustration,
step 4). If it seems too dry and
breaks too much, sprinkle on droplets of water. Do not worry—it will
look as awful as it does here, which is
just the way it should be.

*Step 5. Flipping and folding the rectan-
gle.* When the rectangle is 18 inches
long, flip one end over onto the
middle, using the straight edge of the
pastry sheet (illustration, step 5).

Flip the other end over to cover it,
like folding a business letter. You
now have 3 layers of dough. Scrape
your work surface clean, flour it
lightly, and rotate the dough so the
top flap is at your right (as in step 9).
This first rolling out and folding is
known as the first turn.

*Step 6. Rolling the dough again into a
rectangle.* Flour the top of the dough
lightly, then push, pat, and roll it
again into an 18-inch rectangle (illustration, step 6)—it is looking a little
better. Always keep your rolling pin
clean and lightly floured. (If the
dough has lost its chill, refrigerate it
at once for 20 to 30 minutes.)

3. Blending in the ice water

4. Patting out the dough into a rectangle

5. Using a pastry sheet to help you flip one-third of
the dough onto middle

6. Rolling dough again into a rectangle

7. Flipping dough again to form the 3 layers for
the second turn

8. Folding one-third of the dough rectangle over
the third time

*Step 7. Folding again into 3, the second
turn.* Again fold the dough into 3 layers like a business letter—again
using the pastry sheet to help you (illustration, step 7). Turn 2 is now
completed.

Step 8. Turns 3 and 4. Working fast
to prevent the dough from softening,
make 2 more turns, always cleaning
off and lightly flouring your work
surface and rolling pin. Keep your
rectangle neat, shoring up the ends
and sides with the side of your rolling pin and pastry scraper (illustration, step 8). As you finish the third
turn, your formerly unsightly mess is
beginning to look like a real dough.

9. Completing the 3-layer dough package after the fourth turn

Step 9. Finishing the dough. When you have completed the fourth turn (illustration, step 9), you do have a real dough. It now needs a rest of at least 45 minutes in the refrigerator to relax the gluten and to recongeal the butter. Following its rest, give the dough 2 more turns and it is ready to roll out, form, and bake.

*Ahead-of-time notes: After either the fourth or the sixth turn you may refrigerate the dough for 2 to 3 days—longer, and its unbleached flour will turn grayish. On the other hand, puff pastry dough will keep perfectly in the freezer for several months—if you are planning a high-rising baked pastry, however, you may find it best to freeze a four-turn dough, and complete the final turns just before baking. In any case, be sure to mark on the package how many turns have been given.

RECIPES USING FRENCH PUFF PASTRY

Here are just some of the attractive items you can make using puff pastry.

Puffed Rectangles: Feuilletés

A stack of puff pastry rectangles in your freezer is a marvelously useful resource for quick and elegant first courses, luncheon dishes, and desserts. Take them from your freezer—there's the raw dough on the left—pop them into the oven, and in 15 minutes—by the time you've made your filling—the pastry has baked into the lightly browned, flaky, buttery wonder you see on the right.

For 6 rectangles, 2½ by 5 inches. Roll out a third of the master recipe into an 8- by 10-inch rectangle ¼ inch

Raw and baked puff pastry rectangles

thick. Cut into 6 even rectangles, and arrange upside down on a dampened baking sheet. Chill 30 minutes before baking, or wrap and freeze.

Baking—15 minutes at 450°F. Just before baking, plunge a sharp skewer down through each pastry in 3 places—this helps stabilize the layers. Paint the tops with 2 coats of egg glaze (1 egg beaten with 1 tsp water), and cut shallow cross-hatchings on the surface, going down into the dough with the point of a small knife. Bake in the preheated oven until nicely puffed and brown, as in the illustration—the sides should feel crisp.

SERVING SUGGESTIONS:

As a First Course or Luncheon Dish

Split the rectangle crosswise in two. On the bottom half place several cooked asparagus spears, or a group of cooked broccoli florets, or sautéed wild mushrooms, lobster, or crab. Spoon over it a delicious white butter sauce, page 272, or hollandaise, page 87; cover with the pastry top; and serve at once.

Puff pastry rectangle with hollandaise

(continued)

Puff pastry rectangle with strawberries and whipped cream

Puffed Rectangles: Feuilletés (*continued*)

As a Dessert

Strew sliced strawberries, sliced fresh peaches, or a big handful of raspberries over the hot bottom half of the pastry, sugar lightly, and top it with whipped cream or the Zabaione Sauce on page 453. See also the wonderful combination of caramelized pears, pastry cream, and puff pastry on page 436.

INSTANT PIES AND TARTS FROM YOUR FREEZER

Top any humble pie with a puff pastry crust, and you'll have a winner, like the chicken pot pie described on page 148. To have toppings or pastry shell makings always on hand, roll out disks of puff pastry 10 inches

Puff pastry tops this chicken pot pie.

across and ¼ inch thick, then stack between sheets of plastic in the freezer. They defrost and soften enough to use in the few minutes required to fix the trimmings—and you're then ready to bake them. They're easy to form—here's an apple tart waiting to be baked at left, and an onion tart at right. Puff pastry makes a crust quite different from pastry dough—especially tender, buttery, and flaky.

Baking note: Although the pastries are described as baking on a pastry sheet, you'll always have the best crust when you use the preheated baking stone system for pizza on page 55. Form the open-faced tart on heavy buttered foil set on a paddle, then slip the tart-on-foil onto the hot stone.

Apple tart at left ready for the oven: onion tart at right

Variations

Fillings and toppings are almost infinite—see the ideas for quiches starting on page 384.

SPECIAL NOTE

Mock Puff Pastry: Flaky Pastry

For tarts, for little appetizers and puffs, for the caramelized sugar cookies, Couques, on page 490, a mock puff pastry does nicely. Make it from butter pastry dough (page 381) or from puff pastry dough scraps.

As an example, roll the dough into a rectangle ¼ inch thick, 14 inches long, and 5 inches wide. Spread the top two-thirds with 2 tablespoons of softened butter and fold the unbuttered bottom third up to the middle, then fold the buttered top third over to cover it, making 3 neat layers. Repeat with another 2 tablespoons of butter, then wrap and refrigerate for 45 minutes or so. Give it 2 more turns, without the butter this time, and the dough is ready to use.

Folding buttered rectangle of dough into 3 layers

Fruit Tarts

A 10-inch pastry disk makes an 8-inch tart, which will serve 4 people nicely. Place it on a lightly dampened baking sheet, then, leaving a 1-inch border free, prick the bottom of the dough all over at ¼-inch intervals with the tines of a table fork. Paint the fork-marked bottom with apricot glaze (page 427), and arrange slices of apple or pear attractively on top. Then crimp the edges to hold the fruit, and sprinkle the fruit with a tablespoon of sugar. Bake 30 to 40 minutes in the middle level of a pre-heated 450°F oven, until the bottom of the pastry is crisp and brown. Paint the finished tart with apricot glaze.

Glazed apple tart

An Onion Tart: Pissaladière

Cook 4 cups of sliced onions slowly for 25 minutes or so in 3 tablespoons of olive oil, with salt to taste and a sprinkling of Provençal herb mixture. When thoroughly tender carefully correct seasoning and let cool to tepid. Meanwhile prepare the pastry disk as for the fruit tarts. Spread on a tablespoon of grated Swiss or Parmesan cheese, then the onions. Strew 3 more tablespoons of cheese over the onions, and arrange severai anchovy fillets decoratively on top. Crimp the edges of the pastry to enclose the filling. Bake 30 to 40 minutes as for the fruit tart.

Onion Tart: Pissaladière

OPEN-FACED FREE-FORM PUFF PASTRY TARTS

Like the open-faced free-form tarts made from butter pastry dough on page 382, puff pastry shells may be any size and shape—a tart made with puff pastry is particularly succulent, buttery, and elegant in the mouth. I favor the rectangular shape just because it is easy to serve and produces a minimum of dough scraps.

To Form an Open-Faced Tart Shell

Roll out a rectangle of puff pastry ⅛ inch thick. Roll it up on your pin and unroll it upside down on a lightly dampened pastry sheet. Prick its entire surface with the tines of a table fork—the rectangle illustrated here is about 16 inches long and 10 inches across. For edging, cut inch-wide strips ¼ inch thick: their rapid puff in the oven will hold in the filling. Paint a 1-inch border of cold water around the rectangle.

Press the strips in place, slightly overlapping at the corners as illustrated, step 1.

Seal the outside edges by pressing the top with your fingers while pressing the sides with the back of a fork.

1. Laying pastry strips over dampened dough edges

Then press a design on the tops with the tines of the fork, step 2.

Cover and chill 30 minutes—or freeze.

2. Sealing and decorating dough strip with a fork

Roquefort Cheese Tart

For a 10- by 16-inch tart, serving 12, or serving at least double that amount as cocktail appetizers

Crumble a cup or so of Roquefort cheese into the tart. Whisk 3 egg yolks with 1½ cups of light cream, season with salt, pepper, and drops of Worcestershire; pour over the cheese. Bake about 40 minutes at 450°F, until the bottom is browned and the sides are crisp.

VARIATION

Other Cheeses

Use other cheeses in the same way, especially Swiss or Cheddar, or make a mixture such as cream cheese and blue cheese, or cream or goat cheese and herbs.

Apple or Pear Tart

Use the same system here as for the previous round puff pastry disk apple tart, painting the bottom of the dough with apricot glaze (page 427), arranging the apples on top, and sprinkling them with 2 tablespoons or so of sugar. Bake 40 minutes at 450°F, then another 15 or 20 at 400°F, until the bottom is nicely browned and the sides are crisp.

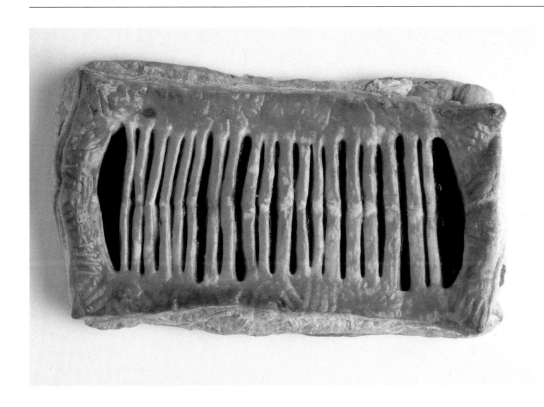

Baking—about 1 hour at 450°F and 400°F. Bake in the lower middle level of the preheated oven. When puffed and lightly brown, in 20 minutes or so, reduce heat to 400°F and bake about 30 minutes more, until the sides are crisp.

Puffed Tidbits: Fleurons

These are attractive accompaniments to clear soups, sauced appetizers, and fancy fish dishes. Roll the reconstituted dough (see next page) ¼ inch thick, and cut into shapes, as illustrated. Cover and chill 20 minutes.

Making decorative cross-hatch marks

Preheat the oven to 450°F. Paint with egg glaze (1 egg beaten with 1 teaspoon water), and make cross-hatch marks through the glaze into the dough with the point of a small knife. Bake 15 minutes at 450°F, until puffed, browned, and the sides are crisp.

To Form and Bake a Peekaboo Tart

The French name for this is the *jalousie,* or Venetian blind, which in a way it could resemble. This system is attractive for cheese tarts and is especially useful for jam tarts.

Forming. Cut off three fifths of your recipe for chilled puff pastry dough, and roll out into a 14- by 16-inch rectangle ⅛ inch thick. Roll it up on your pin and unroll upside down on a slightly dampened baking sheet. Prick the dough all over at ¼-inch intervals with the tines of a table fork, going down through the dough to the baking sheet. Leaving a ⅛-inch border all around, spread on a filling such as the preceding Roquefort cheese but with half the amount of cream, which is added after the sides are folded over the cheese, the next step. Or spread the tart with raspberry jam. Fold the edges of the

dough up and over the filling, as shown. Then roll out a second slightly smaller rectangle of pastry; flour the top, fold in half lengthwise, and cut the central portion into strips as in the illustration. Paint the edges of the bottom dough lightly with cold water, unfold, and press the top piece in place. Wrap and chill 30 minutes.

Assembling the tart

Baked Cheese Appetizers, and Fleurons

Cheese Appetizers

When reconstituting the dough, sprinkle 2 to 3 tablespoons of grated Swiss cheese rather than butter over the rectangle. Fold in 3, roll out, and again sprinkle with cheese before folding. Roll out a final time, cut into shapes or twists, cover, and chill 20 minutes. Glaze and bake as for the preceding tidbits.

SPECIAL NOTE

To Reconstitute Leftover Puff Pastry

Always keep puff pastry scraps flat, to preserve their layers. Paint the edges lightly with cold water and press them together into a rectangular sheet. Roll out to seal, then spread on a tablespoon of soft butter. Fold into 3, like the usual business letter, then roll out and fold again. Chill for an hour, and the pastry is ready to use for tarts and informal pieces that need no dramatic rise.

CREAM PUFFS, FROM VERY LARGE TO VERY SMALL, BOTH SWEET AND SAVORY

The pastry that makes cream puffs, chocolate éclairs, and the romantic giant shell known as the Saint-Honoré is the pastry that makes crisp little stuffed appetizers. It can also become a dumpling or a gnocchi, and is the substance that holds together fish mousses and quenelles. The official culinary name, *pâte-à-choux,* translates as "the pastry for forming little cabbage shapes," and that is indeed what a cream puff resembles.

Choux pastry is one of the basics, in other words. Happily it is also one of the easiest pastries to make: bring a little water and butter to the simmer in a saucepan, dump in flour, beat over heat to thicken it, and whip in a few eggs. That's all there is to it— the eggs make it puff up in the oven.

◀■▬■▶ MASTER RECIPE

Choux Pastry

Cream Puff Pastry: *Pâte-à-Choux*

Here is the basic pastry for whatever recipe you are using, be it for cream puffs, gougères, dumplings, or quenelles.

For 2½ cups of pastry

1 cup water
3 ounces (¾ stick) unsalted butter cut into 6 pieces
Seasoning: *for desserts,* **⅛ tsp salt and 1 Tbs sugar;** *for savories,* **1 tsp salt**
1 cup all-purpose flour (scooped and leveled)
Exactly 1 cup eggs—about 5 "large" eggs (blend them together thoroughly with a fork before measuring)

SPECIAL EQUIPMENT SUGGESTED: *A heavy-bottomed 2-quart stainless saucepan; a stout wooden spatula or spoon; a 3-quart round-bottomed bowl; a cake rack*

MANUFACTURING NOTE. *Hand beating with a whip or portable mixer produces the lightest and puffiest pastry. The food processor is not recommended because it goes so fast and mixes so thoroughly that you cannot add all the egg you need; yet it is egg that makes the puff. And for the puffiest results, form and bake as soon as possible after the pastry is made, since it firms as it cools and that holds down the puff.*

1. Pastry beginning to film bottom of pan

2. Beating egg into pastry with wooden spoon

3. The pastry just holds its shape.

Preliminaries. Set out all the ingredients listed; prepare all the baking pans, pastry bags, and so forth called for in whatever recipe you are using. Preheat the oven, place the racks where needed, and you are ready to begin.

The initial dough. Bring the water to the boil in the 2-quart pan, with the butter and seasoning. As soon as the butter has melted, remove the pan from heat, pour in all the flour at once, and vigorously beat it in—it will be lumpy at first but smoothes out rapidly as you beat. As soon as blended, beat over moderate heat for a minute or more, until the pastry balls up, cleans itself off the sides of the pan, and begins to film its bottom as illustrated (step 1). (This step evaporates excess moisture, so that the pastry will absorb as much egg as possible.)

Adding the eggs. Turn the pastry into the 3-quart bowl and stir with a wooden spatula or spoon for 30 seconds to cool it off briefly. Then make a well in the center of the warm pastry and beat in ¼ cup of the beaten egg; when blended (it will look strangely separated at first, step 2), repeat with another ¼ cup of egg, then another, and half the final bit of egg. The pastry should just hold its shape when lifted in the spoon, step 3—thus you'll probably want all of the remaining egg, but beat it in by dribbles to be sure the pastry is not too loose.

The *pâte-à-choux* is now ready to use. First here's how to form and bake a variety of shells.

To Form and Bake Small Puffs

These are the kind you can fill with something delicious like crab meat, ice cream, or pastry cream.

For 30 to 36 puffs, 1¼ inches across

Egg glaze (1 egg, 1 tsp water, and a pinch of salt blended together and strained into a small bowl)
The master recipe for warm, freshly made choux pastry

SPECIAL EQUIPMENT SUGGESTED: *2 baking sheets about 11 by 17 inches and preferably no-stick; a flexible vinyl pastry bag with ½-inch round tube opening; a pastry brush. (See The Right Way to Use a Pastry Bag, page 460.)*

Preliminaries. Preheat the oven to 425°F, arranging racks in the upper and lower middle levels. Lightly butter the baking sheets; ready the pastry bag and the egg glaze.

Forming the puffs. Fill the pastry bag with the warm choux paste. Spacing them 1½ inches apart, squeeze round blobs of it 1 inch high onto the baking sheets, step 1. Dip the pastry brush into the egg glaze and rapidly

1. Squeezing out blobs of pastry for small puffs

2. Shaping up blobs while painting with egg glaze

3. Slashing baked puffs to let out steam

To Form and Bake Small Puffs (*continued*)

paint each blob, shaping it up nicely with the brush if necessary, step 2—be careful not to dribble egg down the puff onto the baking sheet, as this could glue blob to sheet and prevent puffing.

Baking—about 20 minutes at 425°F. Immediately place the puffs in the preheated oven and shift sheets halfway through. Bake until the puffs have about doubled in size, are a nice golden brown, and are crisp to the touch. Rapidly remove from the oven and make a slash in each to let out steam, step 3; return to the turned-off oven for 5 minutes. Arrange on the rack to cool.

Storing. To keep them crisp, store the puffs in a warming oven, or when thoroughly cooled in an airtight tin; or freeze them.

To Form and Bake Large Puffs

The standard cream puff can be just slightly larger than the preceding small puffs, or twice the size.

Forming. Form them in exactly the same way as the small puffs, but pipe out the blobs 1½ to 2 inches across.

Baking. Bake at 425°F for 20 minutes; lower the thermostat to 375°F, and bake them 10 to 15 minutes more, until they feel crisp. Then pierce and return them to the oven for 5 minutes to let off steam. Then, to insure crispness, I always split them horizontally, fork out the damp interiors, and let them crisp, inside sides up, 5 minutes more in the turned-off oven.

To Form and Bake Éclairs

Éclairs are the loaf-shaped puffs at lower left in the cooked pastry display on page 396. Pipe out cylinder shapes 2½ inches long and ¾ inch across, as illustrated. Bake them 20 minutes at 425°F, then 7 to 10 minutes, or until crisp, at 375°F. Pierce and return them to the oven for 5 minutes. They usually need not be split for final crisping.

Forming éclairs

To Form and Bake a Giant Puff Shell

Make a giant ring, fill it with whipped cream, and douse each serving with warm chocolate sauce—a dramatic presentation that always brings forth great smiles of pleasure. On the other hand, you can use the same idea for a lunch party—fill a giant ring with a Salade Niçoise, as described and illustrated on page 365.

For a giant ring 12 to 14 inches in diameter

¼ cup flour (for the pastry sheet)
The master recipe for warm choux pastry
Egg glaze (leftover egg or a fresh one, beaten with a pinch of salt and droplets of water)

SPECIAL EQUIPMENT SUGGESTED:
A lightly buttered baking sheet; a pastry bag with ½-inch plain tube opening; a pastry brush

Forming the shell. (Preheat the oven to 450°F, and set a rack in the lower middle level.) Sprinkle the flour on the buttered baking sheet and shake to cover it with a light even dusting; turn the sheet upside down and bang off excess flour. Using a 12- to 14-inch pot lid as guide, trace a circle in

1. Piping out the 3rd ring

Enormous Cream Puff au Chocolat
With whipped cream filling

For 8 servings

The preceding baked giant puff ring, cooled

2 cups heavy cream, whipped fairly stiff, sweetened with confectioners sugar, and flavored with pure vanilla extract (page 440)

2 cups warm chocolate sauce (page 422)

Fill the ring with the whipped cream shortly before serving. Spoon warm chocolate sauce over the top; pass the rest of the sauce separately. Cut into portions with a serrated knife.

Another filling

The Crème Chiboust—custard sauce with beaten egg whites—farther along, on page 402, would also go well here, with or without pralin—pulverized caramelized nuts, page 423. Rather than chocolate, you might use the caramel sauce on page 420.

---

the flour on the baking sheet. Pipe a circle of warm choux paste to cover the circular guide, pipe another circle outside the first, and a third to top them both, as illustrated, step 1. Paint the pastry with the egg glaze, evening out any bumps with the flat of your brush.

Baking—20 to 25 minutes at 450°F. Bake until the pastry has puffed to almost triple in height and is nicely browned. Reduce heat to 400°F and continue baking 10 minutes. Pierce the sides of the puff in several places to let out steam. Lower heat to 350°F and bake 10 minutes more. Turn off the oven and leave its door ajar for another 10 minutes—all of this in the interest of drying out the puff, but there will still be damp pastry inside. Remove the puff from the oven, and carefully slice in half horizontally. Scrape uncooked pastry out of the bottom and top, step 2. To crisp the pastry, set the pieces, inside sides up, on the baking sheet in a 350°F oven for 5 minutes.

Serving Suggestions

Here are brief résumés of two splendid dessert ideas—assembly jobs, using standard recipes that appear elsewhere in this book.

2. Scraping out uncooked pastry

Gâteau Paris-Brest

Pastry cream and almond filling

For 8 servings

½ cup pralin (pulverized
  caramelized almonds, page 423)
4 cups of filling
  Either: 2 cups chilled pastry cream
    (page 402) folded with 2 cups of
    whipped cream (1 cup heavy
    cream, whipped)
  Or: 4 cups Crème Chiboust
    (pastry cream with Italian
    meringue, page 402)
The giant puff, preceding recipe
  topped with ½ cup slivered
  almonds spread over the glaze
  before baking
Optional accompaniment: fresh
  raspberries or strawberries, or
  sliced peaches tossed with lemon
  and sugar

Shortly before serving, gently fold
the pralin into the filling. Spoon the
filling into the bottom of the giant
choux circle, and gently replace the
top of the ring. Cut into portions
with a serrated knife, and accompany
with the optional fruit.

The Giant Niçoise Salade Ring

This unusual presentation is described and illustrated on page 366,
in the salad chapter.

Le Gâteau Saint-Honoré

A ring of puffs set on a pastry disk

This is a fantasy pastry shell, where
the bottom is a crisp disk of pastry
onto which a puff ring is glued with
caramel. Resting on the ring is a garland of little puffs, all decorated with
strands of caramel (see photo, page
396, middle). Except for the caramel, you can have all parts of this
charming construction stored in your
freezer, ready for a quick assembly.

MANUFACTURING NOTE. *You can fill
the shell with anything you deem appropriate, from berries to sauced fruits, to
dessert cream. If you decide on a pastry
cream base, see the shortcut suggestion at
the end of this recipe.*

For a 10-inch shell, serving 8

**A 10- by ³⁄₁₆-inch baked disk of your
  best butter pastry dough, such as
  the formula on page 381**
¾ cup warm caramel (page 421)
**A single baked ring of choux pastry
  (the first ring of the 3 piped out
  for the preceding giant puff)**
**20 to 24 small baked puffs (page
  397)**

Forming the shell. Place the disk of
dough on a serving platter. Dot the
bottom of the puff ring with blobs of
warm caramel and place on the disk.
Dip the bottoms of the puffs in the
caramel, and arrange them on top of
the ring.

*Ahead-of-time note: May be prepared
several hours ahead; store in a warm
dry place.

Final assembly. Shortly before serving, dribble warm caramel decora-

tively over the tops of the puffs, and
fill the shell—suggestions follow.

Serving. Cut the shell into wedges
like a pie, scooping up the filling
along with it.

Leftover choux paste becomes pastry cream

If you are planning a custard filling
for the Saint-Honoré, make the full
amount of choux paste called for in
the master recipe on page 396. After
forming the ring, bring the rest to
the simmer with enough milk to thin
it into a thick sauce that will hold its
shape softly in a spoon—and you
have made a reasonable facsimile of
the pastry cream described farther
on.

VARIATIONS

Fruit Fillings

Fill the shell with ripe strawberries
or raspberries, or sliced peaches or
mangoes, and pass sugar, lemon, and
whipped cream separately.

Whipped Cream or Pastry Cream

Or follow the filling suggestions for
the Paris-Brest, using whipped
cream, or pastry cream (page 402)
folded with whipped cream, or the
pastry cream variation, Crème Chiboust—pastry cream with beaten egg
whites. You may wish to pass berries
separately, or a strawberry or raspberry sauce (page 419).

FOUR EXAMPLES OF SMALL FILLED PUFFS

VARIATIONS

Profiteroles: Ice Cream Puffs

After baking and just before serving, slit the puffs in half horizontally, rapidly spoon slightly softened vanilla ice cream into the bottom half of each, replace the cap, and set 3 or 4 on each dessert dish. Dribble a good spoonful of warm chocolate sauce (page 422) over each, and serve.

Whipped Cream Filling

Substitute fairly stiffly beaten whipped cream, sweetened with confectioners sugar and flavored with vanilla (page 440), for the vanilla ice cream. In this case you may wish to slit the side of the puff and pipe in the cream through a pastry bag; you need not rush to serve them, but don't dally too long or the puffs will lose their crisp.

Pastry Cream Filling—the Classic Cream Puff

When you need a group of do-ahead puffs, rather than whipped cream substitute the pastry cream at the end of this section, or its variation with beaten egg whites, and glaze them with the royal icing on page 487.

Cocktail Puffs Filled with Crab Meat
Or other shellfish

You will want about a half tablespoon of impeccably flavored filling per small puff.

For 36 small puffs, about 2½ cups of filling

2 cups (1 pound) fine, fresh-smelling cooked shellfish meat
3 Tbs very finely minced tender celery stalks
1 Tbs very finely minced shallots or scallions
1 lemon
Salt and freshly ground white pepper
2 to 3 Tbs finely minced fresh parsley, and/or chives or dill
¼ to ⅓ cup best-quality mayonnaise
36 small baked puffs (see page 397)

The filling. Blend the shellfish meat in a bowl with the celery and shallots or scallions. Flavor carefully with drops of lemon juice, salt and pepper to taste, and herbs. Fold in just enough mayonnaise to bind.

*Ahead-of-time note: Cover and refrigerate until shortly before serving.

Filling the puffs. Shortly before serving, split the puffs in half horizontally and spoon in the filling.

Cream Puff Fillings: Pastry Creams

Ice cream and whipped cream are lovely fillings for cream puffs, but you have to serve them soon or the cream softens and soggifies the puff. That's why pastry cream came along, a thick custard sauce flavored with vanilla and/or liqueur.

Manufacturing notes

Cornstarch vs. flour. Pastry cream needs an additional thickening besides egg yolks, and that thickener is either flour or cornstarch. You may use either one or a mixture of half starch and half flour. Cornstarch produces a more delicate custard, but I find it a bit lump prone when cold, unless mixed with whipped cream or meringue.

A lighter touch. The basic recipe to follow can be made either with milk or with half-and-half, and I need not say which is the tastier version. You can lighten the custard by folding in a bit of whipped cream, as suggested in the recipe, or of meringue, as described in the variation following.

Pastry Cream: Crème Pâtissière

For about 2½ cups

6 egg yolks
½ cup sugar
A pinch of salt
½ cup all-purpose flour or
    cornstarch, or a mixture of both,
    in a sifter
2 cups milk or half-and-half, heated
A little additional milk, if needed
Flavoring: 1 Tbs pure vanilla
    extract, or ½ Tbs vanilla and 2
    Tbs rum or kirsch
2 Tbs unsalted butter, optional

SPECIAL EQUIPMENT SUGGESTED:
*A wire whisk; a 2-quart stainless sauce-
pan; a wooden spatula or spoon*

The custard mixture. Whisk the yolks
in the saucepan, gradually beating in
the sugar and salt; continue whisking
2 to 3 minutes, until the mixture is
thick and lemon colored. Sift on the
flour and/or cornstarch and whisk it
in. Then, by dribbles at first, blend
in the hot milk or cream.

The cooking. Whisk rather slowly
over moderate heat. As the custard
comes to the boil, it will start to
lump—beat vigorously to smooth it.
Then change from whisk to wooden
spoon, and stir over moderately low
heat, reaching all over the bottom of
the pan, for 2 minutes, to cook the
flour. You will have a thick sauce that
holds its shape softly in a spoon—if
it seems too thick, set again over
heat, whisking in droplets more of
milk. Remove from heat and blend
in the flavoring and the optional butter. Pass the sauce through a fine-
meshed sieve into a bowl.

Chilling. Stir up frequently until
cool; then clean off the sides of the
bowl, press a sheet of plastic wrap
into the surface to keep a skin from
forming, and refrigerate.

Ahead-of-time note: May be refrigerated for 2 to 3 days; may be frozen.

Before using. Whisk up the chilled
pastry cream and taste carefully: you
may want to correct the flavoring, or
you may wish to lighten it by folding
in a little whipped cream—⅓ cup
heavy cream should be enough to
whip for a moderate lightening.

VARIATION

Crème Chiboust: Pastry Cream with Italian Meringue
A filling for cream puffs, tarts, and cakes

Chiboust—that odd name belonged,
it is rumored, to the Parisian pastry
chef who invented this cream in the
1800's, and we must be thankful to
this genius for creating a perfect and
delicious do-ahead custard filling.

Italian meringue is boiling sugar
syrup whipped into beaten egg
whites—it's good old American
boiled white mountain frosting, in
other words. Fold a cup or more of
the meringue into the recipe for pastry cream and you have lightened the
custard, as well as giving it more
volume and staying power.

*For about 4 cups of filling, which would
do nicely for the preceding Saint-
Honoré or the Paris-Brest*

For the Italian meringue
**The egg whites: ⅓ cup (2 "large")
    egg whites; a small pinch of salt; a
    big pinch of cream of tartar**

**The sugar syrup: ⅔ cup sugar; ¼
    cup water**

**2½ cups pastry cream (see preceding
    recipe)**
**Additional pure vanilla extract and/
    or liqueur, if needed**

SPECIAL EQUIPMENT SUGGESTED:
*A table-model electric mixer with whip
attachment*

The Italian meringue. Following the
detailed directions on page 462, beat
the egg whites to soft peaks and leave
the mixer running at low speed.
Meanwhile boil the sugar and water
to the soft-ball stage (page 421),
and, with the mixer going, dribble
the hot syrup into the egg whites.
Beat at high speed for 5 minutes or
more, until the egg whites are cool to
the touch and form beautifully stiff
shining peaks.

Combining meringue and pastry cream.
Beat up the pastry cream to loosen it,
pile the meringue on top, and fold
the two together. Fold in a little more
flavoring if you think it needed.

Ahead-of-time note: Will keep under
refrigeration in a covered bowl for a
day or more.

*Two top-notch recipes for
leftover Crème Chiboust*

A Simple Trifle

Serve leftover Crème Chiboust in individual coupes, the cream folded
with smallish pieces of sponge cake
that have been imbibed in the rum
syrup on page 459.

French Vanilla Custard
Ice Cream

Fold leftover Crème Chiboust with
an equal amount of lightly whipped
cream and freeze in a covered bowl;
when almost set, beat vigorously to
break up any crystals. Return the ice
cream to the freezer until set.

TWO PUFFED CHEESE
APPETIZERS AND A BATCH
OF TENDER DUMPLINGS

Beat cheese into your ready-made
warm choux pastry, and it will bake
into cheese puffs, little ones for cock-
tails or the great big gougères that
makes an amusing first course.

Small Cheese Puffs

For about 36 pieces, beat 1 cup of
finely grated Swiss cheese into the
master recipe for 2 cups of warm
choux pastry. Form and bake the
puffs as for the small puffs on page
397, but top each with a pinch of
cheese rather than egg glaze. Bake 15
minutes in a preheated 425°F oven,
until puffed, crisp, and brown. They
freeze and reheat beautifully.

The Gougères
A cheese puff crown

Using the same mixture as for the
small cheese puffs, nudge large gobs
of the pastry in a circle on a lightly
buttered baking sheet, as illustrated.
Top with a sprinkling of cheese, and
set in the middle level of a preheated

Forming a circle of blobs, for cheese puff crown

425°F oven for 20 minutes, or until
puffed and browned. Turn the oven
down to 400°F and continue baking
10 minutes or so more, until the
sides feel crisp. You might accompany the gougères, as a first course or
luncheon dish, with a small salad of
curly endive with garlic and bacon
dressing (page 353).

Tender Cheese and Parsley
Dumplings: Gnocchi

Warm choux pastry mixed with
cheese and parsley—squeeze and cut
small shapes out of a pastry bag (or
nudge them off a teaspoon) to poach
gently in simmering water. Served
with melted butter and grated cheese,
or gratinéed, gnocchi can be a hot
first course or luncheon dish, or let
them accompany steaks or roasts or a
vegetable plate.

*For 4 to 6 servings as a first course or
as an accompaniment*

**2 cups warm choux pastry (the
master recipe on page 396, but
made with 4 rather than 5 eggs)**
½ cup finely minced fresh parsley
**1 cup finely grated Parmesan or
other hard cheese**
3 or more Tbs melted butter
**½ cup finely grated Parmesan or
other hard cheese**

Forming and preliminary cooking. Beat
into the warm pastry the parsley and
the 1 cup of cheese. Turn the mixture
into a pastry bag and, using kitchen

(*continued*)

Clipping off bits of pastry into the barely simmering water

Tender Cheese and Parsley Dumplings:
Gnocchi (*continued*)

shears dipped in hot water as illustrated, rapidly clip off ¾-inch bits of
the pastry into a pan of lightly salted
barely simmering water. They will
sink at first, and then rise to the surface. Clock them 6 to 7 minutes from
the time they rise, and keep the water
at the bare simmer.

Ahead-of-time note: They may sit in
the hot water for ½ hour or so before
serving. Or, for advance cooking,
drop them into a bowl of cold water,
let them sink, then remove and drain
on paper towels.

Serving.

Immediate serving. Dip the gnocchi
out of the hot water with a wire
skimmer or slotted spoon; let each
group drain well before arranging on
warm plates or a platter. Baste with
the melted butter, sprinkle on the ½
cup of cheese, and serve at once.

Gratinéed. Arrange the drained
gnocchi in a buttered baking dish,
baste with the butter, spread on the
cheese, and bake 20 minutes or so in
the upper third level of a preheated
400°F oven, until bubbling hot and
the cheese has browned lightly.

Clockwise from upper left: Rolled crêpes stuffed with mushroom; Classic Crêpes Suzette; Crêpes Soufflé Mariposa; Tower of Crêpes with lobster

CRÊPES

The crêpe, that famous thin
light French pancake, is any
cook's good friend. Crêpes cook in a
minute or less, and can be made
hours before serving. Not only
hours, but weeks and months ahead
since crêpes freeze perfectly.

The following section gives recipes
and ideas both for main-course dishes
and desserts, and formulae for the
all-purpose crêpe batter which will
serve both, plus a lighter and more
delicate crêpe for desserts alone.

In the first among the main-course
dishes the crêpes are rolled with a
cheese and chicken filling. The second example is a tower of crêpes each
with its own filling—or how to be
dramatic on dressier occasions.

For dessert there are two easy apple
crêpes, a very dressy souffléed crêpe
with strawberry sauce, and the finale
is that marvelously buttery, caramelized, orange- and Cognac-flavored
all-time favorite, Crêpes Suzette.

An All-Purpose Crêpe Formula

This is the crêpe that goes around, under, or on top of almost anything, from entrée to dessert—the formula you want in your freezer.

MANUFACTURING NOTE. *I like instant-blending flour (that sandy-feeling granular flour) for crêpes since the batter is ready to use after only a 10-minute rest, which is needed for the flour granules to absorb the liquid and make a tender crêpe. Regular flour wants a rest of an hour or more.*

For 20 crêpes 5½ inches across, or 8 to 10 crêpes 8 inches across

1 cup flour (instant-blending preferred, but all-purpose, scooped and leveled, will do; see preceding note)
⅔ cup each milk and cold water
3 "large" eggs
¼ tsp salt
6 Tbs clear melted butter (butter spooned off the milky residue)

SPECIAL EQUIPMENT SUGGESTED: *A whisk; a 2-quart measuring pitcher is useful; a frying pan with 5½ to 6 inches bottom diameter—I like heavy-duty no-stick, but a well-seasoned cast-iron pan works well, too; a large cake rack*

The crêpe batter. Measure the flour into the pitcher or a bowl, then whisk in by dribbles the milk and water to make a perfectly smooth blend (if using regular flour, after mixing pour the batter through a fairly fine-meshed sieve to remove any lumps). Whisk in the eggs, salt, and 3 table-spoons of melted butter. Let rest 10 minutes—1 hour or more in the refrigerator for regular all-purpose flour.

Cooking the crêpes. Heat the crêpe pan until drops of water dance on it, then brush lightly with melted butter. Pour ¼ cup of crêpe batter into the center of the hot pan and tilt it in all directions. The batter should cover the pan with a light coating; pour out any excess. After 30 seconds or so, the bottom of the crêpe should be lightly browned—lift an edge with a spatula to see, as illustrated.

Lifting an edge of crêpe to see underside

Shake and jerk the pan by its handle to dislodge the crêpe, then turn it over either with your fingers or a spatula, or flip it over by a toss of the pan. Cook it 15 to 20 seconds—this underside is the nonpublic side, and is never more than a spotty brown.

Storing. Transfer the crêpes as done to the rack and, when thoroughly cool, you may stack them with no fear of their sticking. Slip them into a plastic bag; store in the refrigerator up to 2 days, or freeze for several weeks.

VARIATION

Large Crêpes (for 8 to 10)

Cook large crêpes in exactly the same manner—I like the 10-inch no-stick pan here.

Dessert Crêpe Formula

This recipe produces a lighter and more delicate crêpe, designed especially for dessert. It is made and cooked the same way as the all-purpose crêpes.

For 8 to 10 crêpes 5½ inches across, or 4 to 5 crêpes 8 inches across

½ cup flour (instant-blending suggested; otherwise see note preceding the master recipe)
1 "large" egg and 1 egg yolk
¼ cup each milk and water
1½ Tbs melted butter
1 Tbs kirsch, orange liqueur, bourbon whiskey, or rum
1 Tbs sugar
A big pinch of salt

ENTRÉE CRÊPES
For appetizers, luncheons, first courses

Roulades are the quick-and-easy crêpe dishes—fold almost anything handy into an all-purpose cheese sauce, roll it up in a crêpe, top with a little more sauce and a sprinkle of cheese, and it's ready for the oven.

All-Purpose Cheese Sauce
For crêpe fillings and toppings

This is our friend the white sauce—the béchamel, with the addition of whole egg and egg yolks, which give the sauce sufficient body to hold a filling in suspension. Make enough so that you can dilute what is left over, to be used as sauce for the topping.

For 2 cups of sauce

½ cup all-purpose flour (scooped and
    leveled)
1¼ cups milk
4 Tbs butter, optional
1 "large" egg and 2 egg yolks,
    whisked to blend in a bowl with
    ¼ tsp salt
Seasonings: salt, freshly ground
    white pepper, drops of hot pepper
    sauce, and a speck of nutmeg
⅔ cup grated Swiss cheese

SPECIAL EQUIPMENT SUGGESTED:
A heavy-bottomed 2-quart stainless saucepan; a whisk and a wooden spoon

The sauce base. Measure the flour into the saucepan and whisk in the milk by dribbles; when well blended and smooth, set over moderately high heat. Add the butter if you are using it, and bring to the simmer, stirring with a wooden spoon. As the sauce thickens, beat vigorously with the whisk to smooth out lumps. Simmer, stirring with the wooden spoon, for 2 minutes to cook the flour. The sauce will be very thick.

In go the eggs. Remove from heat and vigorously beat the egg mixture into the hot sauce; beat in salt and pepper to taste, hot pepper sauce, and nutmeg—carefully correct seasoning. Let cool several minutes, whisking occasionally, then stir in the cheese.

*Ahead-of-time note: If not to be used almost at once, lay a piece of plastic wrap on top to prevent a skin from forming. May be stirred over hot water to warm and reheat—but just to tepid, only to loosen and decongeal.

Chicken and Mushroom Roulades

For 4 servings, 2 roulades each

1½ cups sliced onions
⅓ cup dry white French vermouth
⅓ cup chicken broth
1 cup fresh mushrooms, washed,
    dried, and sliced
2 skinless and boneless raw chicken
    breast halves, diced
Salt and freshly ground pepper
1⅓ cups of the preceding All-
    Purpose Cheese Sauce
8 crêpes, 5½ inches across (see
    master recipe, page 405)
A little milk, as needed
3 Tbs grated Swiss cheese

SPECIAL EQUIPMENT SUGGESTED:
A 10-inch frying pan; a lightly buttered baking and serving dish

The filling. Simmer the onions in the frying pan with the vermouth and broth for 8 to 10 minutes, until tender and translucent. Stir in the mushrooms, cover the pan, and let cook 2 minutes while they render their juices. Fold the diced raw chicken into the mushrooms and onions, season lightly with salt and pepper, cover the pan again, and let simmer 1 minute. Uncover the pan and boil rapidly uncovered until all liquid has almost evaporated—1 to 2 minutes. Fold in just enough of the cheese sauce to enrobe the ingredients—½ to ⅔ cup. Taste carefully and correct seasoning.

Rolling up a crêpe with filling

Forming the roulades. Place 2 to 3 tablespoons of filling on the bottom third of each crêpe—on the under and less attractive side. Roll into a fat sausage shape, as illustrated, and place seam side down in the buttered baking dish. Bring ½ cup of the cheese sauce to the simmer, and add droplets of milk, thinning it so that it coats the back of a spoon nicely. Spoon the sauce over each roulade, and sprinkle cheese over each.

*Ahead-of-time note: May be completed to this point in advance; cover and refrigerate.

Baking—25 minutes at 400°F. Bake in the upper third level of the preheated oven just until bubbling hot and the cheese has browned lightly on top.

VARIATIONS

Other Fillings

Chicken livers or sweetbreads and mushrooms make excellent fillings, as does lobster or crab meat, broccoli or spinach, or diced ham—and you'll think of many more combinations. All are done in about the same way.

A Tower of Crêpes

A more dressy presentation is the tower of crêpes, where they are layered upon each other with filling in between—all the same filling, or different ones as suggested here. Of course you don't have to include lobster—crab, shrimp, or chicken will do nicely—but the tower is a relatively economical way to serve lobster to 6 or 8 very important people.

For 6 to 8 servings

2 cups cooked lobster meat
3 or more Tbs butter
3 Tbs minced shallots or scallions
Salt and freshly ground pepper
¼ cup dry white French vermouth
2 cups of the All-Purpose Cheese Sauce
2 cups lightly cooked broccoli florets
3 cups fresh mushrooms, trimmed, washed, and quartered
The juice of ½ lemon
7 crêpes, 8 inches across (see master recipe, page 405)
Droplets of milk, as needed
3 to 4 Tbs grated Swiss Cheese
2 cups fresh tomato sauce (page 358)
1 cup fresh parsley sprigs, optional

The fillings. Sauté the lobster briefly with a spoonful of butter and shallots, season lightly, add the vermouth, and rapidly boil down to

evaporate it almost completely. Fold in ½ cup of the cheese sauce. Warm the broccoli in a spoonful of butter, seasoning lightly and folding in ½ cup of the sauce. Simmer the mushrooms for 2 minutes in a covered pan with a tablespoon each of lemon juice and cold water; uncover, and rapidly boil down to evaporate the liquid, then fold in ½ cup of sauce.

Assembling. Center a crêpe in the baking dish, spoon on half of one filling, as illustrated, cover with a crêpe and half of another filling, and so on, ending with a crêpe. Simmer the remaining ½ cup of sauce with a little milk to thin it slightly, and pour over the tower of crêpes; top with a sprinkling of cheese.

Layering on the fillings

*Ahead-of-time note: May be completed to this point; cover with an upturned bowl and refrigerate.

Baking—about 30 minutes at 400°F. Bake in the lower middle level of the preheated oven until bubbling hot and lightly browned on top.

Serving. Serve surrounded by the tomato sauce and, if you wish, a garland of parsley sprigs. Cut into wedges, like a cake.

CRÊPES FOR DESSERT

Suzette is not the only crêpe dessert—remember the apple, and the strawberry, and the soufflé. Here are examples of each.

Flaming Apple Crêpes

Flaming Apple Crêpes make an easy and appealing dessert, especially when you have crêpes in the freezer and baked apple slices in the fridge. It is also something that will come to mind if you do the apple desserts starting on page 424.

For 4 servings, 2 crêpes each

32 to 48 Oven-Baked Apple Slices (page 428) or the sautéed apples in the next recipe

8 crêpes, 8 inches across (see the master recipe, page 405, or the dessert crêpes following)

2 Tbs sugar

¼ cup melted butter

½ cup bourbon whiskey, rum, or Cognac

SPECIAL EQUIPMENT SUGGESTED: *An attractive lightly buttered baking and serving dish; an attractive small saucepan for the flaming spirits; a heat-proof tray; matches; a long-handled spoon and fork*

Assembling apple crêpes

Assembling. Arrange 4 to 6 apple slices on one half of the under side of each crêpe; fold the other half over, as illustrated. As you fill the crêpes, place them slightly overlapping in the buttered baking dish. Sprinkle on the sugar, and drizzle on the butter.

*Ahead-of-time note: May be prepared several hours in advance; cover and refrigerate.

Baking—about 5 minutes at 425°F. Shortly before serving, bake in the upper third level of the preheated oven until hot through and the sugar topping is beginning to caramelize.

To serve. Warm the spirits in the small saucepan and bring it on a tray with the hot crêpes to the table. Ignite the spirits, pour them flaming onto the crêpes, and spoon over all until the flames subside.

Giant Flip-Flop Fruit-Filled Crêpes
Les Douces et Grandes Sauterelles

The giant crêpe makes a quick dessert, and an amusing informal one, which as a final touch can also be flamed for fun and drama. Sauterelles—sweet large grasshoppers—is the fanciful French here, referring to the act of tossing the giant crêpe over by a flip of the pan. If you happen to have oven-baked apple slices on hand, it's an even quicker dish; otherwise cook them as indicated here.

For 4 servings

Apple topping

2 or 3 apples that will hold their shape (such as Goldens or Granny Smiths), cored, peeled, and sliced

2 Tbs butter, plus more for greasing the crêpe pan

¼ cup sugar

A big pinch of clove, cinnamon, or mace

3 Tbs bourbon whiskey

The master recipe for all-purpose crêpe batter (page 405)—you probably will not use all of it

The flaming finish

2 Tbs melted butter

2 Tbs sugar

¼ cup bourbon whiskey

SPECIAL EQUIPMENT SUGGESTED: *Two no-stick frying pans, one 10 and one 12 inches*

The apples. Sauté the apple slices in the smaller no-stick frying pan for several minutes with the butter. When tender, toss with the sugar and continue cooking a minute or so, until nicely caramelized. Fold in the spices and bourbon; boil briefly to evaporate moisture.

To make the giant crêpe. When you are almost ready to serve, film the larger frying pan with a little butter, heat until almost smoking, then pour in a thin layer of the crêpe batter. Immediately spread the apples over the batter, and spoon a thin coating of batter over the filling. Lower heat to moderate, cover the pan, and let cook slowly for about 2 minutes, until the crêpe batter has set on top.

Either flip the crêpe over in the pan and brown lightly for a minute on the other side, flip over again, and slide out onto a hot serving dish.

Or brown the top of the crêpe lightly under a hot broiler and then slide it out onto the dish.

The flaming finish. At once melt the 2 tablespoons of butter in the hot pan, pour the butter over the crêpe, sprinkle on the 2 tablespoons of sugar, and pour the ¼ cup of bourbon in the pan; heat briefly, ignite with a lighted match, pour over the crêpe, and serve.

VARIATIONS

Other Fillings

Pear Filling. Use the same system for firm ripe pears full of flavor.

Prune and Almond Filling. Simmer ⅔ cup of tenderized pitted prunes with ½ cup of dry vermouth, a big pinch of cinnamon or mace, the grated rind of ½ lemon, and 1 tablespoon of butter. When tender and the liquid has almost entirely evaporated, fold in ½ cup of toasted chopped almonds.

Dried Apricot and Almond or Walnut Filling. Use tenderized dried apricots rather than prunes, and, if you wish, chopped walnuts rather than almonds.

Crêpes Soufflé Mariposa
Crêpes with lemon-almond soufflé and strawberry sauce

Anything goes in crêpes, including a soufflé, and this dramatic dish makes a dashing dessert. Although the soufflé mixture may be done in advance, you must watch the final cooking to be sure of the puff.

For 4 servings

The soufflé base

3 egg yolks
¼ cup sugar
¼ cup flour
¾ cup hot milk
⅓ cup pulverized blanched almonds (page 474)
2 Tbs butter, optional
1 tsp pure vanilla extract
¼ tsp almond extract
2 Tbs freshly squeezed lemon juice
A pinch of salt

The egg whites

5 egg whites (⅔ cup)
¾ cup sugar

2 dessert crêpes, 8 inches across (page 405)
Confectioners sugar in a fine-meshed sieve
Fresh strawberry sauce (page 419)
A small handful of candied lemon peel (page 415), optional but dressy

SPECIAL EQUIPMENT SUGGESTED: *A 2-quart stainless saucepan, a whisk, and a wooden spoon for the soufflé base; egg-white beating equipment; a 12-inch lightly buttered baking and serving dish*

The soufflé base—almond pastry cream. Whisk the egg yolks in the saucepan, sprinkling in the sugar as you beat, until the mixture is thick and pale yellow. Beat in the flour and, when thoroughly blended, whisk in by dribbles the hot milk, then the almonds. Stir with a wooden spoon over moderately high heat until the mixture comes to the boil; whisk vigorously to avoid lumps, then reduce heat to moderate and stir, reaching all over the bottom and sides of pan, for 2 minutes. Remove from heat; stir in the optional butter, the vanilla and almond extracts, lemon juice, and salt.

*Ahead-of-time note: If made ahead, press a sheet of plastic wrap on top of the sauce; before proceeding, reheat just to tepid, stirring over a pan of almost-simmering water.

Crêpes Soufflé Mariposa (*continued*)

Finishing the soufflé mixture. Beat the egg whites until they form soft peaks, then continue beating at high speed as you sprinkle in the sugar; continue beating until the egg whites form stiff shining peaks. Stir a quarter of them into the warm soufflé base to lighten it; delicately fold in the rest.

*Ahead-of-time note: You can cover the mixture now and proceed in ½ hour or so. Preheat the oven to 375°F before proceeding.

Baking—about 20 minutes at 375°F. Fold the two crêpes in half, best sides out, and arrange back to back on the buttered baking dish. Unfold the crêpes one at a time, scoop half the soufflé mixture into each, and lay the top crêpe half back in place. At once, set in the lower middle level of the preheated oven and turn it down to 350°F. Bake until the soufflés have puffed open the crêpes. Rapidly, sieve confectioners sugar over the top of each and bake a few minutes more to be sure the soufflés have puffed to their maximum—but don't overcook or they will collapse.

To serve. As soon as the soufflés are done, remove from the oven; rapidly surround with the strawberry sauce, and decorate with the optional lemon peel. Serve at once, delicately tearing them in two with serving spoon and fork held back-to-back.

Classic Crêpes Suzette

Classic indeed, but the taste is far from outmoded—delicate French pancakes bathed in caramelized orange butter, then flamed in orange liqueur and Cognac. I, for one, who have eaten and demonstrated Crêpes Suzette many dozens of times, am always ready for another heavenly bite. This recipe is essentially that of my beloved French chef and teacher Max Bugnard—of course in those days he didn't have a food processor for the orange butter, but I know he would have approved this speedy modern touch.

For 6 servings

Orange butter (about 3 cups)
The zests (orange part only) of 2 large bright fresh navel oranges
½ cup sugar
8 ounces (2 sticks) unsalted butter, quartered lengthwise and diced
½ cup strained freshly squeezed orange juice
3 Tbs orange liqueur

At the table
18 dessert crêpes, 5 to 6 inches across (page 405), on a plate
A bowl of sugar
Bottles of Cognac and orange liqueur
The bowl of orange butter

SPECIAL EQUIPMENT SUGGESTED: *A food processor; attractive bowls for the orange butter and the sugar; a serving skillet or wide chafing dish; a long-handled fork and spoon; the heat source (see notes at end of recipe); a ladle for the liqueur; warm dessert plates*

The orange butter. Purée the orange zest in the processor with the sugar. Add the pieces of butter and process until creamy and fluffy, scraping down the sides of the container as necessary. Then, by driblets, add the orange juice and the liqueur. Pack into the attractive bowl, cover, and refrigerate.

*Ahead-of-time note: May be refrigerated for 2 days; may be frozen.

Finishing the dish —in the dining room.

Heating the butter. Have at your side the utensils, warm plates, crêpes, sugar bowl, liqueurs, and orange butter. Light the flame, set the dish upon it, and turn in the orange butter. Let it cook until it boils and bubbles, and finally thickens into a syrup—a good 5 minutes or more. Meanwhile busy yourself among your bottles, bowls, and crêpes, keeping up an animated conversation.

In go the crêpes. One by one, rapidly and adeptly, with long-handled spoon and fork, bathe the crêpes on each side in the orange butter; fold in half best side out, then in half again to make a wedge shape. Lay each, as folded, around the edge of the pan.

To flambé with flair: Flambéing is fun for guests and cooks alike, but it is embarrassing for everyone when the steak Diane won't sear, or the crêpes won't flame, and things just splutter along. I've run into a peck of troubles here and there, having had to flambé live in public and on the TV. These are my ground rules:

The heat source. If you are really cooking something, like a steak, or bananas, or orange butter, you must have a strong heat source. A small alcohol wick is of no use at all—you need a butane gas flame, or a wide-mouthed container filled to the brim with Sterno.

Hot food. When it comes time to flambé, be sure the food is bubbling hot or the liqueur won't light. If you have any qualms, heat the liqueur first in a separate little pan and then pour it in. Or heat the liqueur, flambé it in its pan, then pour it flaming over the food.

Protecting the table. You don't need a fire extinguisher around when you are flambéing, but it is a good idea to set the apparatus on a large tray to catch any spills and/or flaming particles.

Never pour from the bottle. Flames can leap up the stream of alcohol and right into the bottle—which can then explode! It has happened. Always pour from bottle into ladle, and from ladle into chafing dish.

Secret practice. Try it out several times on your family so that you will be at ease, and can set your own particular style before your first public performance. Aim for fun and informal but high drama—bring out a little of your own elegant native ham.

The flaming finale. When all are done, sprinkle 2 tablespoons of sugar over the crêpes. Pour a good ⅓ cup of Cognac from the bottle into the ladle, then over the crêpes—never pour from bottle to pan; it's dangerous! Ladle on ⅓ cup of orange liqueur, and let bubble up for several seconds. Tilt the pan into the flame (or ignite with a flaming match) and, dramatically from on high, spoon the flaming liquid over the crêpes for a minute or so, and serve.

Desserts

**Frozen Desserts, Ice Creams,
and Sherbets**

**Apple Desserts, Including
Apple Snow and Apple Crisp,
Caramel Apple Mountain,
and Apple Pizza**

**Dessert Pies and Tarts—
Compotes and Custards**

**Chocolate Mousse, Christmas Pudding,
and the Immense Fruit Bowl**

You can get away with serving a simple fruit and cheese dessert or ice cream from the freezer for informal dinners, but when you are entertaining important company you usually want to show off. It should look sumptuous even though it's easy to make, like the ice-cream cake pictured here. It's store-bought ice cream, all right, and it's a store-bought cake, but imbibing a cake with rum syrup gives it that certain sophistication of taste. And when decorated with whipped cream and chopped walnuts, and served with a strawberry sauce, it looks and tastes like a million.

But the main thrust of this chapter is how to produce the basics—the hows of frozen desserts, the forming and baking of handsome fruit tarts, the perfect chocolate mousse and Christmas pudding. Knowing the way to the basics and how to put them together means knowing what can be prepared in advance, and that saves time and worry.

FROZEN DESSERTS: ICE CREAMS AND SHERBETS

People of a certain ancient age always remember the Sunday chore of chipping at the big block of ice to make pieces of freezer-fitting size, and of hand cranking for what seemed like hours until at last it would crank no more. How easy it is now to make ice creams and sherbets, and we have such a choice of machines, from the luxurious self-contained models to the simple small hand-crankers that you stick in the freezer itself.

I shall not go into the mechanics of freezing, but shall concentrate on a handful of formulae that I have found successful. Although you can freeze almost anything containing the right proportions, just because it has frozen well does not mean it will be a delight to eat. Fresh pineapple, for instance—what a great perfume when it is fully ripe; freeze it as is, however, and the perfume has almost disappeared. Freeze a Cranshaw melon and you have nothing at all, but freeze a strawberry purée and you have the essence of the fruit. In other words, success depends on the fruit itself and its intensity of flavor, and I hope the following will give you ideas to experiment with on your own.

Terminology Note:
Sorbet vs. sherbet.

I know there is sometimes a distinction made that the one contains milk and the other does not, or vice versa. As far as I am concerned they are one and the same, except that sorbet is contemporary cuisine chic-speak.

🏛 MASTER RECIPE

Fresh Lemon Sherbet

It's lemon sherbet in party dress when you serve it in balloon-shaped goblets, top it with a julienne of home-candied lemon peel, and pour around it a shallow pool of aquavit. I first had this splendid combination in Venice.

For 2 quarts, serving 10 to 12

4 to 6 large lemons—enough to make ½ scant cup of zests (yellow part of peel only) and 1 cup of juice
2½ cups sugar
4 cups water
2 egg whites lightly beaten into a foam with ⅛ tsp salt
1 cup or so iced aquavit (2 hours in the freezer)
Candied lemon peel, optional (see Special Note on next page)

SPECIAL EQUIPMENT SUGGESTED:
A vegetable peeler; an electric blender—more efficient for this purée than the food processor; a 2-quart saucepan with tight-fitting cover; an ice cream scoop; a mixing bowl with a tray of ice cubes and water to cover them, for a quick chill; chilled goblets

The sherbet. Remove the zests from the lemons with the vegetable peeler. To extract their flavor, pulverize them 2 minutes with 1 cup of the sugar in the electric blender; add 1½ cups of the water and pulverize 2 minutes more. Pour into the saucepan, add the rest of the sugar, bring to the simmer, and swirl the pan by its handle for several seconds, until you are sure the sugar has completely dissolved. Remove from heat. Pour in the cup of lemon juice and the rest of the water; stir for several minutes over the ice cubes and water until well chilled. Whisk in the egg whites, and freeze according to your machine directions.

Serving. The moment of serving, scoop a ball or two of sherbet into each chilled goblet, pour around it a big spoonful of iced aquavit, and, if you wish, fork out a half dozen strands of the candied peel for decoration.

VARIATIONS

Fresh Orange Sherbet

Follow the general directions for lemon sherbet, using 5 or 6 large fine navel oranges. After cutting off the zests, squeeze the juice—you'll want a quart of juice rather than water. Purée half the zests with the sugar, as described, and complete the sherbet. Candy the rest of the zests. Serve the sherbet with a big spoonful of iced orange liqueur.

Pink Grapefruit Sherbet

Follow the general directions for the lemon sherbet, using 3 or 4 large fine pink grapefruit, and make the following exceptions. Purée half the zests for the sherbet, and reserve the rest for candying. Then cut off all the white part of the peel to expose the grapefruit flesh. Cut the segments from the dividing membranes, and place in a quart measure, adding to it enough juice from the remains to fill the measure—all juice and pulp, but no water. Proceed with the recipe. Serve the sherbet with a big spoonful of iced kirsch.

Fresh Pineapple Sherbet in the Half Shell

Fresh pineapple by itself, even though beautifully ripe, loses its taste when frozen. You need therefore to intensify it but still keep that pure pineapple flavor, and a judicious use of the canned fruit achieves that desired effect. Serve it in the pineapple shell.

For about 1 quart, serving 4 to 6

A 10-ounce can of pineapple slices in syrup
1 cup sugar
1 very ripe fresh pineapple
3 Tbs white rum
The grated peel and juice of 1 lemon

SPECIAL EQUIPMENT SUGGESTED:
A grapefruit knife or pineapple corer; a 6-cup saucepan with tight-fitting cover; an electric blender or a food processor; a bowl of ice cubes and water, for rapid chilling

Candying the canned pineapple. Drain the juice from the canned pineapple and bring it to the simmer in the saucepan with the sugar, swirling the pan until the sugar has dissolved completely. Then cover tightly and boil the syrup to the "crack" stage (238°F—when bubbles are thick). Add 3 pineapple slices and boil again to 238°F—to candy them. Remove the slices from the syrup and, when cool, cover and chill them.

The makings of a pineapple sherbet

The fresh pineapple. Cut a cap off the side of the pineapple as shown. Using a grapefruit knife or pineapple corer, remove the meat and hard central core from the pineapple—except for preserving the pineapple shell intact, you don't have to be neat here.

The sherbet. In a blender or processor, purée the pulp and the uncooked canned pineapple slices with the boiled-down pineapple syrup, the rum, and the grated lemon peel and lemon juice. Stir for several minutes over ice and water to chill, then freeze according to your machine directions. Cover and chill the pineapple shell.

Serving. Let the sherbet soften 15 minutes or so in the refrigerator, then pack into the chilled shell. Decorate with the candied pineapple slices.

Ahead-of-time note: You may fill and freeze the shell, but let the sherbet soften 15 to 20 minutes in the refrigerator before decorating and serving.

SPECIAL NOTE

Candied Lemon, Orange, or Grapefruit Peel

Candied citrus peel is a charming edible decoration for sherbets, puddings, and many fruit desserts. Once made, refrigerate in a covered jar, where it will keep for weeks.

Enough for at least 12 servings

The zests (colored part of peel only) of 4 large fine lemons, 3 oranges, or 2 grapefruit
1 cup sugar
⅓ cup water

SPECIAL EQUIPMENT SUGGESTED:
A vegetable peeler; a 6-cup saucepan with tight-fitting cover

Remove the zests with the vegetable peeler and cut them into neat julienne strips 1½ inches long and less than ⅛ inch wide. Simmer in 1 quart of water 6 minutes, drain, rinse in cold water, and set aside. Bring the sugar and water to the simmer in the saucepan, and when the sugar has dissolved completely, cover the pan tightly and boil a moment or two, until the last drops of syrup to fall from the end of a metal spoon form a thread. Remove from heat, stir in the peel, let steep for an hour, and it is ready to use.

Fresh Strawberry Sherbet with Fresh Strawberries

It's just a purée of strawberries with sugar and a touch of lemon, but when you freeze it you have the marvelous essence of pure strawberry. I don't know a better formula for strawberry sherbet.

For 1 quart, serving 6 to 8

For the sherbet
1½ quarts fine fresh ripe
    strawberries
2 cups sugar
3 Tbs freshly squeezed lemon juice

For decoration
1 quart or so fine fresh ripe
    strawberries
2 Tbs freshly squeezed lemon juice
1 tsp red wine vinegar
¼ cup or more sugar

SPECIAL EQUIPMENT SUGGESTED:
*A food processor; a bowl of ice cubes
and water for quick chilling*

The sherbet mixture. Stem the strawberries, drop them into a large bowl of cold water, swish gently, and drain immediately. Purée them in the processor with the sugar and lemon juice, continuing until the sugar has dissolved completely—taste analytically to be sure. Stir over the ice and water to chill thoroughly; freeze according to your machine directions.

The strawberry garnish. An hour or so before serving, wash and stem the second group of strawberries and drain thoroughly on a rack; quarter or halve them lengthwise. Toss gently

in a bowl with the lemon juice, wine vinegar, and sugar to taste. Cover and chill.

Serving. Spoon the sliced strawberries around each portion of sherbet; the almond wafers on page 483 make an attractive accompaniment.

VARIATIONS

Fresh Raspberry Sherbet

Substitute fresh raspberries for strawberries, but strain the purée to eliminate seeds before freezing the sherbet.

Frozen Strawberries and Raspberries

Purée the frozen berries in a food processor, adding a little freshly squeezed lemon juice. When thoroughly defrosted, strain if you wish, then freeze the purée. Two 10-ounce packages will serve 4 to 5 people.

Instant Strawberry or Raspberry Ice Cream
From frozen berries

Purée a 10-ounce package of frozen strawberries or raspberries in a food processor with 1 cup of chilled heavy cream, and you have an instant soft ice cream. Serve at once, decorating each portion, if you wish, with a few fresh berries or a big spoonful of puréed berries. This will serve 4 or 5 people.

Nesselrode Ice Cream

Nesselrode, an old-fashioned mixture of puréed chestnuts, glacéed fruits, and liqueur, is named after Count Carl von Nesselrode (1780–1862), one-time chancellor of the Russian Empire. He was evidently something of a gastronome since a game consommé and a barley-rice soup also bear his name. It is this rich and wonderful holiday ice cream, however, that ranks him among the immortals. The formula here is adapted from one given by our friend Maggie Mah, whose father always made it for Christmas dinner.

MANUFACTURING NOTES.

Custard base. This is a French custard ice cream, with a *crème anglaise* custard base. Use the base for any number of other flavorings, such as chocolate, caramel, coffee, strawberry, and so forth.

Warning on glacéed fruits. Here's a warning from sad experience—some run-of-the-mill glacéed fruits are terrible, cheap, chemical-tasting junk. Buy the best and taste analytically to be sure they are top quality, or you will ruin your whole expensive batch of ice cream. If you cannot find the right quality, substitute best-quality glacéed cherries, or white raisins, or pitted prunes.

For about 3½ quarts of ice cream

The custard base

4 "large" eggs
2 cups sugar
¼ tsp salt
3 cups whole milk, heated

The Nesselrode flavoring

**¾ cup canned chestnut purée or
almond paste**
1 cup currants (small black raisins)
**1 cup best-quality mixed glacéed
fruits, rinsed in boiling water (see
also preceding notes)**
**12 stemmed maraschino cherries
and ½ cup of their juice**
¼ cup dark Jamaican rum
1 Tbs pure vanilla extract

2 cups half-and-half, chilled
1½ cups heavy cream, chilled
**½ cup crumbs from amaretti
cookies, or crumbed toasted
macaroons**

SPECIAL EQUIPMENT SUGGESTED:
*A stainless 3-quart saucepan; a food
processor; a bowl of ice cubes and water,
for fast chilling*

Custard base. Whisk the eggs, sugar,
and salt in the saucepan for several
minutes, until the mixture is pale yellow. By dribbles, stir in the hot
milk—but do not beat it because you
do not want to create foam. Stir

rather slowly with a wooden spoon
over moderate heat, reaching all over
the bottom and sides of the pan, until
the cream gradually thickens and
coats the spoon lightly—do not bring
near the simmer or you will curdle
the eggs, but you must heat it enough
so that it thickens. Remove from heat
and at once whisk in the chestnut
purée or almond paste, to cool the
custard.

Nesselrode flavoring. Place the fruits
and 2 cups of the custard in the food
processor and pulse several times to
chop but not purée them. Strain, returning the liquid to the saucepan.
Toss the chopped fruits in a metal
bowl with the rum and vanilla, stir
over the ice and water to chill, cover,
and refrigerate.

Freezing. Stir all the custard and two
creams over ice to chill; turn it into
your machine and freeze it—you
may have to divide everything in half
and freeze in two batches. When the
ice cream is set but still soft, fold in
the well-chilled Nesselrode flavoring
and the ground cookies.

Curing. Pack into sealed containers
and freeze at 0°F for at least 4 hours.

Serving. Let the ice cream soften 20
minutes in the refrigerator before
serving. Almond wafers or sugar
cookies would go nicely, or holiday
fruitcake.

Mocha-Chocolate Sour Cream Sherbet

This rich chocolate ice cream, or
semi-sherbet, is less opulent than it
tastes, since it contains only 2 cups of
cream—and sour cream at that.

For about 2 quarts

The mocha-chocolate

8 ounces sweet baking chocolate
3 cups best-quality strong coffee
⅛ tsp salt
1 cup sugar

2 cups chilled sour cream
1 Tbs pure vanilla extract
2 Tbs dark Jamaican rum
**Optional decorations per serving:
swirls of lightly whipped cream,
or a sprinkling of pralin (page
423), or a spoonful of iced coffee
liqueur; 2 sugar cookies**

SPECIAL EQUIPMENT SUGGESTED:
*A 2½-quart stainless saucepan; a spoon
and a whisk; a bowl of ice cubes and
water for a fast chill*

The mixture. Break up the chocolate
and add to the saucepan along with
the coffee, salt, and sugar; bring to
the simmer. Simmer slowly, stirring
and whisking until the chocolate is
well melted and the liquid is perfectly smooth and lightly thickened—
5 minutes or more. Stir for several
minutes over ice to chill; stir in the
sour cream, vanilla, and rum; then
freeze according to your machine
directions.

Serving. Let soften 15 minutes or so
in the refrigerator, then scoop into
bowls or goblets. Spoon around the
iced liqueur if you are using it, decorate with whipped cream or pralin,
and flank with cookies.

Some Sweet Creations from the Supermarket

A little creative dash can do wonders with store-bought dessert ingredients.

Mocha-Rum Quick Fix

Here's a winner when you're in a hurry—super quick and everyone loves it.

Per serving

A large scoop of vanilla, chocolate, or coffee ice cream
1 Tbs dark rum or bourbon whiskey
A big pinch each of cocoa powder and powdered instant coffee (pulverize instant coffee granules in the blender)

Drop the scoop of ice cream into a wide-mouthed stemmed glass and pour around it the rum or bourbon, sprinkle on the cocoa and coffee, and serve at once.

The Multi-Layered Ice-Cream Cake

When you need a fancy-looking formal dessert, a layered ice-cream cake is easy to make and impressive to serve. The handsome example here is made from good supermarket ice creams, and bought yellow cake—either one or two round cakes, or a big sheet from the bakery department, cut to the size of a 9-inch spring-form pan.

For a 9- by 3-inch spring-form pan, serving 12 to 16

A *liqueur syrup for the cake layers*
⅓ cup sugar
⅓ cup hot water in a 2-cup measure
⅓ cup cold water
¼ cup dark rum or orange liqueur

3 cake layers, 9 inches in diameter and ⅜ inch thick (yellow cake, spongecake, genoise)
3 quarts ice cream, such as 1 quart each of coffee, chocolate, and vanilla

Optional decorative suggestions

1 cup chilled heavy cream, whipped, and sweetened with confectioners sugar (page 440)
½ cup chopped walnuts, or crumbled amaretti cookies, or pralin (page 423)
2 cups strawberry sauce (page 419) or chocolate sauce (page 422), optional
Maraschino cherries, optional

SPECIAL EQUIPMENT SUGGESTED:
*A 9- by 3-inch round spring-form
mold, bottom and sides lined with wax
paper*

The liqueur syrup. Stir the sugar into
the hot water; when dissolved, stir in
the cold water and the rum or orange
liqueur.

Imbibing the cake layers. Arrange the
cake layers on wax-paper-lined cookie
sheets. Drizzle the syrup over the
layers and freeze an hour or so.
Meanwhile, let the ice cream soften
to spreadable consistency in the refrigerator—20 minutes or so.

Spreading chocolate ice cream over first cake layer
in spring-form pan

To assemble. Fit a cake layer into the
pan, spread on a layer of ice cream,
cover with another cake layer, then
another layer of softened ice cream,

SPECIAL NOTE

Strawberry or Raspberry Sauce

The sauce of many uses—to accompany ice creams, puddings, custards,
and soufflés, to mention a few. Fresh
berries are the most desirable, of
course, but the packaged frozen ones
do nicely out of season.

For about 2 cups

**1 quart of fresh strawberries or
raspberries (or 2 packages of
frozen berries, partially defrosted)**
**Sugar to taste, "instant" quick
dissolving recommended—about
1 cup for fresh berries, 1 Tbs or
so for frozen berries**
**3 to 4 Tbs freshly squeezed lemon
juice**

---

and so forth, ending with ice cream.
Cover with plastic wrap and freeze at
0°F for at least 6 hours.

Decoration. Release the spring-form
and peel the wax paper off the sides
of the cake. Transfer the frozen cake
from the pan's bottom disk to a
chilled serving platter. Decorate the
top with swirls of whipped cream and
chopped nuts, crumbled cookies, or
pralin.

SPECIAL EQUIPMENT SUGGESTED:
*A food processor or electric blender; a
sieve if needed*

Purée the berries, half the sugar
called for, and 3 tablespoons of
lemon juice in the machine, continuing until the sugar is completely dissolved—2 to 3 minutes. Taste
carefully to be sure there are no tiny
undissolved granules. Purée in more
sugar by spoonful if needed and more
lemon juice by droplets. Sieve if necessary, to remove seeds and seed
residue.

*Ahead-of-time note: Refrigerate in a
covered bowl, where the sauce will
keep for a day or two.

---

*Ahead-of-time note: Cover and store
in the freezer; let soften 20 minutes
in the refrigerator before serving.

Serving. Surround each portion, if
you wish, with strawberry or chocolate sauce, and top with a cherry.

Vanilla Ice-Cream Loaf

Another good idea for a dramatic presentation—it's a loaf pan lined with ladyfingers, filled with ice cream, then frozen solid, and finally unmolded on a sea of raspberry or strawberry sauce. But bought pack-aged ladyfingers are so dismally and disgracefully lifelessly limp! Your own (page 487) will be crisp, light, and lovely.

For a 6-cup loaf pan, serving 8

1½ quarts best-quality vanilla ice cream
About 2 dozen ladyfingers
¼ cup confectioners sugar, moistened to a paste in a small bowl with droplets of water
Raspberry or strawberry sauce (see Special Note, page 419)

SPECIAL EQUIPMENT SUGGESTED:
A 6-cup loaf pan; an electric mixer

Preparing the pan. Remove the ice cream from the freezer and let it soften 15 to 20 minutes. Meanwhile, line the length and width of the loaf pan with double thicknesses of plastic wrap, leaving 2½-inch overhangs for easy unmolding. To line the pan with the ladyfingers, paint a dab of the confectioners sugar paste on the outside bottom of a ladyfinger and anchor it upright, its curved side against a side of the pan. Continue, making an even border all around.

Spooning ice cream into ladyfinger-lined pan

Filling the pan. Beat the ice cream briefly with the electric mixer to re-move any air. Spoon it rapidly into the pan, pressing it gently against the ladyfingers. (You will trim off pro-truding ladyfinger ends later, when the ice cream has firmed.) Cover and freeze at least 6 hours.

**Ahead-of-time note:* Unmold the ice cream loaf onto a chilled platter sev-eral hours before serving; cover and return to the freezer.

Serving. Remove the loaf from the freezer to the refrigerator 20 minutes before serving. Spoon a little of the sauce around the ice cream loaf, and at the table cut the loaf into crosswise slices. For each serving, spoon a pool of sauce slightly to one side of a chilled plate, and lay a slice of ice cream in the center.

Caramel Sauce

Easy to make, and handy to have on hand, this caramel sauce is the best I know.

For about 1½ cups

Caramel (see Special Note on next page)
1 cup heavy cream
A pinch of salt
2 tsp pure vanilla extract

When the caramel has cooled but is still liquid, blend in the cream, which will partially congeal the cara-mel. Simmer, stirring, for several minutes over moderate heat while the caramel dissolves. Remove from heat; stir in the salt and the vanilla. Serve warm or cool.

**Ahead-of-time note:* Refrigerated in a covered jar, the sauce will keep for weeks. To serve warm or to liquefy, heat the jar in a pan of simmering water.

Sugar Syrups

Boiling sugar and making sugar syrups and caramel are essential to creating desserts and cakes. Just hearing the words "caramel" and "sugar syrup at the soft-ball stage" makes some novice cooks quiver. But fear not—you will never have trouble when you follow the few basic directions here.

To make a sugar syrup

Sugar syrups are sugar and water—⅓ cup of water per cup of sugar—boiled to various stages of sugar concentration, beginning with the simple syrup, where the sugar and water are heated just until the sugar is dissolved. The syrup is then usually flavored with vanilla or liqueur and used to imbibe the layers of a cake, or to poach fruit. Boiled a little longer, the last drops to fall from the tip of a spoon into a cup of cold water will form threads. This is the sugar syrup that is beaten into egg yolks for the butter cream on page 468, or beaten into the egg whites for the Italian meringue on page 462. As the water continues to evaporate you go through the hard-ball and the hard-crack stages, then finally the syrup begins to turn into caramel, and eventually it burns black.

Simple syrups are no problem, but, when you get into serious boiling for the soft-ball and caramel stages, you want to be sure that sugar crystals do not form on the sides of the pan—if they do, you are in for trouble because the whole syrup can crystallize. Prevention is simple.

First. Provide yourself with a moderately heavy pan that has a tight-fitting cover, so that the steam condensing on its lid will wash down the sides of the pan and prevent sugar crystals from forming.

Second. Be sure, at the outset, that the sugar has completely dissolved and the syrup is perfectly, limpidly clear before you start in on your serious boiling.

Third. Once you start boiling, never stir the syrup; however, you may swish it, holding the pan by its handle.

To clean pan and utensils, fill the pan with water, add any utensils, and simmer a few minutes to melt the caramel.

Syrup forming soft ball in fingers

To Make Caramel

1 cup sugar
⅓ cup water

SPECIAL EQUIPMENT SUGGESTED:
A heavy 6-cup saucepan with tight-fitting cover; a large pan of cold water at your side

Preliminaries to boiling. Blend the sugar and water in the saucepan and bring to the simmer. Remove from heat, and swirl the pan by its handle to be sure that the sugar has dissolved completely and that the liquid is perfectly clear.

Caramelizing the syrup. Cover the pan tightly and boil the syrup for several minutes over moderately high heat—keep peeking, after a minute or so, and boil until the bubbles are thick. Uncover the pan and continue boiling, swirling the pan slowly by its handle. In a number of seconds the syrup will begin to color. Continue boiling and swirling a few seconds more, until it is a light caramel brown, then remove from heat and continue swirling—it will darken more. Set the bottom of the pan in the cold water to cool it and stop the cooking.

Hot Fudge Sauce—Warm Chocolate Sauce

This is that fine type of chocolate sauce that strings up off the ice cream as you lift it in your spoon. It's the boiled corn syrup that does the trick.

For about 2½ cups

⅔ cup white corn syrup
⅔ cup water
½ cup unsweetened cocoa powder
1½ cups sugar
2 ounces (2 squares) unsweetened baking chocolate, chopped
6 Tbs unsalted butter
½ cup heavy cream
A big pinch of salt
2 tsp pure vanilla extract

The sauce. Boil the corn syrup in a small saucepan for a minute or two, until it forms heavy strands as you drop it off a spoon. Remove from heat and stir in the water. Sieve together the cocoa and sugar, then whisk them in. Simmer, stirring, for several seconds, until you are sure the sugar has dissolved completely—very important since undissolved sugar will cause the sauce to crystallize later. Add the baking chocolate and simmer, stirring, until melted; blend in the butter and heavy cream. Bring to the full boil for 15 seconds. Remove from heat, and blend in the salt and vanilla. Serve warm.

*Ahead-of-time note: Refrigerate in a covered jar, and place the jar in a pan of simmering water to reheat.

1. Pouring hot caramel and nuts onto oiled surface

Peanut Brittle

If you can make caramel, you can make your own peanut brittle—it's as easy as that, but you'd better keep it hidden since one bite is never enough.

For a goodly quantity, a sheet almost the size of 2 jelly-roll pans

4½ cups sugar
1½ cups water
3 cups regular-style roasted and salted and skinned peanuts
½ tsp baking soda

SPECIAL EQUIPMENT SUGGESTED:
2 large metal kitchen spoons; a flexible-blade metal spatula; a very large oiled metal tray, or 2 jelly-roll pans, or a large oiled marble slab; a heavy 2-quart saucepan with tight-fitting cover

Preliminaries. Have all the listed ingredients and equipment right by your side and at the ready since this goes very fast once the caramel is made.

The caramel. Following the detailed directions in the boxed caramel recipe, bring the sugar and water to the simmer, swirl the pan to dissolve the sugar completely, then boil the syrup to the light caramel stage.

The peanuts go in. At once remove from heat and blend in the peanuts; turn them vigorously with a metal spoon for a few seconds, and as soon as the nuts are coated with caramel stir in the soda. The mixture will immediately foam and whiten.

Out onto the work surface. At once, while still hot, turn it out onto your oiled surface, as illustrated, step 1. Now spread the hot mixture with a spoon. Continue spreading and thinning—lifting under the mass with the spatula, pulling it out with the bowl of a spoon. When cool enough, stretch out the caramel base with your fingers to a thickness of about ⅛ inch. When cold and brittle, break it into serving pieces, step 2.

*Ahead-of-time note: Wrap in a plastic bag and store in an airtight container.

2. Breaking cooled brittle into serving pieces

VARIATION

Hazelnut or Almond Brittle— Pralin

Substitute toasted hazelnuts or blanched toasted almonds for the peanuts in the preceding recipe, omitting the soda but adding ½ teaspoon salt to the sugar when making the caramel. See the Special Note on this page for toasting the nuts.

SPECIAL NOTE

Toasted Hazelnuts

Toasting gives hazelnuts much added flavor. Taste before toasting, to make sure they are fresh and fine.

Spread them in a jelly-roll pan, and roast for 20 minutes or so in a 350°F oven, tossing them several times. As they toast, their irresistible new aroma slowly emerges, and they are done when lightly browned. Then rub by handfuls in a rough towel or double thicknesses of paper toweling to remove loose skin—you won't get it all off, which is normal.

Toasted Almonds

Almonds also take on their optimum flavor when toasted. Buy blanched (skinless) almonds, spread them in a jelly-roll pan, and roast to a toasty light brown in a 350°F oven, tossing several times.

*Ahead-of-time notes for toasted nuts: When thoroughly cool, pack into a screw-topped jar and freeze.

1. Chopped brittle being folded into cream

Biscuits Tortoni

A splendid use for almond pralin. When you have an abundance of almond pralin in your freezer, that's when to think about biscuits Tortoni—charming frozen frilly desserts that you can have on hand or whip up in a flash. Tortoni was an Italian ice cream genius whose concoctions became all the rage in the Paris of the early 1800's, when the French went mad over frozen desserts of all kinds.

For 8 servings

For the almond pralin
½ cup granulated sugar
3 Tbs water
⅔ cup toasted blanched almonds

1 cup heavy cream
⅓ cup confectioners sugar
1 Tbs dark rum
1 tsp pure vanilla extract
1 egg white

SPECIAL EQUIPMENT SUGGESTED:
A blender or food processor for pulverizing the pralin; a bowl of ice cubes and water for whipping the cream; a clean bowl and beater for the egg white; frilled paper cups, ⅓-cup capacity; a muffin tin to hold them; twistems or toothpicks to protect them

2. Assembling the Tortoni

The mixture. Make the pralin as described in the variation to the recipe for Peanut Brittle; when cold and brittle, break it up and pulverize rather coarsely. Whip the cream into soft peaks over the ice. Sift and beat in the confectioners sugar, then the rum and vanilla; fold in two thirds of the pralin as illustrated (step 1)— save the rest for topping. In a clean dry bowl, whip the egg white into stiff peaks; fold it into the mixture.

Filling the cups. Place the frilled paper cups in the muffin tins. Spoon in the filling, dust the tops with the remaining pralin, step 2. To leave a ½-inch space between the Tortoni surfaces and their plastic cover to come, insert twistems or toothpicks between the paper frills and the muffin cups. Cover with plastic wrap and slip the tins into a large plastic bag. Freeze at least 2 hours—or for several weeks.

Serving. Arrange the Tortoni on dessert plates. You may wish to serve them with sugar or almond cookies.

APPLE DESSERTS

It's hard to beat an apple—something as one of America's favorite desserts. Although we don't have Mom's Apple Pie here, we do have, among other creations, two splendid apple tarts, an apple and almond pizza, an apple crisp, and a caramelized apple mountain. But in the beginning, there was applesauce.

◢▙ MASTER RECIPE

Applesauce

This is a fine, full-bodied applesauce that stands proudly on its own but can be used in a number of other preparations, including those that follow.

For about 4 cups

3½ to 4 pounds apples (6 to 8 apples)—Granny Smith, or others from the following list
1 medium lemon
½ tsp cinnamon
½ cup sugar, plus more if needed
½ tsp pure vanilla extract

SPECIAL EQUIPMENT SUGGESTED:
A heavy-bottomed saucepan with cover; a vegetable mill with medium screen

Preparing the apples. Wash and quarter the apples, core out the seeds, and halve the quarters but do not peel them—the peel gives flavor and body to the sauce.

Preliminary cooking. Place the apples in the saucepan along with the zest of the lemon (the yellow part of the peel removed with a vegetable peeler), the juice of the lemon, and the cinnamon. Cover the pan and set over moderately low heat; the apples will slowly soften and render their juices. Stir and mash them frequently until they are tender throughout—about 30 minutes in all.

Finishing the applesauce. Purée through the vegetable mill, return the applesauce to the pan, and stir in the sugar. Boil slowly, stirring and adding more sugar to taste, until the purée is thick enough to hold its shape quite solidly in a spoon. Stir in the vanilla.

*Ahead-of-time note: When cold, cover and put in the refrigerator, where the applesauce will keep perfectly several days.

Recipes Featuring Applesauce

Two good uses for applesauce are Apple Snow and Apple Charlotte. See also the Apple and Almond Pizza farther on.

SPECIAL NOTE

Apple Information

Choose the right apple: When you are making just a plain applesauce to use up apples, it makes little difference what apples you choose. But if you want a thick, full-bodied sauce, or apple slices that hold their shape after cooking, pick one of these varieties:

The old faithfuls: Golden Delicious and Granny Smiths are always reliable and always available.

Other varieties, depending upon where you live: Baldwin, Northern Spy, Newtown Pippin, Rhode Island Greening, Rome Beauty, York Imperial.

Apple Amounts (approximations)

1 medium apple, 2½ by 2½ inches = 5½ ounces
1 large apple, 3 by 3 inches = 8 ounces
1 pound apples peeled, cored, and sliced = 2⅔ cups
3 pounds sliced apples = 8 cups raw = 3½ cups sauce

Isabella Beeton's Apple Snow

Mrs. Beeton calls this "a pretty supper dish" and indeed it is, especially when topped with your own caramel sauce. In addition, it could hardly be easier to make—applesauce beaten into egg whites. I never thought such a thing would work, but, rather than collapsing the egg whites as I would have suspected, it stiffens them. Apple snow was not such a fast dish, of course, when Isabella's great *Book of Household Management* appeared in 1861 and all the beating was done by hand. But those were the days of the downstairs scullery maid, who beat her little heart out for the folks upstairs.

For about 6 cups, serving 6 to 8

4 "large" egg whites (½ to almost ⅔ cup), at room temperature
½ tsp cream of tartar
3 cups cold, thick, delicious applesauce (the preceding recipe)
½ to ⅔ cup homemade caramel sauce (page 420)

SPECIAL EQUIPMENT SUGGESTED: *A table-model electric mixer with very clean dry bowl and beater; wide-mouthed goblets; a wide-mouthed preserving funnel—to fill them neatly*

The apple snow. Start beating the egg whites at slow speed for a minute or so, until they foam throughout; beat in the cream of tartar and gradually increase speed to fast, until the egg whites form stiff shining peaks. Reduce speed to moderate and add the applesauce by ½ cupfuls. Continue beating at high speed for a minute or so, until the mixture is stiff enough to hold its shape softly in a spoon.

*Ahead-of-time note: Apple snow will hold several hours in the refrigerator; fill the goblets just before serving.

Serving. Spoon servings through the preserving funnel into each goblet, and dribble a generous spoonful of caramel sauce over each.

Apple Charlotte

Simmer a fine thick applesauce with a
dollop of butter, flavor it nicely with
rum and apricot, and pack it into a
mold lined with strips of butter-
dipped bread. Bake it until the wall
of bread strips is crisply brown, unmold it, and you have apple charlotte, one of the greatest of the apple
desserts.

MANUFACTURING NOTE. *It is essential here to have the right apple, as discussed in the notes preceding the master
recipe. The wrong apple will give you
the partially collapsed charlotte pictured
farther along. However, you can bolster
up a weak sauce by folding in toasted
and buttered bread crumbs.*

For a 6-cup baking dish, serving 6 to 8

The applesauce

**8 pounds of apples—Granny Smiths
    or Golden Delicious
The zests and juice of 2 lemons
½ cup apricot jam
1 cup sugar
1 Tbs pure vanilla extract
¼ cup dark Jamaican rum
3 Tbs butter, optional but nice**

**16 to 18 slices of firm homemade
    type sandwich bread, crusts off
8 ounces (2 sticks) melted butter,
    clear yellow liquid poured off
    from milky residue
½ cup apricot glaze (see directions
    at end of recipe)
Optional decoration: A sprig of
    greenery, or a candied cherry
Optional accompaniment: 2 cups
    custard sauce (crème anglaise,
    page 446), sour cream, sweetened
    whipped cream (page 440), or
    vanilla ice cream**

SPECIAL EQUIPMENT SUGGESTED:
*A heavy-bottomed 3- to 4-quart sauce-
pan with cover; a vegetable mill; a 6-
cup cylindrical baking dish, such as the
charlotte mold pictured here; a pizza
pan to catch juices in the oven*

The applesauce. Start the applesauce as
described in the master recipe, and
when the apples are thoroughly tender and mashed, stir in the apricot
jam, then purée the sauce. Return it
to the saucepan, add the sugar, the
vanilla, rum, and optional butter.
Raise heat and boil, stirring almost
continuously, until the applesauce has
become very thick, almost stiff, and
holds its shape quite solidly in a
spoon—15 minutes or more, and see
the manufacturing note at the beginning of this recipe. Correct seasoning: this should be an absolutely
delicious concoction—but definitely
thick!

Lining the baking dish.

1. Lining baking dish with butter-dipped bread
strips

The bottom. Arrange 4 pieces of
the crustless bread in a square, center
the cylindrical baking dish on top,
and cut around the bottom of the dish
to make 4 pie-shaped pieces to fit inside the dish, as shown in the photograph. Cut a 1½-inch circle out of a
bread scrap. Sauté the 4 pieces and
the circle in a spoonful or two of the
melted butter, to brown very lightly.
Fit the pie-shaped pieces in the bottom of the dish. Reserve the circle.

The sides. Cut the rest of the bread into strips 1¼ inches wide, dip in the melted butter, and fit them, slightly overlapping, around the inside of the dish, as illustrated, step 1.

2. Spooning in the thick applesauce

In goes the applesauce. Spoon a 1-inch layer of applesauce into the dish, step 2, and cover with bits of butter-dipped bread. Continue in layers, letting the filling hump up ¾ inch in the center for the final layer. Cut off any protruding bread-strip ends and press them, along with several buttery bread strips, on top of the sauce. Pour any remaining butter, if you wish, over the tops of the bread strips lining the dish.

Baking—30 to 40 minutes at 425°F. Set in the middle level of the preheated oven, and place the pizza pan on a rack below, to catch any buttery juices. The charlotte is done when you slip a knife between the bread strips and the dish, and see that the bread has browned nicely.

Unmolding. Set a serving platter on top of the charlotte and reverse the two; leave the baking dish in place for 30 minutes. Reverse again, and run a thin knife between the browned bread strips and the sides of the dish. Reverse a final time, the baking dish

upside down over the charlotte. Now lift the dish up slowly an inch or two and wait a bit; lift up more, and if there is the slightest suggestion of bulging sides, slip the dish back down and wait 10 minutes more. Try again; the charlotte may bulge, but it should hold if your sauce was firm enough.

Final decoration. Paint the glaze over the top and sides of the charlotte, center the reserved toast circle on top and glaze it also. Decorate, if you wish, with a sprig of greenery and a red berry or cherry.

3. Partial collapse after the winning serving

Serving. Serve the charlotte warm or at room temperature. Cut into wedges, step 3, and pass the sauce, cream, or ice cream separately. It is quite possible to have a partial charlotte collapse after the first serving—particularly if it is still warm. But if it held up for its initial presentation, you have won!

Apricot Glaze

For glazing tarts, cakes, and fruit toppings (see also Red Currant Glaze, page 437)

Apricot glaze is what makes tarts shimmer and charlottes glitter—nothing but sieved apricot jam boiled down to the thread stage with a little sugar. Make a double or triple amount while you are at it, since it keeps for months.

For 1 cup

1 cup apricot jam
3 Tbs sugar
3 Tbs dark rum, optional

Push the jam through a sieve to remove pulp and skin. Blend it in a small saucepan with the sugar and optional rum, then bring it to the boil, stirring. Boil several minutes until the last drops to fall from the tip of a spoon are thick and sticky—228°F. Use while still warm, or rewarm it; apply it with a pastry brush, with a table knife, or with the back of a spoon.

Storing. Store in a screw-top jar; it does not need refrigeration.

APPLES IN SLICES

◢◣ MASTER RECIPE

Oven-Baked Apple Slices

When you slice your apples and bake them in a dish, basting them all the while with butter, cinnamon, and their own juices, you can well serve them just as they are, or consider them a base for other concoctions as suggested farther on.

For about 3 cups, serving 4 to 6

3 pounds (6 to 8) apples, the kind that will hold their shape when cooked in slices—Goldens are particularly recommended, but see other suggestions from the list on page 424
¼ cup sugar blended with ¼ tsp cinnamon
1 Tbs lemon juice
4 Tbs unsalted butter, melted

SPECIAL EQUIPMENT SUGGESTED:
A 4-quart mixing bowl; a large rubber spatula; a 6-quart baking dish such as one about 12 by 7 by 2 inches; a bulb baster

Preparing the apples. Quarter, core, and peel the apples; cut the quarters into lengthwise thirds to make slices ½ inch wide at the outside edge. Toss in a bowl with the sugar mixture, then with the lemon juice, and finally with the melted butter. Let sit 3 or 4 minutes to render juices and absorb flavor. Taste, and fold in a little more sugar, if needed.

Baking—30 to 40 minutes at 375°F. Turn the apples into the baking dish and bake in the middle level of the preheated oven, sucking up accumulated cooking juices with the bulb baster and distributing them over the apples every 8 to 10 minutes. The apples are done when the slices are thoroughly tender but hold their shape; they should color lightly, and should be perfectly delicious—taste

to check, and baste with more seasonings if necessary. (If the juices have not reduced to a thick syrup, remove them with the bulb baster and boil down in a small saucepan, then pour over the apples.)

*Ahead-of-time note: May be baked a day or two in advance; cover and refrigerate.

Serving. Serve warm or cold with heavy cream, sour cream, ice cream, or custard sauce. Or try one of the following suggestions.

Apple Slices Baked with Bourbon Cream

A simple topping makes for a dressier dessert.

The preceding Oven-Baked Apple Slices
1 egg yolk
¼ cup sugar
3 Tbs bourbon whiskey
½ cup heavy cream

Preparing the apples. Preheat the oven to 400°F. If the apples have been cooked in advance, heat them in the oven until bubbling—about 10 minutes. For the bourbon cream, whisk the egg yolk in a smallish bowl, gradually adding the sugar. Continue beating for several minutes until lightly thickened, then beat in the bourbon, and finally the cream. Spread the topping over the apples, shaking the baking dish so that the cream will sink down into the apples.

Baking. Bake about 5 minutes in the upper middle level of the preheated oven, just until the cream has set and is beginning to brown in places. Serve warm or cold.

Apple Crisp

Apple crisp is an old-fashioned brown-betty type of dessert—sliced apples baked on a bed and under a blanket of streusel—brown sugar, butter, flour, and, in this case, oatmeal flakes. The apples then have a certain crispness over and under, and a sumptuously soft inner core.

For 6 servings

Ingredients for Oven-Baked Apple Slices, minus the butter

The streusel crisp
½ cup flour
¾ cup brown sugar, sieved to remove lumps
⅛ tsp salt
6 Tbs chilled unsalted butter, cut into ½-inch pieces
1 cup rolled oats (instant oatmeal-flake cereal)

Optional accompaniment: vanilla ice cream, sour cream, whipped cream, or *crème anglaise* (custard sauce, page 446)

SPECIAL EQUIPMENT SUGGESTED:
A food processor; a buttered 2½-quart baking dish such as a round one 9¾ by 2¾ inches, with cover

The apples. As directed in the master recipe, quarter, core, peel, and slice the apples; toss in a large mixing bowl with the lemon and the sugar-cinnamon mixture.

The streusel crisp. Process the flour, sugar, salt, and butter in the machine with several on-off pulses, only until the mixture looks like coarse meal. Add the oat flakes and pulse in with 2 or 3 flicks, to break them up roughly.

Assembling. Spread half the streusel in the bottom of the buttered baking dish, turn in the sliced apples and their accumulated juices, and cover with the remaining streusel.

Baking—about 1 hour at 350°F. Bake, covered, in the middle level of the preheated oven until the apples are slowly bubbling—about 20 minutes. Uncover and continue baking, until a knife point goes into them very easily. The streusel topping will have browned lightly.

Serving. Serve warm or cold just as it is, or with ice cream, sour cream, whipped cream, or custard sauce.

VARIATION

Cranberry Crisp

Cranberries in a gently crunchy cloak—serve this with the Thanksgiving turkey, or accompany it with cream or ice cream for a pleasantly tart dessert. It is so rich and concentrated, however, that this recipe can well make a dozen portions.

For an 8-inch square pan, making 12 rectangular pieces

The cranberries
1 package (3½ to 4 cups) fresh cranberries
1 orange
1 cup sugar
½ cup apple cider or apple juice
½ tsp cinnamon
½ cup heavy cream

The preceding streusel for the Apple Crisp
Suggested dessert accompaniment: sweetened whipped cream (page 440), or vanilla ice cream

Cranberry Crisp (*continued*)

SPECIAL EQUIPMENT SUGGESTED:
A food processor; a buttered 8-inch square cake pan, no-stick recommended, otherwise line the pan with buttered wax paper

The cranberries. Pick over and wash the cranberries; place in a 2-quart saucepan. With a vegetable peeler remove the zest (orange part of skin only) of the orange, and pulverize in the processor with ⅓ cup of the sugar. Add this to the cranberries along with the rest of the sugar, the strained juice of the orange, the cider or apple juice, and the cinnamon. Cover the pan and bring to the boil for 3 to 4 minutes, or until the cranberries have burst. Add the cream and boil down several minutes to thicken lightly. Set aside.

*Ahead-of-time note: May be made several days in advance.

Assembling. Butter the cake pan and turn half of the streusel crisp mixture into it, pressing it against the bottom of the pan. Scrape in the cranberries, and spread the remaining crisp over them, pressing them in lightly.

Baking—50 to 60 minutes at 350°F. Bake in the middle level of the preheated oven until the flan is slowly bubbling in several places, and is beginning to brown lightly on top. Cool 20 minutes.

Serving. Run a knife around the edge of the pan, and unmold onto a pastry sheet; immediately set a serving plate over it and reverse the two, ending with the flan top side up. Serve warm, or cold, and, if it is a dessert, accompany with the cream or vanilla ice cream.

Caramel Apple Mountain

Caramel Apple Mountain

This recipe takes oven-baked apples to the summit—the baked slices are rebaked in a caramelized bowl, and unmolded only to be bathed in a cloak of caramel, and surrounded by a gentle cloud of whipped cream.

For an 8-cup mold, serving 10 to 12

The Oven-Baked Apple Slices (page 428)

The caramel
1½ cups sugar
½ cup water
¾ cup heavy cream
½ tsp vanilla

4 "large" eggs plus 1 egg white
¼ cup bourbon whiskey
2 cups sweetened whipped cream (page 440)

SPECIAL EQUIPMENT SUGGESTED:
A 6-cup pan with tight-fitting cover; a round-bottomed 8-cup stainless bowl for the apples; a casserole with rack to hold the bowl in the oven

The apple slices. Bake the apple slices as directed, making sure they are perfectly tender and deliciously flavored. Let cool 10 minutes before assembling; meanwhile prepare the caramel.

The caramel—for the mold and the sauce. Following the recipe for caramel on page 421, bring the sugar and water to the boil, and when the sugar has dissolved completely cover the pan and boil to the light caramel stage. Pour a third into the 8-cup bowl; to coat the bottom and sides, protect your hands with potholders and turn the bowl in all directions for several minutes until the caramel ceases to run. Use the remaining caramel for the sauce, simmering it with the cream and adding the vanilla at the end, as described in the Caramel Sauce recipe on page 420.

Assembling. Whisk the eggs and egg white with the bourbon in a roomy mixing bowl. By large spoonfuls, gently fold the warm apples into the egg mixture. Turn the apples into the caramelized bowl.

Baking—30 to 40 minutes at 325°F. Set the bowl on the rack in the casserole and pour in enough boiling water into the casserole to come halfway up the bowl. Place in the lower middle level of the preheated oven. Regulate heat so the water in the casserole is barely bubbling, not boiling. (Be sure there is always water in the casserole!) The dessert is done in about 30 minutes—when a skewer plunged down through the center comes out almost clean. Remove the bowl from the casserole, and let cool 30 minutes. Unmold onto a serving platter. Serve warm or cold.

Serving. Since it slides off rapidly, spoon the caramel sauce over the apples just before bringing the dessert to the table. Pass the whipped cream separately.

A VARIATION ELSEWHERE:

Apple Crêpes

Another use for Oven-Baked Apple Slices—the Flaming Apple Crêpes on page 408.

DESSERT TARTS

Three Apple Tarts

The open-faced apple tart is always a visual treat, and here are three very different versions, one informal, one classic, and the third, a famous tour de force.

Apple and Almond Pizza

An informal apple tart, this starts with your best pastry dough, which is spread with thick fine applesauce, topped with oven-baked apple slices, strewn with chopped almonds, then slid into the oven to bake like the real-McCoy pizza.

(continued)

Apple and Almond Pizza (*continued*)

For 6 servings

**About 1 pound chilled butter pastry
dough, such as the recipe on page
381**
¼ **cup strained apricot jam**
1¼ **to** 1½ **cups chilled, thick,
delicious applesauce (page 424)**
**30 to 40 Oven-Baked Apple Slices
(page 428)**
1 Tbs dark rum
⅓ **cup blanched almonds coarsely
ground with 3 Tbs sugar (page
474)**
3 to 4 Tbs melted butter

SPECIAL EQUIPMENT SUGGESTED:
*A pizza baking stone or tiles, and a pizza
paddle (described for French bread on
page 37)—you can bake on a pizza pan
but the crust will never be as crisp; buttered heavy-duty foil*

Preliminaries. Preheat the oven to
425°F, set the rack in the lower
middle level, and place the pizza
stone or tiles upon it.

The dough. Roll the chilled dough
into a disk 13 inches in diameter and
⅛ inch thick; unroll onto the buttered foil and slide it onto the pizza
paddle. Working rapidly, paint a ½-
inch border of cold water around the
edge of the dough and fold it over to
make a rim, pressing it in place with
your fingers. Prick the interior of the
pastry disk all over going down to
the pastry sheet at ½-inch intervals
with the tines of a fork.

Assembling the pizza

Assembling the pizza. Paint the interior
of the disk with a thin layer of the
jam. Spread the applesauce over the
jam and strew the apple slices informally but attractively on top as illustrated. Sprinkle the rum over the
apples, spread on the almond-sugar,
and drizzle melted butter over all.

Baking—20 to 25 minutes at 425°F.
Slide the pizza, on its foil, onto the
hot stone or tiles. Bake 15 minutes,
reduce the thermostat to 400°F, and
bake 5 to 10 minutes more, until the
pastry has crisped and browned
lightly on the bottom. Slide onto a
serving board. To serve, cut into
wedges, like a pizza.

A Free-Form
Fresh Apple Tart

The basically blissful simple elemental open-faced apple tart has sliced
apples on a buttery brown crust with
a little sugar to sweeten them up and
a glaze of apricot to make them glitter. Bake it on a free-form rectangular shell for easy serving.

MANUFACTURING NOTE. *Rather than
forming and baking the tart on a pastry
sheet, you will always get a crisper
crust when you form it on foil on a pizza*

*paddle, and slide it onto a hot baking
stone, as for the preceding Apple and
Almond Pizza.*

*For a 14- by 4½-inch tart, serving 4
to 6*

**About 1 pound chilled butter pastry
dough, such as the recipe on page
381**
**2 to 4 apples, depending on the
arrangement you have chosen—
Goldens or Granny Smiths, or
others from the list on page 424**
¼ **cup sugar**
1 cup apricot glaze (page 427)

SPECIAL EQUIPMENT SUGGESTED:
*A buttered baking sheet; a table fork; a
melon baller; a pastry brush*

The free-form tart shell. Roll the
chilled dough into a rectangle ⅛ inch
thick and trim it to 15 by 5½ inches.

Chicken Pipérade (page 138) with apple tart—the
perfect dessert

Roll it up on your pin, and unroll it
onto the lightly buttered baking surface. Working rapidly so the dough

1. Turning up edges of dough rectangle

2. Sealing edges with tines of fork

3. Coring apples with a melon baller

Preparing the apples. Halve and peel the apples. Neatly dig out the core with the melon baller, and the stem with a small knife, step 3. Slice the apple halves crosswise or lengthwise, depending on the effect you wish— they are pictured both ways in the following photographs.

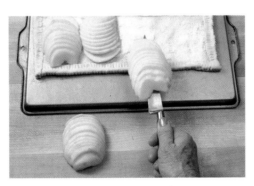

4. Transferring apple slices to sugared pastry surface

Baking—30 to 35 minutes at 375°F. Bake the tart in the upper middle level of the preheated oven. It is done when the pastry is lightly browned on the bottom; the apples will color slightly and should be perfectly tender.

5. Painting the baked tart with apricot glaze

Glazing. Slide the tart onto a rack, and paint with a light coating of warm apricot glaze, step 5.

Serving. Transfer the tart to a board, and serve warm or cold, cutting it into crosswise portions.

*Ahead-of-time and storage notes: The tart may be made several hours ahead, and although it is at its best when fresh, any leftovers may be wrapped and refrigerated or frozen. Reheat the tart in the oven or micro-wave, if you wish, and give an addi-tional coat of glaze before serving.

won't soften, lightly paint a 1-inch strip of cold water on the border of the rectangle all around. Cut a ½-inch square out of each corner, then fold ½ inch of the dough down against the sides and ends, making an edging for the shell as illustrated, step 1. Seal the turned-down edges of dough to the bottom of the pastry with the tines of a table fork held flat, pressing firmly. Then, holding the fork upright, its back to the edges, press it also around the outside of the tart, step 2. Prick the inside surface of the dough all over at ½-inch in-tervals with the fork, going down through the dough to the baking sur-face. Refrigerate the shell for ½ hour at least; the dough must relax, or it may bake out of shape.

*Ahead-of-time note: Or wrap and freeze the shell on its baking sheet; no need to thaw it before baking.

Placing the apples on the shell. Sprinkle 2 tablespoons of sugar in the tart shell. Arrange the apple slices over the sugar. In the illustration, step 4, the apples have been cut crosswise and are slid in place off the knife; if they are a little too wide to fit neatly, shave a bit off the sides of each group. Only 2 apples are needed when you slice them this way and the tart serves 4 people, while the verti-cal slices arranged the length of the tart are more flexible. Sprinkle the remaining sugar over the apples.

VARIATION

Pear Tart

Substitute firm ripe pears for apples—Bartletts are my favorite here.

A famous upside-down apple tart.

Tarte Tatin is the French name for this famous dessert invented years ago by the Demoiselles Tatin, in their restaurant at Lamotte-Beuvron on the Loire River. It is caramelized sliced apples oven-baked in a skillet with the pastry on top; when done, it is turned upside down so the crust is on the bottom and the apple slices—wonderfully brown, buttery, and glazed with caramel—remain in a design on the top.

Historical Note. The following version is my fourth and, so far as I am concerned, definitive recipe for this wonderful tart. It can be tricky—the caramel juices can refuse to thicken, the apples can be either so loose the tart collapses when unmolded, or so stiff they stick to the pan, and so forth. But after numerous trials with my colleagues Nancy Barr and Beth Gurney, I think we have worked out the bugs.

As an example, Nancy and our television cooking team managed to present the making and serving of a tarte

Tatin between 8:55 and 8:58:30 a.m. one day on "Good Morning America." To show it all in our short amount of allotted time, we had prepared the tart in various stages—plenty of sliced raw apples at the ready, then caramel and butter cooking in one frying pan and apples going into it. Switch to ready-arranged apples in another frying pan, which had to be tipped to show the perfect thickness of the caramel syrup before the pastry went on top, and finally the ready-baked tart to be unmolded successfully before the camera. In addition and in case of disaster and retakes, there were three standbys—an apple-filled frying pan and two ready-baked tarts—a real hassle to get all of that ready so early in the morning. Whether many of our viewers were able to follow the final intricate proceedings, I don't know—but we did it all in one take, in 3½ minutes, and we felt triumphant.

La Tarte Tatin

For an 8-inch tart, serving 6

5 to 6 apples, Golden Delicious recommended—the right apple is essential here (see also other suggestions on page 424)
The grated rind and juice of 1 lemon
1½ cups sugar
3 ounces (6 Tbs) unsalted butter, cut into ½-inch pieces
8 ounces butter pastry dough (about half the recipe on page 381)
Optional accompaniment: whipped cream, sour cream, or vanilla ice cream

SPECIAL EQUIPMENT SUGGESTED:
A heavy ovenproof frying pan, such as cast-iron, 9 by 2 inches with fairly straight sides, or heavy no-stick aluminum; a bulb baster; a cover for the pan; a large enough flat-bottomed serving dish

Preparing the apples. Quarter, core, and peel the apples; cut the quarters in half lengthwise. Toss in a bowl with the lemon and ½ cup of sugar, and let steep 20 minutes so they will exude their juices. Drain them.

The caramel. Set the frying pan over moderately high heat with the butter, and when melted blend in the remaining sugar. Stir about with a wooden spoon for several minutes, until the syrup turns a bubbly caramel brown—it will smooth out later, when the apple juices dissolve the sugar.

1. Arranging the apple slices over the caramel

Arranging the apples in the pan. Remove from heat and arrange a layer of apple slices nicely in the bottom of the pan to make an attractive design, as illustrated, step 1. Arrange the rest of the apples on top, close packed and only reasonably neat. Add enough so they heap up 1 inch higher than the rim of the pan—they sink down as they cook.

Preliminary stove-top cooking—20 to 25 minutes. (Preheat the oven to 425°F for the next step, placing the rack in the lower middle level.) Set the pan again over moderately high heat, pressing the apples down as they soften, and drawing the accumulated juices up over them with the bulb baster—basting gives the whole apple mass a deliciously buttery caramel flavor. In several minutes, when the apples begin to soften, cover the pan and continue cooking 10 to 15 minutes, checking and basting frequently until the juices are thick and syrupy. Remove from heat, and let cool slightly while you roll out the dough.

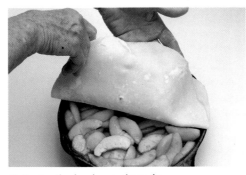

2. Laying the dough over the apples

The dough cover. Roll the chilled dough into a circle ³⁄₁₆ inch thick and 1 inch larger than the top of your pan. Cut 4 steam holes, ¼-inch size, 1½ inches from around the center of the dough. Working rapidly, fold the dough in half, then in quarters; center the point over the apples. Unfold the dough over the apples, step 2. Press the edges of the dough down between the apples and the inside of the pan, step 3.

3. Pressing edges of dough down sides of pan

Baking—about 20 minutes at 425°F. Bake until the pastry has browned and crisped. Being careful of the red-hot pan handle, remove from the oven.

Verification. Tilt the pan, and if the juices are runny rather than a thick syrup, boil down rapidly on top of the stove, but be sure not to evaporate them completely or the apples will stick to the pan.

Serving. Still remembering that the pan is red-hot, turn the serving dish upside down over the apples and reverse the two to unmold the tart. If not quite neat in design—which does happen—rearrange slices as necessary. Serve hot, warm, or cold, with the optional cream or ice cream.

VARIATIONS

Upside-Down Pear Tart

Substitute firm ripe unblemished pears for the apples—Bartletts, Comice, or Bosc.

Caramelized Pears in Puff Pastry
Feuilletés aux Poires

When peeled pear halves are sliced almost to the stem and simmered in caramel butter, the slices slowly fan out in a most attractive way. Serve them in puff pastry with pastry cream, whipped cream, and caramel for a very special dessert.

MANUFACTURING NOTE. *This is a good party item since the puff pastry and pastry cream can be on hand in your larder. Then, besides the pears, which you may caramelize in advance, you have only the cream to whip—but that can wait a while in the refrigerator until you are ready for a quick assembly just before serving. I shall not give details for pastry cream, pastry, or whipped cream since they appear elsewhere in this book. The only new technique is that for the caramelized pears.*

For 6 feuilletés

3 fine ripe unblemished pears (Comice, Bartlett, or Bosc)
Freshly squeezed lemon juice
4 ounces (1 stick) unsalted butter, cut into ½-inch pieces
¾ cup sugar
3 Tbs dark Jamaican rum
A pinch of salt
6 baked puff pastry rectangles (page 391)
1 cup rum-flavored pastry cream (page 402)
½ cup chilled heavy cream, whipped, sweetened, and flavored with rum or vanilla (page 440)

SPECIAL EQUIPMENT SUGGESTED: *A melon baller; a heavy 10-inch frying pan, no-stick recommended; a cover for the pan; a bulb baster*

The pears. Halve the pears one at a time lengthwise, halving the stem also (if possible). Remove the core with the melon baller and the bud end (bottom) with a small knife. Peel the pear halves. Again with a small knife, and starting below the stem, slice the pear half, keeping the slices attached at the stem end. Brush lightly with lemon juice to prevent discoloration, and set aside on a plate while doing the rest.

Pears fanning out as they cook

Caramelizing the pears. Melt the butter in the frying pan, stir in the sugar, and cook several minutes over moderately high heat, stirring slowly and constantly until the butter foams and begins to turn a caramel brown. Don't worry if it lumps. Remove the pan from heat, and add the pears, cut side down (domed side up), in a single layer. Bring to the bubble, cover the pan, and regulate heat so pears are slowly simmering. Every several minutes baste the pears with the caramel. As they cook, the caramel will clear of lumps and foam, and the pear slices will gradually fan out as illustrated. They will be tender in 5 minutes or so. Remove them to a no-stick surface.

Caramel sauce. Boil down the caramel with the rum and pinch of salt until it is a fairly thick syrup; pour into a smallish saucepan and reserve.

*Ahead-of-time note: Both pears and caramel sauce may be cooked a day in advance; cover and refrigerate.

Assembling —an arrangement that I found attractive.

The puff pastry rectangles. The pastries must be fine and fresh-tasting— crisp them in the oven if necessary. They are to be split into 2 layers, the bottom for the filling, and the top for edible decoration. Split them, and remove some of the central portion— the layers should be about ⅜ inch thick.

Arranging each serving. Shortly before serving, drop a pool of caramel sauce in the center of each plate— about 1½ tablespoons. Place the bottom of a pastry layer a little to the side of the sauce. Spread a layer of pastry cream over the pastry, then lift a pear half crosswise onto the cream, letting the slices fan out. Anoint the pear with a good spoonful of caramel sauce, and drop a big spoonful of whipped cream at one side of the pastry, placing the pastry top at the other side. Serve promptly.

FRESH FRUIT TARTS

Fresh Berry Tarts

How lovely, and how very easy to make, are the fresh strawberry tart and tartlets pictured here, and they need no formal recipe except that for the making of the shells on page 382. Paint the inside of the shells with the warm red currant glaze (see Special Note), arrange beautiful ripe stemmed strawberries over the glaze, brush glaze over the strawberries themselves, and dessert is ready to serve. Pass whipped cream separately if you wish, or, rather than passing whipped cream, before arranging the strawberries over the bottom of the glazed tart or tartlet shells, spread on a quarter inch or so of the pastry cream on page 402. Treat raspberries or a collection of wild berries in exactly the same way.

VARIATIONS

Using sugar-cookie dough

Instead of serving a big fruit tart and having leftovers, make charming individual tarts using the sweet cookie dough for *sablés,* as described and illustrated on page 489.

SPECIAL NOTE

Red Currant Glaze
To glaze tarts, cakes, and red fruits (see also Apricot Glaze, page 427)

Boil down 1¼ cups of red currant jelly for several minutes in a small saucepan with 2 tablespoons of sugar until the last drops to fall from a spoon are thick and syrupy. Use while still warm, or let cool and reheat when needed.

Using Meringue-Nut Cookies: Dacquoise Tartlets

For 6 servings, replace the sugar cookie dough with the meringue-nut mixture on page 474, formed into a dozen 3½-inch disks. Just before serving, arrange half the disks on dessert plates, spread a thin layer of whipped cream over the top of each, and cover with sliced strawberries. Pipe swirls of whipped cream over the sliced berries and arrange a fine large whole strawberry in the center. Using a serrated knife, carefully saw the remaining 6 disks into quarters and push quarters at a slant around the central strawberry. Purée a dozen berries with sugar and lemon to taste, and spoon around the tartlets.

TWO THANKSGIVING SPECIALS

A Fluffy Pumpkin Pie

It's creamy, it's even light; it's a pumpkin soufflé in a pie crust. (See also the cold pumpkin soufflé, page 449.)

For an 11-inch pie (or two 9-inch pies), serving 16 to 20

Chilled butter pastry dough (page 381), using 3½ cups of flour

The basic pumpkin mixture

3½ cups cooked or canned (solid pack) pumpkin
1 cup light brown sugar
1 cup granulated sugar
1 tsp salt
3 Tbs light molasses
3 Tbs bourbon whiskey or dark Jamaican rum
3 tsp each cinnamon and ground ginger
¼ tsp each nutmeg and ground cloves
4 egg yolks
1 cup heavy cream
¾ cup milk, or more if needed

5 egg whites
Optional garnish: whipped cream (see Special Note, page 440) or vanilla ice cream; 1 cup or more pulverized pralin (nut brittle) (page 423)

SPECIAL EQUIPMENT SUGGESTED:
A buttered pie pan 11 inches in diameter (or two buttered 9-inch pans)

Preliminaries. Preheat the oven to 450°F. Roll out the chilled dough and fit it into the pie pan, making a strong, fluted rim that extends about

½ inch above the top of the pan. (Do not prick the bottom of the pastry.)

The pumpkin mixture. Blend the basic pumpkin ingredients together in a mixing bowl; the mixture should hold its shape softly in a spoon; beat in droplets more milk if it seems stiff. Beat the egg whites into stiff peaks (page 461), and beat a quarter of them into the pumpkin mixture. Delicately fold in the rest.

Filling the shell. At once, ladle the mixture into the pie shell, filling only to the rim of the pan. Proceed at once to the baking.

Baking—about 1 hour, starting at 450°F. Keep your eye on things here, since if the filling cooks too fast it can turn watery.

Start. Immediately after the shell is filled, set the pie in the middle level of the preheated oven and bake for 15 minutes.

Minute 15. When the rim of the crust colors lightly, reduce heat to 375°F and bake 15 minutes more. (Lower heat if the pastry begins to brown too much.)

Minute 30. Turn thermostat down to 350°F, and continue baking another 15 minutes or so, until a skewer comes out clean when you insert it 2 inches from the edges of the pie.

Minute 45 to 50. Turn the oven off, and leave the door ajar for 20 to 30 minutes more.

*Ahead-of-time note: Serve the pie warm or cold.

Serving. You may wish to accompany each serving with whipped cream or vanilla ice cream; dusting it with a sprinkle of nut brittle is an appetizing touch.

A Mincemeat Pie-Tart for Thanksgiving

Mince pie is a tart when it stands proud and free in a crusty shell, and this recipe uses store-bought mincemeat enhanced with a number of good suggestions to make it your very own creation.

For a 9-inch tart, serving 8 to 10

A 9-inch partially baked pie shell (page 382), and about 2 cups of the chilled raw dough for top decoration

4 to 6 cups (2 to 2½ pounds) bottled or reconstituted dehydrated mincemeat

Suggested additions—any or all, to your taste

Chopped raw apples or pears
Chopped nuts such as walnuts, almonds, hazelnuts, and pecans
Chopped raisins
Seasonings: cinnamon, ground cloves, mace, nutmeg, salt, and pepper
½ cup very finely chopped beef or pork tenderloin
¼ to ½ cup very finely chopped beef suet (fat from around the kidneys)
Several Tbs of good brandy, dark Jamaican rum, or bourbon whiskey

Egg glaze (1 egg beaten with 1 tsp water and a pinch of salt)
Optional accompaniment: vanilla ice cream

SPECIAL EQUIPMENT SUGGESTED:
A ravioli wheel and a pastry brush

Dough strips for the top decoration. Roll out the chilled raw dough into a rectangle ⅛ inch thick and cut into 10-inch strips ¼ inch wide. Arrange on a lightly floured baking sheet; cover and chill or freeze until needed.

The mincemeat. By having previously poured dried beans or rice into the empty form you baked the pie shell in, and having measured the amount, you will know how much filling you need. Pour the mincemeat into a saucepan and bring to the simmer; remove from heat and taste very analytically for seasoning. Stir in such additions as you wish—the chopped beef or pork and the suet, by the way, are for more body and oomph—that's where the mincemeat title comes in.

*Ahead-of-time note: May be prepared a day or more in advance to this point.

Weaving the lattice pattern

Filling the shell. Shortly before baking, turn the filling into the prebaked shell. Paint the pastry rim with egg glaze and weave a raw-dough lattice pattern over the top, as illustrated. Paint the dough strips with egg glaze.

Baking—25 to 30 minutes at 400°F. Bake in the middle level of the preheated oven until the filling is bubbling and the pastry topping has browned nicely. Let cool 20 minutes, then slide the tart onto a serving dish. Whether it is warm or cold, you may wish to accompany your mincemeat tart with great scoops of vanilla ice cream.

OTHER TARTS IN OTHER PLACES

Dessert tarts using French puff pastry (pages 391–5)

Making pastry shells with pie dough (pages 382–5)

Whipped Cream:
A Dessert Essential

To Whip Cream

Perfectly whipped cream, the kind to serve with desserts, rises to twice its original volume, is light and airy, but holds its shape softly—a heavenly edible cloud. It is usually subtly sweetened and flavored with confectioners sugar and vanilla or liqueur.

MANUFACTURING NOTES.

Ice. You will never have trouble whipping cream if you always do it in chilled conditions—in other words, whip the cream in a metal bowl set over a larger bowl of ice cubes and water.

The type of cream. Whether or not it is ultra-pasteurized, always choose "heavy" or "whipping" cream.

The mechanism. I don't recommend table-model mixers since they do not beat in as much air as you can incorporate yourself by hand, using either the big balloon whip or the portable electric mixer.

Lightly Whipped Cream: Crème Chantilly

For 2 cups

1 cup (½ pint) chilled heavy or whipping cream

Optional sweetening and flavoring
½ cup confectioners sugar in a sieve
1 tsp pure vanilla extract, or ½ tsp vanilla and 1 tsp rum, Cognac, or other liqueur

SPECIAL EQUIPMENT SUGGESTED:
A 2½- to 3-quart round-bottomed stainless bowl set in a larger bowl of ice cubes with water to cover; a large balloon-shaped wire whip (page 464) or a portable electric mixer

Whipping the cream. Pour the cream into the metal bowl set over ice. If you are using the large whip, incorporate as much air as possible, sweeping inside the bowl, lifting the whip above the surface for each rapid plunge, rotating the bowl, etc. For the portable mixer, circulate it around and through the bowl with vigorous movements. In 3 to 4 minutes the cream will begin to thicken—it is not a fast operation. For most uses, the cream is done when the beater leaves light traces on the surface, and holds softly when lifted in the beater or a spoon.

Optional sugar and flavoring. Just before serving, sift on the sugar, add the vanilla or liqueur, and fold them in with a large rubber spatula.

*Ahead-of-time note: If the wait is about ½ hour, refrigerate the cream in its bowl of ice, and beat it up briefly before adding the optional sugar. If the wait is an hour or two it is a good idea to turn the cream into a large sieve lined with well-washed cheesecloth, and set over a bowl to catch drippings; store in the refrigerator.

VARIATION

Stiffly Whipped Cream—for Cakes and Flourishes

You will sometimes want stiffer cream for decorating cakes, or for piping through a pastry tube. In this case, simply whip it until it forms soft peaks—if you go too far it will begin turning into butter.

APPLE AND PEAR COMPOTES AND CUSTARDS

Fresh fruit compotes—that is, fruits poached in vanilla syrup—make lovely refreshing desserts when you are looking for one that is simple and fat-free. Compotes are also a useful device for fruits that would otherwise over-ripen, or for fruits that are just not quite ripe enough to eat raw. Serve them just as they are with a little of their poaching syrup, or with cream or a custard sauce, or bake them handsomely in a custard tart as described at the end of this section.

The Rule for Poaching Syrup.
The proportions for a fruit-poaching syrup are always 1½ cups of sugar for each quart of liquid—water or wine; or 6 tablespoons of sugar per cup of liquid.

MASTER RECIPE

Apple Compote
Apples poached in vanilla syrup

For 6 apples

1 quart of water, or 2 cups of water and 2 cups of dry white wine
1½ cups sugar
2 lemons
2 Tbs pure vanilla extract
6 firm ripe unblemished apples— Goldens, Granny Smiths, or other apples that will hold their shape during cooking (page 424)

SPECIAL EQUIPMENT SUGGESTED: *A 2½- to 3-quart stainless saucepan roomy enough to hold the apples in 1 layer; an apple corer*

The poaching syrup. Bring the liquid and sugar to the simmer in the saucepan. Meanwhile cut the zests (yellow part of peel) off the lemons in strips and add to the pan, along with the strained juice of the lemons, and the vanilla. Remove from heat and swirl the pan to dissolve the sugar completely.

Preparing the apples. Set the pan beside your apple preparation area. One at a time, neatly peel and core the apples, and to prevent discoloration drop them into the syrup as you go. The syrup should cover the fruit by ½ inch; measure out and add more water if necessary, blending in 6 tablespoons of sugar per cup.

Poaching the apples. Bring to just below the simmer—actually simmering or boiling will burst the fruit. Maintain at below the simmer for 12 to 15 minutes, or until tender throughout when pierced with a skewer. Let cool in the syrup for 30 minutes so the apples will absorb its flavor.

*Ahead-of-time note: The apples may be cooked several days in advance; refrigerate them in their poaching liquid.

Serving suggestions. Serve warm or cold, either with a little of their poaching syrup or with cream or custard sauce.

VARIATION

Pear Compote

Substitute pears for apples, but do not core them; leave the stems on while peeling them, and shave a bit off the bottoms so they will stand upright.

Glazed Poached Apples or Pears

Here is a dressier presentation, where the poached fruits are set on croutons, and napped with a glazing syrup made from their poaching liquid.

For 6 servings

The preceding apple or pear compote
¾ cup apricot jam, sieved to remove skin and pulp
6 slices of white sandwich bread
3 to 4 Tbs clarified butter (page 139)
Optional accompaniment: lightly whipped cream (page 440), or sour cream, or custard sauce (page 446)

The glazing syrup. Blend 1 cup of the poaching liquid with ½ cup of the sieved apricot jam, and boil down for several minutes in a small saucepan until the last drops to fall from a spoon are thick and sticky. Set aside, and reheat briefly to re-liquefy before using.

The croutons. Cut the bread slices into 6 rounds with a 3-inch cutter. Sauté in the clarified butter to brown lightly on each side.

**Ahead-of-time note:* The glazing syrup and croutons may be prepared in advance.

Serving. Spread a thin coating of sieved apricot jam over each crouton and arrange on serving plates. Just before serving, top each with a well-drained poached apple or pear, and pour a spoonful of glazing syrup over each. Pass the optional cream or custard sauce separately.

VARIATIONS

Sugar Cookies or Meringues. Rather than arranging the poached fruit on croutons, use either the sugar cookies on page 489, or the meringue-nut cookies described for the fruit tarts on page 437. Paint these with sieved apricot glaze as also described. Place the well-drained fruit on top, anoint with the glazing syrup, and pass whipped cream separately. See also the recipe following, where the poached fruit is baked in a pastry shell.

Ice Cream. Or serve the fruits over a good spoonful of vanilla ice cream, topping them with the glazing syrup.

Pear Clafouti
A custard fruit tart

This is actually a clafouti spin-off, the original being a puddinglike, peasanty dish that originated around Limoges in east central France. My French colleague, Simca, and I worked on a lighter version with plums for *Mastering II*, and this is a spin-off of that, being my interpretation of a charming dessert we admired and were served at an old-fashioned hotel in Nemours, south of Paris. It was a tart—large whole poached and glazed pears sitting serenely upright, surrounded by a custard in a deep pie shell.

Expandable baking ring

MANUFACTURING NOTE. *Of course you could bake and serve the dessert in a dish rather than a free-form pastry shell and you would call it a flan rather than a tart. However, the charm of the crust cannot be denied. You'll need a deep shell here, which may be formed and baked in a 9- by 2-inch cake pan, but better yet is the expandable ring 2 inches high being held up in the illustration. Used for cakes as well as pastry shells, these useful items are carried in bakery supply stores, which you'll find listed in the yellow pages.*

The glaze. While the custard bakes, blend the poaching syrup and sieved jam in a small saucepan and boil down until the last drops to fall from a spoon are thick and sticky—reheat briefly to liquefy before using.

Serving. When the custard is done, remove it from the oven and let cool 20 minutes, tightening the foil collar if necessary to prevent the warm shell from spreading out. After its rest the custard will have firmed up sufficiently for you to slide it gently, still wearing its collar, onto the serving dish. Then remove the collar, and spoon the caramel over the pears as shown. Serve warm or cold.

VARIATIONS

Clafouti with stuffed pears

In the preceding recipe the pears are not cored, but they could be cored and stuffed, as in the following suggestion for apples.

Apple Clafouti
Apple Custard Tart

Choose Golden Delicious apples. Peel and core them, and poach as described on page 441. Before arranging the poached apples in the pastry shell, stuff the cored centers with a mixture of chopped walnuts and brown sugar mixed to a paste with a little unsalted butter. Then proceed with the recipe.

For 6 servings

6 whole pears poached in vanilla syrup, Pear Compote; see Variation on preceding page

The custard
2 Tbs flour
2 Tbs sugar
½ cup cool pear-poaching liquid
2 "large" eggs
⅓ cup heavy cream or sour cream
1 tsp pure vanilla extract

A prebaked pastry shell 9 inches in diameter and 2 inches deep (page 382), plus a little leftover raw dough if needed for patching

The glaze
1 cup pear-poaching liquid
½ cup sieved apricot jam

SPECIAL EQUIPMENT SUGGESTED:
A lightly buttered baking sheet; a double-thickness foil strip to surround the tart shell during baking; straight pins to hold the foil in place; a serving dish of sufficient size

The custard. Blend the flour and sugar in a mixing bowl and gradually whisk in the cool pear-poaching liquid. Beat in the eggs, cream, and vanilla.

Assembling the tart. (Preheat the oven to 350°F.) Place the shell on the baking sheet, and surround the shell with the foil strip, pinning it closely in place. Patch any breaks or cracks in the shell from the inside, with the raw dough. Stand 6 poached pears in the shell and pour the custard around them. Proceed at once to the next step.

Baking—about 30 minutes at 350°F. Bake in the middle level of the preheated oven until a trussing needle plunged into the center of the custard comes out almost clean. Do not overcook—the custard should remain tender.

CUSTARD DESSERTS

How lovely is the smooth and tender beauty of a caramel custard, carefully baked, unmolded, and standing high. A flavored liquid bound with eggs and heated just enough for the eggs either to hold the mixture softly in shape or to thicken it into a cream, the custard idea is among the oldest of the dessert techniques.

Caramel Custard

A baking dish is lined with caramel, and when the custard is baked in the dish, it emerges with a caramel coating. For maximum drama, bake the custard in a deep dish. The tinned charlotte mold pictured here is the perfect shape, its little ears placed at just the right distance from the rim of the dish so you can get your fingers around them for unmolding.

For an 8-cup baking dish, serving 8 to 10

¾ **cup sugar**
3 **Tbs water**

For the custard
6 **"large" eggs**
5 **egg yolks**
¾ **cup sugar**
1 **quart hot milk**
2 **or more tsp pure vanilla extract**
A pinch of salt

SPECIAL EQUIPMENT SUGGESTED:
A 6-cup stainless saucepan with tight-fitting cover for the caramel; an 8-cup baking dish 4 inches deep, preferably of metal; a tea strainer; a larger dish to hold the baking dish in the oven

The caramel. Following the detailed directions on page 421, bring the sugar and water to the simmer in the saucepan, swirling the pan to dissolve the sugar completely. Cover the pan, boil to the caramel stage, and proceed directly to the next step. Note: If the caramel hardens while waiting for you, rewarm it briefly until liquefied.

Caramelizing the baking dish. Pour half the caramel into the baking dish, and swirl it around slowly for several minutes, running the caramel over the bottom and halfway up the sides until it stops moving.

Caramel sauce. Pour ⅓ cup of water into the cooking pan and simmer 2 to 3 minutes to dissolve the caramel. Set the syrup aside until serving time.

The custard mixture. (Preheat the oven to 350°F.) Blend the eggs, yolks, and sugar in a bowl with a whip—stir; do not beat and create foam. Gradually blend in the hot milk to dissolve the sugar completely, again stirring rather than beating to minimize foam. Add the vanilla and salt; pour through the tea strainer into the caramelized dish. Skim any bubbles off the top of the custard.

Baking—¾ to 1¼ hours at 350°F. Set the baking dish in the larger dish and place in the lower third of the oven; pour boiling water around to come halfway up the baking dish. In 10 minutes check the water in the larger dish and regulate the heat so the water is at the not-quite-simmer—if it boils the custard will be grainy, but the water must be almost simmering or the custard will take hours to cook.

When is it done? It is done when a skewer plunged down an inch from the edge comes out clean; the center should still tremble slightly.

Unmolding. Remove the custard pan from the hot water and let it settle for at least 30 minutes, or until serving time. To unmold, run a thin, sharp knife between custard and dish; turn the serving dish upside down over the mold and reverse the two—the custard will slowly slip out. Pour the extra caramel syrup around.

*Ahead-of-time note: Do not unmold the custard; when it has cooled, cover and put in the refrigerator, where the custard will keep nicely for a day or two. Unmold before serving, as described.

VARIATIONS

Individual Caramel Custards

To each his own custard—bake them in individual ramekins, such as small Pyrex bowls 3½ inches across and 2¾ inches deep, holding ⅔ cup. The caramel custard recipe proportions will fill 12 of these, but you may wish less, as follows.

For 8 ramekins, ⅔-cup size

2½ cups milk
½ cup sugar
3 "large" eggs
3 egg yolks
1 tsp pure vanilla extract

Following the directions for Caramel Custard, line the ramekins with caramel, fill with the custard mixture, and set in a roasting pan. Surround with boiling water, and bake 20 to 25 minutes, until a skewer plunged ⅛ inch from the edge comes out clean but the centers tremble slightly. Remove from the water, and let settle at least 10 minutes before unmolding.

Cinnamon Toast Flan

You could call this a bread-and-butter pudding, but that title bespeaks nursery food to me. Besides, this is not a bread-and-butter base but a cinnamon toast base, and the flan is baked in a shallow dish—this is the kind of first-class grown-up dessert that even a child will enjoy.

For 6 to 8 servings

4 Tbs softened butter
6 or 7 slices white sandwich bread about ⅜ inch thick, crusts left on
¼ cup sugar mixed with 2 tsp ground cinnamon

The custard
5 "large" eggs
5 egg yolks
¾ cup sugar
3¾ cups hot milk
1½ Tbs pure vanilla extract

Optional accompaniments: strawberry or raspberry sauce (page 419); caramel sauce (page 420); or cut-up fresh fruits

SPECIAL EQUIPMENT SUGGESTED: *A 6-cup baking dish 2 inches deep; a fine-meshed sieve; a roasting pan large enough to hold the baking dish*

The cinnamon toast. Use half the butter to spread on the bread; arrange buttered side up on the rack of a broiling pan. Sprinkle the cinnamon-sugar over each slice and, watching carefully that the bread does not burn, set under the broiler until the sugar bubbles up. Cut each slice into 4 triangles. Smear the baking dish with the remaining butter, and crowd in the toast triangles, sugared side up.

The custard mixture. Prepare the custard mixture according to the directions on the next page.

Assembling. (Preheat the oven to 350°F.) Ladle half the custard through the sieve over the cinnamon toast; let sit 5 minutes while the toast absorbs it. Ladle on the rest.

Baking—25 to 30 minutes at 350°F. Place the dish in the roasting pan and set in the lower middle level of the oven; pour boiling water into the pan to come halfway up the custard dish. Regulate the oven heat during baking so that the water in the pan never actually simmers.

When is it done? It is done when a trussing needle comes out clean if plunged within an inch of the sides; it should come out almost clean, with a few custardy bits clinging, when plunged into the central section.

Serving. Serve as is, hot, tepid, or cold, and accompany, if you wish, with one of the listed suggestions.

THREE DESSERTS BASED ON CRÈME ANGLAISE

Custard sauce—*crème anglaise*—is certainly one of the most useful items to have in your dessert repertoire, since it is often your best choice to serve with puddings, and fruits either fresh or poached; it can be the main ingredient for ice cream, as well as being the base for the three desserts here.

⚏ MASTER RECIPE

Crème Anglaise: Custard Sauce

Crème anglaise is a lightly thickened pale yellow dessert sauce made of egg yolks, sugar, and milk heated together into a warm cream. The only trick is to heat the mixture slowly in order for the yolks to poach and thicken, but not scramble.

For about 2 cups

6 egg yolks
⅔ cup sugar
1½ cups hot milk
1 Tbs pure vanilla extract
3 Tbs unsalted butter, optional
2 Tbs rum, Cognac, or other
   liqueur, optional

SPECIAL EQUIPMENT SUGGESTED:
A 2-quart stainless saucepan; a wire whisk and a wooden spoon

Preliminaries. Whisk the egg yolks in the saucepan, adding the sugar by fairly rapid spoonfuls—if it goes in all at once the yolks can turn grainy.

Continue beating 2 to 3 minutes, until the mixture is pale yellow and thick. By dribbles, stir in the hot milk—stirring, not beating, because you do not want the sauce to foam.

Heating the sauce. Set the saucepan over moderately low heat, stirring rather slowly with the wooden spoon, and reaching all over the bottom and sides of the pan. The sauce should gradually come near—but not to—the simmer. You must be careful not to overheat it and scramble the yolks, but you must have the courage to heat it enough so that it thickens. Indications that it is almost ready are that surface bubbles begin to subside, and almost at once you may see a whiff of steam rising. Watch out at this point, you are almost there!

The finger test

When is it done? The sauce is done when it coats the wooden spoon with a light creamy layer thick enough to hold when you draw your finger across it, as shown.

Finishing. Beat in the vanilla, and the optional butter and rum. Serve warm, tepid, or cold.

**Ahead-of-time note:* The sauce may be refrigerated in a covered container for several days.

Crème Anglaise as the Principal Sauce for a Handsome Dessert

Floating Island

Egg whites and sugar are whipped together into a meringue, piled into a casserole, and baked slowly to form a soft, sweet noncollapsible soufflé. Unmold it, carve it into iceberg chunks, and plop it into a sea of custard sauce. A delicate web of caramel finishes the picture-perfect dessert—spectacular, but easy on the cook.

For 6 to 8 servings

1 Tbs softened butter
¼ cup sifted confectioners sugar

The meringue

1⅔ cups egg whites (about 12 egg
   whites)
A big pinch of salt
½ tsp cream of tartar
1½ cups granulated sugar
1 tsp pure vanilla extract

The caramel

1 cup granulated sugar
⅓ cup water

2 cups of the preceding master recipe
   for Crème Anglaise

SPECIAL EQUIPMENT SUGGESTED:
A straight-sided 4-quart baking dish 3 inches deep; a table-model electric mixer (page 461) or portable beater

The meringue —which may be baked several days in advance, and served tepid or chilled.

Preliminaries. Butter the baking dish; dust it with confectioners sugar, knocking out excess. Preheat the oven to 250°F.

Beating the egg whites. Following the detailed directions on page 461, start beating the egg whites at moderate speed until they foam throughout, beat in the salt and cream of tartar, then gradually increase the speed to fast until soft peaks are formed.

Beating in the sugar. Beat in the sugar by big spoonfuls and continue until stiff shining peaks are formed. Beat in the vanilla, and turn the meringue into the baking dish.

Baking—35 to 40 minutes at 250°F. Set in the lower middle of the oven and bake until the meringue has risen 3 to 4 inches.

1. The skewer test

When is it done? A skewer or straw plunged through it comes out clean, as illustrated, step 1.

Cooling. Set the casserole on a rack. The meringue will sink down to about its original height as it cools.

*Ahead-of-time note: Covered airtight, it will keep several days in the refrigerator or several weeks in the freezer.

Caramel for decorations. Somewhat in advance of serving, make the caramel (page 421); reheat when needed.

Serving. Pour the custard sauce into a serving platter. Run a knife around the edge of the meringue dish and push with a rubber spatula to loosen. Unmold the meringue onto a cookie sheet. Cut it into 6 to 8 big chunks and arrange them over the sauce, step 2.

Caramel-thread decorations. Just before serving, reheat the caramel until you can lift the syrup with a fork and dribble thick strands over meringue.

2. Cutting the meringue into islands

*Crème Anglaise Makes a
Bavarian Cream*

Louisiana Bavarian

Bavarian creams are molded desserts—custard sauce lightened with whipped cream and bound with just enough gelatin so that it will softly and creamily hold its shape when unmolded. Our example here is actually a sophisticated rice pudding flavored with rum and raisins.

For 6 to 8 servings

A little tasteless oil (pure fresh vegetable or almond oil, for instance), or no-stick spray, for the mold

The rice

½ cup plain raw rice, medium-grain suggested for tenderness, but long-grain will do
1⅔ cups milk, plus more, if needed
⅓ cup sugar
2 Tbs butter
1 tsp pure vanilla extract
A pinch of freshly grated nutmeg
A pinch of salt

The rum and raisins

¾ cup currants (small black raisins)
1½ Tbs unflavored gelatin
¼ cup dark Jamaican rum

The crème anglaise

¾ cup sugar
6 egg yolks
1½ cups hot milk

1 cup chilled whipping cream
1½ cups Caramel Sauce (page 420)

SPECIAL EQUIPMENT SUGGESTED:
A 6-cup fancy mold, or a square or cylindrical metal container; a heavy 2-quart stainless saucepan for simmering rice and milk; a wide bowl of ice cubes with water to cover, for quick chilling

The container. Brush or spray the mold lightly and, if the design permits, line the bottom with oiled or sprayed wax paper for ease in unmolding.

Cooking the rice—about 45 minutes. Bring 3 quarts of water to the boil in a saucepan, sprinkle in the rice, and boil 5 minutes; drain. Turn the rice into the heavy saucepan and bring to the simmer with the milk, sugar, butter, vanilla, nutmeg, and salt. Cover and cook very slowly for about 35 minutes, stirring gently once in a while and adding droplets more milk if needed, until the rice is deliciously tender and the liquid has been absorbed.

The raisins and rum. Meanwhile rinse the raisins in hot water, drain well, and blend in a bowl with the gelatin and rum. Set aside.

The crème anglaise. Following the master recipe, beat the sugar into the egg yolks, and when thick and pale yellow, gradually whisk in the milk; stir over moderate heat until thickened.

**Ahead-of-time note:* All parts of the recipe may be completed in advance to this point. Gently reheat the rice and the sauce over hot water before proceeding.

Combining raisins, sauce, and rice. Fold the rum-soaked raisins into the hot custard sauce, stirring to be sure the gelatin has completely dissolved. Slowly fold the sauce into the saucepan of rice.

The whipped cream. Whip the cream over ice until the beater leaves light traces on the surface, following the detailed directions on page 440.

Final assembly. Replace the bowl of whipped cream with the pan of rice and custard in the ice. Fold with a rubber spatula for several minutes, just until the mixture is cool to your finger—careful here, since if it chills it will start to set and you will have to reheat and rechill it. As soon as it is cool, remove immediately from the ice and rapidly fold into it the whipped cream. At once, before it can set, turn the dessert into the prepared mold.

Chilling—3 to 4 hours. Cover with plastic wrap, and refrigerate for several hours, until fully set.

Serving. Dip the mold into hot water, loosen the edges with a small sharp knife, and unmold onto a chilled serving platter. Spoon the caramel sauce over the dessert just before serving.

*Ahead-of-time note: The refrigerated dessert in its mold will keep 2 to 3 days, and the unmolded but unsauced dessert may be covered with an upturned bowl and refrigerated for several hours.

VARIATION

Cold Pumpkin Soufflé

Take the pumpkin out of the pie shell, treat it like a Bavarian beauty with egg whites, cream, and other good things—and you have a splendid dessert for Thanksgiving or any time of the year, including the Fourth of July. *Note:* See also the Fluffy Pumpkin Pie (page 438).

For a 6-cup dish, serving 12

The pumpkin base
6 egg yolks
½ cup dark brown sugar
1¼ cups hot milk
1¾ cups cooked or canned solid-pack pumpkin purée
Flavorings: salt, cinnamon, ground ginger and/or cloves, and nutmeg
1½ Tbs unflavored gelatin, dissolved in ½ cup dark rum or in cider, plus drops of pure vanilla extract
¾ cup ginger marmalade

6 egg whites (¾ cup), stiffly beaten with ¼ cup sugar (page 462)
¾ cup heavy cream, lightly whipped (page 440)
Accompaniment: 1 cup heavy cream, lightly whipped, flavored with confectioners sugar and pure vanilla extract (page 440)

SPECIAL EQUIPMENT SUGGESTED:
A bowl of ice cubes with water to cover; a 6-cup fairly straight-sided baking dish 3 to 3½ inches deep with a 3-inch collar of wax paper (illustrated on page 72)

The pumpkin base. Whisk the egg yolks and brown sugar in a heavy 3-quart pan until thick and pale yellow; by dribbles whisk in the hot milk, then the pumpkin. Beat in flavorings to taste. Stir over moderate heat until hot but not simmering. Mix in the dissolved gelatin and the ginger marmalade. Fold over ice until cool but not chilled, and proceed at once to the next step before the gelatin sets.

Cold Pumpkin Soufflé (*continued*)

Completing the soufflé mixture. Beat the egg whites as directed; stir a dollop of them into the pumpkin mixture to soften it; delicately fold in the rest. Beat the cream over the ice; fold it in. Fill the dish with the pumpkin mixture, which should extend an inch or more into the paper collar. Cover and chill 6 hours or more.

Ahead-of-time note: The dessert may be frozen at this point; thaw several hours in the refrigerator.

Serving. Remove the collar. Decorate the dessert with whipped cream, passing the rest separately.

Crème Anglaise Makes a Tipsy Trifle

The Kiwi Trifle

This deliciously simple tipsy dessert consists of jam-spread spongecake drenched in sherry and brandy, cloaked in custard sauce, chilled, and topped with whipped cream, almonds, and tiny macaroons.

Kiwi caution. Kiwis, that decorative and formerly trendy fruit, are an attractive decoration if you are serving the dessert in a see-through bowl, but if you use them don't make the dessert more than a few hours in advance since there is an enzyme in kiwis that can, in time, turn a custard watery.

For a 2-quart bowl, serving 6

The cake

An 8- by 1½-inch spongecake, genoise, or best-quality store-bought yellow cake
1 cup best-quality raspberry jam
1½ cups excellent sherry
⅓ cup good-quality Cognac or brandy

For the custard sauce (4 cups)

2½ cups milk
The rind (yellow part only) of 1 lemon
1 medium imported bay leaf
9 egg yolks
1 cup granulated sugar
1½ Tbs pure vanilla extract
¼ cup heavy cream
3 Tbs unsalted butter, optional

1 cup additional heavy cream, chilled, whipped, and lightly flavored with confectioners sugar and drops of vanilla (page 440)
Optional decorative suggestions: 3 or 4 kiwis, peeled and sliced crosswise; a handful of shaved almonds, skins on, and another of miniature macaroons ½ inch in diameter (sometimes called Ratafias, or amarettis)

Preparing the cake. Slice the cake in half horizontally (page 460), spread the bottom half with jam, re-form the cake, and cut into wedges to fit the bottom of the bowl. If you are using them, place a row of kiwi slices, laid flat, around the inside bottom of the bowl. Pack the cake wedges in one close layer into the bowl, pour on the sherry and brandy, and let imbibe while you prepare the custard.

The custard sauce. Bring the milk to below the simmer in a small saucepan with the lemon rind and bay leaf; cover and let steep 5 minutes or more. Meanwhile start beating the egg yolks in a stainless saucepan, gradually beating in the sugar until thick and lemon colored. Slowly beat the hot milk into the yolks, then thicken over moderate heat as described in the master recipe on page 446. Remove from heat and beat in the vanilla, the ¼ cup of cream, then by spoonfuls the optional butter. Stir over cold water for a few minutes until tepid, then strain over the sherry-soaked spongecake.

Chilling—5 to 6 hours. Cover and chill until softly set.

Ahead-of-time note: May be made a day or two in advance—unless you use kiwis.

Serving. Spread the whipped cream over the custard, and decorate with whatever tidbits you have chosen.

FINAL MISCELLANY

Including Chocolate Mousse, Plum Pudding with Whiskey Sauce, and an Immense Fruit Bowl

Chocolate Mousse

This uncomplicated but first-rate chocolate mousse features, of course, chocolate, plus butter for body, egg yolks for tenderness, beaten egg whites for lightness, and whipped cream for the extra calories and certain smooth richness that only whipped cream can give.

NOTE: *The master recipe for whipping cream is on page 440; for beating egg whites, on page 461; for melting chocolate, on page 464.*

For about 5 cups, serving 6 to 8

8 ounces sweet or semisweet baking chocolate, melted with ¼ cup strong coffee
3 ounces (6 Tbs) softened unsalted butter
3 egg yolks
1 cup heavy cream
3 egg whites
¼ cup "instant" (finely ground) sugar
Optional accompaniment: whipped cream

SPECIAL EQUIPMENT SUGGESTED: *A smallish saucepan with tight-fitting cover for the chocolate, and a larger pan of almost-simmering water to hold it; a 3-quart metal bowl for the cream, and a larger bowl with ice cubes and water to hold it; a clean dry bowl and beater for the egg whites*

Butter and egg yolks. Beat the soft butter into the smoothly melted chocolate. One by one, beat in the egg yolks.

The whipped cream. Beat the cream over the ice until it leaves light traces on the surface.

The egg whites. Beat the egg whites until they form soft peaks. While beating, sprinkle in the sugar by spoonfuls and continue beating until stiff shining peaks are formed.

Finishing. Scrape the chocolate mixture down the side of the egg-white bowl, and delicately fold them together. When almost blended fold in the whipped cream.

Chilling and serving. Turn the mousse into an attractive serving bowl, or into individual coupes or containers. Cover and chill several hours. You may wish to decorate the mousse with swirls of whipped cream, or to pass whipped cream separately.

A Glorious Plum Pudding for Christmas

While plowing about in my cookbook collection for the best-eating but not-too-onerous-to-make plum pudding, I found what I was looking for in the facsimile of the 1861 edition of Mrs. Beeton's *Book of Household Management* (New York: Farrar Straus and Giroux). That remarkable culinary bible called for the traditional English trappings of suet, pudding cloth, pudding basin, and a boiling session. I have taken the liberty of substituting butter for suet, and a covered bowl and steamer for the pudding cloth and basin. Otherwise Isabella's recipe was the sole inspiration for this modern American version, and I think it's one of the better Christmas puddings—so good in fact, that I would gladly eat it of a cool mid-summer evening.

For about 6 cups baked in an 8-cup mold, serving 12 or more

The pudding mixture

3 cups (lightly packed down) crumbs from homemade type white bread—a ½-pound loaf, crust on, will do it

1 cup each: black raisins, yellow raisins, and currants, chopped

1⅓ cups sugar

½ tsp each: cinnamon, mace, and nutmeg—more if needed

8 ounces (2 sticks) butter, melted

4 "large" eggs, lightly beaten

A few drops of almond extract

½ cup bitter orange marmalade

Serving

½ cup rum or bourbon whiskey, heated before serving

Sprigs of holly, optional

2 cups Zabaione Sauce (see Special Note on next page)

SPECIAL EQUIPMENT SUGGESTED:
A food processor is useful for making the bread crumbs and chopping the raisins; an 8-cup pudding container, such as a round-bottomed metal mixing bowl; a cover for the bowl; a steamer basket or trivet; a roomy soup kettle with tight-fitting cover to hold bowl, cover, and basket

TIMING NOTE. *Like a good fruitcake, a plum pudding develops its full flavor when made at least a week ahead. Count on 6 hours for the initial, almost unattended steaming, and 2 hours to reheat before serving.*

The pudding mixture. Toss the bread crumbs in a large mixing bowl with the raisins, sugar, and spices. Then toss with the melted butter, and finally with the rest of the ingredients. Taste carefully for seasoning, adding more spices if needed.

Steaming—about 6 hours. Pack the pudding mixture into the container; cover with a round of wax paper and the lid. Set the container on the steaming contraption in the kettle, and add enough water to come a third of the way up the sides of the container. Cover tightly; bring to the simmer, and let steam about 6 hours. *Warning:* Check now and then to be sure the water hasn't boiled off!

When is it done? When it is a dark walnut-brown color and fairly firm.

Curing and storing. Let the pudding cool in its container. Store it in a cool wine cellar, or in the refrigerator.

*Ahead-of-time note: It will keep nicely for several months.

Resteaming. A good 2 hours before you plan to serve, resteam the pudding—it must be quite warm indeed for successful flaming. Unmold onto a hot serving platter and decorate, if you wish, with sprigs of holly.

Flaming and serving. Pour the hot rum or whiskey around the pudding. Either ignite it in the kitchen or flame it at the table. Serve the following Zabaione Sauce separately.

Microwaving

I've had good luck with the microwave oven, although the color of the finished cake is pale walnut rather than mahogany. Choose a 2-quart glass pitcher, smoothly line the bottom and ⅓ up the sides with buttered wax paper, and pack the pudding in. Cover with plastic wrap pierced in 4 places with a small knife.

Timing: 30 minutes on *Defrost* or *Low*, 6 minutes on *High*. Rotating the pudding every 5 to 8 minutes is not necessary if your microwave has a revolving plate. When done, cover with a lid and let sit for 20 minutes.

The Immense Fruit Bowl

A beautiful finish to any meal is a lush collection of ripe, colorful fresh fruits, all cut up, flavored, and ready to eat. Your selection will depend on what's available, and out of season don't hesitate to include canned figs and plums along with whatever fresh fruits are on hand. Here is our selection for the big bowl illustrated.

For a dozen or more servings

The fruits we used

1 fresh ripe fragrant pineapple, cut into thin wedges
2 pink or white grapefruit, cut into skinless segments
2 or 3 navel oranges, peel cut off to expose flesh, oranges sliced thin crosswise
1 pint strawberries, stemmed and halved or quartered lengthwise
2 or 3 ripe peaches, peeled and sliced
1 cup each seedless red and green grapes
1 medium cantaloupe, cut into balls
3 or 4 ripe kiwis, peeled and sliced crosswise

Flavoring

½ cup sugar, or to taste
¼ cup or more freshly squeezed lemon juice
¼ cup or more freshly squeezed lime juice
Accompaniments: cookies such as the almond bars (page 482), almond or hazelnut wafers (page 483), madeleines (page 488), or a best-quality store-bought selection

Macerating the fruits—1 hour before serving. Fold the fruits in their bowl with ½ cup of sugar, and ¼ cup each of lemon and lime juice. Refrigerate, folding gently several times, and adding more flavors if you think them needed.

*Ahead-of-time note: Although the fruits will hold longer than an hour, they are at their best when served reasonably soon.

OTHER DESSERTS IN OTHER PLACES

Crêpes (pages 408–11)

Soufflés (pages 76–7)

Cream Puffs, Saint-Honorés, and others made with choux paste (pages 399–401)

Zabaione Sauce

A foamy sauce for puddings and warm fruit desserts.

For about 2 cups

1 "large" egg
2 egg yolks
A small pinch of salt
⅓ cup rum or bourbon whiskey (or Marsala or sherry)
⅓ cup dry white French vermouth
½ cup sugar

Whisk all the ingredients together for 1 minute in a stainless saucepan. Then whisk over moderately low heat for 4 to 5 minutes, until the sauce becomes thick, foamy, and warm to your finger—do not bring it to the simmer and scramble the eggs, but you must heat it enough for it to thicken. Serve warm or cold.

*Ahead-of-time note: The sauce will remain foamy for 20 to 30 minutes, and if it separates simply beat it briefly over heat. If you wish to re-foam the sauce, whisk in a stiffly beaten egg white.

Cakes & Cookies

**All About Making Sponge Cakes
and Genoises**

**Flavorings, Frills, and Essential
Techniques**

**Layer Cakes, Almond Cakes,
Sponge Sheets, Loaf Cakes**

A Selection of Cookies

Cakes, more than any part of cooking it seems to me, are an assembly job. You have several cake formulae up your ample sleeve, plus a number of fillings, frostings, flavorings, and decorative frills; put them together as occasions arise and you can concoct a different cake every time. Perhaps you're on a chocolate binge, or caramel is on your mind, or you're dreaming of a great fluffy cloud of meringue. This chapter hopes to satisfy those cravings by giving a small but select choice, since cakes abound in my other books.

We start with two basic cake formulae and a variation, touch on the subject of store-bought plain yellow cakes—which can be very good—then delve into frostings and fillings before going into two splendid layer cakes. Three almond cakes and a jelly roll precede two loaf cakes and a tenfold cookie finish.

TWO ALL-PURPOSE YELLOW CAKES

A butter spongecake, or *biscuit au beurre*, the kind where beaten egg whites are folded into the batter, is one of the two standard cakes for frosting and filling. For the second cake, the genoise, whole eggs are beaten into a creamy foam and then combined with the other ingredients; it is a little drier in texture and a bit trickier to make. The two are interchangeable for most purposes, but both should be in any good cook's repertoire since their special techniques are part of one's essential culinary baggage.

SPONGECAKE: PÂTE À BISCUIT

In many ways you can think of a spongecake as a noncollapsible soufflé. You make a base of beaten egg yolks and sugar, then you fold in stiffly beaten egg whites alternating with sprinkles of flour. For the soufflé there is only enough flour to hold the egg-white bubbles in a magnificent puff while the soufflé is warm—then plop! But for a cake there is sufficient flour so that when the egg-white bubbles puff in the oven, the flour coagulates around them and the puff stays put. Thus when you have mastered the one, you are automatically master of the other.

■ MASTER RECIPE

To Make the Spongecake Batter

For cakes, petits fours, and sponge sheets

For a 4-cup pan, such as an 8-inch round or square one; or an 11- by 17-inch sponge sheet

The batter base

3 egg yolks
½ cup sugar
1½ tsp pure vanilla extract

The egg whites

3 egg whites
A pinch of salt
A scant ¼ tsp cream of tartar
1½ Tbs additional sugar

Completing the batter

⅓ cup plus ¼ cup (9 Tbs total) plain bleached cake flour, scooped and leveled into a sifter set over wax paper
3 Tbs tepid melted butter

SPECIAL EQUIPMENT SUGGESTED: *A 3-quart mixing bowl; a wire whisk or portable mixer; a clean dry bowl and beater for the egg whites; a large rubber spatula*

MANUFACTURING NOTES. *If you need more details on measuring flour, beating egg yolks and sugar, beating egg whites and folding them into a batter, see pages 461 and 463.*

Preliminaries. Preheat the oven, prepare the pan (see Special Note on the opposite page), and measure out all the ingredients listed so that you can go right through the motions without stopping.

The egg yolks and sugar. Start beating the egg yolks in the mixing bowl, and gradually beat in the sugar by tablespoons; continue for several minutes, until the mixture is thick, pale yellow, and forms the ribbon. Beat in the vanilla.

Beating the egg whites. Beat the egg whites separately, starting at slow speed, until they foam throughout. Add the salt and cream of tartar, and continue until soft peaks are formed; sprinkle in the sugar and beat to stiff peaks.

Finishing the batter. At once stir a quarter of the egg whites into the egg yolks and sugar, to lighten the mixture. Rapidly plop a third of the remaining whites on top, and sift on a quarter of the flour. Delicately and rapidly fold them together, and when almost blended repeat the sequence with a third of the remaining egg whites and a third of the remaining flour, then half of each, and when you have almost blended the last of each, add and fold in the tepid melted butter—do not overblend or you will deflate the batter. Proceed at once to the baking, either in a cake pan as described here, or as the sponge sheet on page 477.

To Bake a Round or Square Cake

The oven has been preheated to 350°F, with the rack in the lower middle level. An 8-inch round or square cake pan, bottom lined with wax paper, has been buttered and floured (see Special Note on this page), and a cake rack is at hand. The preceding spongecake batter has just been completed.

Into the cake pan. Immediately pour and scoop the batter into the prepared

1. Pouring batter into prepared pan

cake pan, which it should fill to within ¼ inch of the rim (see illustration, step 1). If by chance you have too much batter, scoop it out to prevent a possible overflow, or a top with an overhanging ridge. Tilt the pan in all directions to run the batter up to the rim all around, thus discouraging a humped-up center. Bang the pan once lightly on your work surface to deflate any big bubbles, and set the pan at once in the preheated oven. (A square pan is filled in exactly the same way.)

Baking—25 to 30 minutes at 350°F. The cake will slowly rise a little above the rim and will begin to brown.

2. Drawing cake from edges of pan

When is it done? It is almost done when its puff starts to sink very slightly. Gently press the top, which should be springy; the sides should show a faint line of shrinkage from the edges of the pan. It is definitely done when you can gently pull it from the sides of the pan, as shown in step 2.

Cooling and unmolding. Remove the cake pan from the oven and set it on a rack to cool for 15 to 20 minutes. Run a small sharp knife between the cake and against the edge of the pan all around to be sure the cake is loose. Then set the rack over the pan and reverse the two, giving a gentle but sharp shake to dislodge the cake from the pan onto the rack as illus-

3. Cake turned out onto rack—don't worry if bottom surface is rough as shown

trated, step 3. If the wax paper has adhered, neatly peel it off the bottom of the cake. Carefully turn the cake

right side up and let it cool completely—an hour or more. It is now ready for filling and icing.

*Ahead-of-time note: If you are baking the cake well in advance, slip it into an airtight plastic bag when thoroughly cool. Refrigerate it for 2 to 3 days, or you may freeze it for several weeks.

SPECIAL NOTE

To Prepare a Cake Pan
Buttered, floured, and lined with wax paper

Whatever size or shape your cake pan, from round to square to jelly-roll, and whether or not it is no-stick, prepare it as follows.

First, smear the baking surface (bottom and sides) lightly but evenly with soft butter. If the bottom is to be lined with wax paper, cut a sheet to fit it exactly and press it in place, then butter the paper. Finally pour in a half cup or so of all-purpose flour, shake and turn the pan in all directions to film the bottom and sides completely, then bang the pan upside down over the sink to dislodge excess flour. If by chance the kitchen is hot, refrigerate the pan until you are ready to fill it.

VARIATION

Orange-Almond Spongecake Batter

An orange and almond flavoring makes a delightful plain cake or cup cakes, served just with a powdering of confectioners sugar. Or use it for jelly rolls or filled cakes. You will note that folding in the egg whites is easier here, since orange juice softens the base.

For an 8-inch round or square cake, or a sponge sheet

The batter base

3 egg yolks
½ cup sugar
The grated rind of 1 medium orange and ¼ to ⅓ cup of its strained juice
¾ cup blanched almonds pulverized in a blender with 3 Tbs sugar
¼ tsp almond extract
½ cup plain bleached cake flour in a sifter (scooped and leveled)

The egg whites

3 egg whites
A pinch of salt
A scant ¼ tsp cream of tartar
1 Tbs sugar

The batter base. Beat the egg yolks in a mixing bowl, gradually sprinkling in the sugar. When thick and pale yellow, beat in the orange rind and juice, the pulverized almonds, and the almond extract. Slowly sift and beat in the flour.

The egg whites, and finishing the batter. In a clean, dry separate bowl, beat the egg whites to soft peaks with the salt and tartar, sprinkle in the sugar, and continue beating to stiff, shining peaks. Stir a quarter of the egg whites into the batter; delicately fold in the rest.

Forming and baking. Immediately proceed to the baking, in either a round or a square pan as previously described, or as the sponge sheet on page 477.

▤ MASTER RECIPE

Genoise Cake Batter: Pâte à Génoise
Especially recommended for layer cakes and petits fours

The genoise or whole-egg technique is quite different from the separated eggs of the spongecake, in that here you beat whole eggs and sugar over warm water until they have swelled to a fine warm yellow foam—exactly like a zabaione but minus the wine flavoring. You then beat until the eggs are cool, thick, and form a fat ribbon when dropped off the beater. Finally in goes the flour and lastly the butter—all without deflating the egg volume. It's not a tricky batter, but it is exacting; when you feel comfortable with it, you have mastered some of the prime culinary techniques.

MANUFACTURING NOTES. *If you need more details on measuring flour see page 380, beating eggs and sugar see page 461, and folding flour into a batter see page 459.*

For a 6-cup pan, such as a round one 9 by 1½ inches, or an 8- by 2-inch square pan

½ cup plus ⅓ cup plain bleached cake flour (scooped and leveled), set over a sheet of wax paper
1 Tbs sugar
¼ tsp salt
6 Tbs unsalted butter
4 "large" eggs—a generous ¾ cup of eggs
½ cup sugar
1 tsp pure vanilla extract

SPECIAL EQUIPMENT SUGGESTED:
A 6-cup cake pan, bottom lined with wax paper, buttered, and floured (see Special Note, page 457); a 3-quart stainless bowl and a saucepan of almost simmering water to hold it; a balloon whip or portable electric mixer; an electric mixer on a stand—please see an important note on bowl shapes (page 461); a flour sifter

Preliminaries. Preheat the oven to 350°F and place the rack in the middle level. Sift the flour with the tablespoon of sugar and the salt onto the wax paper and return to the sifter. Melt the butter; remove ¼ cup of the clear yellow liquid and reserve, leaving the milky residue behind. Set out the rest of the ingredients and equipment listed.

1. Whisking the eggs over hot water to thicken

Beating eggs and sugar. Blend the eggs, ½ cup of sugar, and vanilla in the stainless bowl, and set it in the pan of almost simmering water. Start

2. Eggs and sugar form the ribbon.

beating as illustrated, step 1, and continue until the eggs feel warm to your finger and have thickened—4 to 5 minutes. Remove the bowl from the water and either continue beating by hand or transfer the eggs to a mixer. Beat at moderately fast speed until the mixture has tripled in volume, is cool, and forms a fat ribbon when some is lifted and dropped back into the bowl as illustrated, step 2— 8 to 10 minutes.

3. Sifting on and folding in the flour

Folding in the flour. Immediately sift a quarter of the flour over the egg mixture, and fold it in rapidly with a large rubber spatula, rotating the bowl and scooping the egg up over the flour, step 3. When almost blended, rapidly fold in a third of the remaining flour, repeat with half of what remains, then the last of the flour. Aim to deflate the egg volume as little as possible—don't overdo the

4. Blending gob of batter into cool melted butter

folding: the batter must retain its volume.

The butter, and completing the batter. The butter should be cool but liquid. Plop a large blob of the egg-flour batter into it; fold it in rapidly and gently, step 4, then fold the butter/ batter mixture rapidly into the eggs and flour. (This clever technique keeps the butter in suspension; otherwise it tends to sink to the bottom of the cake pan.)

Baking—30 to 35 minutes at 350°F. Following the preceding directions for spongecake, immediately turn the batter into the prepared pan and bake until the cake has puffed, browned, and shows a faint line of shrinkage from the sides of the pan.

Cooling, unmolding, and storing. Let cool 20 minutes, then unmold, as described for the spongecake.

FLAVORINGS, FRILLS, AND SOME ESSENTIAL TECHNIQUES

Such everyday essentials as how to beat egg whites, make meringue, melt chocolate, as well as the best way to fill a pastry bag, slice a cake in half, and so forth, are always with us. Since it is cumbersome and boring to repeat them every time they come up, I am giving detailed directions here, and shorthand reminders in the recipes themselves, referring to these pages if you need the details.

Imbibing Syrup
Liqueur flavoring for layer cakes

Every cake benefits from a sprinkling of liqueur syrup that sinks into the layers and gives a pleasant moistness and subtle extra flavor as you bite through the filling and into the body of the cake.

For about 1 cup, enough for 2 or 3 cake layers, 8- to 9-inch size

⅓ **cup hot water**
¼ **cup sugar in a 2-cup measure**
½ **cup cold water**
3 to 4 **Tbs white rum, orange liqueur, or other spirits; or 1 Tbs pure vanilla extract**

Stir the hot water into the sugar, and when the sugar has dissolved completely, stir in the cold water, then the rum or other flavoring. To use, sprinkle a third to half of the syrup over the cut half of each layer.

To Slice a Cake into Two Layers

You will note that the layer cakes in this section are made from one cake 1½ to 2 inches high, cut in two or three horizontal layers—the usual system for French cakes. However, you may, of course, use 2 cakes and have a towering 4 layers.

Slicing a cake into 2 layers

First cut a shallow vertical wedge somewhere in the circumference of the cake; then you will know how to line up the layers for re-forming.

Place the middle of a long thin knife—I'm using a serrated ham slicer—evenly one third or halfway up the cake, and rotate the cake against it as you slice (see illustration); aiming your eye at the tip end of the knife seems to help in keeping the layers even.

The Right Way to Use a Pastry Bag

A pastry bag has many uses—from forming rosettes, swags, and swirls on a cake frosting to making cream puffs, mashed potato borders, and filling hard-boiled eggs. Don't waste your time with the foolish little cookie pushers offered in many cookware departments; get yourself professional equipment—look under Cake Decorating in the yellow pages. Ask for a flexible vinyl bag 16 inches long, and an assortment of tubes from round to flat to fluted.

1. Inserting metal tube into bag

Insert the tube of your choice inside the bag, pushing the tip through the hole at the small end for a snug fit as illustrated, step 1. To fill the bag easily, fold the tube end up against the bag to prevent the filling from oozing out, then set the bag tube end

2. Filling the bag

down in a 2-cup measure, and drape the sides around the outside of the cup. Scoop in the filling with a rubber spatula, step 2.

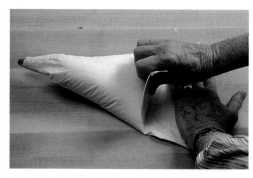

3. Scraping the filling down toward the tip

Lay the filled bag on your work surface, and push the filling tightly down into it, using a pastry scraper, step 3. Twist the top of the bag with one hand to keep steady pressure on

4. The way to hold the bag

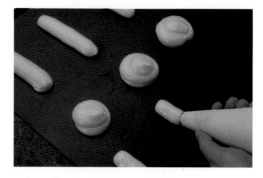

5. Squeezing out the filling

the filling as you squeeze, step 4. Squeeze out the shape, step 5, and, at the end, stop pressure, rotate the bag and tube tip sharply, and raise it up. (Practice first, scoop the practice back into the bag, and go to it.)

EGG-BEATING TECHNIQUES

Egg beating, whether it be egg whites, or whole eggs, is one of the keys to success in making cakes and soufflés because it is the egg that gives the puff. Egg yolks, too, have their special requirements so that they remain smooth and creamy.

For successful beating, the whole egg mass must be in motion at once, thus the right size whip for the bowl you are using is critical. The giant whip and copper bowl, at left, are ideal for hand beating, and the highly efficient heavy-duty mixer, at right, for machine beating.

To Beat Egg Yolks and Sugar
"Forming the ribbon"

This is when your recipe says, "Beat the egg yolks in a bowl, adding the sugar by tablespoons, and continue beating for several minutes until the mixture is thick, pale yellow, and when a bit falls from the wires of the beater it forms a ribbon that slowly dissolves on the surface, as illustrated." The sugar is added slowly because too much at once can cause the yolks to speckle. You beat long enough to dissolve the sugar—it's dissolved when the mixture forms the ribbon. Recipe shorthand will simply direct you to beat the yolks and sugar until they are thick, pale yellow, and form the ribbon.

Eggs and sugar forming the familiar ribbon

To Beat Whole Eggs and Sugar

Whole eggs and sugar beaten to a beautiful foamy yellow cream are the base for genoise cakes, zabaione sauce, and other sweet delights. They triple in volume, and fall from the beater in a thick, slowly dissolving ribbon. Norwegian cooks judge them to be just right when they dribble the name "OLE" off the wires of the beater and the "O" is still standing on the surface as the "E" is completed.

It is most important here that your beating equipment be perfectly clean, since oil or grease can prevent the eggs from mounting. You may use a copper bowl and giant balloon whip or a stainless bowl that is round bottomed and narrow rather than wide; in either case the whole mass of egg should be in motion at once as you beat.

Blend the eggs and sugar in the bowl, then set the bowl in a pan of almost simmering water and beat with a balloon whip or hand-held electric mixer, circulating the mixer about the bowl as though it were a whip. Beat until the eggs are warm to your finger and foaming through-out—4 to 5 minutes; this indicates

that the sugar has dissolved. Remove the bowl from heat and continue beating either by hand or in a mixer on a stand for 8 to 10 minutes more, until the eggs are cool and form a thick, slowly dissolving ribbon.

SPECIAL NOTE

Beating Egg Yolks and Sugar a Faster Way

Beating the yolks and sugar for a genoise cake can be simplified if you have a heavy-duty mixer with hot-water jack that attaches to the bowl. Fill the jack with boiling water, re-plenishing as necessary while you beat until the warm eggs form the ribbon; empty out the jack, fill with ice cubes and water, and continue beating until cool.

To Beat Egg Whites into Stiff Shining Peaks

Stiffly beaten egg whites have mul-tiple uses, from spongecakes to float-ing island to soufflés. Again the bowl and beater are of great importance. They must be clean, with no trace of oil or grease, and not even a speck of egg yolk should be among the whites since oil, grease, and yolk prevent the whites from mounting into a mass of tiny bubbles.

Whether or not you are using a cop-per bowl, it's a good idea to pour a tablespoon of vinegar into the bowl and a teaspoon of salt. Rub the bowl clean with paper towels, but do not wash it—the traces of vinegar and salt help stabilize the egg whites.

Beating Egg Whites (*continued*)

Turn the egg whites into the bowl and if they are chilled, set the bowl in a larger bowl of warm water for a minute or two, until your impeccably clean finger feels them to be of room temperature. Chilled whites do not mount well, and tend to fleck.

Using a giant balloon whip, or a hand-held electric mixer, or a mixer on a stand, start beating the egg whites at moderately slow speed until they are foaming throughout—2 minutes or so. Add a pinch of salt (unless you have rubbed the bowl with salt before you started in), and for 4 egg whites, add ¼ teaspoon of cream of tartar—a stabilizer. Gradually increase the speed to fast (moderately fast if you have a heavy-duty mixer) and continue until stiff shining peaks are formed.

Adding sugar. In most dessert and cake recipes a tablespoon or more of sugar is beaten in at the point where the egg whites form soft peaks; they are then beaten to stiff peaks. Sugar stiffens and stabilizes the whites.

Perfectly beaten egg whites

Overbeating. Egg whites will not perform as they should when they lose their smooth sheen and begin to look grainy. You can usually reconstitute them by adding another egg white and beating briefly until they are smoothly reconstituted.

VARIATION

Italian Meringue
White mountain frosting: boiled icing

Italian meringue is beaten egg whites into which boiling sugar syrup is incorporated; this stabilizes the whites so you may use the meringue as a cake frosting. It is wonderfully useful since besides being a frosting, it may be combined with whipped butter for a cake filling or with heavy cream for vanilla ice cream, or, again, you may form and bake it as meringues. The Bûche de Noël on page 478, for instance, uses Italian meringue not only for frosting and filling, but for baked meringue decorations as well.

For frosting a 9-inch cake

The egg whites
⅔ cup egg whites (4 to 5 egg whites)
A pinch of salt
¼ tsp cream of tartar

The sugar syrup
1⅓ cups sugar
½ cup water

SPECIAL EQUIPMENT SUGGESTED:
A clean dry bowl and beater for the egg whites; a heavy 8-cup saucepan with tight-fitting cover, and a 4-cup measure with 2 cups cold water for the sugar syrup; an electric mixer on a stand

Meringue egg whites in stiff upstanding shining peaks

The egg whites. Following detailed directions in the preceding recipe, beat the egg whites at slow speed until they foam throughout, add the salt and cream of tartar, gradually increase speed to fast, and beat to soft peaks, as illustrated. Turn the machine to slow as you complete the sugar syrup.

The sugar syrup. Following detailed directions on page 421, bring the sugar and water to the simmer, swirl the pan to dissolve the sugar completely, cover tightly, and boil to the soft-ball stage.

Sugar syrup into egg whites. Beating the egg whites at moderately slow speed, dribble into them the boiling syrup—trying to avoid the wires of the whip. Increase speed to moderately fast and beat until cool and the egg whites form stiff, shining, upstanding peaks. The meringue is now ready to use as your recipe directs.

*Ahead-of-time note: It is best to use the meringue within an hour; it remains stable on a cake but may thin out with rebeating.

VARIATIONS

Here are some of the ways to use an Italian meringue for fillings and frostings. In the interests of discretion if not gastronomy, I am leaving the proportions of butter or cream to meringue up to you—in other words, you may use less than indicated.

Meringue Butter-Cream Filling

Beat 4 ounces (1 stick) of softened unsalted butter in a bowl until soft and fluffy, fold in 1 to 1½ cups of Italian meringue, and season with 1 tablespoon of white rum or 2 teaspoons of pure vanilla extract. Enough to fill a 2-layer 9-inch cake.

Meringue Cream Filling and Frosting

Fold 2 cups of whipped cream into 2 cups of Italian meringue, and flavor with 1 tablespoon of white rum or 2 teaspoons of pure vanilla extract. Enough to fill and frost a roulade (jelly roll).

Chocolate Meringue Filling or Frosting

Beat 2 ounces (½ stick) of softened unsalted butter in a bowl until soft and fluffy, fold in 2 cups of Italian meringue, 4 ounces of tepid smoothly melted chocolate, and 2 tablespoons of dark rum. Enough to frost a 9-inch cake or a roulade (jelly roll).

Folding: To Fold Egg Whites into a Cake Batter, etc.

You can beat your egg whites to perfection, but unless you fold them rapidly and expertly into your cake or soufflé batter, you will deflate them and neither your cake nor your soufflé will rise to its proper height. Here's how:

Spatula plunging in, to bring batter up over egg whites

Have your cake or soufflé batter in a roomy pan or bowl. Stir a quarter of the egg whites into the batter to loosen it—an important point, since if the batter is stiff you will deflate the egg whites as you attempt to blend them. Then turn the rest of the egg whites on top. Plunge a large rubber spatula sideways, like a knife, down through the center of the egg whites to the bottom of the pan, as illustrated. Rapidly bring the spatula to the near edge of the pan, and rotate it so its flat side brings some of the batter up over the egg whites. Rotate the pan slightly, and rapidly repeat the plunging-scooping turn of the spatula 7 to 8 times, until the egg whites and batter are blended—do not overblend or you will deflate the egg whites.

TO MELT CHOCOLATE

Chocolate can be a complicated subject when you are making candies or chocolate coverings that must be utterly professional, clear, and shining. Fortunately we are not going into such mysteries here—the main concern is that the chocolate be smoothly melted, and that means not overheating it. Overheating will cause it to seize, to turn hard and grainy; it will melt smoothly at around 100°F. I know that some cooks swear by the microwave, but I prefer the following simple and straightforward system, where I am in complete control.

To Melt Chocolate with Liquid Flavoring

Most of the recipes in this book call for chocolate melted in a small amount of liquid flavoring, such as coffee or rum. The minimum amount of liquid is 1 tablespoon per 2 ounces of chocolate—you can add more but not less or the chocolate will stiffen.

For 1¼ cups

8 ounces sweet or semisweet chocolate; or 6 ounces sweet chocolate and 2 ounces bitter or unsweetened chocolate
¼ cup rum or strong coffee

Melting chocolate slowly in a covered pan set over hot water

SPECIAL EQUIPMENT SUGGESTED:
A 2-cup moderately heavy saucepan with tight-fitting lid; a larger saucepan or frying pan to hold it

Break up the chocolate into the 2-cup pan and add the rum or coffee. Pour 2 to 3 inches of water into the larger pan and bring to the simmer. Remove from heat, let cool 15 seconds, cover the chocolate pan tightly, and

set it in the hot water. In 5 minutes the chocolate should be smoothly melted—if not, reheat the water in the larger pan to below the simmer, remove from heat, return the chocolate pan to it, and stir until the chocolate is smooth and glistening.

To Melt Plain Chocolate

For small amounts, up to about 8 ounces, break up the chocolate in a perfectly dry pan and use the foregoing system (but with no liquid). For large amounts, place the covered chocolate pan in a 100°F oven, where it will be melted and smooth in 20 to 30 minutes.

Remedy for stiffened chocolate. If you have overheated your chocolate and it has seized and stiffened, you can often smooth it out by beating in a little water, setting the pan in hot water, and stirring it about. It will usually not smooth out enough to become a frosting, but will often be suitable for use in cakes or puddings.

Other Techniques Elsewhere

Sugar syrups and caramel (page 421), and caramel sauce (page 420)

Apricot Glaze and Red Currant Glaze (see Special Notes, pages 427 and 437)

To whip cream (page 440)

Royal icing: *glace royale* (page 487)

Baker's Tools

The right equipment always makes a job easier. Except for the serrated ham slicing knife, which you will find in a fine cutlery store, the rest of the items will be in a pastry supply store—look under Cake Decorating in the yellow pages.

Revolving stand to hold cake while decorating

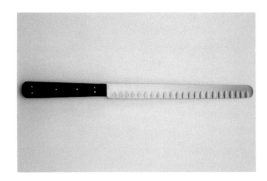

Serrated ham knife with 12-inch blade for slicing cake into layers

Large balloon whip and small whisk

Cardboard rounds in various sizes to hold cakes while decorating

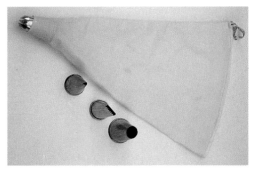

Flexible vinyl pastry bag and metal tubes

Straight-sided aluminum cake pans 2 inches deep

Flexible-blade metal spatulas both bent and straight

SPONGE AND GENOISE LAYER CAKES

Here are two layer cakes. One is an informal sponge-cake with apricot filling and white mountain icing, and the other, a very dressy genoise walled in chocolate, filled and frosted with real French butter cream, and decorated with a chocolate bow. You don't have to make the basic cakes yourself—although you never need admit it—since a good store-bought yellow cake will do nicely under such trimmings.

The Santa Clara

Three-layer cake with apricot filling and white mountain frosting

The Santa Clara is a dessert cake with billowing white frosting, and although you can make it in the conventional two layers, three seem more appropriate here with the moist apricot filling.

CAKE TALK. *An 8- to 9-inch cake 2 inches thick would furnish 3 layers, or make 2 sponge or genoise cakes 1½ inches thick, slice each in half and freeze the fourth half for petits fours or trifle. Slicing a cake into layers is illustrated on page 460.*

Ingredients for an 8- to 9-inch cake, serving 8 to 12

The apricot filling

3 cans, 17 ounces each, unpeeled apricot halves
3 Tbs unsalted butter
½ tsp cinnamon
⅓ cup sugar
The grated zest (yellow part only) and strained juice of 1 lemon

1 cup rum-flavored imbibing syrup (¼ cup sugar, ¾ cup water, 3 to 4 Tbs white rum, page 459)

The white mountain icing—Italian meringue

⅔ cup egg whites (4 to 5 eggs)
A pinch of salt
¼ tsp cream of tartar
1⅓ cups sugar
½ cup water

3 cake layers (see discussion at top of recipe)
4 ounces (1 stick) softened unsalted butter, optional
1 to 2 Tbs white rum
8 to 10 well-formed canned apricot halves and their syrup

The apricot filling. Pour the contents of the cans of apricot halves into a sieve set over a saucepan. Let drain thoroughly, then chop them and set aside. Add the butter, cinnamon, ⅓ cup of sugar, and the lemon peel and juice to the syrup and bring to the boil. When thick and almost syrupy, add the chopped apricots and boil several minutes, stirring frequently,

The Santa Clara (*continued*)

until they form a thick mass that holds its shape softly in a spoon.

The white mountain icing. Following the detailed directions on page 461, beat the egg whites to soft peaks. Turn speed to slow while you boil the sugar and water to the soft-ball stage (page 421). Immediately, while beating the egg whites at moderately slow speed, dribble in the hot syrup; increase speed to moderately fast, and continue beating 5 minutes or more, until the meringue is cool and forms stiff shining upstanding peaks.

If using it, beat all or part of the stick of butter in a bowl until soft and fluffy; fold in 1 cup of the Italian meringue frosting and season with the rum—reserve for the filling. (Or reserve 1⅓ cups butterless meringue.)

1. Half the apricots going over the meringue filling

Filling and frosting the cake. Center one cake layer on strips of wax paper arranged on your serving platter—they will be pulled out after frosting. Dribble several spoonfuls of the imbibing syrup onto the cake. Spread half of the meringue icing over the

2. Frosting top of cake with meringue

cake layer; cover with half of the cooked apricots (see illustration, step 1). Set a second layer of cake over the first and repeat with imbibing syrup, meringue, and apricots. Sprinkle syrup over the third layer, but not enough to soften it, and set it in place. Swirl meringue over the entire cake, step 2.

The apricot topping. Drain the apricot halves and set them domed side up in a lightly buttered baking pan. Boil down ½ to ⅔ cup of their syrup until thick and syrupy and pour it over the apricots. Set them 6 to 8 inches below a hot broiler. Broil, basting them several times with the syrup, for 5 minutes; set aside. When cool, arrange them on top of the cake. Cover the cake with an upside-down bowl and refrigerate until serving time.

**Ahead-of-time note:* Will keep nicely for several hours in the refrigerator.

The Cambridge Cake
Genoise layer cake with mocha buttercream frosting, chocolate walls, and bow

For this sumptuous creation, the 2-inch-high cake is split in half, and each layer is lightly imbibed with a rum syrup to make a moist cake with delicious flavor. If you are generous with that luscious butter cream, the slices can be less than huge—meaning you can serve more people. I'd certainly rather have the thinnest possible sliver of this beauty than several helpings of diet carrot cake!

For 10 to 12 servings

An 8- by 2-inch round yellow cake, homemade or store-bought, split in half horizontally (page 460)
Imbibing syrup (¼ cup sugar, ¾ cup water, 3 Tbs dark Jamaican rum, page 459)
3 cups butter cream (see recipe following)

Chocolate decorations
4 ounces sweet chocolate
1 ounce unsweetened chocolate

SPECIAL EQUIPMENT SUGGESTED: *See the baker's tools illustrated on page 464.*

3. Spreading thin preliminary frosting on sides

Preliminary frosting. Brush crumbs off the outside of the cake. Plop ¾ cup of butter cream on top of the cake. Spread it thinly over the top and sides, step 3—this seals down the crumbs and keeps the final frosting clean and smooth. (Clean off your spatula after using it here, for the same reason.)

1. Spooning imbibing syrup over cake layer

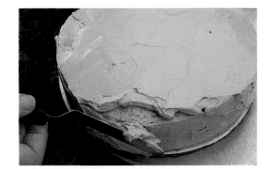

2. Lining up the cake layer with the wedge

4. Frosting top and sides

Imbibing the cake layers. Set the bottom cake layer cut side up on a cardboard cutout or on your upturned cake pan. Turn the top layer cut side up, as shown. Spoon driblets of syrup over both layers, as illustrated, step 1—not too generous on the top, or you may soften it too much for re-forming the cake!

Re-forming the cake. Remove 1½ cups of the butter cream and reserve it for the final decoration. Spread about ½ cup of the butter cream over the bottom layer—a large bent spatula is useful here. Carefully lift the top layer and arrange it over the bottom, lining it up with the wedge, step 2.

Final coat of butter cream. Spread ½ cup of the reserved butter cream around the sides with the bent spatula, step 4, and 1 cup smoothly over the top with the straight spatula.

Interim refrigeration. Refrigerate the cake, uncovered, while you prepare the chocolate for the next step.

(continued)

5. Almost-set chocolate strip trimmed

The Cambridge Cake (*continued*)

Preparing the chocolate strips. Break the chocolate into a small, tightly covered pan set in hot water. When melted, in about 5 minutes, stir until smooth and cool. Spread 2 strips, 3½ by 30 inches and ⅛ inch thick, on wax paper. Chill. When almost set, cut through the chocolate and paper to make two 2- by 27-inch strips, step 5.

6. Applying chocolate strip still attached to wax paper backing

Applying the chocolate wall. Chill the strips a few moments, until set. Meanwhile, remove the cake from the refrigerator so that the frosting will soften slightly. Carefully lift a strip of paper with chocolate, press it around the side of the cake, and peel off the paper—don't touch the chocolate or you'll leave finger marks. Apply the second strip, step 6, and glue the overlaps with a little butter cream.

7. Making rosettes of butter cream

Final decorations. Make chocolate strips and a bow with leftover chocolate. Chill the remaining butter cream until it is stiff enough to push through a pastry bag fitted with a star tube. Finish off the cake with rosettes of butter cream, step 7.

Storing and serving. Transfer the cake to a platter, cover with an upturned bowl, and refrigerate until serving time. Remove from the refrigerator 10 minutes before serving, and cut it with a knife dipped in hot water.

*Ahead-of-time note: The cake will keep under refrigeration for a day or two.

French Butter-Cream Filling and Frosting

This is the ambrosial filling for cakes and petits fours. I so well remember my first taste. It was when we arrived in France after World War II, and I had been used to our native commercial frostings made of vegetable shortening and confectioners sugar— I didn't like cakes, then, and no wonder. But a little petit four, filled and frosted with mocha butter cream and

walled in chocolate, changed my mind forever more. Needless to say, this is hardly diet food—it's binge indulgence of the most exquisite sort. Remember, however, that you can have a completely fat-free, yolk-free icing on the preceding Santa Clara Cake, with the Italian meringue.

MANUFACTURING NOTE. *Another butter-cream version is that made with Italian meringue, described for the Bûche de Noël on page 478. Still another method is to beat softened butter into a cool custard sauce, crème anglaise. The following method is the most stable, that of beating boiling sugar syrup into eggs, and then adding the butter.*

For about 3 cups

The sugar syrup
1½ cups sugar
½ cup water

The eggs
2 "large" eggs
6 egg yolks

1 pound unsalted softened butter, plus more, if needed
2 tsp pure vanilla extract
The flavoring: 2 to 3 Tbs rum, kirsch, or orange liqueur; *or* 2 to 4 ounces melted chocolate; *or* mocha flavoring (2 ounces unsweetened baking chocolate, smoothly melted with 2 Tbs instant coffee and 3 Tbs dark rum)

SPECIAL EQUIPMENT SUGGESTED:
A 4-cup saucepan with tight-fitting cover for the syrup; a stainless bowl (such as that for your electric mixer) and a pan of simmering water to hold it; a large balloon whip or hand-held electric mixer; a mixer on a stand is useful

The sugar syrup. Following detailed directions on page 421, bring the sugar and water to the simmer, swirl the pan to dissolve the sugar completely, cover tightly, and boil to the soft-ball stage. Meanwhile break the eggs and yolks into the stainless bowl, and whip briefly to blend yolks and whites.

Beating the syrup into the eggs. As soon as it is ready, beat the hot syrup in a thin stream into the eggs and yolks, using a large whip or hand-held electric mixer.

Whisking hot sugar syrup into eggs

Beating the eggs over hot water. To cook the egg mixture and thus insure the safekeeping of the butter cream, set the bowl in the pan of almost simmering water and beat for 4 to 5 minutes or more, until the mixture is too hot for your finger and forms a slowly dissolving ribbon when a bit is lifted in the beater and dropped on the surface.

Beating until cool. Remove from heat and beat either by hand or in an electric mixer until cool—5 minutes or more.

Beating creamed butter into eggs

The butter and flavoring. Beat the butter in a bowl until fluffy and creamy. Then, by 2-tablespoon gobs, beat the butter into the egg mixture. When smoothly incorporated, beat in the vanilla and the flavoring. If the cream turns a little grainy or looks separated after the flavoring goes in, beat in a tablespoon or so of additional softened butter.

Cooling the butter cream. Beat over a bowl of ice cubes and water until the cream firms to easy spreading consistency. It is now ready to use.

*Ahead-of-time note: Butter cream will keep several days under refrigeration, or may be frozen for several weeks. In either case, let it come to room temperature, then beat to smooth it. If it looks grainy beat in a spoonful or so of softened butter, and if still grainy, beat it over hot water to smooth and cream it.

TWO FAMOUS ALMOND CAKES

The Genoa and the Queen of Sheba

The Genoa, or *Pain de Gênes*, is a white almond cake, so good in itself that it needs no filling and frosting. The Queen of Sheba, or *Reine de Saba*, usually becomes the favorite chocolate cake of anyone who tastes it, and I must admit to having a version in at least two of my books. This third version is on our video cassettes, and sports a clever chocolate-leaf topping.

The Genoa Cake: Le Pain de Gênes

This is a whole-egg cake, like the genoise, but with a difference: the butter, rather than being melted, is first creamed—or beaten into a *pommade*, as the French say—then combined with a little of the egg mixture before being incorporated into the batter at the end. This is a useful system when you have a relatively large amount of butter, as in this recipe, because it homogenizes with the batter rather than falling to the bottom of the cake pan.

For a 6-cup pan, such as a round one 9 by 1½ inches, or for 10 cup cakes

(continued)

The Genoa Cake: Le Pain de Gênes
(*continued*)

¾ cup (4 ounces) blanched almonds
    pulverized with 3 Tbs sugar (page
    423)
⅓ cup all-purpose flour (scooped and
    leveled, page 380), in a sifter
3 "large" eggs
⅔ cup granulated sugar
2 tsp pure vanilla extract
¼ tsp almond extract
A big pinch of salt
4 ounces (1 stick) softened unsalted
    butter, at room temperature
Optional final decoration:
    confectioners sugar in a sieve

SPECIAL EQUIPMENT SUGGESTED:
*A 9- by 1½-inch round cake pan, but-
tered and floured, bottom lined with
wax paper (page 457); an electric
mixer with the right bowl, on a stand
(page 461); a pan of almost simmering
water to hold the bowl; a metal mixing
bowl for creaming butter*

Preliminaries. Preheat oven to 350°F
and set the rack in the lower middle
level. Set out all the ingredients and
equipment listed. Fluff the almond/
sugar mixture in a bowl to remove
any lumps; sift in the flour and blend
gently together.

The eggs and sugar. Following the detailed directions on page 461, beat
the eggs and sugar in the mixer bowl
for several minutes over the almost
simmering water until foaming and
warm to your finger. Transfer to the
mixer; add the vanilla and almond
extracts, and salt; continue beating
for 6 to 8 minutes, until the mixture
forms a heavy ribbon and is the consistency of thick mayonnaise.

The butter. Beat the butter with a
wooden spoon in the metal mixing
bowl until fluffy and creamy. Using a
rubber spatula, blend a fairly large
dollop (about one fifth) of the eggs/
sugar into the butter—it should now
be about the same consistency as the
eggs/sugar.

Finishing the batter. Rapidly and
lightly start folding the almonds and
flour into the eggs and sugar by
rather large sprinkles; when almost
incorporated, alternate with scoops of
the creamed butter mixture.

Baking—about 30 minutes at 350°F.
At once turn the batter into the prepared cake pan and set in the preheated oven.

When is it done? The cake is done
when the top feels springy, and you
can see the faintest line of shrinkage
between the cake and the pan. Remove the pan to a rack.

Unmolding. Let cool 15 minutes.
Run a thin knife between cake and
pan, unmold onto a rack, remove the
wax paper, and carefully turn right
side up. Let cool for an hour or so.

Maturing—24 hours. The cake develops its full almond flavor if allowed to mature for at least a day.
Wrap airtight when cool, and
refrigerate.

Serving. If you like, powder the top
with a light dusting of confectioners
sugar, or serve as is.

VARIATION

Small Almond Cakes

These make attractive tea cakes, or
serve them with a fruit dessert, or
take them on a picnic.

Use muffin tins with cups of ⅓-cup
capacity. To prevent sticking, brush
the cups lightly with a paste of clarified butter and flour (2 Tbs melted
butter and 2 Tbs flour). Bake about
15 minutes in a preheated 350°F
oven, until puffed and lightly
browned. Let cool 15 minutes, then
unmold. Again, they develop their
best flavor if held for a day or more.
Dust with confectioners sugar before
serving.

The Queen of Sheba: Reine de Saba

A chocolate almond cake

A very special cake of almonds, butter, and chocolate that is somewhat moist in the center—it literally melts in the mouth. This was the first French cake I ever ate, prepared by my French colleague, Simca, and I have never forgotten it. Like most French cakes, it is only an inch and a half high, which makes it easy to serve.

MANUFACTURING NOTE. *This is the spongecake type—separated eggs— where beaten egg whites are folded into the batter. You want to be sure here that the melted chocolate is still warm and smooth so that the egg whites can be folded in easily.*

For a 4-cup pan, such as a round one 8 by 1½ inches, serving 6 to 8

3 ounces sweet baking chocolate
1 ounce unsweetened chocolate
2 Tbs dark rum or strong coffee
4 ounces (1 stick) softened unsalted
    butter, at room temperature
½ cup sugar
3 egg yolks

The egg whites

3 egg whites (a scant ½ cup)
¼ tsp cream of tartar
A pinch of salt
2 Tbs sugar

⅓ cup blanched almonds pulverized
    with 2 Tbs sugar (see Special
    Note, page 474)
¼ tsp almond extract
½ cup plain bleached cake flour
    (scooped and leveled, page 380),
    in a sifter set on wax paper

SPECIAL EQUIPMENT SUGGESTED:
An 8- by 1½-inch round cake pan, buttered and floured (page 457); a 6-cup saucepan with tight-fitting cover, and a larger pan of simmering water, for melting chocolate; a 3-quart mixing bowl for the batter; a hand-held electric mixer is useful; egg-white beating equipment (page 461)

Preliminaries. Preheat the oven to 350°F, and set the rack in the lower middle level. Set out all the ingredients and equipment listed, and melt the chocolate in the rum or coffee (page 464).

Butter, sugar, and egg yolks. Cut the butter into pieces and cream it in the mixing bowl—the portable mixer is useful here. When soft and fluffy, add the sugar and beat 1 minute, then beat in the egg yolks.

(continued)

The Queen of Sheba (*continued*)

Egg whites. Following detailed directions on page 461, beat the egg whites until foaming throughout, beat in the cream of tartar and salt, and continue until soft peaks are formed. Gradually beat in the 2 tablespoons of sugar and continue until stiff shining peaks are formed.

Finishing the batter. At once blend the warm, smoothly melted chocolate and the coffee into the yolk mixture, then the almonds and almond extract. Stir a quarter of the egg whites into the chocolate to lighten it. Scoop the rest of the whites over the chocolate and, alternating with sprinkles of flour, rapidly and delicately fold in the egg whites.

Baking—25 minutes at 350°F. Immediately turn the batter into the prepared pan, tilting it in all directions to run it up to the rim all around, and set in the preheated oven.

When is it done? The cake is done when it has puffed to the top of the pan and a toothpick plunged into the cake 2 and 3 inches from the edges of the pan comes out clean. The center, however, should move slightly when the pan is gently shaken. (Chocolate cakes of the French type should not be cooked dry.)

Cooling and unmolding. Remove the pan to the rack and let cool 15 minutes; unmold onto the rack. Let cool completely—2 hours—before storing or icing.

*Ahead-of-time note: May be wrapped airtight and refrigerated for 2 to 3 days, or may be frozen for several weeks. That limit is for the safe side.

However, during the taping of our videocassettes in California we made quite a number. I took two home to Massachusetts and didn't serve one of them until a year later—delicious.

Serving note. French chocolate cakes are at their best when served at near room temperature—chilled, the chocolate is partly congealed rather than being softly yielding.

Icing and decorating the cake. You may serve the cake simply with a dusting of confectioners sugar, or with the soft chocolate icing described here and a design of whole or shaved almonds on top. Or for the full treatment try decorating the iced cake with chocolate leaves (see Special Note on next page).

Soft Chocolate Icing

If you are also making the chocolate-leaf decorations, do the leaves (recipe following) in advance since they should go onto a still-soft icing.

For an 8-inch cake

2 ounces sweet chocolate
1 ounce unsweetened chocolate
1½ Tbs rum or strong coffee
A pinch of salt
3 ounces (6 Tbs) unsalted softened butter, at room temperature

SPECIAL EQUIPMENT SUGGESTED:
A 6-cup saucepan with tight-fitting lid; a pan of almost simmering water to hold it, for melting chocolate

Following the directions on page 464, melt the chocolates with the rum or coffee. When smooth and glistening, beat in the salt, then the

butter a tablespoon at a time. Beat over cold water until firm enough to spread. Turn the icing on top of the cake; spread it over the top and sides.

MERINGUE-NUT LAYER CAKE

Quite a different cake from the genoise and the spongecake is the meringue-nut layer cake—much easier to make than the conventional cake, and an absolute marvel to eat. The layers are Swiss meringue—beaten egg whites and granulated sugar—folded with pulverized almonds and/or hazelnuts. You form the layers with a pastry bag in any shape you wish, from round to square to rectangular to heart-shaped, and bake them slowly about an hour. Use any filling you wish, too. Here we have a chocolate butter cream for one filling layer, an amaretti butter cream for the second layer, and rum butter cream for the frosting. Toasted almonds cover the sides, and shaved chocolate dusts the top.

Historical Notes. The great Fernand Point, reputed father of La Nouvelle Cuisine, was chef-owner of the famous Pyramide restaurant, which flourished under his leadership pre– and just post–World War II at Vienne, south of Lyons. One of his most famous dessert cakes was Le Marjolaine, a four-layer almond and hazelnut meringue cake with chocolate, whipped cream, and pralin fillings. (Note for the record: The generic French name for these cake layers is *fonds parisiens,* but they are also called *fonds de succès* or *fonds de progrès* after the classic cakes, *Le Succès* and *Le Progrès,* that contain them.)

ALMONDS AND HAZELNUTS

Toasting nuts to a light walnut brown always gives them more flavor, particularly when they are used in fillings and frostings. Toasting directions are in the Special Note (page 423). Note that almonds are blanched (peels removed) before toasting, while hazelnuts need to have their skins rubbed off after toasting— something of a chore.

Hazelnuts vs. almonds. Hazelnuts have a more distinctive flavor than almonds, particularly when toasted, as described on page 423. Sample several from every batch you plan to buy to be sure they are fresh. Store the nuts in the freezer. Use either hazelnuts or almonds, or a portion of each, in the meringue layers.

SPECIAL NOTE

Chocolate-Leaf Decorations

2 ounces sweet chocolate
1 ounce unsweetened chocolate
Cocoa powder in a fine-meshed
   sieve, optional

SPECIAL EQUIPMENT SUGGESTED:
A 6-cup moderately heavy saucepan with tight-fitting lid, and a large pan of almost simmering water to hold it; a heavy flexible plastic sheet is useful here, or wax paper

Following the directions on page 463, melt the chocolates to smooth and glistening. Spread a 1/16-inch layer on the plastic sheet or wax paper, step 1. Chill until set. Break the chocolate into large irregular leaves. Arrange shiny side (bottom side) up on the cake, step 2, using an instrument so as not to leave finger-prints. If you wish, dust the top of the cake with cocoa powder.

*Ahead-of-time note: Chocolate leaves and decorations may be made well in advance and stored in the refrigerator.

VARIATION

Chocolate Shapes

Melt and spread out the chocolate in the same way. When firm but not brittle cut into hearts, figures, letters, numbers, etc. Paper patterns are useful here.

1. Spreading melted chocolate on plastic sheet

2. Placing chocolate leaf on cake

To Form and Bake Almond or Hazelnut Meringue Layers

For 3 meringue-nut layers, about 16 by 4 inches, and ⅜ inch thick

1½ cups toasted hazelnuts and/or almonds pulverized with 1½ cups sugar (see preceding notes)

The Swiss meringue
¾ cup egg whites (5 to 6 egg whites)
A big pinch of salt
¼ tsp cream of tartar
3 Tbs sugar
1 Tbs pure vanilla extract
¼ tsp almond extract

SPECIAL EQUIPMENT SUGGESTED:
A blender or processor for the nuts; egg-white beating equipment for the meringue; a 16-inch pastry bag with ½-inch round tube opening; 2 no-stick pastry sheets about 17 by 12 inches, buttered and floured

Preliminaries. Measure and set out all the ingredients listed. Prepare the baking sheets and mark with a ruler three 16- by 4-inch rectangles upon them. Preheat the oven to 250°F, and place the racks in the upper and lower third levels. Fluff up the pulverized nuts and sugar to be sure there are no lumps.

The meringue-nut mixture. Following the detailed directions on page 461, beat the egg whites, starting at slow speed, until they foam throughout. Add the salt and cream of tartar, and continue until soft peaks are formed; continue beating as you sprinkle in the sugar, then the vanilla and almond extracts; beat to stiff shining peaks. With a big rubber spatula, rapidly and delicately fold in the nut/sugar mixture by generous sprinkles.

Squeezing out meringue for second rectangle

Forming the cake layers. Scoop the meringue mixture into the pastry bag. (Pastry bag directions are on page 460.) Starting at the outside edges and working around inward, squeeze rectangular shapes ⅜-inch thick into the spaces you have outlined, as shown in the photograph. Smooth them with a flexible-blade spatula. (Make individual meringue cakes or cookies with any leftovers—and they can bake on the free section of the second pastry sheet.)

Baking—about 1 hour at 250°F. Immediately set the meringues in the preheated oven, and switch levels every 20 minutes for even baking.

When are they done? They are done when you can push them loose gently—but don't force them since they will take their own time. They should color only lightly, and will not change shape.

**Ahead-of-time note:* Meringues soften rapidly in a humid atmosphere. They keep best wrapped airtight in the freezer, where they may remain for several weeks. They defrost in a few minutes at room temperature while you are setting out the ingredients for your cake.

SPECIAL NOTE

To pulverize nuts. You can grate them fine, if you have such a specialized machine. Otherwise pulverize not more than ½ cup at a time in a blender, or ¾ cup at a time in a food processor with steel blade—always adding 1 tablespoon or more of granulated sugar to prevent the nuts from turning oily. Don't overpulverize—they should be dry and powdery; otherwise they will lump when you fold them into a batter or egg whites.

Le Délice de Montecito

Meringue-nut cake with chocolate and amaretti filling

One of the beauties of the rectangular cake is that after you have sliced off as many servings as you wish, you can refrost and redecorate the cut end, and serve it forth again as a fresh construction. This could be served in half slices as a tea cake—but I'd prefer coffee to tea. However, it makes a magnificent dessert for an important dinner, accompanied by a late-harvest riesling or Sauternes.

For a 16- by 4-inch cake, serving 16 to 24

3 cups French butter cream (page 468)

Butter-cream flavorings

3 Tbs white rum

3 Tbs smoothly melted sweet chocolate (page 464)

2 Tbs pulverized amaretti cookies or toasted macaroons

2 Tbs Amaretto liqueur

3 baked meringue-nut layers, 16- by 4-inch size—the preceding recipe

1 cup warm apricot glaze (sieved apricot jam boiled down with 2 Tbs sugar until thick and sticky, page 427)

Final decoration

1 cup shaved almonds (bought in packages), toasted

2 ounces (2 squares) shaved or grated sweet chocolate

SPECIAL EQUIPMENT SUGGESTED:
3 medium-size mixing bowls for the butter creams; a rectangular serving board or platter of ample size to hold the cake; strips of wax paper

The butter cream. Scoop a quarter of the butter cream into one of the mixing bowls, and another quarter into the second bowl. Beat the rum into the remaining half portion of butter cream and reserve for frosting the cake. Beat the melted chocolate into the first bowl, and the amaretti cookies and liqueur into the second bowl.

Assembling the cake layers. With a serrated knife, trim the edges of the meringue layers to make them even. Paint the top of each layer with a thin coating of warm apricot glaze. Arrange strips of wax paper on the platter in such a way that they may be slipped out after frosting the cake.

1. Spreading on chocolate filling

Arrange one meringue layer over the strips, and spread on the chocolate filling, as illustrated, step 1. Cover with a second meringue layer and spread on the amaretti cream. Cover with the third meringue layer, and spread the rum-flavored butter cream over the top and sides of the rectangle.

2. Spreading shaved almonds along sides

Decorations. Brush shaved almonds against the sides and ends of the cake, step 2. Strew a decorative but rather sparse layer of the shaved or grated chocolate on top.

Chilling before serving—3 to 4 hours. Refrigerate for several hours to soften the meringue and to set the frosting and filling—covering the cake with a box, or a tent of foil.

*Ahead-of-time note: The cake will keep several days under refrigeration. It can be frozen.

VARIATIONS

Other Fillings and Frostings

You may use many other frostings, such as Italian meringue with chocolate or other flavorings, or the pastry cream with whipped cream or meringue—Chiboust (page 402). See another chocolate idea in the Special Note.

Ganache
Chocolate cream filling or frosting

This extremely easy and versatile chocolate filling was not around when I was doing my classic French training in the early 1950's. Now I often wonder why not, who introduced it, etc., etc.

For about 2 cups

**8 ounces sweet chocolate (or 6
  ounces sweet and 2 ounces
  unsweetened)**
1 cup heavy whipping cream
2 tsp pure vanilla extract
2 to 3 Tbs rum, optional
Confectioners sugar

SPECIAL EQUIPMENT SUGGESTED:
*A moderately heavy stainless saucepan;
a large stainless mixing bowl set in a
larger bowl of ice cubes and water; a
large balloon whip or hand-held electric
mixer*

Melting the chocolate. Break up the chocolate, turn it into the saucepan, add the cream, and stir over moderate heat until the chocolate has melted and the cream is almost at the simmer. Stir quite vigorously until the chocolate and cream have melded into a smooth brown mass; stir in the vanilla and/or rum.

Chilling. Turn the chocolate into the mixing bowl, set it in the bowl of ice, and whisk several minutes until it has firmed to spreading consistency. Sieve in confectioners sugar to taste.

*Ahead-of-time note: May be made ahead, but do not bother to beat it over ice; reheat to decongeal before using and then beat over ice if necessary.

VARIATIONS

Chocolate Ganache Truffles

Make the ganache mixture quite stiff, adding a little less cream or a little more chocolate. When well chilled, roll into rough balls, roll in cocoa powder, and drop into frilled paper cups. Keep under refrigeration until serving time.

Ganache Chocolate Mousse or Ice Cream

Use double the amount of cream in the master recipe, to make a mass that holds itself softly in a spoon when chilled over ice. Pack into a serving bowl or individual bowls and chill 2 to 3 hours for a mousse, or freeze for ice cream.

ROULADES—SPONGE SHEETS—JELLY ROLLS

Three terms for the same thing, a cake batter spread in a jelly-roll pan, baked until it just holds its shape, then rolled up with jelly or whipped cream and dusted with confectioners sugar, or slathered with a rich and fancy filling and decorated with frostings and frills.

Manufacturing Notes. A spongecake batter is the one to choose here, either the plain formula on page 456 or the orange-almond variation following it. Use any of the fillings and frostings described in this chapter, and since roulades are so flexible, I'm giving suggestions with only page references for fillings, etc., but full details on how to bake a cake in a jelly-roll pan.

Julia with her Bûche de Noël (recipe, page 478)

Holiday Roulade

This is a dressy suggestion, fine for a party or a holiday meal. I like the orange-almond cake formula here, and an enriched Italian meringue for the filling and frosting.

For an 11- by 17-inch sponge sheet, serving 8 to 10

2 Tbs softened butter and ⅓ cup flour, for the jelly-roll pan
The orange-almond spongecake batter on page 458
Confectioners sugar in a fine-meshed sieve
2 cups whipped cream (page 440)
1 Tbs pure vanilla extract
2 cups Italian meringue (2 egg whites, ¾ cup sugar, and ¼ cup water boiled to the soft-ball stage, page 421)
1 cup pulverized almond or hazelnut pralin (page 423) (save out 2 Tbs for final decoration)
1 cup rum imbibing syrup (¼ cup sugar, ¾ cup water, 3 Tbs white rum, page 459)
Decorative suggestions: Angelica and candied cherries

SPECIAL EQUIPMENT SUGGESTED:
A standard jelly-roll pan about 11 by 17 inches; wax paper; a large tray or baking sheet to help in unmolding; a serving board

Preparing the jelly-roll pan and other preliminaries. Rub the inside of the jelly-roll pan with soft butter; line it with a sheet of wax paper, leaving 2 inches extra at each end. Butter the paper. Roll flour in the pan and knock out excess. Preheat the oven to 375°F and set the rack in the lower middle level. Measure out all the in-gredients listed and have the prepared cake batter ready.

Baking the sponge sheet—about 10 minutes at 375°F. Immediately turn the batter into the prepared pan; bang once firmly but not roughly on your work surface to settle it, and place at once in the preheated oven.

When is it done? It is done when very lightly colored and the top feels springy. It must just hold together; if overcooked and dried out it will crack when you roll it up.

Cooling and unmolding. Remove from the oven, and slice ¼ inch off the long sides of the sponge sheet—they may be brittle and will crack, later. The following maneuvers are to pre-vent the cake from becoming dry and impossible to roll. Sprinkle the top with a ¹⁄₁₆-inch layer of confectioners

(continued)

1. Covering sugared cake with wax paper and dampened towel

2. Rolling up the filled cake with help of towel

Holiday Roulade (*continued*)

sugar. Cover with a sheet of wax paper and a lightly dampened towel (see illustration, step 1). Turn a tray or baking sheet upside down over the cake, and reverse the two. Unmold the cake by holding an end of the wax paper while you lift off the jelly-roll pan. Neatly and carefully peel the wax paper off the cake. Sift another ¹⁄₁₆-inch layer of sugar over the cake and roll it up in the damp towel, then in plastic wrap.

*Ahead-of-time note: The cake may be baked a day or two in advance and refrigerated; if you freeze it, be sure to let it thaw an hour or more or it will break.

Meringue cream for filling and frosting. Fold the whipped cream and vanilla into the cool Italian meringue. Then fold a third of the meringue cream into the pralin—this is the filling.

Filling the sponge sheet. Unroll the sponge sheet and sprinkle with the imbibing syrup. Spread on the pralin cream filling, and roll up the cake, starting at a small end and using the towel to help you, step 2.

Frosting, decorating, and serving. Place the roll seam side down on the serving board and slip pieces of wax paper under the edges all around. Frost the cake with the remaining meringue cream and decorate it. Here I've used a sprinkling of pralin, angelica cut into leaf shapes, and candied cherries. Keep refrigerated until serving and, of course, remove the platter-protecting wax paper strips before presenting your masterpiece.

VARIATION

A Bûche de Noël: A Yule Log Cake

It's easy indeed to turn the preceding roulade into the traditional Yule log cake. Just add one more egg to the Italian meringue mixture for the mushrooms, add chocolate to the rest of the meringue, and boil up some sugar for the spun caramel veil. To serve more people, by the way, double the recipe, making 2 roulades; set them end to end and frosting will hide their joining.

For a 10-inch cake, serving 8 to 10

Ingredients and equipment for the preceding roulade, adding 1 more egg white to the Italian meringue

For filling and frosting

12 ounces semisweet baking chocolate melted with ¹⁄₃ cup strong coffee (page 464)
¹⁄₃ cup, more or less, sifted unsweetened cocoa

For decoration

2 to 3 Tbs unsweetened cocoa in a tea strainer
Confectioners sugar in a fine-meshed sieve

For the spun caramel veil

1 cup sugar
3 Tbs white corn syrup
¹⁄₃ cup water

Sprigs of holly, optional

ADDITIONAL EQUIPMENT:
A buttered and floured pastry sheet for the mushrooms; a 16-inch flexible vinyl pastry bag with ¹⁄₂-inch and ¹⁄₈-inch tubes; a washed and oiled broomstick suspended between 2 chairs, for the caramel veil

2. Inserting cake scrap to make bump on log

Meringue mushrooms. Preheat the oven to 200°F. Scoop a quarter of the plain Italian meringue into a pastry bag and squeeze out 8 to 10 ½-inch domes on the pastry sheet, to serve as mushroom caps. Hold the ⅛-inch tube over the end of the pastry bag and squeeze out 8 to 10 conical shapes ¾ inch high, for the stems, see illustration, step 1. Bake about 1 hour in the middle level of the oven, until the meringues push easily off

1. Forming mushroom stems

the pastry sheet—they should color no more than a darkish cream. Return unused meringue to the main mixture.

*Ahead-of-time note: Meringues may be made in advance and frozen.

The frosting and filling. Before beating the whipped cream into the Italian meringue, as described in the master recipe, beat in the smoothly melted chocolate. Then fold in the whipped cream. Remove two thirds of the mixture to a bowl and refrigerate; this is the frosting.

Filling the cake. Spread the filling over the top of the sponge sheet, roll it up from one of the long sides, and you have made the log shape. Neatly slice a narrow slanting piece from each end of the log. Place the log

seam side down on the serving board and slip double sheets of wax paper under the edge of each side and the two ends—to catch spills.

Frosting the log. Beat 2 or more spoonfuls of sifted cocoa into the frosting mixture to make it of spreadable consistency. (Reserve 2 tablespoons of frosting for the mushrooms.) Leaving the two ends free, frost the cake using a flexible metal spatula, then scumble it with the spatula and a fork to give it a rough, barklike look. With a small knife dig a hole in an upper side of the log and insert a piece of the scrap to simulate a bump or a branch, step 2.

*Ahead-of-time note: Refrigerate the log if you are not continuing; it will keep nicely for a day or even two—if you can find a nonmashing cover for it.

(continued)

3. Inserting mushroom stem into cap

4. Waving forkful of caramel over broomstick

Bûche de Noël (*continued*)

Final decorations, just before serving.

The mushrooms. With a small knife, pierce a hole in the bottom of each meringue mushroom cap, insert a bit of the frosting (or softened butter) into the hole, and then the pointed end of a meringue stem, step 3. Arrange the mushrooms in tasteful clusters upon the log. Dust the log with a sparse coating of confectioners sugar to give a snowy effect. Dust the mushroom tops with cocoa powder tapped from the sieve.

The caramel veil. Shortly before serving, bring the sugar to the simmer with the corn syrup and water in a small saucepan; when completely dissolved and clear, cover tightly and boil to the caramel stage (page 421).

Let it cool 2 to 3 minutes, until it forms thick strands when lifted with a fork. Then, dipping the fork into the syrup, wave it over the broomstick, to form long hanging threads of caramel, step 4.

The finale. Lift the caramel strands off the broomstick; drape them over the yule log. Decorate the serving board with sprigs of holly, if you wish, and the Bûche de Noël is ready to serve.

TWO LOAF CAKES

Loaf cakes are easy to serve, and these two go nicely with any informal meal, be it breakfast, a picnic, or a holiday luncheon. An added advantage is that they keep nicely, so that you can have something on hand for emergencies. They are attractive Christmas gifts, too, if you are one who enjoys making your own presents.

Honey Spice Cake: Pain d'Épices

Every region in France seems to have its own special spice cake, but this is the pick of the lot, to my mind. While the dough can be made and baked at once, you'll find that a honey spice cake improves with age—if you make it in mid-December and give it at Christmas, it will be in perfect flavor for New Year's Day. Although you can prepare the dough by hand, a heavy-duty mixer with flat beater attachment makes light work of it, particularly when you are baking a large number.

For an 8-cup loaf, serving 12 or more

The basic dough
1⅓ cups (1 pound) honey
1 cup sugar
¾ cup boiling water
½ tsp salt
1 Tbs baking soda
3 to 4 cups rye flour, as needed

Additions
⅔ cup blanched almonds, pulverized (page 474)
1 tsp each almond and anise extracts
¼ cup dark rum or bourbon whiskey
½ tsp each: cinnamon, ground cloves, and mace
1 cup mixed glacéed fruits (diced, and rinsed in boiling water)

SPECIAL EQUIPMENT SUGGESTED: *A heavily buttered 8-cup loaf pan, bottom lined with buttered wax paper; a heavy-duty mixer with flat beater is especially welcome here*

Applesauce Fruitcake

Maggie Mah, whose father's Nesselrode ice cream is on page 416, has also given us her grandmother's holiday cake with nuts, multiple spices, and an unusual applesauce base. It's a moist, serious, spicy loaf in the old-fashioned tradition.

For a 9-inch, 6-cup loaf pan

2 cups golden seedless raisins
1½ cups all-purpose flour (scooped and leveled, page 380)
½ cup brown sugar
½ cup granulated sugar
1 tsp each: ground cloves, cinnamon, and allspice
1 tsp salt
1 cup hazelnuts or walnuts, toasted
1 Tbs double-acting baking powder
4 Tbs melted butter
1 cup cool, thick applesauce (page 424), or boiled-down canned applesauce

SPECIAL EQUIPMENT SUGGESTED:
A big mixing bowl and wooden spoon; a pan or bowl for the applesauce; a heavily buttered 9-inch, 6-cup loaf pan, bottom lined with buttered wax paper

(continued)

The cake dough. Preheat the oven to 325°F. Beat the honey, sugar, and boiling water in the mixer bowl until the sugar is dissolved. Beat in the salt and soda, and 3 cups of rye flour. Beat in as much more flour as the dough will take, to make a heavy, sticky mass that you can still manipulate. Beat in the additional ingredients.

Into the loaf pan. Turn the batter into the prepared pan, filling it by about two-thirds. Dip your fingers in cold water to smooth the top nicely.

Baking—1 to 1¼ hours or more at 325°F. Timing depends on the shape of the pan. Bake in the middle level of the preheated oven. *Warning:* Do not open the oven door for 45 minutes, and do not shake the pan—this could release the soda-engendered gases and deflate the cake! The dough will rise to fill the pan, and the top of the cake will crack.

When is it done? The cake is done when a skewer plunged to the bottom of the pan comes out completely clean; the cake should also show a slight line of shrinkage from the sides of the pan—better slightly overcooked than undercooked.

Cooling and storing. Let the cake cool for 20 minutes in its pan; then unmold onto a rack, peel the paper off the bottom, and gently turn the cake right side up. When thoroughly cold, wrap airtight and store for a week or more before serving. It will keep for at least several months under refrigeration.

Thick batter goes into prepared pan.

Applesauce Fruitcake (*continued*)

The cake batter. Preheat the oven to 300°F, and set the rack in the middle level. Toss the raisins in the mixing bowl with the flour, add the sugars, seasonings, nuts, and baking powder. Beat the butter into the thick applesauce; blend all the ingredients together in the bowl. Turn the batter into the prepared pan, as illustrated.

Baking—about 1½ hours at 300°F. Set the cake in the preheated oven—do not press, poke, or shake the cake for an hour at least, or it may deflate.

   When is it done? The cake is done when nicely browned, and a skewer, plunged down through it, comes out clean.

Cooling and curing—24 hours at least. Set the pan on a rack and cool 20 minutes, then unmold onto the rack and turn it right side up. When thoroughly cold, wrap airtight and let cure at least a day before serving. It will keep several weeks under refrigeration.

Serving. Serve the cake as is with fruits, or tea, or as a dessert with vanilla ice cream.

A SELECTION OF COOKIES

A varied selection of cookies ends this chapter, including a near cousin of the biscotti family and two kinds of chocolate truffles, sugar cookies you can use for dessert tarts, Proustian madeleines, as well as complete directions for making your own gingerbread men.

Almond Bar Cookies

These are dry, crisp, spicy cookies, twice baked, closely related to the biscotti of Italy. They keep beautifully and are ever-useful to have on hand in the cookie jar.

For 3 to 5 dozen, depending on how you cut them

The first mixture

1 cup granulated white sugar
¾ cup dark brown sugar
1 tsp pure vanilla extract
2 "large" eggs
⅓ cup fresh peanut oil
2 Tbs cold water

The dry ingredients

2½ cups all-purpose flour (scooped and leveled, page 380)
1 tsp salt
1 tsp cardamom
2 tsp cinnamon
2 tsp baking powder
2 cups slivered almonds, toasted (page 423)

Optional: confectioners sugar in a fine-meshed sieve

SPECIAL EQUIPMENT SUGGESTED: *A medium mixing bowl; a larger mixer bowl; a heavy-duty mixer with flat beater is useful; a jelly-roll pan about 11 by 17 inches, buttered, lined with buttered wax paper, and floured (page 477); 2 pastry sheets for final baking; a large cake rack*

The dough. Beat the sugars, vanilla, eggs, oil, and water in the smaller mixing bowl to dissolve the sugar. Blend the dry ingredients in the larger mixer bowl and beat in the sugar mixture, using the heavy-duty mixer or a strong arm. This is a heavy dough. If it is too thick to spread in the next step, beat in droplets more water.

Into the pan. Preheat the oven to 325°F. Turn the dough into the pan and press it in place with wet hands. Cover with a sheet of plastic wrap and smooth the dough under it with your hands. Remove the plastic.

First baking at 325°F—25 minutes or more. Bake in the middle level of the preheated oven until firm to the touch and lightly browned.

Cutting. Remove the pan from the oven and cool 10 minutes. Unmold onto a board, and peel off the wax paper. Cut into even strips, then cut

Cutting the cookies

each strip crosswise, as illustrated, making pieces of any size you wish—1¼ by 3 inches, for example.

Second baking at 300°F—40 minutes or more. Arrange the cookies on the pastry sheets and bake until a nice walnut brown, crisp to the touch, and crunchy to the tooth—eat one to make sure, and return the pan to the oven if necessary. This second baking also gives the cookies their interesting taste.

Serving and storing. Cool on a rack. Serve them as is, or decorate with a dusting of confectioners sugar. Unsugared cookies keep for weeks in an airtight container.

Almond Wafers: Tuiles aux Amandes

Almond wafers are the perfect accompaniment to sherbets, ice creams, and fruit desserts. Delicate, crisp, light—your own freshly baked wafers will be hard to beat.

For 45 wafers, 3 inches across

3½ Tbs unsalted butter
½ cup sugar
¼ cup egg whites (scant 2 egg whites)
⅓ cup plain bleached cake flour (scooped and leveled, page 380), in a sifter set over wax paper
⅓ cup blanched almonds, pulverized (page 474)
¼ tsp almond extract
½ tsp pure vanilla extract
⅔ cup or so shaved almonds (bought in packages)

SPECIAL EQUIPMENT SUGGESTED:
2 or 3 buttered baking sheets; a 2-quart mixing bowl, wooden spoon, and rubber spatula; a flexible-blade spatula; a rolling pin braced so it won't roll; a large cake rack

Preliminaries. Preheat the oven to 425°F, and set the rack in the middle level. Butter the baking sheets, and measure out all the ingredients listed.

The cookie batter. Cream the butter and sugar together in a bowl with a wooden spoon. When soft and fluffy, add the egg whites, stirring only enough barely to blend. Sift on the flour and begin folding it in with a rubber spatula; when almost blended, fold in the ground almonds, almond extract, and vanilla.

(continued)

Almond Wafers (*continued*)

Onto the baking sheets. Drop 1-tablespoon gobs of batter onto a prepared baking sheet, spacing the gobs 3 inches apart. With the back of a spoon, smear out each into a thin, almost transparent disk 2½ inches in diameter. Top each with a pinch of the shaved almonds.

Cookies crisp into shape on rolling pin.

Baking at 425°F—about 4 minutes. Set a filled sheet in the preheated oven and bake until a ⅛-inch border around the cookies has browned lightly. (Form a new sheet while the first is baking.) Open the oven door and set the baking sheet on it, to keep the cookies flexible during the unmolding process. Quickly slide the flexible spatula under a cookie; lift it off and onto the rolling pin as shown. Continue rapidly with the rest—they crisp in a few seconds. Close the oven door and let the temperature return to 425°F before baking the next batch.

Serving and storing. The wafers lose their crisp in humid atmosphere. It's best to serve them soon after baking, or to keep them in a warming oven at 100°F. However, since the curved roof-tile *tuile* shape is difficult to store, you may wish to crisp them flat on a rack if you are making them ahead and freezing them.

Chocolate Lace Wafers

An unusual cookie—caramelized, crisply chewy, and chocolaty—it's somewhat persnickety to make but worth the trouble.

For about 2½ dozen 4-inch wafers

4 ounces (1 stick) unsalted butter
¼ cup dark molasses
¼ cup light brown sugar
¼ cup heavy cream
2 Tbs white corn syrup
1 tsp ground ginger
A big pinch of salt
1 cup plain bleached cake flour (scooped and leveled, page 380), in a sifter set over wax paper
⅓ cup small chocolate bits (available in a bag, or break up sweet chocolate and chop roughly in the processor)

SPECIAL EQUIPMENT SUGGESTED:
An 8-cup saucepan and a pan of barely simmering water to hold it; 2 baking sheets about 11 by 17 inches; heavy-duty wide aluminum foil; a can of no-stick spray, or almond oil; a cake rack

Preliminaries. Preheat the oven to 375°F and set a rack in the middle level. Line the baking sheets smoothly with the foil, its shiny side up, tucking it in under the edges of the sheets all around; spray with the no-stick solution, or brush with oil.

The batter. Cut up the butter and bring it just to the simmer in the saucepan, with all the ingredients except the flour and the chocolate. Remove from heat and whisk in the flour. Set the pan in the larger pan of almost simmering water.

Forming and baking—4 wafers at a time. Place 4 tablespoon-size blobs, spaced well apart, on a foil-covered baking sheet. Spread them out with the back of a spoon into even 2-inch disks. Bake about 3 minutes, until bubbling—even them out with the back of a spoon if necessary. Rapidly sprinkle ½ teaspoon of chocolate over each. Bake 3 to 4 minutes more, until the bubbling has almost ceased and the cookies have browned nicely. (Prepare another sheet while the first is baking—respray or oil the foil for each batch.)

Unmolding and storing. Remove the baking sheet from the oven and let cool 3 minutes, then peel the cookies off the foil and let them crisp on the rack. Store in a warming oven, or for several days in an airtight container, or freeze.

Chocolate Amaretti Truffles

Chocolate truffles have been trendy items for a number of years and no wonder. They most eminently satisfy the chocolate urge, and they're easy to make. The following recipe is for a fairly sturdy truffle that will sit on the sideboard for a while without softening.

For a dozen or more, depending on size

8 ounces sweet chocolate melted with ¼ cup Amaretto liqueur and 2 Tbs strong coffee (page 464)
4 ounces (1 stick) unsalted softened butter
1 Tbs pure vanilla extract
¾ cup pulverized amaretti cookies

Final powdering: ½ cup each powdered cocoa and instant coffee powder (pulverize granular instant coffee in a blender), mixed in a bowl

SPECIAL EQUIPMENT SUGGESTED:
A 6-cup saucepan with tight-fitting cover and a pan of almost-simmering water to hold it—for melting chocolate; a wire whisk and a wooden spoon; a bowl of ice cubes with water to cover; frilled bonbon cups

The mixture. When the chocolate is melted and smooth, whisk in the butter by tablespoon pieces, then the vanilla, and finally beat in the pulverized cookies. Set over the ice and stir until chilled and fairly firm.

Forming. Dig into the mixture with a teaspoon, gather up a gob, and form into a rough rocklike truffle shape. Roll it in the cocoa/coffee powder and drop it into a frilled paper cup.

Storing and serving. Refrigerate in an airtight container, where they will keep several weeks, or you may freeze them.

VARIATIONS

Other Flavors

Use, for instance, bourbon whiskey or dark rum for the liqueur, and pulverized gingersnaps for the cookies.

Chocolate Ganache Truffles

These high-class but perishable truffles made of heavy cream and chocolate are described in the Special Note on page 476.

GINGERBREAD MEN

Make your own Christmas cookies and let the whole family in on the decorating. First here's the dough for the cookies, then the icing.

Spiced Cookie Dough

To make gingerbread cut-outs, houses, and cookie molds.

TIMING NOTE. *The dough needs a day at least to cure before using.*

For about 3 cups, enough for 30 small-ish shapes, or a 20-inch giant

6 ounces (1½ sticks) unsalted butter
⅔ cup each dark brown sugar and granulated sugar
2 "large" eggs
1½ tsp each: ground cardamom, ginger, cinnamon, and cumin
½ tsp each ground cloves and nutmeg
¼ tsp each salt and pepper
1 tsp double-acting baking powder
2 to 2½ cups all-purpose flour
2 to 2½ cups rye flour

SPECIAL EQUIPMENT SUGGESTED:
A heavy-duty mixer with flat beater is useful here, or a strong arm; buttered and floured baking sheets; a large cake rack

The mixture. Cream the butter and sugars in the mixer. When soft and fluffy, beat in the eggs, then the spices, seasonings, baking powder, and enough of the white and rye flours to make a firm dough. Wrap and chill 24 hours.

To form and bake the dough. Roll it out ¼ inch thick.

Using paper pattern for special shapes

Cut-outs. For metal cutters or paper patterns you fashion yourself, cut the dough to the general size of the design. Roll the dough up on your rolling pin, and unroll it on a buttered and floured baking sheet. Then cut it.

Using cookie molds

Wooden or plastic molds. Flour wooden or plastic molds. Cut a piece of dough the general shape of the design, unroll the dough onto the mold, press it into place, and work off excess dough with your fingers. Knock out the molded dough onto a buttered and floured pastry sheet, and correct the design if necessary with a small knife or other object.

Baking—about 15 minutes at 350°F. Bake in the middle level (or the upper and lower middle levels) of the preheated oven.

When are they done? When dry and firm to the touch. Cool on a rack.

SPECIAL NOTE

Royal Icing: Glace Royale

This standard icing for éclairs, cakes, and cookies hardens as it cools, making it fairly indestructible, and therefore most desirable for Christmas cookies.

For about 1⅓ cups

1 egg white
¼ tsp freshly squeezed lemon juice
2 cups sifted confectioners sugar, plus more, if needed
Food coloring tubes or bottles

SPECIAL EQUIPMENT SUGGESTED:
A 2-quart mixing bowl; a portable electric mixer

The mixture. Beat the egg white, lemon juice, and 2 cups of the confectioners sugar for 2 minutes or more, until the mixture forms stiff peaks—"makes the beak," as cooks say. If it doesn't beak, and you feel you have really given it reasonable time, beat in more sugar by sprinkles.

*Ahead-of-time note: May be made somewhat ahead but do not let it dry out—transfer to a small bowl, then cover with a slightly dampened paper towel and plastic wrap.

For decorations. Place spoonfuls of the icing in small bowls. Leave one as is for white, and add drops of food coloring to the others. Either push the icing out using a paper cone, or apply it with a small spatula.

Ladyfingers: Biscuits à la Cuiller

Ladyfingers, little finger-shaped spongecakes, are delightful accompaniments to sherbets and fruit desserts, or on the tea table. However, one of their most useful functions is to line dessert molds, as pictured here. Unfortunately all the packaged store-bought ones I've sampled have been of a miserably flabby quality—better to use store-bought sugar cookies. However, why not make your own ladyfingers? It's not much of a trick, and they freeze beautifully, too.

For 2 to 2½ dozen

3 egg yolks
⅓ cup sugar
A pinch of salt
1½ tsp pure vanilla extract
½ cup plain bleached cake flour (scooped and leveled, page 380), in a sifter set over wax paper
3 egg whites
A pinch of salt
Scant ¼ tsp cream of tartar
3 additional Tbs sugar
1½ cups confectioners sugar, in a fine-meshed sieve

SPECIAL EQUIPMENT SUGGESTED:
2 baking sheets about 11 by 17 inches, buttered and floured (page 477); a pastry bag with ½-inch tube opening; a portable electric mixer; a 3-quart mixing bowl; egg-white beating equipment (page 461); a large cake rack

Preliminaries. Preheat the oven to 350°F and place the racks in the upper and lower middle levels. Draw horizontal lines on the baking sheets with a pencil eraser or chopstick to make spaces 4 inches deep and with lines 1 inch apart. Prepare the pastry bag. Measure out all the ingredients listed. Work fast so that the batter will stay puffed.

The batter. Beat the egg yolks with the mixer in the 3-quart bowl, gradually adding the ⅓ cup sugar, until the mixture is thick, pale yellow, and forms the ribbon (page 461). Beat in the salt and vanilla. Sift in the flour by thirds, beating it in with the mixer after each addition.

The egg whites. Beat the egg whites separately, starting at slow speed until they foam throughout. Add the salt and cream of tartar, and continue until soft peaks are formed; sprinkle in the additional 3 tablespoons of sugar and beat to stiff shining peaks. With a large rubber spatula, stir a quarter of the egg whites into the yolk mixture to make it smooth and light, then scoop the remaining egg whites over the yolks. Quickly but delicately fold them together—the batter will remain puffed and hold its shape if you've worked quickly. At once transfer the batter to the pastry bag and proceed to the next step.

(continued)

Ladyfingers (*continued*)

Forming and baking. Into the 4-inch spaces marked on the baking sheet, rapidly squeeze out finger shapes, slanting them and spacing them 1 inch apart. Sieve on a generous (¹⁄₁₆-inch) layer of confectioners sugar, and place immediately in the pre-heated oven. Bake 12 minutes; rapidly switch the pans to alternate them on the racks. Bake 5 to 6 minutes more, until lightly browned and crisp under their coating of sugar. (Homemade ladyfingers do not puff a great deal because, unlike commercial ones, they contain no baking powder. In contrast, they are tenderly crisp.) Scoop them off the baking sheets with a spatula, and let them cool on the rack.

Forming note. Accomplished cooks can form ladyfinger shapes with a spoon—*à la cuiller.* It takes a little practice, so they say, to achieve the perfect finger shape.

Serving. Just before serving, dust the ladyfingers with confectioners sugar.

*Ahead-of-time note: Ladyfingers may be refrigerated for a day or two in an airtight container, or frozen. Do not sugar them until after they have defrosted: 10 to 15 minutes at room temperature.

Madeleines
Little shell-shaped cakes

This is presumably the true madeleine from Commercy, the one Marcel Proust dipped in his tea. It's a charming little cake, perfect with tea, sherbets, and fruits.

MANUFACTURING NOTE. *A strange method, this—it was developed by the bakers of Commercy to insure a little shell-shaped cake that humped in the middle. You can buy madeleine molds in most gourmet shops or through mail-order catalogues—or you can bake them in scallop shells. You can also bake the batter in muffin tins, and would then call them Commercy Cupcakes.*

For 24 madeleines, 3 inches long

2 "large" eggs, lightly beaten in a 2-cup measure
²⁄₃ cup sugar
1 cup all-purpose flour (scooped and leveled, page 380), plus 1 Tbs extra for preparing the molds
5 ounces (1¼ sticks) unsalted butter, cut into 6 pieces
A pinch of salt
The grated rind of ½ lemon
Drops of freshly squeezed lemon juice
Drops of pure vanilla extract
Confectioners sugar, for sprinkling

SPECIAL EQUIPMENT SUGGESTED: *A mixing bowl and wooden spoon; a bowl with a tray of ice cubes and water to cover; a pastry brush; 2 madeleine pans, 12 cups each; a large cake rack*

The batter. Measure ¼ cup of the eggs into a bowl, then beat in the sugar and the cup of flour. When thoroughly blended, let rest 10 minutes. Meanwhile, melt the butter in a 6-cup saucepan, bring it to the boil, and let it brown lightly. Place the 1 tablespoon of flour in a small bowl and blend in 1½ tablespoons of the browned butter; set aside for preparing the madeleine pans. Stir the rest of the butter over ice until cool but liquid; blend it and the last of the eggs into the batter along with the salt, lemon rind and juice, and vanilla. Preheat the oven to 375°F, and

1. Lumps of madeleine batter going into cups

set the racks in the upper and lower middle levels.

Molding. Paint the madeleine cups with the reserved butter-flour mixture. Divide the batter into 24 lumps of a generous tablespoon each, and drop them into the madeleine cups, step 1.

Baking—about 15 minutes at 375°F. Bake in the preheated oven until the cakes are lightly browned around the edges, humped in the middle, and slightly shrunk from the cups. Unmold onto a rack.

2. Traditional madeleines and Commercy cupcakes

Serving and storing. When cool, turn shell side up and dust with confectioners sugar for serving, step 2. They will keep in the refrigerator for a day or two in an airtight container, and they freeze perfectly.

SUGAR COOKIES MADE FROM PASTRY DOUGHS

▤ MASTER RECIPE

Sweet Pastry and Cookie Dough: Pâte Sablée

A lovely sweet buttery dough, and when you use the larger amounts of sugar it is a cookie dough, just right for the strawberry tartlets pictured here. The more sugar, of course, the more friable, stickier, and more difficult the dough is to form, but also the more delicious to eat.

For a 9- to 10-inch tart shell, or 12 to 14 medium cookie shapes

¾ cup all-purpose flour (scooped and
   leveled, page 380)
¼ cup plain bleached cake flour
¼ tsp salt
4 ounces (1 stick) chilled unsalted
   butter, cut into 16 pieces
3 Tbs to ½ cup granulated sugar
   (the smaller amount for most pie
   and tart doughs; the larger, for
   cookies)
1 egg yolk
1 tsp pure vanilla extract
1 Tbs cold water, plus droplets more
   water, if needed

SPECIAL EQUIPMENT SUGGESTED:
A food processor with steel blade

Measure the flours, salt, and butter into the container of the machine and process about a minute, until the butter is thoroughly blended. Add and process in the sugar, then the egg yolk, vanilla, and water. Continue processing for several seconds, until the dough masses. Turn it out onto your work surface, form into a rough ball, then push out 2-tablespoon bits with the heel of your hand in 6-inch smears. Gather together into a cake, enclose in plastic wrap, and refrigerate until cold and hard—2 hours at least.

*Ahead-of-time note: The dough will keep 2 to 3 days in the refrigerator before it may turn grayish, but will keep perfectly for weeks in the freezer.

Sugar Cookies: Sablés

WARNING. *Because of the high butter and sugar content, the dough softens easily. Work fast to prevent it from becoming sticky; on a hot day it is wise to roll and cut half or even only a third of it at a time, keeping the rest chilled.*

Forming. Beat the chilled dough with a rolling pin to soften it. Flour the top lightly and flour your rolling surface; rapidly roll out the dough ⅛ inch thick and cut into shapes. Transfer as cut onto a buttered baking sheet; chill 20 minutes while preheat-

Pricking cookie dough with tines of fork

ing the oven to 400°F. As illustrated, prick the surface of each, going down to the baking surface, to keep the cookies from rising.

Note. If the dough breaks or splits, push it together and smooth it out with the rolling pin or your fingers.

Baking—8 to 10 minutes at 400°F. Bake in the middle level of the preheated oven, until the edges begin to brown and the cookies themselves have taken on a light color. Carefully, because they're fragile when hot, transfer the cookies with a wide flexible spatula to a rack; they crisp as they cool.

Storing. They will keep 2 to 3 days in an airtight container, or they may be frozen.

Strawberry Tartlets: Sablés aux Fraises

When is a cookie not a cookie? When it becomes a strawberry tartlet, and how easy it is to make them when you have the preceding sugar cookies in your freezer. You'll want them 3 to 3½ inches in diameter, and they may be square, round, or heart-shaped.

Assembly ideas —as in the photograph.

Open faced. Paint a cookie with warm red currant glaze (page 437), arrange thinly sliced strawberries around the edge, and plop a large fine bright berry in the middle; paint more glaze over the strawberries. Or arrange one or several whole strawberries over the glazed surface of a cookie, paint the berries with glaze, and sprinkle lightly with confectioners sugar.

Strawberry sandwich. Cover an open-faced cookie of sliced and glazed strawberries with a second cookie, sprinkle with confectioners sugar, and top with a big bright berry.

SUGAR COOKIES MADE FROM PUFF PASTRY: COUQUES AND PALMIERS

That wonder dough, French puff pastry, with its hundreds of paper-thin layers of dough between hundreds of paper-thin layers of butter, makes the most glorious of sugar cookies. I imagine they were invented by clever French bakers to deal with their puff pastry leftovers—use leftover puff pastry or make a mock puff pastry out of leftover butter pastry dough. Recipes for both are on pages 389 and 392.

Couques: Elephant Tongues

Big, long, light, crisp caramelized oval cookies to eat by themselves, or to serve with fruit desserts.

A 3-inch disk of dough ½ inch thick, for 8 couques

Chilled puff pastry leftovers, or mock puff pastry dough (pages 389 and 392)
Several cups of granulated sugar

SPECIAL EQUIPMENT SUGGESTED: *A flexible-blade metal spatula; clean dry baking sheets; a large cake rack*

WARNING. *Keep the dough chilled. If the dough begins to soften, stop where you are and refrigerate it. Warm sticky dough is impossible to work with.*

Rolling and stretching round of dough in sugar

Palmiers—Palm Leaves— Elephant Ears

These, too, are superior cookies eaten just by themselves, or with tea, or with fruits. Those pictured here are the small baby elephant ears, but you can make them twice the size if you wish.

A piece of dough 5½ by 2 by 1½ inches, for 2 dozen 3-inch palmiers

Several cups of granulated sugar
Chilled puff pastry leftovers, or
    mock puff pastry dough (pages
    389 and 392)

SPECIAL EQUIPMENT SUGGESTED:
A flexible-blade metal spatula; clean dry baking sheets; a large cake rack

WARNING: *Keep the dough chilled. If the dough begins to soften, stop where you are and refrigerate it. Warm sticky dough is impossible to work with.*

Preliminary rolling in sugar. Spread a generous rectangle of sugar ⅛ inch thick on your work surface. Place the dough upon it, and roll the dough into a rectangle ³⁄₁₆ inch thick. Fold in three, as for a business letter, then rotate the dough so the top flap is to your right. Place again on a layer of sugar, roll out to a rectangle, and again fold in three. Wrap and refrigerate 30 minutes, to firm the butter and relax the dough.

Final rolling and cutting. Again, over a layer of sugar, roll the dough into a rectangle, this time 8 inches wide on its short side and ¼ inch thick. Fold

Stages in manufacturing palmiers

the two long sides to meet at the center, as shown in the illustration. Sprinkle on more sugar and press it into the dough with your rolling pin. Fold the dough in 2 lengthwise, as in the second rectangle to the right of the first—you now have 4 layers of sugary dough. Press them together with your rolling pin, then cut into crosswise pieces ⅜ inch thick.

Shaping. To produce the palmier (or palm-leaf) shape, turn the slices of dough cut side up and bend the two ends outward, as shown at lower right. Place them on the baking sheets, cover, and refrigerate at least 30 minutes. Preheat the oven to 450°F before proceeding.

Baking—6 minutes, then 3 to 4 minutes, at 450°F. Set in the middle level of the preheated oven and bake 6 minutes, or until the bottoms have turned a caramel brown. Turn them over with the spatula, sprinkle with a ¹⁄₁₆-inch layer of sugar, and bake 3 to 4 minutes more, until nicely caramelized. Cool on a rack.

Storing. The cookies will keep a day or two in a 100°F warming oven or an airtight container, or you may freeze them.

Forming. Roll the dough ⅛ inch thick and cut into 2-inch rounds. Spread a 12-inch oval of sugar ⅛ inch thick on your work surface. Lay a round of dough on the sugar and roll it out into a tongue shape about 6 inches long and ¹⁄₁₆ inch thick, as illustrated. Reverse the shape and, holding the other end, roll it again. Turn it upside down (sugared side up) and sprinkle more sugar on top—you need a ¹⁄₁₆-inch layer of sugar for the cookies to caramelize. Lift with a clean dry spatula onto a dry baking sheet. Continue with the rest, spacing the shapes 1 inch apart on the baking sheets. (Ball up and re-roll scraps.) Cover and chill 30 minutes. Preheat the oven to 450°F before the next step.

Baking—7 to 8 minutes at 450°F. Set in the oven. The couques should brown lightly and the sugar topping should melt and caramelize—remove them one by one to the rack as they are done.

Storing. The cookies will keep a day or two in a 100°F warming oven or an airtight container, or you may freeze them.

Beef Chart

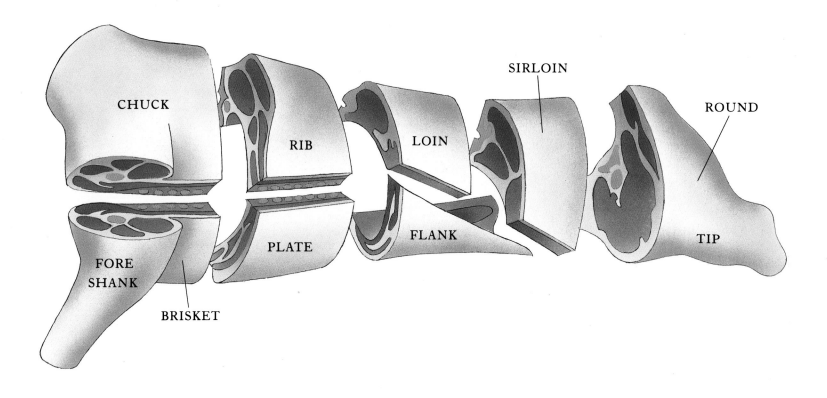

Index

M indicates a master recipe

B a boxed special note

M indicates a master recipe

M indicates a master recipe

B a boxed special note

M indicates a master recipe

B a boxed special note

M indicates a master recipe

A Note About the Author

Julia Child was born in Pasadena, California. She was graduated from Smith College and worked for the OSS during World War II in Ceylon and China. Afterwards she lived in Paris, studied at the Cordon Bleu, and taught cooking with Simone Beck and Louisette Bartholle, with whom she wrote the first volume of *Mastering the Art of French Cooking*, published in 1961.

In 1963 Boston's WGBH launched "The French Chef" television series, which made Julia Child a national celebrity, earning her the Peabody award in 1965 and an Emmy in 1966; subsequent public television shows were "Julia Child & Company" (1978), "Julia Child & More Company" (1980), and "Dinner at Julia's" (1983). In the early 80's, Mrs. Child wrote a monthly feature for *Parade* magazine.

Julia Child is married to Paul Child, who has worked closely with her as an artist and photographer. The Childs live in Massachusetts and in California.